Dear Student,

You are about to embark in the study of one of the most important subjects in your college career. In fact, Chapter 1 argues that it is the most important course you will take. Why? Because in modern business, knowledge of information systems is the key to obtaining and succeeding in interesting and rewarding professional jobs.

Like all college students, you have many claims on your time: friends, family, sports, hobbies, love-life, whatever, but you owe it to your future to take time to consider seriously how you want to spend the bulk of your waking hours for the next 30 to 40 years. You want a job that you find so satisfying that you can hardly wait to get to work in the morning. There are such jobs, believe it or not, and there is one for you. But, it won't just be handed to you at graduation. You have to prepare for it, find it, obtain it in an intensely competitive job market, and then know enough to thrive in it.

This course is key because information systems are the major influence on the modern economy, an influence that has not been beneficial for everyone. Bank lobbies were once filled with bookkeepers, accountants, and accounting managers. Those jobs disappeared with computer systems. Half-asleep, mediocre business school graduates once held managerial jobs over rooms full of typists and clerical workers. Those jobs disappeared as attorneys, auditors, and, indeed, all business professionals conduct their own correspondence using email, texting, and videoconferencing.

The trick to turning information systems to your advantage is to get ahead of their impact. During your career, you can find many opportunities for the innovative application of information systems in business and government, but only if you know how to look for them. Once found, those opportunities become your opportunities when you, as a skilled, nonroutine problem solver, apply emerging technology to improve your organization, whether your job is in marketing, operations, sales, accounting, finance, entrepreneurship, or another discipline.

Congratulations on your decisions so far. Congratulations on deciding to go to college, congratulations on deciding to study business. Now, double down on those good decisions, and use this course to help you obtain and then thrive in an interesting and rewarding career. Start in Chapter 1 by learning how Jennifer lost her job and what you can do to ensure that never happens to you! After that, learn more than just the MIS terminology; understand the ways information systems are transforming business and the many, many ways you can participate.

In this endeavor, I wish you, a future business professional, the very greatest success!

David Kroenke
Whidbey Island, WA

Why This Fourth Edition?

The changes in this 4th edition listed in Figure 1 reflect the changes that information systems are making in business and government today. Chapters 1–6 are introduced with a new case involving an emerging online retailer, GearUp, which sells discontinued sporting goods items and last year's seasonal items at rock-bottom prices. GearUp seeks ways to use IS to better meet its competitive strategy, as you will learn. Chapters 7–12 are introduced with PRIDE, the Performance Recording, Integration, Delivery, and Evaluation system that uses cloud technology and a wide array of mobile devices to integrate patient exercise data with health care providers, health clubs, insurance agencies, and employers.

GearUp is based on a real business, and PRIDE is based on a real business opportunity, but neither is an actual company. To work in a textbook, to teach the material that you need to learn, real businesses must be simplified in ways that actual businesses find objectionable. For an actual business such as GearUp, go to *www.Zulily.com*. For a real business that uses the same technology as PRIDE, go to *www.Endomondo.com*.

As you can tell in the table below, changes have been made to all chapters. The more substantial changes are the following: Chapter 2 has a new discussion of business process and the ways that information systems can improve process quality. Cloud technology changes content in almost all of the chapters. Mobile applications are also a major new discussion throughout. Eleven of the 12 chapters have new chapter-ending cases, and four chapters have new InClass exercises. BigData and Hadoop are featured in Chapters 5 and 9. An entirely new discussion of social media information systems and their role in organizations replaces the 3rd edition's Chapter 8.

Concerning the chapter extensions, the first two collaboration extensions have been rewritten, and in the process the material in the prior edition's Chapter Extension 3 was merged into them. Chapter Extension 4 has been updated and merged with the social media chapter extension to become Chapter Extension 11. Chapter Extensions 7 and 16 are brand new. Chapter Extension 7 discusses mobile application development and BYOD policy, while Chapter Extension 16 discusses agile development technology and scrum. Numerous other changes are made, as listed in the table below.

Chapter	Description of Change
1–6	New GearUp Case
7–12	New PRIDE Case
1	Add employment data
1	New Amazon case at end
2	Revision of new process diagrams and a discussion of process quality
2	New discussion of relationship of IS and processes
2	Introduction of BPMN symbols
2	New discussion of information/data
2	Revised InClass Exercise
2	New Amazon FBA case at end
3	Updated competitive analysis for GearUp Case
4	Modernized discussion including Windows 8 and mobile operating systems
4	Updated application software section, including mobile device application development
4	New discussion of thin versus thick mobile app custom development
4	Two new guides
4	New InClass exercise regarding Google Mobility, Microsoft Surface, and Apple
4	New Apple case at end
5	New GearUp Case to start and throughout
5	New section on NoSQL
5	New NoSQL case at end
6	New Questions on the Cloud
6	Simplified connections discussion
6	New security guide on packet sniffing
6	New Case on Microsoft Cloud
7	New discussion of inter-enterprise systems and the integration of information silos at the enterprise level
7	New case on cloud databases
8	New material addressing social media fundamentals
8	New case focusing on the role of social media policy development for city Chamber of Commerce
9	Complete reorganization, with a new introduction and new discussion of BigData, Hadoop and MapReduce
9	New InClass Exercise
9	New case on data mining of third-party cookies
10	New PRIDE case examples woven throughout
10	New case on cost estimating (for PRIDE)
11	New PRIDE case examples woven throughout
11	New InClass on PRIDE
11	New case on iOS app development
12	PRIDE exam
	Example illustrating design for security
12	New model of security threats
12	New case and collaboration exercise

Chapter Extensions	Description of Change
1	New material focusing on the purposes of collaboration in business: informing, deciding, solving, managing
2	New material focusing on student collaboration needs in Q1 and then evaluating collaboration tool sets in Q5
Prior edition CE 3	Delete and combine with CE 1
Prior edition CE 4	Modernize with social media impact, Enterprise 2.0, and merge into new CE 11
7	New; discussions of mobile systems development and BYOD policies
8	Update examples for PRIDE
9	Update sales data, new section on ERP in the cloud and related questions
10	Add inter-enterprise IS/cloud-based solutions
11	New; discussions hyper-social organization and places KM in the perspective of the hyper-social organization
16	New extension on Agile Development and scrum
17	Revision of functional systems to remove mistaken idea of 1:1 for systems and processes and fix throughout

The Guides

Each chapter includes two unique guides that focus on current issues in information systems. In each chapter, one of the guides focuses on an ethical issue in business. The other guide focuses on the application of the chapter's contents to other business aspects. The content of each guide is designed to stimulate thought, discussion, and active participation to help *you* develop your problem-solving skills and become a better business professional.

LEARNING AIDS FOR STUDENTS

We have structured this book so you can maximize the benefit from the time you spend reading it. As shown in the table below, each chapter includes a series of learning aids to help you succeed in this course.

Resource	Description	Benefit	Example
Question-Driven Chapter Learning Objectives	These queries, and the subsequent chapter sections written around them, focus your attention and make your reading more efficient.	Identifies the main point of the section. When you can answer each question, you've learned the main point of the section.	p. 26
Guides	Each chapter includes two guides that focus on current issues relating to information systems. One of the two deals with an ethical issue.	Stimulates thought and discussion. Helps develop your problem-solving skills. Helps you learn to respond to ethical dilemmas in business.	p. 62
Experiencing MIS InClass Exercise	Each chapter of this text includes an exercise called *Experiencing MIS InClass*. This feature contains exercises, projects, and questions for you and a group of your fellow students to perform in class. Some of those exercises can be done in a single class period; others span several class sections with out-of-class activities in between. For example, see the first Experiencing MIS InClass Exercise on online dating, page 11.	These exercises help you relate the knowledge you are learning in the chapter to your everyday life.	p. 91
How Does the Knowledge in This Chapter Help You? (near the end of each chapter)	This section revisits the opening scenario and discusses what the chapter taught you about it.	Summarizes the "takeaway" points from the chapter as they apply to the company or person in the story, and to you.	p. 37
Active Review	Each chapter concludes with a summary-and-review section, organized around the chapter's study questions.	Offers a review of important points in the chapter. If you can answer the questions posed, you will understand the material.	p. 42

Resource	Description	Benefit	Example
Key Terms and Concepts	Highlights the major terms and concepts with their appropriate page reference.	Provides a summary of key terms for review before exams.	p. 216
Using Your Knowledge	These exercises ask you to take your new knowledge to the next step by applying it to a practice problem.	Tests your critical-thinking skills and keeps reminding you that you are learning material that applies to the real world.	p. 125
Collaboration Exercise	A team exercise that focuses on the chapter's topic.	Use Google Drive, Windows Live SkyDrive, Microsoft SharePoint, or some other tool to collaborate on collective answers.	p. 247
Case Study	A case study closes each chapter. You will reflect on the use in real organizations of the technology or systems presented in the chapter and recommend solutions to business problems.	Requires you to apply newly acquired knowledge to real situations.	p. 248
Application Exercises (at the end of the book)	These exercises ask you to solve business situations using spreadsheet (Excel) database (Access) applications, and other Office applications.	Helps develop your computer skills.	p. 610
MyMISLab	MyMISLab contains a Microsoft Office 2010 simulation environment with tutorials, SharePoint collaboration tools and assignments, student assessments, and classroom videos.	Expands the classroom experience with valuable hands-on activities and tools.	*www.mymislab.com*
SharePoint Hosting	Pearson will host Microsoft SharePoint site collections for your university. Students need only a browser to participate.	Enables students to collaborate using the world's most popular collaboration software.	*www.pearsonhighered.com /kroenke*

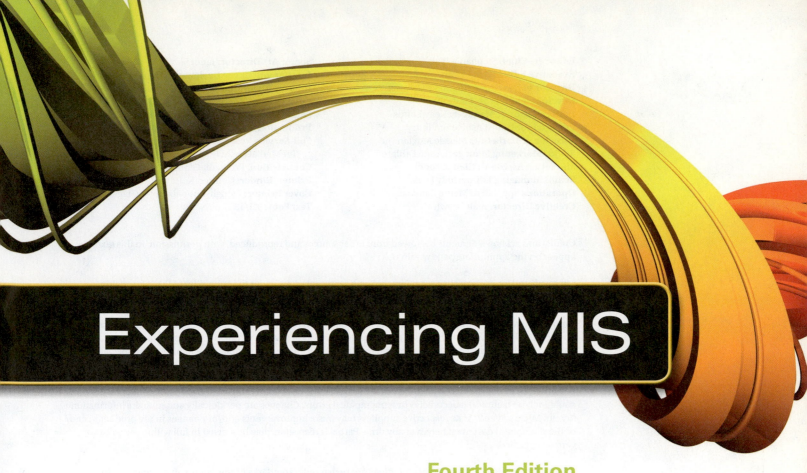

Experiencing MIS

Fourth Edition

David M. Kroenke

PEARSON

Boston   Columbus   Indianapolis   New York   San Francisco   Upper Saddle River
Amsterdam   Cape Town   Dubai   London   Madrid   Milan   Munich   Paris   Montreal   Toronto
Delhi   Mexico City   Sao Paulo   Sydney   Hong Kong   Seoul   Singapore   Taipei   Tokyo

Editor-in-Chief: Stephanie Wall
Executive Editor: Bob Horan
Director of Development: Steve Deitmer
Development Editor: Laura Town
Editorial Project Manager: Kelly Loftus
Editorial Assistant: Ashlee Bradbury
Director of Marketing: Maggie Moylan
Senior Marketing Manager: Anne Fahlgren
Marketing Assistant: Gianna Sandri
Senior Managing Editor: Judy Leale
Operations Specialist: Maura Zaldivar
Creative Director: Blair Brown

Senior Art Director: Janet Slowik
Interior and Cover Designer: Karen Quigley
Interior Illustrations: Simon Alicea
Cover Art/Photo: Julien Tromeur/fotolia
Senior Editorial Media Project Manager: Alana Coles
Production Media Project Manager: Lisa Rinaldi
Full-Service Project Management: Nancy Kincade/
    PreMediaGlobal USA Inc.
Composition: PreMediaGlobal USA Inc.
Printer/Binder: Courier/Kendallville
Cover Printer: Lehigh-Phoenix Color/Hagerstown
Text Font: 9.5/13 Utopia

Credits and acknowledgments borrowed from other sources and reproduced, with permission, in this textbook appear on the appropriate page within text.

Library of Congress Cataloging-in-Publication Data is available on request from the Library of Congress.

10 9 8 7 6 5 4 3 2 1

PEARSON

ISBN 10: 0-13-296748-0
ISBN 13: 978-0-13-296748-8

To C.J., Carter, and Charlotte

CONTENTS OVERVIEW

Experiencing MIS offers basic topic coverage of MIS in its 12 chapters and more in-depth, expanded coverage in its chapter extensions. This modular organization allows you to pick and choose among those topics. Here, chapter extensions are shown below the chapters to which they are related. You will preserve continuity if you use each of the 12 chapters in sequence. In most cases, a chapter extension can be covered any time in the course after its related chapter. You need not use any of the chapter extensions if time is short.

CONTENTS

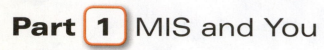

Part ② Information Technology

Part 3 Using IS for Competitive Advantage

Part 4 Information Systems Management

CHAPTER EXTENSIONS

If you were to walk into my office today and ask me for advice about how to use this book, here's what I'd say:

1. This class may be the most important course in the business school. Don't blow it off. See the first few pages of Chapter 1.

2. This class is much broader than you think. It's not just about Excel or Web pages or computer programs. It's about business and how businesses can be more successful with computer-based systems.

3. The design of this book is based on research into how you learn. Every chapter or extension starts with a list of questions. Read the material until you can answer the questions. Then, go to the Active Review and do the tasks there. If you're successful with those tasks, you're done. If it takes you 5 minutes to do that, you're done. If it takes you 5 hours to do that, you're done. But you aren't done until you can complete the Active Review tasks.

4. Pay attention to the issues raised by the opening cases. Those cases are based on real people and real companies and real stories. I changed the names to protect the innocent, the guilty, the publisher, and me.

5. Read the guides. Those stories are what my own students tell me teach them the most.

6. To make it easy to pick up and read, this book includes a lot of colorful and interesting art. However, don't forget to read.

7. I have worked in the computer industry for more than 40 years. There isn't anything in this text that a business professional might never use. It's all relevant, depending on what you decide to do.

8. However, this book contains more than you can learn in one semester. All of the content in this book will be needed by someone, but it may not be needed by you. Pay attention to what your professor says you should learn. He or she knows the job requirements in your local area.

9. With the national unemployment rate for young adults over 10 percent, your primary task in college is to learn something that will get you a job. Many exercises ask you to prepare something for a future job interview. Do those exercises!

10. Technology will create wonderfully interesting opportunities in the next 10 years. Get involved, be successful, and have fun!

David Kroenke
Whidbey Island, WA

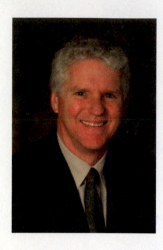

David Kroenke has many years of teaching experience at Colorado State University, Seattle University, and the University of Washington. He has led dozens of seminars for college professors on the teaching of information systems and technology; in 1991 the International Association of Information Systems named him Computer Educator of the Year. In 2009, David was named Educator of the Year by the Association of Information Technology Professionals-Education Special Interest Group (AITP-EDSIG).

David worked for the U.S. Air Force and Boeing Computer Services. He was a principal in the startup of three companies, serving as the vice president of product marketing and development for the Microrim Corporation and as chief of database technologies for Wall Data, Inc. He is the father of the semantic object data model. David's consulting clients have included IBM, Microsoft, and Computer Sciences Corporations, as well as numerous smaller companies. Recently, David has focused on using information systems for teaching collaboration and teamwork.

His text *Database Processing* was first published in 1977 and is now in its 12th edition. He has authored and coauthored many other textbooks, including *Database Concepts*, 6th ed. (2013), *Using MIS*, 6th ed. (2014), *MIS Essentials*, 3rd ed. (2014), *SharePoint for Students* (2012), *Office 365 in Business* (2012), and *Processes, Systems, and Information: An Introduction to MIS* (2013). David lives in Seattle. He is married and has two children and three grandchildren. He enjoys woodworking, and his wife tells him he enjoys gardening as well.

part 1

MIS and You

Knowledge of information systems will be critical to your success in business. If you major in accounting, marketing, management, or in another less technical major, you may not yet know how important such knowledge will be to you. The purpose of Part 1 is to demonstrate why this subject is so important to every business professional. We begin with an example case.

GearUp is a three-year-old, privately owned company that sells quality brand-name athletic gear and clothing at deep discount over the Web. GearUp is a private buying club; before customers can purchase, they must first register.

Each day, GearUp sends emails to its customers announcing that day's sales event. Because events typically last 72 hours, GearUp normally has three events running simultaneously. Members buy until the sale ends or until the maximum quantity that GearUp can obtain has been sold. Because the total quantity is limited, customers are incentivized to buy early.

When the sale ends, GearUp buys the quantity it sold from its supplier, receives the goods in its inventory in Indianapolis, and then repackages the merchandise and ships orders to customers.

GearUp buyers negotiate with suppliers for maximum item quantities, sales prices, and costs. For example, a buyer might agree to purchase up to 5,000 soccer balls, sell them at a price of $22 each, and purchase them for $14 each. Buyers also negotiate shipping costs to the GearUp warehouse.

Source: julien tromeur/Fotolia

Once the terms are agreed upon, operations personnel contact the vendor for photos and descriptions of the goods needed to create attractive displays on computer browsers and mobile devices.

Kelly Summers is GearUp's founder and CEO. During her 20s, Kelly played professional soccer, but after a serious knee injury she retired and began working in sales for a national sports retailer. After three years, she moved to corporate marketing, where she worked two more years before leaving that position to start GearUp.

She took several key employees with her, including Lucas Massey, GearUp's director of IT services, who keeps the Web and sales sites running. Emily Johnson came over as CFO; Drew Mills as manager of event operations; and Addison Lee, who started as GearUp's first buyer, is now the lead buyer for the company.

"Every day is a new world for our customers," according to Kelly. "When you come to our site, you don't know whether you'll find a great deal on volleyballs and nets, hot fashions in ski wear, or premium golf clubs."

Sales revenue the first three years was $3 million, $11 million, $26 million. At present, sales are restricted to the United States. "We're just not ready to get into international shipping, pricing, currencies, etc."

According to Emily Johnson, "Our biggest problem is margins. We're selling more, but not seeing the economies of scale that we should. Our profit, as a percent of sales, has actually gone down. Not much, but a little, and it should be going up. I don't know why that is, but I told Kelly we've got to get on top of it."

Information systems are key to GearUp's success, as you are about to learn.

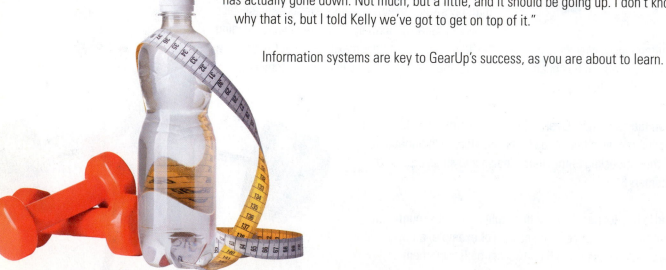

chapter

1

The Importance of MIS

"Fired? You're firing me?"

"Well, *fired* is a harsh word, but . . . well, GearUp has no further need for your services."

"But, Kelly, I don't get it. I really don't. I worked hard, and I did everything you told me to do."

"Jennifer, that's just it. You did everything *I* told you to do."

"I put in so many hours. How could you fire me????"

"Your job was to find ways we can reduce operational expenses without curtailing our effectiveness."

"Right! And I did that."

"No, you didn't. You followed up on ideas *that I gave you*. But we don't need someone who can follow up on my plans. We need someone who can figure out what we need to do, create her own plans, and bring them back to me . . . and others."

"How could you expect me to do that? I've only been here 6 months!!!"

"It's called teamwork. Sure, you're just learning our business, but I made sure all of our senior staff would be available to you . . ."

"I didn't want to bother them."

"Well, you succeeded. I asked Drew what he thought of the plans you're working on. 'Who's Jennifer?' he asked."

"But, doesn't he work down at the warehouse?"

"Right. He's the operations manager . . . and it would seem to be worth talking to him."

"I'll go do that!"

"Jennifer, do you see what just happened? I gave you an idea and you said you'd do it. That's not what I need. I need you to find solutions on your own."

"I worked really hard. I put in a lot of hours. I've got all these reports written."

"Has anyone seen them?"

STUDY QUESTIONS

Q1 WHY IS INTRODUCTION TO MIS THE MOST IMPORTANT CLASS IN THE BUSINESS SCHOOL?

Q2 WHAT IS AN INFORMATION SYSTEM?

Q3 WHAT IS MIS?

Q4 WHY IS THE DIFFERENCE BETWEEN INFORMATION TECHNOLOGY AND INFORMATION SYSTEMS IMPORTANT TO YOU?

Q5 WHAT IS YOUR ROLE IN IS SECURITY?

How does the **knowledge** in this chapter help **you?**

"But today, they're not enough."

"I talked to you about some of them. But, I was waiting until I was satisfied with them."

"Right. That's not how we do things here. We develop ideas and then kick them around with each other. Nobody has all the smarts. Our plans get better when we comment and rework them . . . I think I told you that."

"Maybe you did. But I'm just not comfortable with that."

"Well, it's a key skill here."

"I know I can do this job."

"Jennifer, you've been here almost 6 months; you have a degree in business. Several weeks ago, I asked you for your first idea about how to identify problematic vendors. Do you remember what you said?"

"Yes, I wasn't sure how to proceed. I didn't want to just throw something out that might not work."

"But how would you find out if it would work?"

"I don't want to waste money . . .'"

"No, you don't. So, when you didn't get very far with that task, I backed up and asked you to send me a diagram of the life cycle for one of our events . . . how we select the vendors, how we negotiate with them, how we create the Web pages, run the events, ship the goods. Not details, just the overview."

"Yes, I sent you that diagram."

"Jennifer, it made no sense. Your diagram had vendors sending us sales materials before we finished negotiating with them."

"I know that process, I just couldn't put it down on paper. But, I'll try again!"

"Well, I appreciate that attitude, but times are tight. We don't have room for trainees. When the economy was strong, I'd have been able to look for a spot for you, see if we can bring you along. But, to get our margins up, we can't afford to do that now."

"What about my references?"

"I'll be happy to tell anyone that you're reliable, that you work 40 to 45 hours a week, and that you're honest and have integrity."

"Those are important!"

"Yes, they are. But today, they're not enough."

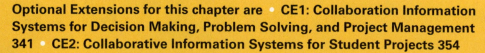

CE

Optional Extensions for this chapter are • **CE1: Collaboration Information Systems for Decision Making, Problem Solving, and Project Management 341** • **CE2: Collaborative Information Systems for Student Projects 354**

WHY IS INTRODUCTION TO MIS THE MOST IMPORTANT CLASS IN THE BUSINESS SCHOOL?

Introduction to MIS is the most important class in the business school. That statement was not true in 2005, and it may not be true in 2025. But it is true in 2013.

Why?

The ultimate reason lies in a principle known as **Moore's Law**. In 1965, Gordon Moore, co-founder of Intel Corporation, stated that because of technology improvements in electronic chip design and manufacturing, "The number of transistors per square inch on an integrated chip doubles every 18 months." His statement has been commonly misunderstood to be, "The speed of a computer doubles every 18 months," which is incorrect, but captures the sense of his principle.

Because of Moore's Law, the ratio of price to performance of computers has fallen from something like $4,000 for a standard computing device to less than a penny for that same device. See Figure 1-1.

As a future business professional, however, you needn't care how fast a computer your company can buy for $100. That's not the point. Here's the point:

> **Because of Moore's Law, the cost of data communications and data storage is essentially zero.**

Think about that statement before you hurry to the next paragraph. What happens when those costs are essentially zero? Here are some consequences:

- YouTube
- iPad
- Facebook
- Second Life
- Pandora
- Twitter
- LinkedIn
- Hulu

None of these was prominent in 2005, and, in fact, most didn't exist in 2005.

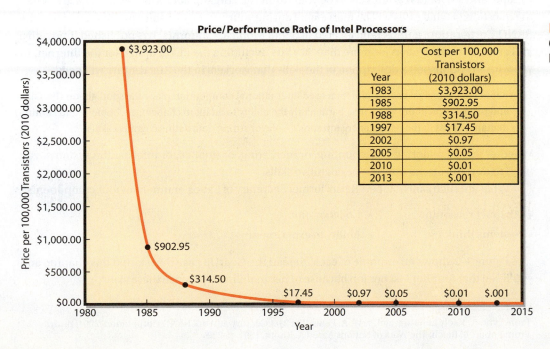

Price/Performance Ratio of Intel Processors

Year	Cost per 100,000 Transistors (2010 dollars)
1983	$3,923.00
1985	$902.95
1988	$314.50
1997	$17.45
2002	$0.97
2005	$0.05
2010	$0.01
2013	$.001

Figure 1-1
Computer Price/Performance Ratio Decreases

WHAT ARE COST-EFFECTIVE BUSINESS APPLICATIONS OF FACEBOOK AND TWITTER OR WHATEVER WILL SOON APPEAR?

Social networking is the rage. Go to any Web page and you'll find the Facebook "Like" and the Twitter "Follow" buttons. The question is, are these applications cost-effective? Do they generate revenue worth the time and expense of running them? Someone needs to be examining that question, and that person works in marketing . . . not in a technical field. We'll examine this question in more depth in Chapter 8. For now, think about the first businesses that saw the potential of Facebook and Twitter. They gained a competitive advantage by being ahead of the crowd in adopting these new technologies.

It's not over. Facebook and Twitter are not the end. Right now, GearUp, and PRIDE (an application you'll study in Chapters 7–12) are employing new processing capabilities called *the cloud* in innovative ways . . . using technology and techniques that have never been seen before. All of this leads us to the first reason Introduction to MIS is the most important course in the business school today:

> **Future business professionals need to be able to assess, evaluate, and apply emerging information technology to business.**

You need the knowledge of this course to attain that skill, and having that skill will lead to greater job security.

HOW CAN I ATTAIN JOB SECURITY?

Many years ago, I had a wise and experienced mentor. One day I asked him about job security, and he told me that the only job security that exists is "a marketable skill and the courage to use it." He continued, "There is no security in our company, there is no security in any government program, there is no security in your investments, and there is no security in Social Security." Alas, how right he turned out to be.

So what is a marketable skill? It used to be that one could name particular skills, such as computer programming, tax accounting, or marketing. But today, because of Moore's Law, because the cost of data storage and data communications is essentially zero, any routine skill can and will be outsourced to the lowest bidder. And if you live in the United States, Canada, Australia, Europe, and so on, that is unlikely to be you. Numerous organizations and experts have studied the question of what skills will be marketable during your career. Consider two of them. First, the RAND Corporation, a think tank located in Santa Monica, California, has published innovative and groundbreaking ideas for more than 60 years, including the initial design for the Internet. In 2004, RAND published a description of the skills that workers in the 21st century will need[1]:

> Rapid technological change and increased international competition place the spotlight on the skills and preparation of the workforce, particularly the ability to adapt to changing technology and shifting demand. Shifts in the nature of organizations . . . favor strong nonroutine cognitive skills.

Whether you're majoring in accounting, or marketing, or finance, or information systems, you need to develop strong nonroutine cognitive skills.

What are such skills? Robert Reich, former Secretary of Labor, enumerates four components[2]:

- Abstract reasoning
- Systems thinking
- Collaboration
- Ability to experiment

Figure 1-2 shows an example of each. Reread the GearUp case that started this chapter, and you'll see that Jennifer lost her job because of her inability to practice these skills.

---

[1]From Lynn A. Kaoly and Constantijn W. A. Panis, The 21st Century at Work RAND Corporation, 2004, p. xiv.
[2]From Robert B. Reich, The Work of Nations Alfred A. Knopf, 1991, p. 229

Figure 1-2
Examples of Critical Skills for
Nonroutine Cognition

Skill	Example	Jennifer's Problem
Abstract reasoning	Construct a model or representation.	Inability to model the event life cycle.
Systems thinking	Model system components and show how components' inputs and outputs relate to one another.	Confusion about when vendors provide collateral material for events.
Collaboration	Develop ideas and plans with others. Provide and receive critical feedback.	Unwilling to work with others with work-in-progress.
Ability to experiment	Create and test promising new alternatives, consistent with available resources.	Fear of failure prohibited discussion of new ideas.

HOW CAN INTRO TO MIS HELP YOU LEARN NONROUTINE SKILLS?

Introduction to MIS is the best course in the business school for learning these four key skills, because every topic will require you to apply and practice them. Here's how.

Abstract Reasoning

Abstract reasoning is the ability to make and manipulate models. You will work with one or more models in every course topic and book chapter. For example, later in this chapter you will learn about all of the five components of an information system. Chapter 2 will describe how to use this model to assess the scope of any new information system project; other chapters will build upon this model.

In this course, you will not just manipulate models that your instructor or I have developed, you will also be asked to construct models of your own. In Chapter 5, for example, you'll learn how to create data models, and in Chapter 10 you'll learn to make process models.

Systems Thinking

Can you go down to a grocery store, look at a can of green beans, and connect that can to U.S. immigration policy? Can you watch tractors dig up a forest of pulpwood trees and connect that woody trash to Moore's Law? Do you know why one of the major beneficiaries of YouTube is Cisco Systems?

Answers to all of these questions require systems thinking. **Systems thinking** is the ability to model the components of the system, to connect the inputs and outputs among those components into a sensible whole that reflects the structure and dynamics of the phenomenon observed.

As you are about to learn, this class is about information *systems*. We will discuss and illustrate systems; you will be asked to critique systems; you will be asked to compare alternative systems; you will be asked to apply different systems to different situations. All of those tasks will prepare you for systems thinking as a professional.

Collaboration

Collaboration is the activity of two or more people working together to achieve a common goal, result, or work product. Chapter Extensions 1 and 2 will teach you collaboration skills and illustrate several sample collaboration information systems. Every chapter of this book includes collaboration exercises that you may be assigned in class or as homework.

Here's a fact that surprises many students: Effective collaboration isn't about being nice. In fact, surveys indicate the single most important skill for effective collaboration is to give and receive critical feedback. Advance a proposal in business that challenges the cherished program of the VP of marketing, and you'll quickly learn that effective collaboration skills differ from party manners at the neighborhood barbeque. So, how do you advance your idea in the face of the VP's resistance? And without losing your job? In this course, you can learn both skills and information systems for such collaboration. Even better, you will have many opportunities to practice them.

The first two chapter extensions on pages 341–370 discuss collaboration in detail and guide you how to collaborate with your peers.

Ability to Experiment

"I've never done this before."

"I don't know how to do it."

"But will it work?"

"Is it too weird for the market?"

Fear of failure paralyzes many good people and many good ideas. In the days when business was stable, when new ideas were just different verses of the same song, professionals could allow themselves to be limited by fear of failure.

Think about GearUp's margin problem. Is there a way it could use social networking within the company to reduce expenses? Could buyers use Facebook or Twitter to share ideas on negotiating the best price? Or, would Google+ be a better choice? Is there anyone in the world who can tell you what to do? How to proceed? No. As Reich says, professionals in the 21st century need to be able to experiment.

Successful experimentation is not throwing buckets of money at every crazy idea that enters your head. Instead, **experimentation** is making a reasoned analysis of an opportunity, envisioning potential solutions, evaluating those possibilities, and developing the most promising ones, consistent with the resources you have.

In this course, you will be asked to use products with which you have no familiarity. Those products might be Microsoft Excel or Access, or they might be features and functions of Blackboard that you've not used. Or, you may be asked to collaborate using Microsoft SharePoint or Google Drive. Will your instructor explain and show every feature of those products that you'll need? You should hope not. You should hope your instructor will leave it up to you to experiment, to envision new possibilities on your own, and experiment with those possibilities, consistent with the time you have available.

JOBS

Employment is the third factor that makes the Introduction to MIS course vitally important to you. During most of 2012, the U.S. unemployment rate averaged 8.3 percent over all ages and job categories. In November 2011, the *Wall Street Journal* reported that unemployment was 16.7 percent for those under 24.[3] Employment was better for college graduates than for those without degrees, but even college grads had a high rate of unemployment. Hope Yen, writing for the Associated Press in April 2012, stated that one in two college graduates are either unemployed or underemployed.[4] But, not in all job categories. If you have a degree in creative writing or European history, jobs may be hard to find. However, the situation is dramatically different for computer-related information systems jobs.

Spence and Hlatshwayo studied employment in the United States from 1990 to 2008.[5] They defined a *tradable job* as one that was not dependent on a particular location; this distinction

---

[3]Joe Light and Lauren Weber, "Generation Jobless," *Wall Street Journal,* November 7, 2011. http://online.wsj.com/article/SB10001424052970203733504577022110945459408.html

[4]http://news.yahoo.com/1-2-graduates-jobless-underemployed-140300522.html

[5]Michael Spence and Sandile Hlatshwayo. *The Evolving Structure of the American Economy and the Employment Challenge.* Council on Foreign Relations, New York, NY, 2011.

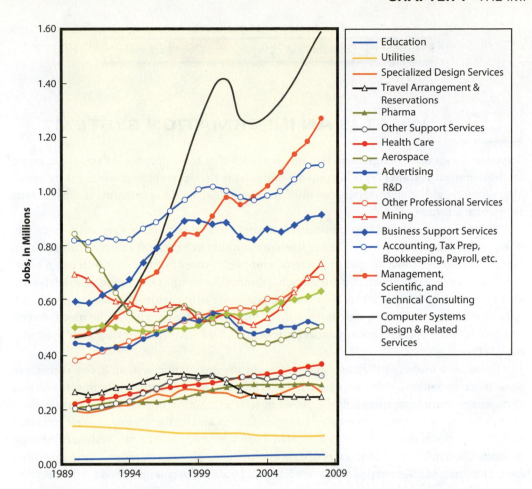

Figure 1-3
Job Growth over the Past Twenty Years

Source: From *The Evolving Structure of the American Economy and the Employment Challenge* by Michael Spence and Sandile Hlatshwayo. Copyright © 2011 by The Council on Foreign Relations Press. Reprinted with permission.

is important because such jobs can be outsourced overseas. As shown in Figure 1-3, Computer Systems Design and Related Services had the strongest growth of any job type in that category. The number of jobs dipped substantially after the dot-com bust in 2000; since 2003, however, job growth has not only recovered but has accelerated dramatically. While this category includes technical jobs like computer programmer and database administrator, it also includes nontechnical sales, support, and business management jobs as well. By the way, because this graph shows tradable jobs, it puts an end to the myth that all the good computer jobs have gone overseas. According to their data analysis, sourced from the U.S. Bureau of Labor Statistics, that simply has not happened (see Figure 1-3).

WHAT IS THE BOTTOM LINE?

The bottom line? This course is the most important course in the business school because

1. **It will give you the background you need to assess, evaluate, and apply emerging information systems technology to business.**
2. **It can give you the ultimate in job security—marketable skills—by helping you learn abstraction, systems thinking, collaboration, and experimentation.**
3. **It introduces you to careers that will have strong job growth.**

Finally, throughout your career you may from time to time be faced with ethical issues involving your use of information systems. To help you prepare for those challenges, in every chapter of this book we have included an *Ethics Guide*. These Guides will get you to start thinking about ethical dilemmas, which will help you clarify your values and make you ready to respond authentically to future ethical challenges.

With that introduction, let's get started!

See the guide on page 18 for more thoughts on how you might consider a MIS-related job.

Figure 1-4
Five Components of an
Information System

Five-Component Framework

Hardware	Software	Data	Procedures	People

WHAT IS AN INFORMATION SYSTEM?

The Ethics Guide in each
chapter of this book considers
the ethics of information
system use. The guides
challenge you to think deeply
about how to apply ethical
standards to unfamiliar
situations. Use these guides
to start interesting discussions
with your classmates. The
Ethics Guide on pages 16–17
considers the ethics of using
information that is not
intended for you.

A **system** is a group of components that interact to achieve some purpose. As you might guess, an **information system (IS)** is a group of components that interact to produce information. That sentence, although true, raises another question: What are these components that interact to produce information?

Figure 1-4 shows the **five-component framework** of computer hardware, software, data, procedures, and people. These five components are present in every information system—from the most simple to the most complex. For example, when you use a computer to write a class report, you are using hardware (the computer, storage disk, keyboard, and monitor), software (Word, WordPerfect, or some other word-processing program), data (the words, sentences, and paragraphs in your report), procedures (the methods you use to start the program, enter your report, print it, and save and back up your file), and people (you).

Consider a more complex example; say, an airline reservation system. It, too, consists of these five components, even though each one is far more complicated. The hardware consists of dozens or more computers linked together by telecommunications hardware. Further, hundreds of different programs coordinate communications among the computers, and still other programs perform the reservations and related services. Additionally, the system must store millions upon millions of characters of data about flights, customers, reservations, and other facts. Hundreds of different procedures are followed by airline personnel, travel agents, and customers. Finally, the information system includes people, not only the users of the system, but also those who operate and service the computers, those who maintain the data, and those who support the networks of computers.

These five components also mean that building information systems requires many different skills besides those of hardware technicians or computer programmers. See the guide starting on page 18 for more.

Before we move forward, note that we have defined an information system to include a computer. Some people would say that such a system is a **computer-based information system**. They would note that there are information systems that do not include computers, such as a calendar hanging on the wall outside of a conference room that is used to schedule the room's use. Such systems have been used by businesses for centuries. Although this point is true, we focus on *computer-based* information systems. To simplify and shorten the book, we will use the term *information system* as a synonym for *computer-based information system*.

WHAT IS MIS?

Today, there are thousands, even millions, of information systems in the world. Not all relate to business. In this textbook, we are concerned with **MIS**, or **management information systems**. MIS is the management and use of information systems that help businesses achieve their strategies. This definition has three key elements: *management and use, information systems*, and *strategies*. We just discussed *information systems*. Now consider *management and use* and *achieving strategies*.

Experiencing MIS

Information Systems and Online Dating

Source: 3Dstock/Shutterstock

"Why should I go to a bar and take the risk that nobody I'm interested in will be there during the 2 hours I'm there, when I can spend half an hour searching online for people that I am likely to be interested in? At worst, I've wasted half an hour. And at least I didn't have to blow-dry my hair."[1]

■ **Lori Gottlieb,** *The Atlantic,* **February 7, 2006, www.theatlantic.com/doc/200602u/online-dating**

Some online dating services match couples using a proprietary algorithm (method) based on a theory of relationships:

- **Chemistry (*www.chemistry.com*)**. Matches are made on the basis of a personality test developed by Dr. Helen Fisher.
- **eHarmony (*www.eHarmony.com*)**. Matches are made on the basis of a test entitled the "Compatibility Matching System" by Dr. Neil Clark Warren.
- **PerfectMatch (*www.PerfectMatch.com*)**. Matches made on the basis of a test based on Duet, a system developed by Dr. Pepper Schwartz.
- **Plenty of Fish (*www.pof.com*)**. Matches made on the basis of a chemistry predictor of five personality factors.

Other sites match people by limiting members to particular groups or interests:

Political interests:

- **Conservative Dates (*www.republicanpeoplemeet. com*)**—"Creating Relationships, Connecting Lives"
- **Liberal Hearts (*www.liberalhearts.com*)**—"Uniting Democrats, Greens, animal lovers & environmentalists who are like in mind and liberal in love."

Common social/economic interests:

- **Good Genes (*www.goodgenes.com*)**—"[Helping] Ivy Leaguers and similarly well-educated graduates and faculty find others with matching credentials."

- **MillionaireMatch (*www.millionairematch.com*)**—"Where you can add a touch of romance to success and achievement!"

Common activity interests:

- **Golfmates (*www.golfmates.com*)**—"The world's premier online dating service designed specifically for the golfing community."
- **FarmersOnly (*www.farmersonly.com*)**—"Because city folks just don't get it."
- **CowboyCowgirl (*www.cowboycowgirl.com*)**—"Join thousands of singles that share your love for the country way of life."
- **Single FireFighters (*www.singlefirefighters.com*)**—"The ONLY place to meet firefighters without calling 911!"
- **Asexual Pals (*www.asexualpals.com*)**—"Because there is so much more to life!"

INCLASS GROUP EXERCISE

1. Visit one of the proprietary method sites and one of the common interest sites.

2. Summarize the matching process that is used by each site.

3. Describe the revenue model of each site.

4. Using general terms, describe the need these sites have for:
   a. Hardware
   b. Software
   c. Data
   d. Procedures
   e. People

5. People sometimes stretch the truth, or even lie, on matching sites. Describe one innovative way that one of the two companies your team chose could use information systems to reduce the impact of this tendency. As you prepare your team's answer, keep the availability of nearly free data communications and data storage in mind.

6. Suppose that the company in your answer to step 5 has requested your team to implement your idea on reducing the impact of lying. Explain how having strong personal skills for each of Reich's four abilities (i.e., abstract thinking, systems thinking, experimentation, and collaboration) would enable each of you to be a better contributor to that team.

7. Working as a team, prepare a 3-minute verbal description of your answers to steps 5 and 6 that all of you could use in a job interview. Structure your presentation to illustrate that you have the four skills in step 6.

8. Deliver your answer to step 7 to the rest of the class.

---

[1]Lori Gottlieb, in "Logging On For Love" interview by Elizabeth Wasserman, The Atlantic, February 7, 2006.

MANAGEMENT AND USE OF INFORMATION SYSTEMS

The next element in our definition of MIS is the *management and use* of information systems. Here, we define management to mean develop, maintain, and adapt. Information systems do not pop up like mushrooms after a hard rain; they must be developed. They must also be maintained and, because business is dynamic, they must be adapted to new requirements.

You may be saying, "Wait a minute, I'm a finance (or accounting or management) major, not an information systems major. I don't need to know how to manage information systems." If you are saying that, you are like a lamb headed for shearing. Throughout your career, in whatever field you choose, information systems will be built for your use, and sometimes under your direction. To create an information system that meets your needs, you need to take an *active role* in that system's development. Even if you are not a programmer or a database designer or some other IS professional, you must take an active role in specifying the system's requirements and in managing the system's development project. Without active involvement on your part, it will only be good luck that causes the new system to meet your needs.

As a business professional, you are the person who understands business needs and requirements. If you want to apply social networking to your products, you are the one who knows how best to obtain customer responses. The technical people who build networks, the database designers who create the database, the IT people who configure the computers—none of these people know what is needed and whether the system you have is sufficient or whether it needs to be adapted to new requirements. You do!

In addition to management tasks, you will also have important roles to play in the *use* of information systems. Of course, you will need to learn how to employ the system to accomplish your goals. But you will also have important ancillary functions as well. For example, when using an information system, you will have responsibilities for protecting the security of the system and its data. You may also have tasks for backing up data. When the system fails (most do, at some point), you will have tasks to perform while the system is down as well as tasks to accomplish to help recover the system correctly and quickly.

ACHIEVING STRATEGIES

The last part of the definition of MIS is that information systems exist to help businesses *achieve their strategies*. First, realize that this statement hides an important fact: Businesses themselves do not "do" anything. A business is not alive, and it cannot act. It is the people within a business who sell, buy, design, produce, finance, market, account, and manage. So, information systems exist to help people who work in a business to achieve the strategies of that business.

Information systems are not created for the sheer joy of exploring technology. They are not created so that the company can be "modern" or so that the company can show it has a social networking presence on the Web. They are not created because the information systems department thinks it needs to be created or because the company is "falling behind the technology curve."

This point may seem so obvious that you might wonder why we mention it. Every day, however, some business somewhere is developing an information system for the wrong reasons. Right now, somewhere in the world, a company is deciding to create a Facebook presence for the sole reason that "every other business has one." This company is not asking questions such as:

- "What is the purpose of our Facebook page?"
- "What is it going to do for us?"

- "What is our policy for employees' contributions?"
- "What should we do about critical customer reviews?"
- "Are the costs of maintaining the page sufficiently offset by the benefits?"

But that company should ask those questions! Chapter 3 addresses the relationship between information systems and strategy in more depth. Chapter 8 addresses social media and strategy specifically.

Again, MIS is the development and use of information systems that help businesses achieve their strategies. Already you should be realizing that there is much more to this class than buying a computer, working with a spreadsheet, or creating a Web page.

 ## WHY IS THE DIFFERENCE BETWEEN INFORMATION TECHNOLOGY AND INFORMATION SYSTEMS IMPORTANT TO YOU?

Information technology and information systems are two closely related terms, but they are different. **Information technology (IT)**[4] refers to the products, methods, inventions, and standards that are used for the purpose of producing information. IT pertains to the hardware, software, and data components. As stated in the previous section, an *information system (IS)* is an assembly of hardware, software, data, procedures, and people that produces information.

Information technology drives the development of new information systems. Advances in information technology have taken the computer industry from the days of punched cards to the Internet, and such advances will continue to take the industry to the next stages and beyond.

Why does this difference matter to you? Knowing the difference between IT and IS can help you avoid a common mistake: Do not try to buy an IS; you cannot do it.

You can buy IT; you can buy or lease hardware, you can license programs and databases, and you can even obtain predesigned procedures. Ultimately, however, it is *your* people who execute those procedures to employ that new IT.

For any new system, you will always have training tasks (and costs), you will always have the need to overcome employees' resistance to change, and you will always need to manage the employees as they use the new system. Hence, you can buy IT, but you cannot buy IS.

Consider a simple example. Suppose your organization decides to develop a Facebook page. Facebook provides the hardware and programs, the database structures, and standard procedures. You, however, provide the data to fill your portion of the Facebook database, and you must extend Facebook's standard procedures with your own procedures for keeping that data current. Those procedures need to provide, for example, a means to review your page's content regularly and a means to remove content that is judged inappropriate. Furthermore, you need to train employees on how to follow those procedures and manage those employees to ensure that they do.

Managing your own Facebook page is as simple an IS as exists. Larger, more comprehensive information systems that involve many, even dozens, of departments and thousands of employees require considerable work. Again, you can buy IT, but you can never buy an IS!

---

[4]You may see the term ICT, for information and communications technology, used synonymously with IT. ICT just emphasizes the important role of communications hardware. ICT is more common in academics; IT is more common in industry.

WHAT IS YOUR ROLE IN IS SECURITY?

As you have learned, information systems create value. However, they also create risk. For example, Amazon.com maintains credit card data on millions of customers and has the responsibility to protect that data. If Amazon.com's security system were breached and that credit card data stolen, Amazon.com would incur serious losses—not only lost business, but also potentially staggering liability losses. Because of the importance of information security, we will consider it throughout this textbook. Additionally, Chapter 12 is devoted to security.

However, you have a role in security that is too important for us to wait until you read that chapter. Like all information systems, security systems have the five components, including people. Thus, every security system ultimately depends on the behavior of its users. If the users do not take security seriously, if they do not follow security procedures, then the hardware, software, and data components of the security system are wasted expense. So, before we proceed further, we will address how you should create and use a strong password, which is an essential component of computer security.

Almost all security systems use user names and passwords. As a user of information systems in a business organization, you will be instructed to create a strong password and to protect it. *It is vitally important for you to do so.* You should already be using such passwords at your university. (According to a 2010 article in the *New York Times*,[5] 20 percent of people use an easily guessed password like 12345. Don't be part of that 20 percent!)

STRONG PASSWORDS

So what is a strong password, and how do you create one? Microsoft, a company that has many reasons to promote effective security, defines a **strong password** as one with the following characteristics:

- Has ten or more characters, twelve is even better
- Does not contain your user name, real name, or company name
- Does not contain a complete dictionary word in any language
- Is different from previous passwords you have used
- Contains both upper- and lowercase letters, numbers, and special characters (such as ˜ ! @; # $ % ^; &; * ( ) _ +; – =; { } | [ ] \ : " ; ' <; >;?, . /)

Examples of good passwords are:

- Qw37^T1bb?at
- 3B47qq5!7b

The problem with such passwords is that they are nearly impossible to remember. And the last thing you want to do is write your password on a piece of paper and keep it near the workstation where you use it. Never do that!

One technique for creating memorable, strong passwords is to base them on the first letter of the words in a phrase. The phrase could be the title of a song or the first line of a poem or one based on some fact about your life. For example, you might take the phrase, "I was born in Rome, New York, before 1990." Using the first letters from that phrase and substituting the character for the word *before*, you create the password *IwbiR,NY<1990*.

---

[5]Ashley Vance, "If Your Password Is 123456, Just Make It HackMe," *New York Times*, January 21, 2010, p. A1. Available at www.nytimes.com/2010/01/21/technology/21password.html?hp

That's an acceptable password, but it would be better if all of the numbers were not placed on the end. So, you might try the phrase, "I was born at 3:00 AM in Rome, New York." That phrase yields the password *Iwba3:00AMiR,NY*, which is a strong password that is easily remembered.

PASSWORD ETIQUETTE

Once you have created a strong password, you need to protect it with proper behavior. Proper password etiquette is one of the marks of a business professional. Never write down your password, and do not share it with others. Never ask others for their passwords, and never give your password to someone else.

But what if you need someone else's password? Suppose, for example, you ask someone to help you with a problem on your computer. You sign on to an information system, and for some reason you need to enter that other person's password. In this case, say to the other person, "We need your password," and then get out of your chair, offer your keyboard to the other person, and look away while he or she enters the password. Among professionals working in organizations that take security seriously, this little "do-si-do" move—one person getting out of the way so that another person can enter a password—is common and accepted.

If someone asks for your password, do not give it out. Instead, get up, go over to that person's machine, and enter your password yourself. Stay present while your password is in use, and ensure that your account is logged out at the end of the activity. No one should mind or be offended in any way when you do this. It is the mark of a professional.

How does the **knowledge** in this chapter help **you?**

It's too late for Jennifer, at least at GearUp. However, it's not too late for you, and it's not too late for Jennifer at her next job. So, what are the takeaways from this chapter?

First, learn Reich's four key skills: abstract thinking, systems thinking, experimentation, and collaboration. And practice, practice, practice them. This class is the best one in the b-school for teaching those skills, so engage in it. As you study and perform assignments, ask yourself how your activity relates to those four abilities and endeavor to improve your proficiency at them.

Second, realize that the future belongs to businesspeople who can creatively envision new applications of information systems and technology. You don't have to be an IS major (though it is a very good major with excellent job prospects), but you should be able to innovate the use of MIS into the discipline in which you do major. How can management, marketing, accounting, production, and so on take advantage of the benefits of Moore's Law?

Next, learn the components of an IS and understand that every business professional needs to take an active role in new information systems development. Such systems are created for your needs and require your involvement. Know the difference between IT and IS. Finally, learn, now, how to create a strong password and begin using such passwords and proper password etiquette.

We're just getting started; there's lots more to come that can benefit Jennifer (in her next job) and you!

Ethics Guide

Ethics of Information from Misdirected Data

Consider the following situations:

Situation A: Suppose you are buying a condo and you know that at least one other party is bidding against you. While agonizing over your best strategy, you stop at a local Starbucks. As you sip your latte, you overhear a conversation at the table next to yours. Three people are talking so loudly that it is difficult to ignore them, and you soon realize that they are the real estate agent and the couple who is competing for the condo you want. They are preparing their offer. Should you listen to their conversation? If you do, do you use the information you hear to your advantage?

Situation B: Consider the same situation from a different perspective—instead of overhearing the conversation, suppose you receive that same information in an email. Perhaps an administrative assistant at the agent's office confuses you and the other customer and mistakenly sends you the terms of the other party's offer. Do you read that email? If so, do you use the information that you read to your advantage?

Situation C: Suppose that you sell computer software. In the midst of a sensitive price negotiation, your customer accidentally sends you an internal email that contains the maximum amount that the customer can pay for your software. Do you read that email? Do you use that information to guide your negotiating strategy? What do you do if your customer discovers that the email may have reached you and asks, "Did you read my email?" How do you answer?

Situation D: Suppose a friend mistakenly sends you an email that contains sensitive personal medical data. Further, suppose you read the email before you know what you're reading and you're embarrassed to learn something very personal that truly is none of your business. Your friend asks you, "Did you read that email?" How do you respond?

Situation E: Finally, suppose that you work as a network administrator and your position allows you unrestricted access to the mailing lists for your company. Assume that you have the skill to insert your email address into any company mailing list without anyone knowing about it. You insert your address into several lists and, consequently, begin to receive confidential email that no one intended for you to see. One of those emails indicates that your best friend's department is about to be eliminated and all of its personnel fired. Do you forewarn your friend?

1. Consider the questions in situations A and B. Do your answers differ? Does the medium by which the information is obtained make a difference? Is it easier to avoid reading an email than it is to avoid hearing a conversation? If so, does that difference matter?

2. Consider the questions in situations B and C. Do your answers differ? In situation B, the information is for your personal gain; in C, the information is for both your personal and your organization's gain. Does this difference matter? How do you respond when asked if you have read the email?

3. Consider the questions in situations C and D. Do your answers differ? Would you lie in one case and not in the other? Why or why not?

4. Consider the question in situation E. What is the essential difference between situations A through D and situation E? Suppose you had to justify your behavior in situation E. How would you argue? Do you believe your own argument?

5. In situations A through D, if you access the information you have done nothing illegal. You were the passive recipient. Even for item E, although you undoubtedly violated your company's employment policies, you most likely did not violate the law. So for this discussion, assume that all of these actions are legal.

a. What is the difference between legal and ethical? Look up both words in a dictionary, and explain how they differ.

b. Make the argument that business is competitive and that if something is legal, then it is acceptable to do it if it helps to further your goals.

c. Make the argument that it is never appropriate to do something unethical.

6. Summarize your beliefs about proper conduct when you receive misdirected information.

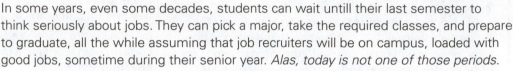

Guide

Five-Component Careers

In some years, even some decades, students can wait untill their last semester to think seriously about jobs. They can pick a major, take the required classes, and prepare to graduate, all the while assuming that job recruiters will be on campus, loaded with good jobs, sometime during their senior year. *Alas, today is not one of those periods.*

In the current employment situation, you need to be proactive and aggressive in your job search. Think about it: you will be spending one-third of your waking life in your job. One of the best things you can do for yourself is to begin to think seriously about your career prospects, now. You don't want to find yourself working as a barista after four years of business school, unless, of course, you're planning on starting the next Starbucks.

So, start here. Are you interested in a career in MIS? At this point, you don't know enough to know, but, Figure 1-3 should catch your attention. With job growth like that, in a category of jobs that is net of outsourcing, you should at least ponder whether there is career for you in IS and related services.

But, what does that mean? If you go to the U.S. Bureau of Labor Statistics, you can find that there are over a million computer programmers in the United States today, and that there are more than 600,000 systems analysts. You probably have some notion of what a programmer does, but you don't yet know what a system analyst is. Examine the five components in Figure 1-4, however, and you can glean some idea. Programmers work primarily with the software component, and systems analysts work with the entire system, with all five components. So, as a system analyst, you work with businesses to determine what the organization needs from an information system, and then with technical people (and others) to help develop that system. You work as a cultural broker; translating the culture of technology into the culture of business, and the reverse.

	Hardware	Software	Data	Procedures	People
Sales & Marketing	Vendors (IBM Cisco, etc.)	Vendors (Microsoft, Oracle, etc.)	Vendors (Acxiom, Google, etc.)	Vendors (SAP, Infor, Oracle)	Recruiters (Robert Half, Lucas Group)
Support	Vendors Internal MIS	Vendors Internal MIS	Database administration Security	Vendor and Internal Customer support	Customer support Training
Development	Computer Engineering Internal MIS	Application programmer Quality test Engineer	Data modeler Database design	Business process management Process re-engineering	Training, Internal MIS recruiting
Management	Internal MIS	Internal MIS	Data administration	Project management	Technical management
Consulting and Training	Pre- and post-sale support. Development and project management. Training for users and developers.				

Fortunately for you, many interesting jobs are not captured by the bureau's data. Why fortunate? Because you can use what you're learning in this course to identify and obtain jobs that other students may not think about, or even know about. If so, you've gained a competitive advantage.

The figure above provides a framework for thinking about careers in an unconventional way. As you can see, there are technical jobs in MIS, but there are fascinating, challenging, and high-paying, nontechnical ones as well. Consider for example, professional sales. Suppose you have the job of selling enterprise-class software to the Mayo Clinic. You will sell to intelligent, highly motivated professionals, with tens of millions of dollars to spend. Or, suppose you are working for the Mayo Clinic, on the receiving end of that sales pitch. How will you spend your tens of millions? You will need knowledge of your business, and you will also need to understand enough technology to ask intelligent questions, and interpret the responses.

Give this some thought by answering the boxed questions, even if they aren't assigned for a grade!

? DISCUSSION QUESTIONS

1. What does the phrase *in a category of jobs that is net of outsourcing* mean? Reread the discussion of Figure 1-3 if you're not certain. Why is this important to you?

2. Examine the Five-Component Careers figure and choose the row that seems most relevant to your interests and abilities. Describe a job in each component column of that row. If you are uncertain, Google the terms in the cells of that row.

3. For each job in your answer to question 2, describe what you think are the three most important skills and abilities for that job.

4. For each job in your answer to question 2, describe one innovative action that you can take this year to increase your employment prospects.

ACTIVE REVIEW

Use this Active Review to verify that you understand the ideas and concepts that answer the chapter's study questions.

Q1 WHY IS INTRODUCTION TO MIS THE MOST IMPORTANT CLASS IN THE BUSINESS SCHOOL?

Define *Moore's Law* and explain why its consequences are important to business professionals today. State how business professionals should relate to emerging information technology. Give the text's definition of *job security* and use Reich's enumeration to explain how this course will help you attain that security. Summarize three reasons why this course is the most important in the business school.

Q2 WHAT IS AN INFORMATION SYSTEM?

List the components of an information system. Explain how knowledge of these components guides business professionals (not just techies) as they build information systems.

Q3 WHAT IS MIS?

List the three elements in the definition of MIS. Why does a nontechnical business professional need to understand all three? Why are information systems developed? Why is part of this definition misleading?

Q4 WHY IS THE DIFFERENCE BETWEEN INFORMATION TECHNOLOGY AND INFORMATION SYSTEMS IMPORTANT TO YOU?

Define *IT*. Does IT include IS, or does IS include IT? Why does technology, by itself, not constitute an information system? What does ICT stand for? How is it different from IT?

Q5 WHAT IS YOUR ROLE IN IS SECURITY?

Summarize the importance of security to corporations such as Amazon.com. Define *strong password*. Explain an easy way to create and remember a strong password. Under what circumstances should you give someone else your password?

How does the knowledge in this chapter help you?

Summarize how mastery of Reich's four skills will serve you in your career. Explain why every business professional needs to learn the basics of IS.

KEY TERMS AND CONCEPTS

Abstract reasoning 7
Collaboration 7
Computer-based information system 10
Experimentation 8
Five-component framework 10
Information system (IS) 10
Information technology (IT) 13
Management information systems (MIS) 10
Moore's Law 5
Strong password 14
System 10
Systems thinking 7

USING YOUR KNOWLEDGE

1. Do you agree that this course is the most important course in the business school? Isn't accounting more important? No business can exist without accounting. Or, isn't management more important? After all, if you can manage people why do you need to know how to innovate with technology? You can hire others to think innovatively for you.

   On the other hand, what single factor will affect all business more than IS? And, isn't knowledge and proficiency with IS and IT key to future employment and success?

Give serious thought to this question and write a single page argument as to why you agree or disagree.

2. Describe three to five personal goals for this class. None of these goals should include anything about your GPA. Be as specific as possible, and make the goals personal to your major, interests, and career aspirations. Assume that you are going to evaluate yourself on these goals at the end of the quarter or semester. The more specific you make these goals, the easier it will be to perform the evaluation.

3. Consider costs of a system in light of the five components: costs to buy and maintain the hardware; costs to develop or acquire licenses to the software programs and costs to maintain them; costs to design databases and fill them with data; costs of developing procedures and keeping them current; and finally, human costs both to develop and use the system.

   a. Over the lifetime of a system, many experts believe that the single most expensive component is people. Does this belief seem logical to you? Explain why you agree or disagree.

   b. Consider a poorly developed system that does not meet its defined requirements. The needs of the business do not go away, but they do not conform themselves to the characteristics of the poorly built system. Therefore, something must give. Which component picks up the slack when the hardware and software programs do not work correctly? What does this say about the cost of a

poorly designed system? Consider both direct money costs as well as intangible personnel costs.

   c. What implications do you, as a future business manager, recognize after answering parts a and b? What does this say about the need for your involvement in requirements and other aspects of systems development? Who eventually will pay the costs of a poorly developed system? Against which budget will those costs accrue?

4. The U.S. Department of Labor publishes descriptions of jobs, educational requirements, and the outlook for many jobs and professions. Go to their site at *www.bls.gov* and answer the following questions:

   a. Search for the job title *systems analyst*. Describe what such people do. Is this a job that interests you? What education do you need? What is the median pay and job growth projection? Why or why not?

   b. Click the Similar Occupations link at the bottom of this page. Find another job that you might want. Describe that job, median salary, and educational requirements.

   c. The BLS data is comprehensive, but it is not up to date for fast-changing disciplines such as IS. For example, one very promising career today is social media marketing, a job that does not appear in the BLS data. Describe one way that you might learn employment prospects for such emerging job categories.

   d. Considering your answer to question c, describe an IS-related job that would be the best match for your skills and interests. Describe how you can learn if that job exists.

COLLABORATION EXERCISE 1

Before you start this exercise, read Chapter Extensions 1 and 2, which describe collaboration techniques as well as tools for managing collaboration tasks. In particular, consider using Google Drive, Google+, Windows Live SkyDrive, Microsoft SharePoint, or some other collaboration tool.

Collaborate with a group of fellow students to answer the following questions. For this exercise do not meet face to face. Coordinate all of your work using email and email attachments, only. Your answers should reflect the thinking of the entire group, and not just one or two individuals.

1. Abstract reasoning.
   a. Define *abstract reasoning*, and explain why it is an important skill for business professionals.

   b. Explain how a list of items in inventory and their quantity on hand is an abstraction of a physical inventory.

   c. Give three other examples of abstractions commonly used in business.

   d. Explain how Jennifer failed to demonstrate effective abstract-reasoning skills.

   e. Can people increase their abstract-reasoning skills? If so, how? If not, why not?

2. Systems thinking.
   a. Define *systems thinking*, and explain why it is an important skill for business professionals.

   b. Explain how you would use systems thinking to explain why Moore's Law caused a farmer to dig up a field of pulpwood trees. Name each of the elements in the system and explain their relationships to each other.

   c. Give three other examples of the use of systems thinking with regard to consequences of Moore's Law.

   d. Explain how Jennifer failed to demonstrate effective systems-thinking skills.

   e. Can people improve their systems-thinking skills? If so, how? If not, why not?

3. Collaboration.

   a. Define *collaboration*, and explain why it is an important skill for business professionals.

   b. Explain how you are using collaboration to answer these questions. Describe what is working with regard to your group's process and what is not working.

   c. Is the work product of your team better than any one of you could have done separately? If not, your collaboration is ineffective. If that is the case, explain why.

   d. Does the fact that you cannot meet face to face hamper your ability to collaborate? If so, how?

   e. Explain how Jennifer failed to demonstrate effective collaboration skills.

   f. Can people increase their collaboration skills? If so, how? If not, why not?

4. Experimentation.

   a. Define *experimentation*, and explain why it is an important skill for business professionals.

   b. Explain several creative ways you could use experimentation to answer this question.

   c. How does the fear of failure influence your willingness to engage in any of the ideas you identified in part b?

   d. Explain how Jennifer failed to demonstrate effective experimentation skills.

   e. Can people increase their willingness to take risks? If so, how? If not, why not?

5. Job security.

   a. State the text's definition of *job security*.

   b. Evaluate the text's definition of job security. Is it effective? If you think not, offer a better definition of job security.

   c. As a team, do you agree that improving your skills on the four dimensions in Collaboration Exercises 1 through 4 will increase your job security?

   d. Do you think technical skills (accounting proficiency, financial analysis proficiency, etc.) provide job security? Why or why not? Do you think students in 1990 would have answered this differently? Why or why not?

CASE STUDY 1

The Amazon of Innovation

On November 29, 2010, Amazon.com customers ordered 13.7 million items worldwide, an average of 158 items per second. On its peak order-fulfillment day, Amazon shipped over 9 million units, and over the entire 2010 holiday season it shipped to 178 countries.[6] Such performance is only possible because of Amazon's innovative use of information systems. Some of its major innovations are listed in Figure 1-5.

You may think of Amazon as simply an online retailer, and that is indeed where the company achieved most of its success. To do this, Amazon had to build enormous supporting infrastructure—just imagine the information systems and fulfillment facilities needed to ship 9 million items on a single day. That infrastructure, however, is only needed during the busy holiday season. Most of the year, Amazon is left with excess infrastructure capacity. Starting in 2000, Amazon began to lease some of that capacity to other companies. In the process, it played a key role in the creation of what are termed *cloud*

services, which you will learn about in Chapter 4. For now, just think of cloud services as computer resources somewhere out in the Internet that are leased on flexible terms. Today, Amazon's business lines can be grouped into three major categories:

- Online retailing
- Order fulfillment
- Cloud services, including Kindles and online media

Consider each.

Amazon created the business model for online retailing. It began as an online bookstore, but every year since 1998 it has added new product categories. In 2011, the company sold goods in 29 product categories. Undoubtedly, there will be more by the time you read this.

Amazon is involved in all aspects of online retailing. It sells its own inventory. It incentivizes you, via the Associates program, to sell its inventory as well. Or, it will help you sell your inventory within its product pages or via one of its

---

[6]Amazon, "Third-Generation Kindle Now the Bestselling Product of All Time on Amazon Worldwide," News release, December 27, 2010. Available at http://phx.corporate-ir.net/phoenix.zhtml?c=176060&p=irol-newsArticle&ID=1510745&highlight= (accessed June 2011).

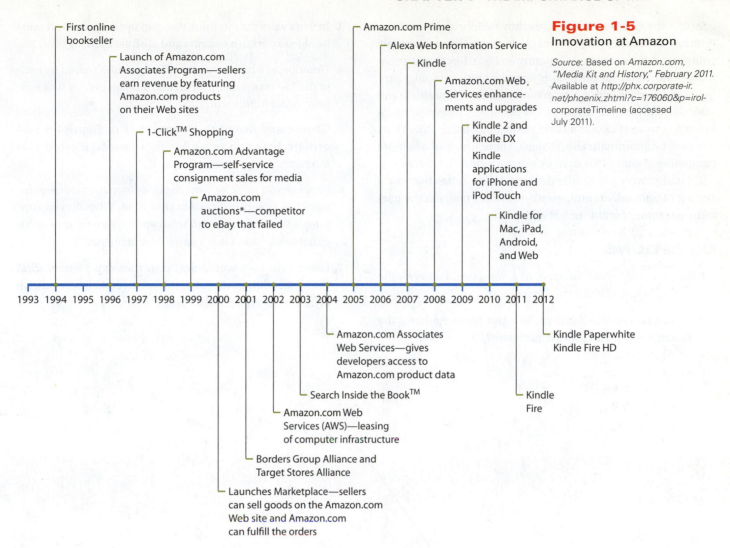

Figure 1-5
Innovation at Amazon

Source: Based on *Amazon.com*, "Media Kit and History," February 2011. Available at *http://phx.corporate-ir. net/phoenix.zhtml?c=176060&p=irol-corporateTimeline* (accessed July 2011).

Timeline labels above the line (1993–2012):
- First online bookseller
- Launch of Amazon.com Associates Program—sellers earn revenue by featuring Amazon.com products on their Web sites
- 1-Click™ Shopping
- Amazon.com Advantage Program—self-service consignment sales for media
- Amazon.com auctions*—competitor to eBay that failed
- Amazon.com Prime
- Alexa Web Information Service
- Kindle
- Amazon.com Web Services enhancements and upgrades
- Kindle 2 and Kindle DX / Kindle applications for iPhone and iPod Touch
- Kindle for Mac, iPad, Android, and Web

Timeline labels below the line:
- Amazon.com Associates Web Services—gives developers access to Amazon.com product data
- Search Inside the Book™
- Amazon.com Web Services (AWS)—leasing of computer infrastructure
- Borders Group Alliance and Target Stores Alliance
- Launches Marketplace—sellers can sell goods on the Amazon.com Web site and Amazon.com can fulfill the orders
- Kindle Paperwhite / Kindle Fire HD
- Kindle Fire

consignment venues. Online auctions are the major aspect of online sales in which Amazon does not participate. It tried auctions in 1999, but it could never make inroads against eBay.[7]

Today, it's hard to remember how much of what we take for granted was pioneered by Amazon. "Customers who bought this, also bought that;" online customer reviews; customer ranking of customer reviews; books lists; Look Inside the Book; automatic free shipping for certain orders or frequent customers; and Kindle books and devices were all novel concepts when Amazon introduced them.

Amazon's retailing business operates on very thin margins. Products are usually sold at a discount from the stated retail price, and 2-day shipping is free for Amazon Prime members (who pay an annual fee of $80). How do they do it? For one, Amazon drives its employees incredibly hard. Former employees claim the hours are long, the pressure is severe, and

the workload is heavy. But what else? It comes down to Moore's Law and the innovative use of nearly free data processing, storage, and communication.

In addition to online retailing, Amazon also sells order fulfillment services. You can ship your inventory to an Amazon warehouse and access Amazon's information systems just as if they were yours. Using technology known as Web services, (discussed in Chapter 6), your order processing information systems can directly integrate, over the Web, with Amazon's inventory, fulfillment, and shipping applications. Your customers need not know that Amazon played any role at all. You can also sell that same inventory using Amazon's retail sales applications.

Amazon Web Services (AWS) allows organizations to lease time on computer equipment in very flexible ways. Amazon's Elastic Cloud 2(EC2) enables organizations to expand and

[7]For a fascinating glimpse of this story from someone inside the company, see "Early Amazon: Auctions" at http://glinden.blogspot.com/2006/04/early-amazon-auctions.html (accessed August 2012).

contract the computer resources they need within minutes. Amazon has a variety of payment plans, and it is possible to buy computer time for less than a penny an hour. Key to this capability is the ability for the leasing organization's computer programs to interface with Amazon's to automatically scale up and scale down the resources leased. For example, if a news site publishes a story that causes a rapid ramp-up of traffic, that news site can, programmatically, request, configure, and use more computing resources for an hour, a day, a month, whatever.

Finally, with the Kindle devices, Amazon has become a vendor of both tablets and, even more importantly in the long term, a vendor of online music and video.

QUESTIONS

1. In what ways does Amazon, as a company, evidence the willingness and ability to collaborate?

2. In what ways does Amazon, as a company, evidence the willingness and ability to experiment?

3. In what ways do you think the employees at Amazon must be able to perform systems and abstract thinking?

4. Describe, at a high level, the principal roles played by each of the five components of an information system that supports order fulfillment.

5. Choose any five of the innovations in Figure 1-5 and explain how you think Moore's Law facilitated that innovation.

6. Suppose you work for Amazon or a company that takes innovation as seriously as Amazon does. What do you suppose is the likely reaction to an employee who says to his or her boss, "But, I don't know how to do that!"?

7. Using your own words and your own experience, what skills and abilities do you think you need to have to thrive at an organization like Amazon?

chapter 2

Business Processes, Information Systems, and Information

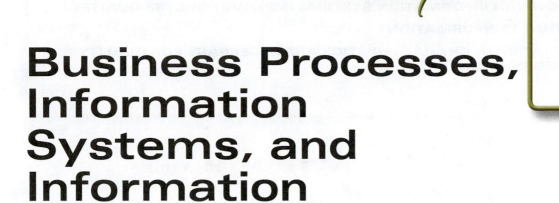

"Drew, what's your hurry?" Addison Lee jumps out of the way as Drew comes barreling out of his office.

"Workload, Addison, workload. They've given me the operations responsibility for *all* the soccer sales. I've got events coming out of my ears!" Drew sounds exhausted.

"All the soccer sales events? Why?" Addison looks closely at him and realizes that he really is exhausted.

"All part of getting our operations costs down. You know, like Kelly's always saying, 'we've got to have the lowest prices on the Net.'"

"So . . . "

"So, to make any money at those low prices, we've got to get costs down. We can negotiate better deals with the vendors, but that only goes so far. After that, we take it out of our hide."

"Ouch."

"Yeah, and these people at General Sports are driving me nuts!"

"General Sports? They're always a problem. I can't tell you how much time I've wasted with them. I had an event completely negotiated, and they pulled the plug at the last minute." Addison has fire in her voice.

"You did? How come nobody told me?" Drew's surprised.

"I don't know. Why didn't you ask me?"

"Well, I didn't know you'd been working with them. I wonder who else has . . . "

"Sarah had much the same experience as I did. Check with her."

"I will. But, really, even if I knew ahead of time about your problems, I doubt it would help."

STUDY QUESTIONS

Q1 WHY DOES THE GEARUP TEAM NEED TO UNDERSTAND BUSINESS PROCESSES?

Q2 WHAT IS A BUSINESS PROCESS?

Q3 HOW CAN INFORMATION SYSTEMS IMPROVE PROCESS QUALITY?

Q4 WHAT IS INFORMATION?

Q5 WHAT DATA CHARACTERISTICS ARE NECESSARY FOR QUALITY INFORMATION?

How does the **knowledge** in this chapter help **you?**

"No?"

"No. Nobody ever asks operations before they start negotiating their deal. They think that if they can buy soccer shoes for $14 and sell them for $24, we've made 10 bucks."

"Haven't we?"

"Yes and no. I mean we've made 10 bucks a pair on the surface, but having to deal with General is twice as expensive for operations as dealing with, say, San Diego Sports."

"Yeah, they're great to work with, aren't they?"

"I'm telling you, any deal with General is not making us the money Kelly thinks it is. Not by the time you factor in all the operational expenses of dealing with those jerks."

"I never thought of it like that, but I guess you're right."

"You buyers ought to change the way you pick these vendors. Sure, the products and their prices matter, but you should think about our costs, too."

"How would we do that? Where's the data?" Addison sounds intrigued, but skeptical.

"How would we do that? Where's the data?"

Q1 WHY DOES THE GEARUP TEAM NEED TO UNDERSTAND BUSINESS PROCESSES?

Kelly, Drew, Addison, Sarah, and the rest of the team at GearUp need to understand business processes, and, even more important, they need to know how to improve business processes. Judging from Drew's frustration in this conversation, they need a better way of sharing vendor data, which will mean changes to their existing business processes, as you are about to learn.

Addison tells Drew he should ask her and Sarah for data about vendors. While such conversations might help Drew with problems concerning General Sports, the organization needs more. What happens when personnel change? Perhaps one of those three is promoted, or

In all meetings, it is important to demonstrate empathetic thinking. The Ethics Guide on pages 38–39 discusses the difference between empathetic and egocentric thinking.

GearUp goes through major growth and hires many new employees? And should every buyer be expected to know whom in operations to contact to warn about problematic vendors?

Furthermore, while hallway conversations might avoid a problem here and there, it doesn't help GearUp negotiate with its vendors. If GearUp can record the frequency and severity of its vendor problems, then buyers can use this data to their advantage during negotiations. Or, they may decide to avoid working with the most problematic vendors. Finally, it might be that Drew and Addison are only having temporary bad luck. They think GearUp has a systematic problem, but without data, it will be hard to know. Kelly, for example, will need evidence, not a few stories, to allocate resources for fixing this problem.

Obtaining that data is possible and most likely very desirable. To do so in a systematic way, in a way so that every buyer and every operations manager can benefit, GearUp needs first to understand its existing processes and to identify the problems they have. Then, they need to design improved processes.

We will use the example at GearUp to help you understand the nature of business processes and how information systems support them. We begin by describing and documenting GearUp's procurement and sales process and then, in the next question, we will show how an information system can help GearUp to record problems and thus better negotiate with or avoid its problematic vendors.

WHAT IS A BUSINESS PROCESS?

A **business process** is a network of activities for accomplishing a business function. Companies have business processes for buying inventory, for selling to customers, for managing inventory, for paying bills, for collecting revenue and for literally, hundreds of other business functions. Before we consider one of GearUp's processes, you should first understand GearUp's relationship to its vendors and customers.

HOW GEARUP WORKS

Vendors agree to sell a certain quantity of items to GearUp at very low prices. Typically these items are discontinued, or out of season or out of style, or overstocked. For example, a vendor might sell GearUp thousands of soccer balls at the end of the summer (Figure 2-1), or hundreds of last year's tennis dresses. Such vendors have dozens of business processes for deciding what

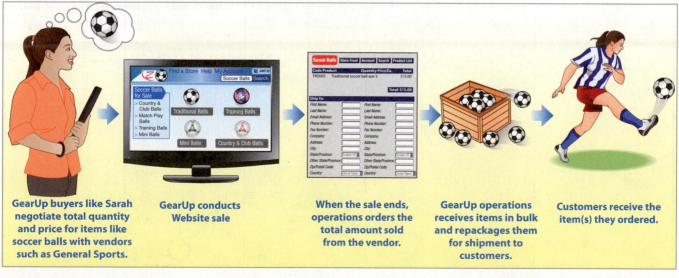

Figure 2-1
GearUp Ordering Activities

items and quantities to sell, what price, and to support shipping, billing, and revenue collection. We will not be concerned with those vendor processes in this chapter.

Once GearUp has negotiated the price and the number of items the vendor will sell at that price, it then conducts an auction on its Web site. Any bidder must register with GearUp before bidding on an item. GearUp uses customer email addresses to solicit bids for its auction items. (You can see an example of such a site in action by visiting *www.zulily.com*.)

After GearUp closes an auction, it orders the total number of items it sold, which might be less than the maximum the vendor agreed to provide. GearUp then receives those items in bulk from the vendor, and repackages them in the quantities ordered by its customers and ships them to the customers.

THE EXISTING GEARUP PROCESS

Figure 2-2 shows a diagram of the existing GearUp process. This diagram, which is a model or an abstraction of GearUp's activities, is constructed using the symbols of **business process**

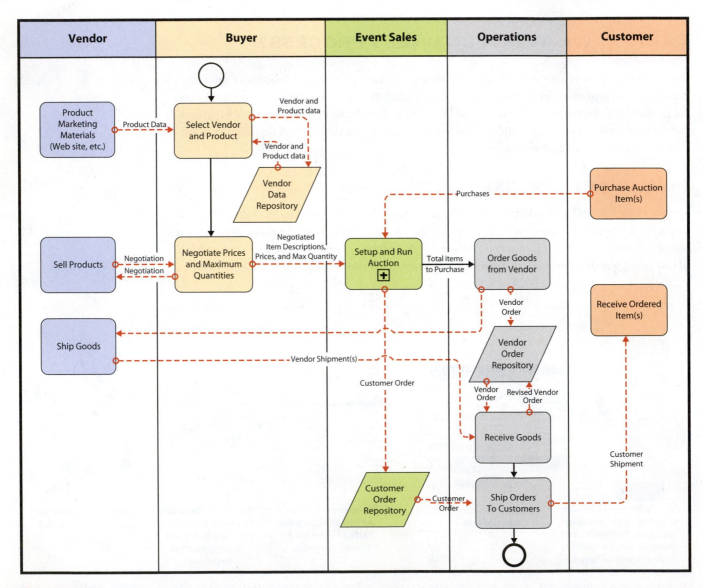

Figure 2-2
Existing GearUp Business Process Using BPMN

modeling notation or **BPMN**. This notation is an international standard for creating business process diagrams.[1] A key to these symbols is shown in Figure 2-3.

Figure 2-2 is organized in what is called **swimlane format**, which is a graphical arrangement in which all of the activities for a given role are shown in a single vertical or horizontal lane. Each swimlane has **activities**, which are specific tasks that need to be accomplished as part of the process. A **role** is a subset of the activities in a business process that is performed by an **actor**, which is a person, group, department, or organization. Figure 2-2 shows the roles of Vendor, Buyer, Event Sales, Operations, and Customer.

Notice that we do not write people's names such as Addison or Sarah at the top of swimlane, but rather we write the name of the role. This is because a given role may be fulfilled by many people, and also because a given employee may play many roles. Furthermore, over time, the organization may change the people who are assigned a given role. In some cases, a role can be fulfilled by an information system.

According to the BPMN standard, the start of a business process is symbolized by a circle having a narrow border. The end of a business process is symbolized by a circle having a thick border. So, in Figure 2-2, the process starts with the Buyer role, or we can also say that a Buyer starts the process.

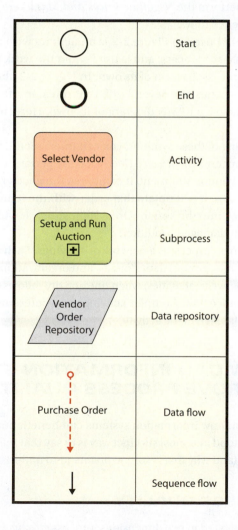

Figure 2-3
Process Symbols (BPMN Standard)

---

[1]These symbols are included with Microsoft's Visio Professional edition. If your university is a member of Microsoft DreamSpark (formerly known as the Microsoft Academic Alliance), you can obtain a license-free copy of Visio and use it to make your own BPMN diagrams.

Activities within a business process are shown in rectangles. The first activity for the Buyer role is *Select a Vendor and Product*. According to this diagram, buyers use the Internet to search for vendors and products to include in an auction. They also obtain vendor and product data from the Vendor Data Repository. A **repository** is a collection of data that is stored within the business process. Repositories can be computer databases, or they can be collections of files in the cloud (think *on the Internet* for now), or they can be printed records stored in a file cabinet or a shoebox. For the purpose of documenting a business process, the particular medium in which repository data is stored is unimportant. The Vendor Data Repository contains data from prior auctions and prior Buyer searches of vendor and product data.

The labeled dashed lines in Figure 2-2 are called **data flows**. They represent the movement of data from one activity to another. The data can be delivered via email, text message, over the phone, by fax, or by some other means. The medium of the data delivery is also unimportant. For the level of our discussion, the format of the data item is also not important. Hence, according to Figure 2-2, Buyers both read and write Vendor and Product data from and to the Vendor Data Repository.

The solid line between the activities *Select Vendor Product* and *Negotiate Prices and Maximum Quantities* means that after a Buyer finishes the *Select Vendor and Product* activity, the Buyer's next action is to perform the *Negotiate Prices and Maximum Quantities* activity. Such solid lines are called **sequence flows**.

The final BPMN symbol used in Figure 2-2 is an activity with a boxed plus sign inside it. This notation indicates a subprocess, and is used when the work to be done is sufficiently complex as to require a process diagram of its own. In Figure 2-2, the *Setup and Run Auction* activity involves many activities and several different roles. In the complete set of process documentation, it would have a BPMN diagram of its own. Here, we will not be concerned with those details.

With the understanding of these symbols, you can interpret the rest of Figure 2-2 on your own. One point to note concerns the *Receive Goods* activity performed by the Operations Role. When GearUp receives a Vendor Shipment, it compares the goods received to those ordered on the original Vendor Order. It will notate that order with the items received and place the Revised Vendor Order back into the Vendor Order Repository. It will also note the items that were missing or received in damaged condition.

To summarize, a business process is a network of activities. Each activity is performed by a role. Roles are taken by people, groups, departments, and organizations. Repositories are collections of data. Data flows between activities; when one activity follows directly after another, the flow is shown with a sequence flow. Complex activities are represented by a separate diagram and denoted by a boxed plus sign in the activity.

HOW CAN INFORMATION SYSTEMS IMPROVE PROCESS QUALITY?

Many ways exist to explain how information systems can benefit business processes. For our purposes, the best understood and most succinct way is to say that *information systems improve process quality*. To understand why that is so, you first need to understand process quality.

WHAT IS PROCESS QUALITY?

Process quality can be measured in two dimensions: process *effectiveness* and process *efficiency*. An **effective business process** is one that enables the organization to accomplish its strategy. According to the dialog at the start of this chapter, GearUp's current process, the one shown in Figure 2-2, is not effective. GearUp wants to provide the lowest possible prices, and Kelly and

Emily think its operational costs are too high. Drew believes that if buyers knew about the problems caused by certain vendors, buyers could negotiate compensation for the cost of the problems, or avoid those vendors entirely.

Examine Figure 2-2 again and you can see the source of the ineffectiveness. The Receive Goods activity of Operations stores the results of vendor shipments in the Vendor Order Repository. However, when Buyers are deciding which vendors and products to sell, and when they are negotiating with the chosen vendor, they use only the Vendor Data Repository; they do not have access to the data in the Vendor Order Repository.

So, one way to make this process more effective, and hence raise process quality, is to change its structure. Figure 2-4 shows a different version of this business process, one in which Buyers and Operations share a single, integrated repository of vendor data. With this business process, buyers will be able to determine which vendors are problematic, and even how much extra work with particular vendors costs.

The second dimension of process quality is efficiency. **Efficiency** is the ratio of benefits to costs. Consider two versions of a business process for accomplishing some function. If both versions create the same benefit, but one costs more than the other does, then the higher-cost

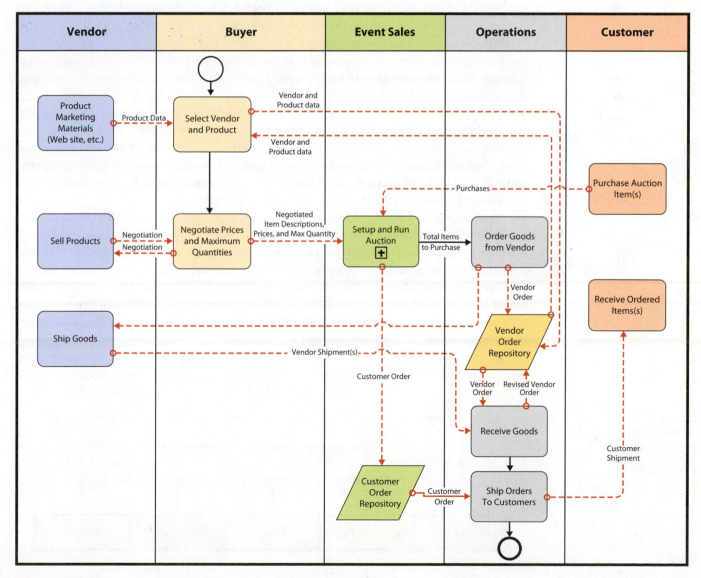

Figure 2-4
Revised GearUp Process Using BPMN

version is less efficient than the lower-cost version. Or, if both versions cost the same, but one generates less benefit than the other does, then the lower-benefit one is less efficient.

If you look at the business processes in Figures 2-2 and 2-4, you won't see any costs, not directly anyway. So, where are they? One major source of cost is the time of the employees who perform the process activities. If it takes someone 10 hours to perform the *Select Vendor and Product* activity, then the cost of that activity is the cost of those 10 labor hours. Behind the scenes, there are also infrastructure costs. Data doesn't just flow automatically from one activity to another. Some type of computer network, email, or other system needs to exist to support those data flows. The cost of that infrastructure is part of the costs of the business process.

USING INFORMATION SYSTEMS TO IMPROVE PROCESS QUALITY

To understand how information systems improve process quality, consider Figure 2-5, which shows the five components of an information system. Notice the symmetry of these components; the outermost components, hardware and people, are both actors; they take action. The software and procedure components are both sets of instructions. Software is instructions for hardware, and procedures are instructions for people. Finally, data is the bridge between the computer side on the left and the human side on the right.

When an activity in a business process is automated, work formerly done by people following procedures has been moved to computers that perform the work by following instructions in software. Thus, the automation of a process activity consists of moving work from the right-hand side of Figure 2-5 to the left.

To understand this, consider the *Select Vendor and Product* activity in Figure 2-2. That process could be entirely manual. The buyer could use the Internet (for this example, ignore the fact that she is using a computer system to access the Internet), gather data about vendors and products, make analyses of costs and margins by hand, and store the results of those analyses on paper in a file folder in her desk. When she wants to access past records for a particular vendor, she would manually search through her desk to find those records.

One way to automate the process would be to use a product such as Excel to make the vendor and product analyses and to store the results of those analyses in a computer database. If this were done, the buyer would have a faster and more reliable means of finding relevant data. The time required to perform the analysis and locate past analyses would be reduced, the cost of the process would decrease, the process would be more efficient, and hence process quality would increase. Furthermore, it would be possible for many buyers to share the same database; thus, they could benefit from one another's work. The process would thus generate greater benefits and would be even more efficient.

But wait . . . labor costs would go down with this example of automation, but the information system that provides that automation would cost something to develop and operate. Those

Figure 2-5
Characteristics of the Five Components

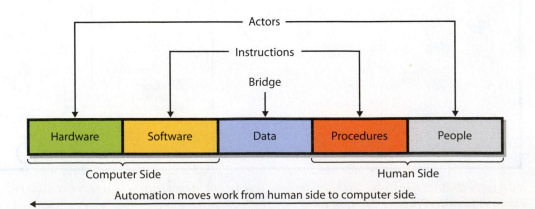

Figure 2-6
GearUp Data on General
Sports

Vendor

VendorID	1
VendorName	General Sports
City	Los Angeles
State	CA
ContactName	Maria Jepperson
ContactEmail	MJ@GenSports.com
ContactPhone	(212) 722-5555

OrderHistory

OrderDate	BuyerName	ReceivedBy	ItemName	QuantityOrdered	QuantityReceived	QuantityDamaged	NetSellable
4/10/2011	Addison	Drew	Ashford Soccer Balls	500	500	0	500
7/15/2011	Addison	Drew	Soccer Nets	100	100	0	100
1/14/2012	Addison	Drew	Blitz Basketballs	1000	855	75	780
3/17/2012	Sarah	Jackson	Ashford Soccer Balls	1500	1200	85	1115
5/19/2012	Addison	Drew	Nonsuch Soocer Jerseys	2000	1200	0	1200
7/11/2012	Sarah	Jackson	Abbotsfield Field Hockey Sticks	1000	700	125	575

costs must also be considered before the organization can decide if making such a change is worthwhile. You can see from this simple example why it is vital that business professionals be involved in the development of information systems. If systems development is left solely to technical personnel, they may develop a system that is technically elegant, but cost inefficient.

In addition to improving process efficiency, information systems can also improve process effectiveness. Drew believes that GearUp could better achieve its strategy (lowest prices) if it negotiated compensation for the costs it incurs when dealing with problematic vendors.

Using information systems, GearUp can track the number of times that vendors fail to ship the quantity of goods they have agreed to ship, the quantity of unshipped items, and the number of items that have been damaged in shipment. Information systems can be developed to automatically generate this data and to make it available to buyers, prior to and even during negotiations.

Figure 2-6 shows an example for General Sports. In 2012, General Sports consistently shipped fewer items (Quantity Received) than it agreed to ship (Quantity Ordered). Further, some items have been damaged. With this data, buyers can negotiate price concessions on future orders to compensate for the extra operational expense of these short-shipments. If so, GearUp can pass those lower prices on to its customers, and thus better achieve its strategy. Therefore, the report shown in Figure 2-6 makes this process more effective.

The bottom line: information systems can increase process quality by increasing both process efficiency and effectiveness. Of course, we are assuming that the data in Figure 2-6 is correct. But is it? Before we close this chapter, you need to understand the factors that lead to quality information, and to do that, you first need to understand the difference between information and data. We discuss that topic next.

WHAT IS INFORMATION?

Information is one of those fundamental terms that we use every day but that turns out to be surprisingly difficult to define. Defining *information* is like defining words such as *alive* and *truth*. We know what those words mean, we use them with each other without confusion, but they are nonetheless difficult to define.

DEFINITIONS VARY

In this text, we will avoid the technical issues of defining information and will use common, intuitive definitions instead. Probably the most common definition is that **information** is knowledge derived from data, whereas *data* is defined as recorded facts or figures. Thus, the facts that employee James Smith earns $17.50 per hour and that Mary Jones earns $25.00 per hour are *data*. The statement that the average hourly wage of all the aerobics instructors is $22.37 per hour is *information*. Average wage is knowledge that is derived from the data of individual wages.

Another common definition is that *information is data presented in a meaningful context*. The fact that Jeff Parks earns $10.00 per hour is data.[2] The statement that Jeff Parks earns less than half the average hourly wage of the aerobics instructors, however, is information. It is data presented in a meaningful context.

Another definition of information that you will hear is that *information is processed data*, or sometimes, *information is data processed by summing, ordering, averaging, grouping, comparing, or other similar operations*. The fundamental idea of this definition is that we do something to data to produce information.

For the purposes of this text, any of these definitions of information will do. Choose the definition that makes sense to you. The important point is that you discriminate between data and information. You also may find that different definitions work better in different situations.

Yet a fourth definition of *information* is presented in the Guide on pages 40–41. There, *information* is defined as "a difference that makes a difference."

WHERE IS INFORMATION?

Suppose you create a graph of Amazon.com's stock price and net income over its history. Does that graph contain information? Well, if it presents information in a meaningful context, or if it shows a difference that makes a difference, then it fits two of the definitions of information, and it's tempting to say that the graph contains information.

However, show that graph to your family dog. Does your dog find information in that graph? Well, nothing about Amazon.com, anyway. The dog might learn what you had for lunch, but it won't obtain any information about Amazon.com's stock price over time.

Reflect on this experiment and you will realize that the graph is not, itself, information. The graph is data that you and other humans perceive, and from that perception you conceive information. In short, if it's on a piece of paper or on a digital screen, it's data. If it's in the mind of a human, it's information.

Why, you're asking yourself, do I care? Well, for one, it explains why you, as a human, are the most important part of any information system you use. The quality of your thinking, of your ability to conceive information from data, is determined by your cognitive skills. The data is the data, the information you conceive from it is the value that you add to the information system.

Furthermore, people have different perceptions and points of view. Not surprisingly, then, they will perceive different information from the same data. You cannot say to someone, "Look, it's right there in front of you, in the data," because it's not right there in the data. Rather, it's in your head, and your job is to explain what you have conceived so that others can understand it.

Finally, once you understand this, you'll understand that all kinds of common sentences make no sense. "I sent you that information," cannot be true. "I sent you the data, from which you conceived the information," is the most we can say. During your business career, this observation will save you untold frustration if you remember and apply it.

---

[2]Actually the word *data* is plural; to be correct we should use the singular form *datum* and say, "The fact that Jeff Parks earns $10 per hour is a datum." The word datum, however, sounds pedantic and fussy, and we will avoid it in this text.

Experiencing MIS   INCLASS EXERCISE 2

How Much Is a Quarter Worth?

Source: W.Scott/Fotolia

The Ohio State University, UCLA, University of Washington, Oregon State University . . .

All of these universities operate on the quarter system, in which the academic year is broken into four terms (including summer) of about 10 weeks each. Most students at these schools attend three quarters a year: Fall, Winter, and Spring. Other universities (in fact, the majority in the United States) operate on the semester system, where the year is broken into three terms (Fall, Spring, and Summer) of about 15 weeks each. Most students attend only the Fall and Spring semesters. One unit of credit in the quarter systems is worth two-thirds a unit of credit in the semester system.

Students and faculty have different opinions on the relative merits of the two systems. The following table summarizes most of these arguments.

	Pros	Cons
Quarters	Can take more classes	Too fast paced
	Opportunity cost of a frivolous class (ball-room dancing) lower	Exams too frequent
		Don't get ill for a week!
	Bad class experience shorter	Not enough time for serious projects
	Exposure to more professors	More work for professors
	More flexibility for professors	Out of sync with majority of universities
Semester	More opportunity to focus on difficult subjects	Some subjects don't need a full semester
	Less frenetic course pace	Too long to remember course content for final
	More time for serious projects	
	More time to meet fellow students	Bad class lasts forever

Few of the arguments that you'll find on the Web focus on costs. In a time of burgeoning educational expense, this omission seems odd. Perhaps costs are too pragmatic for proper consideration within ivy-covered walls? We in the College of Business, however, need not be so constrained.

Consider the following business processes, all of which are necessary for every new term (quarter or semester):

- Schedule classes
- Allocate classrooms and related equipment
- Staff classes
- Enroll students
- Prepare and print course syllabi
- Adjust enrollments via add/drop
- Schedule finals
- Allocate final exam rooms
- Grade finals
- Record final grades

Each of these processes has associated costs, and many of those costs are substantial. Given that a semester system pays these costs one fewer time per year than a quarter system, it would seem cost prudent for all universities to adopt the semester system. Indeed, Ohio State plans to switch from quarters to semesters sometime soon; undoubtedly, other universities on the quarter system are considering such conversions as well.

Suppose you attend a university on the quarter system that has just undergone a substantial tuition hike. You decide to initiate a campus movement to save the process costs of the extra term each year. Working with a group as directed by your professor, answer the following questions:

You have been asked by the president of a quarter-system university to prepare a position report on the possibility of a switch to semesters. In preparation, answer the following questions:

1. Use Google or Bing (or another Internet search engine) to search for the phrase "quarter versus semester." Read several of the opinions, then adjust and augment the table of pros and cons.

2. List business processes involved in starting a new term. Examples are processes to develop the roster of classes, to staff classes, and to enroll students. Name as many more of the processes required as you can. Examine the list of processes presented in the case study above and add processes that you think may have been omitted, if any.

3. List the sources of costs for each of the two processes you chose in your answer to step 2.

4. Considering just the College of Business at your university, estimate each of the costs for the processes in step 3. Make and justify assumptions about labor rates and other factors.

5. Assuming that costs for other colleges are the same as for the College of Business (an unrealistic assumption; law and medicine probably have higher costs), what is the total cost for the two processes you selected for your university, in total?

6. List and describe five factors that you think could be keeping a university that is on a quarter system from converting to a semester system.

7. Suppose you actually did this at your university. Explain how you could use this experience to demonstrate your capabilities in a job interview.

Q5 WHAT DATA CHARACTERISTICS ARE NECESSARY FOR QUALITY INFORMATION?

You have just learned that humans conceive information from data. As stated, the quality of the information that you can create depends, in part, on your thinking skills. It also depends, however, on the quality of the data that you are given. If, for example, the data in Figure 2-6 is incorrect, there is no way the decision makers at GearUp can make good decisions about problematic vendors. Figure 2-7 summarizes critical data characteristics.

ACCURATE

First, good information is conceived from accurate, correct, and complete data, and it has been processed correctly, as expected. Accuracy is crucial; business professionals must be able to rely on the results of their information systems. The IS function can develop a bad reputation in the organization if a system is known to produce inaccurate data. In such a case, the information system becomes a waste of time and money as users develop work-arounds to avoid the inaccurate data.

A corollary to this discussion is that you, a future user of information systems, ought not to rely on data just because it appears in the context of a Web page, a well-formatted report, or a fancy query. It is sometimes hard to be skeptical of data delivered with beautiful, active graphics. Do not be misled. When you begin to use a new information system, be skeptical. Cross-check the data you are receiving. After weeks or months of using a system, you may relax. Begin, however, with skepticism. Again, you cannot conceive accurate information from inaccurate data.

TIMELY

Good information requires that data be timely—available in time for its intended use. A monthly report that arrives six weeks late is most likely useless. The data arrives long after the decisions that needed your information have been made. An information system that sends you a poor customer credit report after you have shipped the goods is unhelpful and frustrating. Notice that timeliness can be measured against a calendar (6 weeks late) or against events (before we ship).

When you participate in the development of an IS, timeliness will be part of the requirements you specify. You need to give appropriate and realistic timeliness needs. In some cases, developing systems that provide data in near real time is much more difficult and expensive than producing data a few hours later. If you can get by with data that is a few hours old, say so during the requirements specification phase.

Consider an example. Suppose you work in marketing and you need to be able to assess the effectiveness of new online ad programs. You want an information system that not only will deliver ads over the Web, but that also will enable you to determine how frequently customers click on those ads. Determining click ratios in near real time will be very expensive; saving the data in a batch and processing it some hours later will be much easier and cheaper. If you can live with data that is a day or two old, the system will be easier and cheaper to implement.

Figure 2-7
Characteristics of Good Data

- Accurate
- Timely
- Relevant
  - To context
  - To subject
- Just barely sufficient
- Worth its cost

RELEVANT

Data should be relevant both to the context and to the subject. Considering context, you, the CEO, need data that is summarized to an appropriate level for your job. A list of the hourly wage of every employee in the company is unlikely to be useful. More likely, you need average wage information by department or division. A list of all employee wages is irrelevant in your context.

Data should also be relevant to the subject at hand. If you want data about short-term interest rates for a possible line of credit, then a report that shows 15-year mortgage interest rates is irrelevant. Similarly, a report that buries the data you need in pages and pages of results is also irrelevant to your purposes.

JUST BARELY SUFFICIENT

Data needs to be sufficient for the purpose for which it is generated, but just barely so. We are inundated with data; one of the critical decisions that each of us has to make each day is what data to ignore. The higher you rise into management, the more data you will be given, and, because there is only so much time, the more data you will need to ignore. So, data should be sufficient, but just barely.

WORTH ITS COST

Data is not free. There are costs for developing an information system, costs of operating and maintaining that system, and costs of your time and salary for reading and processing the data the system produces. For data to be worth its cost, an appropriate relationship must exist between the cost of data and its value.

Consider an example. What is the value of a daily report of the names of the occupants of a full graveyard? Zero, unless grave robbery is a problem for the cemetery. The report is not worth the time required to read it. It is easy to see the importance of economics for this silly example. It will be more difficult, however, when someone proposes new technology to you. You need to be ready to ask, "What's the value of the information that I can conceive from this data?" "What is the cost?" "Is there an appropriate relationship between value and cost?" Information systems should be subject to the same financial analyses to which other assets are subjected.

How does the knowledge in this chapter help you?

Drew, Addison, and others at GearUp have an intuition about what needs to be done: share data. They do not know, however, how to make that intuition more specific. With the knowledge of this chapter, they would be able to document GearUp's business processes, and explain in a professional way how GearUp should develop new or adjust existing information systems. With that documentation, they could approach Kelly and other managers at GearUp with their ideas. In doing so, they would demonstrate, using the terms from Chapter 1, their ability to engage in systems thinking, abstraction, collaboration and experimentation. Hence, this knowledge would not only help GearUp, it would help them with their career prospects as well.

If GearUp were to move forward with these ideas, the next steps would likely involve working with IS professionals—either in-house or outside contractors. The knowledge of this chapter would help Drew, Addison, and others to communicate effectively with those professionals. Such communication will not only result in a better solution, it will also enable the IS professionals to understand more quickly the business needs, hence saving GearUp cost. Think about how their experience can help you, as you will likely encounter similar issues in your career.

Ethics Guide

Egocentric Versus Empathetic Thinking

According to one definition, a *problem* is a perceived difference between what is and what ought to be. When creating or adapting business processes and information systems to support them, it is critical for the development team to have a common definition and understanding of the problem. This common understanding, however, can be difficult to achieve.

Cognitive scientists distinguish between egocentric and empathetic thinking. Egocentric thinking centers on the self; someone who engages in egocentric thinking considers his or her view as "the real view" or "what really is." In contrast, those who engage in empathetic thinking consider their view as one possible interpretation of the situation and actively work to learn what other people are thinking.

Different experts recommend empathetic thinking for different reasons. Religious leaders say that such thinking is morally superior; psychologists say that empathetic thinking leads to richer, more fulfilling relationships. In business, empathetic thinking is recommended because it's smart. Business is a social endeavor, and those who can understand others' points of view are always more effective. Even if you do not agree with others' perspectives, you will be much better able to work with them if you understand their views.

Consider an example. Suppose you say to your MIS professor, "Professor Jones, I couldn't come to class last Monday. Did we do anything important?" Such a statement is a prime example of egocentric thinking. It takes no account of your professor's point of view and implies that your professor talked about nothing important. As a professor, it's tempting to say, "No, when I noticed you weren't there, I took out all the important material."

To engage in empathetic thinking, consider this situation from the professor's point of view. Students who do not come to class cause extra work for their professors. It doesn't matter how valid your reason for not coming to class was; you may actually have been contagious with a fever of 102°F. But no matter what, your absence is more work for your professor. He or she must do something extra to help you recover from the lost class time.

Using empathetic thinking, you would do all you can to minimize the impact of your absence on your professor. For example, you could say, "I couldn't come to class, but I got the class notes from Mary. I read through them, and I have a question about business processes and how they relate to information. . . . Oh, by the way, I'm sorry to trouble you with my problem."

Before we go on, let's consider a corollary to this scenario: Never, ever, send an email to your boss that says, "I couldn't come to the staff meeting on Wednesday. Did we do anything important?" Avoid this for the same reasons as those for missing class. Instead, find a way to minimize the impact of your absence on your boss.

Now what does this have to do with MIS? Suppose that you buy a new laptop computer and within a few days, it fails. Repeated calls to customer support produce short-term fixes, but no one remembers who you are or what has been suggested to you in the past. Assume the keyboard continues to lock up every few days. In this scenario, there are a few views of the problem: (1) Customer support reps do not have data about prior customer contacts; (2) the customer support rep recommended a solution that did not work; and (3) the company is shipping too many defective laptops. The solution to each of these problem definitions requires a different information system.

Now imagine yourself in a meeting about this situation, and suppose that different people in the meeting hold the three views of the problem. If everyone engages in egocentric thinking, what will happen? The meeting will be argumentative and likely will end with nothing accomplished.

Suppose, instead, that the attendees think empathetically. In this case, people will make a concerted effort to understand the different points of view, and the outcome will be much more positive—possibly a definition of all three problems ranked in order of priority. In both scenarios, the attendees have the same information; the difference in outcomes results from the attendees' thinking style.

Empathetic thinking is an important skill in all business activities. Skilled negotiators always know what the other side wants; effective salespeople understand their customers' needs. Buyers who understand the problems of their vendors get better service. And students who understand the perspective of their professors get better . . .

DISCUSSION QUESTIONS

1. In your own words, explain the difference between egocentric and empathetic thinking.

2. Suppose you and another person differ substantially on a problem definition. Suppose she says to you, "No, the real problem is that . . . ," followed by her definition of the problem. How do you respond?

3. Again, suppose you and another person differ substantially on a problem definition. Assume you understand his definition. How can you make that fact clear?

4. Explain how you could use Figures 2-2, 2-4, and 2-6 to define GearUp's problem.

5. Suppose you're in a meeting to discuss GearUp's problem and it appears to you that someone differs with you, but does not understand Figures 2-2 and 2-4. How would you respond?

6. Suppose you're in a meeting to discuss GearUp's problem, and you're the one who doesn't understand Figure 2-2 and 2-4. What would you do?

Guide

Understanding Perspectives and Points of View

Every human being speaks and acts from the perspective of a personal point of view. Everything we say or do is based on—or biased by—that point of view. Thus, everything you read in any textbook, including this one, is biased by the author's point of view. Authors may think that they are writing unbiased accounts of neutral subject material. But no one can write an unbiased account of anything, because we all write from a particular perspective.

Similarly, your professors speak to you from their points of view. They have experience, goals, objectives, hopes, and fears, and, like all of us, they use those elements to provide a framework from which they think and speak.

Sometimes, when you read or hear an editorial or opinion-oriented material, it is easy to recognize a strongly held point of view. It does not surprise you to think that such opinions might contain personal biases. But what about statements that do not appear to be opinions? For example, consider the following definition of *information*: "Information is a difference that makes a difference." By this definition, there are many differences, but only those that make a difference qualify as information.

This definition is obviously not an opinion, but it nevertheless was written from a biased perspective. The perspective is just less evident because the statement appears as a definition, not an opinion. But, in fact, it is the definition of information according to the well-known psychologist Gregory Bateson.

I find his definition informative and useful. It is imprecise, but it is a pretty good guideline, and I have used it to my advantage when designing reports and queries for end users. I ask myself, "Does this report show people a difference that makes a difference to them?" So I find it to be a useful and helpful definition.

My colleagues who specialize in quantitative methods, however, find Bateson's definition vapid and useless. They ask, "What does it say?" or "How could I possibly use that definition to formalize anything?" or "A difference that makes a difference to what or whom?" Or they say, "I couldn't quantify anything about that definition; it's a waste of time."

And they are right, but so am I, and so was Gregory Bateson. The difference is a matter of perspective, and surprisingly, conflicting perspectives can all be true at the same time.

Source: Warren Goldswain/Shutterstock

One last point: Whether it is apparent or not, authors write and professors teach not only from personal perspectives, but also with personal goals. I write this textbook in the hope that you will find the material useful and important and that you will tell your professor that it is a great book so that he or she will use it again. Whether you (or I) are aware of that fact, it and my other hopes and goals bias every sentence in this book.

Similarly, your professors have hopes and goals that influence what and how they teach. Your professors may want to see light bulbs of recognition on your face, they may want to win the Professor of the Year award, or they may want to gain tenure status in order to be able to do some advanced research in the field. Whatever the case, they, too, have hopes and goals that bias everything they say.

So, as you read this book and as you listen to your professor, ask yourself, "What is her perspective?" and "What are his goals?" Then compare those perspectives and goals to your own. Learn to do this not just with your textbooks and your professors, but with your colleagues as well. When you enter the business world, being able to discern and adapt to the perspectives and goals of those with whom you work will make you much more effective.

Source: Sergey/Fotolia

? DISCUSSION QUESTIONS

1. Consider the following statement: "The quality of your thinking is the most important component of an information system." Do you agree with this statement? Do you think it is even possible to say that one component is the most important one?

2. Although it does not appear to be so, the statement "There are five components of an information system: hardware, software, data, procedures, and people" is an opinion based on a perspective. Suppose you stated this opinion to a computer engineer who said, "Rubbish. That's not true at all. The only components that count are hardware and maybe software." Contrast the perspective of the engineer with that of your MIS professor. How do those perspectives influence their opinions about the five-component framework? Which is correct?

3. Consider Bateson's definition, "Information is a difference that makes a difference." How can this definition be used to advantage when designing a Web page? Explain why someone who specializes in quantitative methods might consider this definition to be useless. How can the same definition be both useful and useless?

4. Some students hate open-ended questions. They want questions that have one correct answer, like "7.3 miles per hour." When given a question like that in question 3, a question that has multiple, equally valid answers, some students get angry or frustrated. They want the book or the professor to give them the answer. How do you feel about this matter?

5. Do you think individuals can improve the quality of their thinking by learning to hold multiple, contradictory ideas in their minds at the same time? Or do you think that doing so just leads to indecisive and ineffective thinking? Discuss this question with some of your friends. What do they think? What are their perspectives?

ACTIVE REVIEW

Use this Active Review to verify that you understand the ideas and concepts that answer the chapter's study questions.

Q1 WHY DOES THE GEARUP TEAM NEED TO UNDERSTAND BUSINESS PROCESSES?

Summarize the ways knowledge of business processes will help Drew and Addison develop a systematic solution to Gear-Up's vendor problem. Explain why knowledge of the role of information systems is important as well.

Q2 WHAT IS A BUSINESS PROCESS?

Define *business process* and give three examples. Define BPMN, swimlane format, activity, role, actor, repository, data flow, sequence flow and subprocess. Describe the BPMN symbols used for each. Review Figure 2-2 and ensure you can explain how this business process works.

Q3 HOW CAN INFORMATION SYSTEMS IMPROVE PROCESS QUALITY?

Define two dimensions of process quality. Explain how information systems can improve both of these dimensions. Give an example of an information system that improves both.

Q4 WHAT IS INFORMATION?

Give four definitions of *information*. Using your own experience and judgment, rank those definitions in the order of usefulness in business. Justify your ranking. Describe where both data and information are located.

Q5 WHAT DATA CHARACTERISTICS ARE NECESSARY FOR QUALITY INFORMATION?

Name and describe five data characteristics that are needed to produce quality information. Explain why each is required.

How does the knowledge in this chapter help you?

Summarize how knowledge and consideration of business processes will enable the GearUp team to accomplish its goal. Explain the differences between Figures 2-2 and 2-4 and describe how the process shown in Figure 2-4 will help GearUp deal with problematic vendors. Explain the meaning of the data in Figure 2-6 and discuss how GearUp can use it during vendor negotiations. Discuss how an understanding of business processes will help you in your career.

KEY TERMS AND CONCEPTS

Actor 29
Activities 29
Business process 27
Business process modeling notation
   (BPMN) 28–29

Data Flows 30
Effective business process 30
Efficiency 31
Information 33

Repository 30
Role 29
Sequence flows 30
Swimlane format 29

USING YOUR KNOWLEDGE

1. Consider the four definitions of *information* presented in this chapter. The problem with the first definition, "knowledge derived from data," is that it merely substitutes one word we don't know the meaning of (*information*) for a second word we don't know the meaning of (*knowledge*). The problem with the second definition, "data presented

in a meaningful context," is that it is too subjective. Whose context? What makes a context meaningful? The third definition, "data processed by summing, ordering, averaging, etc.," is too mechanical. It tells us what to do, but it doesn't tell us what information is. The fourth definition, "a difference that makes a difference," is vague and unhelpful.

Also, none of these definitions helps us to quantify the amount of information we receive. What is the information content of the statement that every human being has a navel? Zero—you already know that. However, the statement that someone has just deposited $50,000 into your checking account is chock-full of information. So, good information has an element of surprise.

Considering these points, answer the following questions:

a. What is information made of?

b. If you have more information, do you weigh more? Why or why not?

c. If you give a copy of your transcript to a prospective employer, is that information? If you show that same transcript to your dog, is it still information? Where is the information?

d. Give your own best definition of *information.*

e. Explain how you think it is possible that we have an industry called the *information technology industry*, but we have great difficulty defining the word *information.*

2. The text states that data should be worth the cost required to produce it. Both cost and value can be broken into tangible and intangible factors. *Tangible* factors can be measured directly; *intangible* ones arise indirectly and are difficult to measure. For example, a tangible cost is the cost of a computer monitor; an intangible cost is the lost productivity of a poorly trained employee.

Give five important tangible and five important intangible costs of an information system. Give five important tangible and five important intangible measures of the value of an information system. If it helps to focus your thinking, use the example of the class scheduling system at your university or some other university information system. When determining whether an information system is worth its cost, how do you think the tangible and intangible factors should be considered?

3. Suppose you manage the Buyers at GearUp and that you have been asked to help determine the requirements for a new vendor selection information system. As you think about those requirements, you wonder how much autonomy you want your employees to have in selecting the vendors and products to sell. You can develop a system that will make the vendor/product selection automatically, or you can build one that allows employees to make that selection. Explain how this characteristic will impact:

a. The skill level required for your employees

b. The number of employees you will need

c. Your criteria for hiring employees

d. Your management practices

e. The degree of autonomy for your employees

f. Your flexibility in managing your department

4. Suppose management has left you out of the requirements definition process. Explain how you could use the knowledge you developed in answering this question to justify your need to be involved in the requirements definition.

COLLABORATION EXERCISE 2

Before you start this exercise, read Chapter Extensions 1 and 2, which describe collaboration techniques as well as tools for managing collaboration tasks. In particular, consider using Google Drive, Google+, Windows Live SkyDrive, Microsoft SharePoint, or some other collaboration tool.

Many students, especially those with limited business experience, have difficulty understanding how important business processes are and how complex even simple processes can become. The following business situation and exercises will help you understand the need for business processes, the importance of process design, and the role that information systems play in support of such processes.

Suppose you work for a supplier of electric and plumbing supplies, equipment, and tools. Your customers are home builders and construction companies that are accustomed to buying on credit. When you receive an order, you need to evaluate it and approve any special terms before you start removing items from inventory and packaging them for shipment. Accordingly, you have developed the order-approval process shown in Figure 2-8 on the next page. (In this figure, the diamond represents a decision. Flow out of the diamond depends on the answer that is labeled on the arrow.)

As you can see, your order-approval process consists of several stages: prepare quotation, adjust quotation for requested terms, check inventory, check credit, and evaluate special terms. You check inventory and credit on every order, but you need to approve special terms only if the customer asks for something special, such as free shipping, an extra discount, or unusually fast service and delivery.

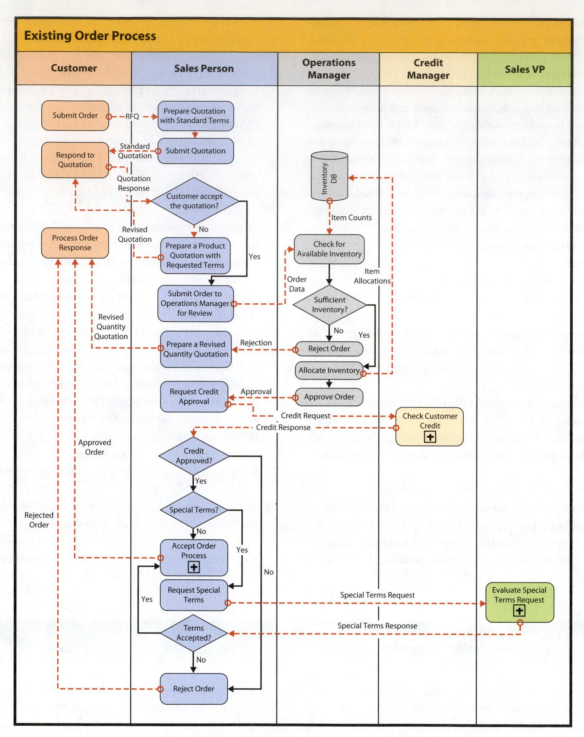

Figure 2-8
Existing Order Process

As you will see, even a business process this simple has unexpected complexity. For one, are the checks in the proper order? This business process checks inventory before it checks credit. Does it make sense to check inventory before you check credit? Would checking credit first make more sense? And, if it turns out that you are going to reject the special terms of an order, would it make sense to check them first, before evaluating inventory and credit?

Notice that if sufficient inventory does exist, the needed inventory is allocated to that order. But, if the customer's credit or special terms is rejected, that inventory is not released. In that case, you or one of your employees will need to remember to free the allocated inventory.

We can't tell this from this diagram, but if customer credit is increased if credit checking is approved, then a similar comment pertains to credit. If special terms are not approved, the allocated credit needs to be returned to the customer somehow.

Other problems occur because you are most likely processing many orders at the same time. Suppose two orders include one Kohler Supreme kitchen sink, but you have just one in inventory. You want to sell the sink to the first customer, but that means you must allocate that sink to it. Otherwise, both orders will be processed for the same sink. But suppose that the special terms of the order to which you've allocated the sink are disapproved. You would like to reassign the sink to the second order if it is still around to be processed. How can you accomplish that?

This scenario ignores another possibility. Suppose you have two order requests for the same sink; one is from a retail customer who wants it for her mountain home, and the second is from Big Sky Construction, a customer that buys 500 sinks a year from you. To which customer do you want to allocate that single sink? And how do you know how to do that?

Working with your team, answer the following questions:

1. In Figure 2-8, explain why inventory must be allocated.

2. Using Figure 2-8, explain why credit must be allocated to customers. What is the business consequence if these allocations are not adjusted when special terms are not approved?

3. Recommend a process for adjusting credit for orders for which credit or special terms are not approved. Indicate which role makes the adjustment and how they receive the data for doing so.

4. Change the process in Figure 2-8 so that allocated inventory is returned when credit or special terms are not approved. Indicate which role makes the adjustment and how they obtain the data for doing so.

5. There are six different sequences for the three approval tasks in Figure 2-8. Name each and select what your team considers to be the most promising three.

6. Evaluate each of the three sequences that you selected in question 5. Identify which sequence you think is best.

7. State the criteria that you used for making your selections in questions 5 and 6.

8. So far, we haven't considered the impact of this process on the salesperson. What information do salespeople need to maintain good relationships with their customers?

9. *Optional extension.* Download the Visio diagram version of Figure 2-8 from this book's Web site, *www.pearson highered.com/kroenke*. Modify the diagram to illustrate the sequence of tasks you chose as best in your answer to question 6.

CASE STUDY 2

Fulfillment by Amazon (FBA)

As stated in Case 1 (page 22), Amazon has three primary product offerings: an online retail store, computing infrastructure that it leases on an elastic basis, and order fulfillment services. In this case, you'll examine whether a company like GearUp might be able to advantageously use Amazon's order fulfillment services.

First, notice that GearUp's business model differs substantially from Amazon's retail model. Amazon retail buys goods, takes both ownership and physical possession, and places those goods into inventory. It then sells from that inventory. Amazon also sells goods on a consignment basis, but such sales are not its primary offering.

GearUp, on the other hand, buys items only after it has sold them at auction. It does not place an order until it knows how many of which goods it has sold. At that point, it orders in bulk, takes ownership and delivery, and then repackages the orders for shipment in small lots to its customers.

With the understanding of these differences, consider the use of Amazon's fulfillment services at GearUp. First, what is it?

Fulfillment by Amazon (FBA) is an Amazon service by which other sellers can ship goods to Amazon warehouses for stocking, order packaging, and shipment. FBA customers pay a fee for the service as well as for inventory space. Amazon uses its own inventory management and order fulfillment business processes and information systems to fulfill the FBA customers' orders.

FBA customers can sell their goods on Amazon.com, sell them via their own sales channels, or both. If the FBA customer sells on Amazon.com, Amazon will provide customer service for order processing (handling returns, fixing erroneously packed orders, answering customer order queries, and the like)

The table on the next page summarizes the FBA fees for products like sporting goods as of May 2012[3]:

---

[3]http://www.amazonservices.com/content/fulfillment-by-amazon.htm#!pricing, accessed May 2012.

	Sold via Amazon.com	Sold elsewhere
Order handling (per order)	$1.00	$4.75 (+)
Pick & pack (per item)	$1.00	$0.75
Weight handling (per pound)	$0.37	$0.45 (+)
Storage (cubic foot per month)	Minimum $0.45 (rates vary by time of year)	Minimum $.045 (rates vary by time of year)

Source: Courtesy of Amazon.com or its affiliates. All rights reserved.

If goods are sold via Amazon.com, Amazon uses its own information systems to drive the order fulfillment process. However, if the goods are sold via an FBA customer's sales channel, then the FBA customer must connect its own information systems with those at Amazon. Amazon provides a standardized interface by which this is done called Amazon Marketplace Web Service (MWS). Using Web-standard technology (see Chapter 6), FBA customers' order and payment data is directly linked to Amazon's information systems.

FBA enables companies to outsource order fulfillment to Amazon, thus avoiding the cost of developing their own processes, facilities, and information systems for this purpose. Is FBA right for GearUp?

QUESTIONS

1. In your own words, summarize the differences in the sales models of Amazon retail and GearUp.

2. Is GearUp able to sell its goods on Amazon.com? Why or why not?

3. Compute GearUp's cost of using FBA to process:
   a. An order of 10 soccer balls weighing a total of 25 pounds.
   b. An order of a single soccer ball weighing 2.5 pounds.
   c. The cost of a tennis outfit weighing 10 ounces.
   d. The cost of storing 1,000 soccer balls for three months. Make your own assumptions.

4. If GearUp were to use FBA, what business processes would it not need to develop? What costs would it save?

5. If GearUp were to use FBA, what information systems would it not need to develop? What costs would it save?

6. If GearUp were to use FBA, how would it integrate its information systems with Amazon's? (To add depth to your answer, search for the term *Amazon MWS*.)

7. In your opinion, does it make sense for GearUp to use FBA? Justify your answer.

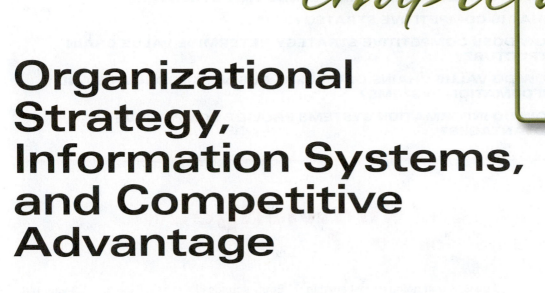

Organizational Strategy, Information Systems, and Competitive Advantage

Kelly Summers, CEO of GearUp, has called a meeting with Emily Johnson, CFO, Lucas Massey, IT director, Drew Mills, manager of Event Operations, and Addison Lee, lead buyer.

"Kelly, you hate meetings. This must be important!" Drew was one of Kelly's first hires and he knows her well.

"Drew, you are right—on both counts. I hate meetings because they consume expensive employee labor hours, and you're also right that I think this is important." Kelly nods at him as she says this.

"OK, then, what's up?" Drew looks back at her.

"Expenses, that's what. Emily just showed me last month's operations expenses and the news is bad. Emily?" Kelly looks around the group as she says this.

"Yes," Emily says, "Every month our operations expenses creep up . . . not just in dollars, but as a percent of our revenue. If this keeps up, we're going to have to raise prices."

"Well, I think our products are too cheap. I know our customers would pay more if they thought it was worth it. Why don't we add value to justify a price increase?" says Lucas, the IT director.

"Like *what*?" Clearly Emily doesn't like that response.

"Well, if we offer something they want, something extra, maybe, for example, we add an equipment selection feature to our site . . . you know, search for an item, then see what we've sold in the past and have reviews . . ."

STUDY QUESTIONS

How does the knowledge in this chapter help you?

"OK, but give me real data. I want solid grounding."

"Lucas, is that going to cost anything?" Emily sounds like she's talking to her 2-year old. "Well, sure . . ."

Kelly jumps in. "Look, everyone. We got into this business to provide the absolute lowest, rock-bottom prices on everything we sell. That's who we are. That's what our customers expect. If we want to be something else, we should start another business."

Lucas backs off. "OK, Kelly, sorry. Just thought I'd throw that in."

Kelly ignores his comment. "What I *do* want us to do is to figure out innovative ways to save money. Reduce expenses. In fact, Lucas, my goal would be to take another 10 percent off the prices we're charging now. I think we'll need that to stay competitive with WebGearNow."

"Those people aren't any good. Their site's a mess."

"Doesn't matter to our customers. They want cheap sporting goods and they'll switch to them in a New York minute if they can get lower prices."

"So much for customer loyalty . . ."

"Right, Lucas. There isn't any." Kelly is certain of that. "Besides, most of our new business comes from impulse buys. We need super-low prices to get new customers."

"Kelly, Drew and I were talking about something the other day." Addison speaks for the first time, softly, reluctant to get into this foray . . .

"It better save costs!" Lucas jumps in.

"I think it might. But, you'd know better than I," Addison pushes back.

"What do you mean?"

"Well, you've got the data. At least I think you must."

Lucas is puzzled. "What data are you talking about?"

"Maybe I can add something here." Drew knows what Addison has in mind and wants to support her. "We know that some vendors cause problems . . . take General Sports, for example . . ."

The name of General Sports catches Emily's attention . . . she knows that General provides goods for more than 15 percent of their business. "We do a lot of business with General. I hope you're not saying we shouldn't."

"Should, shouldn't. I don't know. I do know they're a pain in the neck!"

Kelly is surprised at this response. "Why is that, Drew?"

"Because they don't send us what they say they will. They commit to sending 1,000 soccer balls, we sell 1,000, and then they deliver 850 . . . we have to cancel orders for the missing 150, which is a terrible customer experience! I had to hire temporary staff just to deal with the customer calls last week."

"Why cancel? Why not buy 150 elsewhere?" Lucas is curious now.

Addison sees the problems with that. "We could do that, but where? And by when? And more expense because we'll never get the same low prices."

"On the other hand, what's the cost of a lost customer? Maybe we change our information system to automatically order more when that happens, drop-ship to the customer. Hey, Kelly, can we get chairs somewhere? I'm tired of standing." Lucas wants to outline his idea.

"No. Lucas, we cannot. I don't want this meeting to go on much longer, so don't get comfortable. . ." Kelly pauses while she gathers her thoughts.

"Here's what I *do* want. Addison, I want you and Drew and Lucas to get together and find out if we've got the data to determine who the problematic vendors are."

"OK." Addison likes Kelly's decisiveness just as the meeting was about to drag.

"Then, let's see what we've got. With that data, Emily, you can go back and talk with the problematic vendors. Try to get some cash or price concessions . . . at least put them on notice that we're watching."

"OK, but give me real data. I want solid grounding."

"Or, maybe do something else." Drew is thinking about having the buyers negotiate better deals with problematic vendors.

"Maybe. But here's the key and don't forget it: *We are the lowest price source of the sporting goods we carry, anywhere!*" Kelly just keeps drumming that in.

"But, we need to be profitable . . ." Emily adds.

"Yeah, and we do that by reducing costs." Kelly can't say that enough. "Everyone got it?"

HOW DOES ORGANIZATIONAL STRATEGY DETERMINE INFORMATION SYSTEMS REQUIREMENTS?

Kelly assigned the GearUp team the task of finding ways of reducing costs so that GearUp can "provide the absolute, rock-bottom prices on everything we sell." That sensible and appropriate task starts in the middle of the story. In this chapter, we will back up to understand how Kelly and GearUp arrived at that assignment.

Figure 3-1 summarizes a planning process used by many organizations. In short, organizations examine the structure of their industry and, from that, develop a competitive strategy. That strategy determines value chains, which, in turn, determine business processes like those we discussed in Chapter 2. As you saw in that chapter, the nature of business processes determines the requirements and functions of information systems.

Michael Porter, one of the key researchers and thinkers in competitive analysis, developed three different models that help us understand the elements of Figure 3-1. We begin with his five forces model.

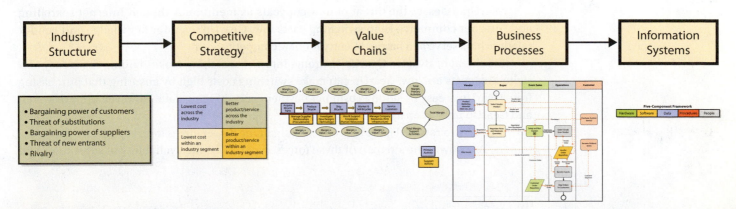

Figure 3-1

Organizational Strategy Determines Information Systems

Q2 WHAT FIVE FORCES DETERMINE INDUSTRY STRUCTURE?

Porter developed the **five forces model**[1] to help organizations determine the potential profitability of an industry. Over the years, this model has been applied for another purpose: As a way of understanding organizations' competitive environments. That understanding is then used to formulate a competitive strategy, as you will see.

Porter's five competitive forces can be grouped into two types: forces related to competition and forces related to supply chain bargaining power.

Competitive Forces
- **Competition from vendors of substitutes**
- **Competition from new competitors**
- **Competition from existing rivals**

Bargaining Power Forces
- **Bargaining power of suppliers**
- **Bargaining power of customers**

Porter assesses these five forces to determine the characteristics of an industry, how profitable it is, and how sustainable that profitability will be. Here, we will use this model for a different purpose: to identify sources of strong competition and use that knowledge to create a competitive strategy to combat those strong forces. We will apply this technique to GearUp and see, in the process, that Kelly's assignment to the team was exactly right.

Each of the three competitive forces concerns the danger of customers taking their business elsewhere. As shown in the first column of Figure 3-2, two strength factors that relate to all three of these forces are switching costs and customer loyalty. If the costs of switching to another vendor are high, then the strength of the competitive forces is low. Similarly, if customers are loyal to the company or brand, then the strength of the competitive forces is low.

Now consider each of the three competitive forces individually. The threat of a substitute is stronger if the substitute's price is lower and if the perceived benefits of the substitute are similar. As shown in Figure 3-2, GearUp views sporting goods stores as substitution threats.

GearUp judges the threat from sporting goods store substitutes to be weak, primarily because such stores must carry inventory and need to lease retail space, costs that GearUp does not incur. However, GearUp must do everything it can to keep prices low to counter the disadvantage of delay that its customers have in receiving their goods.

GearUp assesses the threat of new copycats as medium. Although Internet searching and Internet commerce keep switching costs low, GearUp's vendor knowledge and vendor relationships serve as a barrier to entry for new competitors.

The threat of rivals to GearUp is strong. Internet searching makes finding rivals easy and switching costs are low. GearUp can make switching costs high by ensuring that purchasing from GearUp is easy by storing customer payment and shipping data. However, price drives all and GearUp must keep its prices low.

The last two rows of Figure 3-2 concern bargaining power forces from suppliers or from customers. As shown, the strength of these forces depends on the availability of substitutes and

---

[1]Michael Porter, *Competitive Strategy: Techniques for Analyzing Industries and Competitors* (New York: Free Press, 1980).

Type (Strength Factors)	Competitive Force (Strength Factors)	GearUp Threat (Factors Assessment)	GearUp's Strength Assessment
Competitve (Switching costs, customer loyalty)	**Substitutes** (Lower price and perceived benefits the same)	**Sporting goods store** (Moderate switching costs, costs of carrying inventory and of retail space should mean higher prices than GearUp)	**weak**
	New Entrants (Barriers to entry, capital requirements, noncapital resources)	**New copycats** (Low switching costs, customers moderately loyal to GearUp, capital requirements medium, knowledge of vendors and vendor relationships is barrier to entry)	**medium**
	Rivalry (Price, quality, innovation, marketing)	**Rivals** (Low switching costs, customers moderately loyal to GearUp, customers influenced by price/quality/innovation/marketing)	**strong**
Supply chain bargaining power (Availabilty of substitutes, relative size)	**Supplier**	**Vendors** (Seasonal and brand cycles ensure vendor excess inventory, GearUp must beat competition to it, though.)	**medium**
	Customer	**Customers** (Impulse buys common. Most purchases are elective. Price is everything.)	**strong**

Figure 3-2
Five Forces and GearUp

the relative size of the firm (here, it's GearUp) compared to the size of suppliers or customers. A Nobel–prize-winning scientist has strong bargaining supplier power at your university because such scientists are rare. In contrast, a temporary part-time instructor has little bargaining power, because many people can fill that role. If such instructors were to form a union, however, then that union would have greater bargaining power because of its relative size.

Similarly, you, as an individual, have little bargaining power as a customer to your university. Your application can be readily replaced with another, and you are an individual attempting to bargain with a large organization. In contrast, a large organization such as Oracle, Microsoft, or Google would have much stronger bargaining power for its employees at your university.

The bargaining power of GearUp's vendors is weak. There are many of them and because of the seasonality of sports and the obsolescence of sports products, they all have excess inventory. As an aside, note that the better they can use information systems to predict sales and manage inventory, the lower that excess will be.

Finally, the bargaining power of GearUp's customers is strong. Most buying on GearUp's site is impulsive, driven by super-low prices. Most customers do not need to buy the items that they purchase, so if GearUp cannot keep its prices low, they won't buy. Repeat customers also know that GearUp takes a long time to deliver, so extra-low prices must compensate for those delays.

Review Figure 3-2 and you can see why Kelly is so concerned to keep GearUp's costs as low as possible.

Figure 3-3
Porter's Four Competitive
Strategies

Source: Based on "How Competitive
Forces Shape Strategy" by Michael
Porter, Harvard Business Review,
July–August 1997.

	Cost	Differentiation
Industry-wide	Lowest cost across the industry	Better product/service across the industry
Focus	Lowest cost within an industry segment	Better product/service within an industry segment

WHAT IS COMPETITIVE STRATEGY?

An organization responds to the structure of its industry by choosing a competitive strategy. As shown in Figure 3-3, Porter defined four fundamental competitive strategies.[2] An organization can be the cost leader and provide products at the lowest prices, or it can focus on adding value to its products to differentiate them from those of the competition. Further, the organization can employ the cost or differentiation strategy across an industry, or it can focus its strategy on a particular industry segment. In this text, we define **competitive strategy** to be one of the four alternatives shown in Figure 3-3.

Consider the car rental industry, for example. According to the first column of Figure 3-3, a car rental company can strive to provide the lowest-cost car rentals across the industry, or it can seek to provide the lowest-cost car rentals to a "focused" industry segment—say, U.S. domestic business travelers.

As shown in the second column, a car rental company can seek to differentiate its products from the competition. It can do so in various ways—for example, by providing a wide range of high-quality cars, by providing the best reservation system, by having the cleanest cars or the fastest check-in, or by some other means. The company can strive to provide product differentiation across the industry or within particular segments of the industry, such as U.S. domestic business travelers.

According to Porter, to be effective the organization's goals, objectives, culture, and activities must be consistent with the organization's strategy. To those in the MIS field, this means that all information systems in the organization must facilitate the organization's competitive strategy.

Consider competitive strategy at GearUp. Its primary competitive threat is from rivals and GearUp wants to address that threat with the lowest possible prices. With regard to bargaining power, customers have strong power and that, too, can be addressed with low prices. Thus, GearUp must be the cost leader in their segment, which is sporting goods.

HOW DOES COMPETITIVE STRATEGY DETERMINE VALUE CHAIN STRUCTURE?

Organizations analyze the structure of their industry, and, using that analysis, they formulate a competitive strategy. They then need to organize and structure the organization to implement that strategy. If, for example, the competitive strategy is to be a *cost leader*, then business activities need to be developed to provide essential functions at the lowest possible cost.

---

[2]Michael Porter, *Competitive Strategy* (New York: Free Press, 1980).

A business that selects a *differentiation* strategy would not necessarily structure itself around least-cost activities. Instead, such a business might choose to develop more costly systems, but it would do so only if those systems provided benefits that outweighed their risks. Porter defined **value** as the amount of money that a customer is willing to pay for a resource, product, or service. The difference between the value that an activity generates and the cost of the activity is called the **margin**. A business with a differentiation strategy will add cost to an activity only as long as the activity has a positive margin.

A **value chain** is a network of value-creating activities. That generic chain consists of five primary activities and four support activities. **Primary activities** are business functions that relate directly to the production of the organization's products or services. **Support activities** are business functions that assist and facilitate the primary activities. Value chain analysis is most easily understood in the context of manufacturing, so we will leave the GearUp case for now and switch to the example of a bicycle manufacturer.

PRIMARY ACTIVITIES IN THE VALUE CHAIN

To understand the essence of the value chain, consider a small bicycle manufacturer (see Figure 3-4). First, the manufacturer acquires raw materials using the inbound logistics activity. This activity concerns the receiving and handling of raw materials and other inputs. The accumulation of those materials adds value in the sense that even a pile of unassembled parts is worth something to some customer. A collection of the parts needed to build a bicycle is worth more than an empty space on a shelf. The value is not only the parts themselves, but also the time required to contact vendors for those parts, to maintain business relationships with those vendors, to order the parts, to receive the shipment, and so forth.

In the operations activity, the bicycle maker transforms raw materials into a finished bicycle, a process that adds more value. Next, the company uses the outbound logistics activity to deliver the finished bicycle to a customer. Of course, there is no customer to send the bicycle

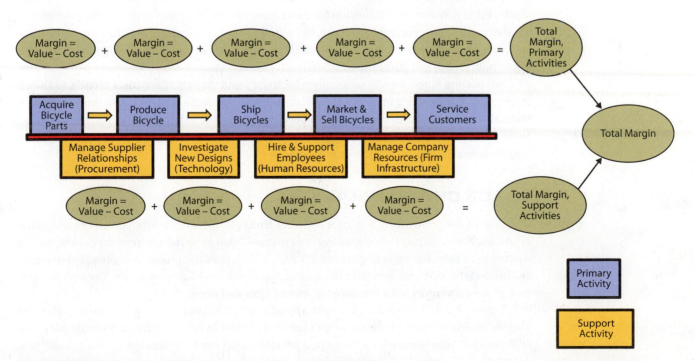

Figure 3-4
Bicycle Manufacturer's Value Chain

Figure 3-5

Task Descriptions for Primary Activities of the Value Chain

Primary Activity	Description
Inbound Logistics	Receiving, storing, and disseminating inputs to the product
Operations/Manufacturing	Transforming inputs into the final product
Outbound Logistics	Collecting, storing, and physically distributing the product to buyers
Sales and Marketing	Inducing buyers to purchase the product and providing a means for them to do so
Customer Service	Assisting customer's use of the product and thus maintaining and enhancing the product's value

to without the marketing and sales value activity. Finally, the service activity provides customer support to the bicycle users.

Each stage of this generic chain accumulates costs and adds value to the product. The net result is the total margin of the chain, which is the difference between the total value added and the total costs incurred. Figure 3-5 summarizes the primary activities of the value chain.

SUPPORT ACTIVITIES IN THE VALUE CHAIN

The support activities in the generic value chain facilitate the primary activities and contribute only indirectly to the production, sale, and service of the product. They include procurement, which consists of the processes of finding vendors, setting up contractual arrangements, and negotiating prices. (This differs from inbound logistics, which is concerned with ordering and receiving in accordance with agreements set up by procurement.)

Porter defined technology broadly. It includes research and development, but it also includes other activities within the firm for developing new techniques, methods, and procedures. He defined human resources as recruiting, compensation, evaluation, and training of full-time and part-time employees. Finally, firm infrastructure includes general management, finance, accounting, legal, and government affairs.

Supporting functions add value, albeit indirectly, and they also have costs. Hence, as shown in Figure 3-4, supporting activities contribute to a margin. In the case of supporting activities, it would be difficult to calculate the margin because the specific value added of, say, the manufacturer's lobbyists in Washington, is difficult to know. But there is a value added, there are costs, and there is a margin, even if it is only in concept.

VALUE CHAIN LINKAGES

Porter's model of business activities includes **linkages**, which are interactions across value activities. For example, manufacturing systems use linkages to reduce inventory costs. Such a system uses sales forecasts to plan production; it then uses the production plan to determine raw material needs and then uses the material needs to schedule purchases. The end result is just-in-time inventory, which reduces inventory sizes and costs.

Value chain analysis has a direct application to manufacturing businesses like the bicycle manufacturer. However, value chains also exist in service-oriented companies. The difference is that most of the value in a service company is generated by the operations, marketing and sales, and service activities. Inbound and outbound logistics are not typically as important.

HOW DO VALUE CHAINS DETERMINE BUSINESS PROCESSES AND INFORMATION SYSTEMS?

As you learned in the last chapter, a business process is a network of activities, resources, facilities, and information that accomplish a business function. Now we can be more specific and say that business processes implement value chains or portions of value chains. Thus, each value chain is supported by one or more business processes.

For example, Figure 3-6 shows a portion of a bike rental value chain for a bicycle rental company. The top part of this figure shows how a company having a competitive strategy of providing low-cost rentals to college students might implement this portion of its operations value

Before leaving the topic of competitive strategy, consider the issues raised in the Ethics Guide on pages 62–63. This guide illustrates the impact of a change in strategy on the employees of one bicycle manufacturer.

	Value Chain Activity	Greet Customer	Determine Needs	Rent Bike	Return Bike & Pay
Low-Cost Rental to Students	Message that implements competitive strategy	"You wanna bike?"	"Bikes are over there. Help yourself."	"Fill out this form, and bring it to me over here when you're done."	"Show me the bike." "OK, you owe $23.50. Pay up."
	Supporting business process	None.	Physical controls and procedures to prevent bike theft.	Printed forms and a shoebox to store them in.	Shoebox with rental form. Minimal credit card and cash receipt system.
High-Service Rental to Business Executives at Conference Resort	Message that implements competitive strategy	"Hello, Ms. Henry. Wonderful to see you again. Would you like to rent the WonderBike 4.5 that you rented last time?"	"You know, I think the WonderBike Supreme would be a better choice for you. It has . . ."	"Let me just scan the bike's number into our system, and then I'll adjust the seat for you."	"How was your ride?" "Here, let me help you. I'll just scan the bike's tag again and have your paperwork in just a second." "Would you like a beverage?" "Would you like me to put this on your hotel bill, or would you prefer to pay now?"
	Supporting business process	Customer tracking and past sales activity system.	Employee training and information system to match customer and bikes, biased to "up-sell" customer.	Automated inventory system to check bike out of inventory.	Automated inventory system to place bike back in inventory. Prepare payment documents. Integrate with resort's billing system.

Figure 3-6
Operations Value Chains for Bicycle Rental Companies

chain. The bottom part shows how a company with a competitive strategy of providing high-quality rentals to business executives at a conference resort might implement this portion of that same value chain.

Note that the value chain activities are the same for both companies. Both greet the customer, determine the customer's needs, rent a bike, and return the bike. However, each company implements these activities in ways that are consistent with its competitive strategy.

The low-cost vendor has created barebones, minimum processes to support its value chain. The high-service vendor has created more elaborate business processes (supported by information systems) that are necessary to differentiate its service from that of other vendors. As Porter says, however, these processes and systems must create sufficient value that they will more than cover their costs. If not, the margin of those systems will be negative.

If a value chain's margin is negative, the company must make some change. Either the value must be increased, or the costs of the value chain need to be reduced. To investigate this principle further, consider Collaboration Exercise 3 on pages 68–69.

Before we continue, review Figure 3-1 again. The material in these first three chapters is presented from the right to the left in this figure. We began with the components of an information system in Chapter 1. We then considered business processes in Chapter 2. In this chapter, we have considered value chains, competitive strategy, and industry structure.

HOW DO INFORMATION SYSTEMS PROVIDE COMPETITIVE ADVANTAGES?

In your business strategy class, you will study the Porter models in greater detail than we have discussed here. When you do so, you will learn numerous ways that organizations respond to the five competitive forces. For our purposes, we can distill those ways into the list of principles shown in Figure 3-7. Keep in mind that we must apply these principles within the context of the organization's competitive strategy.

Some of these competitive techniques are created via products and services, and some are created via the development of business processes. Consider each.

COMPETITIVE ADVANTAGE VIA PRODUCTS

The first three principles in Figure 3-7 concern products or services. Organizations gain a competitive advantage by creating *new* products or services, by *enhancing* existing products or services, and by *differentiating* their products and services from those of their competitors. As you think about these three principles, realize that an information system can be part of a product or it can provide support for a product or service.

Consider, for example, a car rental agency like Hertz or Avis. An information system that produces information about the car's location and provides driving instructions to destinations

Figure 3-7
Principles of Competitive Advantage

| **Product Implementations** |
| 1. Create a new product or service |
| 2. Enhance products or services |
| 3. Differentiate products or services |
| **Process Implementations** |
| 4. Lock in customers and buyers |
| 5. Lock in suppliers |
| 6. Raise barriers to market entry |
| 7. Establish alliances |
| 8. Reduce costs |

Experiencing MIS

Competitive Strategy Over the Web

Source: NetPhotos/Alamy (both photos)

As shown in Figure 3-1, information systems' requirements are a logical consequence of an organization's analysis of industry structure via the chain of models. Consequently, you should be able to combine your knowledge of an organization's market, together with observations of the structure and content of its Web storefront, to infer the organization's competitive strategy and possibly make inferences about its value chains and business processes. The process you use here can be useful in preparing for job interviews as well.

Form a three-person team (or as directed by your professor) and perform the following exercises. Divide work as appropriate, but create common answers for the team.

1. The following pairs of Web storefronts have market segments that overlap in some way. Briefly visit each site of each pair:
   * *www.sportsauthority.com* vs. *www.soccer.com*
   * *www.target.com* vs. *www.sephora.com*
   * *www.woot.com* vs. *www.amazon.com*
   * *www.petco.com* vs. *www.wag.com*
   * *www.llbean.com* vs. *www.rei.com*

2. Select two pairs from the list. For each pair of companies, answer the following questions:
   a. How do the companies' market segments differ?
   b. How do their competitive pressures differ?
   c. How do their competitive strategies differ?
   d. How is the "feel" of the content of their Web sites different?
   e. How is the "feel" of the user interface of their Web sites different?
   f. How could either company change its Web site to better accomplish its competitive strategy?
   g. Would the change you recommended in step f necessitate a change in one or more of the company's value chains? Explain.

3. Use your answers in step 2 to explain the following statement: "The structure of an organization's information system (here a Web storefront) is determined by its competitive strategy." Write your answer so that you could use it in a job interview to demonstrate your overall knowledge of business planning.

4. Present your team's answers to the rest of the class.

---

is part of the car rental, and thus is part of the product itself (see Figure 3-8a). In contrast, an information system that schedules car maintenance is not part of the product, but instead supports the product (Figure 3-8). Either way, information systems can achieve the first three objectives in Figure 3-7.

The remaining five principles in Figure 3-7 concern competitive advantage created by the implementation of business processes.

COMPETITIVE ADVANTAGE VIA BUSINESS PROCESSES

Organizations can *lock in customers* by making it difficult or expensive for customers to switch to another product. This strategy is sometimes called establishing high **switching costs**. Organizations can *lock in suppliers* by making it difficult to switch to another organization, or, stated

Figure 3-8
Two Roles for Information
Systems Regarding Products

a. Information System as Part of a Car Rental Product

b. Information System That Supports a Car Rental Product

Daily Service Schedule — November 17, 2012

StationID 22
StationName Lubrication

ServiceDate	ServiceTime	VehicleID	Make	Model	Mileage	ServiceDescription
11/17/2012	12:00 AM	155890	Ford	Explorer	2244	Std. Lube
11/17/2012	11:00 AM	12448	Toyota	Tacoma	7558	Std. Lube

StationID 26
StationName Alignment

ServiceDate	ServiceTime	VehicleID	Make	Model	Mileage	ServiceDescription
11/17/2012	9:00 AM	12448	Toyota	Tacoma	7558	Front end alignment inspect

StationID 28
StationName Transmission

ServiceDate	ServiceTime	VehicleID	Make	Model	Mileage	ServiceDescription
11/17/2012	11:00 AM	155890	Ford	Explorer	2244	Transmission oil change

positively, by making it easy to connect to and work with the organization. Competitive advantage can be gained by *creating entry barriers* that make it difficult and expensive for new competition to enter the market.

Another means to gain competitive advantage is to *establish alliances* with other organizations. Such alliances establish standards, promote product awareness and needs, develop market size, reduce purchasing costs, and provide other benefits. Finally, by creating better business processes, organizations can gain competitive advantage by *reducing costs*. Such reductions enable the organization to reduce prices and/or to increase profitability. Increased profitability means not just greater shareholder value, but also more cash, which can fund further infrastructure development for even greater competitive advantage.

All of these principles of competitive advantage make sense, but the question you may be asking is, "How do information systems help to create competitive advantage?" To answer that question, consider a sample information system.

HOW DOES AN ACTUAL COMPANY USE IS TO CREATE COMPETITIVE ADVANTAGES?

ABC, Inc.,[3] is a worldwide shipper with sales well in excess of $1 billion. From its inception, ABC invested heavily in information technology and led the shipping industry in the application of information systems for competitive advantage. Here we consider one example of an information system that illustrates how ABC successfully uses information technology to gain competitive advantage.

ABC maintains customer account data that include not only the customer's name, address, and billing information, but also data about the identity of that customer and the locations to which the customer ships. Figure 3-9 shows a Web form that an ABC customer is using to

---

[3]The information system described here is used by a major transportation company that does not want to be identified.

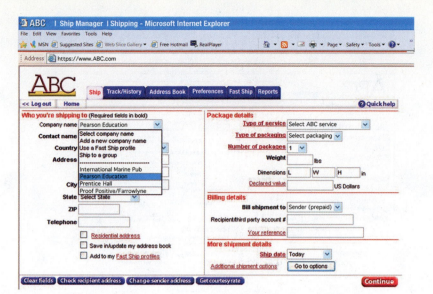

Figure 3-9
ABC, Inc., Web Page to
Select a Recipient from the
Customer's Records

schedule a shipment. When the ABC system creates the form, it fills the Company name drop-down list with the names of companies that the customer has shipped to in the past. Here, the user is selecting Pearson Education.

When the user clicks the Company name, the underlying ABC information system reads the customer's contact data from a database. The data consist of names, addresses, and phone numbers of recipients from past shipments. The user then selects a Contact name, and the system inserts that contact's address and other data into the form using data from the database, as shown in Figure 3-10. Thus, the system saves customers from having to reenter data for people to whom they have shipped in the past. Providing the data in this way also reduces data entry errors.

Figure 3-11 shows another feature of this system. On the right-hand side of this form, the customer can request that ABC send email messages to the sender (the customer), the recipient, and others as well. The customer can choose for ABC to send an email when the shipment

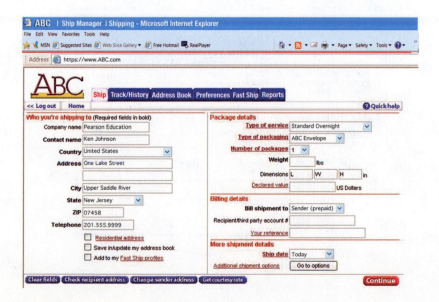

Figure 3-10
ABC, Inc., Web Page to
Select a Contact from the
Customer's Records

Figure 3-11
ABC, Inc., Web Page to
Specify Email Notification

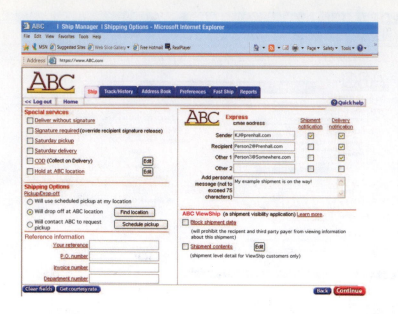

is created and when it has been delivered. In Figure 3-11, the user has provided three email addresses. The customer wants all three addresses to receive delivery notification, but only the sender will receive shipment notification. The customer can add a personal message as well. By adding this capability to the shipment-scheduling system, ABC has extended its product from a package-delivery service to a package- *and* information-delivery service.

Figure 3-12 shows one other capability of this information system. It has generated a shipping label, complete with bar code, for the user to print. By doing this, the company not only reduces errors in the preparation of shipping labels, but it also causes the customer to provide the paper and ink for document printing! Millions of such documents are printed every day, resulting in a considerable savings to the company.

Figure 3-12
ABC, Inc., Web Page to
Print a Shipping Label

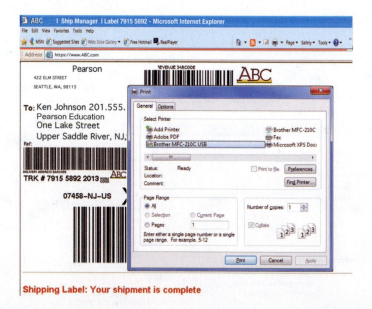

Shipping Label: Your shipment is complete

HOW DOES THIS SYSTEM CREATE A COMPETITIVE ADVANTAGE?

Now consider the ABC shipping information system in light of the competitive advantage factors in Figure 3-7. This information system *enhances* an existing product because it eases the effort of creating a shipment to the customer while reducing errors. The information system also helps to *differentiate* the ABC package delivery product from competitors that do not have a similar system. Further, the generation of email messages when ABC picks up and delivers a package could be considered to be a *new* product.

Because this information system captures and stores data about recipients, it reduces the amount of customer work when scheduling a shipment. Customers will be *locked in* by this system: If a customer wants to change to a different shipper, he or she will need to rekey recipient data for that new shipper. The disadvantage of rekeying data may well outweigh any advantage of switching to another shipper.

This system achieves a competitive advantage in two other ways as well. First, it raises the barriers to market entry. If another company wants to develop a shipping service, it will not only have to be able to ship packages, but it will also need to have a similar information system. In addition, the system reduces costs. It reduces errors in shipping documents, and it saves ABC paper, ink, and printing costs. (Of course, to determine if this system delivers a *net savings* in cost, the cost of developing and operating the information system will need to be offset against the gains in reduced errors and paper, ink, and printing costs. It may be that the system costs more than the savings. Even still, it may be a sound investment if the value of intangible benefits, such as locking in customers and raising entry barriers, exceeds the net cost.)

Before continuing, review Figure 3-7. Make sure that you understand each of the principles of competitive advantage and how information systems can help achieve them. In fact, the list in Figure 3-7 probably is important enough to memorize, because you can also use it for non-IS applications. You can consider any business project or initiative in light of competitive advantage.

How does the **knowledge** in this chapter help **you?**

Reread the opening dialog of this chapter. Explain how Kelly's comments are consistent with GearUp's competitive strategy. Explain why Lucas' idea of adding value to justify a price increase is inconsistent with GearUp's strategy. Identify another statement that Lucas makes that is inconsistent with their strategy. Develop guidance for yourself about the relationship between competitive strategy and information systems requirements. Summarize what you have learned from this example in a statement that you could make in a job interview. Ensure your statement demonstrates your understanding of the relationship of business strategy and the use of information technology and systems.

The Guide on pages 64–65 helps you understand how to use the principles of competitive advantage in a personal way.

Ethics Guide

Yikes! Bikes

Suppose you are an operations manager for Yikes! Bikes, a manufacturer of high-end mountain bicycles with $20 million in annual sales. Yikes! has been in business over 25 years, and the founder and sole owner recently sold the business to an investment group, Major Capital. You know nothing about the sale until your boss introduces you to Andrea Parks, a partner at Major Capital, who is in charge of the acquisition. Parks explains to you that Yikes! has been sold to Major Capital and that she will be the temporary general manager. She explains that the new owners see great potential in you, and they want to enlist your cooperation during the transition. She hints that if your potential is what she thinks it is, you will be made general manager of Yikes!

Parks explains that the new owners decided there are too many players in the high-end mountain bike business, and they plan to change the competitive strategy of Yikes! from high-end differentiation to lowest-cost vendor. Accordingly, they will eliminate local manufacturing, fire most of the manufacturing department, and import bikes from China. Further, Major Capital sees a need to reduce expenses and plans a 10 percent across-the-board staff reduction and a cut of two-thirds of the customer support department. The new bikes will be of lesser quality than current Yikes! bikes, but the price will be substantially less. The new ownership group believes it will take a few years for the market to realize that Yikes! bikes are not the same quality as they were. Finally, Parks asks you to attend an all-employee meeting with the founder and her.

At the meeting, the founder explains that due to his age and personal situation, he decided to sell Yikes! to Major Capital and that starting today Andrea Parks is the general manager. He thanks the employees for their many years of service, wishes them well, and leaves the building. Parks introduces herself to the employees and states that Major Capital is very excited to own such a great company with a strong, quality brand. She says she will take a few weeks to orient herself to the business and its environment and plans no major changes to the company.

You are reeling from all this news when Parks calls you into her office and explains that she needs you to prepare two reports. In one, she wants a list of all the employees in the manufacturing department, sorted by their salary (or wage for hourly employees). She explains that she intends to cut the most costly employees first. "I don't want to be inflexible about this, though," she says. "If there is someone whom you think we should keep, let me know, and we can talk about it."

She also wants a list of the employees in the customer support department, sorted by the average amount of time each support rep spends with customers. She explains, "I'm not so concerned with payroll expense in customer support. It's not how much we're paying someone; it's how much time they're wasting with customers. We're going to have a barebones support department, and we want to get rid of the gabby chatters first."

You are, understandably, shocked and surprised . . . not only at the speed with which the transaction has occurred, but also because you wouldn't think the founder would do this to the employees. You call him at home and tell him what is going on.

"Look," he explains, "when I sold the company, I asked them to be sure to take care of the employees. They said they would. I'll call Andrea, but there's really nothing I can do at this point; they own the show."

In a black mood of depression, you realize that you no longer want to work for Yikes!, but your wife is 6 months pregnant with your first child. You need medical insurance for her at least until the baby is born. But what miserable tasks are you going to be asked to do before then? And you suspect that if you balk at any task, Parks won't hesitate to fire you, too.

As you leave that night you run into Lori, the most popular customer support representative and one of your favorite employees. "Hey," Lori asks you, "what did you think of that meeting? Do you believe Andrea? Do you think they'll let us continue to make great bikes?"

DISCUSSION QUESTIONS

1. In your opinion, did the new owners take any illegal action? Is there evidence of crime in this scenario?

2. Was the statement that Parks made to all of the employees unethical? Why or why not? If you questioned her about the ethics of her statement, how do you think she would justify herself?

3. What do you think Parks will tell the founder if he calls as a result of your conversation with him? Does he have any legal recourse? Is Major Capital's behavior toward him unethical? Why or why not?

4. Parks is going to use information to perform staff cuts. What do you think about her rationale? Ethically, should she consider other factors, such as number of years of service, past employee reviews, or other criteria?

5. How do you respond to Lori? What are the consequences if you tell her what you know? What are the consequences of lying to her? What are the consequences of saying something noncommittal?

6. If you actually were in this situation, would you leave the company? Why or why not?

7. In business school, we talk of principles like competitive strategy as interesting academic topics. But, as you can see from the Yikes! case, competitive strategy decisions have human consequences. How do you plan to resolve conflicts between human needs and tough business decisions?

8. How do you define *job security*?

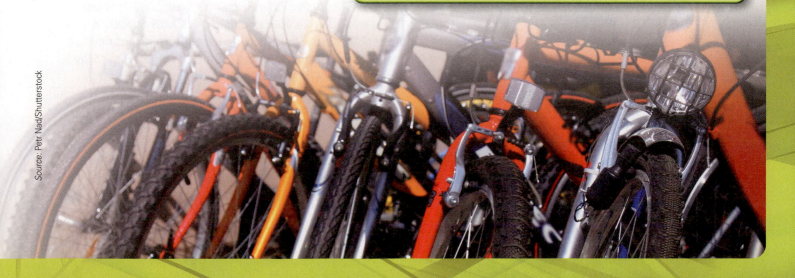

Guide

Your Personal Competitive Advantage

Consider the following possibility: After working hard to earn your degree in business, you graduate, only to discover that you cannot find a job in your area of study. You look for 6 weeks or so, but then you run out of money. In desperation, you take a job waiting tables at a local restaurant. Two years go by, the economy picks up, and the jobs you had been looking for become available. Unfortunately, your degree is now 2 years old; you are competing with students who have just graduated with fresh degrees (and fresh knowledge). Two years of waiting tables, good as you are at it, does not appear to be good experience for the job you want. You're stuck in a nightmare that will be hard to get out of—and one that you cannot allow to happen.

Examine Figure 3-7 again, but this time consider those elements of competitive advantage as they apply to you personally. As an employee, the skills and abilities you offer are your personal product. Examine the first three items in the list and ask yourself, "How can I use my time in school—and in this MIS class, in particular—to create new skills, to enhance those I already have, and to differentiate my skills from the competition?" (By the way, you will enter a national/international market. Your competition is not just the students in your class; it's also students in classes in Ohio, California, British Columbia, Singapore, New York, and everywhere else they're teaching MIS today.)

Suppose you are interested in a sales job. Perhaps you want to sell in the pharmaceutical industry. What skills can you learn from your MIS class that will make you more competitive as a future salesperson? Ask yourself, "How does the pharmaceutical industry use MIS to gain competitive advantage?" Use the Internet to find examples of the use of information systems in the pharmaceutical industry. How does Pfizer, for example, use a customer information system to sell to doctors? How can your knowledge of such systems differentiate you from your competition for a job there? How does Pfizer use a knowledge management system? How does the firm keep track of drugs that have an adverse effect on each other?

The fourth and fifth items in Figure 3-7 concern locking in customers, buyers, and suppliers. How can you interpret those elements in terms of your personal competitive advantage? Well, to lock in a relationship, you first have to have one. So do you have an internship? If not, can you get one? And once you have an internship, how can you use your knowledge of MIS to lock in your job so that you get a job offer? Does the company you are interning for have an information systems for managing customers (or any other information system that is important to the company)? If users are happy with the system, what characteristics make it worthwhile? Can you lock in a job by becoming an expert user of this system? Becoming an expert user not only locks you into your job, but it also raises barriers to entry for others who might be competing for the job. Also, can you suggest ways to improve the system, thus using your knowledge of the company and the system to lock in an extension of your job?

Human resources personnel say that networking is one of the most effective ways of finding a job. How can you use this class to establish alliances with other students?

Does your class have a Web site? Is there an email list server for the students in your class? How about a Facebook group? How can you use these to develop job-seeking alliances with other students? Who in your class already has a job or an internship? Can any of those people provide hints or opportunities for finding a job?

Don't restrict your job search to your local area. Are there regions of your country where jobs are more plentiful? How can you find out about student organizations in those regions? Search the Web for MIS classes in other cities, and make contact with students there. Find out what the hot opportunities are in other cities.

Finally, as you study MIS, think about how the knowledge you gain can help you save costs for your employers. Even more, see if you can build a case that an employer would actually save money by hiring you. The line of reasoning might be that because of your knowledge of IS, you will be able to facilitate cost savings that more than compensate for your salary.

In truth, few of the ideas that you generate for a potential employer will be feasible or pragmatically useful. The fact that you are thinking creatively, however, will indicate to a potential employer that you have initiative and are grappling with the problems that real businesses have. As this course progresses, keep thinking about competitive advantage, and strive to understand how the topics you study can help you to accomplish, personally, one or more of the principles in Figure 3-7.

Source: ER_09/Shutterstock

? DISCUSSION QUESTIONS

1. Summarize the efforts you have taken thus far to build an employment record that will lead to job offers after graduation.

2. Considering the first three principles in Figure 3-7, describe one way in which you have a competitive advantage over your classmates. If you do not have such competitive advantage, describe actions you can take to obtain one.

3. In order to build your network, you can use your status as a student to approach business professionals. Namely, you can contact them for help with an assignment or for career guidance. For example, suppose you want to work in banking and you know that your local bank has a customer information system. You could call the manager of that bank and ask him or her how that system creates a competitive advantage for the bank. You also could ask to interview other employees and go armed with the list in Figure 3-7. Describe two specific ways in which you can use your status as a student and the list in Figure 3-7 to build your network in this way.

4. Describe two ways that you can use student alliances to obtain a job. How can you use information systems to build, maintain, and operate such alliances?

ACTIVE REVIEW

Use this Active Review to verify that you understand the ideas and concepts that answer the chapter's study questions.

Q1 HOW DOES ORGANIZATIONAL STRATEGY DETERMINE INFORMATION SYSTEMS REQUIREMENTS?

Diagram and explain the relationship among industry structure, competitive strategy, value chains, business processes, and information systems. Working from the bottom up, explain how the knowledge you've gained in these first three chapters pertains to that diagram.

Q2 WHAT FIVE FORCES DETERMINE INDUSTRY STRUCTURE?

Describe the original purpose of the five forces model and the different purpose for which it is used in this chapter. Name two types of forces and describe the strength factors for each. Name three competitive forces and describe the strength factors for each. Name two bargaining power forces. Summarize the five forces operating on GearUp.

Q3 WHAT IS COMPETITIVE STRATEGY?

Describe four different strategies, as defined by Porter. For each strategy, offer an example of a company that uses that strategy. Describe GearUp's competitive strategy and justify it.

Q4 HOW DOES COMPETITIVE STRATEGY DETERMINE VALUE CHAIN STRUCTURE?

Define the terms *value, margin,* and *value chain.* Explain why organizations that choose a differentiation strategy can use

value to determine a limit on the amount of extra cost to pay for differentiation. Name the primary and support activities in the value chain and explain the purpose of each. Explain the concept of linkages.

Q5 HOW DO VALUE CHAINS DETERMINE BUSINESS PROCESSES AND INFORMATION SYSTEMS?

What is the relationship between a value chain and a business process? How do business processes relate to competitive strategy? How do information systems relate to competitive strategy? Justify the comments in the two rows labeled "Supporting business process" in Figure 3-6.

Q6 HOW DO INFORMATION SYSTEMS PROVIDE COMPETITIVE ADVANTAGES?

List and briefly describe eight principles of competitive advantage. Consider your college bookstore, and list one application of each of the eight principles. Strive to include examples that involve information systems.

How does the knowledge in this chapter help you?

Summarize why the knowledge in this chapter indicates that GearUp is on the right track in its search for cost savings. Explain the importance of Figure 3-1. Discuss how the principles of competitive advantage apply to you personally.

KEY TERMS AND CONCEPTS

Competitive strategy 52
Five forces model 50
Linkages 54

Margin 53
Primary activities 53
Support activities 53

Switching costs 57
Value 53
Value chain 53

USING YOUR KNOWLEDGE

1. Suppose you decide to start a business that recruits students for summer jobs. You will match available students with available jobs. You need to learn what positions are available and which students are available for filling those positions. In starting your business, you know you will be competing with local newspapers, Craigslist (*www.craigslist.org*), and with your college. You will probably have other local competitors as well.

   a. Analyze the structure of this industry according to Porter's five forces model.

   b. Given your analysis in part a, recommend a competitive strategy.

   c. Describe the primary value chain activities as they apply to this business.

   d. Describe a business process for recruiting students.

   e. Describe information systems that could be used to support the business process in part d.

   f. Explain how the process you described in part d and the system you described in part e reflect your competitive strategy.

2. Consider the two different bike rental companies in Figure 3-6. Think about the bikes that they rent. Clearly, the student bikes will be just about anything that can be ridden out of the shop. The bikes for the business executives, however, must be new, shiny, clean, and in tip-top shape.

   a. Compare and contrast the operations value chains of these two businesses as they pertain to the management of bicycles.

   b. Describe a business process for maintaining bicycles for both businesses.

   c. Describe a business process for acquiring bicycles for both businesses.

   d. Describe a business process for disposing of bicycles for both businesses.

   e. What roles do you see for information systems in your answers to the earlier questions? The information systems can be those you develop within your company or they can be those developed by others, such as Craigslist.

3. Samantha Green owns and operates Twigs Tree Trimming Service. Samantha graduated from the forestry program of a nearby university and worked for a large landscape design firm, performing tree trimming and removal. After several years of experience, she bought her own truck, stump grinder, and other equipment and opened her own business in St. Louis, Missouri.

   Although many of her jobs are one-time operations to remove a tree or stump, others are recurring, such as trimming a tree or groups of trees every year or every other year. When business is slow, she calls former clients to remind them of her services and of the need to trim their trees on a regular basis.

   Samantha has never heard of Michael Porter or any of his theories. She operates her business "by the seat of her pants."

   a. Explain how an analysis of the five competitive forces could help Samantha.

   b. Do you think Samantha has a competitive strategy? What competitive strategy would seem to make sense for her?

   c. How would knowledge of her competitive strategy help her sales and marketing efforts?

   d. Describe, in general terms, the kind of information system that she needs to support sales and marketing efforts.

4. YourFire, Inc., is a small business owned by Curt and Julie Robards. Based in Brisbane, Australia, YourFire manufactures and sells a lightweight camping stove called the YourFire. Curt, who previously worked as an aerospace engineer, invented and patented a burning nozzle that enables the stove to stay lit in very high winds—up to 90 miles per hour. Julie, an industrial designer by training, developed an elegant folding design that is small, lightweight, easy to set up, and very stable. Curt and Julie manufacture the stove in their garage, and they sell it directly to their customers over the Internet and via phone.

   a. Explain how an analysis of the five competitive forces could help YourFire.

   b. What does YourFire's competitive strategy seem to be?

   c. Briefly summarize how the primary value chain activities pertain to YourFire. How should the company design these value chains to conform to its competitive strategy?

   d. Describe business processes that YourFire needs in order to implement its marketing and sales and also its service value chain activities.

   e. Describe, in general terms, information systems to support your answer to part d.

COLLABORATION EXERCISE 3

Before you start this exercise, read Chapter Extensions 1 and 2, which describe collaboration techniques as well as tools for managing collaboration tasks. In particular, consider using Google Drive, Google+, Windows Live SkyDrive, Microsoft SharePoint, or some other collaboration tool.

Figure 3-13 shows the business process and related information systems for the high-value bike rental company described in Figure 3-6. The small cylinders (⬭) represent a computer database, the most common type of repository.

In terms of Porter's value chain model, this process involves both the sales and operations activities. The bike rental company uses information systems to maintain customer data in the Customer database and bike inventory data in the Bike Inventory database and to transmit hotel charge data to the Hotel Billing system.

Each information system consists of all five IS components. Consider, for example, the information system for processing the Bike Inventory database. With regard to hardware, the database itself will be stored on a computer, and it will be accessed from other computers or computing devices, such as cash registers or handheld scanning devices (possibly used to check bikes in). Computer programs will provide forms for the system users to query and update the database. Other computer programs will be used to manage the database. (You will

learn about such programs in Chapter 5.) Data, the third component of an information system, will be stored in the database. Each employee will be trained on procedures for using the system. For example, the sales clerk will learn how to query the database to determine what bikes are available and how to determine promising up-sell candidates. Finally, the people component will consist of the clerks in the rental shop as well as any support personnel for maintaining the inventory system.

Information systems that support the Customer database and those that interface with the Hotel Billing system will also have the five IS components. (By the way, whenever you consider the development or use of an information system, it is good practice to think about these five components.)

As stated in this chapter, business processes must generate more value than their cost. If they do not—if the margin of a business process is negative—then either costs must be reduced or the value increased. Considering the business process in Figure 3-13, one possibility for reducing costs is to eliminate rental personnel. Bicycles could be placed on racks having locks that customers can open with their hotel room keys; the bike would be rented until the customer places the bike back on the rack. Another possibility is to increase the value of the process. The rental agency could decide to rent additional types of equipment or perhaps to sell clothing or food and beverages.

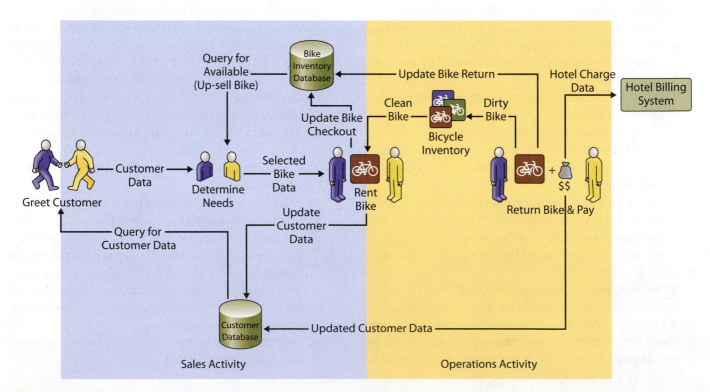

Figure 3-13
Rental Process for High-Value Bike Rental

Collaborate with your team to answer the following questions.

1. Explain the relationship between value and cost according to the Porter model. When does it make sense to add cost to a business process?

2. Suppose you are told that the business process in Figure 3-13 has a negative margin. Explain what that means. Suppose the margin of some business process is a negative $1 million. If costs are reduced by $1.2 million, will the margin necessarily be positive? Explain why or why not.

3. Consider the alternative of replacing the rental personnel from the business process in Figure 3-13.
   a. Describe changes that will need to be made to the process documented in Figure 3-13. You can download a copy of this Visio diagram from this text's Web site at *www.pearsonhighered.com/kroenke.*
   b. Would eliminating the rental personnel change the competitive strategy of this company? Is it possible to be a high-value company with no rental personnel? Explain why or why not.
   c. Would eliminating the rental personnel necessarily reduce costs? What costs would increase as a result of this change?

4. Consider the alternative of increasing the value delivered by existing rental personnel. The text suggests possibly renting more kinds of equipment or selling items of use to guests who are renting bicycles, but consider other options as well.
   a. Describe five ways that you think the existing personnel could increase the value of this business process.
   b. For the five alternatives you developed in part a, name and describe criteria for selecting among them.
   c. Using your criteria in part b, evaluate the alternative you identified in part a and select the best one. Explain your selection.
   d. Redraw Figure 3-13 for the alternative you selected in part c.

CASE STUDY 3

BOSU® Balance Trainer

The BOSU® Balance Trainer is a device for developing balance, strength, and aerobic conditioning. Invented in 1999, the BOSU Balance Trainer has become popular in leading health clubs, in athletic departments, and in homes. BOSU® stands for "both sides up," because either side of the equipment can be used for training. Figure 3-14 shows a BOSU Balance Trainer in use.

BOSU is not only a training device; it also reflects a new philosophy in athletic conditioning that focuses on balance. According to the BOSU® inventor, David Weck, "The BOSU Balance Trainer was born of passion to improve my balance. In my lifelong pursuit of enhanced athleticism, I have come to understand that balance is the foundation on which all other performance components are built." In order to obtain broad market acceptance both for his philosophy as well as for the BOSU product, Weck licensed the sales and marketing of BOSU products to Fitness Quest in 2001.

The BOSU Balance Trainer has been very successful, and that success has attracted copycat products. Fitness Quest has successfully defeated such products using a number of techniques, but primarily by leveraging its alliances with professional trainers.

According to Dustin Schnabel, BOSU® product manager,

We have developed strong and effective relationships with more than 10,000 professional trainers. We do all we can to make sure those trainers succeed with BOSU® Balance Trainer and they in turn encourage their clients to purchase our product rather than some cheap imitation.

It's all about quality. We build a quality product, we create quality relationships with the trainers, and we make sure those trainers have everything they need from us to provide a quality experience to their clients.

That strategy has worked well. Early on, Fitness Quest had a serious challenge to the BOSU Balance Trainer from a large sports equipment vendor that had preexisting alliances with major chains such as Target and Walmart. The competitor introduced a BOSU copycat at a slightly lower price. Within a few months, in an effort to gain sales, the competitor reduced the copycat's price, eventually several times, until the copycat was less than half the price of the BOSU product. Today, that copycat product is not to be seen. According to Schnabel, "They couldn't give that product away. Why? Because customers were coming in the store to buy the BOSU product that their trainers recommended."

Fitness Quest maintains a database of trainer data. It uses that database for email and postal correspondence, as well as for other marketing purposes. For example, after a marketing message has been sent, Schnabel and others watch the database for changes in trainer registration. Registrations increase after a well-received message, and they fall off when messages are off target.

Figure 3-14
The BOSU® Balance Trainer

Figure 3-15
The Indo-Row

Fitness Quest and Schnabel introduced a new piece of cardio-training equipment called the Indo-Row (shown in Figure 3-15) for which they intend to use the same marketing strategy. First, they will leverage their relationships with trainers to obtain trainer buy-in for the new concept. Then, when that buy-in occurs, they will use it to sell Indo-Row to individuals.

Go to *www.indorow.com* and watch the video. As you'll see, Indo-Row competes directly with other equipment-based forms of group exercise, such as Spinning. Schnabel states that many clubs and workout studios are looking for a new, fun, and innovative group training medium, and Indo-Row meets that need.

You can learn more about BOSU devices at *www.bosu. com*, more about Indo-Row at *www.indorow.com*, and more about Fitness Quest at *www.fitnessquest.com*.

Sources: BOSU®, *www.bosu.com* (accessed June 2012); Indo-Row, *www.indorow.com* (accessed June 2012); and conversation with Dustin Schnabel, July 2009.

QUESTIONS

1. Review the principles of competitive advantage in Figure 3-7. Which types of competitive advantage has BOSU used to defeat copycat products?

2. What role did information systems play in your answer to question 1?

3. What additional information systems could Fitness Quest develop to create barriers to entry to the competition and to lock in customers?

4. In the beginning, Fitness Quest had alliances with trainers and its main competitor had alliances with major retailers. Thus, both companies were competing on the basis of their alliances. Why do you think Fitness Quest won this competition? To what extent did its success in leveraging relationships with trainers depend on information systems? On other factors?

5. The case does not state all of the ways that Fitness Quest uses its trainer database. List five applications of the trainer database that would increase Fitness Quest's competitive position.

6. Describe major differences between the BOSU product and the Indo-Row product. Consider product use, product price, customer resistance, competition, competitive threats, and other factors related to market acceptance.

7. Describe information systems that Fitness Quest could use to strengthen its strategy for bringing Indo-Row to market. Consider the factors you identified in your answer to question 6 in your response.

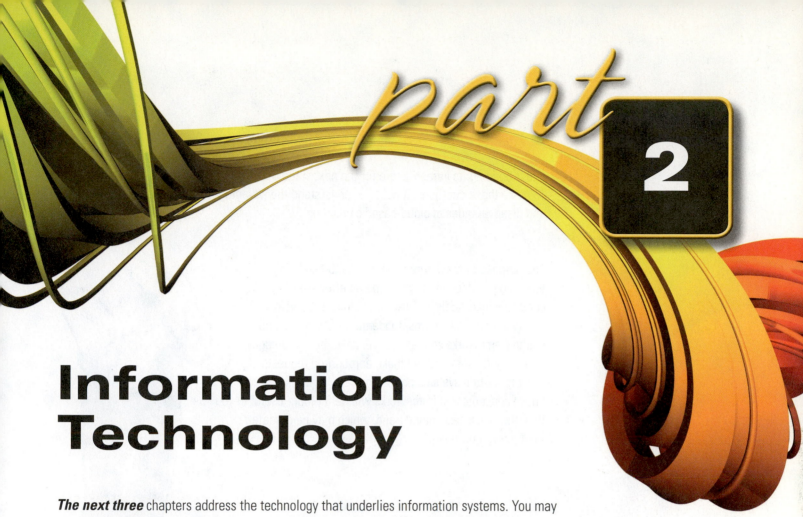

part 2

Information Technology

The next three chapters address the technology that underlies information systems. You may think that such technology is unimportant to you as a business professional. However, as you will see, today's managers and business professionals work with information technology all the time, as consumers, if not in a more involved way.

Chapter 4 discusses hardware and software and defines basic terms and fundamental computing concepts. You will see that GearUp has important decisions to make about a critical software development project.

Chapter 5 addresses the data component of information technology by describing database processing. You will learn essential database terminology and will be introduced to techniques for processing databases. We will also introduce data modeling, because you may be required to evaluate data models for databases that others develop for you.

Chapter 6 continues the discussion of computing devices begun in Chapter 4 and describes data communications and Internet technologies. GearUp needs to make decisions

Source: julien tromeur/Fotolia

about building its infrastructure for the next stage of its growth. To make those decisions, it needs to understand the advantages and disadvantages of cloud-based computing.

The purpose of these three chapters is to teach you technology sufficient for you to be an effective IT consumer, like Addison, Drew, and Emily at GearUp. You will learn basic terms, fundamental concepts, and useful frameworks so that you will have the knowledge to ask good questions and make appropriate requests of the information systems professionals who will serve you. Those concepts and frameworks will be far more useful to you than the latest technology trend, which may be outdated by the time you graduate!

Source: Gresei/Fotolia

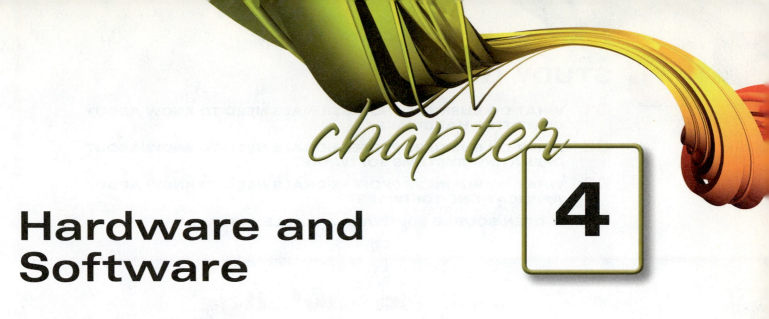

Hardware and Software

Emily Johnson, GearUp's CFO; Lucas Massey, IT director; and Drew Mills, events operations manager, are having an impromptu meeting in the company's lunchroom. Drew continues to text while they talk.

"We don't have the resources," Lucas says in response to a question from Drew. Lucas is looking at the top of Drew's head.

"What do you mean?" Drew looks up . . . his short response sounds angry.

"As in money, you know. *Dinero.* Budget. Don't have it."

"Emily, is that right?" Drew looks at Emily while he texts.

"Well, this sounds important. We might be able to . . ." She can't finish her sentence before Lucas jumps back in.

"Wait a minute; weren't we talking about *reducing* expenses last week?" Lucas' face is turning red.

"Lucas, I don't know about budget, but what I'm telling you is that if we don't have an iPad app, we don't have a business." Drew furiously texts on his phone . . .

"OK, let's talk about it for a second. You want an iPhone app, too?"

"Yes."

"Which version of iOS do you want?"

"You're not listening. I don't want iOS . . . I don't even know what that is. I want an iPad app."

"iOS . . . it's the iPad's operating system, you nitwit."

"Hold it, guys, hold it. Let's all calm down." Emily's thinking about their voices carrying down the hall.

"OK, sorry," Drew actually sounds contrite. "Are there different versions? Why does it matter?"

"Well, iOS 6 has features and functions that earlier versions don't. So, you need to tell me if we need those new features."

"Can we build for both . . . new and old?"

STUDY QUESTIONS

Q1 WHAT DO BUSINESS PROFESSIONALS NEED TO KNOW ABOUT COMPUTER HARDWARE?

Q2 WHAT DO BUSINESS PROFESSIONALS NEED TO KNOW ABOUT OPERATING SYSTEMS SOFTWARE?

Q3 WHAT DO BUSINESS PROFESSIONALS NEED TO KNOW ABOUT APPLICATIONS SOFTWARE?

Q4 IS OPEN SOURCE SOFTWARE A VIABLE ALTERNATIVE?

How does the **knowledge** in this chapter help **you?**

". . . if we don't have an iPad app, we don't have a business."

"Sure, it just comes down to . . ." Lucas is trying to stay calm.

"Resources." Drew finishes his sentence for him.

"Yup."

"Look, it's not just me. I was just texting Addison, and she says she's having a hard time with San Diego Sports."

"No! Not San Diego!" Emily jumps in, "We need them. What's going on?" Emily knows they're a key supplier in this year's revenue plan.

"Addison says they brought up the iPad issue in her negotiations for the golf clubs. They said they didn't think we were competitive . . . because we don't have an iPad app."

"Well, customers can order on Safari." Lucas offers this lamely; by now he knows this issue isn't going away.

"Yeah, they can, Lucas. But they don't want to! They want to use applications on their iPads and iPhones."

There's a pause in the conversation. Then Emily continues, "Lucas, have you looked into international development?" Emily's realizing they have to do something about this, too.

"You mean India?"

"Yeah, or some Asian company somewhere. Jerome over at Pickins.com told me that's what they did."

"We know nothing about it. What are we gonna do, run an ad in a New Delhi newspaper?" Lucas stares at the ceiling.

"No, but I can find out what Jerome did." Emily ignores his sarcasm.

Lucas realizes he needs to chill out. "I was looking into Indian developers last week, Emily . . . for another project. It's pretty scary."

"Why?"

"Like I said, we don't know what we're doing. We could waste a lot of money and time."

"Well . . ."

"One site had bad grammar and misspelled words," but as he says this, he's getting more interested.

"Does that matter?"

"Maybe not. It doesn't inspire confidence, though. I wonder about open source. . . . Nah," Lucas muses.

Optional Extension for this chapter is CE3: Introduction to Microsoft Excel 2010 371

Emily interrupts him, "I've heard about it, but what exactly is open source?"

"It's when a bunch of amateurs get together over beer and munchies and write computer programs for a hobby." Drew sounds irritated as he puts his phone away. That's more than Lucas can stand.

"Drew, you know that's ludicrous. What about Linux? Huh? Seems to work pretty well for us. But I don't think open source will work here . . ."

"Linux, Schmenix. I've got to go. I'm setting up tomorrow's golf club event . . . assuming we get the deal. I'm telling you two, you want to stay in business, get us an iPad app . . . like this week."

Drew strides out of the room, leaving Lucas and Emily staring at one another.

"Lucas, I think we better do something."

"OK, I'll look into it. How much money you got?"

"Nice try. Send me a proposal and we'll see." Emily didn't get to be a CFO by falling for that question.

"OK, give me a week to look around. Meanwhile, would you find out what Pickens.com did?"

"Sure."

WHAT DO BUSINESS PROFESSIONALS NEED TO KNOW ABOUT COMPUTER HARDWARE?

As discussed in the five-component framework, **hardware** consists of electronic components and related gadgetry that input, process, output, and store data according to instructions encoded in computer programs or software. Figure 4-1 shows the components of a generic computer. You will find these components in all types of computers: desktops, laptops, phones, iPads and other slates, Xbox and other games, etc.

BASIC COMPONENTS

Typical **input hardware** devices are the keyboard, mouse, document scanners, and bar-code (Universal Product Code) scanners like those used in grocery stores. Microphones and cameras are also input devices; with tablet PCs, human handwriting can be input as well. Older input devices include magnetic ink readers (used for reading the ink on the bottom of checks) and scanners such as the Scantron test scanner.

Processing devices include the **central processing unit (CPU)**, which is sometimes called "the brain" of the computer. Although the design of the CPU has nothing in common with the

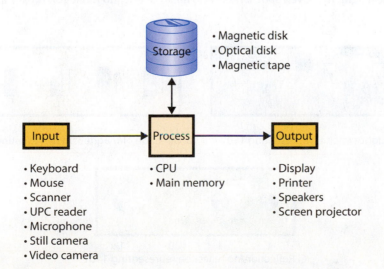

Figure 4-1
Input, Process, Output, and Storage Hardware

anatomy of animal brains, this description is helpful, because the CPU does have the "smarts" of the machine. The CPU selects instructions, processes them, performs arithmetic and logical comparisons, and stores results of operations in memory. Some computers have two or more CPUs. A computer with two CPUs is called a **dual-processor** computer. **Quad-processor** computers have four CPUs. Some high-end computers have 16 or more CPUs.

CPUs vary in speed, function, and cost. Hardware vendors such as Intel, Advanced Micro Devices, and National Semiconductor continually improve CPU speed and capabilities while reducing CPU costs (as discussed under Moore's Law in Chapter 1). Whether you or your department needs the latest, greatest CPU depends on the nature of your work, as you will learn.

The CPU works in conjunction with **main memory**. The CPU reads data and instructions from memory, and it stores results of computations in main memory. We will describe the relationship between the CPU and main memory later in the chapter. Main memory is sometimes called **RAM**, for random access memory.

Output hardware consists of video displays, printers, audio speakers, overhead projectors, and other special-purpose devices, such as large flatbed plotters.

Storage hardware saves data and programs. Magnetic disk is by far the most common storage device, although optical disks such as CDs and DVDs also are popular. Thumb drives are small, portable magnetic storage devices that can be used to back up data and to transfer it from one computer to another. In large corporate data centers, data is sometimes stored on magnetic tape.

In the past, many different plug receptacles were required to connect keyboards, mice, printers, cameras, and so on. Starting in 2000, all of these were replaced with **Universal Serial Bus (USB)** connectors. USB connectors simplified the connection of peripheral gear to computers for both manufacturers and users.

COMPUTER DATA

Most computers today also have hardware for connecting to networks. See Chapter 6.

Before we can further describe hardware, we need to define several important terms. We begin with binary digits.

Binary Digits

Computers represent data using **binary digits**, called **bits**. A bit is either a zero or a one. Bits are used for computer data because they are easy to represent physically, as illustrated in Figure 4-2. A switch can be either closed or open. A computer can be designed so that an open switch represents zero and a closed switch represents one. Or the orientation of a magnetic field can represent a bit; magnetism in one direction represents a zero, magnetism in the opposite direction represents a one. Or, for optical media, small pits are burned onto the surface of the disk so that they will reflect light. In a given spot, a reflection means a one; no reflection means a zero.

Figure 4-2
Bits are Easy to Represent Physically

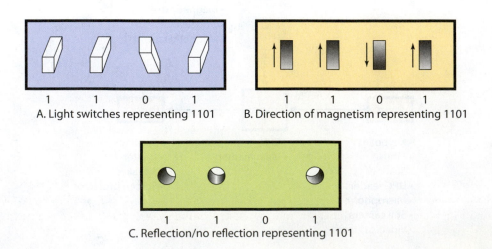

A. Light switches representing 1101   B. Direction of magnetism representing 1101

C. Reflection/no reflection representing 1101

Term	Definition	Abbreviation
Byte	Number of bits to represent one character	
Kilobyte	1,024 bytes	K
Megabyte	1,024 K = 1,048,576 bytes	MB
Gigabyte	1,024 MB = 1,073,741,824 bytes	GB
Terabyte	1,024 GB = 1,099,511,627,776 bytes	TB
Petabyte	1,024 TB = 1,125,899,906,842,624 bytes	PB
Exabyte	1,024 PB = 1,152,921,504,606,846,976 bytes	EB

Figure 4-3
Important Storage—Capacity Terminology

Sizing Computer Data

All forms of computer data are represented by bits. The data can be numbers, characters, currency amounts, photos, recordings, or whatever. All are simply a string of bits.

For reasons that interest many people but are irrelevant for business professionals, bits are grouped into 8-bit chunks called **bytes**. For character data, such as the letters in a person's name, one character will fit into one byte. Thus, when you read a specification that a computing device has 100 million bytes of memory, you know that the device can hold up to 100 million characters.

Bytes are used to measure sizes of noncharacter data as well. Someone might say, for example, that a given picture is 100,000 bytes in size. This statement means the length of the bit string that represents the picture is 100,000 bytes or 800,000 bits (because there are 8 bits per byte).

The specifications for the size of main memory, disk, and other computer devices are expressed in bytes. Figure 4-3 shows the set of abbreviations that are used to represent data-storage capacity. A **kilobyte,** abbreviated **K**, is a collection of 1,024 bytes. A **megabyte**, or **MB**, is 1,024 kilobytes. A **gigabyte,** or **GB**, is 1,024 megabytes, a **terabyte**, or **TB**, is 1,024 gigabytes, a **petabyte**, or **PB**, is 1,024 terabytes, and an **exabyte**, or **EB**, is 1,024 petabytes.

Sometimes you will see these definitions simplified as 1K equals 1,000 bytes and 1MB equals 1,000K. Such simplifications are incorrect, but they do ease the math. Also, disk and computer manufacturers have an incentive to propagate this misconception. If a disk maker defines 1MB to be 1 million bytes—and not the correct 1,024K—the manufacturer can use its own definition of MB when specifying drive capacities. A buyer may think that a disk advertised as 100MB has space for 100 × 1,024K bytes, but in truth the drive will have space for only 100 × 1,000,000 bytes. Normally, the distinction is not too important, but be aware of the two possible interpretations of these abbreviations.

IN FEWER THAN 300 WORDS, HOW DOES A COMPUTER WORK?

Figure 4-4 shows a snapshot of a computer in use. The CPU is the major actor. To run a program or process data, the computer first transfers the program or data from disk to *main memory*. Then, to execute an instruction, it moves the instruction from main memory into the CPU via the **data channel** or **bus**. The CPU has a small amount of very fast memory called a **cache**. The CPU keeps frequently used instructions in the cache. Having a large cache makes the computer faster, but the cache is expensive.

Main memory of the computer in Figure 4-4 contains program instructions for Microsoft Excel, Adobe Acrobat, and a browser (Microsoft Internet Explorer or Mozilla Firefox). It also contains a block of data and instructions for the **operating system (OS)**, which is a program that controls the computer's resources.

Figure 4-4
Computer Components, in Use

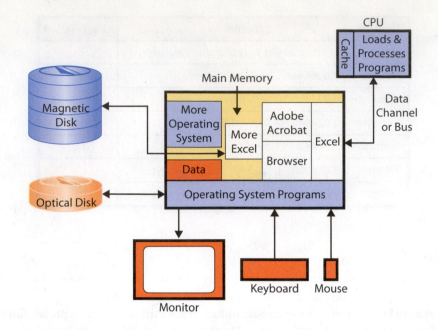

Over the course of your career, application software, hardware, and firmware will change, sometimes rapidly. The Guide on pages 96–97 challenges you to choose a strategy for addressing this change.

Main memory is too small to hold all of the programs and data that a user might want to process. For example, no personal computer has enough memory to hold all of the code in Microsoft Word, Excel, and Access. Consequently, the CPU loads programs into memory in chunks. In Figure 4-4, one portion of Excel was loaded into memory. When the user requested additional processing (say, to sort the spreadsheet), the CPU loaded another piece of Excel code.

If the user opens another program (say, Word) or needs to load more data (say, a picture), the operating system will direct the CPU to attempt to place the new program or data into unused memory. If there is not enough memory, it will remove something, perhaps the block of memory labeled More Excel, and then it will place the just-requested program or data into the vacated space. This process is called **memory swapping**.

WHY DOES A BUSINESS PROFESSIONAL CARE HOW A COMPUTER WORKS?

You can order computers with varying sizes of main memory. An employee who runs only one program at a time and who processes small amounts of data requires very little memory—1GB will be adequate. However, an employee who processes many programs at the same time (say, Word, Excel, Firefox, Access, Acrobat, and other programs) or an employee who processes very large files (pictures, movies, or sound files) needs lots of main memory, perhaps 3GB or more. If that employee's computer has too little memory, then the computer will constantly be swapping memory, and it will be slow. (This means, by the way, that if your computer is slow and if you have many programs open, you likely can improve performance by closing one or more programs. Depending on your computer and the amount of memory it has, you might also improve performance by adding more memory.)

You can also order computers with CPUs of different speeds. CPU speed is expressed in cycles called *hertz*. In 2012, a slow personal computer has a speed of 1.5 Gigahertz. A fast personal computer has a speed of 3+ Gigahertz, with dual processors. As predicted by Moore's Law, CPU speeds continually increase.

Additionally, CPUs today are classified as **32-bit** or **64-bit**. Without delving into the particulars, a 32-bit is less capable and cheaper than a 64-bit CPU. The latter can address more main memory; you need a 64-bit processor to effectively use more than 4GB of memory. 64-bit processors have other advantages as well, but they are more expensive than 32-bit processors.

An employee who does only simple tasks such as word processing does not need a fast CPU; a 32-bit, 1.5 Gigahertz CPU will be fine. However, an employee who processes large, complicated spreadsheets or who manipulates large database files or edits large picture, sound, or movie files needs a fast computer like a 64-bit, dual processor with 3.5 Gigahertz or more.

One last comment: The cache and main memory are **volatile**, meaning their contents are lost when power is off. Magnetic and optical disks are **nonvolatile**, meaning their contents survive when power is off. If you suddenly lose power, the contents of unsaved memory—say, documents that have been altered—will be lost. Therefore, get into the habit of frequently (every few minutes or so) saving documents or files that you are changing. Save your documents before your roommate trips over the power cord.

WHAT IS THE DIFFERENCE BETWEEN A CLIENT AND A SERVER?

Before we can discuss computer software, you need to understand the difference between a client and a server. Figure 4-5 shows the computing environment of the typical user. Users employ **client** computers for word processing, spreadsheets, database access, and so forth. Most client computers also have software that enables them to connect to a network. It could be a private network at their company or school, or it could be the Internet, which is a public network. (We will discuss networks and the cloud in Chapter 6. Just wait!)

Servers, as their name implies, provide some service. Some servers process email; others process Web sites; others process large, shared databases; and some provide all of these functions or other, similar functions.

A server is just a computer, but, as you might expect, server computers must be fast and they usually have multiple CPUs. They need lots of main memory, at least 4GB, and they require very large disks—often a terabyte or more. Because servers are almost always accessed from another computer via a network, they have limited video displays, or even no display at all. For the same reason, many have no keyboard.

Business professionals also need to be aware of how malware can affect productivity—both theirs and their organization's. For more information on malware, see Ethics Guide on pages 94–95.

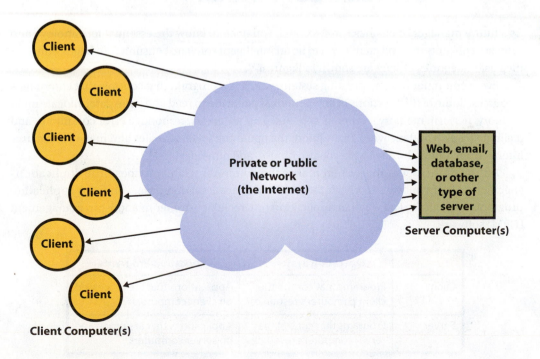

Figure 4-5
Client and Server Computers

Figure 4-6
Server Farm

Source: Amy Walters/Shutterstock.

For sites with large numbers of users (e.g., Amazon.com), servers are organized into a collection of servers called a **server farm** like the one shown in Figure 4-6. Servers in a farm coordinate their activities in an incredibly sophisticated and fascinating technology dance. They receive and process hundreds, possibly thousands, of service requests per minute. For example, as you learned in Case 1, on November 29, 2010, Amazon.com processed an average of 158 items per second for 24 hours. In this dance, computers hand off partially processed requests to each other while keeping track of the current status of each request. They can pick up the pieces when a computer in the farm fails. All of this is done in the blink of an eye, with the user never knowing any part of the miracle underway. It is absolutely gorgeous engineering!

Increasingly, server infrastructure is delivered as a service in what is termed *the cloud*. We will discuss cloud computing in Chapter 6, after you have some knowledge of data communications.

 ## WHAT DO BUSINESS PROFESSIONALS NEED TO KNOW ABOUT OPERATING SYSTEMS SOFTWARE?

As a future manager or business professional, you need to know the essential terminology and software concepts that will enable you to be an intelligent software consumer. To begin, consider the basic categories of software shown in Figure 4-7.

Every computer has an operating system, which is a program that controls that computer's resources. Some of the functions of an operating system are to read and write data, allocate main memory, perform memory swapping, start and stop programs, respond to error conditions, and facilitate backup and recovery. In addition, the operating system creates and manages the user interface, including the display, keyboard, mouse, and other devices.

Although the operating system makes the computer usable, it does little application-specific work. If you want to check the weather or access a database, you need application programs such as an iPad weather application or Oracle's customer relationship management (CRM) software.

Figure 4-7
Categories of Computer Software

	Operating System	**Application Programs**
Client	Programs that control the client computer's resources	Applications that are processed on client computers
Server	Programs that control the server computer's resources	Applications that are processed on server computers

Both client and server computers need an operating system, though they need not be the same. Further, both clients and servers can process application programs. The application's design determines whether the client, the server, or both, process it.

You need to understand two important software constraints. First, in most cases, a particular operating system works only with a particular type of hardware. iOS works only on the iPhone and iPad hardware. Mac OS X works only on the Mac. However, in some cases, multiple versions of the operating system are available for different computer types. There is a version of Linux (see Figure 4-8 below) for just about everything, including your kitchen blender. Android, a version of Linux, runs on the Kindle Fire, many slates and many smartphones as well.

Second, application programs are written to use a particular operating system. That fact is problematic for GearUp. They want to build a phone application for their auctions, but because applications only run on particular operating systems, they'll have to create one version for Apple devices, and other versions for other types, such as Android or Windows phones. Consider operating systems and application programs in more detail.

WHAT ARE THE MAJOR OPERATING SYSTEMS?

The major operating systems are listed in Figure 4-8.

Category	Operating System	Used for	Remarks
Nonmobile Clients	Windows	Personal Computer Clients	Most widely used operating system in business. Current version is Windows 8. Metro-style applications provide a touch interface.
	Mac OS X	Macintosh Clients	First used by graphic artists and others in arts community; now used more widely. First desktop OS to provide a touch interface.
	Unix	Workstation Clients	Popular on powerful client computers used in engineering, computer-assisted design, architecture. Difficult for the nontechnical user.
	Linux	Just about anything	Open-source variant of Unix. Adapted to almost every type of computing device. On a PC, used with Open Office application software.
Mobile Clients	Symbian	Nokia, Samsung, and other phones	Popular world-wide, but less so in North America.
	Blackberry OS	Research in Motion Blackberries	Device and OS developed for use by business. Very popular in beginning, but strongly challenged by iPhone and others
	iOS	iPhone, iPod Touch, iPad	Rapidly increasing installed base with success of the iPhone and iPad. Based on Max OS X.
	Android	T-Mobile and other phones. Tablets and e-readers like the Kindle Fire	Linux-based phone/tablet operating system from Google. Rapidly increasing market share.
	Windows RT	Windows 8 for ARM devices	Windows 8 tailored specifically for ARM devices, mostly tablets, but some PCs, too.
Servers	Windows Server	Servers	Businesses with a strong commitment to Microsoft.
	Unix	Servers	Fading from use. Replaced by Linux.
	Linux	Servers	Very popular. Aggressively pushed by IBM.

Figure 4-8
Major Operating Systems

Figure 4-9
Metro Interface

Source: Microsoft Corporation

Nonmobile Client Operating Systems

Nonmobile client operating systems are used on desktops and laptop computers. The most popular is **Microsoft Windows**. Some version of Windows resides on more than 85 percent of the world's desktops, and, if we consider just business users, the figure is more than 95 percent.

The most recent client version of Windows is Windows 8, a major re-write of prior versions. Windows 8 is distinguished by what Microsoft calls **Metro-style applications**. These applications are touch-screen oriented and provide context-sensitive, pop-up menus. They can also be used with a mouse and keyboard. Microsoft claims that Metro-style applications work just as well on portable, mobile devices such as slate computers as they do on desktop computers. One key feature of Metro applications is the minimization of menu bars, status lines, and other visual overhead. Figure 4-9 shows an example of a Metro-style version of searching for images in Windows Explorer.

For more on Metro-style interfaces, see Chapter Extension 7, Mobile Systems.

Apple Computer, Inc., developed its own operating system for the Macintosh, **Mac OS**. The current version is Mac OS X Lion. Apple touts it as the world's most advanced desktop operating system, and until Windows 8, it was. Now OS X and Windows 8 compete neck and neck for that title.

Until recently, Mac OS was used primarily by graphic artists and workers in the arts community. But for many reasons, Mac OS has made headway into the traditional Windows market. According to Apple, Mac sales increased 28 percent in 2010 while sales of Windows personal computers fell 1 percent.[1] Others claim that Windows has stopped the loss and is regaining market share.[2]

Mac OS was designed originally to run the line of CPU processors from Motorola. In 1994, Mac switched to the PowerPC processor line from IBM. As of 2006, Macintosh computers are available for both PowerPC and Intel CPUs. A Macintosh with an Intel processor is able to run both Windows and the Mac OS.

Most industry observers would agree that Apple has led the way, both with the Mac OS and the iOS, in creating easy-to-use interfaces. Certainly, many innovative ideas have first appeared in a Macintosh or iSomething and then later been added, in one form or another, to Windows or one of the mobile operating systems.

Today, both Mac OS X Lion and Windows 8 include many of the features that Apple made popular on the iPhone and iPad. It seems clear that touch-based interfaces, on all devices, are the future.

---

[1] Steve Jobs presentation in June 2011.
[2] http://www.netmarketshare.com/os-market-share.aspx?qprid=9, accessed May, 2012.

Unix is an operating system that was developed at Bell Labs in the 1970s. It has been the workhorse of the scientific and engineering communities since then. Unix is generally regarded as being more difficult to use than either Windows or Mac. Many Unix users know and employ an arcane language for manipulating files and data. However, once they surmount the rather steep learning curve, most Unix users become fanatic supporters of the system. Sun Microsystems and other vendors of computers for scientific and engineering applications are the major proponents of Unix. In general, Unix is not for the business user.

Linux is a version of Unix that was developed by the open source community (discussed on page 90). This community is a loosely coupled group of programmers who mostly volunteer their time to contribute code to develop and maintain Linux. The open source community owns Linux, and there is no fee to use it. Linux can run on client computers, but usually only when budget is of paramount concern. Linux is by far most popular as a server OS.

Mobile Client Operating Systems

Figure 4-8 also lists the five principal mobile operating systems. **Symbian** is popular on phones in Europe and the Far East, but less so in North America. **BlackBerry OS** was one of the most successful early mobile operating systems and was used primarily by business users on BlackBerry devices. It is now losing market share to iOS and Android.

iOS is the operating system used on the iPhone, iPod Touch, and iPad. When first released, it broke new ground with its ease of use and compelling display, features that are now being copied by the BlackBerry OS and Android. With the popularity of the iPhone and iPad, Apple has been increasing its market share of iOS and now claims that it is used on 44 percent of all mobile devices.

Android is a mobile operating system licensed by Google. Android devices have a very loyal following, especially among technical users. Recently, Android has been gaining market share over the BlackBerry OS on phones, and it received a big boost when it was selected for the Amazon Kindle Fire.

Windows RT is a version of Windows for use on ARM devices. **ARM** is a computer architecture and instruction set that is designed for portable devices such as phones and slates. Windows RT is a version of Windows 8 that is specifically designed to provide a touch-based interface for devices that use this architecture. Windows RT places some restrictions on applications to preserve device power and prolong battery life. As of August 2012, it appears that some vendors will offer personal computers based on the ARM architecture that include Windows RT, and possibly include new versions of Office Word, Excel, PowerPoint, and OneNote with the operating system. By the time you read this, much more will be known. Search *Windows RT* on the Internet to learn the most recent news.

The smartphone market has always been huge, but recently, e-book readers and tablets have substantially increased the market for mobile client operating systems. As of early 2012, one in four Americans owned at least one of these devices.[3]

Server Operating Systems

The last three rows of Figure 4-8 show the three most popular server operating systems. **Windows Server** is a version of Windows that has been specially designed and configured for server use. It has much more stringent and restrictive security procedures than other versions of Windows and is popular on servers in organizations that have made a strong commitment to Microsoft.

Unix can also be used on servers, but it is gradually being replaced by Linux.

Linux is frequently used on servers by organizations that want, for whatever reason, to avoid a server commitment to Microsoft. IBM is the primary proponent of Linux and in the past has used it as a means to better compete against Microsoft. Although IBM does not own Linux, IBM

[3]http://betanews.com/2012/01/23/one-in-four-americans-own-an-e-book-reader-or-tablet/, accessed August 30, 2012.

has developed many business systems solutions that use Linux. By using Linux, neither IBM nor its customers have to pay a license fee to Microsoft.

VIRTUALIZATION

Virtualization is the process by which one computer hosts the appearance of many computers. One operating system, called the **host operating system**, runs one or more operating systems as applications. Those hosted operating systems are called **virtual machines (vm).** Each virtual machine has disk space and other resources allocated to it. The host operating system controls the activities of the virtual machines it hosts to prevent them from interfering with one another. With virtualization, each vm is able to operate exactly the same as it would if it were operating in a stand-alone, nonvirtual environment.

Three types of virtualization exist:

- PC virtualization
- Server virtualization
- Desktop virtualization

With **PC virtualization**, a personal computer, such as a desktop or portable computer, hosts several different operating systems. Say a user needs, for some reason, to have both Linux and Windows 8 running on his or her computer. In that circumstance, the user can install a virtual host operating system and then both Linux and Windows 8 on top of it. In that way, the user can have both systems on the same hardware. VMWare Workstation is a popular PC virtualization product that can run both Windows and Linux operating systems.

With **server virtualization**, a server computer hosts one (or more) other server computers. In Figure 4-10, a Windows Server computer is hosting two virtual machines. Users can log on to either of those virtual machines, and they will appear as normal servers. Figure 4-11 shows how virtual machine VM3 appears to a user of that server. Notice that a user of VM3 is running a browser that is accessing SharePoint. In fact, this virtual machine was used to generate many of the SharePoint figures in Chapter Extension 2. Server virtualization plays a key role for cloud vendors, as you'll learn in Chapter 6.

PC and server virtualization are important and interesting, but it is possible that desktop virtualization will revolutionize desktop processing. With **desktop virtualization**, a server hosts

Figure 4-10
Windows Server Computer
Hosting Two Virtual Machines

Source: Microsoft Corporation

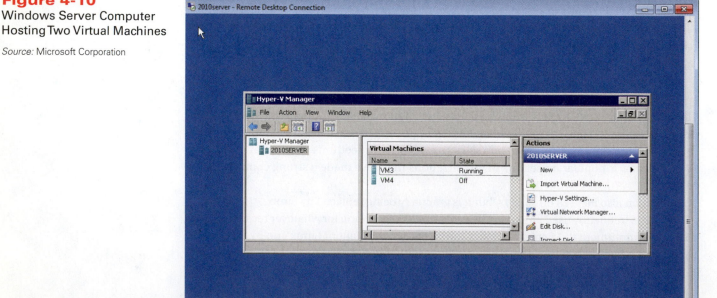

Figure 4-11
Virtual Machine Example

many versions of desktop operating systems. Each of those desktops has a complete user environment and appears to the user to be just another PC. However, the desktop can be accessed from any computer to which the user has access. Thus, you could be at an airport and go to a computer and access your virtualized desktop. To you, it appears as if that airport computer is your own personal computer. Later, you could do the same to a utility computer while sitting in your hotel room. Meanwhile, many other users could have accessed the computer in the airport, and each thought he or she had his or her personal computer. IBM offers PC virtualization for as low as $12 a month, per PC. Desktop virtualization is in its infancy, but it could have a major impact during the early years of your career.

Own Versus License

As you read this chapter, understand that when you buy a computer program, you are not actually buying that program. Instead, you are buying a **license** to use that program. For example, when you buy a Windows license, Microsoft is selling you the right to use Windows. Microsoft continues to own the Windows program. Large organizations do not buy a license for each computer user. Instead, they negotiate a **site license**, which is a flat fee that authorizes the company to install the product (operating system or application) on all of that company's computers or on all of the computers at a specific site.

In the case of Linux, no company can sell you a license to use it. It is owned by the open source community, which states that Linux has no license fee (with certain reasonable restrictions). Large companies such as IBM and smaller companies such as RedHat can make money by supporting Linux, but no company makes money selling Linux licenses.

WHAT DO BUSINESS PROFESSIONALS NEED TO KNOW ABOUT APPLICATIONS SOFTWARE?

During your professional career, it is highly unlikely that you'll have much influence over the operating system chosen by your organization. That decision will be made by others. However, you will have a choice about your own devices and their operating systems, so such knowledge will matter to you when selecting them.

The situation is different for **application software**, which is software that runs on top of the operating system and performs particular services and functions. Most such software is for your use and for the use of those whom you employ, work with, or sell to. Because this is so, you will likely have a greater role in participating in the selection and possibly the development of application software. For example, at GearUp, Drew has strong opinions regarding the applications that GearUp builds for phones, and GearUp management will pay attention to him. In fact, those opinions are a significant part of his professional value to GearUp. The same situation could pertain to you, so you need to pay close attention to relevant applications, both now and throughout your career.

What Categories of Application Programs Exist?

Application software is a broad category. On the one hand, it includes powerful and complicated applications like Microsoft Office that are used for a wide array of purposes. On the other hand, application software includes smaller, single-function applications such as LocalEats, an iOS application that provides local restaurant recommendations and nothing else. To organize this broad category, three types of application software have been defined.

Horizontal-market application software provides capabilities common across all organizations and industries. Word processors, graphics programs, spreadsheets, and presentation programs are all horizontal-market application software.

Examples of such software are Microsoft Word, Excel, and PowerPoint. Examples from other vendors are Google Drive, Adobe's Acrobat, Photoshop, PageMaker, and Jasc Corporation's Paint Shop Pro. These applications are used in a wide variety of businesses, across all industries. They are purchased off-the-shelf, and little customization of features is necessary (or possible).

To learn more about Microsoft Excel, see Chapter Extension 3.

Vertical-market application software serves the needs of a specific industry. Examples of such programs are those used by dental offices to schedule appointments and bill patients, those used by auto mechanics to keep track of customer data and customers' automobile repairs, and those used by parts warehouses to track inventory, purchases, and sales.

Vertical applications usually can be altered or customized. Typically, the company that sold the application software will provide such services or offer referrals to qualified consultants who can provide this service.

One-of-a-kind application software is developed for a specific, unique need. The IRS develops such software, for example, because it has needs that no other organization has. Additionally, with the increased importance of phone and tablet applications, many companies have developed one-of-a-kind applications for their particular business. Vanguard has mobile applications for iOS and Android, for example. GearUp needs to do the same, at least according to Drew.

Thin Clients Versus Thick Clients

When you use an application such as Adobe Photoshop, it runs only on your computer and does not need to connect to any server to run. Such programs are called **desktop programs** and are not considered clients.

Applications that process code on both the client and the server are called **client-server applications**. A **thick-client application** is an application program that must be preinstalled on the client. A **thin-client application** is one that runs within a browser and does not need to be preinstalled. When the user of a thin-client application starts that application, if any code is needed, the browser loads that code dynamically from the server.

For example, the Office Web Applications that come with Windows Live SkyDrive and Office 365 are thin clients, whereas the Office 2010 versions are thick clients. Thus, the Word Web Application is thin; the full version of Office 2010 Word is thick. The latter application needs to be installed.

Note this category pertains to personal computers as well as mobile devices such as phones and tablets. Thin applications run only within a browser on the device; thick applications are purchased, usually from a store such as iTunes.

To summarize, the relationship of application types is as follows:

- Desktop application
- Client-server application
  - Thick client
  - Thin client

Thick and thin clients each have their own advantages and disadvantages. Because thick clients can be larger (they don't have to be downloaded while the user waits), they can have more features and functions. However, they do have to be installed, as when you buy a new application for your iPhone or other mobile device. Periodically, you update to new versions when you synch your phone or otherwise connect to the source of the application. To you, as an individual, this isn't much of a problem. However, in a large organization, where it is important that everyone use the same version of the same application, such installation and version management is an expensive administrative burden.

Thin-client applications are sometimes preferred to thick-client applications because they require only a browser; no special client software needs to be installed. This also means that when a new version of a thin-client application is created, the browser automatically downloads that new code. However, because the code is downloaded during use, thin clients need to be smaller.

Today, organizations use a wide mixture of applications and operating systems. Figure 4-12 shows a typical situation. Two clients are running Windows; one is running the Mac OS,

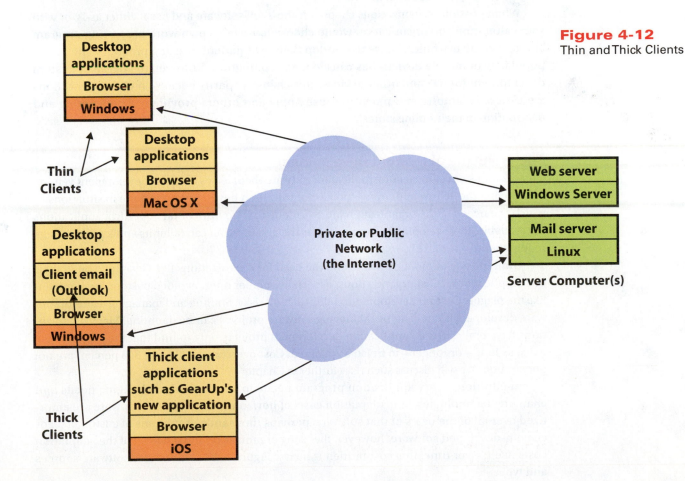

Figure 4-12
Thin and Thick Clients

and the other is running iOS on an iPhone. Two thin clients are running only a browser, like Google Chrome. The thick clients each have a thick-client email application installed; one is running Microsoft Office Outlook, and the other is running GearUp's new application and other thick applications.

Figure 4-12 also shows two servers; the Windows Server computer is supporting a Web server, and the Linux server is supporting email.

HOW DO ORGANIZATIONS ACQUIRE APPLICATION SOFTWARE?

You can acquire application software in exactly the same ways that you can buy a new suit. The quickest and least risky option is to buy your suit off-the-rack. With this method, you get your suit immediately, and you know exactly what it will cost. You may not, however, get a good fit. Alternately, you can buy your suit off-the-rack and have it altered. This will take more time, it may cost more, and there's some possibility that the alteration will result in a poor fit. Most likely, however, an altered suit will fit better than an off-the-rack one.

Finally, you can hire a tailor to make a custom suit. In this case, you will have to describe what you want, be available for multiple fittings, and be willing to pay considerably more. Although there is an excellent chance of a great fit, there is also the possibility of a disaster. Still, if you want a yellow and orange polka-dot silk suit with a hissing rattlesnake on the back, tailor-made is the only way to go. You can buy computer software in exactly the same ways: **off-the-shelf software**, **off-the-shelf with alterations software**, or tailor-made. Tailor-made software is called **custom-developed software**.

When possible, organizations choose off-the-shelf software and use it either as-is, or with some alteration. No organization would choose to write its own word processing program and few dentists would choose to develop their own patient tracking program. The rise in popularity of mobile devices has caused many companies, however, to engage in custom development for iOS and other devices. This change is partly because mobile applications are generally simpler and partly because Apple and others provide wide marketing and distribution in their online stores.

The Problems of Custom Development

Organizations develop custom application software themselves or hire a development vendor. Like buying the yellow and orange polka-dot suit, such development is done in situations in which the needs of the organization are so unique that no horizontal or vertical applications are available. By developing custom software, the organization can tailor its application to fit its requirements.

Until the rise of mobile devices and the need for organizations like GearUp to build their own applications, most organizations, especially smaller ones, avoided custom development like the plague. Custom development is difficult and risky. Staffing and managing teams of software developers is challenging. Managing software projects can be daunting. Many organizations have embarked on application development projects only to find that the projects take twice as long—or longer—to finish as planned. Cost overruns of 200 and 300 percent are not uncommon. We will discuss such risks further in Chapter 10.

In addition, every application program needs to be adapted to changing needs and changing technologies. The adaptation costs of horizontal and vertical software are amortized over all of the users of that software, perhaps thousands or millions of customers. For custom-developed software, however, the using organization must pay all of the adaptation costs itself. Over time, this cost burden is heavy. Figure 4-13 summarizes software sources and types.

Figure 4-13
Software Sources and Types

	Software Source		
Software Type	Off-the-shelf	Off-the-shelf and then customized	Custom-developed
Horizontal applications	🟩		
Vertical applications	🟧	🟧	
One-of-a-kind applications			🟦

Thin-client Versus Thick-client Mobile Custom Software

In most cases, it is easier to build a thin-client custom application than a thick-client one. The programming languages are simpler, and fewer skills are required to develop them. However, until recently, the user experience of a thin-client application was not as fully featured or as interesting as on a thick-client. New technology is on the horizon that may make thin clients' user experience competitive with thick ones. Having a better user experience is one reason Drew wants GearUp to build a thick-client application.

There is another reason for organizations to develop thick-client applications; they create switching costs. If I use LocalEats' thick-client application to find restaurants, it is far less likely that I'll try some other restaurant review service. If I use the LocalEats' thin-client on Safari, there is little cost for me to switch to another source of reviews.

Apple set the stage for the acquisition of mobile thick-clients when it created the iTunes store. Apple tests and certifies applications before it places them in the store, and then it sells the applications to customers, on behalf of the developer. That model has been a screaming success, as you can read in Case 4 (page 101). However, it poses problems for mobile applications that are developed in-house, for in-house use. If, say, a major corporation like 3M develops an application for employee insurance applications that will run on a mobile device, how do those employees obtain that application? 3M is naturally reluctant to place it in the iTunes store (and will view Apple's testing of 3M's own application as unnecessary and even patronizing). So, how do employees obtain mobile custom applications? We don't know. Not as of 2012, anyway. This question lies right on the edge of today's technology. Stay tuned.

To learn about this new technology including HTML5 and CSS3, see Chapter Extension 7.

WHAT IS FIRMWARE?

Firmware is computer software that is installed into devices such as printers, print servers, and various types of communication devices. The software is coded just like other software, but it is installed into special, read-only memory of the printer or other device. In this way, the program becomes part of the device's memory; it is as if the program's logic is designed into the device's circuitry. Users do not need to load firmware into the device's memory.

Firmware can be changed or upgraded, but this is normally a task for IS professionals. The task is easy, but it requires knowledge of special programs and techniques that most business users choose not to learn.

IS OPEN SOURCE SOFTWARE A VIABLE ALTERNATIVE?

To answer this question, you first need to know a bit about the open source movement and process. Most computer historians would agree that Richard Matthew Stallman is the father of the movement. In 1983, he developed a set of tools called **GNU** (a self-referential acronym meaning

GNU Not Unix) for creating a free Unix-like operating system. Stallman made many other contributions to open source, including the **GNU general public license (GPL) agreement,** one of the standard license agreements for open source software. Stallman was unable to attract enough developers to finish the free Unix system, but continued making other contributions to the open source movement.

In 1991, Linus Torvalds, working in Helsinki, began work on another version of Unix, using some of Stallman's tools. That version eventually became Linux, the high-quality and very popular operating system discussed previously.

The Internet proved to be a great asset for open source, and many open source projects became successful, including:

- Open Office (a Microsoft Office look-alike)
- Firefox (a browser)
- MySQL (a DBMS, see Chapter 5)
- Apache (a Web server, see Chapter 6)
- Ubuntu (a Windows-like desktop operating system)
- Android (a mobile-device operating system)
- Cassandra (a NoSQL DBMS, see Chapter 5)
- Hadoop (a BigData processor, see Chapter 8)

WHY DO PROGRAMMERS VOLUNTEER THEIR SERVICES?

To anyone who has never written computer programs, it is difficult to understand why anyone would donate their time and skills to contribute to open source projects. Programming is, however, an intense combination of art and logic, and designing and writing a complicated computer program is exceedingly pleasurable (and addictive). Like many programmers, at times in my life I have gleefully devoted 16 hours a day to writing computer programs—day after day—and the days would fly by. If you have an artistic and logical mind, you ought to try it.

Anyway, the first reason that people contribute to open source is that it is great fun! Additionally, some people contribute to open source because it gives them the freedom to choose the projects upon which they work. They may have a programming day job that is not terribly interesting, say, writing a program to manage a computer printer. Their job pays the bills, but it's not fulfilling.

In the 1950s, Hollywood studio musicians suffered as they recorded the same style of music over and over for a long string of uninteresting movies. To keep their sanity, those musicians would gather on Sundays to play jazz, and a number of high-quality jazz clubs resulted. That's what open source is to programmers. A place where they can exercise their creativity while working on projects they find interesting and fulfilling.

Another reason for contributing to open source is to exhibit one's skill, both for pride as well as to find a job or consulting employment. A final reason is to start a business selling services to support an open source product.

HOW DOES OPEN SOURCE WORK?

The term *open source* means that the source code of the program is available to the public. **Source code** is computer code as written by humans and that is understandable by humans. Figure 4-14 shows a portion of the computer code that I wrote for the phone application shown on page 221. Source code is compiled into **machine code** that is processed by a computer. Machine code is, in general, not understandable by humans and cannot be modified. When the

Experiencing MIS

Place Your Bets Now!

Source: dozornaya/Fotolia

June 18, 2012, Milk Studios, Los Angeles

Microsoft announces Microsoft **Surface**, a tablet device to compete with the iPad and Kindle.

Just another hardware announcement? Not quite. For the first time in Microsoft's 37 year history it decided to manufacture its own hardware. (Except for keyboards, mice, and the Xbox, that is.)

Microsoft has been notorious for not manufacturing hardware. In the early PC days, Microsoft expressly left hardware manufacturing to IBM, Compaq, Hewlett-Packard, Dell, etc. It gained considerable market share over Apple because that decision enabled those powerful companies to succeed selling Microsoft Windows on their hardware, which in turn set the stage for Microsoft Office. In the 1980s, Bill Gates famously wrote Steve Jobs telling him that he needed to give up hardware and focus on software.

But, was Steve Jobs right all along? At the announcement, Steve Ballmer, Microsoft CEO, indicated there were features that Microsoft could build, or at least build better, if it controlled the hardware. Is owning manufacturing one of the keys for Apple's ability to create such beautiful, easily used, and highly functional devices? Maybe so.

Meanwhile, that same month, Google finalized its acquisition of Motorola Mobility, thus becoming a manufacturer of smartphone hardware. Is its manufacture of tablet hardware just around the corner? Or, perhaps by the time you read this, Google will have announced that it is manufacturing its own tablet.

But Google and Microsoft have a problem (or is it an advantage?) that Apple doesn't have: channel conflict. Apple is the only manufacturer of Apple hardware. But, numerous companies other than Google make Android phones and tablets, and several companies other than Microsoft make Windows phones and tablets. What happens to those businesses? Have they been thrown under the technology bus?

So now it's a three-way race for market share: Apple far in the lead, Google following up, and Microsoft struggling for footing back in the dust. They're all strong horses; all have deep technical staff, knowledge, and patents, and plenty of money. Place your bets now!

Form a group as directed by your professor and answer the following questions:

1. Apple held its Worldwide Developers Conference on June 11, 2012. OS Mountain Lion and a new, lightweight Mac were announced. By Apple standards, not much. Exactly one week later, Microsoft announced Surface. Invitations to Microsoft's announcement went to the press on June 14, 2012. Interpret the timing of those events.

2. Microsoft held the press conference at a movie studio in Los Angeles. Why there? It was probably not the only location in the United States available on short notice. Why did they choose that particular location? Was there to have been a Surface media announcement that fell through at the last minute? Search for news since June 2012 that may explain what happened.

3. Update the table on the next page with the latest announcements and data. Go to http://finance.yahoo.com and update the financial data. Add new devices as appropriate. Search the Internet, using terms such as *iPhone vs. Android market share* to update the market share data.

4. According to the latest data, how has the market share of these three companies changed? Has Apple made continued inroads on Android phones? Has Surface made inroads on the iPad? What's happened to the Kindle? And what about Microsoft's measly 2 percent of the phone market? Has Surface helped? Or has Microsoft finally given up on smartphones?

5. Unlike Apple and Google, Microsoft controls Windows Server, a server operating system. Does that provide an advantage to Microsoft in this race? There are rumors, in fact, that Apple runs Windows Server in its iCloud data center. If true, does it matter?

6. In October 2011, Microsoft purchased Skype. Does Skype contribute to Surface? Can you find announcements that indicate there is some convergence there?

7. Microsoft makes and sells the Xbox with motion-sensing Kinect. Can you envision a way for Microsoft to use either of those to help increase market share of its Surface/phone devices? If so, what?

8. The name *Microsoft Surface* had been used in the past by Microsoft for another product, one that is now called PixelSense (see the collaboration exercise). Surface is a great name; PixelSense is terrible. Do you think the choice of names says anything important about how Microsoft values the two products? Why or why not?

9. Suppose your group has $500,000 to invest in AAPL, GOOG, or MSFT. You must put all of it in one stock. Which stock do you choose and why?

	Apple		Google		Microsoft	
Device	iPhone	iPad	Android Phones	Kindle Fire[1]	Windows Phones	Surface
Hardware Manufacturer	Apple	Apple	Google & Others	Others	Others	Microsoft & Others
OS	iOS	iOS	Android	Android	Windows 8 RT	Windows 8 Windows 8 RT
Market Share	30%[2]	68%	46%	13%	2%	0%
Camera	Yes	Yes	Yes	No	Yes	No
Keyboard	Internal	Internal	Internal	Internal	Internal	External
Revenue	$146 billion		$40 billion		$73 billion	
Cash 6/18/2012	$29 billion		$47 billion		$58 billion	
Market Cap 6/18/2012	$547 billion		$186 billion		$250 billion	
Share Price 6/18/2011	$320		$485		$24	
Share Price 6/18/2012	$586		$571		$30	
Annual Price Growth	86%		17%		25%	

[1] Device is manufactured and sold by Amazon. By the time you read this, Google will likely have its own tablet, not as of August 2012, however.

[2] Meaning, 30 percent of the cell phone market.

Source of Financial Data: finance.yahoo.com

application runs, the machine code version of the program in Figure 4-14 runs on the phone's computer. We do not show machine code in a figure because it would look like this:

1101001010010111111001110111100100011100000111111011101111100111 . . .

In a **closed source** project, say Microsoft Office, the source code is highly protected and only available to trusted employees and carefully vetted contractors. The source code is protected like gold in a vault. Only those trusted programmers can make changes to a closed source project.

With open source, anyone can obtain the source code from the open source project's Web site. Programmers alter or add to this code depending on their interests and goals. In most cases, programmers can incorporate open source code into their own projects. They may be able to re-sell those projects depending on the type of license agreement the project uses.

Open source succeeds because of collaboration. A programmer examines the source code and identifies a need or project that seems interesting. He or she then creates a new feature, redesigns or reprograms an existing feature, or fixes a known problem. That code is then sent to others in the open source project who then evaluate the quality and merits of the work and add it to the product, if appropriate.

Typically, there is a lot of give and take. Or, as described in Chapter Extension 1, there are many cycles of iteration and feedback. Because of this iteration, a well-managed project with strong peer reviews can result in very high-quality code, like that in Linux.

Figure 4-14
Source Code Sample

```
/// <summary>
/// Allows the page to draw itself.
/// </summary>
private void OnDraw(object sender, GameTimerEventArgs e)
{
    SharedGraphicsDeviceManager.Current.GraphicsDevice.Clear(Color.CornflowerBlu

    SharedGraphicsDeviceManager.Current.GraphicsDevice.Clear(Color.Black);

    // Render the Silverlight controls using the UIElementRenderer.
    elementRenderer.Render();

    // Draw the sprite
    spriteBatch.Begin();

    // Draw the rectangle in its new position
    for (int i = 0; i < 3; i++)
    {
        spriteBatch.Draw(texture[i], bikeSpritePosition[i], Color.White);
    }

    // Using the texture from the UIElementRenderer,
```

SO, IS OPEN SOURCE VIABLE?

The answer depends on to whom and for what. Open source has certainly become legitimate. According to *The Economist*, "It is now generally accepted that the future will involve a blend of both proprietary and open-source software."[6] During your career, open source will likely take a greater and greater role in software. However, whether open source works for a particular situation depends on the requirements and constraints of that situation. You will learn more about matching requirements and programs in Chapter 10.

In some cases, companies choose open source software because it is "free." It turns out that this advantage may be less important than you'd think, because in many cases support and operational costs swamp the initial licensing fee.

How does the **knowledge** in this chapter help **you?**

In the world of today's commerce, you will be involved with the use of technology in business. You have no real choice; the only choice you do have is whether to be a passive participant or to become actively involved. The knowledge of this chapter will help you choose the latter. From it, you know enough about hardware and software to ask good questions, and to avoid embarrassing gaffs as when Drew didn't know that iOS is the operating system of the iPad. You also now know sources of application software, and the reasons for choosing one source over another. Finally, you know that open source is not just a "bunch of amateurs" but a movement that has created numerous quality software products, and is a viable alternative for many situations. However, all of this knowledge is perishable, just like tomatoes at the farmers' market. You'll need to follow some of the techniques in the Keeping Up to Speed Guide to continually refresh your knowledge.

---

[6]"Unlocking the Cloud," *The Economist*, May 28, 2009. Available at http://www.economist.com/node/13740181, accessed August 30, 2012.

Guide

Keeping Up to Speed

Have you ever been to a cafeteria where you put your lunch tray on a conveyor belt that carries the dirty dishes into the kitchen? That conveyor belt reminds me of technology. Like the conveyor, technology just moves along, and all of us run on top of the technology conveyor, trying to keep up. We hope to keep up with the relentless change of technology for an entire career without ending up in the techno-trash.

Technology change is a fact, and the only appropriate question is, "What am I going to do about it?" One strategy you can take is to bury your head in the sand: "Look, I'm not a technology person. I'll leave it to the pros. As long as I can send email and use the Internet, I'm happy. If I have a problem, I'll call someone to fix it."

That strategy is fine, as far as it goes, and many businesspeople have used it. Following that strategy won't give you a competitive advantage over anyone, and it will give someone else a competitive advantage over you, but as long as you develop your advantage elsewhere, you'll be OK—at least for yourself.

What about your department, though? If an expert says, "You should be buying your employees Windows 8 RT slate devices," are you going to nod your head and say, "Great. Sell 'em to me!" Or are you going to know enough to realize that it may be too early to know what the success of Windows 8 RT will be? Or to know that maybe you'll have problems getting home-grown, in-house applications down from whatever store Microsoft sets up?

At the other end of the spectrum are those who love technology. You'll find them everywhere—they may be accountants, marketing professionals, or production-line supervisors who not only know their field, but also enjoy information technology. Maybe they were IS majors or had double majors that combined IS with another area of expertise (e.g., IS with accounting). These people read CNET News and ZDNet most days, and they can tell you the latest on desktop virtualization or html5 or Windows 8 RT. Those people are sprinting along the technology conveyor belt; they will never end up in the techno-trash, and they will use their knowledge of IT to gain competitive advantage throughout their careers.

Many business professionals fall in between these extremes. They don't want to bury their heads, but they don't have the desire or interest to become technophiles (lovers of technology) either. What to do? There are a couple of strategies. For one, don't allow yourself to ignore technology. When you see a technology article in the *Wall Street Journal*, read it. Don't just skip it because it's about technology. Read the technology ads, too. Many vendors invest heavily in ads that instruct without seeming to. Another option is to take a seminar or pay attention to professional events that combine your specialty with technology. For example, when you go to the banker's convention, attend a session or two on "Technology Trends for Bankers." There are always sessions like that, and you might make a contact with similar problems and concerns in another company.

Probably the best option, if you have the time for it, is to get involved as a user representative in technology committees in your organization. At a company like

GearUp, get involved in the specifications for the iOS app. Or, if your company is doing a review of its CRM system, see if you can get on the review committee. When there's a need for a representative from your department to discuss needs for the next-generation help-line system, sign up. Or, later in your career, become a member of the business practice technology committee, or whatever they call it at your organization.

Just working with such groups will add to your knowledge of technology. Presentations made to such groups, discussions about uses of technology, and ideas about using IT for competitive advantage will all add to your IT knowledge. You'll gain important contacts and exposure to leaders in your organization as well.

It's up to you. You get to choose how you relate to technology. But be sure you choose; don't let your head fall into the sand without thinking about it.

Source: WavebreakMediaMicro/Fotolia

DISCUSSION QUESTIONS

1. Do you agree that the change of technology is relentless? What do you think that means to most business professionals? To most organizations?

2. Think about the three postures toward technology presented here. Which camp will you join? Why?

3. Write a two-paragraph memo to yourself justifying your choice in question 2. If you chose to ignore technology, explain how you will compensate for the loss of competitive advantage. If you're going to join one of the other two groups, explain why, and describe how you're going to accomplish your goal.

4. Given your answer to question 2, assume that you're in a job interview and the interviewer asks about your knowledge of technology. Write a three-sentence response to the interviewer's question.

ACTIVE REVIEW

Use this Active Review to verify that you understand the ideas and concepts that answer the chapter's study questions.

Q1 WHAT DO BUSINESS PROFESSIONALS NEED TO KNOW ABOUT COMPUTER HARDWARE?

List categories of hardware and explain the purpose of each. Define *bit* and *byte*. Explain why bits are used to represent computer data. Define the units of bytes used to size memory. In general terms, explain how a computer works. Explain how a manager can use this knowledge. Explain why you should save your work from time to time while you are using your computer. Define *server farm* and summarize the technology dance that occurs on a server farm.

Q2 WHAT DO BUSINESS PROFESSIONALS NEED TO KNOW ABOUT OPERATING SYSTEMS SOFTWARE?

Review Figure 4-8 and explain the meaning of each cell in this table. Describe the competition between Apple's OS X and Microsoft's Windows 8. Define Metro-style application. Describe three kinds of virtualization, and explain the use of each. Explain the difference between software ownership and software licenses.

Q3 WHAT DO BUSINESS PROFESSIONALS NEED TO KNOW ABOUT APPLICATIONS SOFTWARE?

Explain the difference in roles that business professionals play regarding the choice of operating system and applications software. Explain the differences among horizontal-market, vertical-market, and one-of-a-kind applications. Compare thin- and thick-clients and give an example of each on an iPhone. Describe the three ways that organizations can acquire software. Summarize the problems of custom development, and explain two reasons that an organization might choose to develop a thick-client mobile application. Explain how the traditional method of selling and distributing mobile applications fails for organizations that develop their own mobile apps for their own employees.

Q4 IS OPEN SOURCE SOFTWARE A VIABLE ALTERNATIVE?

Define *GNU* and *GPL*. Name three successful open source projects. Describe four reasons programmers contribute to open source projects. Define *open source, closed source, source code,* and *machine code*. In your own words, explain why open source is a legitimate alternative but may or may not be appropriate for a given application.

How does the knowledge in this chapter help you?

State the choice you have with regard to your involvement with technology in commerce. List the topics that you have learned about hardware and software. Explain how you can use knowledge of application software sources. Briefly describe open-source software and explain why it is sometimes, but not always, a viable option. Explain why this knowledge is perishable and state what you can do about that fact.

KEY TERMS AND CONCEPTS

USING YOUR KNOWLEDGE

1. Suppose that your roommate, a political science major, asks you to help her purchase a new laptop computer. She wants to use the computer for email, Internet access, and for note-taking in class. She wants to spend less than $1,000.
   a. What CPU, memory, and disk specifications would you recommend?
   b. What software does she need?
   c. Shop *www.dell.com*, *www.hp.com*, and *www.lenovo.com* for the best computer deal.
   d. Which computer would you recommend, and why?

2. Suppose that your father asks you to help him purchase a new computer. He wants to use his computer for email, Internet access, downloading pictures from his digital camera, uploading those pictures to a shared photo service, and writing documents to members of his antique auto club.
   a. What CPU, memory, and disk specifications would you recommend?
   b. What software does he need?
   c. Shop *www.dell.com*, *www.hp.com*, and *www.lenovo.com* for the best computer deal.
   d. Which computer would you recommend, and why?

3. Microsoft offers free licenses of certain software products to students at colleges and universities that participate in its DreamSpark program (formerly known as the Microsoft Developer Network (MSDN) Academic Alliance (AA)). If your college or university participates in this program, you have the opportunity to obtain hundreds of dollars of software, for free. Here is a partial list of the software you can obtain:
   - Microsoft Access 2010
   - OneNote 2010
   - Expression Studio 4
   - Windows 2008 Server
   - Microsoft Project 2010
   - Visual Studio Developer
   - SQL Server 2008
   - Visio 2010
   a. Search *www.microsoft.com*, *www.google.com*, or *www.bing.com* and determine the function of each of these software products.
   b. Which of these software products are operating systems, and which are application programs?
   c. Which of these programs are DBMS products (the subject of the next chapter)?
   d. Which of these programs should you download and install tonight?

e. Either (1) download and install the programs in your answer to part d, or (2) explain why you would not choose to do so.

f. Does DreamSpark provide an unfair advantage to Microsoft? Why or why not?

4. Suppose you work at GearUp and Emily asks you to create a list of the top five features needed by the GearUp iOS application. Visit a company similar to GearUp, say Woot (*www.woot.com*), or MyHabit (*www.myhabit.com*) to get a sense of the requirements. If you have access to

an iPhone or an iPad, download the Woot or MyHabit iOS application and study it. List what you think are the application's top five features and functions and briefly describe each.

5. Visit *www.apple.com*, *www.microsoft.com*, and *www.ibm.com*. Summarize differences in the look and feel of each of these sites. Do you think one of these sites is superior to the others? If not, say why. If so, do you think the look and feel of the superior site should be copied by the other companies? Why or why not?

COLLABORATION EXERCISE 4

Before you start this exercise, read Chapter Extensions 1 and 2, which describe collaboration techniques as well as tools for managing collaboration tasks. In particular, consider using Google Drive, Google+, Windows Live SkyDrive, Microsoft SharePoint, or some other collaboration tool.

In the past few years, Microsoft has been promoting **PixelSense**, a new hardware–software product that enables people to interact with data on the surface of a table. PixelSense initiates a new product category, and the best way to understand it is to view one of Microsoft's promotional videos at *www.PixelSense.com*.

PixelSense paints the surface of the 30-inch table with invisible, near-infrared light to detect the presence of objects. It can respond to up to 52 different touches at the same time. According to Microsoft, this means that four people sitting around the PixelSense table could use all 10 of their fingers to manipulate up to 12 objects, simultaneously.

PixelSense uses wireless and other communications technologies to connect to devices that are placed on it, such as cameras or cell phones. When a camera is placed on PixelSense, pictures "spill" out of it, and users can manipulate those pictures with their hands. Products can be placed on PixelSense, and their product specifications are displayed. Credit cards can be placed on PixelSense, and items to be purchased can be dragged or dropped onto the credit card.

Currently, Microsoft PixelSense is marketed and sold to large-scale commercial organizations in the financial services, healthcare, hospitality, retail, and public service business sectors. Also, smaller organizations and individuals can purchase a PixelSense unit from Samsung. (*www.samsunglfd.com /solution/sur40.do*)

One of the first implementers of PixelSense was the iBar lounge at Harrah's Rio All-Suite Hotel and Casino in Las Vegas, Nevada. The subtitle for the press release announcing iBar's system read, "Harrah's Reinvents Flirting and Offers New Uninhibited Fun and Play to iBar Patrons."[8]

The potential uses for PixelSense are staggering. Maps can display local events, and consumers can purchase tickets to those events by just using their fingers. PixelSense can also be used for new computer games and gambling devices. Children can paint on PixelSense with virtual paintbrushes. Numerous other applications are possible. At the product's announcement, Steve Ballmer, CEO of Microsoft, said, "We see this as a multibillion dollar category, and we envision a time when surface computing technologies will be pervasive, from tabletops and counters to the hallway mirror. PixelSense is the first step in realizing that vision."[9]

As you can see at the PixelSense Web site, this product can be used for many different purposes in many different places, such as restaurants, retail kiosks, and eventually at home. Probably most of the eventual applications for PixelSense have not yet been envisioned. One clear application, however, is in the gambling and gaming industry. Imagine placing your credit card on a PixelSense gambling device and gambling the night away. Every time you lose, a charge is made against your credit card. Soon, before you know it, you've run up $15,000 in debt, which you learn when PixelSense tells you you've reached the maximum credit limit on your card.

Recall the RAND Study cited in Chapter 1 that stated there will be increased worldwide demand for workers who can apply new technology and products to solve business problems in innovative ways. PixelSense is an excellent example of a new technology that will be applied innovatively.

---

[8]"Harrah's Entertainment Launches Microsoft Surface at Rio iBar, Providing Guests with Innovative and Immersive New Entertainment Experiences." Microsoft Press Release, http://www.microsoft.com/presspass/press/2008/jun08/06-11HETSurfacePR.mspx, accessed June 2012.
[9]Microsoft Press Release, May 29, 2007.

1. Consider uses for PixelSense at your university. How might PixelSense be used in architecture, chemistry, law, medicine, business, geography, political science, art, music, or any other discipline in which your team has interest? Describe one potential application for PixelSense for five different disciplines.

2. List specific features and benefits for each of the five applications you selected in question 1.

3. Describe, in general terms, the work that needs to be accomplished to create the applications you identified in question 1.

4. Until June 2012, PixelSense was called Surface. At that time, Microsoft repurposed the name to use on its tablet devices. Surface was changed to PixelSense. What conclusions do you draw from these naming decisions?

5. You will sometimes hear the expression, "Emerging technology is constantly leveling the playing field," meaning that technology eliminates competitive advantages of existing companies and enables opportunities for new companies. How does this statement pertain to Surface, Windows 8, and Apple?

CASE STUDY 4

The Apple of Your i

A quick glance at Apple's stock history in Figure 4-15 will tell you that Apple, Inc., is a very successful company. You might be surprised to learn, however, just *how* successful. In roughly 4 years, Apple has quadrupled its market capitalization (the number of outstanding shares times the stock price) to more than $600 billion, making Apple the largest public company in the world. To put that number in perspective, Microsoft—for years the market capitalization leader of software companies—has a market capitalization of $266.3 billion, and Google has a market capitalization of $225.0 billion.[10]

In late June 2011, numerous market analysts were predicting that the then $332 stock would increase another $100 within

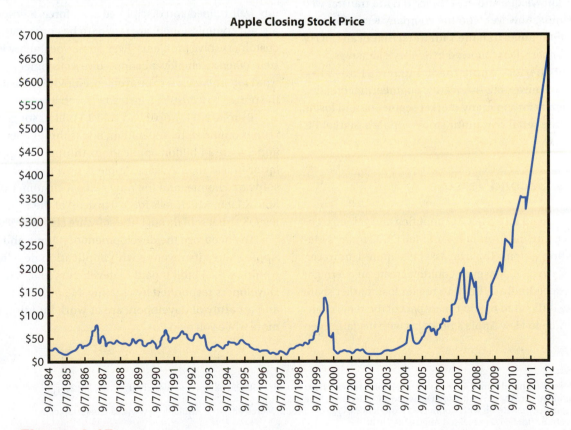

Figure 4-15
Growth in Apple Stock Price

Source: Reprinted with permission from Yahoo! Inc. © 2012 Yahoo! Inc. YAHOO! and the YAHOO! logo are trademarks of Yahoo! Inc.

---

[10]http://finance.yahoo.com, accessed August 29, 2012.

6 months. In fact, by August 2012, it was trading over $600. Apple has been so successful that the NASDAQ stock exchange concluded that it was overinfluential in the computation of the NASDAQ-100 Index and reduced Apple's weight in that index from 20 to 12 percent. That's success!

Alas, it wasn't always that way.

Early Success and Downfall

At the dawn of the personal computer age, in the early 1980s, Apple pioneered well-engineered home computers and innovative interfaces with its Apple II PC for the home and its Macintosh computer for students and knowledge workers. At one point, Apple owned more than 20 percent of the PC market, competing against many other PC vendors, most of which are no longer relevant (or in business).

However, Apple lost its way. In 1985, Steve Jobs, Apple's chief innovator, lost a fight with the Apple board and was forced out. He founded another PC company, NeXT, which developed and sold a groundbreaking PC product that was too groundbreaking to sell well in that era. Meanwhile, Apple employed a succession of CEOs, starting with John Sculley, who was hired away from Pepsi-Cola where he'd enjoyed considerable success. Sculley's knowledge and experience did not transfer well to the PC business, however, and the company went downhill so fast that CNBC named him the 14th worst American CEO of all time.[11] Two other CEOs followed in Sculley's footsteps.

During this period, Apple made numerous mistakes, among them not rewarding innovative engineering, creating too many products for too many market segments, and losing the respect of the retail computer stores. Apple's market PC share plummeted.

Steve Jobs, Second Verse

In 1996, Apple bought Jobs' NeXT Computing and gained technology that became the foundation of Mac OS X, today's Macintosh operating system. The true asset it acquired, however, was Steve Jobs. Even he, however, couldn't create an overnight miracle. It is exceedingly difficult to regain lost market share and even more difficult to regain the respect of the retail channel that had come to view Apple's products with disdain. Even

by 2011, Apple's PC market share was in the range of 10 to 12 percent, down from a high of 20 percent in the 1980s.

In response to these problems, Apple broke away from the PC and created new markets with its iPod, iPhone, and iPad. It also countered retailer problems by opening its own stores. In the process, it pioneered the sale of music and applications over the Internet.

iPod, iPhone, and iPad devices are a marvel of creativity and engineering. They exude not only ease of use, but also now/wow/fun coolness. By selling hot music for the iPod, Apple established a connection with a dynamic segment of the market that was willing to spend lots of money on bright, shiny objects. The ability to turn the iPhone on its side to rotate images probably sold more iPhones than anything else. With the iPad, portable devices became readable, and the market responded by awarding Apple a 44 percent (and growing) share of the mobile market.[12]

All of this success propelled Apple's stores not only beyond vanilla retailers like Best Buy, but also beyond the lofty heights of Tiffany & Co. In 2011, Apple stores were grossing more than $4,000 per square foot, compared to $3,000 for Tiffany and a mere $880 for Best Buy. As of 2012, Apple operates over 350 such retail outlets and has welcomed over 1 billion customer visits.[13]

Apple encourages customer visits and loyalty with its open and inviting sales floor, its Genius Bar help desk, and its incredibly well-trained and disciplined sales force. Salespeople, who are not commissioned, are taught to be consultants who help customers solve problems. Even some vocabulary is standardized. When an employee cannot solve a customer's problem, the word *unfortunately* is to be avoided; employees are taught to use the phrase *as it turns out,* instead.[14] Try that on your next exam!

By mid-2011, Apple had sold 15 billion songs through its iTunes online store, 130 million books through its iBookstore, and a mere 14 billion applications through its App Store, the latter in less than 3 years. Apple is now the number one PC software channel and the only place a customer can buy the Mac X Lion, which sells for $30 instead of the $130 for the earlier OS X that sold through the software channel.[15]

To encourage the development of iPhone and iPad apps, Apple shares its revenue with application developers. That would be $2.5 billion paid to developers in less than 3 years! Developers responded by creating 445,000 iOS applications, and an army of developers are at work building thousands more while you read this.

---

[11]"Portfolio's Worst CEOs of All Time," CNBC.com. Available at www.cnbc.com/id/30502091?slide=8, accessed August 30, 2012.

[12]Apple presentation at the Apple Worldwide Developers Conference, June 6, 2011.

[13]Carl Howe, "Apple Reboots Retail with Connected Experiences," Yankee Group, March 23, 2011. Available at www.yankeegroup.com/ResearchDocument.do?id=56472, accessed August 30, 2012.

[14]Yukari Iwatani Kane and Ian Sherr, "Secrets from Apple's Genius Bar: Full Loyalty, No Negativity," *Wall Street Journal,* June 15, 2011. Available at http://online.wsj.com/article/SB10001424052702304563104576364071955678908.html, accessed August 30, 2012.

[15]Apple presentation at the Apple Worldwide Developers Conference, June 6, 2011.

By the way, if you want to build an iOS application, what's the first thing you need to do? Buy a Macintosh. Apple closed its development to any other development method. Adobe Flash? No way. Apple claims that Flash has too many bugs, and perhaps so. Thus, Flash developers are excluded. Microsoft Silverlight? Nope. Microsoft developers are out in the cold, too. The non-Apple development community was furious, and Apple's response was, in essence, "Fine, we'll pay our $2.5 billion to someone else."

The bottom line? Every sales success feeds every other sales success. Hot music fed the iPod. The iPod fed iTunes and created a growing customer base that was ripe for the iPhone. Sales of the iPhone fed the stores, whose success fed the developer community, which fed more applications, which fed the iPhone and set the stage for the iPad, which fed the App Store, which enabled the $30 price on the OS X Lion, which led to more loyal customers, and, of course, to more developers. No wonder some shareholders want Steve Ballmer to resign as CEO over at Microsoft![16]

QUESTIONS

1. Which of Porter's four competitive strategies (from Chapter 3) does Apple engage in? Explain.

2. What do you think are the three most important factors in Apple's incredible success? Justify your answer.

3. Steve Jobs passed away in October 2011. Until his death, he had been the heart and soul of Apple's innovation. Today, 35,000 Apple employees continue onward in his absence. A huge question for many investors is whether the company can be successful without him. As of 2012, the stock has continued its rapid climb, so his death hasn't hurt stock price so far. What is your opinion? What role did he play? How can Apple respond to his loss? Would you be willing to invest in Apple without his leadership? Why or why not?

4. Microsoft took an early lead in the development of slate devices (like the iPad), and it had the world's leading operating system and applications for over 20 years. Provide five reasons why Microsoft was not able to achieve the same success that Apple has. Most industry analysts would agree that the skills and abilities of Microsoft's 88,000 employees are as good, on average, as Apple's.

5. Considering your answers to the four questions above, as well as the current stock price, if you had a spare $5,000 in your portfolio and wanted to buy an equity stock with it, would you buy AAPL (Apple)? Why or why not?

[16]Sharon Pian Chan, "Steve Ballmer Pre-Announces 2011 Earnings for Microsoft," *Seattle Times,* June 30, 2011. Available at http://seattletimes.nwsource.com/html/businesstechnology/2015465692_microsoftballmer30.html, accessed August 30, 2012.

Database Processing

Kelly Summers, CEO of GearUp, assigned Drew Mills and Addison Lee the task of finding ways to reduce operational costs. Drew and Addison know that one source of inefficiency is order cancellations that happen when suppliers don't ship the inventory they say they will. Even though Drew and Addison know this is a problem, they don't know how big of a problem, and they can't convince Kelly on the basis of a hunch.

Accordingly, Drew and Addison set up a meeting with Lucas Massey, the director of GearUp's IT department, to request a report that they need.

"This looks like trouble! The two of you at once, I mean." Lucas is only partly kidding as he looks at them.

"Oh, come on, Lucas, you can handle us just fine," Drew responds as he sits down. "Besides, if you have trouble, it's standing right over there," he says, nodding at Addison.

"OK, here's the deal," Addison doesn't have patience for this small talk. "We're trying to get our operational costs down and we know some vendors are causing us a ton of extra expense."

"For example," Drew jumps in, "we know that General Sports routinely tells us they have inventory they don't have."

"So what happens?" Lucas knows the answer, but he wants to hear how Drew or Addison understands it.

"We have to cancel any of the customer orders that depended on that inventory, which I think you know . . ." Drew's in mid-sentence when Addison finishes his thought.

"Or, make a partial shipment of what we do have, but even that's got problems. You know, if you buy a kayak and a paddle from us, and we only send you the paddle . . . well, you get the picture."

STUDY QUESTIONS

Q1 WHAT IS THE PURPOSE OF A DATABASE?

Q2 WHAT IS A DATABASE?

Q3 WHAT IS A DATABASE MANAGEMENT SYSTEM (DBMS)?

Q4 HOW DO DATABASE APPLICATIONS MAKE DATABASES MORE USEFUL?

Q5 WHAT IS A NoSQL DBMS?

How does the **knowledge** in this chapter help **you?**

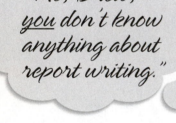

"No, Drew, you don't know anything about report writing."

"And no matter what," continues Drew, "even if the cancellation is clean, we have extra costs as well as lost customer goodwill."

"So where do I come in?" asks Lucas.

"We need data. We know that General causes us problems, but we don't know how much. So we want a report of all the cancellations caused by General's short shipments." Addison is pleased to finally get to the point.

"Actually, it's not just General. We know other vendors ship shortages that cause cancellations as well. But we really don't know which ones and how much," Drew adds.

"So," Lucas pauses while he ponders his response, "you want a report of all the cancelled orders?"

"No, not all the cancelled orders, just all those that were cancelled because we didn't get the inventory from the supplier."

"Hmmm. We'll have to combine data from our customer order and shipping system with data from accounts payable. It can be done. How soon do you need it?"

"Today." Addison's in a hurry.

"No way. I can't do that. How about I give you a data extract and you create the report. I could do that by Monday."

"We don't know anything about . . ." Drew starts to object when Addison jumps in.

"Can you put the data into Access?"

"Sure."

"All right. We'll take you up on that. What time Monday?"

"Noon?"

"OK."

After the meeting, Addison and Drew are talking quietly on their way back to Drew's cubicle.

"Addison, what are you doing? We don't know anything about creating reports . . . ," Drew whispers.

"No, Drew, *you* don't know anything about report writing. This isn't hard. If he gives me the data, I can munge around in Access to make the report. It's just for us; we're not gonna post it on the Web site."

"Seems hard to me, but I'll go along. I hope that's not a mistake."

"It won't be. Just watch."

Optional Extensions for this chapter are • CE4: Database Design 389 • CE5: Using Microsoft Access 2010 404 • CE6: Using Excel and Access Together 423

Q1 WHAT IS THE PURPOSE OF A DATABASE?

The purpose of a database is to help people keep track of things. When most students learn that, they wonder why we need a special technology for such a simple task. Why not just use a list? If the list is long, put it into a spreadsheet.

In fact, many professionals do keep track of things using spreadsheets. If the structure of the list is simple enough, there is no need to use database technology. The list of student grades in Figure 5-1, for example, works perfectly well in a spreadsheet.

Suppose, however, that the professor wants to track more than just grades. Say that the professor wants to record email messages as well. Or, perhaps the professor wants to record both email messages and office visits. There is no place in Figure 5-1 to record that additional data. Of course, the professor could set up a separate spreadsheet for email messages and another one for office visits, but that awkward solution would be difficult to use because it does not provide all of the data in one place.

Instead, the professor wants a form like that in Figure 5-2. With it, the professor can record student grades, emails, and office visits all in one place. A form like the one in Figure 5-2

For more on Database Design, See Chapter Extension 4.

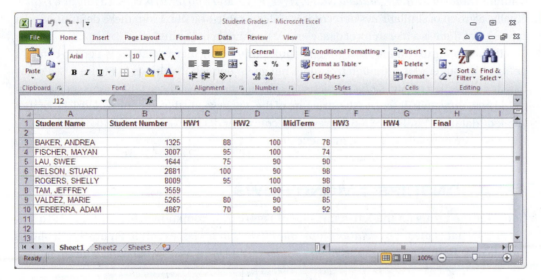

Figure 5-1
A List of Student Grades Presented in a Spreadsheet

Source: Microsoft Excel 2010

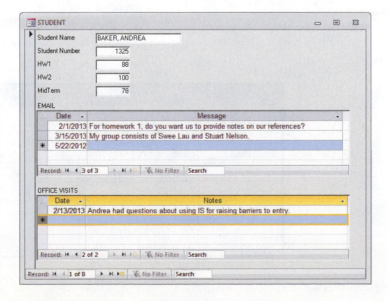

Figure 5-2
Student Data Shown in a Form, from a Database

Source: Microsoft Access 2010

is difficult, if not impossible, to produce from a spreadsheet. Such a form is easily produced, however, from a database.

The key distinction between Figures 5-1 and 5-2 is that the data in Figure 5-1 is about a single theme or concept. It is about student grades only. The data in Figure 5-2 has multiple themes; it shows student grades, student emails, and student office visits. We can make a general rule from these examples: Lists of data involving a single theme can be stored in a spreadsheet; lists that involve data with multiple themes require a database. We will say more about this general rule as this chapter proceeds.

Q2   WHAT IS A DATABASE?

As you will see, databases can be more difficult to develop than spreadsheets; this difficulty causes some people to prefer to work with spreadsheets—or at least pretend to—as described in the Guide on pages 122–123.

A **database** is a self-describing collection of integrated records. To understand the terms in this definition, you first need to understand the terms illustrated in Figure 5-3. As you learned in Chapter 4, a **byte** is a character of data. In databases, bytes are grouped into **columns**, such as *Student Number* and *Student Name*. Columns are also called **fields**. Columns or fields, in turn, are grouped into **rows**, which are also called **records**. In Figure 5-3, the collection of data for all columns (*Student Number*, *Student Name*, *HW1*, *HW2*, and *MidTerm*) is called a *row* or a *record*. Finally, a group of similar rows or records is called a **table** or a **file**. From these definitions, you can see that there is a hierarchy of data elements, as shown in Figure 5-4.

It is tempting to continue this grouping process by saying that a database is a group of tables or files. This statement, although true, does not go far enough. As shown in Figure 5-5, a database is a collection of tables *plus* relationships among the rows in those tables, *plus* special data, called *metadata*, that describes the structure of the database. By the way, the cylindrical symbol labeled "database" in Figure 5-5 represents a computer disk drive. It is used like this because databases are normally stored on magnetic disks.

Access is a common database. For more information on Access, see Chapter Extensions 5 and 6. Chapter Extension 6 covers Excel as well.

RELATIONSHIPS AMONG ROWS

Consider the terms on the left-hand side of Figure 5-5. You know what tables are. To understand what is meant by *relationships among rows in tables*, examine Figure 5-6. It shows sample data from the three tables *Email*, *Student*, and *Office_Visit*. Notice the column named

Figure 5-3
Student Table (also called a file)

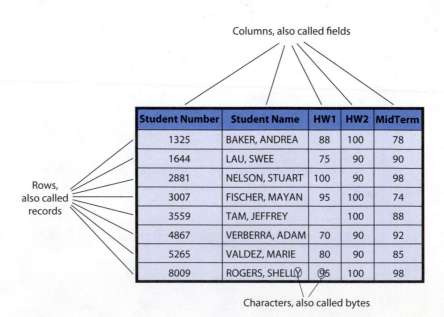

Columns, also called fields

Student Number	Student Name	HW1	HW2	MidTerm
1325	BAKER, ANDREA	88	100	78
1644	LAU, SWEE	75	90	90
2881	NELSON, STUART	100	90	98
3007	FISCHER, MAYAN	95	100	74
3559	TAM, JEFFREY		100	88
4867	VERBERRA, ADAM	70	90	92
5265	VALDEZ, MARIE	80	90	85
8009	ROGERS, SHELLY	95	100	98

Rows, also called records

Characters, also called bytes

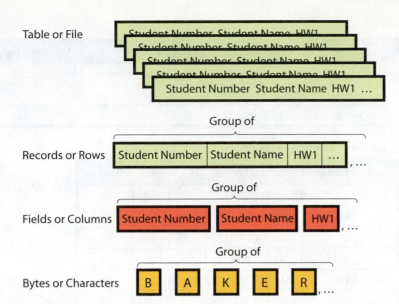

Figure 5-4
Hierarchy of Data Elements

Student Number in the *Email* table. That column indicates the row in *Student* to which a row of *Email* is connected. In the first row of *Email*, the *Student Number* value is 1325. This indicates that this particular email was received from the student whose *Student Number* is 1325. If you examine the *Student* table, you will see that the row for Andrea Baker has this value. Thus, the first row of the *Email* table is related to Andrea Baker.

Now consider the last row of the *Office_Visit* table at the bottom of the figure. The value of *Student Number* in that row is 4867. This value indicates that the last row in *Office_Visit* belongs to Adam Verberra.

From these examples, you can see that values in one table relate rows of that table to rows in a second table. Several special terms are used to express these ideas. A **key** (also called a **Primary Key**) is a column or group of columns that identifies a unique row in a table. *Student Number* is the key of the *Student* table. Given a value of *Student Number*, you can determine one and only one row in *Student*. Only one student has the number 1325, for example.

Every table must have a key. The key of the *Email* table is *EmailNum*, and the key of the *Office_Visit* table is *VisitID*. Sometimes more than one column is needed to form a unique identifier. In a table called *City*, for example, the key would consist of the combination of columns (*City, State*), because a given city name can appear in more than one state.

Student Number is not the key of the *Email* or the *Office_Visit* tables. We know that about *Email* because there are two rows in *Email* that have the *Student Number* value 1325. The value 1325 does not identify a unique row, therefore *Student Number* cannot be the key of *Email*.

Nor is *Student Number* a key of *Office_Visit*, although you cannot tell that from the data in Figure 5-6. If you think about it, however, there is nothing to prevent a student from visiting a professor more than once. If that were to happen, there would be two rows in *Office_Visit* with

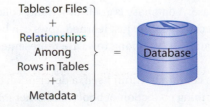

Figure 5-5
Components of a Database

Email Table

EmailNum	Date	Message	Student Number
1	2/1/2012	For homework 1, do you want us to provide notes on our references?	1325
2	3/15/2012	My group consists of Swee Lau and Stuart Nelson.	1325
3	3/15/2012	Could you please assign me to a group?	1644

Student Table

Student Number	Student Name	HW1	HW2	MidTerm
1325	BAKER, ANDREA	88	100	78
1644	LAU, SWEE	75	90	90
2881	NELSON, STUART	100	90	98
3007	FISCHER, MAYAN	95	100	74
3559	TAM, JEFFREY		100	88
4867	VERBERRA, ADAM	70	90	92
5265	VALDEZ, MARIE	80	90	85
8009	ROGERS, SHELLY	95	100	98

Office_Visit Table

VisitID	Date	Notes	Student Number
2	2/13/2012	Andrea had questions about using IS for raising barriers to entry.	1325
3	2/17/2012	Jeffrey is considering an IS major. Wanted to talk about career opportunities.	3559
4	2/17/2012	Will miss class Friday due to job conflict.	4867

Figure 5-6
Example of Relationships Among Rows

the same value of *Student Number*. It just happens that no student has visited twice in the limited data in Figure 5-6.

In both *Email* and *Office_Visit*, *Student Number* is a key, but it is a key of a different table, namely *Student*. Hence, the columns that fulfill a role like that of *Student Number* in the *Email* and *Office_Visit* tables are called **foreign keys**. This term is used because such columns are keys, but they are keys of a different (foreign) table than the one in which they reside.

Before we go on, databases that carry their data in the form of tables and that represent relationships using foreign keys are called **relational databases**. (The term *relational* is used because another, more formal name for a table like those we're discussing is **relation**.) You'll learn about another kind of database in Case Study 5.

METADATA

Recall the definition of database: A database is a self-describing collection of integrated records. The records are integrated because, as you just learned, rows can be tied together by their key/foreign key relationship. Relationships among rows are represented in the database. But what does *self-describing* mean?

It means that a database contains, within itself, a description of its contents. Think of a library. A library is a self-describing collection of books and other materials. It is self-describing

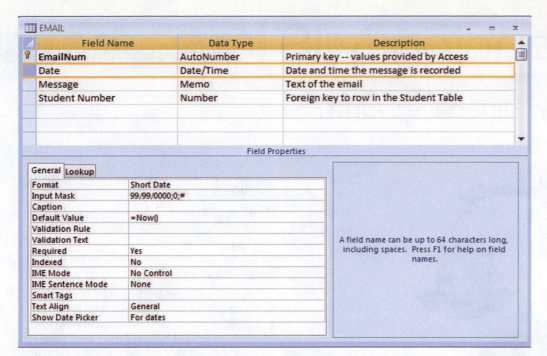

Figure 5-7
Sample Metadata (in Access)

Source: Microsoft Access 2010.

because the library contains a catalog that describes the library's contents. The same idea also pertains to a database. Databases are self-describing because they contain not only data, but also data about the data in the database.

    Metadata are data that describe data. Figure 5-7 shows metadata for the *Email* table. The format of metadata depends on the software product that is processing the database. Figure 5-7 shows the metadata as they appear in Microsoft Access. Each row of the top part of this form describes a column of the *Email* table. The columns of these descriptions are *Field Name*, *Data Type*, and *Description*. *Field Name* contains the name of the column, *Data Type* shows the type of data the column may hold, and *Description* contains notes that explain the source or use of the column. As you can see, there is one row of metadata for each of the four columns of the *Email* table: *EmailNum*, *Date*, *Message*, and *Student Number*.

    The bottom part of this form provides more metadata, which Access calls *Field Properties*, for each column. In Figure 5-7, the focus is on the *Date* column (note the light rectangle drawn around the *Date* row). Because the focus is on *Date* in the top pane, the details in the bottom pane pertain to the *Date* column. The Field Properties describe formats, a default value for Access to supply when a new row is created, and the constraint that a value is required for this column. It is not important for you to remember these details. Instead, just understand that metadata are data about data and that such metadata are always a part of a database.

    The presence of metadata makes databases much more useful. Because of metadata, no one needs to guess, remember, or even record what is in the database. To find out what a database contains, we just look at the metadata inside the database.

Metadata make databases easy to use, for both authorized and unauthorized purposes, as described in the Ethics Guide on pages 120–121.

WHAT IS A DATABASE MANAGEMENT SYSTEM (DBMS)?

A database, all by itself, is not very useful. The tables in Figure 5-6 have all of the data the professor wants, but the format is unwieldy. The professor wants to see the data in a form like that in Figure 5-2 and also as a formatted report. Pure database data are correct, but in raw form they are not pertinent or useful.

Experiencing MIS

How Much Is a Database Worth?

Source: faberfoto/Fotolia

The Firm, a workout studio in Minneapolis (*http://thefirmmpls.com/*), realizes over 15,000 person-visits, an average of 500 visits per day. Neil Miyamoto, one of the two business partners, believes that the database is The Firm's single most important asset. According to Neil:

Take away anything else — the building, the equipment, the inventory — anything else, and we'd be back in business in 6 months or less. Take away our customer database, however, and we'd have to start all over. It would take us another 8 years to get back where we are.[1]

Why is the database so crucial? It records everything the company's customers do. If The Firm decides to offer an early morning kickboxing class featuring a particular trainer, it can use its database to offer that class to everyone who ever took an early morning class, a kickboxing class, or a class by that trainer. Customers receive targeted solicitations for offerings they care about and, maybe equally important, they don't receive solicitations for those they don't care about. Clearly, The Firm database has value and, if it wanted to, The Firm could sell that data.

In this exercise, you and a group of your fellow students will be asked to consider the value of a database to organizations other than The Firm.

1. Many small business owners have found it financially advantageous to purchase their own building. As one owner remarked upon his retirement, "We did well with the business, but we made our real money by buying the building." Explain why this might be so.

2. To what extent does the dynamic you identified in your answer to step 1 pertain to databases? Do you think it likely that, in 2050, some small businesspeople will retire and make statements like, "We did well with the business, but we made our real money from the database we generated?" Why or why not? In what ways is real estate different from database data? Are these differences significant to your answer?

3. Suppose you had a national database of student data. Assume your database includes the name, email address, university, grade level, and major for each student. Name five companies that would find that data valuable, and explain how they might use it. (For example, Pizza Hut could solicit orders from students during finals week.)

4. Describe a product or service that you could develop that would induce students to provide the data in item 3.

5. Considering your answers to items 1 through 4, identify two organizations in your community that could generate a database that would potentially be more valuable than the organization itself. Consider businesses, but also think about social organizations and government offices.

   For each organization, describe the content of the database and how you could entice customers or clients to provide that data. Also, explain why the data would be valuable and who might use it.

6. Prepare a 1-minute statement of what you have learned from this exercise that you could use in a job interview to illustrate your ability to innovate the use of technology in business.

7. Present your answers to items 1–6 to the rest of the class.

---

[1] Personal conversation with the author, May 23, 2012. Reprinted by permission.

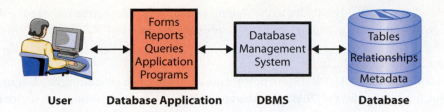

Figure 5-8
Components of a Database
Application System

Figure 5-8 shows the components of a **database application system**. Such systems make database data more accessible and useful. Users employ a database application that consists of forms (like that in Figure 5-2), formatted reports, queries, and application programs. Each of these, in turn, calls on the database management system (DBMS) to process the database tables. We will first describe DBMSs and then discuss database application components in the next question.

A **database management system (DBMS)** is a program used to create, process, and administer a database. As with operating systems, almost no organization develops its own DBMS. Instead, companies license DBMS products from vendors such as IBM, Microsoft, Oracle, and others. Popular DBMS products are **DB2** from IBM, **Access** and **SQL Server** from Microsoft, and **Oracle Database** from the Oracle Corporation. Another popular DBMS is **MySQL**, an open source DBMS product that is license-free for most applications.[2] Other DBMS products are available, but these five process the great bulk of databases today.

Note that a DBMS and a database are two different things. For some reason, the trade press and even some books confuse the two. A DBMS is a software program; a database is a collection of tables, relationships, and metadata. The two are very different concepts.

Creating the Database and Its Structures

Database developers use the DBMS to create tables, relationships, and other structures in the database. The form in Figure 5-7 can be used to define a new table or to modify an existing one. To create a new table, the developer just fills the new table's metadata into the form.

To modify an existing table—say, to add a new column—the developer opens the metadata form for that table and adds a new row of metadata. For example, in Figure 5-9 the developer has added a new column called *Response?*. This new column has the data type *Yes/No*, which means that the column can contain only one value—*Yes* or *No*. The professor will use this column to

Figure 5-9
Adding a New Column to
a Table (in Access)

Source: Microsoft Access 2010

Field Name	Data Type	Description
EmailNum	AutoNumber	Primary key -- values provided by Access
Date	Date/Time	Date and time the message is recorded
Message	Memo	Text of the email
Student Number	Number	Foreign key to row in the Student Table
Response?	Yes/No	True / false value indicates whether or not prof has responded

Field Properties

General | Lookup

Format	Yes/No
Caption	
Default Value	0
Validation Rule	
Validation Text	
Indexed	No
Text Align	General

A field name can be up to 64 characters long, including spaces. Press F1 for help on field names.

---

[2]MySQL was supported by the MySQL company. In 2008, that company was acquired by Sun Microsystems, which was, in turn, acquired by Oracle later that year. However, because MySQL is open source, Oracle does not own the source code.

indicate whether he has responded to the student's email. A column can be removed by deleting its row in this table, though doing so will lose any existing data.

Processing the Database

The second function of the DBMS is to process the database. Such processing can be quite complex, but, fundamentally, the DBMS provides applications for four processing operations: to read, insert, modify, or delete data. These operations are requested in application calls upon the DBMS. From a form, when the user enters new or changed data, a computer program behind the form calls the DBMS to make the necessary database changes. From a Web application, a program on the client or on the server application program calls the DBMS directly to make the change.

Structured Query Language (SQL) is an international standard language for processing a database. All five of the DBMS products mentioned earlier accept and process SQL (pronounced "see-quell") statements. As an example, the following SQL statement inserts a new row into the *Student* table:

```
INSERT INTO Student
([Student Number], [Student Name], HW1, HW2, MidTerm)
VALUES (1000, 'Franklin, Benjamin', 90, 95, 100);
```

As stated, statements like this one are issued "behind the scenes" by programs that process forms. Alternatively, they can be issued directly to the DBMS by an application program.

You do not need to understand or remember SQL language syntax. Instead, just realize that SQL is an international standard for processing a database. SQL can also be used to create databases and database structures. You will learn more about SQL if you take a database management class.

Administering the Database

A third DBMS function is to provide tools to assist in the administration of the database. **Database administration** involves a wide variety of activities. For example, the DBMS can be used to set up a security system involving user accounts, passwords, permissions, and limits for processing the database. To provide database security, a user must sign on using a valid user account before she can process the database.

Permissions can be limited in very specific ways. In the Student database example, it is possible to limit a particular user to reading only *Student Name* from the *Student* table. A different user could be given permission to read the entire *Student* table, but limited to update only the *HW1*, *HW2*, and *MidTerm* columns. Other users can be given still other permissions.

In addition to security, DBMS administrative functions include backing up database data, adding structures to improve the performance of database applications, removing data that are no longer wanted or needed, and similar tasks.

For important databases, most organizations dedicate one or more employees to the role of database administration. Figure 5-10 summarizes the major responsibilities for this function. You will learn more about this topic if you take a database management course.

 ## HOW DO DATABASE APPLICATIONS MAKE DATABASES MORE USEFUL?

A **database application** is a collection of forms, reports, queries, and application programs that process a database. A database may have one or more applications, and each application may have one or more users. Figure 5-11 shows three applications used at GearUp. Buyers use the first one to schedule events; operations personnel use the second to set up the graphics and auction terms and screens; and accounting personnel use the third to process event financial results. These applications have different purposes, features, and functions, but they all process the same GearUp event database.

Category	Database Administration Task	Description
Development	Create and staff DBA function	Size of DBA group depends on size and complexity of database. Groups range from one part-time person to small group.
	Form steering committee	Consists of representatives of all user groups. Forum for community-wide discussions and decisions.
	Specify requirements	Ensure that all appropriate user input is considered.
	Validate data model	Check data model for accuracy and completeness.
	Evaluate application design	Verify that all necessary forms, reports, queries, and applications are developed. Validate design and usability of application components.
Operation	Manage processing rights and responsibilities	Determine processing rights/restrictions on each table and column.
	Manage security	Add and delete users and user groups as necessary; ensure that security system works.
	Track problems and manage resolution	Develop system to record and manage resolution of problems.
	Monitor database performance	Provide expertise/solutions for performance improvements.
	Manage DBMS	Evaluate new features and functions.
Backup and Recovery	Monitor backup procedures	Verify that database backup procedures are followed.
	Conduct training	Ensure that users and operations personnel know and understand recovery procedures.
	Manage recovery	Manage recovery process.
Adaptation	Set up request tracking system	Develop system to record and prioritize requests for change.
	Manage configuration change	Manage impact of database structure changes on applications and users.

Figure 5-10
Summary of Database Administration Tasks

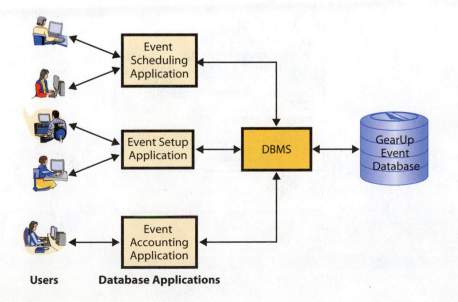

Figure 5-11
Users of Multiple Database Applications

Figure 5-12
Example of a Student
Report

Student Report with Emails

Name	Number	HW1	HW2	MidTerm (= 3 HW)	Total Points
BAKER, ANDRI	1325	88	100	78	422
LAU, SWEE	1644	75	90	90	435

Date	Message
3/15/2013	My group consists of Swee Lau and Stuart Nelson.
2/1/2013	For homework 1, do you want us to provide notes on our references?
3/15/2012	Could you please assign me to a group?

WHAT ARE FORMS, REPORTS, AND QUERIES?

Figure 5-2 shows a typical database application data entry **form,** and Figure 5-12 shows a typical **report**. Data entry forms are used to read, insert, modify, and delete data. Reports show data in a structured context.

Recall from Chapter 1 that one of the definitions of information is "data presented in a meaningful context." The professor can create information from this report because it shows the student data in a context that will be meaningful to the professor. Some reports, like the one in Figure 5-12, also compute values as they present the data. An example is the computation of *MidTerm Total* in Figure 5-12.

DBMS programs provide comprehensive and robust features for querying database data. For example, suppose the professor who uses the Student database remembers that one of the students referred to the topic *barriers to entry* in an office visit, but cannot remember which student or when. If there are hundreds of students and visits recorded in the database, it will take some effort and time for the professor to search through all office visit records to find that event. The DBMS, however, can find any such record quickly. Figure 5-13a shows a **query** form in which the professor types in the keyword for which she is looking. Figure 5-13b shows the results of the query.

WHY ARE DATABASE APPLICATION PROGRAMS NEEDED?

Forms, reports, and queries work well for standard functions. However, most applications have unique requirements that a simple form, report, or query cannot meet. For example, in an order-entry application what should be done if only a portion of a customer's request can be met? If someone wants ten widgets and we only have three in stock, should a backorder for seven more be generated automatically? Or should some other action be taken?

Figure 5-13a
Sample Query Form Used to
Enter Phrase for Search

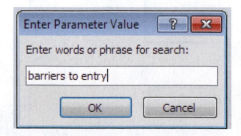

Figure 5-13b
Sample Query Results of
Query Operation

Source: Microsoft Access 2010

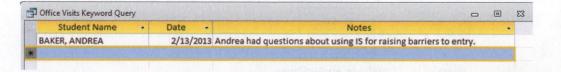

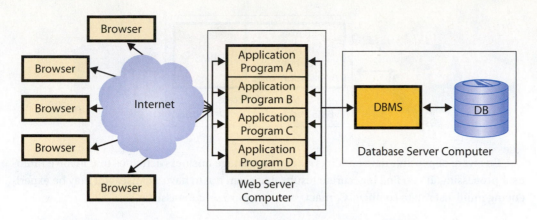

Figure 5-14
Four Application Programs
on a Web Server Computer

Application programs process logic that is specific to a given business need. In the Student database, an example application is one that assigns grades at the end of the term. If the professor grades on a curve, the application reads the break points for each grade from a form, and then processes each row in the *Student* table, allocating a grade based on the break points and the total number of points earned.

Another important use of application programs is to enable database processing over the Internet. For this use, the application program serves as an intermediary between the Web server and the database. The application program responds to events, such as when a user presses a submit button; it also reads, inserts, modifies, and deletes database data.

For example, Figure 5-14 shows four different database application programs running on a Web server computer. Users with browsers connect to the Web server via the Internet. The Web server directs user requests to the appropriate application program. Each program then processes the database as necessary. You will learn more about Web-enabled databases in the next chapter.

MULTI-USER PROCESSING

Figures 5-11 and 5-14 show multiple users processing the database. Such **multi-user processing** is common, but it does pose unique problems that you, as a future manager, should know about. To understand the nature of those problems, consider the following scenario.

Two GearUp customers, Andrea and Jeffrey, are both attempting to buy the last five soccer balls available for a particular event. Andrea uses her browser to access the GearUp Web site and finds that five are available. She places all of them in her shopping cart. She doesn't know it, but when she opened the event form, she invoked an application on GearUp's server that read the database to find that five soccer balls are available. Before she checks out, she takes a moment to verify with her supervisor that she should buy all five.

Meanwhile, Jeffrey uses his browser and also finds that five soccer balls are available because his browser activates that same application that reads the database and finds (because Andrea has not yet checked out) that five are available. He places five in his cart and checks out.

Meanwhile, Andrea learns that she should buy all five, so she checks out. Clearly, we have a problem. Both Andrea and Jeffrey have purchased the same five soccer balls. One of them is going to be disappointed.

This problem, known as the **lost-update problem**, exemplifies one of the special characteristics of multi-user database processing. To prevent this problem, some type of locking must be used to coordinate the activities of users who know nothing about one another. Locking brings its own set of problems, however, and those problems must be addressed as well. We will not delve further into this topic here, however.

Realize from this example that converting a single-user database to a multi-user database requires more than simply connecting another computer. The logic of the underlying application processing needs to be adjusted as well.

Figure 5-15
Personal Database System

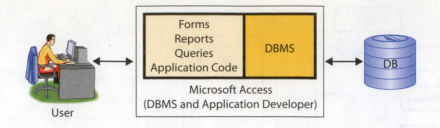

Be aware of possible data conflicts when you manage business activities that involve multi-user processing. If you find inaccurate results that seem not to have a cause, you may be experiencing multi-user data conflicts. Contact your IS department for assistance.

ENTERPRISE DBMS VERSUS PERSONAL DBMS

DBMS products fall into two broad categories. **Enterprise DBMS** products process large organizational and workgroup databases. These products support many, possibly thousands, of users and many different database applications. Such DBMS products support 24/7 operations and can manage databases that span dozens of different magnetic disks with hundreds of gigabytes or more of data. IBM's DB2, Microsoft's SQL Server, and Oracle's Oracle Database are examples of enterprise DBMS products.

Personal DBMS products are designed for smaller, simpler database applications. Such products are used for personal or small workgroup applications that involve fewer than 100 users, and normally fewer than 15. In fact, the great bulk of databases in this category have only a single user. The professor's Student database is an example of a database that is processed by a personal DBMS product.

In the past, there were many personal DBMS products—Paradox, dBase, R:base, and FoxPro. Microsoft put these products out of business when they developed Access and included it in the Microsoft Office suite. Today, about the only remaining personal DBMS is Microsoft Access.

To avoid one point of confusion for you in the future, the separation of application programs and the DBMS shown in Figure 5-11 is true only for enterprise DBMS products. Microsoft Access includes features and functions for application processing along with the DBMS itself. For example, Access has a form generator and a report generator. Thus, as shown in Figure 5-15, Access is both a DBMS *and* an application development product.

 WHAT IS A NOSQL DBMS?

Something unusual occurred recently in the field of database processing. Amazon.com determined that relational database technology wouldn't meet its processing needs, and it developed a nonrelational data store called **Dynamo**.[3] Meanwhile, for many of the same reasons, Google developed a nonrelational data store called **Bigtable**.[4] Facebook took concepts from both of these systems and developed a third nonrelational data store called **Cassandra**.[5] In 2008, Facebook turned Cassandra over to the open source community, and now Apache has dubbed it a Top Level Project (TLP), which is the height of respectability among open source projects.

---

[3]Werner Vogel, "Amazon's Dynamo," All Things Distributed blog, October 2, 2007. Available at www.allthingsdistributed.com/2007/10/amazons_dynamo.html (accessed June 2011).
[4]Fay Chang, Jeffrey Dean, Sanjay Ghemawat, Wilson C. Hsieh, Deborah A. Wallach, Mike Burrows, Tushar Chandra, Andrew Fikes, and Robert E. Gruber, "Bigtable: A Distributed Storage System for Structured Data," OSDI 2006, Seventh Symposium on Operating System Design and Implementation, Seattle, WA, November 2006. Available at http://labs.google.com/papers/bigtable.html (accessed June 2011).
[5]Jonathan Ellis, "Cassandra: Open Source Bigtable + Dynamo." Available at www.slideshare.net/jbellis/cassandra-open-source-bigtable-dynamo (accessed June 2011).

Such nonrelational DBMS have come to be called **NoSQL DBMS**. This term refers to software systems that support very high transaction rates, processing relatively simple data structures, replicated on many servers in the cloud. NoSQL is not the best term; *NotRelational DBMS* would have been better, but the die has been cast. You can learn more about the rationale for NoSQL products and some of their intriguing features in Case Study 5, page 127.

WILL NOSQL REPLACE RELATIONAL DBMS PRODUCTS?

Because of the success of these leading companies, is it likely that others will follow their examples and convert their existing relational databases to NoSQL databases? Probably not. Such conversion would be enormously expensive and disruptive, and in cases where the relational database meets the organization's needs, would also be unnecessary.

However, the rise of NoSQL does mean that, for large organizational IS, choosing a relational DBMS is no longer automatic. For requirements that fit NoSQL's strengths, such products will likely be used for new projects, and, for existing systems with performance problems, some relational database conversions may also occur.

Also, at least with today's features, NoSQL DBMS products are very technical and can be used only by those with a deep background in computer science. Whereas a technology-tolerant business professional can learn to use Microsoft Access effectively (consider Addison at GearUp), it will be impossible for such a person to use a NoSQL DBMS without years of additional training. So, continue to learn Access; it will be an important tool for you as an end-user for years to come. But, at the same time, realize that your organization may choose NoSQL products for specialized applications.

NOSQL'S IMPACT ON THE DBMS PRODUCT MARKET

The emergence of these products is interesting not only from a technical perspective, but also because none of them were developed by software vendors such as Microsoft or Oracle. Instead, they were developed by hugely successful companies that had business requirements unmet by relational DBMS products. Most companies would not be able to afford the costs and risks of such development, but these very rich companies already employed highly skilled technical personnel, and those employees could and did build them. And, having done so, they turned that software over to the open source community, or at least Facebook did in the case of Cassandra.

Using the vocabulary of Chapter 3, for the first time in over 20 years, the database software market experienced viable new entrants. So, will Microsoft and Oracle and other DBMS vendors lose some of their market to NoSQL products and vendors? Or will they follow IBM's path? Become less of a vendor of software and more a seller of services supporting open source software such as Cassandra? Or, will we soon see companies like Oracle, which is rich with cash, purchasing a NoSQL company? Indeed, that may have happened by the time you read this. These are interesting times, so stay tuned!

How does the **knowledge** in this chapter help **you?**

Drew is at a disadvantage vis-à-vis Addison. She knows how to use Access to manipulate the data extract they will be given and how to produce reports with that data. With the knowledge in this chapter, and with some rudimentary knowledge of Access, you'll be able to do the same.

It is common in most companies today for end-users to receive extracts of operational data and to then query and report the results they need from that extracted data. Thus, you can expect to encounter the situation described here sometime during your career. When you do, the knowledge of this chapter will help you succeed.

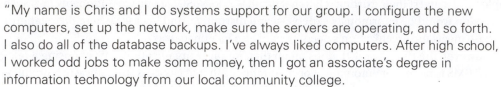

Ethics Guide

Nobody Said I Shouldn't

"My name is Chris and I do systems support for our group. I configure the new computers, set up the network, make sure the servers are operating, and so forth. I also do all of the database backups. I've always liked computers. After high school, I worked odd jobs to make some money, then I got an associate's degree in information technology from our local community college.

"Anyway, as I said, I make backup copies of our databases. One weekend, I didn't have much going on, so I copied one of the database backups to a thumb drive and took it home. I had taken a class on database processing as part of my associate's degree, and we used SQL Server (our database management system) in my class. In fact, I suppose that's part of the reason I got the job. Anyway, it was easy to restore the database on my computer at home, and I did.

"Of course, as they'll tell you in your database class, one of the big advantages of database processing is that databases have metadata, or data that describe the content of the database. So, although I didn't know what tables were in our database, I did know how to access the SQL Server metadata. I just queried a table called *sysTables* to learn the names of our tables. From there it was easy to find out what columns each table had.

"I found tables with data about orders, customers, salespeople, and so forth, and, just to amuse myself, and to see how much of the query language SQL that I could remember, I started playing around with the data. I was curious to know which order entry clerk was the best, so I started querying each clerk's order data, the total number of orders, total order amounts, things like that. It was easy to do and fun.

"I know one of the order entry clerks, Jason, pretty well, so I started looking at the data for his orders. I was just curious, and it was very simple SQL. I was just playing around with the data when I noticed something odd. All of his biggest orders were with one company, Valley Appliances, and even stranger, every one of its orders had a huge discount. I thought, well, maybe that's typical. Out of curiosity, I started looking at data for the other clerks, and very few of them had an order with Valley Appliances. But, when they did, Valley didn't get a big discount. Then I looked at the rest of Jason's orders, and none of them had much in the way of discounts either.

"The next Friday, a bunch of us went out for a beer after work. I happened to see Jason, so I asked him about Valley Appliances and made a joke about the discounts. He asked me what I meant, and then I told him that I'd been looking at the data for fun and that I saw this odd pattern. He just laughed, said he just 'did his job,' and then changed the subject.

"Well, to make a long story short, when I got to work on Monday morning, my office was cleaned out. There was nothing there except a note telling me to go see my boss. The bottom line was, I was fired. The company also threatened that if I didn't return all of its data, I'd be in court for the next 5 years . . . things like that. I was so mad I didn't even tell them about Jason. Now my problem is that I'm out of a job, and I can't exactly use my last company for a reference."

Guide

No, Thanks, I'll Use a Spreadsheet

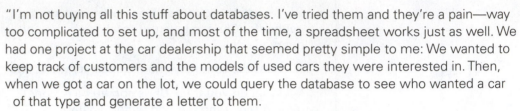

"I'm not buying all this stuff about databases. I've tried them and they're a pain—way too complicated to set up, and most of the time, a spreadsheet works just as well. We had one project at the car dealership that seemed pretty simple to me: We wanted to keep track of customers and the models of used cars they were interested in. Then, when we got a car on the lot, we could query the database to see who wanted a car of that type and generate a letter to them.

"It took forever to build that system, and it never did work right. We hired three different consultants, and the last one finally did get it to work. But it was so complicated to produce the letters. You had to query the data in Access to generate some kind of file, then open Word, then go through some mumbo jumbo using mail/merge to cause Word to find the letter and put all the Access data in the right spot. I once printed over 200 letters and had the name in the address spot and the address in the name spot and no date. And it took me over an hour to do even that. I just wanted to do the query and push a button to get my letters generated. I gave up. Some of the salespeople are still trying to use it, but not me.

"No, unless you are getting billions in government bailouts, I wouldn't mess with a database. You have to have professional IS people to create it and keep it running. Besides, I don't really want to share my data with anyone. I work pretty hard to develop my client list. Why would I want to give it away?

"My motto is, 'Keep it simple.' I use an Excel spreadsheet with four columns: Name, Phone Number, Car Interests, and Notes. When I get a new customer, I enter the name and phone number, and then I put the make and model of cars they like in the Car Interests column. Anything else that I think is important I put in the Notes column—extra phone numbers, address data if I have it, email addresses, spouse names, last time I called them, etc. The system isn't fancy, but it works fine.

"When I want to find something, I use Excel's Data Filter. I can usually get what I need. Of course, I still can't send form letters, but it really doesn't matter. I get most of my sales using the phone, anyway."

DISCUSSION QUESTIONS

1. To what extent do you agree with the opinions presented here? To what extent are the concerns expressed here justified? To what extent might they be due to other factors?

2. What problems do you see with the way that the car salesperson stores address data? What will he have to do if he ever does want to send a letter or an email to all of his customers?

3. From his comments, how many different themes are there in his data? What does this imply about his ability to keep his data in a spreadsheet?

4. Does the concern about not sharing data relate to whether or not he uses a database?

5. Apparently, management at the car dealership allows the salespeople to keep their contact data in whatever format they want. If you were management, how would you justify this policy? What disadvantages are there to this policy?

6. Suppose you manage the sales representatives, and you decide to require all of them to use a database to keep track of customers and customer car interest data. How would you sell your decision to this salesperson?

7. Given the limited information in this scenario, do you think a database or a spreadsheet is a better solution?

ACTIVE REVIEW

Use this Active Review to verify that you understand the ideas and concepts that answer the chapter's study questions.

Q1 WHAT IS THE PURPOSE OF A DATABASE?

State the purpose of a database. Explain the circumstances in which a database is preferred to a spreadsheet. Describe the key difference between Figures 5-1 and 5-2.

Q2 WHAT IS A DATABASE?

Define the term *database*. Explain the hierarchy of data and name three elements of a database. Define *metadata*. Using the example of *Student* and *Office_Visit* tables, show how relationships among rows are represented in a database. Define the terms *primary key, foreign key*, and *relational database*.

Q3 WHAT IS A DATABASE MANAGEMENT SYSTEM (DBMS)?

Explain why a database, by itself, is not very useful to business users. Name the components of a database application system and sketch their relationship. Explain the acronym DBMS and name its functions. List five popular DBMS products. Explain the difference between a DBMS and a database. Summarize the functions of a DBMS. Define *SQL*. Describe the major functions of database administration.

Q4 HOW DO DATABASE APPLICATIONS MAKE DATABASES MORE USEFUL?

Name and describe the components of a database application. Explain the need for application programs. For multi-user processing, describe one way in which one user's work can interfere with another's. Explain why multi-user database processing involves more than just connecting another computer to the network. Define two broad categories of DBMS and explain their differences.

Q5 WHAT IS A NoSQL DBMS?

Define *NoSQL data store* and give three examples. Explain how NoSQL will likely be used in organizations and state why learning Microsoft Access is still important to you. Explain what is unusual about the development of these systems. Describe possible consequences of NoSQL on the DBMS product market.

How does the **knowledge** in this chapter help **you?**

After learning the concepts presented in this chapter and with some rudimentary knowledge of Access, you'll be able to query and extract data to help you know how to solve the problems your organization faces . . . or at least you will be able to pinpoint what the problem is.

KEY TERMS AND CONCEPTS

USING YOUR KNOWLEDGE

1. Suppose you are a marketing assistant for a consumer electronics company and are in charge of setting up your company's booth at trade shows. Weeks before the shows, you meet with the marketing managers and determine what displays and equipment they want to display. Then, you identify each of the components that need to be shipped and schedule a shipper to deliver them to the trade show site. You then supervise convention personnel as they set up the booths and equipment. Once the show is over, you supervise the packing of the booth and all equipment as well as schedule its shipment back to your home office. When the equipment arrives, you check it into your warehouse to ensure that all pieces of the booth and all equipment are returned. If there are problems due to shipping damage or loss, you handle those problems. Your job is important; at a typical show, you are responsible for more than a quarter of a million dollars' worth of equipment.

   a. You will need to track data about booth components, equipment, shippers, and shipments. List typical fields for each type of data.

   b. Could you use a spreadsheet to keep track of this data? What would be the advantages and disadvantages of doing so?

   c. Using your answer to part a, give an example of two relationships that you need to track. Show the keys and foreign keys for each.

   d. Which of the following components of a database application are you likely to need: data entry forms, reports, queries, or application program? Explain one use for each that you will need.

   e. Will your application be for one user or for multiple users? Will you need a personal DBMS or an enterprise DBMS? If a personal DBMS, which product will you use?

2. Samantha Green (the same Samantha we met at the end of Chapter 3, p. 67) owns and operates Twigs Tree Trimming Service. Recall that Samantha has a degree from a forestry program and recently opened her business in St. Louis, Missouri. Her business consists of many one-time operations (e.g., remove a tree or stump), as well as recurring services (e.g., trimming customers' trees every year or two). When business is slow, Samantha calls former clients to remind them of her services and of the need to trim their trees on a regular basis.

   a. Name and describe tables of data that Samantha will need to run her business. Indicate possible fields for each table.

   b. Could Samantha use a spreadsheet to keep track of this data? What would be the advantages and disadvantages of doing so?

   c. Using your answer to question a, give an example of two relationships that Samantha needs to track. Show the keys and foreign keys for each.

   d. Which of the following components of a database application is Samantha likely to need: data entry forms, reports, queries, or application program? Explain one use for each that she needs.

   e. Will this application be for one user or for multiple users? Will she need a personal DBMS or an enterprise DBMS? If a personal DBMS, which product will she use?

3. YourFire, Inc., (the same YourFire we met at the end of Chapter 3, p. 67) is a small business owned by Curt and Julie Robards. Based in Brisbane, Australia, YourFire manufactures and sells YourFire, a lightweight camping stove. Recall that Curt used his previous experience as an aerospace engineer to invent a burning nozzle that enables the stove to stay lit in very high winds. Using her industrial design training, Julie designed the stove so that it is small, lightweight, easy to set up, and very stable. Curt and Julie sell the stove directly to their customers over the Internet and via phone. The warranty on the stove covers 5 years of cost-free repair for stoves used for recreational purposes.

   YourFire wants to track every stove and the customer who purchased it. They want to know which customers own which stoves in case they need to notify customers of safety problems or need to order a stove recall. Curt and Julie also want to keep track of any repairs they have performed.

   a. Name and describe tables of data that YourFire will need. Indicate possible fields for each table.

   b. Could YourFire use a spreadsheet to keep track of this data? What would be the advantages and disadvantages of doing so?

   c. Using your answer to question a, give an example of two relationships that YourFire needs to track. Show the keys and foreign keys for each.

   d. Which of the following components of a database application is YourFire likely to need: data entry forms, reports, queries, or application program? Explain one use for each needed component.

   e. Will this application be for one user or for multiple users? Will YourFire need a personal DBMS or an enterprise DBMS? If a personal DBMS, which product will it use? If an enterprise DBMS, which product can it obtain license-free?

COLLABORATION EXERCISE 5

Before you start this exercise, read Chapter Extensions 1 and 2, which describe collaboration techniques as well as tools for managing collaboration tasks. In particular, consider using Google Drive, Google+, Windows Live SkyDrive, Microsoft SharePoint, or some other collaboration tool.

Figure 5-16 shows a spreadsheet that is used to track the assignment of sheet music to a choir—it could be a church choir or school or community choir. The type of choir does not matter, because the problem is universal. Sheet music is expensive, choir members need to be able to take sheet music away for practice at home, and not all of the music gets back to the inventory. (Sheet music can be purchased or rented, but either way, lost music is an expense.)

Look closely at this data and you will see some data integrity problems—or at least some possible data integrity problems. For one, do Sandra Corning and Linda Duong really have the same copy of music checked out? Second, did Mozart and J. S. Bach both write a Requiem, or in row 15 should J. S. Bach actually be Mozart? Also, there is a problem with Eleanor Dixon's phone number; several phone numbers are the same as well, which seems suspicious.

Additionally, this spreadsheet is confusing and hard to use. The column labeled *First Name* includes both people names and the names of choruses. *Email* has both email addresses and composer names, and *Phone* has both phone numbers and copy identifiers. Furthermore, to record a checkout of music the user must first add a new row and then reenter the name of the work, the composer's name, and the copy to be checked out. Finally, consider what happens when

the user wants to find all copies of a particular work: The user will have to examine the rows in each of four spreadsheets for the four voice parts. In fact, a spreadsheet is ill suited for this application. A database would be a far better tool, and situations like this are obvious candidates for innovation.

1. Analyze the spreadsheet shown in Figure 5-16 and list all of the problems that occur when trying to track the assignment of sheet music using this spreadsheet.

2. The following two tables could be used to store the data in Figure 5-16 in a database:
   ChoirMember (LastName, FirstName, Email, Phone, Part)
   MusicalWork (NameOfWork, Composer, Part, CopyNumber)
   Note: This notation means there are two tables, one named *ChoirMember* and a second named *MusicalWork*. The *ChoirMember* table has five columns: *LastName, FirstName, Email, Phone,* and *Part*; *MusicalWork* has four columns: *NameOfWork, Composer, Part, CopyNumber*.
   a. Redraw the data in Figure 5-16 into this two-table format.
   b. Select primary keys for the *ChoirMember* and *Musical-Work* tables.
   c. The two tables are not integrated; they do not show who has checked out which music. Add foreign key columns to one of the tables to integrate the data.
   d. This two-table design does not eliminate the potential for data integrity problems that occur in the spreadsheet. Explain why not.

	A	B	C	D	E
1	Last Name	First Name	Email	Phone	Part
2	Ashley	Jane	JA@somewhere.com	703.555.1234	Soprano
3	Davidson	Kaye	KD@somewhere.com	703.555.2236	Soprano
4	Ching	Kam Hoong	KHC@overhere.com	703.555.2236	Soprano
5	Menstell	Lori Lee	LLM@somewhere.com	703.555.1237	Soprano
6	Corning	Sandra	SC2@overhere.com	703.555.1234	Soprano
7		B-minor mass	J.S. Bach	Soprano Copy 7	
8		Requiem	Mozart	Soprano Copy 17	
9		9th Symphony Chorus	Beethoven	Soprano Copy 9	
10	Wei	Guang	GW1@somewhere.com	703.555.9936	Soprano
11	Dixon	Eleanor	ED@thisplace.com	703.555.12379	Soprano
12		B-minor mass	J.S. Bach	Soprano Copy 11	
13	Duong	Linda	LD2@overhere.com	703.555.8736	Soprano
14		B-minor mass	J.S. Bach	Soprano Copy 7	
15		Requiem	J.S. Bach	Soprano Copy 19	
16	Lunden	Haley	HL@somewhere.com	703.555.0836	Soprano
17	Utran	Diem Thi	DTU@somewhere.com	703.555.1089	Soprano

Figure 5-16
Spreadsheet Used for Assignment of Sheet Music

3. A three-table database design for the data in the spreadsheet in Figure 5-16 is as follows:

    ChoirMember (LastName, FirstName, Email, Phone, Part)
    MusicalWork (NameOfWork)
    CheckOut (LastName, FirstName, NameOfWork, Part, CopyNumber, DateOut, DateIn)

    a. Redraw the data in Figure 5-16 into this three-table format.
    b. Identify which columns are primary keys for each of these tables.
    c. The foreign keys are already in place; identify which columns are foreign keys and which relationships they represent.

    d. Does this design eliminate the potential for data integrity problems that occur in the spreadsheet? Why or why not?

4. Assume you manage the choir and you foresee two possibilities:
    - Keep the spreadsheet, but create procedures to reduce the likelihood of data integrity problems.
    - Create an Access database and database application for the three-table design.

Describe the advantages and disadvantages of each of these possibilities. Recommend one of these two possibilities and justify your recommendation.

CASE STUDY 5

Fail Away with Dynamo, Bigtable, and Cassandra

As you learned in Case Study 1, Amazon.com processed more than 158 order items per second on its peak day of the 2010 holiday sales season. To do that, it processed customer transactions on tens of thousands of servers. With that many computers, failure is inevitable. Even if the probability of any one server failing is .0001, the likelihood that not one out of 10,000 of them fails is .9999 raised to the 10,000 power, which is about .37. Thus, for these assumptions the likelihood of at least one failure is 63 percent. For reasons that go beyond the scope of this discussion, the likelihood of failure is actually much greater.

Amazon.com must be able to thrive, even in the presence of such constant failure. Or, as Amazon.com engineers stated: "Customers should be able to view and add items to their shopping cart even if disks are failing, network routes are flapping, or data centers are being destroyed by tornados."[6]

The only way to deal with such failure is to replicate the data on multiple servers. When a customer stores a Wish List, for example, that Wish List needs to be stored on different, separated servers. Then, when (notice *when*, not *if*) a server with one copy of the Wish List fails, Amazon.com applications obtain it from another server.

Such data replication solves one problem but introduces another. Suppose that the customer's Wish List is stored on

servers A, B, and C and server A fails. While server A is down, server B or C can provide a copy of the Wish List, but if the customer changes it, that Wish List can only be rewritten to servers B and C. It cannot be written to A, because A is not running. When server A comes back into service, it will have the old copy of the Wish List. The next day, when the customer reopens his or her Wish List, two different versions exist: the most recent one on servers B and C and an older one on server A. The customer wants the most current one. How can Amazon.com ensure that it will be delivered? Keep in mind that 9 million orders are being shipped while this goes on.

None of the current relational DBMS products was designed for problems like this. Consequently, Amazon.com engineers developed Dynamo, a specialized data store for reliably processing massive amounts of data on tens of thousands of servers. Dynamo provides an always-open experience for Amazon.com's retail customers; Amazon.com also sells Dynamo store services to others via its S3 Web Services product offering.

Meanwhile, Google was encountering similar problems that could not be met by commercially available relational DBMS products. In response, Google created Bigtable, a data store for processing petabytes of data on hundreds of thousands of servers.[7] Bigtable supports a richer data model than Dynamo, which means that it can store a greater variety of data structures.

[6]Giuseppe DeCandia, Deniz Hastorun, Madan Jampani, Gunavardhan Kakulapati, Avinash Lakshman, Alex Pilchin, Swami Sivasubramanian, Peter Vosshall, and Werner Vogels, "Dynamo: Amazon's Highly Available Key-Value Store," *Proceedings of the 21st ACM Symposium on Operating Systems Principles*, Stevenson, WA, October 2007.
[7]Fay Chang, Jeffrey Dean, Sanjay Ghemawat, Wilson C. Hsieh, Deborah A. Wallach, Mike Burrows, Tushar Chandra, Andrew Fikes, and Robert E. Gruber, "Bigtable: A Distributed Storage System for Structured Data," *OSDI 2006: Seventh Symposium on Operating System Design and Implementation*, Seattle, WA, November 2006. Available at http://labs.google.com/papers/bigtable.html (accessed June 2011).

Both Dynamo and Bigtable are designed to be **elastic**; this term means that the number of servers can dynamically increase and decrease without disrupting performance.

In 2007, Facebook encountered similar data storage problems: Massive amounts of data, the need to be elastically scalable, tens of thousands of servers, and high volumes of traffic. In response to this need, Facebook began development on Cassandra, a data store that provides storage capabilities like Dynamo with a richer data model like Bigtable.[8,9] Initially, Facebook used Cassandra to power its Inbox Search. By 2008, Facebook realized that it had a bigger project on its hands than it wanted and gave the source code to the open source community. As of 2011, Cassandra is used by Facebook, Twitter, Digg, Reddit, Cisco, and many others.

Cassandra, by the way, is a fascinating name for a data store. In Greek mythology, Cassandra was so beautiful that Apollo fell in love with her and gave her the power to see the future. Alas, Apollo's love was unrequited, and he cursed her so that no one would ever believe her predictions. The name was apparently a slam at Oracle.

Cassandra is elastic and fault-tolerant; it supports massive amounts of data on thousands of servers and provides **durability**, meaning that once data is committed to the data store, it won't be lost, even in the presence of failure. One of the most interesting characteristics of Cassandra is that clients (meaning the programs that run Facebook, Twitter, etc.) can select the level of consistency that they need. If a client requests that all servers always be current, Cassandra will ensure that that happens, but performance will be slow. At the other end of the trade-off spectrum, clients can require no consistency, whereby performance is maximized. In between, clients can require that a majority of the servers that store a data item be consistent.

Cassandra performance is vastly superior to relational DBMS products. In one comparison, Cassandra was found to be 2,500 times faster than MySQL for write operations and 23 times faster for read operations[10] on massive amounts of data on hundreds of thousands of possibly failing computers!

QUESTIONS

1. Clearly, Dynamo, Bigtable, and Cassandra are critical technology to the companies that create them. Why did they allow their employees to publish academic papers about them? Why did they not keep them as proprietary secrets?

2. What do you think this movement means to the existing DBMS vendors? How serious is the NoSQL threat? Justify your answer. What responses by existing DBMS vendors would be sensible?

3. Is it a waste of your time to learn about the relational model and Microsoft Access? Why or why not?

4. Given what you know about GearUp, should it use a relational DBMS, such as Oracle Database or MySQL, or should it use Cassandra?

5. Suppose that GearUp decides to use a NoSQL solution, but a battle emerges among the employees in the IT department. One faction wants to use Cassandra, but another faction wants to use a different NoSQL data store, named MongoDB (www.mongodb.org). Assume that you're Kelly, and Lucas asks for your opinion about how he should proceed. How do you respond?

---

[8]"Welcome to Apache Cassandra," The Apache Software Foundation. Available at http://cassandra.apache.org (accessed June 2011).
[9]Parleys.com—The Cassandra Distributed Database, www.parleys.com/#st=5&id=1866&sl=20 (accessed June 2011).
[10]Slide 21, www.parleys.com/#st=5&id=1866&sl=21 (accessed June 2011).

Data Communication and the Cloud

"What's your plan, Lucas?" Kelly Summers, CEO of GearUp, is meeting with Lucas Massey, IT director, and Emily Johnson, CFO, to discuss GearUp's Web hosting costs.

"Right now, Kelly, we're fine. Our hosting service processes our transactions on time and we've had no real outages, but . . ."

Emily can't stand this. "Well, we're fine until you look at the bills we're running up. Our hosting costs have increased 350 percent *in a year*."

This could happen to you

"Yes, Emily, they have, but our volume's gone up 400 percent."

"True enough, but . . ."

Kelly has had enough: "We've been over this before. No need to rehash it. We all agree that our hosting costs are too high. Lucas, I'd asked you to look into alternatives. What have you got?"

"The cloud."

"The *what*?" Emily hopes he's not losing it.

"The cloud. We move our Web servers and databases to the cloud."

Kelly is curious. "OK, Lucas, I'll bite. What's the cloud?"

"It's a movement—I'd call it a fad, except I think it's here to stay."

"So how does it help us?"

"We lease server capability from a third party."

Emily's confused. "But, we're already doing that from our hosting vendor."

"Well, it's different. We can lease on very, very flexible, pay-as-you-go terms. If we have a popular item, like the golf clubs, we can acquire more resources—they use the term *provision*—we can provision more resources."

"You mean each day? We can change the terms of our lease on a daily basis?" Emily thinks that's not possible because she knows the terms of GearUp's contract with its current hosting vendor.

STUDY QUESTIONS

Q1 WHAT IS A COMPUTER NETWORK?

Q2 WHAT ARE THE COMPONENTS OF A LAN?

Q3 WHAT ARE THE FUNDAMENTAL CONCEPTS YOU SHOULD KNOW ABOUT THE INTERNET?

Q4 WHAT PROCESSING OCCURS ON A TYPICAL WEB SERVER?

Q5 WHY IS THE CLOUD THE FUTURE FOR MOST ORGANIZATIONS?

How does the **knowledge** in this chapter help **you?**

"No, I mean 25 cents an hour."

"No, I mean each hour. We can provision or release server resources by the hour." Lucas is enjoying this.

Emily is surprised. "No way. How do they do that? We have to give our hosting vendor at least a week's notice."

"Yeah, we do. But that's not how the cloud works, at least not how some cloud vendors work."

Emily persists. "I still don't get it."

"They use what's called *virtualization.* They don't actually provision new hardware; they provision new instances of servers on existing hardware."

"So one server is actually many?" Emily's read about this somewhere.

"No, one server is *virtually* many." Lucas is having fun.

"Whatever." Emily does *not* like to be corrected.

"The point is they can do this programmatically, no humans involved. Our programs can tell their programs to give us another 10 servers; we can use them a few hours, and then give them back." Lucas gets serious again.

"OK, so how much does it cost? This can't be cheap." Emily's skeptical.

"How about a quarter an hour?"

Kelly's puzzled at that. "You mean a quarter of an hour? 15 minutes?"

"No, I mean 25 cents an hour." Lucas grins as he says this.

"*What*?" Emily's dumbfounded.

"Yeah, that's it. That's for processing. For databases, we have to commit to a monthly charge. Fifty dollars a month for what we'd need." Lucas isn't quite sure, because these are preliminary prices. He thinks the actual costs could be less.

"Lucas, you've got to be kidding. We can knock thousands off of our hosting fees. This is *huge.*" As Emily says this, in the back of her mind she's thinking, "If it's true."

"Well, it's good; I don't know about huge. We still have development costs on our end. And we need to create the procedures, train people, the whole system thing . . ."

"Lucas, give me a plan. I want a plan." Kelly's thinking what these savings could mean to their next two quarters . . . and beyond.

"I'll give you something next week."

"I want it by Monday, Lucas."

"OK," he says, leaving the room thinking, "There goes the weekend."

Kelly stays seated, pondering. Emily starts to get up.

"Emily, we need to find out if this is real."

"Seems too good to be true."

"It does. But let's find out. Someone else will be doing it, if it's real. What about Blue Nile, what are they doing? They'd talk to me. Find one or two of our friends and let's talk to them. Anyway, I want to know what the downside is."

"You want to go see them?"

"I will if I have to. First, let's talk. Set up a videoconference."

"Will do."

WHAT IS A COMPUTER NETWORK?

A computer **network** is a collection of computers that communicate with one another over transmission lines or wirelessly. As shown in Figure 6-1, the three basic types of networks are local area networks, wide area networks, and internets.

A **local area network (LAN)** connects computers that reside in a single geographic location on the premises of the company that operates the LAN. The number of connected computers can range from two to several hundred. The distinguishing characteristic of a LAN is *a single location*. A **wide area network (WAN)** connects computers at different geographic locations. The computers in two separated company sites must be connected using a WAN. To illustrate, the computers for a College of Business located on a single campus can be connected via a LAN. The computers for a College of Business located on multiple campuses must be connected via a WAN.

The single- versus multiple-site distinction is important. With a LAN, an organization can place communications lines wherever it wants, because all lines reside on its premises. The same is not true for a WAN. A company with offices in Chicago and Atlanta cannot run a wire down the freeway to connect computers in the two cities. Instead, the company contracts with a communications vendor that is licensed by the government and that already has lines or has the authority to run new lines between the two cities.

An **internet** is a network of networks. Internets connect LANs, WANs, and other internets. The most famous internet is **"the Internet"** (with an uppercase letter *I*), the collection of networks that you use when you send email or access a Web site. In addition to the Internet, private networks of networks, called *internets*, also exist. A private internet that is used exclusively within an organization is sometimes called an **intranet**.

The networks that comprise an internet use a large variety of communication methods and conventions, and data must flow seamlessly across them. To provide seamless flow, an elaborate scheme called a *layered protocol* is used. The details of protocols are beyond the scope of this text. Just understand that a **protocol** is a set of rules that programs on two communicating devices follow. There are many different protocols; some are used for LANs, some are used for WANs, some are used for internets and the Internet, and some are used for all of these. We will identify several common protocols in this chapter.

Type	Characteristic
Local area network (LAN)	Computers connected at a single physical site
Wide area network (WAN)	Computers connected between two or more separated sites
The Internet and internets	Networks of networks

Figure 6-1
Basic Network Types

Q2 WHAT ARE THE COMPONENTS OF A LAN?

As stated, a LAN is a group of computers connected together on a single site. Usually the computers are located within a half mile or so of each other. The key distinction, however, is that all of the computers are located on property controlled by the organization that operates the LAN. This means that the organization can run cables wherever needed to connect the computers.

A TYPICAL SOHO LAN

Figure 6-2 shows a LAN that is typical of those in a **small office or a home office (SOHO)**. Typically, such LANs have fewer than a dozen or so computers and printers. Many businesses, of course, operate LANs that are much larger than this one. The principles are the same for a larger LAN, but the additional complexity is beyond the scope of this text.

The computers and printers in Figure 6-2 communicate via a mixture of wired and wireless connections. Computers 1 and 3 and printer 1 use wired connections; computers 2, 4, and 5 as well as printer 2 use wireless connections. The devices and protocols used differ for wired and wireless connectivity.

Wired Connectivity

Computers 1 and 3 and printer 1 are wired to a **switch**, which is a special-purpose computer that receives and transmits wired traffic on the LAN. In Figure 6-2, the switch is contained within the box labeled "LAN Device." When either of these two computers communicates with each other or with printer 1, it does so by sending the traffic over wires to the switch, which redirects the traffic to the other computer or printer 1.

The **LAN device** is a small computer that contains the following networking components. It has a switch, as just described; it also has a device for wireless communication, as you are about to learn. In most cases, it has devices for connecting to a WAN and via the WAN to the Internet.

Figure 6-2
Typical Small Office/Home Office

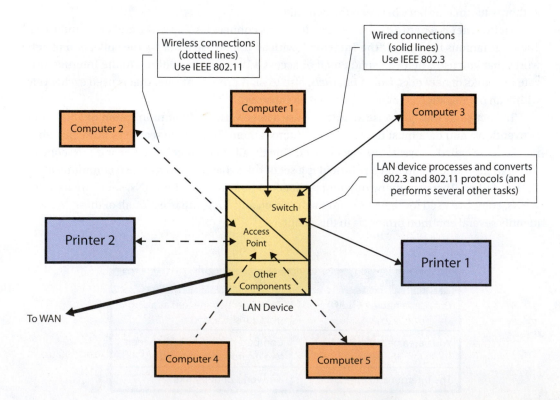

For SOHO applications, LAN devices are usually provided by the phone or cable vendor. They have many different names, depending on the brand.

Each wired computer or printer on the LAN has a **network interface card (NIC)**, which is a device that connects the computer's or printer's circuitry to the network wires. The NIC works with programs in each device to implement the protocols necessary for communication. Most computers today ship from the factory with an **onboard NIC**, which is a NIC built into the computer's circuitry.

The computers, printers, and the switches on a wired LAN are connected using one of two wired media. Most LAN connections are made using **unshielded twisted pair (UTP) cable**. This cable contains sets of wires that are twisted together to improve signal quality. However, if the connection carries a lot of traffic, the UTP cable may be replaced by **optical fiber cables**. The signals on such cables are light rays, and they are reflected inside the glass core of the optical fiber cable.

LANs that are larger than the one in Figure 6-2 use more than one switch. Typically, in a building with several floors, a switch is placed on each floor, and the computers on that floor are connected to the switch with UTP cable. The switches on each floor are connected to each other via the faster-speed optical fiber cable.

Wireless Connections

In Figure 6-2, three of the computers and one printer are connected to the LAN using wireless technology. The wireless computers and printer have a **wireless NIC (WNIC)** instead of a NIC. Today, nearly all personal computers ship from the factory with an onboard WNIC. (By the way, in almost all cases a NIC or WNIC can be added to a computer that does not have one.)

As shown in Figure 6-2, the WNIC devices connect to an **access point**, which is the component of the LAN device that processes wireless traffic and communicates with the wired switch. Thus, with this design every device on the LAN, whether wired or wireless, can communicate with every other device. Wireless devices communicate to each other via the access point. If wireless devices need to connect to a wired device, they do so via the access point, then to the switch, and then to the wired devices. Similarly, wired devices communicate to each other via the switch. If the wired devices need to connect to wireless ones, they do so via the switch, then to the access point, and then to the wireless devices.

LAN Protocols

For two devices to communicate, they must use the same protocol. The Institute for Electrical and Electronics Engineers (IEEE, pronounced "I triple E") sponsors committees that create and publish protocol and other standards. The committee that addresses LAN standards is called the *IEEE 802 Committee*. Thus, IEEE LAN protocols always start with the numbers 802.

The **IEEE 802.3 protocol** is used for wired LAN connections. This protocol standard, also called **Ethernet**, specifies hardware characteristics, such as which wire carries which signals. It also describes how messages are to be packaged and processed for wired transmission over the LAN.

The NICs in most personal computers today support what is called **10/100/1000 Ethernet**. These products conform to the 802.3 specification and allow for transmission at a rate of 10, 100, or 1,000 Mbps (megabits per second). Switches detect the speed that a given device can handle and communicate with it at that speed. If you check computer listings at Dell, Lenovo, and other manufacturers, you will see PCs advertised as having 10/100/1000 Ethernet. Today, speeds of up to 1 Gbps are possible on wired LANs.

By the way, the abbreviations used for communications speeds differ from those used for computer memory. For communications equipment, *k* stands for 1,000, not 1,024 as it does for memory. Similarly, *M* stands for 1,000,000, not 1,024 × 1,024; *G* stands for 1,000,000,000, not 1,024 × 1,024 × 1,024. Thus, 100 Mbps is 100,000,000 bits per second. Also, communications speeds are expressed in *bits*, whereas memory sizes are expressed in *bytes*.

Technology enables cost-effective communicating appliances . . . maybe next year they'll be tweeting one another. But, do you care? See the Guide on pages 154-155 for a discussion of the planning of exponential phenomena.

Wireless LAN connections use the **IEEE 802.11 protocol**. Several versions of 802.11 exist, and as of 2012, the most current one is IEEE 802.11n. The differences among these versions are beyond the scope of this discussion. Just note that the current standard, 802.11n, allows speeds of up to 600 Mbps.

Observe that the LAN in Figure 6-2 uses both the 802.3 and 802.11 protocols. The NICs operate according to the 802.3 protocol and connect directly to the switch, which also operates on the 802.3 standard. The WNICs operate according to the 802.11 protocol and connect to the wireless access point. The access point must process messages using both the 802.3 and 802.11 standards; it sends and receives wireless traffic using the 802.11 protocol and then communicates with the switch using the 802.3 protocol. Characteristics of LANs are summarized in the top two rows of Figure 6-3.

Bluetooth is another common wireless protocol. It is designed for transmitting data over short distances, replacing cables. Some devices, such as wireless mice and keyboards, use Bluetooth to connect to the computer. Smartphones use Bluetooth to connect to automobile entertainment systems.

CONNECTING TO THE INTERNET

Wireless devices can also be used to obtain data from users without their knowledge. See the Ethics Guide on page 152–153 for an example of this and a discussion.

Although you may not have realized it, when you connect your SOHO LAN, phone, iPad, or Kindle to the Internet, you are connecting to a WAN. You must do so because you are connecting to computers that are not physically located on your premises. You cannot start running wires down the street to plug in somewhere.

When you connect to the Internet, you are actually connecting to an **Internet service provider (ISP)**. An ISP has three important functions. First, it provides you with a legitimate Internet address. Second, it serves as your gateway to the Internet. The ISP receives the communications from your computer and passes them on to the Internet, and it receives communications from the Internet and passes them on to you. Finally, ISPs pay

Figure 6-3
Office (SOHO) LAN

Type	Topology	Transmission Line	Transmission Speed	Equipment Used	Protocol Commonly Used	Remarks
Local area network	Local area network	UTP or optical fiber	Common: 10/100/1000 Mbps Possible: 1 Gbps	Switch NIC UTP or optical	IEEE 802.3 (Ethernet)	Switches connect devices, multiple switches on all but small LANs.
	Local area network with wireless	UTP or optical for non-wireless connections	Up to 600 Mbps	Wireless access point Wireless NIC	IEEE 802.11n	Access point transforms wired LAN (802.3) to wireless LAN (802.11).
Connections to the Internet	DSL modem to ISP	DSL telephone	Personal: Upstream to 1 Mbps, downstream to 40 Mbps (max 10 likely in most areas)	DSL modem DSL-capable telephone line	DSL	Can have computer and phone use simultaneously. Always connected.
	Cable modem to ISP	Cable TV lines to optical cable	Upstream to 1 Mbps Downstream 300 Kbps to 10 Mbps	Cable modem Cable TV cable	Cable	Capacity is shared with other sites; performance varies depending on other's use.
	WAN wireless	Wireless connection to WAN	500 K to 1.7 Mbps	Wireless WAN modem	One of several wireless standards	Sophisticated protocol enables several devices to use the same wireless frequency.

for the Internet. They collect money from their customers and pay access fees and other charges on your behalf.

Figure 6-3 shows the three common alternatives for connecting to the Internet. Notice that we are discussing how your computer connects to the Internet via a WAN; we are not discussing the structure of the WAN itself. WAN architectures and their protocols are beyond the scope of this discussion. Search the Web for "leased lines" or "PSDN" if you want to learn more about WAN architectures.

SOHO LANs (like that in Figure 6-2) and individual home and office computers are commonly connected to an ISP in one of three ways: a special telephone line called a DSL line, a cable TV line, or a wireless-phone-like connection. Each of these alternatives uses its own, special protocol.

Digital Subscriber Lines (DSL)

A **digital subscriber line (DSL)** provides an Internet connection that uses the same lines as voice telephones, but they operate so that their signals do not interfere with voice telephone service. Because DSL signals do not interfere with telephone signals, DSL data transmission and telephone conversations can occur simultaneously. A device at the telephone company separates the phone signals from the computer signals and sends the latter signal to the ISP.

Cable Lines

Cable lines provide high-speed data transmission using cable television lines. The cable company installs a fast, high-capacity optical fiber cable to a distribution center in each neighborhood that it serves. At the distribution center, the optical fiber cable connects to regular cable-television cables that run to subscribers' homes or businesses. Cables operate in such a way that their signals do not interfere with TV signals.

Because up to 500 user sites can share these facilities, performance varies depending on how many other users are sending and receiving data. At the maximum, users can download data up to 50 Mbps and can upload data at 512 Kbps. Typically, performance is much lower than this. In most cases, the download speed of cable modems and DSL modems is about the same.

WAN Wireless Connection

A third way that you can connect your computer, iPhone, iPad, Kindle, or other communicating device is via a **WAN wireless** connection. Amazon.com's Kindle, for example, uses a Sprint, Verizon, and other wireless networks to provide wireless data connections. The iPhone uses a LAN-based wireless network if one is available and a WAN wireless network if one is not. The LAN-based network is preferred because performance is considerably higher. As of 2012, WAN wireless provides an average performance of 500 Kbps, with peaks of up to 1.7 Mbps, as opposed to the typical 50 Mbps for LAN wireless.

Before we leave the topic of network connections, you should learn the meaning of two other terms used to classify network speed. **Narrowband** lines typically have transmission speeds less than 56 Kbps. **Broadband** lines have speeds in excess of 256 Kbps. Today, all popular communication technologies provide broadband capability, and so these terms are likely to fade from use.

Experiencing MIS

INCLASS EXERCISE 6

Opening Pandora's Box

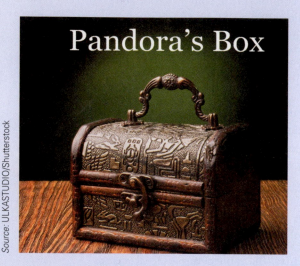

Pandora's Box

Source: ULKASTUDIO/Shutterstock

Nearly free data communications and data storage have created unprecedented opportunities for businesses, as we have described numerous times. Inevitably, such technology will have a revolutionary impact in the home as well. The Guide on page 154 discusses why you should be wary of toasters and microwaves that talk to each other, but home entertainment is another matter.

Sonos is a good example. Sonos has leveraged emerging technologies, especially wireless technology, to develop easy-to-install, high-quality wireless audio systems. Customers hook up one of several different Sonos devices into their home LAN device using a wired Ethernet connection. That device then connects wirelessly to up to 32 other Sonos audio devices around the home. Each device can play its own music or other audio, some can play the same audio, or all can be forced to play the same audio.

Some Sonos devices provide wireless stereo to existing stereo systems; other devices include the wireless receiver and an amplifier, with the customer providing the speakers. Still other devices provide the wireless receiver, amplifier, and speakers in one unit.

Each Sonos device includes a computer running Linux. Those computers communicate wirelessly using a proprietary Sonos protocol. Because every device communicates with every other device, Sonos refers to its network of equipment as a *wireless mesh*. The benefit of this mesh to the consumer is flexibility and ease of installation. The devices find each other and determine their own data communications pathways (akin to, but different from, IP routing on the Internet).

Sonos works with any Internet radio source and with music services such as Pandora. With Pandora (and similar services), you establish a personal radio station by selecting a favorite song or musical work. Pandora then plays music based on your selection. You can vote thumbs up or thumbs down on music that is played. Based on your ratings, Pandora selects similar music based on proprietary algorithms.

Form a group of students and answer the following questions:

1. Imagine that you have graduated, have the job of your dreams, and want to install a wireless stereo system in your new condo. Assume that you have a spare bedroom you use as an office that has a LAN device connected to the Internet. You have an existing stereo system in your living room, a pair of unused speakers, but no other stereo equipment. Assume that you want to play audio and music in your office, your living room, and your bedroom.

   a. Visit the Sonos Web site at *www.sonos.com* and select and price the equipment you will need.

   b. Go to the Web sites of Sonos' competitors at *http://www.logitech.com/en-us/speakers-audio* or *http://soundbridge.roku.com/soundbridge/index.php* and select and price equipment you will need.

   c. Recommend one of the selections you identified in your answers to items a and b and justify your selection.

   d. Report your findings to the rest of the class.

2. Visit the Pandora Web site at *www.pandora.com*. Using the free trial membership, build a radio station for your group. Base your station on whatever song or music your group chooses.

3. The Sonos equipment has no on-off switch. Apparently, it is designed to be permanently on, like your LAN device. You can mute each station, but to turn a station off you must unplug it, an action few people take. Suppose you have tuned a Sonos device to a Pandora station, and you mute that device. Because the Sonos equipment is still on, it will continue downloading packets over the Internet to a device that no one is listening to 13.

   a. Describe the consequences of this situation on the Internet.

   b. You pay a flat fee for your Internet connection. In what ways does such a fee arrangement discourage efficiency?

4. Using your group's imagination and curiosity, describe the consequences of Internet-based audio on each of the following:

   a. Existing radio stations

   b. Vendors of traditional audio receivers

   c. Audio entertainment

   d. Cisco (a vendor of Internet routers)

   e. Your local ISP

   f. Any other companies or entities you believe will be affected by wireless audio systems

Report your conclusions to the rest of the class.

5. Using history as a guide, we can imagine that audio leads the way for video.

   a. Explain how you could use a wireless video system in your new condo.

   b. In the opinion of your group, is having multiple wireless video players in your condo more or less desirable than wireless audio? Explain.

   c. Answer a–f in item 4, but use wireless video rather than audio as the driving factor.

   d. Report your answers to the rest of the class.

6. Considering all of your answers to items 1–5:

   a. What industries are the winners and losers?

   b. What companies are the winners and losers?

   c. How does your answer to parts a and b guide your job search?

7. Use the knowledge you have gained in answering items 1–6 to prepare a 1-minute statement that you could make in a job interview about emerging opportunities in Internet-based audio and video. Assume that with this statement you wish to demonstrate your ability to think innovatively. Deliver your statement to the rest of the class.

WHAT ARE THE FUNDAMENTAL CONCEPTS YOU SHOULD KNOW ABOUT THE INTERNET?

As discussed in Q1, the Internet is an *internet*, meaning that it is a network of networks. As you might guess, the technology that underlies the Internet is complicated and beyond the scope of this text. However, because of the popularity of the Internet, certain terms have become ubiquitous in 21st-century business society. In this question, we will define and explain terms that you need to know to be an informed business professional and consumer of Internet services.

AN INTERNET EXAMPLE

Figure 6-4 illustrates one use of the Internet. Suppose that you are sitting in snowbound Minneapolis and you want to communicate with a hotel in sunny, tropical, northern New Zealand.

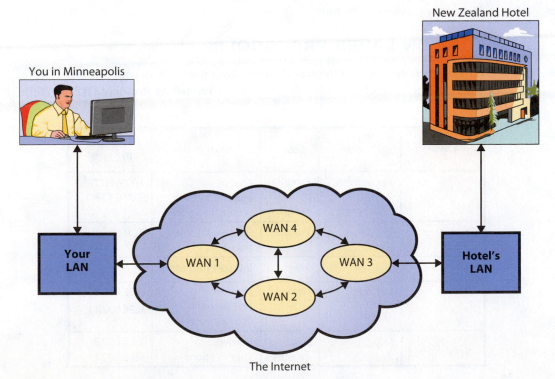

Figure 6-4
Using the Internet for a Hotel Reservation

Maybe you are making a reservation using the hotel's Web site, or maybe you are sending an email to a reservations clerk inquiring about facilities or services.

To begin, note that this example is an internet because it is a network of networks. It consists of two LANs (yours and the hotel's) and four WANs. (In truth, the real Internet consists of tens of thousands of WANs and LANs, but to conserve paper we don't show all of them here.)

Your communication to the hotel involves nearly unimaginable complexity. Somehow, your computer communicates with a server in the New Zealand hotel, a computer that it has never "met" before and knows nothing about. Further, your transmission, which is too big to travel in one piece, is broken up into parts and each part passed along from WAN to WAN in such a way that it arrives intact. Then your original message is reassembled, any parts that were lost or damaged (this happens) are resent, and the reconstructed message delivered to the server for processing. All of this is accomplished by computers and data communications devices that most likely have not interacted before.

What all these devices do know, however, is that they process the same set of protocols. Thus, we need to begin with Internet protocols.

THE TCP/IP PROTOCOL ARCHITECTURE

The protocols used on the Internet are arranged according to a structure known as the **TCP/IP Protocol architecture**, which is a scheme of five protocol types arranged in layers. As shown in Figure 6-5, the top layer concerns protocols for applications like browsers and Web servers. The next two layers concern protocols about data communications across any internet (note the small *i*; this means any network of networks), including the Internet. The bottom two layers involve protocols that concern data transmission within a network. For example, the IEEE 802.3 and 802.11 LAN protocols operate at the bottom two layers.

As stated, a protocol is a set of rules and data structures for organizing communication. One or more protocols are defined at each layer. Data communications and software vendors write computer programs that implement the rules of a particular protocol. (For protocols at the bottom layer, the physical layer, they build hardware devices that implement the protocol.)

You are probably wondering, "Why should I know about this?" The reason is so that you will understand the terms you will hear and the products you will use, buy, or possibly invest in that relate to each other via this architecture.

APPLICATION-LAYER PROTOCOLS

You will directly encounter at least three application-layer protocols in your professional life. (In fact, you have used two of them already.) **Hypertext Transport Protocol (HTTP)** is the

Figure 6-5
TCP/IP Protocol Architecture

Layer	Name	Scope	Purpose	Example Protocol
5	Application	Program to program	Enable communication among programs	HTTP, HTTPS, SMTP, FTP
4	Transport	Internets	Reliable internet transport	TCP
3	Internet	Internets	Internet routing	IP
2	Data Link	Network	Flow among switches and access points	IEEE 802.3 IEEE 802.11
1	Physical	Two devices	Hardware specifications	IEEE 802.3 IEEE 802.11

protocol used between browsers and Web servers. When you use a browser such as Internet Explorer, Safari, or Chrome, you are using a program that implements the HTTP protocol. At the other end, at the New Zealand Hotel for example, there is a server that also processes HTTP, as you will learn in Q4. Even though your browser and the server at the hotel have never "met" before, they can communicate with one another because they both follow the rules of HTTP. Your browser sends requests for service encoded in a predefined HTTP *request format*; the server receives that request, does something, and formats a response in a predefined HTTP *response format*.

As you will learn in Chapter 12, there is a secure version of HTTP called **HTTPS**. Whenever you see *https* in your browser's address bar, you have a secure transmission, and you can safely send sensitive data like credit card numbers. When you are on the Internet, if you do not see *https*, then you should assume that all of your communication is open and could be published on the front page of your campus newspaper tomorrow morning. Hence, when you are using HTTP, email, text messaging, chat, videoconferencing, or anything other than HTTPS, know that whatever you are typing or saying could be known by anyone else. Thus, in your classroom, when you send a text message to a fellow student, that message can be intercepted and read by anyone in your class, including your professor. The same is true of people at a coffee shop, an airport, or anywhere.

Two additional TCP/IP application-layer protocols are common. **SMTP,** or **Simple Mail Transfer Protocol**, is used for email transmissions (along with other protocols as well). **FTP,** or **File Transfer Protocol**, is used to move files over the Internet. One very common use for FTP is to maintain Web sites. When a Web site administrator wishes to post a new picture or story on a Web server, the administrator will often use FTP to move the picture or other item to the server. Like HTTP, FTP has a secure version as well, but do not assume you are using it.

With this knowledge, we can clear up one common misconception. You are using the Internet when you use any of these protocols. However, you are using the Web only when you use either HTTP or HTTPS. Thus, the **Web** is the Internet-based network of browsers and servers that process HTTP or HTTPS. When you send a file using FTP, you are using the Internet, but not the Web. It is incorrect to say you are using the Web to send or receive FTP files.

TCP AND IP PROTOCOLS

You have some idea of the protocols used at the application (top) layer in Figure 6-5, and from the discussion in Q2 you have some idea of the LAN protocols used at the bottom two layers. But what is the purpose of the layers in between, the transport and internet layers? You know these two layers must be important because the architecture is named after their protocols.

These protocols manage traffic as it passes across an internet (including the Internet) from one network to another. The most important protocol in the transport layer is **TCP,** or the **Transmission Control Protocol**. As a transport protocol, TCP has many functions, most of which are beyond the scope of our discussion. One easily understood function, however, is that TCP programs break your traffic up into pieces and send each piece along its way. It then works with TCP programs on other devices in the internet to ensure that all of the pieces arrive at their destination. If one or more pieces are lost or damaged, TCP programs detect that condition and cause retransmission of that piece. Hence, the TCP layer is said to provide *reliable internet transport.*

The primary protocol of the Internet layer is called **IP (Internet Protocol)**, which is a protocol that specifies the routing of the pieces of your message through the networks that comprise any internet (including the Internet). In Figure 6-4, programs on devices at each of the networks (the two LANs and the four WANs) receive a portion of your message and route it to another computer in its network, or to another network altogether. A **packet** is a piece of a message that is handled by programs that implement IP. A **router** is a special-purpose computer that moves packet traffic according to the rules of the IP protocol.

Your message is broken into packets (for simplicity we're leaving a *lot* out here) and each packet is sent out onto the Internet. The packet contains the address of where it is supposed to go. Routers along the way receive the packet, examine the destination IP address, and send it either to the desired destination, or to another router that is closer to the desired destination.

When your message starts on its way to the New Zealand hotel, no device knows what route the pieces will take. Until the last hop, a router just sends the packet to another router that it determines to be closer to the final destination. In fact, the packets that make up your message may take different pathways through the Internet (this is rare, but it does occur). Because of this routing scheme, the Internet is very robust. For example, in Figure 6-4, either WAN 2 or WAN 4 could fail and your packets would still get to the hotel.

To summarize, TCP provides reliable internet transport and IP provides internet routing.

IP ADDRESSING

An **IP address** is a number that identifies a particular device. **Public IP addresses** identify a particular device on the public Internet. Because public IP addresses must be unique, worldwide, their assignment is controlled by a public agency known as **ICANN (Internet Corporation for Assigned Names and Numbers).**

Private IP addresses identify a particular device on a private network, usually on a LAN. Their assignment is controlled within the LAN, usually by the LAN device shown in Figure 6-2. When you sign on to a LAN at a coffee shop, for example, the LAN device loans you a private IP address to use while you are connected to the LAN. When you leave the LAN, it reuses that address.

Use of Private IP Addresses

When your computer uses TCP/IP within a LAN, say to access a private Web server within the LAN, it uses a private IP address. However, and this is far more common, when you access a public site, say *www.pearsonhighered.com*, from within the LAN, your traffic uses your internal IP address until it gets to the LAN device. At that point, the LAN device substitutes your private IP address for its public IP address and sends your traffic out onto the Internet.

This private/public IP address scheme has two major benefits. First, public IP addresses are conserved. All of the computers on the LAN use only one public IP address. Second, by using private IP addresses, you need not register a public IP address for your computer with ICANN-approved agencies. Furthermore, if you had a public IP address for your computer, every time you moved it, say from home to school, the Internet would have to update its addressing mechanisms to route traffic to your new location. Such updating would be a massive burden (and a mess)!

Functions of the LAN Device

Before we continue with IP addressing, note all of the functions of the LAN device. A lot is happening in that little box shown in Figure 6-2:

- Switch processing IEEE 802.3 wired LAN traffic
- Access-point processing IEEE 802.11 wireless LAN traffic
- Translation between IEEE 802.3 and IEEE 802.11

- Modem converting between analog and digital
- Server that assigns private IP addresses
- Private/public IP address translation converting between private and public IP addresses
- Internet router routing packets
- And more that is beyond the scope of this discussion . . .

Public IP Addresses and Domain Names

IP addresses have two formats. The most common form, called **IPv4**, has a four-decimal dotted notation like 173.194.35.177; the second, called **IPv6**, has a longer format that will not concern us here. Because it is longer, however, IPv6 can allow for millions of more IP addresses than IPv4. In your browser, if you enter *http://173.194.35.177/*, your browser will connect with the device on the public Internet that has been assigned to this address. Try it to find out who has this address.

Nobody wants to type IP addresses like *http://173.194.35.177/* to find a particular site. Instead, we want to enter names like *www.pandora.com* or *www.woot.com* or *www.amazon.com*. To facilitate that desire, ICANN administers a system for assigning names to IP addresses. First, a **domain name** is a worldwide-unique name that is affiliated with a public IP address. When an organization or individual wants to register a domain name, it goes to a company that applies to an ICANN-approved agency to do so. Go Daddy *www.godaddy.com* is an example of such a company (Figure 6-6).

Go Daddy, or a similar agency, will first determine if the desired name is unique, worldwide. If so, then it will apply to register that name to the applicant. Once the registration is completed, the applicant can affiliate a public IP address with the domain name. From that point onward, traffic for the new domain name will be routed to the affiliated IP address.

Note two important points: First, several (or many) domain names can point to the same IP address. Second, the affiliation of domain names with IP addresses is dynamic. The owner of the domain name can change the affiliated IP addresses at its discretion.

Before we leave the Internet, you need to know one more term. A **URL (Uniform Resource Locator)** is an address on the Internet. Commonly, it consists of a protocol (like http:// or ftp://)

Figure 6-6
Go Daddy Screenshot

Figure 6-7
Remote Access Using VPN;
Actual Connections

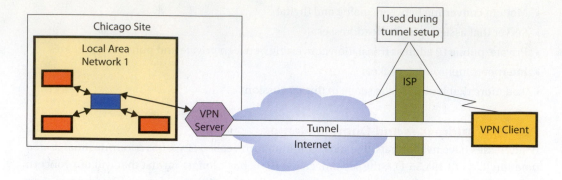

followed by a domain name or public IP address. A URL is actually quite a bit more complicated than this description, but that detailed knowledge is beyond the scope of this text. The preferred pronunciation of URL is to say the letters U, R, L.

VIRTUAL PRIVATE NETWORK

A **virtual private network (VPN)** uses the Internet to create the appearance of private point-to-point connections. As Emily learned, in the IT world the term *virtual* means something that appears to exist but, in fact, does not. Here, a VPN uses the public Internet to create the appearance of a private connection.

A Typical VPN

Figure 6-7 shows one way to create a VPN to connect a remote computer, perhaps an employee working at a hotel in Miami, to a LAN at a Chicago site. The remote user is the VPN client. That client first establishes a connection to the Internet. The connection can be obtained by accessing a local ISP, as shown in the figure, or, in some cases, the hotel itself provides a direct Internet connection.

In either case, once the Internet connection is made, VPN software on the remote user's computer establishes a connection with the VPN server in Chicago. The VPN client and VPN server then have a point-to-point connection. That connection, called a **tunnel**, is a virtual, private pathway over a public or shared network from the VPN client to the VPN server. Figure 6-8 illustrates the connection as it appears to the remote user.

VPN communications are secure, even though they are transmitted over the public Internet. To ensure security, VPN client software *encrypts*, or codes (see Chapter 12, page 321), the original message so that its contents are protected from snooping. Then the VPN client

Figure 6-8
Remote Access Using VPN;
Apparent Connection

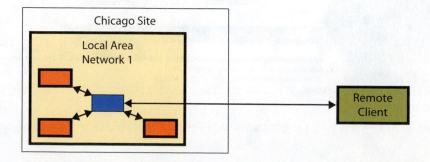

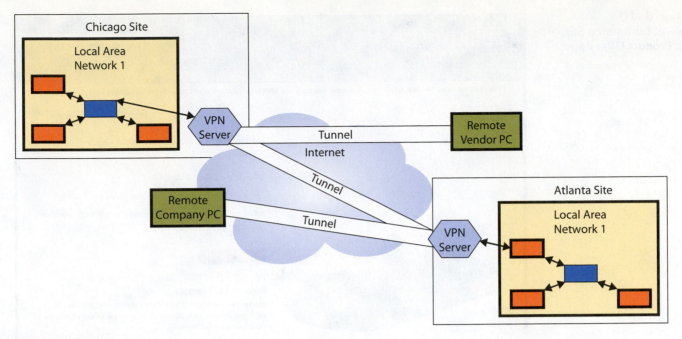

Figure 6-9
WAN Using VPN

appends the Internet address of the VPN server to the message and sends that package over the Internet to the VPN server. When the VPN server receives the message, it strips its address off the front of the message, *decrypts* the coded message, and sends the plain text message to the original address on the LAN. In this way, secure private messages are delivered over the public Internet.

VPNs offer the benefit of point-to-point leased lines, and they enable remote access, both by employees and by any others who have been registered with the VPN server. For example, if customers or vendors are registered with the VPN server, they can use the VPN from their own sites. Figure 6-9 shows three tunnels: one supports a point-to-point connection between the Atlanta and Chicago sites, and the other two support remote connections.

Microsoft has fostered the popularity of VPNs by including VPN support in Windows. All versions of Microsoft Windows have the capability of working as VPN clients. Computers running Windows Server can operate as VPN servers.

 WHAT PROCESSING OCCURS ON A TYPICAL WEB SERVER?

At this point, you know basic networking terms and have a high-level view of how internets and the Internet work. To complete this chapter's high-level survey of data communications, you need to know a bit about the processing that occurs on a Web server. For this discussion, we will use the example of a Web storefront, which is a server on the Web from which you can buy products.

Suppose you want to buy an item from Zulily, a company that sells high-end children's clothes. To do so, you go to www.zulily.com and navigate to the product(s) that you want to buy (see Figure 6-10). When you find something you want, you add it to your shopping cart and keep shopping. At some point, you check out by supplying credit card data.

Figure 6-10
Sample of Commerce Server
Pages; Product Offer Pages

Source: Reprinted by permission of
Zulily. *www.zulily.com*

In Q3, we discussed how your traffic crosses over the Internet to arrive at the Zulily server. The next question is: What happens at that server when it arrives? Or, from another perspective, if you want to set up a Web storefront for your company, what facilities do you need?

THREE-TIER ARCHITECTURE

Almost all e-commerce applications use the **three-tier architecture**, which is an arrangement of user computers and servers into three categories, or tiers, as shown in Figure 6-11. The **user tier** consists of computers, phones, and other devices that have browsers that request and process Web pages. The **server tier** consists of computers that run Web servers and process application programs. The **database tier** consists of computers that run a DBMS that processes requests to retrieve and store data. Figure 6-11 shows only one computer at the database tier. Some sites have multicomputer database tiers as well.

When you enter http://www.zulily.com in your browser, the browser sends a request that travels over the Internet to a computer in the server tier at the Zulily site. That request is formatted and processed according to the rules of HTTP. (Notice, by the way, that if you just type *www.zulily.com*, your browser will add the http:// to signify that it is using HTTP.) In response to your request, a server-tier computer sends back a **Web page**, which is a document that is coded in one of the standard page markup languages. The most popular page markup language is the Hypertext Markup Language (HTML), which is described later in this section.

Figure 6-11
Three-Tier Architecture

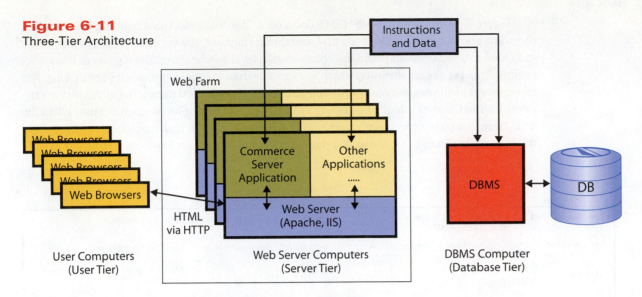

Web servers are programs that run on a server-tier computer and that manage HTTP traffic by sending and receiving Web pages to and from clients. A **commerce server** is an application program that runs on a server-tier computer. A commerce server receives requests from users via the Web server, takes some action, and returns a response to the users via the Web server. Typical commerce server functions are to obtain product data from a database, manage the items in a shopping cart, and coordinate the checkout process. In Figure 6-11, the server-tier computers are running a Web server program, a commerce server application, and other applications having an unspecified purpose.

To ensure acceptable performance, commercial Web sites usually are supported by several or even many Web server computers in a facility called a **Web farm**. Work is distributed among the computers in a Web farm so as to minimize customer delays. Today, organizations commonly outsource their Web farm to a cloud vendor. See Q5 later in this chapter.

HYPERTEXT MARKUP LANGUAGE (HTML)

Hypertext Markup Language (HTML) is the most common language for defining the structure and layout of Web pages. An HTML **tag** is a notation used to define a data element for display or other purposes. The following HTML is a typical heading tag:

```
<h2>Price of Item</h2>
```

Notice that tags are enclosed in < > (called *angle brackets*) and that they occur in pairs. The start of this tag is indicated by <h2>, and the end of the tag is indicated by </h2>. The words between the tags are the value of the tag. This HTML tag means to place the words "Price of Item" on a Web page in the style of a level-two heading. The creator of the Web page will define the style (font size, color, and so forth) for h2 headings and the other tags to be used.

Web pages include **hyperlinks**, which are pointers to other Web pages. A hyperlink contains the URL of the Web page to find when the user clicks the hyperlink. The URL can reference a page on the server that generated the page containing the hyperlink, or it can reference a page on another server.

Figure 6-12a shows a sample HTML document. The document has a heading that provides metadata about the page and a body that contains the content. The tag <h1> means to format the indicated text as a level-one heading; <h2> means a level-two heading. The tag <a> defines a hyperlink. This tag has an **attribute**, which is a variable used to provide properties about a tag. Not all tags have attributes, but many do. Each attribute has a standard name. The attribute for a hyperlink is **href**, and its value indicates which Web page is to be displayed when the user clicks the link. Here, the page *www.pearsonhighered.com/kroenke* is to be returned when the user clicks the hyperlink. Figure 6-12b shows this page as rendered by Internet Explorer.

Figure 6-12a
Sample HTML
Code Snippet

```
<!DOCTYPE html PUBLIC "-//W3C//DTD XHTML 1.0 Transitional//EN" "http://www.w3.org/TR/xhtml1/DTD/xhtml1-transitional.dtd">
<html xmlns="http://www.w3.org/1999/xhtml">
<head>
<meta content="en-us" http-equiv="Content-Language" />  <meta content="text/html; charset=utf-8" http-equiv="Content-Type" />
<title>UMIS Example HTML</title>
<style type="text/css">
.style1 {
    font-size: xx-large;
    text-align: center;
    font-family: Arial, Helvetica, sans-serif;}
.style2 {
    color: #FF00FF;}
.style3 {
    font-size: medium;
    text-align: center;
    font-family: Arial, Helvetica, sans-serif;}
.style5 {
    font-size: medium;
    text-align: left;
    font-family: Arial, Helvetica, sans-serif;}
.auto-style1 {
    color: #FF0000;}
</style>  </head>
<body>
<p class="style1">
    <span class="auto-style1">Experiencing</span><strong>MIS</strong></p>
<p class="style1"> </p>
<p class="style3"><em>Fourth Edition</em></p>
<p class="style3"> </p>
<p class="style5">Example HTML Document</p>
<p class="style5"> </p>
<p class="style5"> </p>
<p class="style5">Click <a href="http://www.PearsonHigherEd.com/kroenke">here</a> for the textbook&#39;s Web site at Pearson Education.</p>
</body>
</html>
```

Figure 6-12b
Document Created from
HTML Code in Figure 6-12a

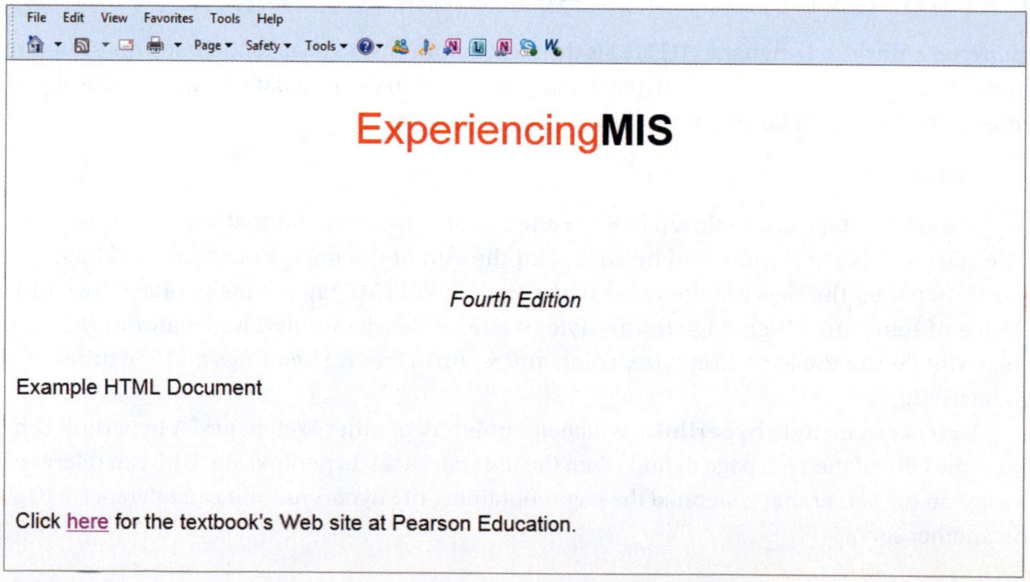

The most current version of html is HTML5. This version adds considerable capability to Web pages, including the ability to show animations and to run on mobile devices. If you are interested in learning html, by all means, learn HTML5.

 WHY IS THE CLOUD THE FUTURE FOR MOST ORGANIZATIONS?

Until 2010 or so, most organizations constructed and maintained their own computing infrastructure. Organizations purchased or leased hardware, installed it on their premises, and used it to support enterprise-wide email, Web sites, e-commerce sites, and in-house applications, such as accounting and operations systems (you'll learn about them in the next chapter). After about 2010, however, organizations began to move their computing infrastructure to the cloud, and it is likely that in the future all, or nearly all, computing infrastructure will be leased from the cloud. So, just what is the cloud, and why is it the future?

See Chapter Extension 7 for a discussion of HTML5 and CSS3.

WHAT IS THE CLOUD?

The **cloud** is the *elastic* leasing of *pooled* computer resources that are accessed via Internet protocols. The term *cloud* is used because most early diagrams of three-tier and other Internet-based systems used a cloud symbol to represent the Internet (see Figure 6-4 for an example), and organizations came to view their infrastructure as being "somewhere in the cloud."

Consider each of the italicized terms in the definition. The term **elastic**, which was first used this way by Amazon.com, means that the amount of resources leased can be increased or decreased dynamically, programmatically, in a short span of time and that organizations pay for just the resources that they use. The resources are **pooled**, because many different organizations use the same physical hardware; they share that hardware through virtualization. Cloud vendors dynamically allocate virtual machines to physical hardware as customer needs increase or decrease. Finally, the resources are accessed via **Internet protocols and standards**, which are additions to TCP/IP that enable cloud-hosting vendors to provide processing capabilities in flexible, yet standardized, ways.

An easy way to understand the essence of this development is to consider electrical power. In the very earliest days of electric power generation, organizations operated their own generators to create power for their company's needs. Over time, as the power grid expanded, it became possible to centralize power generation so that organizations could purchase just the electricity they needed from an electric utility.

Both cloud vendors and electrical utilities benefit from economies of scale. According to this principle, the average cost of production decreases as the size of the operation increases. Major cloud vendors operate enormous Web farms. Figure 6-13 shows the building that contains the computers in the Web farm that Apple constructed in 2011 to support its iCloud offering. This billion-dollar facility contains more than 500,000 square feet.[1] IBM, Google, Amazon.com, Microsoft, Oracle, and other large companies each operate several or many similar farms as well.

---

[1] Patrick Thibodeau, "Apple, Google, Facebook Turn N.C. into Data Center Hub," *Computerworld,* June 3, 2011. Available at www.computerworld.com/s/article/9217259/Apple_Google_Facebook_ turn_N.C._into_data_ center_hub (accessed July 2011).

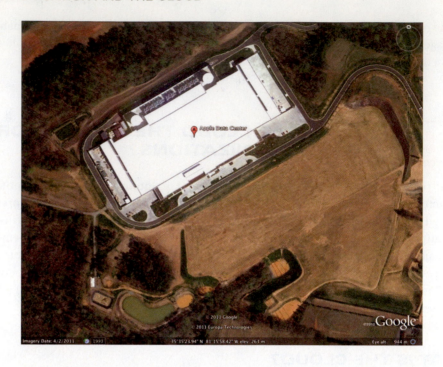

WHY IS THE CLOUD PREFERRED TO IN-HOUSE HOSTING?

Figure 6-14 compares and contrasts cloud-based and in-house hosting. As you can see, the positives are heavily tilted toward cloud-based computing. The cloud vendor Rackspace will lease you one medium server for as little as 1.5 cents per hour. You can obtain and access that server today, actually within a few minutes. Tomorrow, if you need thousands of servers, you can readily scale up to obtain them. Furthermore, you know the cost structure; although you might have a surprise in regard to how many customers want to access your Web site, you won't have any surprises as to how much it will cost.

Another positive is that as long as you're dealing with large, reputable organizations, you'll be receiving best-of-breed security and disaster recovery (discussed in Chapter 12). In addition, you need not worry that you're investing in technology that will soon be obsolete; the cloud vendor is taking that risk. All of this is possible because the cloud vendor is gaining economies of scale by selling to an entire industry, not just to you.

The negatives of cloud computing involve loss of control. You're dependent on a vendor; changes in the vendor's management, policy, and prices are beyond your control. Further, you don't know where your data—which may be a large part of your organization's value—is located. Nor do you know how many copies of your data there are, or even if they're located in the same country as you are. Finally, you have no visibility into the security and disaster preparedness that is actually in place.

The positives and negatives of in-house hosting are shown in the second column of Figure 6-14. For the most part, they are the opposite of those for cloud-based computing; note, however, the need for personnel and management. With in-house hosting, not only will you have to construct your own data center, you'll also need to acquire and train the personnel to run it and then manage those personnel and your facility.

WHY NOW?

A skeptic responds to Figure 6-14 by saying "If it's so great, why hasn't cloud-based hosting been used for years?" Why now?

In fact, cloud-based hosting (or a version of it under a different name) has been around since the 1960s. Long before the creation of the personal computer and networks, time-sharing

Cloud-Based Hosting	In-House Hosting
Positive:	
Small capital requirements	Control of data location
Speedy development	In-depth visibility of security and disaster preparedness
Superior flexibility and adaptability to growing or fluctuating demand	
Known cost structure	
Possibly best-of-breed security/disaster preparedness	
No obsolescence	
Industry-wide economies of scale, hence cheaper	
Negative:	
Dependency on vendor	Significant capital required
Loss of control over data location	Significant development effort
Little visibility into true security and disaster preparedness capabilities	Annual maintenance costs
	Ongoing support costs
	Staff and train personnel
	Increased management requirements
	Difficult (impossible?) to accommodate fluctuating demand
	Cost uncertainties
	Obsolescence

Figure 6-14
Comparison of Cloud-Based Hosting and In-House Hosting

vendors provided slices of computer time on a use-fee basis. However, the technology of that time, continuing up until the first decade of this century, did not favor the construction and use of enormous data centers.

Three factors have made cloud-based hosting advantageous today. First, processors, data communication, and data storage are so cheap as to be nearly free. At the scale of a Web farm of hundreds of thousands of processors, providing a virtual machine for an hour costs essentially nothing, as the 1.5 cents price per hour indicates. Because data communication is so cheap, getting the data to and from that processor is also nearly free.

Second, virtualization technology enables the near instantaneous creation of a new virtual machine. The customer provides (or creates in the cloud) a disk image of the data and programs of the machine it wants to provision. Virtualization software takes it from there.

Finally, new Internet-based protocols and standards have enabled cloud-hosting vendors to provide processing capabilities in flexible, yet standardized, ways. Chief among them are the **Web service standards** that sit on top of HTTP and are used to specify how computers interoperate. The provider of a Web service, such as a cloud-hosting organization, uses these standards to specify the work that it will perform and how it will provide it. Consumers of that service use those standards to request and receive service. The bottom line: Web service standards provide a vocabulary and grammar for programs on different computers to communicate.

When Does the Cloud Not Make Sense?

Cloud-based hosting makes sense for most organizations. The only organizations for which it may not make sense are those that are required by law or by industry standard practice to have physical control over their data. Such organizations might be forced to create and maintain their own hosting infrastructure. A financial institution, for example, might be legally required to maintain physical control over its data.

Even where physical control is a requirement, it is possible for organizations to obtain some of the benefits of cloud computing in what is termed the **private cloud**, which is in-house hosting, delivered via Web service standards, that can be configured dynamically. Some say that there is no such thing as a private cloud, however, because the infrastructure is owned by the using organization and the economies of scale cannot be shared with other companies.

HOW CAN ORGANIZATIONS USE THE CLOUD?

Cloud-based service offerings can be organized into the three categories shown in Figure 6-15. An organization that provides **software as a service (SaaS)** provides not only hardware infrastructure, but also an operating system and application programs on top of that hardware. For example, Salesforce.com provides programs for customer and sales tracking as a service. Similarly, Microsoft provides Office 365 as a service. Exchange, Lync, and SharePoint applications are provided as a service "in the cloud."

Apple's iCloud is probably the most exciting recent SaaS offering. Using iCloud, Apple will automatically sync all of its customers' iOS devices. As of 2012, Apple provides nine free applications in the iCloud. Calendar is a good example. When a customer enters an appointment in her iPhone, Apple will automatically push that appointment into the calendars on all of that customer's iOS devices. Further, customers can share calendars with others that will be synchronized as well. Mail, pictures, applications, and other resources are also synched via iCloud.

An organization can move to SaaS simply by signing up and learning how to use it. In Apple's case, there's nothing to learn. To quote the late Steve Jobs, "It just works."

The second category of cloud hosting is **platform as a service (PaaS)**, where vendors provide hosted computers, an operating system, and possibly a DBMS. Microsoft Windows Azure, for example, provides servers installed with Windows Server. Customers of Windows Azure then add their own applications on top of the hosted platform. Microsoft SQL Azure provides a host with Windows Server and SQL Server. Oracle on Demand provides a hosted server with Oracle Database. Again, for PaaS, organizations add their own applications to the host.

Figure 6-15
Three Fundamental Cloud Types

Cloud Category	Examples
SaaS (software as a service)	Salesforce.com iCloud Office 365
PaaS (platform as a service)	Microsoft Azure Oracle on Demand
IaaS (infrastructure as a service)	Amazon EC2 (Elastic Cloud 2) Amazon S3 (Simple Storage Service)

The most basic cloud offering is **infrastructure as a service (IaaS)**, which is the cloud hosting of a bare server computer or disk drive. The Amazon EC2 provides bare servers, and its Simple Storage Server provides, in essence, an unlimited, reliable disk drive in the cloud. Rackspace provides similar capabilities.

Organizations choose the cloud service they need. Lucas, for example, wants to host GearUp's e-commerce server in the cloud. In terms of Figure 6-15, GearUp needs to put its Web servers and its database server in the cloud using PaaS. To do so, GearUp could use, say, Windows Azure for the Web servers and SQL Azure for the database server. Lucas was thinking of that option when he cited the 25 cents per hour price.

If GearUp wanted to, it could also obtain bare servers from an IaaS vendor like Amazon.com or Rackspace. Were it to do so, GearUp would need to provision an operating system and DBMS on top of the server. Most likely, a small organization like GearUp would use PaaS.

How does the knowledge in this chapter help you?

For one, the knowledge of this chapter provides background for your general knowledge as a business professional. Today, understanding basic networking terms, knowing the purpose and the names of some of the important LAN and Internet protocols, knowing the major functions of Web server hardware and software, and understanding the importance and advantages and disadvantages of the cloud are foundational knowledge for every business professional.

Another reason is more specific. The knowledge of this chapter will help you approve project plans and budgets that involve IT and data communications. It will enable you to be a better consumer of IT professionals' services, and it will help you understand how your organization can weave cloud-based applications into its strategy. In fact, you will see one such application soon . . . at the start of Chapters 7-12.

Ethics Guide

You Said What? About Me? In Class?

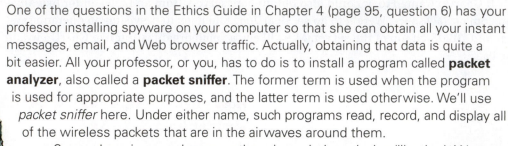

One of the questions in the Ethics Guide in Chapter 4 (page 95, question 6) has your professor installing spyware on your computer so that she can obtain all your instant messages, email, and Web browser traffic. Actually, obtaining that data is quite a bit easier. All your professor, or you, has to do is to install a program called **packet analyzer**, also called a **packet sniffer**. The former term is used when the program is used for appropriate purposes, and the latter term is used otherwise. We'll use *packet sniffer* here. Under either name, such programs read, record, and display all of the wireless packets that are in the airwaves around them.

Somewhere in your classroom there is a wireless device (like the LAN Device in Figure 6-2) that is receiving and sending wireless packets to and from your computer, connecting you to the Internet, and performing other functions as discussed in this chapter. All of those wireless packets have to be broadcast in the open so that they can reach the intended destination (when you send, that's the wireless device; when you receive, that's your computer or mobile device). So, all the packet sniffer does is capture all of the wireless packets floating around the room and format them in an easily accessible manner.

So, anyone in your classroom (and anyone *near* your classroom) can go to *www.wireshark.com* (or a similar site) and download and install a packet sniffer. Learning to use it isn't difficult, and their site provides video and other helpful documentation to speed their learning process. Once they've done that, they can read nearly anything that anyone in the room is sending or receiving over the LAN wireless network. That *anything* includes instant messages, most email, and any http:// Web traffic.

Your professor is too professional to use a packet sniffer for such a violation of your privacy, but the guy sitting next to you may not be. It could be he who asks you, "Does Jennifer know you say such terrible things about her?" or "Did you enjoy looking at those models on VictoriaSecrets.com in class?" or perhaps, "Why were you searching for the term *DUI lawyer* in class today?"

What can you do? Well, for one, you can use https:// instead of http://. If you do so, the packet sniffer will be able to tell that you went to a particular site, but it won't obtain data about what you did when you got there. For example, if you use *https://google.com*, the sniffer will be able to determine you went to Google but it won't be able to record what you searched for. However, for anything other than buying, few sites respond to both http:// and https://. You can use secure email, but almost no one else will, so that's not much help. Of course, if you never send anything that you wouldn't be proud to have published on Page 1 of the campus newspaper tomorrow, you won't have a problem with what *you* say. That doesn't help when flakey friends send you sensational material, however. The ultimate protection is not to use your computer or mobile device for any unauthorized purpose in class.

DISCUSSION QUESTIONS

1. Explain what packet sniffers do and describe the situation that enables them to succeed.

2. Besides your classroom, what other places do you visit for which packet sniffing might be a problem for you?

3. List five ways that you can protect yourself from packet sniffing intrusion.

4. List the evidence you have that your traffic has never been sniffed. You can answer this question with one word.

5. Is packet sniffing illegal? Is it unethical? Explain your answers.

6. If you use a mobile device, but connect with the cell tower wireless instead of the classroom's LAN, are you protected from packet sniffing? Why or why not?

7. Summarize your conclusions about your future behavior regarding wireless use in class.

8. [Optional for high achievers or sniffers-in-training] Go to *www.wireshark.com* and watch the introductory video. Explain how their packet sniffer formats wireless packets for easy consumption. List terms used in the video that you learned in this chapter.

Source: olly/Shutterstock

Guide

Thinking Exponentially Is Not Possible, but . . .

Nathan Myhrvold, the chief scientist at Microsoft Corporation during the 1990s, once said that humans are incapable of thinking exponentially. Instead, when something changes exponentially, we think of the fastest linear change we can imagine and extrapolate from there, as illustrated in the figure on the next page. Myhrvold was writing about the exponential growth of magnetic storage. His point was that no one could then imagine how much growth there would be in magnetic storage and what we would do with it.

This limitation pertains equally well to the growth of computer network phenomena. We have witnessed exponential growth in a number of areas: the number of Internet connections, the number of Web pages, and the amount of data accessible on the Internet. And, all signs are that this exponential growth isn't over.

You might wonder how this will affect you. Well, suppose you are a product manager for home appliances. Because most homes have a wireless network, it would be cheap and easy for appliances to talk to one another. How does that fact affect your existing product line? Will the competition's talking appliances take away your market share? However, talking appliances may not satisfy a real need. If a toaster and a coffee pot have nothing to say to each other, you'll be wasting money to create them.

Every business, every organization, needs to be thinking about the ubiquitous and cheap connectivity that is growing exponentially. What are the new opportunities? What are the new threats? How will our competition react? How should we position ourselves? How should we respond? As you consider these questions, keep in mind that because humans cannot think exponentially, we're all just guessing.

So what can we do to better anticipate changes brought by exponential phenomena? For one, understand that technology does not drive people to do things they've never done before, no matter how much the technologists suggest it might. (Just because we *can do* something does not mean anyone will *want to do* that something.)

Social progress occurs in small, evolutionary, adaptive steps. Right now, for example, if you want to watch a movie with someone, you both need to be in the same room. It needn't be that way. Using data communications, several people can watch the same movie, at the same time, together, but not in the same location. They can have an open audio line to make comments to each other during the movie or even have a Web cam so they can see each other watching the same movie. That sounds like something people might want to do—it's an outgrowth of what people are already doing.

However, emerging network technology enables my dry cleaner to notify me the minute my clothes are ready. Do I want to know? How much do I care to know that my clothes are ready Monday at 1:45 rather than sometime after 4:00 on Tuesday? In truth, I don't care. Such technology does not solve a problem that I have.

So, even if technology enables a capability, that possibility doesn't mean that anyone wants that capability. People want to do what they're already doing, but more easily; they want to solve problems that they already have.

Another response to exponential growth is to hedge your bets. If you can't know the outcome of an exponential phenomenon, don't commit to one direction. Position yourself to move as soon as the direction is clear. Develop a few talking appliances, position your organization to develop more, but wait for a clear sign of market acceptance before going all out.

Finally, notice in the exponential curve that the larger the distance between Now and The Future, the larger the error. In fact, the error increases exponentially with the length of the prediction. So, if you hear that the market for talking kitchen appliances will reach $1 billion in 1 year, assign that statement a certain level of doubt. However, if you hear that it will reach $1 billion in 5 years, assign that statement an exponentially greater level of doubt.

?

DISCUSSION QUESTIONS

1. In your own words, explain the meaning of the claim that no one can think exponentially. Do you agree with this claim?

2. Describe a phenomenon besides connectivity or magnetic memory that you believe is increasing exponentially. Explain why it is difficult to predict the consequences of this phenomenon in 3 years.

3. To what extent do you think technology is responsible for the growth in the number of news sources? On balance, do you think having many news sources of varying quality is better than having just a few high-quality ones?

4. List three products or services, such as remote group movie viewing, that could dramatically change because of increased connectivity. Do not include movie viewing.

5. Rate your answers to question 4 in terms of how closely they fit with problems that people have today.

● **Actual growth**

● **Growth we can imagine**

Now **Future**

Source: S/Fotolia

ACTIVE REVIEW

Use this Active Review to verify that you understand the ideas and concepts that answer the chapter's study questions.

Q1 WHAT IS A COMPUTER NETWORK?

Define *computer network.* Explain the differences among LANs, WANs, internets, and the Internet. Describe the purpose of a protocol.

Q2 WHAT ARE THE COMPONENTS OF A LAN?

Explain the key distinction of a LAN. Describe the purpose of each component in Figure 6-2. Describe the placement of switches in a multistory building. Explain when optical fiber cables are used for a LAN. Define *IEEE 802.3* and *802.11* and explain how they differ. List three ways of connecting a LAN or computer to the Internet. Explain the nature of each.

Q3 WHAT ARE THE FUNDAMENTAL CONCEPTS YOU SHOULD KNOW ABOUT THE INTERNET?

Explain the statement, "The Internet is an internet." Define *TCP/IP* and name its layers. Explain, in general terms, the purpose of each layer. Explain the purpose of HTTP, HTTPS, SMTP, and FTP. Explain why TCP is said to provide *reliable internet transport.* Define *IP, packet,* and *router.* Explain why IP is said to provide internet routing. Describe the advantages of private and public IP addresses. List the purposes of the LAN device. Explain, in general terms, how you would obtain a domain name. Describe the relationship between domain names and public IP addresses. Define *URL.* Explain the purpose of a VPN and describe, in broad terms, how a VPN works.

Q4 WHAT PROCESSING OCCURS ON A TYPICAL WEB SERVER?

Explain what a Web storefront is. Define *three-tier architecture* and name and describe each tier. Explain the function of a Web page, a Web server, and a commerce server. Explain the purpose of a Web farm. Explain the function of each tier in Figure 6-11 as the page in Figure 6-10 is processed. Define *HTML* and explain its purpose. Define *href* and *attribute.* Explain the importance of HTML5.

Q5 WHY IS THE CLOUD THE FUTURE FOR MOST ORGANIZATIONS?

Define *cloud* and explain the three key terms in your definition. Using Figure 6-14 as a guide, compare and contrast cloud-based and in-house hosting. Explain three factors that make cloud computing possible today. When does it not make sense to use a cloud-based infrastructure? Define *SaaS, PaaS,* and *IaaS.* Provide an example of each. For each, describe the requirements for when it would be the most appropriate option.

How does the knowledge in this chapter help you?

Name the principal advantage of the cloud to GearUp. For hosting its Web site, which cloud offering—SaaS, PaaS, or IaaS—makes the most sense, given the size and nature of GearUp's business? If GearUp were larger and employed a more sophisticated IT staff, name another alternative that could make sense. Explain why.

KEY TERMS AND CONCEPTS

USING YOUR KNOWLEDGE

1. Suppose you manage a group of seven employees in a small business. Each of your employees wants to be connected to the Internet. Consider two alternatives:
   - **Alternative A:** Each employee has his or her own modem and connects individually to the Internet.
   - **Alternative B:** The employees' computers are connected using a LAN, and the network uses a single modem to connect to the Internet.
   a. Sketch the equipment and lines required for each alternative.
   b. Explain the actions you need to take to create each alternative.
   c. Compare the alternatives on cost and capability.
   d. Which of these two alternatives do you recommend?

2. Suppose that you have a consulting practice implementing LANs for fraternities and sororities on your campus.
   a. Consider a fraternity house. Explain how a LAN could be used to connect all of the computers in the house. Would you recommend an Ethernet LAN, an 802.11 LAN, or a combination? Justify your answer.
   b. This chapter did not provide enough information for you to determine how many switches the fraternity house might need. However, in general terms, describe how the fraternity could use a multiple-switch system.
   c. Considering the connection to the Internet, would you recommend that the fraternity house use a DSL modem, a cable modem, or WAN wireless? Although you can rule out at least one of these alternatives with the knowledge you already have, what additional information do you need in order to make a specific recommendation?
   d. Should you develop a standard package solution for each of your customers? What advantages accrue from a standard solution? What are the disadvantages?

3. Define *cloud* and explain the three key terms in your definition. Using Figure 6-14 as a guide, compare and contrast cloud-based and in-house hosting. In your opinion, explain the three most important factors that make cloud-based hosting preferable to on-site hosting.

4. Apple invested more than $1 billion in the North Carolina center that will host the iCloud. For Apple to spend such a sum, it must perceive the iCloud as being a key component of its future. Using the principles listed in Figure 3-7 (page 56), explain all the ways that you believe the iCloud will give Apple a competitive advantage over other mobile device vendors.

COLLABORATION EXERCISE 6

Before you start this exercise, read Chapter Extensions 1 and 2, which describe collaboration techniques as well as tools for managing collaboration tasks. In particular, consider using Google Drive, Google+, Windows Live SkyDrive, Microsoft SharePoint, or some other collaboration tool.

The cloud is causing monumental changes in the information systems services industry. Giants like Microsoft need to change, the business model of small companies that support local networking solutions are being turned upside down, and opportunities for new companies and services are emerging. Investigate these changes and identify a potential opportunity by answering the following questions:

1. Read Case Study 6 and answer the questions at the end, paying particular attention to your answers to questions 6 and 7.

2. Suppose you are an independent software vendor (ISV) that is being displaced by Azure and the cloud and you decide to offer consulting services on the use of Office 365.

   Reread Chapter Extension 2.
   List the four major components of Office 365 and describe three services that you could provide for each.

3. Identify a market of particular interest to your group (e.g., accounting firms, government offices, medical practices, etc.). For that market, list and describe four consulting services that you could provide.

4. Considering your answer to question 3, and keeping in mind that up until now you have provided consulting services for the installation and support of Exchange and similar servers, describe the ways that you will need to change your business, in particular personnel.

CASE STUDY 6

Turbulent Air in Those Azure Clouds

"For the Cloud, we're all in."
—Steve Ballmer, Microsoft CEO, March 9, 2010[2]

What exactly does Ballmer mean? When the CEO for Microsoft, the world's leading software vendor, says they're all in for the cloud, what can he mean? How does Microsoft move its $15 billion server business into the cloud?

We can't peek behind the corporate curtain to view what the cloud really means to Microsoft's revenue, nor can we know with any degree of certainty what its strategy is and how it intends to achieve it. We also don't know how much revenue Microsoft earns from particular products in particular channels, so we can't know if we're even in the right ballpark. Nonetheless, let's ponder.

Clearly, Microsoft has a huge problem. Change is in the air, the cloud is real, Apple has the momentum with young and hip customers, and however much Microsoft might want to turn back the clock to 1995, when they dominated everything except their U.S. antitrust lawsuit, they cannot. Here's Ballmer again, in mid-2011:

> The cloud is essentially a buzzword that refers to using the Internet to connect you even more seamlessly to the people and information that's important to you. Those phenomena, in the large, will be the source of so many new companies . . . that it will be a really exciting time over the next 5, 10 years.[3]

If Ballmer were a venture capitalist, we could understand his enthusiasm for so many new companies, but he's the CEO of a company that has to grow and thrive through these turbulent times by outcompeting new, and old, companies.

Essentially, Microsoft has to find a profitable way to put a big part of its business out of business. During the quarterly earnings announcement in April 2011, Peter Klein, Microsoft's CFO, offered this:

> We delivered strong financial results despite a mixed PC environment, which demonstrates the strength and breadth of our businesses. Consumers are purchasing Office 2010, Xbox, and Kinect

---

[2]"Ballmer on the Cloud: We're All In," Microsoft.com, March 9, 2010. Available at www.microsoft.com/showcase/en/us/details/9c8601a 5-a82a-4452-965d-e4a04f38efb6 (accessed July 2011).

[3]Sharon Pian Chan, "Steve Ballmer Pre-Announces 2011 Earnings for Microsoft," *Seattle Times,* June 29, 2011. Available at http://seattletimes.nwsource.com/html/businesstechnology/2015465692_microsoftballmer30.html (accessed July 2011).

at tremendous rates, and businesses of all sizes are purchasing Microsoft platforms and applications.[4]

Parse that statement carefully: "Customers are purchasing Office 2010, the Xbox, and Kinect *at tremendous rates*" (emphasis added). However, businesses are just "*purchasing . . . platforms*." Where's the *tremendous* in that last sentence? Now, this could mistakenly be overemphasizing a few words, but it may not. Run the numbers for a simple example.

Consider a small business that has, say, 20 employees, and suppose that business switches to Office 365 for Small Businesses. The basic version includes Exchange (Microsoft's email server), Lync, SharePoint Online, and Office Web Apps (browser-based, limited functionality versions of Office 2010). Office 365 costs $6 per month, per employee, which for 20 people, is $120 a month, or $1,440 per year.

First, can Microsoft earn profit at that price? Figure 6-16 lists prices for Microsoft Azure, Microsoft's primary cloud offering. As shown, if you're an outsider, you can purchase an hour of a mid-range server for 24 cents. Let's assume the cost of running that server is a little less than half, say, 10 cents. Because Rackspace can sell an hour on a bare server for a penny and a half, it's likely that a big part of that 24 cents is a license for Windows Server, and the true marginal cost to Microsoft is probably much less than 10 cents, but let's assume high.

Each year has 365 times 24 hours, or 8,760 hours. Thus the cost of running that mid-sized server for a year is 10 cents times 8,760, or $876. There are storage costs as well, but they're miniscule. Can Microsoft support 20 people on that one server? Based on typical resource use, it's likely that it can support 200 people, maybe even 2,000 people, on that one server. But certainly it can support 20, so Microsoft's margin equals revenue of $1,440 minus costs of $876, or $564. So, yes, it can make money on Office 365.

EXCEPT, if that customer is typical, Office 365 is replacing an Exchange server. Based on similar situations, the typical installation cost for an Exchange server in a business of 20 people is about $12,000: $3,000 for the hardware, $4,000 for Exchange licenses to Microsoft, and $5,000 to the

Windows Azure
- Compute
  - Extra small instance: $0.05 per hour
  - Small instance (default): $0.12 per hour
  - Medium instance: $0.24 per hour
  - Large instance: $0.48 per hour
  - Extra large instance: $0.96 per hour
- Storage
  - $0.15 per GB stored per month
  - $0.01 per 10,000 storage transactions

- Content Delivery Network (CDN)
  - $0.15 per GB for data transfers from European and North American locations
  - $0.01 per 10,000 transactions

SQL Azure
- Web Edition
  - $9.99 per database up to 1GB per month
  - $49.95 per database up to 5GB per month
- Business Edition
  - $9.99 per database up to 10GB per month
  - $199.98 per database up to 20GB per month
  - $299.97 per database up to 30GB per month
  - $399.96 per database up to 40GB per month
  - $499.95 per database up to 50GB per month

Figure 6-16
Azure Standard Rates

[4]"Microsoft Reports Record Third-Quarter Results," Microsoft Press Release, April 28, 2011. Available at www.microsoft.com/investor/EarningsAndFinancials/Earnings/PressReleaseAndWebcast/FY11/Q3/default.aspx (accessed July 2011).

independent software vendor (ISV) that installs and supports that server.[5]

Office 365 replaces them all. Certainly that's bad news for Dell, as well as for the independent software vendors that install and maintain servers, who'd better find a way to make money supporting Office 365 or they'll be out of business.

But what about Microsoft? It has traded $4,000 in Exchange license fees for $564 in Office 365 profit. Why would it do that?

According to Microsoft's 2010 Annual Report, the server and tools business, which includes Windows Server, SQL Server, Exchange, and Azure, accounted for $15 billion in revenue, which was 24 percent of its total revenue. Azure, if it's successful, will replace Windows Server and SQL Server. Office 365 will replace Exchange.

The bottom line? Microsoft better sell a lot of Azure and Office 365! As in $15 billion worth. No wonder Ballmer says they're "all in for the cloud."

QUESTIONS

1. In your own words, summarize Microsoft's problem.

2. Explain the meaning of the following: ". . . you can purchase an hour of a mid-range server for 24 cents. Let's assume the cost of running that server is a little less than half, say, 10 cents. Because Rackspace can sell an hour on a bare server for a penny and a half, it's likely that a big

part of that 24 cents is a license for Windows Server, and the true marginal cost to Microsoft is probably much less than 10 cents."

3. How does the example Office 365 marginal revenue analysis change if the cost of running that server is 1 cent, not 10?

4. How does the example Office 365 marginal revenue analysis change if that server supports 2,000 users, not 20?

5. As of this writing, Microsoft had just purchased Skype. Its reasons for doing so are unclear at present (August 2012), but most likely involve the problems addressed in this case study. By the time you read this, Microsoft's Skype strategy should be clear. Describe what it is and how it changes this analysis.

6. Over the years, Microsoft has devoted considerable resources and time to building a network of loyal ISVs. It provides training, sales support, conferences, and awards and even has categories of gold-, silver-, and bronze-level partners. From this case study, it appears to be throwing these ISVs under the bus. Do you think that it is? Why or why not? If you were an ISV, what would you do?

7. If you were Microsoft and you had a $15 billion server business that was threatened by the cloud, what would you do?

---

[5]Phil Wainewright, "How Much Does Exchange Really Cost? ZDNet, November 15, 2008. Available at www.zdnet.com/blog/saas/how-much-does-exchange-really-cost/609 (accessed July 2011).

part 3

Using IS for Competitive Advantage

In the previous six chapters, you gained a foundation of IS fundamentals. In the remaining chapters, Chapters 7–12, you will apply those fundamentals to learn ways organizations use information systems to achieve their strategies. Part 3, Chapters 7–9, focuses on application of IS; Part 4, Chapters 10–12, focuses on management of IS.

This could happen to you

Chapters 7–12 are introduced using a cloud-based, mobile application for the health-care industry. To my knowledge, the system does not yet exist. However it is entirely plausible, may be an excellent entrepreneurial opportunity, and features some of today's most exciting emerging technology to one of today's most important industries. Health-care is much in the public debate because it is the source of great benefit, high costs, and many organizational and governmental funding problems. Many people see technology as one potential source of health cost reductions.

The figure on the next page shows the major actors involved in this system, which we will call the Performance Recording, Integration, Delivery, and Evaluation (PRIDE). Using PRIDE, exercise workout data is collected from devices that conform to the ANT[1] protocol, which is a personal network communications protocol implemented by exercise equipment such as treadmills, stationary bikes, heart monitors, footpads, and the like. Using this protocol, data is transmitted from exercise devices to the Internet, either via a local area network or via a

Source: julien tromeur/Fotolia

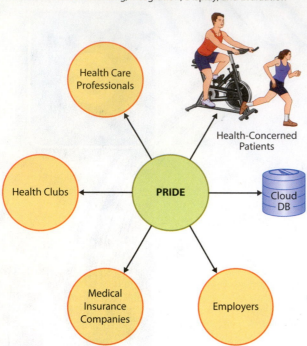

PRIDE:
Performance Recording, Integration, Display, and Evaluation

Health Care Professionals

Health-Concerned Patients

Health Clubs

PRIDE

Cloud DB

Medical Insurance Companies

Employers

cell phone. That exercise data is then stored in a cloud database.[1]

Once the data is stored in the cloud, individuals, health care professionals, health clubs, insurance companies, and employers can query and obtain exercise reports. Doctors can ensure their patients are exercising neither too little nor too much; health clubs can integrate exercise class data with personal exercise data; insurance companies can use that data to adjust policy rates for policy holders with healthy lifestyles, and employers can assess the effectiveness of investments they make into improving employee health.

Of course, privacy is crucial. The PRIDE system needs to be developed to give individuals complete control over the distribution of their data. We will consider this requirement in detail in Part 4.

As you are about to learn, a cardiac surgeon, Dr. Romero Flores, is driving his practice to develop a prototype of the health care and patient portion of the PRIDE system. He is focused on a prototype to learn whether patients will respond and whether he and his partners achieve the benefits they expect. Once they have answers to those questions, they will determine how to proceed to an operational system that involves the other organizations shown in the figure above.

Does the PRIDE system generate sufficient value to be worth its cost? Can existing technology support this system? Is the PRIDE system a good investment? If you were a venture capitalist or an angel investor, would you invest in its development? You will have an opportunity to address these and other important questions on your own as you study the next six chapters. As a successful business professional, you will likely make similar assessments about this or other technology, in other industries, numerous times during your career.

Chapter 1 states that "future business professionals need to be able to assess, evaluate, and apply emerging information technology to business." We will use the PRIDE system to illustrate and allow you to practice that key skill.

Source: Kratka Photography/Shutterstock

[1]See http://www.thisisant.com.

Organizations and Information Systems

Romero Flores, a cardiac surgeon, is calling the daughter of a recent cardiac bypass patient:

"Lindsey, this is Dr. Flores."

"Oh, no! Is Mom OK?" Lindsey panics as she hears Dr. Flores' voice.

"Everything's fine. She was just here and she's doing fine. I have nothing urgent, but I do want to talk."

"Whew." Lindsey sits down on her desk and relaxes her grip on the phone. "What's wrong? Is Mom not taking her meds?"

"Well, in a way. Look, she's doing OK, but not great, and certainly not as well as she could be. She needs to be more active; she needs to start walking and exercising. She's not recovering the way we want her to. We need to get her moving."

This could happen to you

"Dr. Flores, I know. But, she lives alone. She's never been much of an exerciser. I've talked to her about it, and I will again, but I'm not sure it will do much good. I'd go over there every day, but I'm busy at work, I've got young kids that need me and . . ." Lindsey's voice trails off as she tries to imagine finding time to walk with her mom.

"I've got an idea that might help." Dr. Flores sounds optimistic.

"What's that?"

"We're starting a new program in our practice. Your mom would be one of the first. Does she have a treadmill at home?"

"Yes. Ted and I bought her one in February."

STUDY QUESTIONS

Q1 HOW DO INFORMATION SYSTEMS VARY BY SCOPE?

Q2 HOW DO ENTERPRISE SYSTEMS SOLVE THE PROBLEMS OF INFORMATION SILOS?

Q3 HOW DO CRM, ERP, AND EAI SUPPORT ENTERPRISE SYSTEMS?

Q4 HOW DO INTER-ENTERPRISE IS SOLVE THE PROBLEMS OF ENTERPRISE SILOS?

How does the **knowledge** in this chapter help **you?**

"Every morning I get a report about the exercise your mother's getting so I can see how she's doing."

"Good. I know she has a cell phone, so the only other things she'll need are a heart rate monitor and an exercise watch to gather the data."

"How much do they cost?"

"I've got equipment she can borrow. We can try it. If this works like I hope, you can buy it . . . around $100. You think we can do this?"

"Maybe . . . though I'm not completely sure what you're proposing."

"OK. Here's the idea: Your mom wears a heart monitor and puts on the special watch. She gets on the treadmill and does the exercises that I prescribe. Signals about her heart rate and her exercise activities go over the Internet to a database that we access here. Every morning I get a report about the exercise your mother's getting so I can see how she's doing. If she'll give permission, we can set it up so you get the report, too."

"Wow! That's interesting."

"We think so, too. That's why we're investing in this system. It is a trial, though; we're not sure how well it will work."

"It may not make her work out, but at least we'll know sooner that she isn't."

"Right. And there might be some features we can implement that will help her motivation as well."

"So what do we do?"

"Make an appointment here with your mom. We'll explain everything and set up the equipment. You can try it at home and if you need help, we'll send one of our staff members out to get everything working."

"I'll do it." Lindsey wonders how she'll talk her mom into this as she agrees.

"One other thing, we can evaluate her heart rate data and adjust her exercises if necessary. But, we may need your help to ensure she understands that she needs to change."

"You mean you can't program her treadmill from your office?"

"No. At least, not yet!"

 Optional Extensions for this chapter are • CE8: Functional Applications 468 • CE9: Enterprise Resource Planning (ERP) Systems 479 • CE10 Supply Chain Management 494

HOW DO INFORMATION SYSTEMS VARY BY SCOPE?

As shown in Figure 7-1, modern organizations use four types of information systems that vary according to the scope of the organizational unit. We begin by considering each IS type.

PERSONAL INFORMATION SYSTEMS

Personal information systems are information systems used by a single individual. The contact manager in your iPhone or in your email account is an example of a personal information system. Because such systems have only one user, procedures are simple and probably not documented or formalized in any way.

It is easy to manage change to personal information systems. If you switch email from, say MSN to Google, you'll have to move your contact list from one vendor to the other, and you'll have to inform your correspondents of your new address, but you control the timing of that change. Because you will be the sole user of the new system, if new procedures are required, only you need to adapt. And, if there are problems, you can solve them yourself.

Figure 7-1 uses the example of a drug salesperson. Each person has his or her own personal information systems for managing doctors and other customers, appointments, product descriptions and costs, drug companies, and so forth. All of this data exists independently of other salespeople.

WORKGROUP INFORMATION SYSTEMS

A **workgroup information system** is an information system that facilitates the activities of a group of people. At a physicians' partnership, doctors, nurses, and staff use information systems to manage patient appointments, keep patient records, schedule in-office procedures and equipment, and facilitate other workgroup activities.

Workgroup information systems that support a particular department are sometimes called **departmental information systems**. An example is the accounts payable system that is used by the accounts payable department. Other workgroup information systems support a particular business function and are called **functional information systems**. An example of a functional system is a sales application like the Zulily application shown in Chapter 6. Finally, the collaboration information systems discussed in Chapter Extension 2 are also workgroup information systems.

Scope	Example	Characteristics
Personal	Drug Salesperson	Single user; procedures informal; problems isolated; easy to manage change
Workgroup	Physician Partnership	10–100 users; procedures understood within group; problem solutions within group; somewhat difficult to change
Enterprise	Hospital	100–1,000s users; procedures formalized; problem solutions affect enterprise; difficult to change
Inter-enterprise	PRIDE System	1,000s users; procedures formalized; problem solutions affect multiple organizations; difficult to change

Figure 7-1
Information Systems Scope

Workgroup information systems, whether departmental, functional, or collaborative, share the characteristics shown in Figure 7-1. Typically, workgroup systems support 10 to 100 users. The procedures for using them must be understood by all members of the group. Often, procedures are formalized in documentation, and users are sometimes trained in the use of those procedures.

When problems occur, they almost always can be solved within the group. If accounts payable duplicates the record for a particular supplier, the accounts payable group can make the fix. If the Web storefront has the wrong number of widgets in the inventory database, that count can be fixed within the storefront group.

(Notice, by the way, that the *consequences* of a problem are not isolated to the group. Because the workgroup exists to provide a service to the rest of the organization, its problems have consequences throughout the organization. The *fix* to the problem can be usually obtained within the group, however.)

ENTERPRISE INFORMATION SYSTEMS

Enterprise information systems are information systems that span an organization and support activities of people in multiple departments. At a hospital, doctors, nurses, the pharmacy, the kitchen, and others use information systems to track patients, treatments, medications, diets, room assignments, and so forth.

Enterprise information systems typically have hundreds to thousands of users. Procedures are formalized and extensively documented; users undergo formal procedure training. Sometimes enterprise systems include categories of procedures, and users are defined according to levels of expertise with the system as well as by levels of security authorization.

The solutions to problems in an enterprise system usually involve more than one department. Because enterprise systems span many departments and involve potentially thousands of users, they are very difficult to change. Changes must be carefully planned, cautiously implemented, and users given considerable training. Sometimes users are given incentives and other inducements to motivate them to change.

INTER-ENTERPRISE INFORMATION SYSTEMS

Inter-enterprise information systems are information systems that are shared by two or more independent organizations. The PRIDE system introduced at the start of this part is an inter-enterprise system that is shared among patients, health care providers, health clubs, insurance companies, and employers. All of these organizations have an interest in assigning, recording, or viewing individual performance data.

Such systems involve hundreds to thousands of users, and solutions to problems require cooperation among different, usually independently owned, organizations. Problems are resolved by meeting, contract, and sometimes by litigation. Because of the wide span, complexity, and multiple companies involved, such systems can be exceedingly difficult to change. The interaction of independently owned and operated information systems is required.

The development of information systems at any level can lead to problems caused by information silos. We turn to those problems and the ways that IS can be used to solve them next.

HOW DO ENTERPRISE SYSTEMS SOLVE THE PROBLEMS OF INFORMATION SILOS?

Review Chapter Extension 8 for more information on processes, applications, and systems.

An **information silo** is the condition that exists when data are isolated in separated information systems. Silos come into existence as entities at one organizational level create information systems that meet their particular needs only. For example, Figure 7-2 lists six common departments (workgroups) and several information systems applications that support each.

Department	Application
Sales and marketing	• Lead generation • Lead tracking • Customer management • Sales forecasting • Product and brand management
Operations	• Order entry • Order management • Finished-goods inventory management
Manufacturing	• Inventory (raw materials, goods-in-process) • Planning • Scheduling • Operations
Customer service	• Order tracking • Account tracking • Customer support and training
Human resources	• Recruiting • Compensation • Assessment • HR planning
Accounting	• General ledger • Financial reporting • Cost accounting • Accounts receivable • Accounts payable • Cash management • Budgeting • Treasury management

Figure 7-2
Common Departmental
Information Systems

Reflect on these applications for a moment and you'll realize that each application processes customer, sales, product, and other data, but each uses that data for different purposes and will likely store somewhat different data. Sales, for example, will store contact data for customers' purchasing agents, while Accounting will store contact data for customers' accounts payable personnel.

It's completely natural for a workgroup to develop information systems solely for its own needs, but, over time, the existence of these separate systems will result in information silos that cause numerous problems.

WHAT ARE THE PROBLEMS OF INFORMATION SILOS?

Figure 7-3 lists the major problems caused by information silos at the department level, in this case, between the Sales and Marketing department and the Accounting department. First, data are duplicated. Sales and Marketing and Accounting applications maintain separate databases that store some of the same customer data. As you know, data storage is cheap, so the problem with duplication is not wasted file space. Rather, the problem is data inconsistency. Changes to customer data made in the Sales and Marketing application may take days or weeks to be made to the Accounting application's database. During that period, shipments will reach the customer without delay, but invoices will be sent to the wrong address. When an organization has inconsistent duplicated data, it is said to have a **data integrity** problem.

Additionally, when applications are isolated, business processes are disjointed. Suppose a business has a rule that credit orders over $15,000 must be preapproved by the accounts

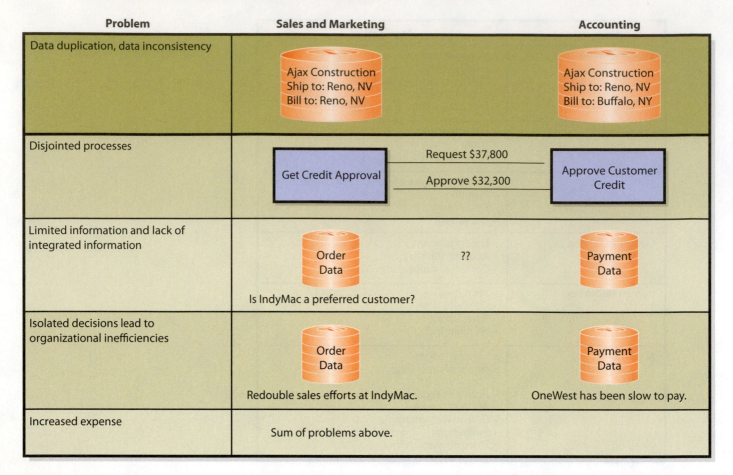

Figure 7-3
Problems Created by Information Silos

receivable department. If the supporting applications are separated, it will be difficult for the two activities to reconcile their data, and the approval will be slow to grant and possibly erroneous.

In the second row of Figure 7-3, Sales and Marketing wants to approve a $20,000 order with Ajax. According to the Sales and Marketing database, Ajax has a current balance of $17,800, so Sales and Marketing requests a total credit amount of $37,800. The Accounting database, however, shows Ajax with a balance of only $12,300, because the accounts receivable application has credited Ajax for a return of $5,500. According to Accounting's records, a total credit authorization of only $32,300 is needed in order to approve the $20,000 order, so that is all they grant.

Sales and Marketing doesn't understand what to do with a credit approval of $32,300. According to their database, Ajax already owes $17,800, so if the total credit authorization is only $32,300, was only $14,500 of the new order approved? And why that amount? Both departments want to approve the order. It will take numerous emails and phone calls, however, to sort this out. The interacting business processes are disjointed.

A consequence of such disjointed systems is the lack of integrated enterprise information. For example, suppose Sales and Marketing wants to know if IndyMac is still a preferred customer. Suppose that determining whether this is so requires a comparison of order history and payment history data. However, with information silos, that data will reside in two different databases and, in one of them, IndyMac is known by the name of the company that acquired it, OneWest Bank. Data integration will be difficult. Making the determination will require manual processes and days, when it should be readily answered in seconds.

This leads to the fourth consequence: inefficiency. When using isolated functional applications, decisions are made in isolation. As shown in the fourth row of Figure 7-3, Sales and Marketing decided to redouble its sales effort with IndyMac. However, Accounting knows that IndyMac was foreclosed by the FDIC and sold to OneWest and has been slow to pay. There are far better prospects for increased sales attention. Without integration, the left hand of the organization doesn't know what the right hand is doing.

Finally, information silos can result in increased cost for the organization. Duplicated data, disjointed systems, limited information, and inefficiencies all mean higher costs.

HOW DO ORGANIZATIONS SOLVE THE PROBLEMS OF INFORMATION SILOS?

As defined, an information silo occurs when data is stored in isolated systems. The obvious way to fix such a silo is to integrate the data into a single database and revise applications (and business processes) to use that database. If that is not possible or practical, another remedy is to allow the isolation, but to manage it to avoid problems.

The arrows in Figure 7-4 show this resolution at two levels of organization. First, isolated data created by workgroup information systems are integrated using enterprise-wide applications.

Second, today isolated data created by information systems at the enterprise level are being integrated into inter-enterprise systems using distributed applications (such as PRIDE) that process data in a single cloud database or that connect disparate, independent databases so that applications can process those databases as if they were one database. We will discuss inter-enterprise systems further in Q4.

For now, to better understand how isolated data problems can be resolved, consider an enterprise system at a hospital.

AN ENTERPRISE SYSTEM FOR PATIENT DISCHARGE

Figure 7-5 shows some of the hospital departments and a portion of the patient discharge process. A doctor initiates the process by issuing a patient discharge order. That order is delivered

Figure 7-4
Information Silo as Drivers

Scope	Example	Example Information Silo	Enabling Technology
Work-group	Physician Partnership	Physicians and hospitals store separated data about patients. Unnecessarily duplicate tests and procedures.	Functional applications.
		⬇	Enterprise applications (CRM, ERP, EAI) on enterprise networks.
Enterprise	Hospital	Hospital and local drug store pharmacy have different prescription data for the same patient.	
		⬇	Distributed systems using Web technologies in the cloud.
Inter-enterprise	Inter-agency prescription application	Doctors, hospitals, pharmacies share patients' prescription and other data.	

Figure 7-5
Some of the Departments
Involved in Patient Discharge

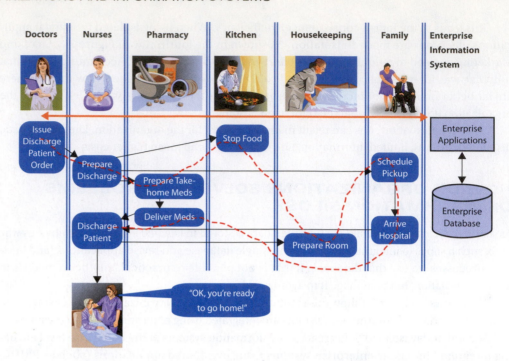

to the appropriate nursing staff, who initiates activities at the pharmacy, the patient's family, and kitchen. Some of those activities initiate activities back at the nursing staff. In this figure, the enterprise information system is represented by a dotted red line.

Prior to the enterprise system, the hospital had developed procedures for using a paper-based system and informal messaging via the telephone. Each department kept its own records. When the new enterprise information system was implemented, not only was the data integrated into a database, but new computer-based forms and reports were created. The staff needed to transition from the paper-based system to the computer-based system. They also needed to stop making phone calls and let the new information system make notifications across departments. These measures involved substantial change, and most organizations experience considerable anguish when undergoing such transitions.

BUSINESS PROCESS REENGINEERING

Enterprise systems like the one in Figure 7-5 were not feasible until network, data communication, and database technologies reached a sufficient level of capability and maturity in the late 1980s and early 1990s. At that point, many organizations began to develop enterprise systems.

As they did so, organizations realized that their existing business processes needed to change—partly to use the shared databases and partly to use new computer-based forms and reports. An even more important reason for changing business processes was that integrated data and enterprise systems offered the potential of substantial operational efficiencies. It became possible to do things that had been impossible before. Using Porter's language (Chapter 3, page 54), enterprise systems enabled the creation of stronger, faster, more effective linkages among value chains.

For example, when the hospital used a paper-based system, the kitchen would prepare meals for everyone who was a patient at the hospital as of midnight the night before. It was not possible to obtain data about discharges until the next midnight. Consequently, considerable food was wasted, at substantial cost.

With the enterprise system, the kitchen can be notified about patient discharges as they occur throughout the day, resulting in substantial reductions in wasted food. But, when should the kitchen be notified? Immediately? And what if the discharge is cancelled before completion? Who will notify the kitchen of the cancelled discharge? Many possibilities and alternatives exist. So, to design its new enterprise system, the hospital needed to determine how best to change its processes to take advantage of the new capability. Such projects came to be known as **business process reengineering**, which is the activity of altering and designing business processes to take advantage of new information systems.

Unfortunately, business process reengineering is difficult, slow, and exceedingly expensive. Systems analysts need to interview key personnel throughout the organization to determine how best to use the new technology. Because of the complexity involved, such projects require high-level, expensive skills and considerable time. Many early projects stalled when the enormity of the project became apparent. This left some organizations with partially implemented systems that had disastrous consequences. Personnel didn't know if they were using the new system, the old system, or some hacked-up version of both.

The stage was set for the emergence of the three major enterprise applications, which we discuss next.

HOW DO CRM, ERP, AND EAI SUPPORT ENTERPRISE SYSTEMS?

When the need for business process reengineering emerged, most organizations were still developing their applications in-house. At the time, organizations perceived their needs as being "too unique" to be satisfied by off-the-shelf or altered applications. However, as applications became more and more complex, in-house development costs became infeasible. As stated in Chapter 4, systems built in-house are expensive, not only because of their initial development, but also because of the continuing need to adapt those systems to changing requirements.

In the early 1990s, as the costs of business process reengineering were coupled with the costs of in-house development, organizations began to look more favorably on the idea of licensing preexisting applications. "Maybe we're not so unique, after all."

Some of the vendors who took advantage of this change in attitude were PeopleSoft, which licensed payroll and limited-capability human resources systems; Siebel, which licensed a sales lead tracking and management system; and SAP, which licensed something new, a system called *enterprise resource management*.

These three companies, and ultimately dozens of others like them, offered not just software and database designs. They also offered standardized business processes. These **inherent processes**, which are predesigned procedures for using the software products, saved organizations from expensive and time-consuming business process reengineering. Instead, organizations could license the software and obtain, as part of the deal, prebuilt procedures, which the vendors assured them were based upon "industry best practices."

Some parts of that deal were too good to be true, because, as you'll learn, inherent processes are almost never a perfect fit. But, the offer was too much for many organizations to resist. Over time, three categories of enterprise applications emerged: customer relationship management, enterprise resource planning, and enterprise application integration. Consider each.

CUSTOMER RELATIONSHIP MANAGEMENT (CRM)

A **customer relationship management (CRM) system** is a suite of applications, a database, and a set of inherent processes for managing all the interactions with the customer, from lead

Some companies may change too often. See the Guide on pages 182–183 for a discussion on how management fads can grow tiresome for employees.

Figure 7-6
The Customer Life Cycle

Source: Used with permission of
Professor Douglas MacLachlan,
Michael G. Foster School of Business,
University of Washington.

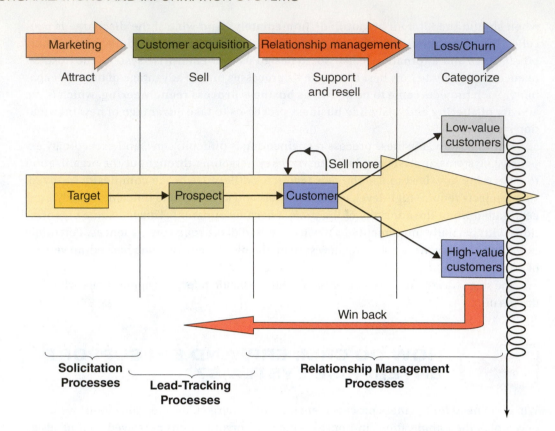

generation to customer service. Every contact and transaction with the customer is recorded in the CRM database. Vendors of CRM software claim using their products makes the organization *customer-centric.* Though that term reeks of sales hyperbole, it does indicate the nature and intent of CRM packages.

Figure 7-6 shows four phases of the **customer life cycle**: marketing, customer acquisition, relationship management, and loss/churn. Marketing sends messages to the target market to attract customer prospects. When prospects order, they become customers who need to be supported. Additionally, relationship management processes increase the value of existing customers by selling them more product. Inevitably, over time the organization loses customers. When this occurs, win-back processes categorize customers according to value and attempt to win back high-value customers.

Figure 7-7 illustrates the major components of a CRM application. Notice that components exist for each stage of the customer life cycle. As shown, all applications process

Figure 7-7
CRM Applications

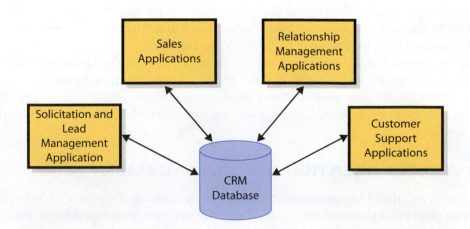

Experiencing MIS

INCLASS EXERCISE 7

Choosing a CRM Product

Source: Inspirestock/Glow Images and FotolEdhar/Fotolia

PROSPECTS

Choosing a CRM product is complicated. Dozens of CRM products exist, and it's difficult to determine their different features and functions, let alone how easy they are to learn and use, how difficult they are to implement, and so forth. Choosing a CRM requires knowing the organization's requirements as well, and often those requirements aren't fully known, or, if they are known, they are changing as the organization grows.

This exercise is designed to give you a sense of the challenges involved when choosing a CRM product. Form a team of students, fire up your browsers, and answer the following questions:

1. Act! and GoldMine are two of the lower-end CRM products. They began as sales lead tracking tools for individuals and small offices but have evolved since then.

   a. To learn about these products, visit *www.act.com* and *www.goldmine.com.*

   b. As you can see, it is difficult to know how these products compare based just on the information on those sites. To learn more, Google or Bing the phrase "Act vs. Goldmine." Read several comparisons.

   c. Summarize your findings in a 2-minute presentation to the rest of the class. Include in your summary the intended market for these products, their costs, and their relative strengths and weaknesses.

2. Salesforce.com and Sugar are CRM products that are intended for use by larger organizations than Act! and GoldMine.

   a. To learn about these products, visit *www.salesforce.com* and *www.sugarcrm.com.*

   b. These two products seem to differ in orientation. To learn how others view these differences, Google or

Bing the phrase "Salesforce vs. Sugar CRM." Read several comparisons.

   c. Summarize your findings in a 2-minute presentation to the rest of the class. Include in your summary the intended market for these products, their costs, and their relative strengths and weaknesses.

3. Of course, the major software vendors have CRM offerings as well. Using a combination of acquisition and internal development, Microsoft created the Dynamics CRM product. Oracle, meanwhile, through acquisition of Siebel Systems and other acquisitions, has developed a suite of CRM applications.

   a. To learn about these products, visit *http://crm.dynamics.com/en-us/Default.aspx* and *www.oracle.com/us/solutions/crm/index.htm.* You may have to search within these sites to find the data you need.

   b. Oracle offers a suite of products. List and briefly describe Oracle's offerings. Briefly describe Microsoft's CRM offering. To learn more, Google or Bing "Microsoft CRM vs. Oracle CRM."

   c. Summarize your findings in a 2-minute presentation to the rest of the class. Include in your summary the intended market for those products, their costs, and their relative strengths and weaknesses.

4. Given your answers to parts 1–3 (and those of other teams, if you have been presenting to each other), consider the desirability of CRM product offerings for a variety of businesses. Specifically, suppose you have been asked to recommend two of the CRM products you've explored for further research. For each of the following businesses, recommend two such products and justify your recommendation:

   a. An independent personal trainer who is working in her own business as a sole proprietor

   b. An online vendor, such as *www.sephora.com*

   c. A musical venue, such as *www.santafeopera.org*

   d. A vendor of consulting services, such as *www.crmsoftwaresolutions.ca*

   e. A vacation cruise ship line, such as *www.hollandamerica.com*

Present your findings to the rest of the class.

5. Summarize what you have learned from this exercise about choosing a CRM product. Formulate your summary as an answer to a job interviewer's question about the difficulties that organizations face when choosing software products.

a common customer database. This design eliminates duplicated customer data and removes the possibility of inconsistent data. It also means that each department knows what has been happening with the customer at other departments. Customer support, for example, will know not to provide $1000 worth of support labor to a customer that has generated $300 worth of business over time. They will also know to bend over backwards for the customers that have generated hundreds of thousands of dollars of business. The result of this integration to the customer is that he or she feels like they are dealing with one entity and not many.

CRM systems vary in the degree of functionality they provide. One of the primary tasks when selecting a CRM package is to determine the features you need and to find a package that meets that set of needs. You might be involved in just such a project during your career.

ENTERPRISE RESOURCE PLANNING (ERP)

You can learn more about ERP applications in Chapter Extension 9.

Despite the clear benefits of inherent processes and ERP, there can be an unintended consequence. See the Ethics Guide on pages 180–181 and consider that risk.

Enterprise resource planning (ERP) is a suite of applications, a database, and a set of inherent processes for consolidating business operations into a single, consistent, computing platform. As shown in Figure 7-8, ERP includes the functions of CRM, but also incorporates accounting, manufacturing, inventory, and human resources applications.

ERP systems are used to forecast sales and to create manufacturing plans and schedules to meet those forecasts. Manufacturing schedules include the use of material, equipment, and personnel and thus need to incorporate inventory and human resources applications. Because ERP includes accounting, all of these activities are automatically posted in the general ledger and other accounting applications.

SAP is the worldwide leader of ERP vendors. In addition to its base ERP offering, SAP offers industry-specific packages that customize its product for particular uses. There is an SAP package for automobile manufacturing, for example, and for many other specialty industries as well.

Figure 7-8
ERP Applications

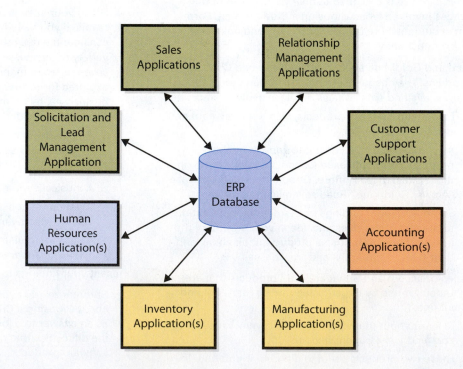

ERP originated in manufacturing and has a definite manufacturing flavor. However, it has been adapted for use in service organizations such as hospitals as well as many other organizations.

ENTERPRISE APPLICATION INTEGRATION (EAI)

ERP systems are not for every organization. For example, some nonmanufacturing companies find the manufacturing orientation of ERP inappropriate. Even for manufacturing companies, some find the process of converting from their current system to an ERP system too daunting. Others are quite satisfied with their manufacturing application systems and do not wish to change them.

Companies for which ERP is inappropriate still have the problems of information silos, however, and some choose to use **enterprise application integration (EAI)** to solve those problems. EAI is a suite of software applications that integrates existing systems by providing layers of software that connect applications together. EAI does the following:

- It connects system "islands" via a new layer of software/system.
- It enables existing applications to communicate and share data.
- It provides integrated information.
- It leverages existing systems—leaving functional applications as is, but providing an integration layer over the top.
- It enables a gradual move to ERP.

The layers of EAI software shown in Figure 7-9 enable existing applications to communicate with each other and to share data. For example, EAI software can be configured to automatically make the conversions needed to share data among different systems. When the CRM applications send data to the manufacturing application system, for example, the CRM system sends its data to an EAI software program. That EAI program makes the conversion and then sends the converted data to the ERP system. The reverse action is taken to send data back from the ERP to the CRM.

Although there is no centralized EAI database, the EAI software keeps files of metadata that describe where data are located. Users can access the EAI system to find the data they need. In some cases, the EAI system provides services that supply a "virtual integrated database" for the user to process.

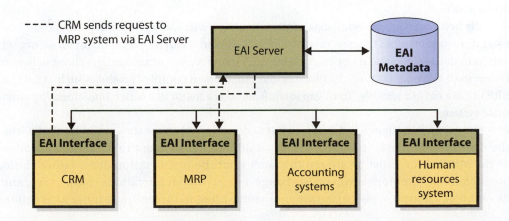

Figure 7-9
Enterprise Application
Integration (EAI) Architecture

The major benefit of EAI is that it enables organizations to use existing applications while eliminating many of the serious problems of isolated systems. Converting to an EAI system is not nearly as disruptive as converting to ERP, and it provides many of the benefits of ERP. Some organizations develop EAI applications as a steppingstone to complete ERP systems.

WHAT ARE THE CHALLENGES WHEN IMPLEMENTING NEW ENTERPRISE SYSTEMS?

Implementing new enterprise systems is challenging, difficult, expensive, and risky. It is not unusual for enterprise systems projects to be well over budget and a year or more late in delivery. The expense and risks arise from four primary factors:

- Collaborative management
- Requirements gaps
- Transition problems
- Employee resistance

Collaborative Management

Unlike departmental systems in which a single department manager is in charge, enterprise systems have no clear boss. Examine the discharge process in Figure 7-5; there is no manager of discharge. The discharge process is a collaborative effort among many departments (and customers).

With no single manager, who resolves disputes that inevitably arise? All of these departments ultimately report to the CEO, so there is a single boss over all of them, but employees can't go to the CEO with a problem about, say, coordinating discharge activities between nursing and housekeeping. The CEO would throw them out of his or her office. Instead, the organization needs to develop some sort of collaborative management for resolving process issues.

Usually this means that the enterprise develops committees and steering groups for providing enterprise process management. Although this can be an effective solution, and in fact may be the *only* solution, the work of such groups is both slow and expensive.

Requirements Gaps

Few organizations today create their own enterprise systems from scratch. Instead, they license an enterprise product that provides specific functions and features and that includes inherent procedures. But, such licensed products are never a perfect fit. Almost always there are gaps between the requirements of the organization and the capabilities of the licensed application.

The first challenge is identifying the gaps. To specify a gap, an organization must know both what it needs and what the new product does. However, it can be very difficult for an organization to determine what it needs; that difficulty is one reason organizations chose to license rather than to build. Further, the features and functions of complex products such as CRM or ERP are not easy to identify. Thus, gap identification is a major task when implementing enterprise systems.

The second challenge is deciding what to do with gaps, once they are identified. Either the organization needs to change the way it does things to adapt to the new application, or the application must be altered to match what the organization does. Either choice is problematic. Employees will resist change, but paying for alterations is expensive, and, as noted in Chapter 4, the organization is committing to maintaining those alternations as the application is changed over time. Here, organizations fill gaps by choosing their lesser regret.

Transition Problems

Transitioning to a new enterprise system is also difficult. The organization must somehow change from using isolated departmental systems to using the new enterprise system, while continuing to run the business. It's like having heart surgery while running a 100-yard dash.

Such transitions require careful planning and substantial training. Inevitably, problems will develop. Knowing this will occur, senior management needs to communicate the need for the change to the employees and then stand behind the new system as the kinks are worked out. It is an incredibly stressful time for all involved employees. We will discuss development techniques and implementation strategies further in Chapter 10.

Employee Resistance

People resist change. Change requires effort and it engenders fear. Considerable research and literature exists about the reasons for change resistance and how organizations can deal with it. Here we will summarize the major principles.

First, senior-level management needs to communicate the need for the change to the organization and must reiterate that, as necessary, throughout the transition process. Second, employees fear change because it threatens their **self-efficacies**, which is a person's belief that he or she can be successful at his or her job. To enhance confidence, employees need to be trained and coached on the successful use of the new system. Word-of-mouth is a very powerful factor, and, in some cases, key users are trained ahead of time to create positive buzz about the new system. Video demonstrations of employees successfully using the new system are also effective.

Third, employees may need to be given extra inducement to change to the new system. As one experienced change consultant said, "Nothing succeeds like praise or cash, especially cash." Straight-out pay for change is bribery, but contests with cash prizes among employees or groups can be very effective at inducing change.

Implementing new enterprise systems can solve many problems and bring great efficiency and cost savings to an organization, but it is not for the faint of heart.

Q4 HOW DO INTER-ENTERPRISE IS SOLVE THE PROBLEMS OF ENTERPRISE SILOS?

The discussions in Q2 and Q3 have shown you some of the primary ways that enterprise systems solve the problems of workgroup information silos. In this question we will use the PRIDE example to show you how inter-enterprise systems can accomplish the same for enterprise silos. (The transition shown by the lower arrow leading to the bottom row in Figure 7-4, page 169.)

Figure 7-10 shows the information silos that exist among health care providers, health clubs, and patients. Providers keep track of patient histories and maintain records of exercise recommendations, called exercise prescriptions in Figure 7-10. Health clubs maintain membership, class, personal trainer and exercise performance data. At the club, the latter is gathered automatically from exercise equipment and member heart monitors and stored in a club database. At home, individuals generate exercise data on

Supply chain systems are a common type of inter-enterprise system that you can learn about in Chapter Extension 10.

Figure 7-10
Information Silos without
PRIDE

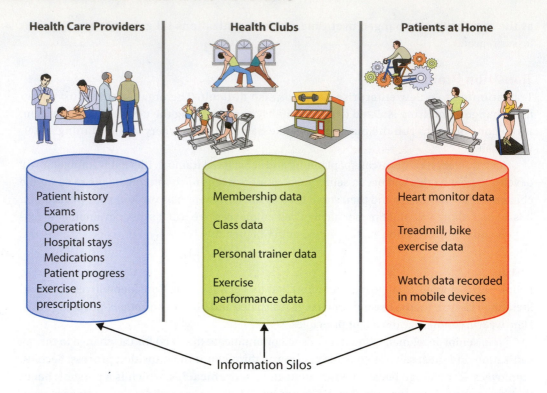

heart monitors and equipment, and that data are recorded in mobile devices using exercise watches.

The isolation of this exercise data causes problems. For example, doctors would like to have reports on exercise data that is stored on patient devices and in health clubs. Patients would like to have prescription data from their providers as well as exercise data from their time at health clubs. Health clubs would like to have exercise prescriptions and home workout data to integrate with the data they have. All three entities would like to produce reports from the integrated data.

Figure 7-11 shows the structure of an inter-enterprise system that meets the goals of the three types of participant. In this figure, the labeled rectangles inside the cloud represent mobile applications that could be native, thin-client, or both. Some of the application processing might be done on cloud servers as well as on the mobile devices. Those design decisions are not shown. As shown, this system assumes that all users receive reports on mobile devices, but, because of the large amount of keying involved, that health care providers submit and manage prescriptions using a personal computer.

As you can see, prescription and exercise data is integrated in the PRIDE database, which is a relational rather than a NoSQL database. (Case 7 shows the structure of major portions of that database.) The integrated data can be processed by a reporting application (Chapter 9) to create and distribute the reports as shown.

Systems like that shown in Figure 7-11 are referred to as **distributed systems** because processing is distributed across multiple computing devices. Standards such as http, https, HTML5, CSS3, JavaScript, and others enable programs on varied and disparate devices to flexibly communicate with the cloud servers and database, and, indirectly communicate with each other.

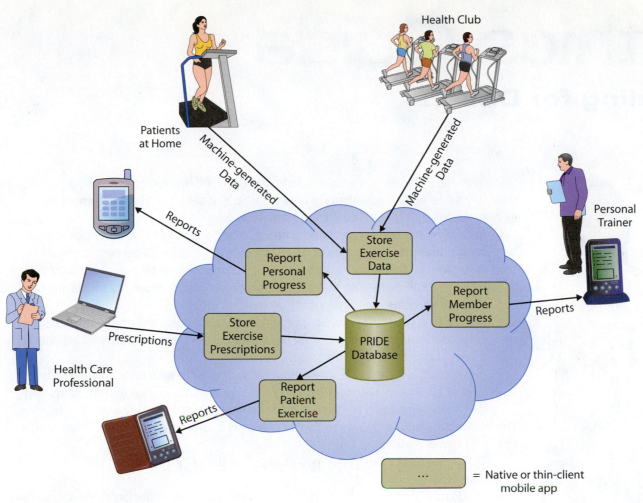

Figure 7-11
Inter-enterprise PRIDE system

How does the **knowledge** in this chapter help **you?**

The knowledge of this chapter will help you understand levels of information systems and the problems that each level can have. It will also help you to put information systems that you use into perspective and to understand how they may or may not be creating information silos. You also know the potential problems of silos and how to resolve them at both the workgroup and enterprise levels. Further, when you encounter CRM, ERP, and EAI applications in your future, you will know what such systems are, what they do, and some of the issues you will run into when using and implementing them. Finally, understanding how PRIDE uses the cloud to support an inter-enterprise system will give you the background for investigating the use of the cloud for other applications as well.

Ethics Guide

Dialing for Dollars

Suppose you are a salesperson, and your company's CRM forecasts that your quarterly sales will be substantially under quota. You call your best customers to increase sales, but no one is willing to buy more.

Your boss says that it has been a bad quarter for all of the salespeople. It's so bad, in fact, that the vice president of sales has authorized a 20-percent discount on new orders. The only stipulation is that customers must take delivery prior to the end of the quarter so that accounting can book the order. "Start dialing for dollars," she says, "and get what you can. Be creative."

Using your CRM, you identify your top customers and present the discount offer to them. The first customer balks at increasing her inventory, "I just don't think we can sell that much."

"Well," you respond, "how about if we agree to take back any inventory you don't sell next quarter?" (By doing this, you increase your current sales and commission, and you also help your company make its quarterly sales projections. The additional product is likely to come back next quarter, but you think, "Hey, that's then and this is now.")

"OK," she says, "but I want you to stipulate the return option on the purchase order."

You know that you cannot write that on the purchase order because accounting won't book all of the order if you do. So you tell her that you'll send her an email with that stipulation. She increases her order, and accounting books the full amount.

With another customer, you try a second strategy. Instead of offering the discount, you offer the product at full price, but agree to pay a 20-percent credit in the next quarter. That way you can book the full price now. You pitch this offer as follows: "Our marketing department analyzed past sales using our fancy new computer system, and we know that increasing advertising will cause additional sales. So, if you order more product now, next quarter we'll give you 20 percent of the order back to pay for advertising."

In truth, you doubt the customer will spend the money on advertising. Instead, they'll just take the credit and sit on a bigger inventory. That will kill your sales to them next quarter, but you'll solve that problem then.

Even with these additional orders, you're still under quota. In desperation, you decide to sell product to a fictitious company that is "owned" by your brother-in-law. You set up a new account, and when accounting calls your brother-in-law for a credit check, he cooperates with your scheme. You then sell $40,000 of product to the fictitious company and ship the product to your brother-in-law's garage. Accounting books the revenue in the quarter, and you have finally made quota. A week into the next quarter, your brother-in-law returns the merchandise.

Meanwhile, unknown to you, your company's ERP system is scheduling production. The program that creates the production schedule reads the sales from your activities (and those of the other salespeople) and finds a sharp increase in product demand. Accordingly, it generates a schedule that calls for substantial production increases and schedules workers for the production runs. The production system, in turn, schedules the material requirements with the inventory application, which increases raw materials purchases to meet the increased production schedule.

DISCUSSION QUESTIONS

1. Is it ethical for you to write the email agreeing to take the product back? If that email comes to light later, what do you think your boss would say?

2. Is it ethical for you to offer the "advertising" discount? What effect does that discount have on your company's balance sheet?

3. Is it ethical for you to ship to the fictitious company? Is it legal?

4. Describe the impact of your activities on next quarter's inventories.

5. Setting aside the ethical issues, would you say the enterprise system is more a help or a hindrance in this example?

Source: koya79/Fotolia

Guide

The Flavor-of-the-Month Club

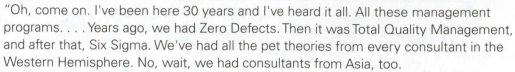

"Oh, come on. I've been here 30 years and I've heard it all. All these management programs. . . . Years ago, we had Zero Defects. Then it was Total Quality Management, and after that, Six Sigma. We've had all the pet theories from every consultant in the Western Hemisphere. No, wait, we had consultants from Asia, too.

"Do you know what flavor we're having now? We're redesigning ourselves to use the cloud. We are going to integrate our systems with our suppliers into a multi-enterprise CRM system to transform the supply chain to be response to our orders!

"You know how these programs go? First, we have a pronouncement at a 'kick-off meeting' where the CEO tells us what the new flavor is going to be and why it's so important. Then a swarm of consultants and 'change management' experts tell us how they're going to 'empower' us. Then HR adds some new item to our annual review, such as, 'Measures taken to achieve customer-centric company.'

"So, we all figure out some lame thing to do so that we have something to put in that category of our annual review. Then we forget about it because we know the next new flavor of the month will be along soon. Or worse, if they actually force us to use the new system, we comply, but viciously. You know, go out of our way to show that the new system can't work, that it really screws things up.

"You think I sound bitter, but I've seen this so many times before. The consultants and rising stars in our company get together and dream up one of these programs. Then they present it to the senior managers. That's when they make their first mistake: They think that if they can sell it to management, then it must be a good idea. They treat senior management like the customer. They should have to sell the idea to those of us who actually sell, support, or make things. Senior management is just the banker; the managers should let us decide if it's a good idea.

"If someone really wanted to empower me, she would listen rather than talk. Those of us who do the work have hundreds of ideas of how to do it better. Now it's inter-enterprise to better serve our customers? As if we haven't been trying to better serve that for years!

"Anyway, after the CEO issues the pronouncements about the new initiative, he gets busy with other things and forgets about it for a while. Six months might go by, and then we're either told we're not doing enough to become multi-enterprise-customer-centric (or whatever the flavor is) or the company announces another new flavor.

"In manufacturing they talk about push versus pull. You know, with push style, you make things and push them onto the sales force and the customers. With pull style, you let the customers' demand pull the product out of manufacturing. You build when you have holes in inventory. Well, they should adapt those ideas to what they call 'change management.' I mean, does anybody need to manage real change? Did somebody have a 'use the mobile device program'? Did some CEO announce, 'This year, we're all going to use mobile devices'? Did the HR department put a line into our annual evaluation form that asked how many times we'd used a mobile device? No, no, no, and no. Customers pulled the mobility through. We wanted it, so we bought and used mobile devices. Hurray for iPhone, Kindle, iPad, and the mobile apps on Twitter and Facebook.

"That's pull. You get a group of workers to form a network, and you get things going among the people who do the work. Then you build on that to obtain true organizational change. Why don't they figure it out?

"Anyway, I've got to run. We've got the kick-off meeting of our new initiative—something called business process management. Now they're going to empower me to manage my own activities, I suppose. Like, after 30 years, I don't know how to do that. Oh, well, I plan to retire soon.

"Oh, wait. Here, take my T-shirt from the knowledge management program 2 years ago. I never wore it. It says, 'Empowering You through Knowledge Management.' That one didn't last long."

DISCUSSION QUESTIONS

1. Clearly, this person is cynical about new programs and new ideas. What do you think might have been the cause of her antagonism? What seems to be her principal concern?

2. What does she mean by "vicious" compliance? Give an example of an experience you've had that exemplifies such compliance.

3. Consider her point that the proponents of new programs treat senior managers as the customer. What does she mean? To a consultant, is senior management the customer? What do you think she's trying to say?

4. What does she mean when she says, "If someone wants to empower me, she would listen rather than talk"? How does listening to someone empower that person?

5. Her examples of "pull change" all involve the use of new products. To what extent do you think pull works for new management programs?

6. How do you think management could introduce new programs in a way that would cause them to be pulled through the organization? Consider the suggestion she makes, as well as your own ideas.

7. If you managed an employee who had an attitude like this, what could you do to make her more positive about organizational change and new programs and initiatives?

Source: Gregory Gerber/Shutterstock

ACTIVE REVIEW

Use this Active Review to verify that you understand the ideas and concepts that answer the chapter's study questions.

Q1 HOW DO INFORMATION SYSTEMS VARY BY SCOPE?

Explain how information systems vary by scope. Provide examples of four levels of information scope other than those in this chapter. Describe characteristics of information systems for each.

Q2 HOW DO ENTERPRISE SYSTEMS SOLVE THE PROBLEM OF INFORMATION SILOS?

Define *information silo,* and explain how such silos come into existence. When do such silos become a problem? Name and describe five common functional applications. Describe data that are likely duplicated among those five applications. Summarize the problems that information silos cause. Summarize the ways that enterprise systems can be used to solve problems of information silos at both the workgroup and the enterprise level. Define business process engineering and explain why it is difficult and expensive.

Q3 HOW DO CRM, ERP, AND EAI SUPPORT ENTERPRISE SYSTEMS?

Explain two major reasons why it is expensive to develop enterprise information systems in-house. Explain the advantages of inherent processes. Define and differentiate among *CRM, ERP,* and *EAI.* Explain how CRM and ERP are more similar to one another than to EAI. Name and describe four sources of challenge when implementing enterprise systems. Describe why enterprise systems management must be collaborative. Explain two major tasks required to identify requirements gaps. Summarize challenges of transitioning to an enterprise system. Explain why employees resist change, and describe three ways of responding to that resistance.

Q4 HOW DO INTER-ENTERPRISE IS SOLVE ENTERPRISE SILOS?

Describe information silos that exist among health care providers, health clubs, and individuals with regard to patient exercise data. Describe problems that those silos create. Explain how the system shown in Figure 7-11 will solve the problems caused by those silos.

How does the knowledge in this chapter help you?

Describe how you can benefit from the information in this chapter. Suppose a job interviewer asked you, "What do you know about ERP?" How would you respond?

KEY TERMS AND CONCEPTS

Business process reengineering 171
Customer life cycle 172
Customer relationship management (CRM) system 171
Data integrity 167
Departmental information systems 165
Distributed systems 178

Enterprise application integration (EAI) 175
Enterprise information system 166
Enterprise resource planning (ERP) 174
Functional information system 165
Information silo 166

Inherent processes 171
Inter-enterprise information system 166
Personal information system 165
Self-efficacy 177
Workgroup information system 165

USING YOUR KNOWLEDGE

1. Using the example of your university, give examples of information systems for each of the four levels of scope shown in Figure 7-1. Describe three workgroup information systems that are likely to duplicate data. Explain how the characteristics of information systems in Figure 7-1 relate to your examples.

2. In your answer to question 1, explain how the three workgroup information systems create information silos. Describe the kinds of problems that those silos are likely to cause. Use Figure 7-3 as a guide.

3. Using your answer to question 2, describe an enterprise information system that will eliminate the silos. Would the implementation of your system require process reengineering? Explain why or why not.

4. Is the information system you proposed in your answer to question 3 an application of CRM, ERP, or EAI? If so, which one and why? If not, explain why not.

5. Explain how the four sources of challenge discussed in Q3 would pertain to the implementation of the PRIDE system. Give specific examples of each. In general, do you think these challenges are more difficult to overcome for an inter-enterprise system like PRIDE or for an enterprise system like CRM?

COLLABORATION EXERCISE 7

Before you start this exercise, read Chapter Extensions 1 and 2, which describe collaboration techniques as well as tools for managing collaboration tasks. In particular, consider using Google Drive, Google+, Windows Live SkyDrive, Microsoft SharePoint, or some other collaboration tool.

The county planning office issues building permits, septic system permits, and county road access permits for all building projects in the county. The planning office issues permits to homeowners and builders for the construction of new homes and buildings and for any remodeling projects that involve electrical, gas, plumbing, and other utilities, as well as the conversion of unoccupied spaces such as garages into living or working space. The office also issues permits for new or upgraded septic systems and permits to provide driveway entrances to county roads.

Figure 7-12 shows the permit process that the county used for many years. Contractors and homeowners found this process to be slow and very frustrating. For one, they did not like its sequential nature. Only after a permit had been approved or rejected by the engineering review process would they find out that a health or highway review was also needed. Because each of these reviews could take 3 or 4 weeks, applicants requesting permits wanted the review processes to be concurrent rather than serial. Also, both the permit applicants and county personnel were frustrated because they never knew where a particular application was in the permit process. A contractor would call to ask how much longer, and it might take an hour or more just to find which desk the permits were on.

Accordingly, the county changed the permit process to that shown in Figure 7-13. In this second process, the permit office made three copies of the permit and distributed one to each department. The departments reviewed the permits in parallel; a clerk would analyze the results and, if there were no rejections, approve the permit.

Unfortunately, this process had a number of problems, too. For one, some of the permit applications were lengthy; some included as many as 40 to 50 pages of large architectural drawings. The labor and copy expense to the county was considerable.

Second, in some cases departments reviewed documents unnecessarily. If, for example, the highway department rejected an application, then neither the engineering nor health departments needed to continue their reviews. At first, the county responded to this problem by having the clerk who analyzed results cancel the reviews of other departments when he or she received a rejection. However, that policy was exceedingly unpopular with the permit applicants, because once an application was rejected and the problem corrected, the permit had to go back through the other departments. The permit would go to the end of the line and work its way back into the departments from which it had been pulled. Sometimes this resulted in a delay of 5 or 6 weeks.

Cancelling reviews was unpopular with the departments as well, because permit-review work had to be repeated. An application might have been nearly completed when it was

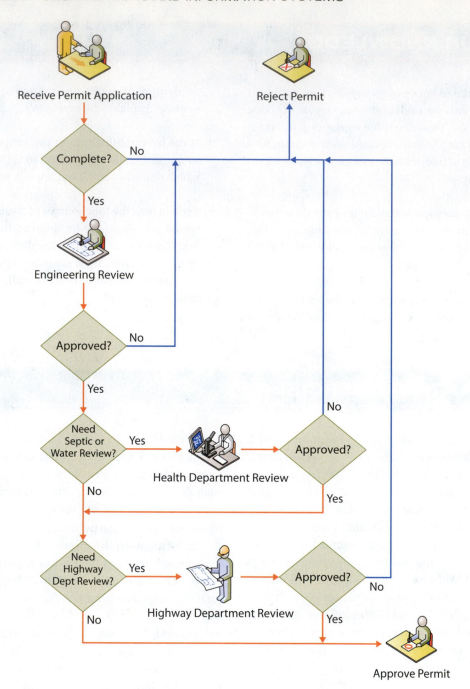

Figure 7-12
Sequential Permit Review Process

cancelled due to a rejection in another department. When the application came through again, the partial work results from the earlier review were lost.

1. Explain why the processes in Figures 7-12 and 7-13 are classified as enterprise processes rather than as departmental processes. Why are these processes not considered to be inter-enterprise processes?

2. Using Figure 7-5 as an example, redraw Figure 7-12 using an enterprise information system that processes a shared database. Explain the advantages of this system over the paper-based system in Figure 7-12.

3. Using Figure 7-5 as an example, redraw Figure 7-13 using an enterprise information system that processes a shared database. Explain the advantages of this system over the paper-based system in Figure 7-13.

4. Assuming that the county has just changed from the system in Figure 7-12 to the one in Figure 7-13, which of your answers in questions 2 and 3 do you think is better? Justify your answer.

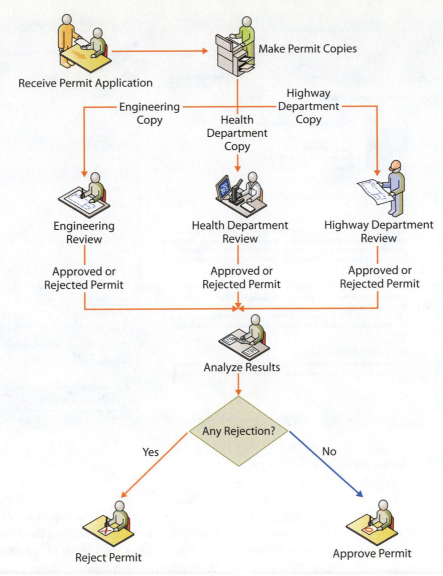

Figure 7-13
Parallel Permit-Review Process

5. Assume your team is in charge of the implementation of the system you recommend in your answer to question 4. Describe how each of the four challenges discussed in Q3 pertain to this implementation. Explain how your team will deal with those challenges. Read the Guide on pages 182–183, if you have not already done so. Assume that person is a key player in the implementation of the new system. How will your team deal with her?

CASE STUDY 7

Using the PRIDE Database

Figure 7-11 shows the PRIDE Database that is located in the cloud. This database symbol hides a world of complexity. In order to make symbols like that more concrete and easier for you to comprehend, we will delve into its structure in this case. To understand this discussion, you will need to use some of the knowledge you gained from Chapter 5. However, as you read this case, don't attempt to remember each detail. Instead, strive to get an overall understanding of the structure and management of a real-world database in the cloud.

Figure 7-14 shows a thin-client application that Microsoft provides for developers to use to create and administer SQL Azure cloud databases. This application is not used to process the database. Instead, the database will be processed using native or thin-client applications like those shown in Figure 7-11.

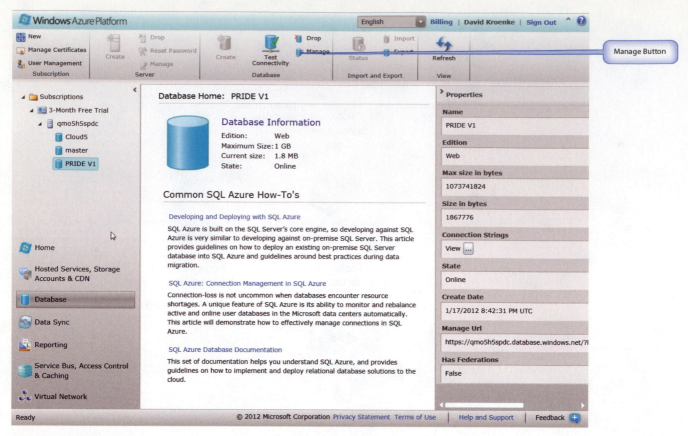

Figure 7-14

Thin-Client Application for Managing a Cloud Database

Source: Microsoft Corporation

In this figure, a database named PRIDE V1 is highlighted. When the developer clicks the Manage icon in the Database section of the menu, SQL Azure opens a thin-client application for working with that particular database. Figure 7-15 shows one page in that application that is used to process queries. Here, the SQL statements required to define a table named Workout are shown. The developer needs to process statements like this for every table in the database.

Figure 7-16 shows three of the PRIDE V1 tables: Person, Workout, and Performance. These diagrams were created by Microsoft Visual Studio, which is a thick-client PC application that developers use to build applications and manage

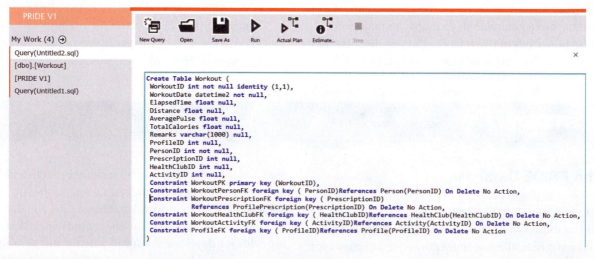

Figure 7-15

Defining the Workout Table with SQL

Source: David Kroenke

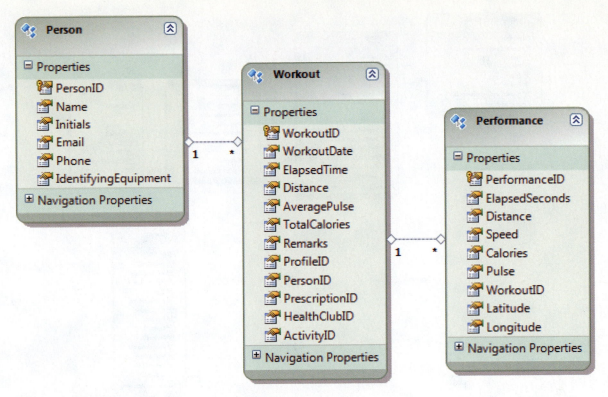

Figure 7-16
PRIDE: Person, Workout, and Performance Tables

Source: David Kroenke

databases. Visual Studio accesses PRIDE V1 in the cloud, reads its metadata and constructs these representations of tables and relationships. The 1. . . * notation on the lines between the tables means the relationship between them is 1:N. Thus a row in Person can relate to many Workout rows, and a row in Workout can relate to many Performance rows.

These tables are used as follows: the Store Exercise data application in Figure 7-11 stores a row in Workout when a workout starts. As the workout proceeds, it periodically stores a row in Performance that records exercise data so far, including Distance, Speed, Calories, Pulse, and so forth. It optionally records latitude and longitude for outside workouts such as runs and bike rides. A given workout might have 100 rows or more of Performance data.

Figure 7-17 shows the tables involved in prescribing workouts. Health care professionals create one or more standard workout profiles in the Profile table. Then that profile is prescribed to a particular person, who then performs one or more workouts according to that profile. Performance data is also stored as just described (not shown). The notation 0..1 on the relationship line between Workout and Profile indicates that a Workout need not relate to any Profile. This rule is needed so that workout data can be stored even if a workout is not governed by a profile.

Figure 7-18 shows all of the tables in this database. The tables with names preceded by the word *Terms_* contain data that PRIDE uses to determine how much, if any, of a person's data can be reported to a particular agency. For example, the table Terms_PersonHealthClub contains

data that specifies how much of the person's data is to be shared with a particular health club. The terms table data is used by the three reporting applications in Figure 7-11 to limit data reported in accordance with each person's preferences.

QUESTIONS

1. Explain the advantages of locating the PRIDE database in the cloud. Dr. Flores and his partners could place it on one of their own servers in the practice. Give reasons why it would be unwise for them to do so.

2. Explain the origin of Figures 7-15 and 7-16. What application created each? Where did the data for constructing the tables in Figure 7-16 arise? Using your intuition and database knowledge, explain how the relationship between Person and Workout is defined in Figure 7-15. What coding in Figure 7-15 ensures that every row in Workout will correspond to some row in Person?

3. Explain how the Store Exercise Prescriptions application in Figure 7-11 will use the tables shown in Figure 7-17.

4. Explain how the Store Exercise Data application in Figure 7-11 will use the tables shown in Figure 7-17.

5. Explain how the Report Patient Exercise application in Figure 7-11 will use the tables shown in Figure 7-17.

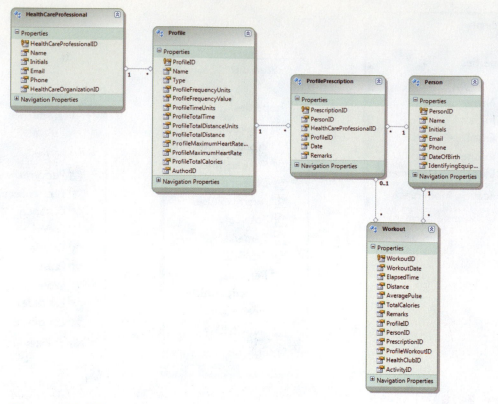

Figure 7-17

PRIDE: Tables Relating to Exercise Prescriptions

Source: David Kroenke

6. Data in the Person table most likely duplicates data in health clubs' membership databases as well as data in health care providers' patient databases. Will this duplication create problems for the health clubs, health care providers, and PRIDE users? If not, say why not. If so, give two examples of problems and suggest ways that those problems can be solved.

7. Explain the ways in which the PRIDE database eliminates possible enterprise-level information silos. Explain ways that it might create another form of information silo.

8. Given what you know so far, do you think the PRIDE system is likely to be successful? Explain your answer.

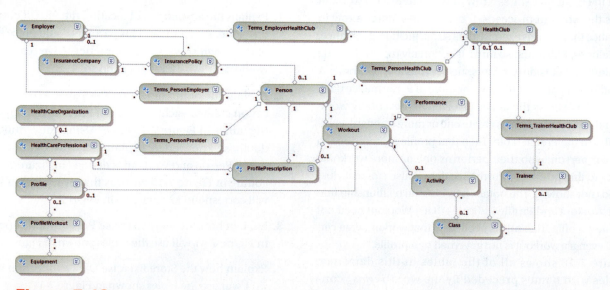

Figure 7-18

PRIDE: All Database Tables

Source: David Kroenke

8

Social Media Information Systems

Dr. Romero Flores, the cardiac surgeon you met in Chapter 7, is on the phone with Lindsey Garrett discussing the exercise activities of her mother, one of Flores' cardiac patients:

"Were you able to access your mother's exercise report?" Dr. Flores is referring to the browser report shown to the right.

"Yes, I was, and it's not good, is it?"

"I'm afraid not—94 calories in 11 treadmill sessions isn't what we want her to be doing."

"Yeah, I know, she's not doing anything. You know, it's a very strange thing, but she lied to me about this...my own mother, who *preached to me* that honesty's the best policy, out and out lied to me about her exercise..."

"I wouldn't go too far with that, Lindsey. She's going through quite a bit, and she's confused and frightened."

"Yeah, I know. But what do we do?"

"Well, first, let's be glad we've got the data and that we know what she's really doing...or not doing."

"Yeah, but where does that get us?"

"Well, we have a new PRIDE feature that involves social networking."

"Mom hates Facebook; I don't know why. Some weird fear or something."

"I don't mean Facebook. We're implementing virtual classes. Your Mom signs up with a group, and we have one of our staff members run group sessions where all the participants are using their own equipment, at home."

"I wonder if she'd do that."

"Go out to Endomondo.com—you'll see an example of how people are sharing their exercise data. We want to do something a little different, but with our own mobile app, or maybe a Facebook app, we're not sure. Again,

This could happen to you

STUDY QUESTIONS

Q1 WHAT IS A SOCIAL MEDIA INFORMATION SYSTEM (SMIS)?

Q2 HOW DO SMIS ADVANCE ORGANIZATIONAL STRATEGY?

Q3 HOW DO SMIS INCREASE SOCIAL CAPITAL?

Q4 HOW CAN ORGANIZATIONS MANAGE THE RISKS OF SOCIAL MEDIA?

Q5 WHERE IS SOCIAL MEDIA TAKING US?

How does the **knowledge** in this chapter help **you**?

"Nobody is going to see pictures of you in your PJs on your treadmill."

though, we're just getting started. Not sure this will work, but we'll provide staff to see if we can make it work."

"OK, I'll talk with her about it."

Later that day, Lindsey is on the phone with her mother. We hear just Lindsey's side of the conversation:

"Mom! I know what you think about Facebook. And it's Twitter, not Bitter. With a T!"

...

"Mother, nobody is going to see pictures of you in your PJs on your treadmill. We're not talking about any pictures."

...

"Look, Mother. It's simple. You go to one session at Dr. Flores'. You meet the other people that will be in your class...people just like you, your age, more or less, and all of whom have had heart surgery."

...

"Yes, I'll put an application on your cell phone. At the scheduled time, you sign in to the application...I'll show you how...and then you do your exercise and your phone will show you how you're doing compared to the others. It will keep a record, too, so you can brag about it later."

...

"Don't tell me bragging's not nice. Little Ms. Mother who tried to deceive her doctor about her exercise..."

"Never mind. Anyway, there will be a little icon on the screen...a little picture-like thing. There won't be any pictures of you shown to anyone. Just a little icon with your first name. Or you can use a fake name, if you want. That doesn't matter."

"Look I'll come over with the kids, and we'll set it up and show you how."

"No, don't bake anything. None of us need food. We need you to start doing your exercises. I'll see you tonight. OK?"

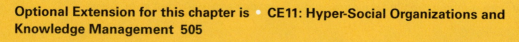

CE Optional Extension for this chapter is • **CE11: Hyper-Social Organizations and Knowledge Management 505**

WHAT IS A SOCIAL MEDIA INFORMATION SYSTEM (SMIS)?

Before we address this question, understand that this chapter makes no attempt to discuss the latest features of Facebook, Twitter, LinkedIn, foursquare, Pinterest, or any other social media service. Most likely you know much about these already, and further, they are changing so fast that whatever particulars you learn today will be old when you graduate and obsolete when you begin work. Instead, this chapter focuses on principles, conceptual frameworks, and models that will last over changes in social media services and technology and be useful when you address the opportunities and risks of social media systems in the early years of your professional career.

That knowledge will also help you avoid mistakes. Every day, you can hear businesspeople saying, "We're using Twitter" and "We've connected our Facebook page to our Web site." Or, creating ads and news releases that say, "Follow us on Twitter." The important question is, for what? To be modern? To be hip? Are they worth their cost? How do they advance the organization's strategy?

Social media (SM) is the use of information technology to support the sharing of content among networks of users. Social media enables people to form **communities**, **tribes**, or **hives**, all of which are synonyms that refer to a group of people related by a common interest. (The latter two terms are in vogue among business and technology writers.) A **social media information system (SMIS)** is an information system that supports the sharing of content among networks of users.

As illustrated in Figure 8-1, social media is the merger of many disciplines. In this book, we will focus on the MIS portion of this diagram by discussing SMIS and how they contribute to organizational strategy. If you decide to work in the SM field as a professional, you will need some knowledge of all these disciplines, except possibly computer science.

THREE SMIS ROLES

Before discussing the components of an SMIS, we need to clarify the roles played by the three organizational units shown in Figure 8-2:

- User communities
- Social media sponsors
- Social media application providers

Figure 8-1
Social Media is a Convergence of Disciplines

Figure 8-2
SMIS Organizational Roles

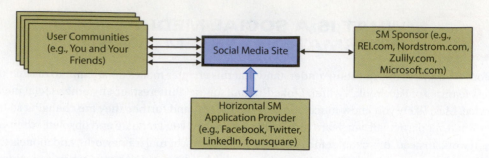

User Communities

Forming communities is a natural human trait; anthropologists claim that the ability to form them is responsible for the progress of the human race. In the past, however, communities were based on family relationships or geographic location. Everyone in the village formed a community. The key difference of SM communities is that they are formed based on mutual interests and transcend familial, geographic, and organizational boundaries.

Because of this transcendence, most people belong to several, or even many, different user communities. Google+ recognized this fact when it created user circles that enable users to allocate their connections (*people,* using Google+ terminology) to one or more community groups. Facebook and other SM application providers are adapting in similar ways.

Figure 8-3 expands on the community–SM site relationship in Figure 8-2. From the point of view of the SM site, Community A is a first-tier community that consists of users

Figure 8-3
SM Communities

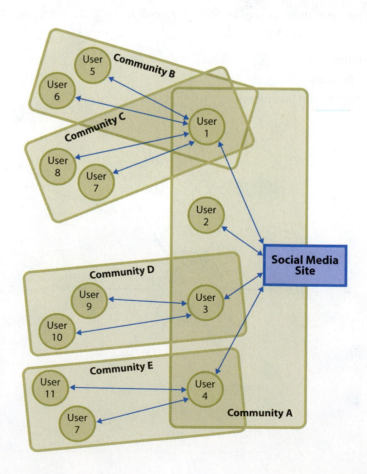

that have a direct relationship to that site. User 1, in turn, belongs to three communities: A, B, and C (these could be, say, classmates, professional contacts, and friends). From the point of view of the SM site, Communities B–E are second-tier communities because the relationships in those communities are intermediated by first-tier users. The number of second- and first-tier community members grows exponentially. If each community had, for example, 100 members, then the SM site will have 100×100, or 10,000, second-tier members and $100 \times 100 \times 100$ third-tier members (not shown in Figure 8-3). However, that statement is not quite true, because communities overlap; in Figure 8-3, for example, user 7 belongs to communities C and E. Thus, these calculations are the maximum number of users.

How the SM site chooses to relate to these communities depends on its goals. If the SM site is interested in pure publicity, it will want to relate to as many tiers of communities as it can. If so, it will create a **viral hook**, which is some inducement, such as a prize or other reward, for passing communications along through the tiers. If, however, the purpose of the SM site is to solve an embarrassing problem, say to fix a product defect, then the sponsors of the SM site would endeavor to constrain, as much as it can, the communications to Community A.

The exponential nature of relationships via community tiers offers sponsoring organizations both a blessing and a curse. An employee who is a member of Community A can share her sincere and legitimate pride in her organization's latest product or service with hundreds or thousands of people in her communities. However, she can also blast her disappointment at some recent development to that same audience, or, worse, inadvertently share private and proprietary organizational data with someone in that audience who works for the competition.

Social media is a powerful tool, and to use it well, organizations must know their goals and plan accordingly, as you'll learn.

Social Media Sponsors

Social media sponsors are companies and other organizations that choose to support a presence on one or more SM sites. Figure 8-4 shows Microsoft's Office365.com page with links to Facebook, Twitter, and LinkedIn in the bottom-left corner of that page. When Microsoft places those icons on its promotional pages, it is making a commitment to invest considerable employee time and other costs to support social media. In particular, it needs to develop procedures and staff and train people to support that site, as you'll learn in the next section.

Figure 8-4
Not a Casual Commitment

Source: Microsoft Corporation

Social Media Application Providers

Social media application providers are the companies that operate the SM sites. Facebook, Twitter, LinkedIn, and Google are all SM application providers. These providers create the features and functions of the site, and they compete with one another for the attention of user communities and SM sponsors.

Social media have evolved in such a way that users expect to use SM applications without paying a license fee or other charge. Sponsors may or may not pay a fee, depending on the application and on what they do with it. On Facebook, for example, creating a company page is free, but Facebook charges a fee to advertise to communities that "Like" that page. Most SM applications earn revenue through some type of advertising model.

In some SMIS, the social media sponsor develops its own provider rather than use one of the standard providers like Facebook or Twitter. A company that wants to use social media internally, say for knowledge management or for employee motivation and morale, might develop its own provider using, say, SharePoint 2013, or some other software that is capable of providing wikis, discussion groups, sharing photos and the like.

SMIS COMPONENTS

Because they are information systems, SMIS have the same five components as all IS: hardware, software, data, procedures, and people. Consider each component for each of the three organizational roles; user, sponsor, and application provider, shown in Figure 8-5.

Hardware

Both community users and employees of SM sponsors process SM sites using desktops, laptops, smartphones, iPads, HTML 5 devices, and, indeed, any intelligent communications device. In most cases, SM application providers host the SM presence using elastic servers in the cloud.

Figure 8-5
Five Components of SMIS

Component	Role	Description
Hardware	User	Any user computing device
	SM Sponsor	Any user computing device
	Application Provider	Elastic, cloud-based servers
Software	User	Browser, iOS and other applications
	SM Sponsor	Browser, application Tools
	Application Provider	Application; NoSQL or other DBMS
Data	User	User-generated content; connection data
	SM Sponsor	Sponsor content
	Application Provider	Content and connection data storage and rapid retrieval
Procedures	User	Informal, copy each other
	SM Sponsor	Create, manage, remove content; extract value from content and connections; manage risk
	Application Provider	Run and maintain application (beyond the scope of this text)
People	User	Adaptive; can be irrational
	SM Sponsor	Key Users
	Application Provider	Staff to run and maintain application (beyond the scope of this text)

Software

Users employ browsers and native mobile applications, such as iOS applications, to read and submit data and to add and remove connections to communities and other users. SM sponsors contribute to the site via browsers or using specialized sponsor applications provided by the SM application provider. In some cases, like, say, Facebook applications, SM sponsors create their own applications and interface those applications with the SM site.

SM application providers develop and operate their own custom, proprietary, social networking application software. As you learned in Chapter 4, supporting custom software is expensive over the long term; SM application vendors must do so because the features and functions of their applications are fundamental to their competitive strategy. They can do so because they spread the development costs over the revenue generated by millions of users.

As you learned in Case Study 5, many social networking vendors use a NoSQL database management system to process their data, although traditional relational DBMS products are used as well. Recall, too, that Facebook began development of Cassandra in-house (Case Study 5, page 127), but donated it to the open-source community when it realized the expense and commitment of maintaining it.

Data

SM data falls into two categories: content and connection. **Content data** is data and responses to data that are contributed by users and SM sponsors. You provide the source content data for your Facebook site, and your friends provide response content when they write on your wall, make comments, tag you, or otherwise publish on your site.

Connection data is data about relationships. On Facebook, for example, the relationships to your friends are connection data. The fact that you've liked particular organizations is also connection data. Connection data differentiates SMIS from Web site applications. Both Web sites and social networking sites present user and responder content, but only social networking applications store and process connection data.

SM application providers store and retrieve SM data on behalf of sponsors and user communities. As explained in Case Study 5, they must do so in the presence of network and server failures, and they must do so rapidly. The problem is made somewhat easier, however, because SM content and connection data have a relatively simple structure.

Procedures

For social networking users, procedures are informal, evolving, and socially oriented. You do what your friends do. When the members of your tribe learn how to do something new and interesting, you copy them. Software is designed to be easy to learn and use.

Such informality makes using SMIS easy; it also means that unintended consequences are common. The most troubling examples concern user privacy. Many people have learned not to post pictures of themselves in front of their house numbers on the same publicly accessible site on which they're describing their new high-definition television. Many others, alas, have not. Others have learned not to post data that can cause them to lose their jobs, or not get jobs in the first place. See the Social Recruiting Guide on pages 214–215.

For SM sponsors, social networking procedures cannot be so informal. Before initiating a social networking presence, organizations must develop procedures for creating content, managing user responses, removing obsolete or objectionable content, and extracting value from content. For an example of the latter, setting up an SMIS to gather data on product problems is a wasted expense unless procedures exist to extract knowledge from that social networking data. Organizations also need to develop procedures to manage SM risk, as described in Q4.

Procedures for operating and maintaining the SM application are beyond the scope of this text.

How honest are people with social media? Reflect on ethical issues for social media in the Ethics Guide on pages 212–213.

People

Users of social media do what they want to do depending on their goals and their personalities. They behave in certain ways and observe the consequences. They may or may not change their behavior. By the way, note that SM users aren't necessarily rational, at least not in purely monetary ways. See, for example, the study by Vernon Smith in which people walked away from free money because they thought someone else was getting more![1]

SM sponsors, however, cannot be casual. Anyone who contributes to an organization's SM site or who uses his or her position in a company to speak for an organization needs to be trained on both SMIS user procedures as well as on the organization's social networking policy. We will discuss such procedures and policies in Q4.

Social media is creating new job titles, new responsibilities, and the need for new types of training. For example, what makes for a good tweeter? What makes for an effective wall writer? What type of person should be hired for such jobs? What education should they have? How does one evaluate candidates for such positions? All of these questions are being asked and answered today. Clearly, it's a hot field, and because social media reinforces inherent human behavior, SM jobs are not likely to disappear anytime soon.

The staff to operate and maintain the SM application is beyond the scope of this text.

Not Free

Before we go on, you will sometimes read that SMIS are free. It is true that Facebook, Twitter, LinkedIn, and other sites do not charge for hardware, software, or data storage. However, unless the SM sponsor takes the foolish and irresponsible posture of letting its social networking presence do whatever it will, someone will need to develop, implement, and manage the social networking procedures just described. Furthermore, employees who contribute to and manage social networking sites will generate direct labor costs.

HOW DO SMIS ADVANCE ORGANIZATIONAL STRATEGY?

In Chapter 3, Figure 3-1 (page 49), you learned the relationship of information systems to organizational strategy. In brief, strategy determines value chains, which determine business processes, which determine information systems. Therefore, when any organization considers using social media, it should ensure that it knows how that social media will contribute to its strategy. In this question we will discuss, in particular, how social media contributes to the primary value chain activities.

Gossieaux and Moran, creators of the **hyper-social organization** theory, identify two kinds of communities that are important to commerce:[2]

- Defenders of belief
- Seekers of the truth

Defenders of belief share a common belief and form their hive around that belief. They seek conformity and want to convince others of the wisdom of their belief. A group that believes that Google+ is far superior to Facebook will engage in behaviors to convince others that this is true. When confronted with contrary evidence, they do not change their opinion, but become more firmly convinced in their belief.[3] Defenders-of-belief communities facilitate activities like

[1]Vernon Smith, *Rationality in Economics: Constructivist and Ecological Forms* (Cambridge, UK: Cambridge University Press, 2007), pp. 247–250.
[2]Francois Gossieaux and Edward K. Moran, *The Hyper-Social Organization* (New York: McGraw-Hill), pp. 22, 23–25.
[3]Daniel Kahneman, Paul Slovic, and Amos Tversky, *Judgment Under Uncertainty: Heuristics and Biases* (Cambridge, UK: Cambridge University Press, 1982), p. 144.

Activity	Community Type	Focus	Dynamic Process	Risks
Sales and Marketing	Defender of Belief	Outward to Prospects	Social CRM Peer-to-peer sales	Loss of Credibility Bad PR
Customer Service	Seeker of Truth	Outward to Customers	Peer-to-peer support	Loss of Control
Inbound Logistics	Seeker of Truth	Upstream Supply Chain providers	Problem Solving	Privacy
Outbound Logistics	Seeker of Truth	Downstream Supply Chain shippers	Problem Solving	Privacy
Manufacturing and Operations	Seeker of Truth	Outward for User design; Inward to Operations and Manufacturing	User-guided design Enterprise 2.0 Knowledge Management	Efficiency/ Effectiveness
Human Relations	Defender of Belief	Employee candidates; Employee Communications	Employee prospecting, recruiting, and evaluation SharePoint & Enterprise 2.0 for employee-to-employee communication	Error Loss of Credibility

Figure 8-6
SM in Value Chain Activities

sales and marketing. They are not effective for activities that involve innovation or problem solving. Such groups can form strong bonds and allegiance to an organization.

Seekers of the truth share a common desire to learn something, solve a problem, or make something happen. Cardiac surgeons who want to learn how to motivate their patients to exercise appropriately seek "the truth." They share a common problem, but not a common solution to that problem. Not surprisingly, such tribes are incredible problem solvers and excel at innovation. They can be useful in customer service activity, as long as they don't conclude that the best way to solve a product problem is to use another company's product, something they might do because such groups seldom form a strong bond to an organization. The only organizational bond seekers of the truth are likely to form occurs when the organization demonstrates behavior that indicates that it, too, is committed to solving the community's shared problem.

Figure 8-6 summarizes how social media contributes to the five primary value chain activities and to the human resources support activity. Consider each row of this table.

SOCIAL MEDIA AND THE SALES AND MARKETING ACTIVITY

In the past, organizations controlled their relationships with customers using structured processes and related information systems. In fact, the primary purpose of traditional CRM was to manage customer touches. Traditional CRM ensured that the organization spoke to customers with one voice and that it controlled the messages, offers, and even the support that customers received based on the value of a particular customer. In 1990, if you wanted to know something about an IBM product, you'd contact its local sales office; that office would classify you as a prospect and use that classification to control the literature, documentation, and your access to IBM personnel.

Social CRM is a dynamic, SM-based CRM process. The relationships between organizations and customers emerge in a dynamic process as both parties create and process content. In addition to the traditional forms of promotion, employees in the organization create wikis, blogs, discussion lists, frequently asked questions, sites for user reviews and commentary, and other dynamic content. Customers search this content, contribute reviews and commentary, ask more questions, create user groups, and so forth. With social CRM, each customer crafts his or her own relationship with the company.

Social CRM flies in the face of the principles of traditional CRM. Because relationships emerge from joint activity, customers have as much control as companies. This characteristic is an anathema to traditional sales managers who want control over what the customer is reading, seeing, and hearing about the company and its products.

Further, traditional CRM is centered on lifetime value; customers that are likely to generate the most business get the most attention and have the most impact on the organization. However, with social CRM, the customer who spends 10 cents but who is an effective reviewer, commentator, or blogger can have more influence than the quiet customer who purchases $10 million a year. Such imbalance is incomprehensible to traditional sales managers.

However, traditional sales managers *are* happy to have defenders-of-belief groups sell their products using peer-to-peer recommendations. A quick look at products and their reviews on Amazon.com will show how frequently customers are willing to write long, thoughtful reviews of products they like or do not like. Amazon.com and other online retailers also allow readers to rate the helpfulness of reviews. In that way, substandard reviews are revealed for the unwary.

However, using social media for sales and marketing does present some risks. In March 2011, Microsoft tweeted the following after the Japanese earthquakes: "How you can #SupportJapan-http://bingedit/fEh7iT. For every retweet, @bing will give $1 to Japan quake victims, up to $100k." The URL was for a page that detailed how to use Bing Maps and other services to help with the disaster. Users expressed their disgust at what they saw as Microsoft using a tragedy to promote its search engine. Seven hours later, Bing apologized with the following tweet: "We apologize the tweet was negatively perceived. Intent was to provide a way for people to help Japan. We have donated $100k."[4] The risks of social media for sales and marketing are loss of credibility and bad public relations.

SOCIAL MEDIA AND CUSTOMER SERVICE

Product users are amazingly willing to help each other solve problems. Even more, they will do so without pay; in fact, payment can warp and ruin the support experience as customers fight with one another. SAP learned that it was better to reward its SAP Developer Network with donations on their behalf to charitable organizations than it was to give them personal rewards.[5]

Not surprisingly, organizations whose business strategy involves selling to or through developer networks have been the earliest and most successful at SM-based customer support. In addition to SAP, Microsoft has long sold through its network of partners. Its MVP (Most Valuable Professional) program is a classic example of giving praise and glory in exchange for customer-provided customer assistance (*http://mvp.support.microsoft.com*). Of course, the developers in their networks have a business incentive to participate because that activity helps them sell services to the communities in which they participate.

However, users with no financial incentive are also willing to help others. Amazon.com supports a program called Vine by which customers can be selected to give pre-release and new product reviews to the buyer community.[6] You'll need your psychology course to explain what drives people to strive for such recognition. MIS just provides the platform!

The primary risk of peer-to-peer support is loss of control. As stated, seekers of the truth will seek the truth, even if that means recommending another vendor's product over yours. We address that risk in Q4.

---

[4]Greg Lamm, "Microsoft Apologizes for Bing Japan Earthquake Tweet," March 13, 2011, www.techflash.com/seattle/2011/03/microsoft-sorry-for-bing-quake-tweet.html, accessed September 7, 2011.
[5]Francois Gossieaux and Edward K. Moran, *The Hyper-Social Organization* (New York: McGraw-Hill), pp. 8, 9.
[6]http://www.amazon.com/gp/help/customer/display.html?ref=hp_200791020_vine?nodeId=200791020#vine, accessed October 8, 2012

SOCIAL MEDIA AND INBOUND AND OUTBOUND LOGISTICS

Companies whose profitability depends on the efficiency of their supply chain have long used information systems to improve both the effectiveness and efficiency of structured supply chain processes. Because supply chains are tightly integrated into structured manufacturing processes, there is less tolerance for the unpredictability of dynamic, adaptive processes like social media.

Problems, however, are an exception. The Japanese earthquake in the spring of 2011 created havoc in the automotive supply chain when major Japanese manufacturers lacked power and, in some cases, facilities to operate. Social media was used to dispense news, allay fears of radioactive products, and solve problems.

Seekers-of-the-truth communities provide better and faster problem solutions to complex supply chain problems. Social media is designed to foster content creation and feedback among networks of users, and that characteristic facilitates the iteration and feedback needed for problem solving, as described in Chapter Extension 1.

Loss of privacy is, however, a significant risk. Problem solving requires the open discussion of problem definitions, causes, and solution constraints. Suppliers and shippers work with many companies; supply chain problem solving via social media is problem solving in front of your competitors.

SOCIAL MEDIA AND MANUFACTURING AND OPERATIONS

Operations and manufacturing activities are dominated by structured processes. The flexibility and adaptive nature of social media would result in chaos if applied to the manufacturing line or to the warehouse. However, social media does play a role in product design as well as in employee knowledge sharing and management.

Crowdsourcing is the dynamic social media process of employing users to participate in product design or product redesign. eBay often solicits customers to provide feedback on their eBay experience. As that site says, "There's no better group of advisors than our customers." User-guided design has been used for the design of video games, shoes, and many other products.

Enterprise 2.0 is the application of social media to facilitate the cooperative work of people inside organizations. Enterprise 2.0 can be used in operations and manufacturing to enable users to share knowledge and problem-solving techniques.

Andrew McAfee, the originator of the term *Enterprise 2.0*, defined six characteristics that he refers to with the acronym **SLATES** (see Figure 8-7).[7] Workers want to be able to *search* for content inside the organization just as they do on the Web. Most workers find that searching is more effective than navigating content structures such as lists and tables of content. Workers want to access organizational content by *link*, just as they do on the Web. They also want to *author* organizational content using blogs, wikis, discussion groups, published presentations, and so on.

Enterprise 2.0 content is *tagged*, just like content on the Web, and tags are organized into structures, as is done on the Web at sites such as Delicious (*www.delicious.com*). These structures organize tags as a taxonomy does, but, unlike taxonomies, they are not preplanned; they emerge. A **folksonomy** is content structure that has emerged from the processing of many user tags. Additionally, Enterprise 2.0 workers want applications to enable them to rate tagged content and to use the tags to predict content that will be of interest to them (as with Pandora), a process McAfee refers to as *extensions*. Finally, Enterprise 2.0 workers want relevant content pushed to them; they want to be *signaled* when something of interest to them happens in organizational content.

---

[7]Andrew McAfee, "Enterprise 2.0: The Dawn of Emergent Collaboration," *MIT Sloan Management Review*, Spring 2006, http://sloanreview.mit.edu/the-magazine/files/saleablepdfs/47306.pdf, accessed August 2011.

Figure 8-7
McAffee's SLATES
Enterprise 2.0 Model

Enterprise 2.0 Component	Remarks
Search	People have more success searching than they do in finding from structured content.
Links	Links to enterprise resources (like on the Web).
Authoring	Create enterprise content via blogs, wikis, discussion groups, presentations, etc.
Tags	Flexible tagging (e.g., Delicious) results in folksonomies of enterprise content.
Extensions	Using usage patterns to offer enterprise content via tag processing (e.g., Pandora).
Signals	Pushing enterprise content to users based on subscriptions and alerts.

The potential problem with Enterprise 2.0 is the quality of its dynamic process. Because the benefits of Enterprise 2.0 result from emergence, there is no way to control for either effectiveness or efficiency. It's a messy process about which little can be predicted.

SOCIAL MEDIA AND HUMAN RESOURCES

The last row in Figure 8-6 concerns the use of social media and human resources. Social media is used for finding employee prospects; for recruiting candidates; and, in some organizations, for candidate evaluation.

Social media is also used for employee communications, using internal, personnel sites such as MySite and MyProfile in SharePoint or other, similar Enterprise 2.0 facilities. SharePoint provides a place for employees to post their expertise in the form of "Ask me about" questions. When employees are looking for an internal expert, they can search SharePoint for people who have posted that desired expertise. SharePoint 2013 greatly extends support for social media beyond that in earlier SharePoint versions.

The risks of social media in human resources concern the possibility of error when using sites such as Facebook to form conclusions about employees. A second risk is that the SM site becomes too defensive as a defender of belief or is obviously promulgating an unpopular management message.

Study Figure 8-6 to understand the general framework by which organizations can accomplish their strategy via dynamic process supported by SMIS. We will now turn to an economic perspective on the value and use of SMIS.

Social media is increasingly used to recruit and evaluate potential employees. See the Guide on pages 214–215.

Q3 HOW DO SMIS INCREASE SOCIAL CAPITAL?

Business literature defines three types of capital. Karl Marx defined **capital** as the investment of resources for future profit. This traditional definition refers to investments into resources such as factories, machines, manufacturing equipment, and the like. **Human capital** is the investment in human knowledge and skills for future profit. By taking this class, you are investing in your own human capital. You are investing your money and time to obtain knowledge that you hope will differentiate you from other workers and ultimately give you a wage premium in the workforce.

According to Nan Lin, **social capital** is the investment in social relations with the expectation of returns in the marketplace.[8] When you attend a business function for the purpose of meeting people and reinforcing relationships, you are investing in your social capital. Similarly, when you join LinkedIn or contribute to Facebook, you are (or can be) investing in your social capital.

WHAT IS THE VALUE OF SOCIAL CAPITAL?

According to Lin, social capital adds value in four ways:

- Information
- Influence
- Social credentials
- Personal reinforcement

Relationships in social networks can provide *information* about opportunities, alternatives, problems, and other factors important to business professionals. They also provide an opportunity to *influence* decision makers at one's employer or in other organizations who are critical to your success. Such influence cuts across formal organizational structures, such as reporting relationships. Third, being linked to a network of highly regarded contacts is a form of *social credential*. You can bask in the glory of those with whom you are related. Others will be more inclined to work with you if they believe critical personnel are standing with you and may provide resources to support you. Finally, being linked into social networks reinforces a professional's image and position in an organization or industry. It reinforces the way you define yourself to the world (and to yourself).

Social networks differ in value. The social network you maintain with your high school friends probably has less value than the network you have with your business associates, but not necessarily so. According to Henk Flap, the **value of social capital** is determined by the number of relationships in a social network, by the strength of those relationships, and by the resources controlled by those related.[9] If your high school friends happened to have been Warren Buffett and Mark Zuckerberg, and if you maintain strong relations with them via your high school network, then the value of that social network far exceeds any you'll have at work. For most of us, however, the network of our current professional contacts provides the most social capital.

So, when you use social networking professionally, consider those three factors. You gain social capital by adding more friends and by strengthening the relationships you have with existing friends. Further, you gain more social capital by adding friends and strengthening relationships with people who control resources that are important to you. Such calculations may seem cold, impersonal, and possibly even phony. When applied to the recreational use of social networking, they may be. But when you use social networking for professional purposes, keep them in mind.

HOW DO SOCIAL NETWORKS ADD VALUE TO BUSINESSES?

Organizations have social capital just as humans do. Historically, organizations created social capital via salespeople, via customer support, and via public relations. Endorsements by high-profile people are a traditional way of increasing social capital, but there are tigers in those woods.

---

[8]Nan Lin, *Social Capital: The Theory of Social Structure and Action* (Cambridge, UK: Cambridge University Press, 2002), Location 310 of the Kindle Edition.

[9]Henk D. Flap, "Social Capital in the Reproduction of Inequality," *Comparative Sociology of Family, Health, and Education*, Vol. 20 (1991), pp. 6179ñ6202. Cited in Nan Lin, *Social Capital: The Theory of Social Structure and Action* (Cambridge, UK: Cambridge University Press, 2002), Kindle location 345.

Today, progressive organizations maintain a presence on Facebook, LinkedIn, Twitter, and possibly other sites. They include links to their social networking presence on their Web sites and make it easy for customers and interested parties to leave comments. In most cases, such connections are positive, but they can backfire, when customers leave excessively critical feedback. See Q4 for more.

To understand how social networks add value to businesses, consider each of the elements of social capital: number of relationships, strength of relationships, and resources controlled by "friends."

USING SOCIAL NETWORKING TO INCREASE THE NUMBER OF RELATIONSHIPS

In a traditional business relationship, a client (you) has some experience with a business, such as a restaurant. Traditionally, you may express your opinions about that experience by word of mouth to your social network. However, such communication is unreliable and brief: You are more likely to say something to your friends if the experience was particularly good or bad; but, even then, you are likely only to say something to those friends whom you encounter while the experience is still recent. And once you have said something, that's it; your words don't live on for days or weeks.

Figure 8-8 shows the same relationships as shown in Figure 8-3 but cast into the framework of a restaurant that specializes in hosting wedding receptions. Users 1–4 in this example are restaurant customers who have a direct relationship with the restaurant's SM site (Facebook, or whatever is popular). Here, communities B–D in Figure 8-3 have been replaced by wedding receptions. (User 1 is a wedding planner who has held two events at the restaurant.)

This diagram indicates that receptions can potentially contribute more than just revenue. If the restaurant can find a way to induce reception attendees to form a direct relationship with it, wedding receptions will contribute substantially to the number of relationships in its social

Figure 8-8
SM Communities

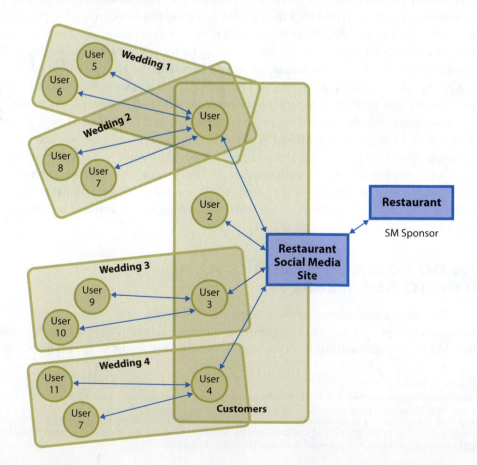

Experiencing MIS   INCLASS EXERCISE 8

Computing Your Social Capital

Source: Andres Rodriguez/Fotolia

Social capital is not an abstract concept that applies only to organizations; it applies to you as well. You and your classmates are accumulating social capital now. What is the value of that capital? To see, form a group as directed by your professor and complete the following items:

1. Define *capital, human capital,* and *social capital.* Explain how these terms differ.

2. How does the expression "It's not what you know, but who you know that matters" pertain to the terms you defined in item 1?

3. Do you, personally, agree with the statement in item 2? Form your own opinion before discussing it with your group.

4. As a group, discuss the relative value of human and social capital. In what ways is social capital more valuable than human capital? Form a group consensus view on the validity of the statement in item 2.

5. Visit the Facebook, LinkedIn, Twitter, or other social networking presence site of each group member.
   a. Using the definition of social capital value in this chapter, assess the value of each group member's social networking presence.
   b. Recommend at least one way to add value to each group member's social capital at each site.

6. Suppose you each decide to feature your Facebook or other social networking page on your professional résumé.
   a. How would you change your presence that you evaluated in item 5 in order to make it more appropriate for that purpose?
   b. Describe three or four types of professionals that you could add to your social network that would facilitate your job search.

7. Imagine that you are the CEO of a company that has just one product to sell: You.
   a. Review the Enterprise 2.0 SLATES principles in Figure 8-7 and assess how each could pertain to the selling of your "product" (i.e., obtaining a quality job that you want). You can find the McAfee article at *http://sloanreview.mit.edu/the-magazine/2006-spring /47306/enterprise-the-dawnof-emergent-collaboration/*
   b. Explain how you could use your social networking presence to facilitate social CRM selling of your product.
   c. Devise a creative and interesting way to use this exercise as part of your social CRM offering.

8. Present your answers to items 4 and 7 to the rest of the class.

network and, depending on the strength and value of those connections, possibly contribute substantially to the restaurant's social capital.

Such relationship sales have been going on by word of mouth for centuries; the difference here is that SMIS allow such sales to scale to levels not possible in the past; SMIS also make those relationships visible and available for other purposes.

USING SOCIAL NETWORKS TO INCREASE THE STRENGTH OF RELATIONSHIPS

To an organization, the **strength of a relationship** is the likelihood that the entity (person or other organization) in the relationship will do something that benefits the organization. An organization has a strong relationship with you if you buy its products, write positive reviews about it, post pictures of you using the organization's products or services, and so on.

As stated earlier, social networks provide four forms of value: influence, information, social credentials, and reinforcement. If an organization can induce those in its relationships to provide more of any of those factors, it has strengthened that relationship.

In his autobiography, Benjamin Franklin provided a key insight.[10] He said that if you want to strengthen your relationship with someone in power, ask him to do you a favor. Before Franklin invented the public library, he would ask powerful strangers to lend him their expensive books. In that same sense, organizations have learned that they can strengthen their relationships with you by asking you to do them a favor. Thus, many organizations develop their SMIS to encourage you to create content as a way of getting you to do them a favor. When you provide that favor, it strengthens your relationship with the organization.

Traditional capital depreciates. Machines wear out, factories get old, technology and computers become obsolete, and so forth. Does social capital also depreciate? Do relationships wear out from use? So far, the answer seems to be both yes and no.

Clearly, there are only so many favors you can ask of someone in power. And, there are only so many times a company can ask you to review a product, post pictures, or provide connections to your friends. At some point, the relationship deteriorates due to overuse. So, yes, social capital does depreciate.

However, frequent interactions strengthen relationships and hence increase social capital. The more you interact with a company, the stronger your commitment and allegiance. But continued frequent interactions occur only when both parties see value in continuing the relationship. Thus, at some point, the organization must do something to make it worth your while to continue to do them a favor.

So, social capital does depreciate, but such depreciation can be ameliorated by adding something of value to the interaction. And, continuing a successful relationship over time substantially increases relationship strength.

CONNECTING TO THOSE WITH MORE ASSETS

The third measure of the value of social capital is the size of the assets controlled by those in the relationships. An organization's social capital is thus partly a function of the social capital of those to whom it relates. The most visible measure is the number of relationships. Someone with 1,000 loyal Twitter followers is usually more valuable than someone with 10. But the calculation is more subtle than that; if those 1,000 followers are college students, and if the organization's product is adult diapers, the value of the relationship to the followers is low. A relationship with 10 Twitter followers who are in retirement homes would be more valuable.

There is no formula for computing social capital, but the three factors would seem to be more multiplicative than additive. Or, stated in other terms, the value of social capital is more in the form of

*Social Capital = Number of Relationships * Relationship Strength * Entity Resources*

Than it is:

Social Capital = Number of Relationships + Relationship Strength + Entity Resources

Again, do not take these equations literally; take them in the sense of the multiplicative interaction of the three factors.

---

[10]Founding father of the United States. Author of *Poor Richard's Almanac*. Successful businessman; owner of a chain of print shops. Discoverer of groundbreaking principles in the theory of electricity. Inventor of bifocals, the potbelly stove, the lightning rod, and much more. Founder of the public library and the postal service. Darling of the French court and salons, and now, contributor to social network theory!

This multiplicative nature of social capital means that a huge network of relationships to people who have few resources may be lower in capital than that of a smaller network with people with substantial resources. Furthermore, those resources must be relevant to the organization. Students with pocket change are relevant to Pizza Hut; they are irrelevant to a BMW dealership.

This discussion brings us to the brink of social networking practice. Most organizations today (2013) ignore the value of entity assets and simply try to connect to more people with stronger relationships. This area is ripe for innovation. You will learn in the next chapter how some organizations use a NoSQL DBMS named Hadoop to process social media data to find patterns and relationships. Also, data aggregators like ChoicePoint and Acxiom maintain detailed data about people, worldwide. Such data could be used by information systems to calculate the potential value of a relationship to a particular individual or class of people. Such applications enable organizations to better understand the value of their social networks as well as guide their behavior with regard to particular individuals.

Stay tuned; many possibilities exist, and some ideas, maybe yours, will be very successful.

 HOW CAN ORGANIZATIONS MANAGE THE RISKS OF SOCIAL MEDIA?

Social media represents a revolution in the way that organizations communicate. Twenty years ago, most organizations managed all public and internal messaging with the highest degree of control. Every press conference, press release, public interview, presentation, and even academic paper needed to be preapproved by both the legal and marketing departments. Such approval could take weeks or months.

Today, progressive organizations have turned that model on its head. Employees are encouraged to engage with communities and, in most organizations, to identify themselves with their employer while doing so. All of this participation, all of this engagement, however, comes with risks. In this question, we will consider risks from employee communication and risks from nonemployee, user-generated content.

MANAGING THE RISK OF EMPLOYEE COMMUNICATION

The first step that any SM-aware organization should take is to develop and publicize a **social media policy**, which is a statement that delineates employees' rights and responsibilities. You can find an index to 100 different policies at the Social Media Today Web site.[11] In general, the more technical the organization, the more open and lenient are the social policies. The U.S. military has, perhaps surprisingly, endorsed social media with enthusiasm, tempered by the need to protect classified data.

Intel Corporation has pioneered open and employee-trusting SM policies, policies that they continue to involve as they gain more experience with employee-written social media. The three key pillars of their policy in 2012 are:

- Disclose
- Protect
- Use Common Sense[12]

[11]"Social Media Employee Policy Examples from Over 100 Organizations," Social Media Today, http://socialmediatoday.com/ralphpaglia/141903/social-media-employee-policy-examples-over-100-companies-and-organizations, accessed June 2012.
[12]"Intel Social Media Guidelines," Intel, www.intel.com/content/www/us/en/legal/intel-social-media-guidelines.html, accessed November 2011.

Figure 8-9

Intel's Rules of Social Media
Engagement

Source: Used with permission from Intel
Corporation

Disclose	Be transparent—real name and employer Be truthful—point out if you have a vested interest Be yourself—stick to your expertise and write what you know
Protect	Don't tell secrets Don't slam the competition Don't overshare
Use Common Sense	Add value—make your contribution worthwhile Keep it cool—don't inflame or respond to every criticism Admit mistakes—be upfront and quick with corrections

Those policies are further developed as shown in Figure 8-9. Visit *http://www.intel.com/content/www/us/en/legal/intel-social-media-guidelines.html,* and read this policy carefully; it contains great advice and considerable wisdom.

Two elements in this list are particularly noteworthy. The first is the call for transparency and truth. As an experienced and wise business professional once told me, "Nothing is more serviceable than the truth." It may not be convenient, but it is serviceable long term. Second, SM contributors and their employers should be open and above board. If you make a mistake, don't obfuscate; instead correct it, apologize, and make amends. The SM world is too open, too broad, and too powerful to fool.

When singer Amy Winehouse died in July 2011, both Microsoft and Apple tweeted messages about where to buy her music that the Twittersphere found distasteful and objectionable.[13] After a loud outcry, both organizations were prompt with apologies, made amends to her family and friends, and the errors were forgotten by day's end. Had they done otherwise, we would still be hearing about them. See also Using Your Knowledge Question 5 on page 217.

MANAGING THE RISK OF USER-GENERATED CONTENT

User-generated content (UGC), which simply means content on your SM site that is contributed by nonemployee users, is the essence of SM relationships. As with any relationship, however, UGC comments can be inappropriate or excessively negative in tone or otherwise problematic. Organizations need to determine how they will deal with such content before engaging in social media.

Problem Sources

The major sources of UGC problems are:

- Junk and crackpot contributions
- Inappropriate content
- Unfavorable reviews
- Mutinous movements

When a business participates in a social network or opens its site to UGC, it opens itself to misguided people who post junk unrelated to the site's purpose. Crackpots may also use the network or UGC site as a way of expressing passionately held views about unrelated topics, such as UFOs, government cover-ups, fantastic conspiracy theories, and so forth. Because of the possibility of such content, SM sponsors should regularly monitor the site and remove objectionable material immediately. Monitoring can be done by employees, or companies like Bazaarvoice

---

[13]Sarah Kessler, "Microsoft Apologizes for 'Crass' Amy Winehouse Tweet," CNN.com, July 26, 2011, www.cnn.com/2011/TECH/social.media/07/25/apology.winehouse.tweet.mashable/index.html?iref=allsearch, accessed August 2011.

offer services not only to collect and manage ratings and reviews, but also to monitor the site for irrelevant content.

Unfavorable reviews are another risk. Research indicates that customers are sophisticated enough to know that few, if any, products are perfect. Most customers want to know the disadvantages of a product before purchasing it so they can determine if those disadvantages are important for their application. However, if every review is bad, if the product is rated 1 star out of 5, then the company is using social media to publish its problems. In this case, some action must be taken as described next.

Mutinous movements are an extension of bad reviews. When President Obama used Twitter to explain and justify one element of the federal budget debate in August 2011, it backfired. He lost 33,000 followers as a result.[14]

Responding to Social Networking Problems

The first task in managing social networking risk is to know the sources of potential problems and to monitor sites for problematic content. Once such content is found, however, organizations must have a plan for creating the organization's response. Three possibilities are:

- Leave it
- Respond to it
- Delete it

If the problematic content represents reasonable criticism of the organization's products or services, the best response may be to leave it where it is. Such criticism indicates that the site is not just a shill for the organization, but contains legitimate user content. Such criticism also serves as a free source of product reviews, which can be useful for product development. To be useful, the development team needs to know about the criticism, so, as stated, processes to ensure that the criticism is found and communicated to the development team are necessary.

A second alternative is to respond to the problematic content. However, this alternative is dangerous. If the response could be construed in any way as patronizing or insulting to the content contributor, the response can enrage the community and generate a strong backlash. Also, if the response appears defensive, it can become a public relations negative.

In most cases, responses are best reserved for when the problematic content has caused the organization to do something positive as a result. For example, suppose a user publishes that he or she was required to hold for customer support for 45 minutes. If the organization has done something to reduce wait times, then an effective response to the criticism is to recognize it as valid and state, nondefensively, what had been done to reduce wait times.

If a reasoned, nondefensive response generates continued and unreasonable UGC from that same source, it is best for the organization to do nothing. Never wrestle with a pig; you'll get dirty and the pig will enjoy it. Instead, allow the community to constrain the user. It will.

Deleting content should be reserved for contributions that are inappropriate because they are contributed by crackpots, because they have nothing to do with the site, or because they contain obscene or otherwise inappropriate content. However, deleting legitimate negative comments can result in a strong user backlash. Nestlé created a PR nightmare on its Facebook account with its response to criticism it received about its use of palm oil. Someone altered the Nestlé logo, and in response Nestlé decided to delete all Facebook contributions that used that altered logo, and did so in an arrogant, heavy-handed way. The result was a negative firestorm on Twitter.[15]

---

[14]http://nation.foxnews.com/president-obama/2011/07/29/obama-twitter-spams-usa-loses-10000-followers Accessed July 18, 2012. Anjali Mullany, Daily News, "Obama Loses 40,000 Twitter Followers."
[15]Bernhard Warner, "Nestlé's 'No Logo' Policy Triggers Facebook Revolt," Social Media Influence, March 19, 2010, http://socialmediainfluence.com/2010/03/19/nestles-no-logo-policy-triggers-facebook-revolt/ accessed August 2010.

A sound principle in business is to never ask a question to which you do not want the answer. We can extend that principle to social networking; never set up a site that will generate content for which you have no effective response!

Q5 WHERE IS SOCIAL MEDIA TAKING US?

So much change is in the air: nearly free storage and communication is enabling relationships among people and organizations that were unimaginable even five years ago. Facebook had the audacity to overprice and oversell its initial public offering, yet it still raised $104 billion. Is there another Facebook out there, right now? We don't know. However, new versions of mobile devices, along with dynamic and agile information systems based on cloud computing, guarantee that monumental changes will continue at least through the early years of your career. The PRIDE system, or one like it, could be a reality soon.

Today, social media applications are limited only by imagination. In Brazil, Unilever placed GPS devices in 50 packages of its Omo detergent.[16] The GPS devices were activated when customers removed the package from the shelf. The devices then reported the customer's home location to Unilever. Unilever employees then contacted the customers at home and gave them pocket video cameras. The point? Promotion. But what's next? Starbucks is concerned enough to have created a position of Chief Digital Officer (CDO), a position responsible for developing and managing innovative social media programs.[17]

Advance the clock 10 years. You're now the product marketing manager for an important new product series for your company…the latest in a line of, say, intelligent home appliances. How are you going to promote your products? GPS, with a team following them home? No, you'll have to do something even more creative by then, something that will involve social media that does not exist today.

Think about your role as a manager in 10 years. Your team has 10 people, 3 of whom report to you; 2 report to other managers; and 5 work for different companies. Your company uses Office Gizmo 2022, augmented by Google Whammo ++ Star, both of which have many features that enable employees to publish their ideas in blogs, wikis, videos, and whatever other means have become available. A few employees, those in specialized positions have company computers, but all of those in your department use their own mobile devices to access the Internet via networks they pay for themselves. Occasionally, when they have to, they use the organization's network as well. Of course, your employees have their own Facebook, Twitter, LinkedIn, foursquare, and other social networking sites to which they regularly contribute.

How do you manage this team? If "management" means to plan, organize, and control, how can you accomplish any of these functions in this emergent network of employees? But, if you and your organization follow the lead of tech-savvy companies like Intel, you'll know you cannot close the door on your employees' SM lives, nor will you want to. Instead, you'll harness the power of the social behavior of your employees and partners to advance your strategy.

In the context of CRM, social media means that the vendor loses control of the customer relationship. Customers use all the vendor's touch points they can find to craft their own relationships. Emergence in the context of management means loss of control of employees. Employees craft their own relationships with their employers, whatever that might mean in 10 years. Certainly it means a loss of control, one that is readily made public to the world.

In the 1960s, when someone wanted to send a letter to Don Draper at Sterling Cooper, his or her secretary addressed the envelope to Sterling Cooper and down at the bottom added, "Attention: Don Draper." The letter was to Sterling Cooper, oh, by the way, also to Don Draper.

---

[16]Laurel Wentz, "Is Your Detergent Stalking You?" *Advertising Age,* July 29, 2010, http://adage.com/globalnews/article?article_id=145183, accessed August 2010.

[17]Jennifer van Grove, "How Starbucks Is Turning Itself into a Tech Company," *VB/Social,* June 12, 2012, http://venturebeat.com/2012/06/12/starbucks-digital-strategy/, accessed June 2012.

Email changed that. Today, someone would send an email to DonDraper@SterlingCooper.com, or even just to Don@SterlingCooper.com. That address is to a person and then to the company.

Social media changes addresses further. When Don Draper creates his own blog, people respond to Don's Blog, and only incidentally do they notice in the "About Don" section of the blog that Don works for Sterling Cooper. In short, the focus has moved in 50 years from organizations covering employee names to employees covering organization names.

Does this mean that organizations go away? Hardly. They are needed to raise and conserve capital and to organize vast groups of people and projects. No group of loosely affiliated people can envision, design, develop, manufacture, market, sell, and support an iPad. Organizations are required.

So what, then? Maybe we can take a lesson from biology. Crabs have an external exoskeleton. Deer, much later in the evolutionary chain, have an internal endoskeleton. When crabs grow, they must endure the laborious and biologically expensive process of shedding a small shell and growing a larger one. They are also vulnerable during the transition. When deer grow, the skeleton is inside and it grows with the deer. No need for vulnerable molting. And, considering agility, would you take a crab over a deer?

In the 1960s, organizations were the exoskeleton around employees. In ten years, they will be endoskeleton, supporting the work of people on the exterior.

Does that analogy offer guidance to the future? Maybe.

How does the knowledge in this chapter help you?

You already know how to use Facebook and Twitter and other social sites for your personal use. This chapter has shown you how to apply some of the knowledge to help organizations. You learned the components of a social media IS and the commitment that an organization makes when it places a Facebook or Twitter icon on its Web page. You also learned how organizations use SMIS to achieve their strategies, across the five primary value chain activities, and how SMIS can increase social capital. Finally, you learned how organizations need to manage the risks of social media and how social media will challenge you in the future.

If Dr. Flores were to hire you to help create the social media site for his cardiac surgery patients, you would be able to apply all of this knowledge to help him and his patients. Stay tuned, however, the story is evolving. When you read about social media developments in the future, think about organizations, and not just your own use.

Ethics Guide

Hiding the Truth?

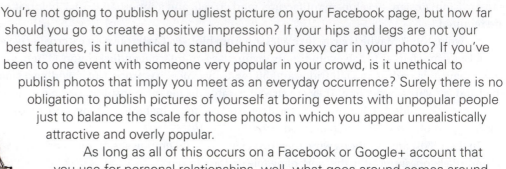

You're not going to publish your ugliest picture on your Facebook page, but how far should you go to create a positive impression? If your hips and legs are not your best features, is it unethical to stand behind your sexy car in your photo? If you've been to one event with someone very popular in your crowd, is it unethical to publish photos that imply you meet as an everyday occurrence? Surely there is no obligation to publish pictures of yourself at boring events with unpopular people just to balance the scale for those photos in which you appear unrealistically attractive and overly popular.

As long as all of this occurs on a Facebook or Google+ account that you use for personal relationships, well, what goes around comes around. But consider social networking in the business arena:

a. Suppose that a river rafting company starts a group on a social networking site for promoting rafting trips. Graham, a 15-year-old high school student who wants to be more grown-up than he is, posts a picture of a handsome 22-year-old male as a picture of himself. He also writes witty and clever comments on the site photos and claims to play the guitar and be an accomplished masseuse. Are his actions unethical? Suppose someone decided to go on the rafting trip, in part because of Graham's postings, and was disappointed with the truth about Graham. Would the rafting company have any responsibility to refund that person's fees?

b. Suppose you own and manage the rafting company. Is it unethical for you to encourage your employees to write positive reviews about your company? Does your assessment change if you ask your employees to use an email address other than the one they have at work?

c. Again, suppose you own and manage the rafting company and that you pay your employees a bonus for every client they bring to a rafting trip. Without specifying any particular technique, you encourage your employees to be creative in how they obtain clients. One employee invites his Facebook friends to a party at which he shows photos of prior rafting trips. On the way to the party, one of the friends has an automobile accident and dies. His spouse sues your company. Should your company be held accountable? Does it matter if you knew about the presentation? Would it matter if you had not encouraged your employees to be creative?

d. Suppose your rafting company has a Web site for customer reviews. In spite of your best efforts at camp cleanliness, on one trip (out of dozens) your staff accidentally served contaminated food and everyone became ill with food poisoning. One of those clients from that trip writes a poor review because of that experience. Is it ethical for you to delete that review from your site?

e. Assume you have a professor who has written a popular textbook. You are upset with the grade you received in his class, so you write a scandalously poor review of that professor's book on Amazon.com. Are your actions ethical?

f. Instead of owner, suppose you were at one time employed by this rafting company and you were, undeservedly you think, terminated. To get even, you use Facebook to spread rumors to your friends (many of whom are river guides) about the safety of the company's trips. Are your actions unethical? Are they illegal? Do you see any ethical distinctions between this situation and that in item d?

g. Again, suppose that you were at one time employed by the rafting company and were undeservedly terminated. You notice that the company's owner does not have a Facebook account, so you create one for her. You've known her for many years and have dozens of photos of her, some of which were taken at parties and are unflattering and revealing. You post those photos along with critical comments that she made about clients or employees. Most of the comments were made when she was tired or frustrated, and they are hurtful, but because of her wit, also humorous. You send friend invitations to people whom she knows, many of whom are the target of her biting and critical remarks. Are your actions unethical?

? DISCUSSION QUESTIONS

1. Read the situations in items a through g, and answer the questions contained in each.

2. Based on your answers in question 1, formulate ethical principles for creating or using social networks for business purposes.

3. Based on your answers in question 1, formulate ethical principles for creating or using user-generated content for business purposes.

4. Summarize the risks that a business assumes when it chooses to sponsor user-generated content.

5. Summarize the risks that a business assumes when it uses social media for business purposes.

Source: W2 Photography/Corbis/Glow Images

Guide

Social Recruiting

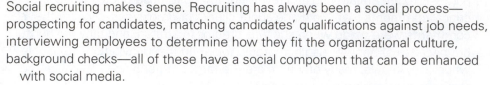

Social recruiting makes sense. Recruiting has always been a social process—prospecting for candidates, matching candidates' qualifications against job needs, interviewing employees to determine how they fit the organizational culture, background checks—all of these have a social component that can be enhanced with social media.

Today, some organizations use their communities to locate prospects. In the recent downturn, some have created communities of "alumni" employees, meaning those who have been laid off, to keep track of them in case an opportunity to rehire good performers occurs. Professional recruiters also build and use existing communities to locate prospects for openings they have.

In addition to prospecting, employers also use candidates' SM sites, particularly LinkedIn, Facebook, and Twitter, to get a sense of the candidate as a person and to find any potential behavior or attitude problems. However, using social data exposes **protected data**, which is data about candidates' sex, race, religion, sexual orientation, and disabilities that is illegal to use for hiring decisions. In most cases, it is clear that none of this data should influence such decisions, but the issues can sometimes be cloudy. Can an organization reject a person shown sitting in a wheelchair for a job that requires walking? The legal precedents are not clear.

What is clear, however, is that by consuming that data the organization loses a common defense against bias lawsuits: "We didn't know." Because the organization does know, it must be careful not to use such data inappropriately and also to appear not to have done so.

The general guideline is to treat every candidate the same. If social media is used for screening for one candidate, use it for all. If social media is used only after the first interview, conduct that same process for all. Furthermore, keep screenshots of every Web page that informs the hiring decision. Finally, when organizations do find worrisome indicators on SM sites, they may want to allow the candidate an opportunity to address any concerns during an interview. Data that appears problematic may be harmless or an error.

Now, put the shoe on the other foot. What should you, as a job candidate, do? First, as of now at least, join LinkedIn and use it only for professional purposes. Fill your profile with appropriate professional data. Strive to ensure that your data indicates an ambitious interest in whatever field you choose. Build your connections and check out LinkedIn tools like the JobsInsider for using your contacts to obtain references inside organizations.

Second, assume that any prospective employer will use all of your SM data that it can find. Remove inappropriate content from sites that can be publicly accessed. You should assume that any prospective employer will use all of your public SM data. In case they might ask for private data, which has happened,[18] some students set up a decoy site. Such a site is a public site that has your most professional and responsible social data. Use a different name and identity for your real social site. On the other hand,

---

[18] http://finance.yahoo.com/news/job-seekers-getting-asked-facebook-080920368.html, accessed May 2012.

you might decide that any company that wants your private social networking data is not a company for which you want to work.

By the way, what is funny or innocent to you and your friends may not appear so to a potential employer. If you're in doubt, ask professional people who are 10 or 20 years older than you to assess your social data.

Finally, keep in mind that social media is a double-edged sword. Check out the blogs, commentary, and any other postings of people who already work at prospective employers. See, for example, the employer reviews on *www.GlassDoor.com*. You're not necessarily looking for organizational dirt; you're looking for a good fit between you and the organization's culture. If, for example, an employee's blog or social data indicates employees travel frequently, that can be good or bad for you, depending on whether you want to travel. But at least you'll know from a reliable source. Human resources may say, "We have flexible working hours," and employees may agree, "Yes, we do. Work any 65 hours a week you want." If you do find employee social data that concerns you, at an appropriate time and in a polite way, review those concerns during your job interview process.

DISCUSSION QUESTIONS

1. Define *protected data*. In your opinion, what kind of protected data should never be used for hiring decisions? Name and describe three situations in which it is at least debatable whether such data should be used.

2. Think of two organizations for which you would like to work. Assume both organizations review job candidates' SM data as part of their initial screening process.
a. Name and describe three positive criteria that both companies could use to evaluate applicants. If you think the companies might use different criteria, explain the difference.
b. Name and describe three indications of problematic issues that both companies could use to evaluate candidates. If you think the companies might use different criteria, explain the difference.
c. If you were rejected because of a lack of social data supporting your criteria for item a or because of the presence of social data in the criteria for item b, would you know it?

3. Evaluate your own social data in light of your answer to question 2.
a. Describe elements in your social data that support positive criteria.
b. Describe elements in your social data that could indicate problematic issues.

4. Ask someone else to evaluate your social data in light of both sets of criteria in question 2. You can ask a friend, but you will likely obtain better information if you pick someone whom you do not know well. Most human resource screening personnel are in their 30s. Try to pick someone in that age group to evaluate your criteria, if you can.

5. Choose the most negative social data according to your answers to questions 3 and 4. Suppose you are in a job interview and you are asked about that problematic data. Explain your response.

6. Consider the job you would most like to obtain after you graduate. Assume you are the hiring decision maker for that job. Name and describe five indications that would positively influence you toward a job candidate.

7. Join LinkedIn if you have not already done so. Build your personal profile in accordance with your answer to question 6.

Source: Rob Wilkinson/Alamy

ACTIVE REVIEW

Use this Active Review to verify that you understand the ideas and concepts that answer this chapter's study questions.

Q1 WHAT IS A SOCIAL MEDIA INFORMATION SYSTEM (SMIS)?

Define *social media, communities, tribes, hives,* and *social media information systems.* Name and describe three SMIS organizational roles. Explain the elements of Figure 8-3. Explain why placing a LinkedIn icon on a company Web site is not a casual decision. In your own words, explain the nature of the five components of SMIS for each of the three SMIS organizational roles.

Q2 HOW DO SMIS ADVANCE ORGANIZATIONAL STRATEGY?

Explain the terms *defenders of belief* and *seekers of the truth.* How do the goals of each type of community differ? Summarize how social media contributes to sales and marketing, customer support, inbound logistics, outbound logistics, manufacturing and operations, and human resources. Name SM risks for each activity. Define *social CRM, crowdsourcing,* and *Enterprise 2.0.* Explain each element in the SLATES model.

Q3 HOW DO SMIS INCREASE SOCIAL CAPITAL?

Define *social capital* and explain four ways that social capital adds value. Name three factors that determine social capital and explain how "they are more multiplicative than additive."

Q4 HOW CAN ORGANIZATIONS MANAGE THE RISKS OF SOCIAL MEDIA?

Name and describe two types of SM risk. Describe the purpose of an SM policy and summarize Intel's six guiding principles. Describe an SM mistake, other than one in this text, and explain the wise response to it. Name four sources of problems of UGC; name three possible responses, and give the advantages and disadvantages of each.

Q5 WHERE IS SOCIAL MEDIA TAKING US?

Summarize possible management challenges when during the first years of your career. Describe the text's suggested response. How does the change in forms of address since the 1960s indicate a change in the relationship of employees and organizations to the business world? Explain the relationship of the differences between crab and deer to this change.

How does the knowledge in this chapter help you?

You know how to use Facebook and Twitter. Explain how each of the questions addressed in this chapter will help you help your employers to use them as well. Summarize the challenges (and opportunities) that social media will present to you, a future manager.

KEY TERMS AND CONCEPTS

USING YOUR KNOWLEDGE

1. Using the Facebook page of a company that you have "Liked" (or would choose to), fill out the grid in Figure 8-5. Strive to replace the phrases in that grid with specific statements that pertain to Facebook, the company you like, and you and users whom you know. For example, if you and your friends access Facebook using an Android phone, enter that specific device.

2. Name a company for which you would like to work. Using Figure 8-6 as a guide, describe, as specifically as you can, how that company could use social media. Include community type, specific focus, processes involved, risks, and any other observations.
   a. Sales and marketing
   b. Customer service
   c. Inbound logistics
   d. Outbound logistics
   e. Manufacturing and operations
   f. Human resources

3. Visit *www.lie-nielsen.com* or *www.sephora.com*. On the site you chose, find links to social networking sites. In what ways are those sites sharing their social capital with you? In what ways are they attempting to cause you to share your social capital with them? Describe the business value of social networking to the business you chose.

4. According to Paul Greenberg, Amazon.com is the master of the 2-minute relationship and Boeing is the master of the 10-year relationship.[19] Visit *www.boeing.com* and *www.amazon.com*. From Greenberg's statement and from the appearance of these Web sites, it appears that Boeing is committed to traditional CRM and Amazon.com to social CRM. Give evidence from each site that this might be true. Explain why the products and business environment of both companies cause this difference. Is there any justification for traditional CRM at Amazon.com? Why or why not? Is there any justification for social CRM at Boeing? Why or why not? Based on these companies, is it possible that a company might endorse Enterprise 2.0 but not endorse social CRM? Explain.

5. Visit *http://socialmediatoday.com/ralphpaglia/141903 /social-media-employee-policy-examples-over-100-companies-and-organizations*. Find an organization with a very restricted employee SM policy. Name the organization and explain why you find that policy restrictive. Does that policy cause you to feel positive, negative, or neutral about that company? Explain.

---

[19]Paul Greenberg, *CRM at the Speed of Light,* 4th ed. (New York: McGraw-Hill, 2010), p. 105.

COLLABORATION EXERCISE 8

Before you start this exercise, read Chapter Extensions 1 and 2, which describe collaboration techniques as well as tools for managing collaboration tasks. In particular, consider using Google Drive, Google+, Windows Live SkyDrive, Microsoft SharePoint, or some other collaboration tool.

Collaborate with a group of fellow students to answer the following questions. For this exercise do not meet face to face. Coordinate all of your work using email and email attachments, only. Your answers should reflect the thinking of the entire group, and not just one or two individuals.

You most likely do not know much about the particular purposes and goals that Flores and his partners and staff have for the social media group they will create to motivate their cardiac patients to maintain their exercise programs. So, you can't realistically create a prototype social media site for that purpose. Instead assume that you and your group are going to create a social media group for maintaining motivation on an exercise program for getting and staying in shape for an intramural soccer or other sports team over the summer. Or, if your group prefers, assume you are going to create a group to maintain discipline for maintaining a diet, or some other program requiring discipline that can be assisted by a social group. Using iteration and feedback, answer the following questions:

1. State the particular goals of your group. Be as specific as possible.

2. Identify five different social media alternatives for helping your group to maintain discipline for the activity you selected. An obvious choice is a Facebook group, but find

other alternatives as well. Visit *www.socialmediatoday.com* for ideas. Summarize each alternative.

3. Create a list of criteria for evaluating your alternatives. Use iteration and feedback to find creative criteria, if possible.

4. Evaluate your alternatives based on your criteria and select one for implementation.

5. Implement a prototype of your site. If, for example, you chose a Facebook group, create a prototype page on Facebook.

6. Describe the five components of the SMIS you will create for your group. Be very specific with regard to the procedure and people components. Your goal should be to produce a result that could be implemented by any group of similarly motivated students on campus.

7. Assess your result. How likely do you think it will help your group members achieve the goals in item 1? If you see ways to improve it, describe them.

8. Write a two-paragraph summary of your work that your group members could use in a job interview to demonstrate their knowledge of the use of social media for employee motivation.

CASE STUDY 8

Sedona Social

Sedona, Arizona, is a small city of 10,000 people that is surrounded by use Coconino National Forest. At an elevation of 4,500 feet, it is considerably higher than the valley cities of Phoenix and Tucson, but 2000 feet below the altitude of Flagstaff. This middle elevation provides a moderate climate that is neither too hot in the summer nor too cold in the winter. Sedona is surrounded by gorgeous sandstone red/orange rocks and stunning red rock canyons, as shown in Figure 8-10.

This beautiful city was the location for more than 60 movies, most of them westerns, between the 1930s and the 1950s.

Figure 8-10
Sedona Red Rocks

Source: © David Kroenke

If you've ever watched an old black-and-white western, it was likely situated in Sedona. Among the well-known movies located in Sedona are *Stagecoach, Johnny Guitar, Angel and the Badman,* and *3:10 to Yuma.*

Many who visit Sedona believe there is something peaceful yet energizing about the area, especially in certain locations known as *vortices,* according to VisitSedona.com.

"Vortex sites are enhanced energy locations that facilitate prayer, meditation, mind/body healing, and exploring your relationship with your Soul and the divine. They are neither electric nor magnetic."[20]

Tests with scientific instruments have failed to identify any unusual readings of known energy types, and yet many people, of all religions and religious persuasions, believe there is something about Sedona that facilitates spiritual practice. For a city of its size, Sedona has many more churches than one might expect, including the Catholic Chapel of the Holy Cross, Protestant churches of many dominations, the Latter Day Saints (Mormon) church, the local synagogue, and the new-age Sedona Creative Life Center. (See Figure 8-11.)

Because it is situated in the middle of a national forest, Sedona is surrounded by hundreds of miles of hiking trails; it is possible to hike every day for a year and not use all the trails. The area was home to Native Americans in the 12th and 13th centuries, and there are numerous cliff dwellings and other native sites nearby.

[20]http://www.visitsedona.com/article/151

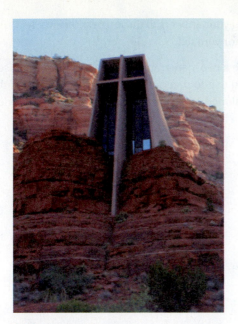

Figure 8-11
Chapel of the Holy Cross

Source: © David Kroenke

As a relatively young modern city, Sedona does not have the cultural history of Santa Fe or Taos, New Mexico. Nonetheless, there is a burgeoning arts community centered around Tlaquepaque, a 1980s-built shopping area modeled on a Mexican city of the same name.

As with many tourist destinations, there are tensions. Pink Jeep Tours runs daily trips of raucous tourists past vortices occupied by meditating spiritual practitioners. With its Hollywood past, Sedona is home to many Los Angeles expatriates, and at the local health food store it's possible to see 50-something blond women wearing tight pants and jewel-studded, fresh-from-Rodeo-drive sandals fighting for the last pound of organic asparagus with aging male hippies shaking their white-gray ponytails off the shoulders of their tie-dyed shirts.

The emerging arts community wants to be serious; the uptown jeep-riding tourists (See Figure 8-12) want to have fun with four-wheel thrills and margaritas (we hope in that sequence). Hikers want to visit petroglyphs, while nature preservers don't want the locations of those sites to be known. Those seeking spiritual guidance want enlightenment in silence, while the locals want to shut out everyone, just as long, that is, as their property values increase at a steady pace, year by year. Meanwhile, the Lear Jets and Citations fly in and out carrying who-knows-who Hollywood celebrity from her home behind the walls of Seven Canyons Resort. And businesses in town want to have reliable, year-round revenue, and not too much competition.

Given all that, let's suppose that the Sedona Chamber of Commerce has just hired you as its first-ever manager of community social media. They want you to provide advice and assistance to local businesses in the development of their social media sites, and they want you to manage their own social media presence as well.

QUESTIONS

1. Search Facebook for *Sedona, Arizona*. Examine a variety of Sedona-area pages that you find. Using the knowledge of this chapter and your personal social media experience, evaluate these pages and list several positive and negative features of each. Make suggestions on ways that they could be improved.

2. Repeat question 1 for another social media provider. As of this writing, possibilities are Twitter, LinkedIn, and Pinterest, but choose another social media provider if you wish.

3. The purpose of a Chamber of Commerce is to foster a healthy business climate for all of the businesses in the community. Given that purpose, your answers to questions 1 and 2, and the knowledge of this chapter, develop a set of 7 to 10 guidelines for local businesses to consider when developing their social media presence.

4. Sedona has quite a number of potentially conflicting community groups. Explain three ways that the Chamber of Commerce can use social media to help manage conflict so as to maintain a healthy business environment.

Figure 8-12
Pink Jeep Tours

Source: © David Kroenke

5. Examine Figure 8-6 and state how the focus of each of the primary value chain activities pertains to the Chamber of Commerce. If one does not pertain, explain why. In your answer, be clear about who the Chamber's customers are.

6. Given your answer to question 5, and considering your responsibility to manage the Chamber's social media presences, state how each applicable row of Figure 8-6 guides the social media sites you will create.

7. Using your answers to these questions, write a job description for yourself.

8. Write a two-paragraph summary of this exercise that you could use to demonstrate your knowledge of the role of social media in commerce in a future job interview.

Business Intelligence Systems

Dr. Flores is talking with Maggie Jensen, one of the IS professionals who is developing the PRIDE system.

"Dr. Flores, check this out." Maggie is clearly excited to show him something.

"What is it?" Flores is busy, as always, but curious to see what she has.

"It's our new, well, I guess you'd call it a report, but it's more than that. It's a screenshot of my phone earlier today. I was on a stationary bike and competing against my last four exercises." Maggie hands him a printout from a phone (similar to the one to the right).

This could happen to you

"So the bicycle icons were moving up the screen?" Flores looks at the phone.

"Exactly. The blue icons are my past workouts, and the green one was my workout this morning. I was spinning against myself." Maggie explains.

"So how could we use this?" Dr. Flores sounds a little skeptical.

Maggie was ready. "Well, for one, we could use it to motivate patients. They would compete against their past workout data."

"Yeah, although we might want to have some control over that. Some of our patients are excessively competitive. I'd hate to encourage them to go overboard." Dr. Flores nods at a very aggressive looking 65-year-old walking out of an exam room.

"OK. Another option is to record the perfect workout for a given recovery stage. Maybe have three or four versions of good workouts for each stage . . . and assign patients prescriptions to work out against those. We could put a red icon on the screen for the optimal workout . . . and reward them on the basis of how close they get to that optimal." Maggie's enthusiasm is infectious.

"I like that. Can you prototype it for me?"

"Sure." As she says this, she wonders how to get it done, but she knows it's possible.

"Meanwhile, I've got another question."

"What's that?" Maggie loves these dialogs.

"Well, the key word is *overboard*. We want our patients to exercise within a narrow range; too little effort and they don't get any benefit, and too much, they're endangering their health." From the expression on his face, Flores is clearly concerned.

"I understand."

"When they work out in a health facility, we control that. But here, we can't. To compensate, one of the docs or nurses checks each patient's previous day's workouts. We call or email if we see a problem."

STUDY QUESTIONS

Q1 HOW DO ORGANIZATIONS USE BUSINESS INTELLIGENCE (BI) SYSTEMS?

Q2 WHAT ARE THE THREE PRIMARY ACTIVITIES IN THE BI PROCESS?

Q3 HOW DO ORGANIZATIONS USE DATA WAREHOUSES AND DATA MARTS TO ACQUIRE DATA?

Q4 WHAT ARE THREE TECHNIQUES FOR PROCESSING BI DATA?

Q5 WHAT ARE THE ALTERNATIVES FOR PUBLISHING BI?

How does the **knowledge** in this chapter help **you?**

"We can make the bits produce any report you want, but you've got to pay for it."

Maggie is curious to know where this is heading. "That's what you wanted, I think."

"Right. But, as they say, 'Be careful what you ask for.' Now that the program is up and running, we're spending too many hours each day looking at patient workouts."

"Hmmm," Maggie pauses, "so you'd like an exception report?"

"Not sure what that is."

"Pretty much like it sounds. With each workout profile, we store bounds of performance, could be percentage under and over. Then, each morning, we create a report for any patients whose workouts are out of bounds. We send you reports about the *exceptions* to those bounds."

"I like the sound of that. But do we have to wait until morning? I mean, for the slackers, we can wait till morning. But if someone is overdoing it, I'd really like to know right away." Flores nods again at the patient exam room.

"You want to know in real time? As it's happening?"

"Is that possible?"

"Sure. It's just bits. We can make the bits produce any report you want, but you've got to pay for it."

"Ah, there's always that."

"There's always that." Maggie says with a chuckle.

CE Optional Extensions for this chapter are • CE12 Database Marketing 518 • CE13 Reporting Systems and OLAP 528 • CE14 Geographic Information Systems (GIS) 540

HOW DO ORGANIZATIONS USE BUSINESS INTELLIGENCE (BI) SYSTEMS?

Business intelligence (BI) systems are information systems that process operational and other data to analyze past performance and to make predictions. The patterns, relationships, and trends identified by BI systems are called **business intelligence**. As information systems, BI systems have the five standard components: hardware, software, data, procedures, and people. The software component of a BI system is called a **BI application**.

In the context of their day-to-day operations, organizations generate enormous amounts of data. According to McKinsey & Company, as of 2009, companies with more than 1,000 employees in "nearly all sectors in the U.S. economy had at least an average of 200 terabytes of stored data."[1] Business intelligence is buried in that data, and the function of a BI system is to extract it and make it available to those who need it.

As shown in Figure 9-1, source data for a BI system can be the organization's own operational databases, it can be data that the organization purchases from data vendors, or it can be social data like that generated by social media IS. The BI application processes the data to produce business intelligence for use by knowledge workers. As you will learn, this definition encompasses reporting applications, data mining applications, and BigData applications.

As shown in Figure 9-2, business intelligence is used for all four of the collaborative tasks described in Chapter Extension 1. Starting with the last row of this figure, business intelligence is used just for informing. Medical staff can use PRIDE to learn how patients are using the new system. At the time of the analysis, the staff may not have any particular purpose in mind, but are just browsing the BI results for some future, unspecified purpose. At GearUp, the company we studied in Chapters 1-6, Kelly may just want to know how GearUp's current sales compare to the forecast; she may have no particular purpose in mind, she just wants to know "how we're doing."

Moving up a row in Figure 9-2, some managers use BI systems for decision making. At the start of this chapter, Flores is concerned that some patients may be exercising too much; he can use BI to determine if anyone is and, if so, who they are. Addison at GearUp may have an opportunity to purchase 10,000 soccer balls; she needs to use business intelligence to determine how many she thinks GearUp can sell prior to her negotiation with the vendor.

(By the way, some authors define BI systems as supporting decision making only, in which case they use the older term **decision support systems** as a synonym for decision-making BI

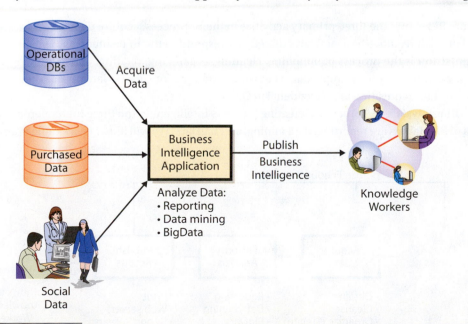

Figure 9-1
Structure of a Business Intelligence System

---

[1]"Big Data: The Next Frontier for Innovation, Competition, and Productivity," McKinsey & Company, May 2011. Available at www.mckinsey.com/mgi/publications/big_data/index.asp, accessed July 2012.

Figure 9-2
Example Uses of Business Intelligence

Task	PRIDE Example	GearUp Example
Project Management	Use PRIDE to reduce medical costs.	Create GearUp Europe.
Problem Solving	How can we get our patients to follow prescriptions better?	How can we reduce operational expenses?
Deciding	Which of our patients are exercising too much?	How many soccer balls can we sell?
Informing	In what ways are patients using the new system?	How do sales compare to our sales forecast?

systems. We take the broader view here to include all four of the tasks in Figure 9-2 and will avoid the term *decision support systems*.)

Problem solving is the next category of business intelligence use. Again, a problem is a perceived difference between what is and what ought to be. Business intelligence can be used for both sides of that definition: determining *what is* as well as *what should be*. Flores and his partner may want to use BI to solve the problem of getting patients to exercise more faithfully according to their plan, and Emily and GearUp staff can use it to find ways of reducing operational expenses.

Finally, business intelligence can be used during project management. PRIDE can be used to support a project to reduce medical costs by reducing office visits. When GearUp decides to open its European office, it can use business intelligence to determine which gear it should sell first and which vendors to contact to obtain that gear.

As you study this figure, recall the hierarchical nature of these tasks. Deciding requires informing; problem solving requires deciding (and informing); and project management requires problem solving (and deciding (and informing)).

Data mining and other business intelligence systems are useful, but they are not without problems, as discussed in the Guide on pages 244–245.

 WHAT ARE THE THREE PRIMARY ACTIVITIES IN THE BI PROCESS?

Figure 9-3 shows the three primary activities in the BI process: acquire data, perform analysis, and publish results. These activities directly correspond to the BI elements in Figure 9-1. **Data acquisition** is the process of obtaining, cleaning, organizing, relating, and cataloging source data. We will illustrate a simple data acquisition example for GearUp later in this question and discuss data acquisition in greater detail in Q3.

BI analysis is the process of creating business intelligence. The three fundamental categories of BI analysis are reporting, data mining, and BigData. We will illustrate a simple example of

Figure 9-3
Three Primary Activities in the BI Process

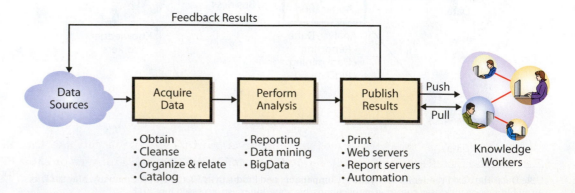

a reporting system for GearUp later in this question, and describe each of the three categories of BI analysis in greater detail in Q4.

Publish results is the process of delivering business intelligence to the knowledge workers who need it. **Push publishing** delivers business intelligence to users without any request from the users; the BI results are delivered according to a schedule or as a result of an event or particular data condition. **Pull publishing** requires the user to request BI results. Publishing media include print as well as online content delivered via Web servers, specialized Web servers known as *report servers*, and BI results that are sent via automation to other programs. We will discuss these publishing options further in Q5.

For now, to better understand the three phases of BI analysis, consider an example of a reporting analysis at GearUp.

USING BUSINESS INTELLIGENCE FOR PROBLEM SOLVING AT GEARUP

At the start of Chapter 5, personnel at GearUp were attempting to reduce operational expenses. Buyers and operations personnel believed that some vendors were causing GearUp lost sales and extra expense when they agreed to deliver more items than they had, resulting in GearUp having to cancel or reduce customer orders. In addition to that problem, some vendors seem to have more goods damaged in shipment than others. However, other than a general notion that some vendors were especially problematic or especially not-problematic, they didn't know how serious this problem was, nor did they know the particular pattern for each vendor. The following summarizes the process and potential problems:

1. GearUp obtains a commitment from a vendor for a maximum number of an item at a given price, say up to 10,000 soccer balls at $15 each.

2. GearUp runs a sales event for the item for which it has a commitment.

3. GearUp sells as many of the items as it can during the 3 days of each event, up to the promised amount (here 10,000).

4. At the end of the event, GearUp orders from the vendor the amount it actually sold (10,000 or fewer).

5. Normally, GearUp receives the number of items that it has ordered. However, some vendors fail to ship the full amount to which they committed or some items are damaged in shipment.

6. If GearUp receives fewer items than it orders, it attempts to ship partial orders. If, for example, a customer ordered 20 pairs of soccer shoes (common for soccer teams, for example), GearUp will call the customer and attempt to sell, say, 15 or some other reduced number. They will do this for enough orders to cover the quantity shortage.

7. Some customers, when told they will receive only some of what they ordered, cancel their entire order.

Addison, a buyer, and Drew, the operations manager, met with Lucas, the IT director, who agreed to provide data that Addison and Drew could analyze. In terms of Figure 9-3, Lucas agreed to acquire data by extracting it from GearUp's customer order and shipping databases as well as its accounts payable system and to deliver that extracted data to Addison in a Microsoft Access database.

ACQUIRE DATA

The top section of Figure 9-4 shows three of the tables in GearUp's operational database that Lucas used to produce the data extract. The *Order_Item* table contains records of items on customer orders. The columns are self-explanatory except for EventItemNumber, which is a number

To learn more about database marketing, see Chapter Extension 12.

Figure 9-4
Tables Used for BI Analysis
at GearUp

Source tables from operational database:

Order_Item (<u>InvoiceNumber, LineItemNumber,</u> EventItemNumber, QuantityOrdered)

Shipment_Item (<u>ShipmentID, EventItemNumber,</u> InvoiceNumber, QuantityShipped)

Item_Received (<u>PurchaseOrderNumber, DateReceived,</u> VendorID, EventItemNumber,
QuantityReceived, QuantityAccepted)

Lucas creates the following tables in an Access BI database:

Item_Shipped (<u>InvoiceNumber, EventItemNumber,</u> QuantityOrdered, QuantityShipped)

Item_Not_Shipped (<u>InvoiceNumber, EventItemNumber,</u> QuantityOrdered)

Quantity_Received (<u>VendorID, EventItemNumber,</u> TotalQuantityReceived,
TotalQuantityAccepted)

Also places the Order_Item in the BI database

Addison creates a new table in the Access BI database:

Item_Summary_Data (VendorID, EventItemNumber, TotalOrdered, TotalReceived,
TotalDamaged, TotalCancelled, NetSold)

Note: Underline indicates primary key.

that identifies an item from a particular vendor that is to be sold during a particular event. Thus, for example, EventItemNumber 10 identifies the purchase of soccer balls from San Diego Sports for the sales event starting July 14, 2013.

Shipment_Item is similar to *Order_Item*, but it contains records of the items that GearUp shipped to customers. If all promised items were delivered to GearUp with no damage, then the QuantityOrdered in *Order_Item* and the QuantityShipped in *Shipment_Item* will be equal.

The data in *Item_Received* is generated when vendor shipments are received at the GearUp loading dock. It shows the number of items received and the number that were accepted; the difference between the number received and the number accepted is the number that were damaged.

Lucas uses the data in these source tables to create the *Item_Shipped, Item_Not_ Shipped,* and *Quantity_Received* tables shown in the middle part of Figure 9-4. He placed those tables into the data extract database along with the *Order_Item* table.

When Addison received that database, she summed quantities from the tables that Lucas had given her to create the *Item_Summary_Data* table shown in the last part of Figure 9-4. We will not explain the SQL statements she used, but you should verify that the source data given is sufficient to be able to construct it. See Using Your Knowledge Questions 1 and 2, page 247.

ANALYZE DATA

Figure 9-5 shows sample data for the *Item_Summary_Data* table. The actual table contains more than 700 rows, but this sample will do for our purposes. TotalOrdered is the number that Gear-Up sold to its customers and, in turn, ordered from the vendor. TotalReceived is the number sent by the vendor, including damaged items. TotalDamaged is the number that were received in damaged condition. NetSold is the number of items that were actually shipped to the customers, taken from shipping records.

Item_Summary_Data

EventItemNumber	VendorID	TotalOrdered	TotalReceived	TotalDamaged	NetSold	TotalCancelled
100	1000	7500	7500	800	5200	1500
200	2000	11000	11000	0	11000	0
300	4000	10000	9000	100	8500	1400
400	1000	10500	10500	6500	3800	200
500	4000	7500	7500	400	6800	300
600	3000	27000	15000	0	9750	17250
700	2000	700	700	0	700	0
800	4000	12000	12000	0	12000	0
900	1000	6300	6300	0	6300	0
1000	2000	19800	19800	600	19800	-600
1100	3000	8000	6500	200	5800	2000
1200	4000	8000	7800	0	7800	200
1300	5000	14500	14500	0	14500	0
1400	1000	900	900	400	475	25
1500	4000	7500	7200	0	6800	700

Figure 9-5
Extract of the ITEM_SUMMARY_Data Table

To discriminate between orders lost to damage and those lost to cancellations, Gear-Up computes TotalCancelled, but it must do so indirectly. To illustrate, in the third row, GearUp knows from shipping records that 8,500 units were actually shipped to customers; so the net unit sales loss is 1,500 units (10,000 ordered – 8,500 shipped). Of those 1,500, GearUp operations knows that 100 items were damaged. So the net loss that can be attributed to shortage cancellations, whether requested by GearUp or demanded by customers, is 1,400.

To determine the extent of sales lost due to short shipments or damage, Addison created an Access report (Figure 9-6) to sum data from the *Item_Summary_Data* table. Sum-OfTotalOrdered is the number of items ordered from each vendor. SumOfNetSold is the total number of items actually shipped to customers for each vendor. SumOfLostSales is the difference between these two. From this report, she can see that vendors 5000 and 2000 have never had a shortage or quality problem. Vendor 4000 has a modest problem, but vendors 1000 and 3000 have caused numerous lost sales, either due to shortages or damaged goods. In fact, more than half of the sales of vendor 3000's items have been lost (19,450/35,000).

Drew wonders if these lost sales are due to one or two events or if they represent a recurring problem. To investigate, Addison creates the report shown in Figure 9-7. From this report, they can see that vendor 3000's problems, although substantial, are primarily due to one problem on EventItemNumber 600. However, vendor 4000 has a regular pattern of shortages or damage, or both. To learn which, Addison creates more reports, as you will see below.

Figure 9-6
Lost Sales Summary Report

Lost Sales Summary

VendorID	SumOfTotalOrdered	SumOfNetSold	SumOfLostSales
5000	14500	14500	0
2000	31500	31500	0
4000	45000	41900	3100
1000	25200	15775	9425
3000	35000	15550	19450

Figure 9-7
Lost Sales Detail Report

Lost Sales Detail

VendorID	EventItemNumber	TotalOrdered	NetSold	LostSales
1000				
	100	7500	5200	2300
	400	10500	3800	6700
	900	6300	6300	0
	1400	900	475	425
2000				
	200	11000	11000	0
	700	700	700	0
	1000	19800	19800	0
3000				
	600	27000	9750	17250
	1100	8000	5800	2200
4000				
	300	10000	8500	1500
	500	7500	6800	700
	800	12000	12000	0
	1200	8000	7800	200
	1500	7500	6800	700
5000				
	1300	14500	14500	0

But first, notice that these reports are difficult to interpret because they show vendor IDs and not vendor names. Also, Figure 9-7 shows items by EventItemNumber and not by item name and event date. Drew, as operations manager, keeps a Microsoft Excel spreadsheet that has event data, including vendor and item names. A sample of that spreadsheet is shown in Figure 9-8.

If Drew's spreadsheet were in tabular format, it would be easy to import this data from Excel to Access. However, it is not, and someone must go through this spreadsheet and either put it into tabular format or extract the data from the spreadsheet and manually enter it into the Access database. This situation is typical of the kinds of data conversion and integration activities that business intelligence requires. We will leave that problem for now, however, and turn to other issues.

Figure 9-8
Event Data Spreadsheet

	A	B	C	D	E	F	G
1							
2		**Event:**	**7/11/2013**	**Addison**			
3							
4			Items:				
5							
6			Soccer Balls	General Sports	$ 12.75	$ 27.00	100
7			Orange Cones	San Diego Sports	$ 17.00	$ 35.00	200
8			Coaching Manuals	Green Lake	$ 3.50	$ 7.00	300
9							
10		**Event:**	**7/12/2013**	**Julie**			
11							
12			Items:				
13							
14			Mountain Tent	General Sports	$112.00	$185.00	400
15			Camp Stove	Americana Sports	$ 37.50	$ 85.00	500

Figure 9-9
Short and Damaged
Shipments Summary

Short and Damaged Summary

VendorID	SumOfItemsShort	SumOfItemsDamaged
5000	0	0
2000	0	600
1000	0	7700
4000	1500	500
3000	13500	200

Drew wants to determine how many of the lost sales are due to short vendor shipments and how many are due to damage. To make that determination, Addison produces the report shown in Figure 9-9. As you can see, all of vendor 1000's problems are caused by damage; that vendor always shipped the appropriate number. This damage could have occurred as the result of catastrophe to a single shipment, or it might be a persistent damage problem. To check out that possibility, Addison prepares the report shown in Figure 9-10. From this report, they determine that vendor 1000 has persistent damage problems. Addison and other buyers can use this knowledge when negotiating with that vendor in the future.

However, if you're reading closely, you see a problem. According to the report in Figure 9-6, vendor 2000 has never had a shortage of any type. However, the report in Figure 9-9 shows that that same vendor, 2000, had 600 units rejected as damaged. Figure 9-10 shows that those damaged items occurred with EventItemNumber 1000.

Look back to the data extraction in Figure 9-5, and you will see the problem. In the row for EventItemNumber 1000 (sixth row from the bottom), the value of TotalCancelled was computed to be –600. This result, an error, occurred because the operational data showed that 19,800 units were ordered and 19,800 units were sold. However, the operational data also showed that

Figure 9-10
Short and Damaged
Shipments Details Report

Short and Damaged Details

VendorID	EventItemNumber	ItemsShort	ItemsDamaged
1000			
	100	0	800
	400	0	6500
	900	0	0
	1400	0	400
2000			
	200	0	0
	700	0	0
	1000	0	600
3000			
	600	12000	0
	1100	1500	200
4000			
	300	1000	100
	500	0	400
	800	0	0
	1200	200	0
	1500	300	0
5000			
	1300	0	0

600 units were damaged. Clearly, something is wrong, somewhere. It could be due to a keying mistake by someone on the receiving dock, it could be that the vendor subsequently shipped replacement items that were not charged and therefore did not appear in the accounts payable database that Lucas queried, or it could be due to some other reason.

Such a discrepancy is not unusual for BI analyses. When data are integrated from several or many different sources, the resulting collection is frequently inconsistent. The only safeguard against inaccurate analyses from such inconsistent data is for the analysts and knowledge workers to know that such inconsistencies are possible, to be on the lookout for them, and to apply a critical eye to BI results.

PUBLISH RESULTS

Addison, Drew, and Lucas would use a process similar to that just discussed to finish their analysis. They would likely add costs to the data they've already gathered and analyze it so as to produce an average cost per item for each vendor and other similar results. The particulars are not important here; just realize they would continue in a similar vein until they were finished.

At that point, according to the process summary in Figure 9-3, they would publish their results. Several possibilities exist:

- Print and distribute the results via email or a collaboration tool
- Publish via a Web server or SharePoint
- Publish on a BI server
- Automate the results via a Web service

We will discuss these alternatives in more detail in Q5. For now, just realize that GearUp would choose among these alternatives according to its needs. If the business intelligence is only created to provide guidance for buyers, Addison and Drew might be content just to print their results and email them to buyers or share them using a collaboration tool. As an alternative, they could also produce the report in HTML and place it on a Web server. As an extension to that option, they could use SharePoint to publish the results. Although we didn't discuss them in Chapter Extensions 1 or 2, SharePoint has extensive features and functions for BI reporting. Addison and Drew could integrate their analyses with these features and functions so that users could go to a SharePoint site for the latest data. Also, they could publish via a BI server, which is a Web server application that is specialized for publishing BI results. Finally, Lucas might assign a programmer in his department to create a Web service that would make it possible for other programs to obtain the BI results programmatically. Most likely, for their situation, they will print the results and email them or share them via a collaboration tool.

With this example in mind, we will now discuss each of the elements of Figure 9-3 in greater detail.

HOW DO ORGANIZATIONS USE DATA WAREHOUSES AND DATA MARTS TO ACQUIRE DATA?

Although it is possible to create basic reports and perform simple analyses from operational data, this course is not usually recommended. For reasons of security and control, IS professionals do not want business analysts like Addison processing operational data. If Addison makes an error, that error could cause a serious disruption in GearUp's operations. Also, operational data is structured for fast and reliable transaction processing. It is seldom structured in a way that readily supports BI analysis. Finally, BI analyses can require considerable processing; placing BI applications on operational servers can dramatically reduce system performance.

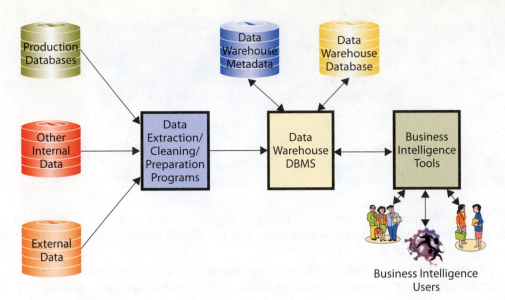

Figure 9-11
Components of a Data Warehouse

Business Intelligence Users

For these reasons, most organizations extract operational data for BI processing. For a small organization like GearUp, the extraction may be as simple as an Access database. Larger organizations, however, typically create and staff a group of people who manage and run a **data warehouse**, which is a facility for managing an organization's BI data. The functions of a data warehouse are to:

- Obtain data
- Cleanse data
- Organize and relate data
- Catalog data

Figure 9-11 shows the components of a data warehouse. Programs read production and other data and extract, clean, and prepare that data for BI processing. The prepared data are stored in a data warehouse database using a data warehouse DBMS, which can be different from the organization's operational DBMS. For example, an organization might use Oracle for its operational processing but use SQL Server for its data warehouse. Other organizations use SQL Server for operational processing but use DBMSs from statistical package vendors such as SAS or SPSS in the data warehouse.

Data warehouses include data that are purchased from outside sources. The purchase of data about other companies is not unusual or particularly concerning from a privacy standpoint. However, some companies, like GearUp, might choose to buy personal, consumer data (like marital status) from data vendors like Acxiom Corporation. Figure 9-12 lists some of the consumer data that can be readily purchased. An amazing (and from a privacy standpoint, frightening) amount of data is available.

Metadata concerning the data—its source, its format, its assumptions and constraints, and other facts about the data—is kept in a data warehouse metadata database. The data warehouse DBMS extracts and provides data to BI applications.

PROBLEMS WITH OPERATIONAL DATA

Most operational and purchased data have problems that inhibit their usefulness for business intelligence. Figure 9-13 lists the major problem categories. First, although data that are critical for successful operations must be complete and accurate, data that are only

Figure 9-12
Examples of Consumer Data
That Can Be Purchased

• Name, address, phone	• Magazine subscriptions
• Age	• Hobbies
• Gender	• Catalog orders
• Ethnicity	• Marital status, life stage
• Religion	• Height, weight, hair and
• Income	eye color
• Education	• Spouse's name, birth date
• Voter registration	• Children's names and
• Home ownership	birth dates
• Vehicles	

marginally necessary need not be. For example, some systems gather demographic data in the ordering process. But, because such data are not needed to fill, ship, and bill orders, their quality suffers.

Problematic data are termed dirty data. Examples are a value of B for customer gender and of 213 for customer age. Other examples are a value of 999–999–9999 for a U.S. phone number, a part color of "gren", and an email address of WhyMe@GuessWhoIAM.org. All of these values can be problematic for BI purposes.

Purchased data often contain missing elements. Most data vendors state the percentage of missing values for each attribute in the data they sell. An organization buys such data because for some uses, some data are better than no data at all. This is especially true for data items whose values are difficult to obtain, such as Number of Adults in Household, Household Income, Dwelling Type, and Education of Primary Income Earner. However, care is required here because for some BI applications, a few missing or erroneous data points can seriously bias the analysis.

Inconsistent data, the third problem in Figure 9-13, is particularly common for data that have been gathered over time. When an area code changes, for example, the phone number for a given customer before the change will not match the customer's number after the change. Likewise, part codes can change, as can sales territories. Before such data can be used, they must be recoded for consistency over the period of the study.

Some data inconsistencies occur from the nature of the business activity. Consider a Web-based order-entry system used by customers worldwide. When the Web server records the time of order, which time zone does it use? The server's system clock time is irrelevant to an analysis of customer behavior. Coordinated Universal Time (formerly called Greenwich Mean Time) is also meaningless. Somehow, Web server time must be adjusted to the time zone of the customer.

Another problem is nonintegrated data. A particular BI analysis might require data from an ERP system, an e-commerce system, and a social networking application. Analysts may wish to integrate that organizational data with purchased consumer data. Such a data collection will likely have relationships that are not represented in primary key/foreign key relationships. It is the function of personnel in the data warehouse to integrate such data, somehow.

Data can also have the wrong **granularity**, a term that refers to the level of detail represented by the data. Granularity can be too fine or too coarse. For the former, suppose we want to analyze the placement of graphics and controls on an order-entry Web page. It is possible to capture the customers' clicking behavior in what is termed *clickstream data*. Those data, however,

Figure 9-13
Possible Problems with
Source Data

• Dirty data	• Wrong granularity
• Missing values	– Too fine
• Inconsistent data	– Not fine enough
• Data not integrated	• Too much data
	– Too many attributes
	– Too many data points

include everything the customer does at the Web site. In the middle of the order stream are data for clicks on the news, email, instant chat, and a weather check. Although all of that data may be useful for a study of consumer browsing behavior, it will be overwhelming if all we want to know is how customers respond to an ad located differently on the screen. To proceed, the data analysts must throw away millions and millions of clicks.

Data can also be too coarse. For example, a file of regional sales totals cannot be used to investigate the sales in a particular store in a region, and total sales for a store cannot be used to determine the sales of particular items within a store. Instead, we need to obtain data that is fine enough for the lowest-level report we want to produce.

In general, it is better to have too fine a granularity than too coarse. If the granularity is too fine, the data can be made coarser by summing and combining. Only analysts' labor and computer processing are required. If the granularity is too coarse, however, there is no way to separate the data into constituent parts.

The final problem listed in Figure 9-13 is to have too much data. As shown in the figure, we can have either too many attributes or too many data points. Think back to the discussion of tables in Chapter 5. We can have too many columns or too many rows.

Consider the first problem: too many attributes. Suppose we want to know the factors that influence how customers respond to a promotion. If we combine internal customer data with purchased customer data, we will have more than a hundred different attributes to consider. How do we select among them? Because of a phenomenon called the *curse of dimensionality*, the more attributes there are, the easier it is to build a model that fits the sample data, but that is worthless as a predictor. There are other good reasons for reducing the number of attributes, and one of the major activities in data mining concerns efficient and effective ways of selecting attributes.

The second way to have too much data is to have too many data points—too many rows of data. Suppose we want to analyze clickstream data on CNN.com. How many clicks does that site receive per month? Millions upon millions! In order to meaningfully analyze such data, we need to reduce the amount of data. One good solution to this problem is statistical sampling. Organizations should not be reluctant to sample data in such situations.

DATA WAREHOUSES VERSUS DATA MARTS

A **data mart** is a data collection, smaller than the data warehouse, that addresses the needs of a particular department or functional area of the business. To understand the difference between data warehouses and data marts, think of a data warehouse as a distributor in a supply chain. The data warehouse takes data from the data manufacturers (operational systems and purchased data), cleans and processes the data, and locates the data on the shelves, so to speak, of the data warehouse. The people who work with a data warehouse are experts at data management, data cleaning, data transformation, data relationships and the like. However, they are not usually experts in a given business function.

If the data warehouse is the distributor in a supply chain, then a data mart is like a retail store in a supply chain. Users in the data mart obtain data that pertain to a particular business function from the data warehouse. Such users do not have the data management expertise that data warehouse employees have, but they are knowledgeable analysts for a given business function.

Figure 9-14 illustrates these relationships. The data warehouse takes data from the data producers and distributes the data to three data marts. One data mart is used to analyze clickstream data for the purpose of designing Web pages. A second analyzes store sales data and determines which products tend to be purchased together. This information is used to train salespeople on the best way to up-sell to customers. The third data mart is used to analyze customer order data for the purpose of reducing labor for item picking from the warehouse. A company like Amazon.com, for example, goes to great lengths to organize its warehouses to reduce picking expenses.

As you can imagine, it is expensive to create, staff, and operate data warehouses and data marts. Only large organizations with deep pockets can afford to operate a system like that shown

Figure 9-14
Data Mart Examples

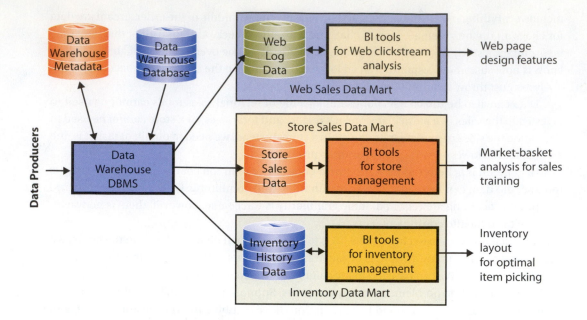

in Figure 9-11. Smaller organizations like GearUp operate subsets of this system, but they must find ways to solve the basic problems that data warehouses solve, even if those ways are informal.

WHAT ARE THREE TECHNIQUES FOR PROCESSING BI DATA?

Figure 9-15 summarizes the goals and characteristics of three fundamental types of BI analysis. In general, reporting analyses are used to create information about past performance, whereas data mining is used primarily for classifying and predicting. There are exceptions, but these statements are reasonable rules of thumb. The goal of BigData analysis is to find patterns and relationships in the enormous amounts of data generated from sources like social media sites or Web server logs. As indicated, BigData data techniques can include reporting and data mining as well. Consider the characteristics of each type.

REPORTING ANALYSIS

Reporting analysis is the process of sorting, grouping, summing, filtering and formatting structured data. **Structured data** is data in the form of rows and columns. Most of the time structured data means tables in a relational database, but it can refer to spreadsheet data as well.

Figure 9-15
Three Types of BI Analysis

BI Analysis Type	Goal	Characteristics
Reporting	Create information about past performance.	Process structured data by sorting, grouping, summing, filtering, and formatting.
Data mining	Classify and predict.	Use sophisticated statistical techniques to find patterns and relationships.
BigData	Find patterns and relationships in BigData.	Volume, velocity, and variety force use of MapReduce techniques. Some applications use reporting and data mining as well.

The GearUp analysis you read in Q2 is an example of a reporting analysis. As Maggie implies at the start of this chapter, **exception reports** are reports produced when something out of predefined bounds occurs. A report that is produced when the Dow Jones falls below a certain level is an exception report.

In the past, reports were printed and therefore needed to be static. With the increasing use of mobile systems, however, many reports, like the exercise progress report on Maggie's smartphone, can be dynamic.

DATA MINING ANALYSIS

Data mining is the application of statistical techniques to find patterns and relationships among data for classification and prediction. Data mining techniques emerged from the combined discipline of statistics, mathematics, artificial intelligence and machine-learning.

To learn more about Reporting Systems and OLAP, see Chapter Extension 13.

Most data mining techniques are sophisticated, and many are difficult to use well. Such techniques are valuable to organizations, however, and some business professionals, especially those in finance and marketing, have become expert in their use. Today, in fact, there are many interesting and rewarding careers for business professionals who are knowledgeable about data mining techniques.

Data mining techniques fall into two broad categories: unsupervised and supervised. We explain both types in the following sections.

UNSUPERVISED DATA MINING

With **unsupervised data mining**, analysts do not create a model or hypothesis before running the analysis. Instead, they apply the data mining technique to the data and observe the results. With this method, analysts create hypotheses after the analysis to explain the patterns found.

One common unsupervised technique is **cluster analysis**. With it, statistical techniques identify groups of entities that have similar characteristics. A common use for cluster analysis is to find groups of similar customers from customer order and demographic data.

For example, suppose a cluster analysis finds two very different customer groups: One group has an average age of 33; owns at least one laptop, at least one cell phone, and one iPad; drives an expensive SUV; and tends to buy expensive children's play equipment. The second group has an average age of 64, owns vacation property, plays golf, and buys expensive wines. Suppose the analysis also finds that both groups buy designer children's clothing.

These findings are obtained solely by data analysis. There is no prior model about the patterns and relationship that exist. It is up to the analyst to form hypotheses, after the fact, to explain why two such different groups are both buying designer children's clothes.

SUPERVISED DATA MINING

With **supervised data mining**, data miners develop a model prior to the analysis and apply statistical techniques to data to estimate parameters of the model. For example, suppose marketing experts in a communications company believe that cell phone usage on weekends is determined by the age of the customer and the number of months the customer has had the cell phone account. A data mining analyst would then run an analysis that estimates the impact of customer and account age. One such analysis, which measures the impact of a set of variables on another variable, is called a **regression analysis**. A sample result for the cell phone example is:

$$CellPhoneWeekendMinutes = 12 + (17.5 \times CustomerAge)$$
$$+ (23.7 \times NumberMonthsOfAccount)$$

Using this equation, analysts can predict the number of minutes of weekend cell phone use by summing 12, plus 17.5 times the customer's age, plus 23.7 times the number of months of the account.

As you will learn in your statistics classes, considerable skill is required to interpret the quality of such a model. The regression tool will create an equation, such as the one shown. Whether that equation is a good predictor of future cell phone usage depends on statistical factors such as *t* values, confidence intervals, and related statistical techniques.

BIGDATA

BigData (also spelled Big Data) is a term used to describe data collections that are characterized by huge *volume*, rapid *velocity*, and great *variety*. Considering volume, BigData refers to data sets that are at least a petabyte in size, and usually larger. A data set containing all Google searches in the United States on a given day is BigData in size. Additionally, BigData has high velocity, meaning that it is generated rapidly. (If you know physics, you know that *speed* would be a more accurate term, but speed doesn't start with a *v*, and the *vvv* description has become a common way to describe BigData.) The Google search data for a given day is generated, in, well, just a day. In the past, months or years would have been required to generate so much data.

Finally, BigData is varied. BigData may have structured data, but it also may have free-form text, dozens of different formats of Web server and database log files, streams of data about user responses to page content, and possibly graphics, audio, and video files.

MAPREDUCE

Because BigData is huge, fast, and varied, it cannot be processed using traditional techniques. **MapReduce** is a technique for harnessing the power of thousands of computers working in parallel. The basic idea is that the BigData collection is broken into pieces, and hundreds or thousands of independent processors search these pieces for something of interest. That process is referred to as the *Map* phase. In Figure 9-16, for example, a data set having the logs of Google searches is broken into pieces, and each independent processor is instructed to search for and count search keywords. This figure, of course, shows just a small portion of the data; here, you can see a portion of the keywords that begin with *H*.

As the processors finish, their results are combined in what is referred to as the *Reduce* phase. The result is a list of all the terms searched for on a given day and the count of each. The process is considerably more complex than described here, but this is the gist of the idea.

By the way, you can visit Google Trends to see an application of MapReduce. There you can obtain a trend line of the number of searches for a particular term or terms. Figure 9-17 shows the search trend for the term *Web 2.0*. The vertical axis is scaled; a value of 1.0 represents the average number of searches over that time period. This particular trend line, by the way, supports the contention that the term *Web 2.0* is fading from use. Go to *www.Google.com/trends* and enter the terms Big Data, BigData, and Hadoop to see why it's a better use of your time to be learning about them!

HADOOP

Hadoop is an open-source program supported by the Apache Foundation[2] that manages thousands of computers and which implements MapReduce. Hadoop could drive the process of finding and counting the Google search terms, but Google uses its own proprietary version of MapReduce to do so, instead.

---

[2]A nonprofit corporation that supports open-source software projects, originally those for the Apache Web server, but today for a large number of additional major software projects.

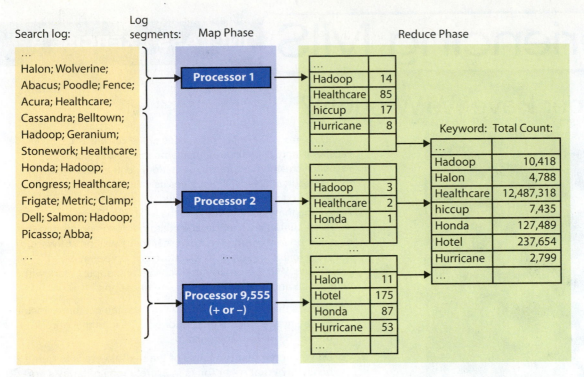

Figure 9-16
MapReduce Processing Summary

Hadoop began as part of Cassandra, but the Apache Foundation split it off to become its own product. Hadoop is written in Java and originally ran on Linux; at this writing, Microsoft is reported to be implementing it on Windows Server as well. Some companies implement Hadoop on server farms they manage themselves, and others run Hadoop in the cloud. Amazon.com supports Hadoop as part of its EC3 cloud offering. Hadoop includes a query language entitled **Pig.**

At present, deep technical skills are needed to run and use Hadoop. Judging by the development of other technologies over the years, it is likely that higher-level, easier-to-use products will be implemented on top of Hadoop. For now, understand that expert programmers are required to use it; you may be involved, however, in planning a BigData study or in interpreting results.

BigData analysis can involve both reporting and data mining techniques. The chief difference is, however, that BigData has volume, velocity, and variation characteristics that far exceed those of traditional reporting and data mining.

Whether an analysis is performed with reporting, data mining, or BigData techniques, the results provide no value until they are delivered to the appropriate users. We turn to that topic next.

Data mining in the workplace can lead to challenging situations. Read the Ethics guide on 242–243 for examples.

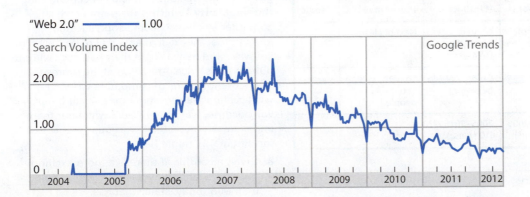

Figure 9-17
Google Trends on the Term Web 2.0

Source: Google Trends™ © 2012 Google

Experiencing MIS

What Wonder Have We Wrought?

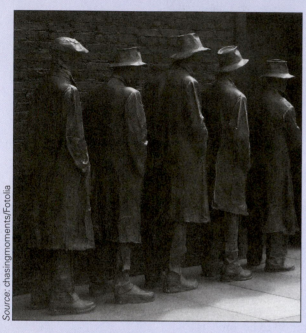

Source: chasingmoments/Fotolia

On May 18, 2012, Facebook went public at a valuation of $104 billion. Many investors found the evaluation unrealistic for an 8-year-old company that was yet to prove it could consistently earn revenue and make product. Still, with 900 million visits in March 2012, Facebook was hard to ignore.

What's next? What's the Next_Big_Thing? If you knew, you could identify the next Facebook or Google for investment or employment or perhaps start it yourself. Of course, no one knows for certain, but let's apply knowledge you already have as a guide.

Figure 1 casts the history of the computer industry into the frame of the five components of an information system. IBM led the hardware era; hardware customers focused on writing their own software to accomplish some function, payroll and other accounting functions were common. Next came the software era that Microsoft led with Windows, but companies like Oracle and SAP contributed by making software licensing a reality. The focus of software customers is to create data.

Data, really BigData, is the focus of the current era. Google, Facebook, and LinkedIn are data companies. As evidence, Facebook created Cassandra and Hadoop, and gave them away to open-source. Clearly, it perceives its value as data and not software. And, what will be the focus of BigData customers? Answering that question is key to the Next_Big_Thing.

Note that at each stage, the customer focus pointed to the next component. Hardware customer focus was on software. Software focus was on data. Data focus is on behavior, or procedures. Will the procedure focus be on people? Work with your group and answer the following questions:

1. Discuss the meaning of "At each stage, the customer focus has pointed at the next component." Restate this phrase in the words of your own group.

2. Do you agree that the focus of the BigData era is to guide behavior? What other focus interpretations of today's era are possible?

3. Assume the next era computer industry will concern procedures and that the focus will be on people. One possible focus is to Eliminate Jobs. If that is the focus, what does it mean for business? For the economy? For you? Discuss your answers among your group and report your conclusions to the rest of the class.

4. Rather than Eliminate Jobs, another possible focus of the procedural component is to Enhance Human Life. Discuss ways in which that might happen. If it does, what opportunities will it create for you? Discuss your answers among your group and report your conclusions to the rest of the class.

5. Working with your group, identify two or three other procedural focus statements other than Eliminate Jobs or Enhance Human Life.

6. Of all the focus statements you've considered, choose the one you think is most likely. Explain your choice. Using that statement, describe three business opportunities that could lead to the Next_Big_Thing.

7. One important question is what happens after the People-component-era? Where does the arrow on the far right go? Ray Kurzweil developed a concept he calls **the singularity**,[3] which is the point at which computer systems become sophisticated enough that they can adapt and create their own software and hence adapt their behavior without human assistance. At that point, he claims that farms of thousands of computers working 24/7 will accelerate away from humanity and humans will become, well, what? Work with your team and state what you think the consequences of the singularity might be.

8. Given all of this, if there is a more exciting, important, and potentially rewarding field than MIS today, state what it is.

	Hardware	Software	(Big)Data	Procedures	People
Leaders	IBM	Microsoft Oracle SAP	Google Facebook LinkedIn	Next big leader	
Customer focus	Write software →	Create data →	Guide behavior →	Something about people ???? →	?
Era	1955–1985 (30 years)	1985–2005 (20 years)	2005–2015 ??? (10 years?)		

Figure 1
Trends in the Computing Industry

3www.Singularity.com

WHAT ARE THE ALTERNATIVES FOR PUBLISHING BI?

For BI results to have value, they must be published to the right user at the right time. In this question, we will discuss the primary publishing alternatives and discuss the functionality of BI servers, a special type of Web server.

CHARACTERISTICS OF BI PUBLISHING ALTERNATIVES

Figure 9-18 lists four server alternatives for BI publishing. **Static reports** are BI documents that are fixed at the time of creation and do not change. A printed sales analysis is an example of a static report. In the BI context, most static reports are published as PDF documents.

Dynamic reports are BI documents that are updated at the time they are requested. A sales report that is current as of the time the user accessed it on a Web server is a dynamic report. In almost all cases, publishing a dynamic report requires the BI application to access a database or other data source at the time the report is delivered to the user.

Pull options for each of the servers in Figure 9-18 are the same. The user goes to the site, clicks a link (or opens an email), and obtains the report. Because they're the same for all four server types, they are not shown in Figure 9-18.

Push options vary by server type. For email or collaboration tools, push is manual; someone, say a manager, an expert, or an administrator, creates an email with the report as an attachment (or URL to the collaboration tool) and sends it to the users known to be interested in that report. For Web servers and SharePoint, users can create alerts and RSS feeds to have the server push content to them when the content is created or changed, with the expiration of a given amount of time, or at particular intervals. SharePoint workflows can also push content.

A BI server extends alert/RSS functionality to support user **subscriptions**, which are user requests for particular BI results on a particular schedule or in response to particular events. For example, a user can subscribe to a daily sales report, requesting that it be delivered each morning. Or, the user might request that analyses be delivered whenever a new result is posted on the server, or, like Dr. Flores, subscribe to an exception report that is generated whenever a patient exceeds his or her exercise prescription.

The skills needed to create a publishing application are either low or high. For static content, little skill is needed. The BI author creates the content, and the publisher (usually the same person) attaches it to an email or puts it on the Web or a SharePoint site, and that's it. Publishing dynamic BI is more difficult; it requires the publisher to set up database access when documents are consumed. In the case of a Web server, the publisher will need to develop or have

Server	Report Type	Push Options	Skill Level Needed
Email or collaboration tool	Static	Manual	Low
Web server	Static Dynamic	Alert/RSS	Low for static High for dynamic
SharePoint	Static Dynamic	Alert/RSS	Low for static High for dynamic
BI server	Dynamic	Alert/RSS Subscription	High

Figure 9-18
BI Publishing Alternatives

a programmer write code for this purpose. In the case of SharePoint and BI servers, program code is not necessarily needed, but dynamic data connections need to be created, and this task is not for the technically faint of heart. You'll need knowledge beyond the scope of this class to develop dynamic BI solutions. You should be able to do this, however, if you take a few more IS courses or major in IS.

WHAT ARE THE TWO FUNCTIONS OF A BI SERVER?

A **BI server** is a Web server application that is purpose-built for the publishing of business intelligence. The Microsoft SQL Server Report manager (part of Microsoft SQL Server Reporting Services) is the most popular such product today, but there are other products as well.

BI servers provide two major functions: management and delivery. The management function maintains metadata about the authorized allocation of BI results to users. The BI server tracks what results are available, what users are authorized to view those results, and the schedule upon which the results are provided to the authorized users. It adjusts allocations as available results change and users come and go.

As shown in Figure 9-19, all management data needed by any of the BI servers is stored in metadata. The amount and complexity of such data depends, of course, on the functionality of the BI server.

BI servers use metadata to determine what results to send to which users and, possibly, on which schedule. Today, the expectation is that BI results can be delivered to "any" device. In practice, *any* is interpreted to mean computers, mobile devices, applications such as Microsoft Office, and cloud services.

Figure 9-19
Components of a Generic
Business Intelligence System

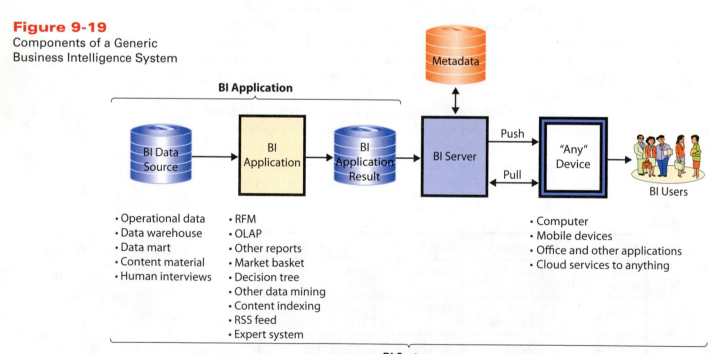

How does the knowledge in this chapter help you?

As a future business professional, business intelligence is a critical skill. According to Jim Goodnight, founder of SAS:

> If you want to be successful in business, make sure you have some understanding of analytics and when to use them. People who can use analytics—such as data mining and forecasting—to turn raw data into better business decisions have never been in greater demand. With all the talk of "Big Data," organizations across industries need people who understand how to use analytics to make sense of it all. I encourage this year's graduates to learn about how and when analytics can support their decisions.[4]

From this chapter, you know the three phases of BI analysis, and you have learned common techniques for acquiring, processing, and publishing business intelligence. This knowledge will enable you to imagine innovative uses for data that your employer generates and also to know some of the constraints of such use. At PRIDE, the knowledge of this chapter will help you understand possible uses for the exercise data that is being generated. If PRIDE becomes a successful product, with millions of users, you know that BigData techniques can be used to analyze minute-by-minute exercise data. Finding a valuable use of such BI, however, will be up to you!

To learn about an additional way technology is being used in health care, see Chapter Extension 14, Geographic Information Systems (GIS).

---

[4]http://lifeinc.today.msnbc.msn.com/_news/2012/06/05/12008767-ceo-advice-for-grads-travel-learn-follow-your-passion?lite, accessed June 18, 2012.

Ethics Guide

Data Mining in the Real World

"I'm not really against data mining. I believe in it. After all, it's my career. But data mining in the real world is a lot different from the way it's described in textbooks.

"There are many reasons it's different. One is that the data are always dirty, with missing values, values way out of the range of possibility, and time values that make no sense. Here's an example: Somebody sets the server system clock incorrectly and runs the server for a while with the wrong time. When they notice the mistake, they set the clock to the correct time. But all of the transactions that were running during that interval have an ending time before the starting time. When we run the data analysis, and compute elapsed time, the results are negative for those transactions.

"Missing values are a similar problem. Consider the records of just 10 purchases. Suppose that two of the records are missing the customer number and one is missing the year part of transaction date. So you throw out three records, which is 30 percent of the data. You then notice that two more records have dirty data, and so you throw them out, too. Now you've lost half your data.

"Another problem is that you know the least when you start the study. So you work for a few months and learn that if you had another variable, say the customer's zip code, or age, or something else, you could do a much better analysis. But those other data just aren't available. Or, maybe they are available, but to get the data you have to reprocess millions of transactions, and you don't have the time or budget to do that.

"Overfitting is another problem, a huge one. I can build a model to fit any set of data you have. Give me 100 data points and in a few minutes, I can give you 100 different equations that will predict those 100 data points. With some techniques, you can create a model of any level of complexity you want, except that none of those 100 equations will predict new cases with any accuracy at all. When using some techniques, you have to be very careful not to overfit the data.

"Then, too, data mining is about probabilities, not certainty. Bad luck happens. Say I build a model that predicts the probability that a customer will make a purchase. Using the model on new-customer data, I find three customers who have a .7 probability of buying something. That's a good number, well over a 50–50 chance, but it's still possible that none of them will buy. In fact, the probability that none of them will buy is $.3 \times .3 \times .3$, or .027, which is 2.7 percent.

"Now suppose I give the names of the three customers to a salesperson who calls on them, and sure enough, we have a stream of bad luck and none of them buys. This bad result doesn't mean the model is wrong. But what does the salesperson think? He thinks the model is worthless and can do better on his own. What should he do? What is the ethical course of action? He tells his manager who tells her associate, who tells the entire Northeast Region, and sure enough, the model has a bad reputation all across the company.

"Another problem is seasonality. Say all your training data are from the summer. Will your model be valid for the winter? Maybe, but maybe not. You might even know that it won't be valid for predicting winter sales, but if you don't have winter data, what do you do?

"When you start a data mining project, you never know how it will turn out. I worked on one project for 6 months, and when we finished, I didn't think our model was any good. We had too many problems with data: wrong, dirty, and missing. There was no way we could know ahead of time that it would happen, but it did.

"When the time came to present the results to senior management, what could we do? How could we say we took 6 months of our time and substantial computer resources to create a bad model? We had a model, but I just didn't think it would make accurate predictions. I was a junior member of the team, and it wasn't for me to decide. I kept my mouth shut, but I never felt good about it.

"However, I'm only talking about my bad experiences. Some of my projects have been excellent. On many, we found interesting and important patterns and information, and a few times I've created very accurate predictive models. It's not easy, though, and you have to be very careful. Also, lucky!"

DISCUSSION QUESTIONS

1. Summarize the concerns expressed by this data miner.

2. Do you think the concerns raised here are sufficient to avoid data mining projects altogether? Why or why not?

3. If this employee had serious misgivings about the team's results, was it unethical for him to do nothing?

4. Suppose he raised his objections with his boss, and she told him to bury his objections and get on with work. Is it ethical for him to do so? Is it ethical for his boss to do so?

5. If you were a junior member of a data mining team and you thought that the model that had been developed was ineffective, maybe even wrong, what

would you do? If your boss disagrees with your beliefs, would you go higher in the organization? What are the risks of doing so? What else might you do?

6. Suppose you were his boss. How would you respond to his concerns? What would you do?

7. Do your answers to questions 5 and 6 depend on whether this application was predicting car purchases or predicting heart attacks? If so, how do they change? Either way, justify your opinion.

Guide
Semantic Security

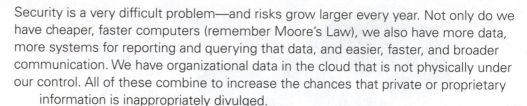

Security is a very difficult problem—and risks grow larger every year. Not only do we have cheaper, faster computers (remember Moore's Law), we also have more data, more systems for reporting and querying that data, and easier, faster, and broader communication. We have organizational data in the cloud that is not physically under our control. All of these combine to increase the chances that private or proprietary information is inappropriately divulged.

Access security is hard enough: How do we know that the person (or program) who signs on as Megan Cho really is Megan Cho? We use passwords, but files of passwords can be stolen. Setting that issue aside, we need to know that Megan Cho's permissions are set appropriately. Suppose Megan works in the HR department, so she has access to personal and private data of other employees. We need to design the reporting system so that Megan can access all of the data she needs to do her job, and no more.

Also, the delivery system must be secure. A BI server is an obvious and juicy target for any would-be intruder. Someone can break in and change access permissions. Or, a hacker could pose as someone else to obtain reports. Application servers help the authorized user, resulting in faster access to more information. But, without proper security reporting, servers also ease the intrusion task for unauthorized users.

All of these issues relate to access security. Another dimension to security is equally serious and far more problematic: **semantic security**. Semantic security concerns the unintended release of protected information through the release of a combination of reports or documents that are independently not protected. The term data triangulation is also used for this same phenomenon.

Take an example from class. Suppose I assign a group project, and I post a list of groups and the names of students assigned to each group. Later, after the assignments have been completed and graded, I post a list of grades on the Web site. Because of university privacy policy, I cannot post the grades by student name or identifier; so instead, I post the grades for each group. If you want to get the grades for each student, all you have to do is combine the list from Lecture 5 with the list from Lecture 10. You might say that the release of grades in this example does no real harm—after all, it is a list of grades from one assignment.

But go back to Megan Cho in HR. Suppose Megan evaluates the employee compensation program. The COO believes salary offers have been inconsistent over time and that they vary too widely by department. Accordingly, the COO authorizes Megan to receive a report that lists *SalaryOfferAmount* and *OfferDate* and a second report that lists *Department* and *AverageSalary*.

Those reports are relevant to her task and seem innocuous enough. But Megan realizes that she could use the information they contain to determine individual salaries—information she does not have and is not authorized to receive. She proceeds as follows.

Like all employees, Megan has access to the employee directory on the Web portal. Using the directory, she can obtain a list of employees in each department,

244

and using the facilities of her ever-so-helpful report-authoring system she combines that list with the department and average-salary report. Now she has a list of the names of employees in a group and the average salary for that group.

Megan's employer likes to welcome new employees to the company. Accordingly, each week the company publishes an article about new employees who have been hired. The article makes pleasant comments about each person and encourages employees to meet and greet them.

Megan, however, has other ideas. Because the report is published on SharePoint, she can obtain an electronic copy of it. It's an Acrobat report, and using Acrobat's handy Search feature, she soon has a list of employees and the week they were hired.

She now examines the report she received for her study, the one that has *SalaryOfferAmount* and the offer date, and she does some interpretation. During the week of July 21, three offers were extended: one for $35,000, one for $53,000, and one for $110,000. She also notices from the "New Employees" report that a director of marketing programs, a product test engineer, and a receptionist were hired that same week. It's unlikely that they paid the receptionist $110,000; that sounds more like the director of marketing programs. So, she now "knows" (infers) that person's salary.

Next, going back to the department report and using the employee directory, she sees that the marketing director is in the marketing programs department. There are just three people in that department, and their average salary is $105,000. Doing the arithmetic, she now knows that the average salary for the other two people is $102,500. If she can find the hire week for one of those other two people, she can find out both the second and third person's salaries.

You get the idea. Megan was given just two reports to do her job. Yet, she combined the information in those reports with publicly available information and was able to deduce salaries, for at least some employees. These salaries are much more than she is supposed to know. This is a semantic security problem.

SALARY INFORMATION

DISCUSSION QUESTIONS

1. In your own words, explain the difference between access security and semantic security.

2. Why do reporting systems increase the risk of semantic security problems?

3. What can an organization do to protect itself against accidental losses due to semantic security problems?

4. What legal responsibility does an organization have to protect against semantic security problems?

5. Suppose semantic security problems are inevitable. Do you see an opportunity for new products from insurance companies? If so, describe such an insurance product. If not, explain why not.

Source: 3D folder, Steve Young/Fotolia; generic report, Pete Linforth/Fotolia; document file, kitkana/Fotolia; hand/funnel, viviamo/Shutterstock

ACTIVE REVIEW

Use this Active Review to verify that you understand the ideas and concepts that answer the chapter's study questions.

Q1 HOW DO ORGANIZATIONS USE BUSINESS INTELLIGENCE (BI) SYSTEMS?

Define *business intelligence* and *BI system*. Explain the elements in Figure 9-1. Give an example, other than in this text, of one way that an organization could use business intelligence for each of the four collaborative tasks in Figure 9-2.

Q2 WHAT ARE THE THREE PRIMARY ACTIVITIES IN THE BI PROCESS?

Name and describe the three primary activities in the BI process. Summarize how Addison and Drew used these activities to produce BI results for GearUp.

Q3 HOW DO ORGANIZATIONS USE DATA WAREHOUSES AND DATA MARTS TO ACQUIRE DATA?

Describe the need and functions of data warehouses and data marts. Name and describe the role of data warehouse components. List and explain the problems that can exist in data used for data mining and sophisticated reporting. Use the example of a supply chain to describe the differences between a data warehouse and a data mart.

Q4 WHAT ARE THREE TECHNIQUES FOR PROCESSING BI DATA?

Name and describe the three techniques. State the goals and characteristics of each. Summarize reporting analysis. Define structured data. Summarize data mining. Explain the difference between supervised and unsupervised data mining. Differentiate between reporting analysis and data mining. Name and explain the three v's of BigData. Describe how MapReduce works and explain the purpose of Hadoop.

Q5 WHAT ARE THE ALTERNATIVES FOR PUBLISHING BI?

Name four alternative types of server used for publishing business intelligence. Explain the difference between static and dynamic reports; explain the term *subscription*. Describe why dynamic reports are difficult to create.

How does the knowledge in this chapter help you?

Summarize the knowledge you learned in this chapter and explain how you might use it as a future business professional. Explain how your knowledge would benefit the PRIDE project and describe one use of BigData and PRIDE.

KEY TERMS AND CONCEPTS

USING YOUR KNOWLEDGE

1. Using words, not SQL, explain the logic of the steps that Lucas must have taken to use the tables in the top part of Figure 9-4 to create the tables in the center part of the figure. Verify that all necessary data are present. Make and justify assumptions, if required.

2. Using words, not SQL, explain the logic of the steps that Addison must have taken to use the tables in the middle part of Figure 9-4 to create the *Item_ Summary_Data* table. Verify that all necessary data are present. Make and justify assumptions, if required.

3. Reflect on the differences between reporting systems and data mining systems. What are their similarities and differences? How do their costs differ? What benefits does each offer? How would an organization choose between these two BI tools?

4. Suppose you are a member of the Audubon Society, and the board of the local chapter asks you to help them analyze its member data. The group wants to analyze the demographics of its membership against members' activity, including events attended, classes attended, volunteer activities, and donations. Describe two different reporting applications and one data mining application that they might develop. Be sure to include a specific description of the goals of each system.

5. Suppose you are the director of student activities at your university. Recently, some students have charged that your department misallocates its resources. They claim the allocation is based on outdated student preferences. Funds are given to activities that few students find attractive, and insufficient funds are allocated to new activities in which students do want to participate. Describe how you could use reporting and/or data mining systems to assess this claim.

6. Describe the characteristics of BigData. Describe three student-related applications at your university that meet BigData characteristics. Describe patterns and relationships that might be found within that data.

COLLABORATION EXERCISE 9

Before you start this exercise, read Chapter Extensions 1 and 2, which describe collaboration techniques as well as tools for managing collaboration tasks. In particular, consider using Google Drive, Windows Live SkyDrive, Microsoft SharePoint, or some other collaboration tool.

Collaborate with a group of fellow students to answer the following questions. For this exercise do not meet face to face. Coordinate all of your work using email and email attachements, only. Your answers should reflect the thinking of the entire group, and not just one or two individuals. Read Case 9 (page 248) if you have not already done so.

Undeniably, third-party cookies offer advantages to online sellers. They also increase the likelihood that consumers will receive online ads that are close to their interests; thus third-party cookies can provide a consumer service as well. But, at what cost to personal privacy? And what should be done about them? Working with your team, answer the following questions:

1. Summarize the ways that third-party cookies are created and processed. Even though cookies are not supposed to contain personally identifying data, explain how such data can readily be obtained. (See Question 4, page 250.)

2. Numerous browser features, add-ins, and other tools exist for blocking third-party cookies. Search the Web for *block third-party cookies for xxx,* and fill in the *xxx* with the name and version of your browser. Read the instructions and summarize the procedures that you need to take to view the cookies issued from a given site.

3. In large measure, ads pay for the free use of Web content and even Web sites themselves. If, because of a fear of privacy, many people block third-party cookies, substantial ad revenue will be lost. Discuss with your group how such a movement would impact the valuation of Facebook and other ad-revenue-dependent companies. Discuss how it would impact the delivery of online content like that provided by *Forbes* or other providers of free online content.

4. Many companies have a conflict of interest with regard to third-party cookies. On the one hand, such cookies help generate revenue and pay for Internet content. On the other hand, trespassing on users' privacy could turn out to be a PR disaster. As you learned in your answer to question 2, browsers include options to block third-party cookies. However, in most cases, those options are turned

off in the default browser installation. Discuss why that might be so. If sites were required to obtain your permission before installing third-party cookies, how would you determine whether or not to grant it? List criteria that your team thinks you would actually use (as opposed to what the team thinks you *should* do). Assess the effectiveness of such a policy.

5. The processing of third-party cookies is hidden; we don't know what is being done behind the scenes with the data about our own behavior. Because there is so much of it and so many parties involved, the possibilities are difficult to comprehend, even if the descriptions were available. And if your privacy is comprised by the interaction of seven different companies working independently, which

is to be held accountable? Summarize consequences of these facts on consumers.

6. Summarize the benefits of third-party cookies to consumers.

7. Given all you have learned about third-party cookies, what does your team think should be done about them? Possible answers are a) nothing; b) require Web sites to ask users before installing third-party cookies; c) require browsers to block third-party cookies; d) require browsers to block third-party cookies by default, but enable them at the users' option; e) something else. Discuss these alternatives among your team and recommend one. Justify your recommendation.

CASE STUDY 9

Hadoop the Cookie Cutter

A **cookie** is data that a Web site stores on your computer to record something about its interaction with you. The cookie might contain data such as the date you last visited, whether or not you are currently signed in, or something else about your interaction with that site. Cookies can also contain a key value to one or more tables in a database that the server company maintains about your past interactions. In that case, when you access a site, the server uses the value of the cookie to look up your history. Such data could include your past purchases, portions of incomplete transactions, or the data and appearance you want for your Web page. Most of the time cookies ease your interaction with Web sites.

Cookie data includes the URL of the Web site of the cookie's owner. Thus, for example, when you go to Amazon, it asks your browser to place a cookie on your computer that includes its name, *www.Amazon.com*. Your browser will do so unless you have turned cookies off.

A **third-party cookie** is a cookie created by a site other than the one you visited. Such cookies are generated in several ways, but the most common occurs when a Web page includes content from multiple sources. For example, Amazon designs its pages so that one or more sections contain ads provided by the ad-servicing company, DoubleClick. When the browser constructs your Amazon page, it contacts Double-Click to obtain the content for such sections (in this case, ads). When it responds with the content, DoubleClick instructs your browser to store a DoubleClick cookie. That cookie is a third-party cookie. In general, third-party cookies do not contain the name or any value that identifies a particular user.

Instead, they include the IP address to which the content was delivered.

On its own servers, when it creates the cookie, Double-Click records that data in a log, and if you click on the ad, it will add that fact of that click to the log. This logging is repeated every time DoubleClick shows an ad. Cookies have an expiration date, but that date is set by the cookie creator, and they can last many years. So, over time, DoubleClick and any other third-party cookie owner will have a history of what they've shown, what ads have been clicked, and the intervals between interactions.

But, the opportunity is even greater. DoubleClick has agreements not only with Amazon, but also with many others, such as Facebook. If Facebook includes any DoubleClick content on its site, DoubleClick will place another cookie on your computer. This cookie is different from the one that it placed via Amazon, but both cookies have your IP address and other data sufficient to associate the second cookie as originating from the same source as the first. So, DoubleClick now has a record of your ad response data on two sites. Over time, the cookie log will contain data to show not only how you respond to ads, but also your pattern of visiting various Web sites on all those sites in which it places ads.

You might be surprised to learn how many third-party cookies you have. The browser FireFox has an optional feature called *Collusion* that tracks and graphs all the cookies on your computer. Figure 9-20 shows the cookies that were placed on my computer as I visited various Web sites. As you can see, in Figure 9-20a, when I started my computer and browser, there were no cookies. The cookies on my computer after I visited *www.msn.com* are shown in Figure 9-20b.

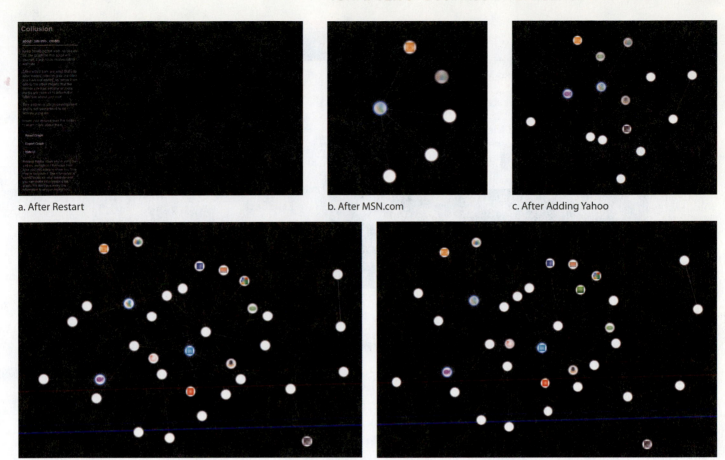

a. After Restart

b. After MSN.com

c. After Adding Yahoo

d. After Adding Seattle Times, LinkedIn, and Facebook

e. After Closing All Browser Windows

Figure 9-20

Third-party Cookie Growth a) After Restart b) After MSN.Com c) After Adding Yahoo d) After Adding Seattle Times, LinkedIn, and Facebook e) After Closing All Browser Windows

Source: © Mozilla

At this point, there are already five third-party cookies tracking my behavior. After I visited *www.yahoo.com* and *www.amazon.com* as well, I had 12 third-party cookies as shown in Figure 9-20c. Finally, Figure 9-20d shows the too-many-to-count third-party cookies on my machine after I visited the Seattle Times, Facebook and LinkedIn as well. All of that is disturbing and bothersome, so I closed all of my browser sessions. Figure 9-20e shows that even after closing I was still being watched by third-party cookies.

Who are these companies that are gathering my browser behavior data? You can find out using Ghostery®, another useful browser add-in feature (*www.ghostery.com*). Figure 9-21 shows the 10 third-party cookies installed by zulily.com when I visited their site. If you click on the name of the third-party cookie owner, it will display the popup shown in this figure. Click on the *What is . . .* and you can find out who that company is and what they do.

Third-party cookies generate incredible volumes of log data. For example, suppose a company, such as DoubleClick, shows 100 ads to a given computer in a day. If it is showing ads

to 10 million computers (possible), that is a total of one billion log entries per day, or 365 billion a year. Truly this is BigData.

Storage is essentially free, but how can they possibly process all that data? How do they parse the log to find entries just for your computer? How do they integrate data from different cookies on the same IP address? How do they analyze those entries to determine which ads you clicked on? How do they then characterize differences in ads to determine which characteristics matter most to you? The answer, as you learned in Q4, is to use parallel processing. Using a MapReduce algorithm, they distribute the work to thousands of processors that work in parallel. They then aggregate the results of these independent processors and then, possibly, move to a second phase of analysis where they do it again. Hadoop, the opensource program that you learned about in Q4, is a favorite for this process. No wonder Amazon offers Hadoop MapReduce as part of EC3. They built it for themselves, and now, given that they have it, why not lease it out?

(See the collaboration exercise on page 247 for a continuation of the third-party cookie problem? Or opportunity?)

Figure 9-21
Ghostery® in Use

QUESTIONS

1. Using your own words, explain how third-party cookies are created.

2. Suppose you are an ad-serving company and you maintain a log of cookie data for ads you serve to Web pages for a particular vendor (say Amazon).

   a. How can you use this data to determine which are the best ads?

   b. How can you use this data to determine which are the best ad formats?

   c. How could you use records of past ads and ad clicks to determine which ads to send to a given IP address?

   d. How could you use this data to determine how well the technique you used in your answer to question c was working?

   e. How could you use this data to determine that a given IP address is used by more than one person?

   f. How does having this data give you a competitive advantage vis-à-vis other ad-serving companies?

3. Suppose you are an ad-serving company and you have a log of cookie data for ads served to Web pages of all your customers (Amazon, Facebook, etc.)

   a. Describe, in general terms, how you can process the cookie data to associate log entries for a particular IP address.

   b. Explain how your answers to question 2 change given that you have this additional data.

   c. Describe how you can use this log data to determine users who consistently seek the lowest price.

   d. Describe how you can use this log data to determine users who consistently seek the latest fashion.

   e. Explain why uses like those in c and d above are only possible with MapReduce or similar technique.

4. As stated, third-party cookies usually do not contain, in themselves, data that identifies you as a particular person. However, Amazon, Facebook, and other first-party cookie vendors know who you are because you signed in. Only one of them needs to reveal your identity to the ad server and your identity can then be correlated with your IP address. At that point, the ad server and potentially all of its clients know who you are. Are you concerned about the invasion of your privacy that third-party cookies enable? Explain your answer.

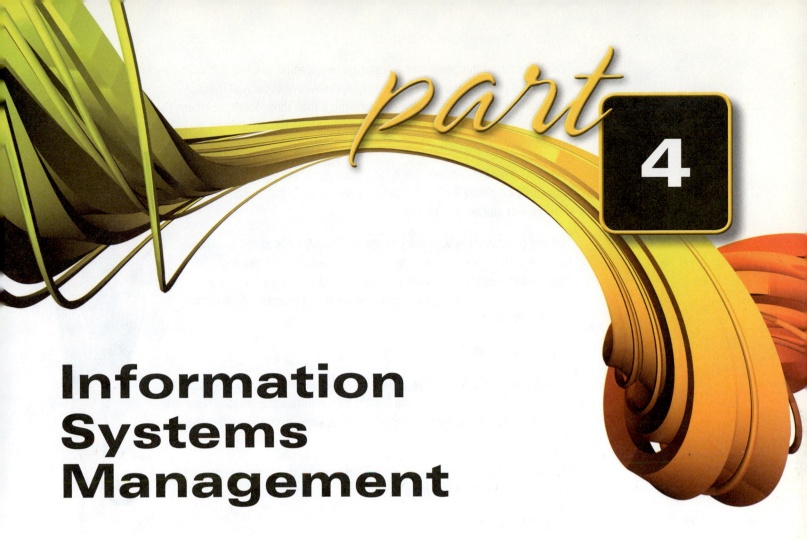

part 4

Information Systems Management

Part 4 addresses the management of information systems development, resources, and security in Chapters 10, 11, and 12, respectively. Even if you are not an IS major, you need to know about these functions so that you can be a successful and effective consumer of IS professionals' services. Here's an example of why:

Dr. Romero Flores is meeting with Maggie Jensen, a business analyst who is part of the team developing the PRIDE system, and with Jason Weber, the office administrator.

"It's a mess. We really didn't know what we were doing." Jason sounds dejected and depressed.

Dr. Flores joins in, "Sunk by our own success. I would never have imagined."

"Hold it, guys. I wouldn't say *sunk*. We're a long ways from sunk. But we do need to turn our attention to procedures and management." Maggie doesn't want this meeting to go too far downhill.

"I'll say. We've got patients calling for instructions on how to maintain their treadmills. OK, that's dumb. But a lot of them have called about problems with the heart monitors. At least those devices have *heart* in their name. Many of them think we should know something about *heart* monitors, given that we're a cardiac surgery practice."

Source: julien tromeur/Fotolia

"OK. We started this project as a prototype; we wanted to know if it would work and if patients would respond to it. And now we know that it does and that many, not all, but many patients, more than three-fourths of them, in fact, will actively use PRIDE." Maggie summarizes the situation in an upbeat way.

"Well, we know that they'll use it for a few months anyway. We don't know how long they'll use it." It's clear from his voice that Jason wishes they'd never started this project.

"So, we have success with the prototype. Now we have to decide what to do next. Clearly, we need to look at our procedures and training, and manage our users better. We might need to add some new players and resources. The help desk at equipment vendors, for example. Also, some local health clubs."

"Health clubs? Why?"

"Didn't you tell me that you're getting a lot of questions on what exercise to do next? Or, how do get the same benefit from a different exercise? Now tha spring is here, people are wanting to exercise, some even to jog, rather than their treadmills."

"There's another issue as well …" Dr. Flores enters the conversation with a heavy sigh, "We need to decide where we're going with this."

"What do you mean?"

"I need to meet with my medical partners and see what they want to do. We've demonstrated that it works with the prototype. Now, do we want this system to be just for our practice and our patients? Do we want to share it with others? Do we want to form a separate company and offer this service to more surgery practices? Maggie, I'm meeting with them next week at the end of the day. Probably around 6:30. I want you there."

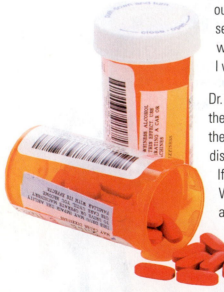

Dr. Flores and his partners need to decide what to do with their new invention. Clearly, they need to know how better to use it in their practice, which means they need to finish the *system* of all five components, and not just the software and database parts. We'll discuss that in Chapter 10, next. Beyond that, how are they going to support it, long-term? If they form a separate company, how does that company run the PRIDE infrastructure? We'll discuss IS management in Chapter 11. Finally, with a system like PRIDE, security and privacy are critical, and not just because patients ask for it. Medical practices have legal requirements to protect patient data. Chapter 12 wraps up IS management by discussing security.

As you can tell from the PRIDE example, you will need this knowledge whether or not you are an IS major.

chapter 10

Information Systems Development

Following the meeting described on page 251, Maggie, Dr. Flores, Dr. Christine Lomar, and Dr. Chris Vesper meet the next week. The three doctors are the partners and sole owners of Austin Cardiac Surgery. The purpose of the meeting is to determine what to do next.

Dr. Flores starts. "Our PRIDE prototype works, and patients are responding to it. The question is, what do we do next? It's not really finished, even for us, and it may cost more than we want to pay to finish it. So?"

Dr. Vesper looks at Flores directly.

"Romero, this has been your pet project and I've gone along with you. I know you think it's fantastic, but I want to focus on surgery. This post-op care, techno stuff really doesn't interest me, and I don't think we should pay much attention to it."

"What are you saying, 'Drop it?'"

"Maybe. Or, if you want to keep playing around with it on your time and money, OK, but I don't really want the partners or the partnership to participate."

"OK, but I'm sorry to hear that. Christine, what do you think?"

"I'm in the middle between you two. I think there is value, and I appreciate treating patients more effectively in our post-op care. But, we are a surgery practice and not a technology company. How much will it cost us to finish?"

"Maggie?"

"Dr. Flores asked me to put together a finish plan. At the minimum, we need to define the business procedures here at your partnership and document them in some way. Then we need to train the staff. We may also need to involve some of our

STUDY QUESTIONS

Q1 WHAT IS SYSTEMS DEVELOPMENT?

Q2 WHY IS SYSTEMS DEVELOPMENT DIFFICULT AND RISKY?

Q3 WHAT ARE THE FIVE PHASES OF THE SDLC?

Q4 HOW IS SYSTEM DEFINITION ACCOMPLISHED?

Q5 WHAT IS THE USERS' ROLE IN THE REQUIREMENTS PHASE?

Q6 HOW ARE THE FIVE COMPONENTS DESIGNED?

Q7 HOW IS AN INFORMATION SYSTEM IMPLEMENTED?

Q8 WHAT ARE THE TASKS FOR SYSTEM MAINTENANCE?

Q9 WHAT ARE SOME OF THE PROBLEMS WITH THE SDLC?

How does the **knowledge** in this chapter help **you?**

partners in this endeavor. I'd estimate that it's probably $25K for that, maybe more, but less than $50K."

"Ouch."

"Well, then there's another matter. Right now we're supporting the Garmin exercise watch and iPhones and iPads. To make this system more generally available, we need to support other watches and mobile devices, and at least Android phones."

"How much is that?" Dr. Lomar is being careful.

"Well, it depends on what devices . . ."

Dr. Vesper can't stand this discussion. "Look, I don't care what else there is. I don't even want to pay the minimum 25K! That's nuts. Let's get back to surgery."

Pandemonium breaks out among the three surgeons. Finally, Maggie breaks in.

"Here's a thought. Why don't we create the PRIDE procedures here so you all have a workable system for the devices we support currently?

"Then, look for outside investors to take the system and technology and form a company around it. You all can take major ownership of the new company, or license your system to it, or something."

"What about the 25K?" Vesper isn't letting that slide.

"Well, you decide. If Drs. Flores and Lomar want to fund it, then they own more, or all, of the interest in the new company, or whatever. You all can figure that out."

"Maggie, thank you. I think we'll need to excuse you now while we sort this out among ourselves."

"I understand. I'll head on home, but call my cell phone if you have any questions."

"Thanks, Maggie," both Lomar and Flores nod in agreement as Maggie leaves the room.

> *"We need to support other watches and mobile devices, and at least Android phones."*

 **CE** **Optional Extensions for this chapter are** • **CE15: Systems Development Project Management 560** • **CE16: Agile Development 573**

WHAT IS SYSTEMS DEVELOPMENT?

Systems development or systems analysis and design as it is sometimes called, is the process of creating and maintaining information systems. Notice that this process concerns *information systems*, not just computer programs. Developing an *information system* involves all five components: hardware, software, data, procedures, and people. Developing a *computer program* involves software programs, possibly with some focus on data and databases. Figure 10-1 shows that systems development has a broader scope than computer program development.

Because systems development addresses all five components, it requires more than just programming or technical expertise. Establishing the system's goals, setting up the project, and determining requirements necessitate business knowledge and management skill. Tasks such as building computer networks and writing computer programs require technical skills; developing the other components requires nontechnical, human relations skills. Creating data models requires the ability to interview users and understand their view of the business activities. Designing procedures, especially those involving group action, requires business knowledge and an understanding of group dynamics. Developing job descriptions, staffing, and training all require human resource and related expertise.

Therefore, do not suppose that systems development is exclusively a technical task undertaken by programmers and hardware specialists. Rather, it requires coordinated teamwork of both specialists and nonspecialists with business knowledge.

In Chapter 4, you learned that there are three sources for software: off-the-shelf, off-the-shelf with adaptation, and tailor-made. Although all three sources pertain to software, only two of them pertain to information systems. Unlike software, *information systems are never off-the-shelf.* Because information systems involve your company's people and procedures, you must construct or adapt procedures to fit your business and people, regardless of how you obtain the computer programs.

As a future business manager, you will have a key role in information systems development. In order to accomplish the goals of your department, you need to ensure that effective procedures exist for using the information system. You need to ensure that personnel are properly trained and are able to use the IS effectively. If your department does not have appropriate procedures and trained personnel, you must take corrective action. Although you might pass off hardware, program, or data problems to the IT department or independent contractor, you cannot pass off procedural or personnel problems to that department. Such problems are your problems. The single most important criterion for information systems success is for users to take ownership of their systems.

WHY IS SYSTEMS DEVELOPMENT DIFFICULT AND RISKY?

Systems development is difficult and risky. Many projects are never finished. Of those that are finished, some are 200 or 300 percent over budget. Still other projects finish within budget and schedule, but never satisfactorily accomplish their goals.

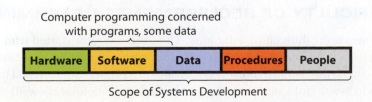

Figure 10-1
Systems Development Versus Program Development

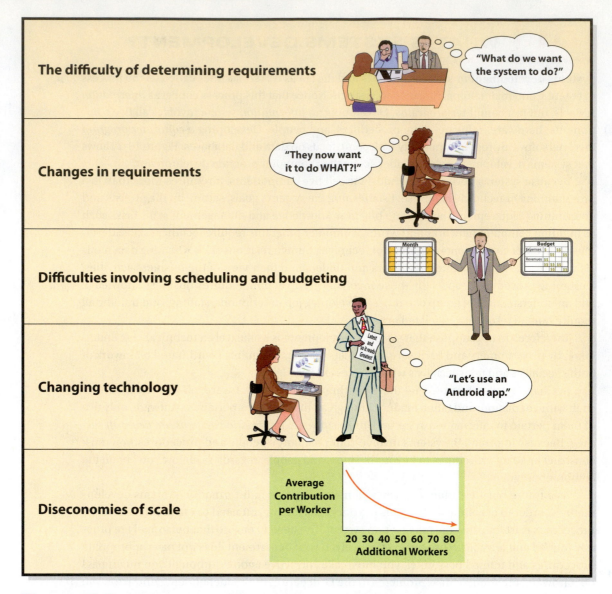

Figure 10-2
Major Challenges to Systems Development

You may be amazed to learn that systems development failures can be so dramatic. You might suppose that with all the computers and all the systems developed over the years that by now there must be some methodology for successful systems development. In fact, there *are* systems development methodologies that can result in success, and we will discuss the primary one in this chapter. But, even when competent people follow this or some other accepted methodology, the risk of failure is still high.

In the following sections, we will discuss the five major challenges to systems development displayed in Figure 10-2.

You can learn about another promising development technique called Agile Development in Chapter Extension 16.

THE DIFFICULTY OF REQUIREMENTS DETERMINATION

First, requirements are difficult to determine. The PRIDE system started with a prototype, which, as you'll learn, is often a good way to begin. But now, as they think about the operational system, what are the true requirements? Will it involve just cardiac surgeons and their patients? Or, will they add health clubs, and insurance companies, and employers as well? Which mobile devices do they want to support? What are the functions of the applications? An answer to that last question is needed to decide whether they need a thin-client or native application.

But these are broad requirements. Before the system can be finalized, detailed requirements also need to be specified. What, exactly, does the report that the doctors receive look like? Will they have both a standard and exception report? Are those reports fixed in structure or can the user adapt them? If the latter, how?

How many practices and how many patients per practice will PRIDE support? Answers to questions like that are needed to decide how much cloud resource is needed. What does privacy mean, in the details? Who sets patient privacy policy? Who can change it? What granularity of permission is needed? And, as any experienced systems analyst knows, there will undoubtedly be important questions that no one knows to ask. Perhaps the requirements are specified in calendar Q1, and there are year-end reporting needs that no one currently remembers.

The questions go on and on. One of the major purposes of the systems development process is to create an environment in which such questions are both asked and answered.

CHANGES IN REQUIREMENTS

Even more difficult, systems development aims at a moving target. Requirements change as the system is developed, and, the bigger the system and the longer the project, the more the requirements change. For example, midway through the development process, a major health club chain approaches Flores with a lucrative contract proposal. But, that proposal necessitates major changes in planned reporting requirements.

When requirements do change, what should the development team do? Stop work and rebuild the system in accordance with the new requirements? If they do that, the system will develop in fits and starts and may never be completed. Or, should the team finish the system, knowing that it will be unsatisfactory the day it is implemented and will, therefore, need immediate maintenance?

SCHEDULING AND BUDGETING DIFFICULTIES

Other challenges involve scheduling and budgeting. How long will it take to build a system? That question is not easy to answer. Suppose you are developing the new PRIDE database. Is the database design in Case 7 sufficient (page 187)? If not, should you create a new data model? If so, how long will it take to create? Even if you know how long it takes to create the data model, others may disagree with you and with each other. How many times will you need to rebuild the data model until everyone agrees? How many labor hours should you plan?

Consider database applications. How long will it take to build the forms, reports, queries, and application programs? How long will it take to test all of them? What about procedures and people? What procedures need to be developed, and how much time should be set aside to create and document them, develop training programs, and train the personnel?

Further, how much will all of this cost? Labor costs are a direct function of labor hours; if you cannot estimate labor hours, you cannot estimate labor costs. Moreover, if you cannot estimate how much a system costs, then how do you perform a financial analysis to determine if the system generates an appropriate rate of return?

CHANGING TECHNOLOGY

Yet another challenge is that while the project is underway, technology continues to change. For example, say that while you are developing the PRIDE application, Apple, Microsoft, and Google and their business partners all release hot, new mobile devices with vastly improved graphics and animation. You know that with these new devices you can create far better animations for comparative exercise, much better than the one on page 221.

Do you want to stop your development to switch to the new technology? Would it be better to finish developing according to the existing plan? Such decisions are tough. Why build an out-of-date system? But, can you afford to keep changing the project?

DISECONOMIES OF SCALE

Unfortunately, as development teams become larger, the average contribution per worker decreases. This is true because as staff size increases, more meetings and other coordinating activities are required to keep everyone in sync. There are economies of scale up to a point, but beyond a workgroup of, say, 20 employees, diseconomies of scale begin to take over.

A famous adage known as **Brooks' Law** points out a related problem: *Adding more people to a late project makes the project later*.[1] Brooks' Law is true not only because a larger staff requires increased coordination, but also because new people need training. The only people who can train the new employees are the existing team members, who are thus taken off productive tasks. The costs of training new people can overwhelm the benefit of their contribution.

In short, managers of software development projects face a dilemma: They can increase work per employee by keeping the team small, but in doing so they extend the project's timeline. Or, they can reduce the project's timeline by adding staff, but because of diseconomies of scale they will have to add 150 or 200 hours of labor to gain 100 hours of work. And, due to Brooks' Law, once the project is late, both choices are bad.

Furthermore, schedules can be compressed only so far. According to one other popular adage, "Nine women cannot make a baby in one month."

IS IT REALLY SO BLEAK?

Is systems development really as bleak as the list of challenges makes it sound? Yes and no. All of the challenges just described do exist, and they are all significant hurdles that every development project must overcome. As noted previously, once the project is late and over budget, no good choice exists. "I have to pick my regrets," said one beleaguered manager of a late project.

The IT industry has over 50 years of experience developing information systems; over those years, methodologies have emerged that successfully deal with these problems. In the next study question, we will consider the systems development life cycle (SDLC), the most common process for systems development.

WHAT ARE THE FIVE PHASES OF THE SDLC?

You can learn more about project planning by reading Chapter Extension 15, Systems Development Project Management.

The **systems development life cycle (SDLC)** is the traditional process used to develop information systems. The IT industry developed the SDLC in the "school of hard knocks." Many early projects met with disaster, and companies and systems developers sifted through the ashes of those disasters to determine what went wrong. By the 1970s, most seasoned project managers agreed on the basic tasks that need to be performed to successfully build and maintain information systems. These basic tasks are combined into phases of systems development.

---

[1]Fred Brooks was a successful executive at IBM in the 1960s. After retiring from IBM, he wrote a classic book on IT project management called *The Mythical Man-Month*. Published by Addison-Wesley in 1975, the book is still pertinent today and should be read by every IT or IS project manager. It's an enjoyable book, too.

Different authors and organizations package the tasks into different numbers of phases. Some organizations use an eight-phase process, others use a seven-phase process, and still others use a five-phase process. In this book, we will use the following five-phase process:

1. **System definition**
2. **Requirements analysis**
3. **Component design**
4. **Implementation**
5. **Maintenance**

Figure 10-3 shows how these phases are related. Development begins when a business-planning process identifies a need for a new system. We address IS planning processes in Chapter 11. For now, suppose that management has determined, in some way, that the organization can best accomplish its goals and objectives by constructing a new information system.

For the PRIDE system, Dr. Flores had the initial idea to connect his practice to patient exercise data in the cloud. With that idea, he hired Maggie Jensen, a business analyst, to develop a prototype to test the desirability of the system to his patients and his practice. At this point, he wants to start a systems development process to create an operational capability.

Developers in the first SDLC phase—**system definition**—use management's statement of the system needs in order to begin to define the new system (for PRIDE, this statement is based on experience with the prototype). The resulting project plan is the input to the second phase—requirements analysis. Here, developers identify the particular features and functions of the new system. The output of that phase is a set of approved user requirements, which become the primary input used to design system components. In phase 4, developers implement, test, and install the new system.

Over time, users will find errors, mistakes, and problems. They will also develop new requirements. The description of fixes and new requirements is input into a system maintenance phase. The maintenance phase starts the process all over again, which is why the process is considered a cycle.

In the following sections, we will consider each phase of the SDLC in more detail.

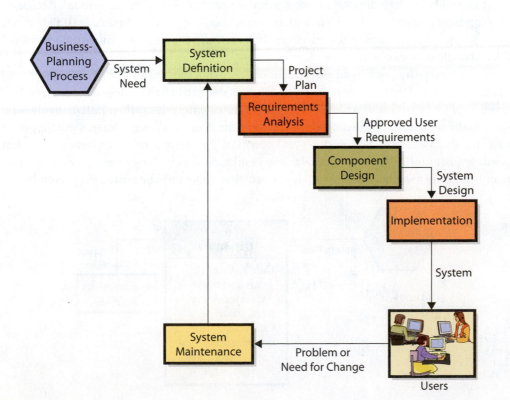

Figure 10-3
Phases in the SDLC

HOW IS SYSTEM DEFINITION ACCOMPLISHED?

In response to the need for the new system, the organization will assign a few employees, possibly on a part-time basis, to define the new system, to assess its feasibility, and to plan the project. Typically, that is someone in IS development, but the members of that initial team are both users and IS professionals. In the case of a small company, Dr. Flores has hired Maggie, an independent expert, to work with his partners, staff, and patients to define the system.

DEFINE SYSTEM GOALS AND SCOPE

As Figure 10-4 shows, the first step is to define the goals and scope of the new information system. Information systems exist to facilitate an organization's competitive strategy by supporting business processes or by improving decision making. At this step, the development team defines the goal and purpose of the new system in terms of these reasons.

Consider PRIDE. The goal of the system is to integrate patient exercise data and make it available in suitable reports to PRIDE participants. But, who are they? In its ultimate form, Flores believes PRIDE can integrate activities of patients, healthcare professionals, health clubs, insurance companies, and employers. But, how many of these organizations need to be involved in the first implementation? The team may choose to limit the scope just to patients and medical practices, or perhaps to include health clubs as well.

In other systems, the scope might be defined by specifying the users who will be involved, or the business processes that will be involved, or the plants, offices, and factories that will be involved.

ASSESS FEASIBILITY

For a discussion of ethical issues relating to estimation, see the Ethics Guide on pages 272–273

Once we have defined the project's goals and scope, the next step is to assess feasibility. This step answers the question, "Does this project make sense?" The aim here is to eliminate obviously nonsensible projects before forming a project development team and investing significant labor.

Feasibility has four dimensions: *cost, schedule, technical, and organizational.* Because IS development projects are difficult to budget and schedule, cost and schedule feasibility can be only an approximate, back-of-the-envelope analysis. The purpose is to eliminate any obviously infeasible ideas as soon as possible.

Cost feasibility involves an assessment of the cost of the project. For PRIDE, this is a difficult assessment (see Case 10, page 279). Clearly, it depends on the scope of the project. Even given an understanding of scope, however, as an inter-enterprise system PRIDE involves numerous different parties with different goals and objectives. What requirements will they deem essential that Flores and Maggie don't yet know? Will they have a native application or a thin-client application? If the former, how many mobile devices will they need to support? How many users will there be, and how much data will they generate to be hosted in the cloud?

Figure 10-4
SDLC: System Definition Phase

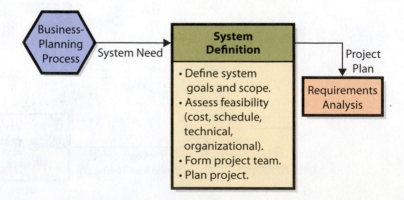

At this point, all the team can do is to make rough estimates. Certainly, any potential investor will scrutinize these estimates, so Maggie will need to do more than guess. Still, at this point, the team doesn't need a precise total; they simply need a range of costs that are close.

Like cost feasibility, **schedule feasibility** is difficult to determine because it is hard to estimate the time it will take to build the system. However, if Maggie determines that it will take, say, no less than 6 months to develop the system and put it into operation, Flores and partners can then decide if they can accept that minimum schedule. At this stage of the project, the organization should not rely on either cost or schedule estimates; the purpose of these estimates is simply to rule out any obviously unacceptable projects.

Technical feasibility refers to whether existing information technology is likely to be able to meet the needs of the new system. Because PRIDE uses new technology (the cloud) and innovative mobile devices (exercise equipment and other devices), Flores decided to build a prototype to test feasibility. As you learned at the start of this chapter, the system seems to be technically feasible.

Finally, **organizational feasibility** concerns whether the new system fits within the organization's customs, culture, charter, or legal requirements. For example, will doctors be willing to use PRIDE? Will they see it as an incursion into their practice? Even more, the critical PRIDE users are sick, older people who may be technology-phobic. Flores needed the prototype to demonstrate that it would work with this audience.

FORM A PROJECT TEAM

If the defined project is determined to be feasible, the next step is to form the project team. Normally the team consists of both IS professionals and user representatives. The project manager and IS professionals can be in-house personnel or outside contractors. In Chapter 11, we will describe various means of obtaining IT personnel using outside sources and the benefits and risks of outsourcing.

Typical personnel on a development team are a manager (or managers for larger projects), business analysts, systems analysts, programmers, software testers, and users. **Business analysts** specialize in understanding business needs, strategies, and goals and helping businesses implement systems to accomplish their competitive strategies. **Systems analysts** are IT professionals who understand both business and technology.

Systems analysts are closer to IT and are a bit more technical, though there is considerable overlap in the duties and responsibilities of business and systems analysts. Both are active throughout the systems development process and play a key role in moving the project through the systems development process. Business analysts work more with managers and executives; systems analysts integrate the work of the programmers, testers, and users. Depending on the nature of the project, the team may also include hardware and communications specialists, database designers and administrators, and other IT specialists.

The team composition changes over time. During requirements definition, the team will be heavy with business and systems analysts. During design and implementation, it will be heavy with programmers, testers, and database designers. During integrated testing and conversion, the team will be augmented with testers and business users.

User involvement is critical throughout the system development process. Depending on the size and nature of the project, users are assigned to the project either full or part time. Sometimes users are assigned to review and oversight committees that meet periodically, especially at the completion of project phases and other milestones. Users are involved in many different ways. *The important point is for users to have active involvement and to take ownership of the project throughout the entire development process.*

The first major task for the assembled project team is to plan the project. Members of the project team specify tasks to be accomplished, assign personnel, determine task dependencies, and set schedules.

Q5 WHAT IS THE USERS' ROLE IN THE REQUIREMENTS PHASE?

The primary purpose of the requirements analysis phase is to determine and document the specific features and functions of the new system. For most development projects, this phase requires interviewing dozens of users and documenting potentially hundreds of requirements. Requirements definition is, thus, expensive. It is also difficult, as you will see.

DETERMINE REQUIREMENTS

Determining the system's requirements is the most important phase in the systems development process. If the requirements are wrong, the system will be wrong. If the requirements are determined completely and correctly, then design and implementation will be easier and more likely to result in success.

Examples of requirements are the contents and the format of Web pages and the functions of buttons on those pages, or the structure and content of a report, or the fields and menu choices in a data entry form. Requirements include not only what is to be produced, but also how frequently and how fast it is to be produced. Some requirements specify the volume of data to be stored and processed.

If you take a course in systems analysis and design, you will spend weeks on techniques for determining requirements. Here, we will just summarize that process. Typically, systems analysts interview users and record the results in some consistent manner. Good interviewing skills are crucial; users are notorious for being unable to describe what they want and need. Users also tend to focus on the tasks they are performing at the time of the interview. Tasks performed at the end of the quarter or end of the year are forgotten if the interview takes place mid-quarter. Seasoned and experienced systems analysts know how to conduct interviews to bring such requirements to light.

As listed in Figure 10-5, sources of requirements include existing systems as well as the Web pages, forms, reports, queries, and application features and functions desired in the new system. Security is another important category of requirements.

If the new system involves a new database or substantial changes to an existing database, then the development team will create a data model. As you learned in Chapter 5, that model must reflect the users' perspective on their business and business activities. Thus, the data model is constructed on the basis of user interviews and must be validated by those users.

Sometimes, the requirements determination is so focused on the software and data components that other components are forgotten. Experienced project managers ensure

Figure 10-5
SDLC: Requirements Analysis Phase

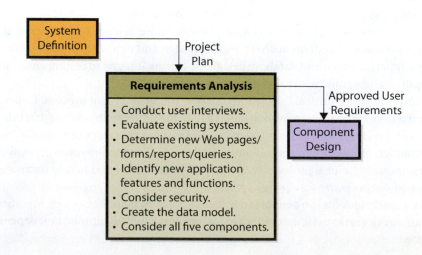

Experiencing MIS

Garden Tracker

Source: Superstock Royalty Free

Suppose that you and two or three other students have decided to start a business that offers landscaping services. Your goal is to develop a list of clients for whom you provide regular and recurring services, such as mowing, weeding, and pool cleaning, as well as one-time specialty services, such as pruning, garden preparation, tree removal, sprinkler installation and repair, and the like.

You know that it will be critical for your success to have an information system for tracking customers, services you have provided, and services you are scheduled to provide in the future. As a new small business, you want a simple and

affordable system based on Excel or Access. You name your new system *GardenTracker*.

Form a team of three or four students and, given what you know about lawn and garden maintenance and your intuition and business knowledge, complete the following tasks:

1. Explain how you would use the SDLC to develop GardenTracker.

2. Define the scope of your system.

3. Explain the process you would use to determine the feasibility of GardenTracker. List data you need for such an assessment, and explain how you might obtain or estimate that data.

4. Consider just the tracking of recurring services, and list all of the requirements that you can imagine for that functionality. Be specific and answer at least the following:
   a. What data will you need?
   b. How will you input that data? Show a mockup of a data entry screen, and describe how it will be used.
   c. Using your mockup, describe how you will modify recurring service data.
   d. Using your mockup, describe how you will cancel a recurring service.
   e. Specify any other requirements you believe are important for tracking recurring services.

5. Present your answers to item 4 to the rest of the class and obtain feedback from your classmates.

6. Modify your answer to item 4 based upon feedback you received in item 5.

7. Considering just the recurring services functionality, do you think it would be better to use Excel or Access for this project? List the criteria you used to answer that question. Summarize the consequences of making a poor choice between these two products.

8. What does this short exercise tell you about information systems development? Answer this question in such a way that you could use your answer to demonstrate your critical-thinking skills in a job interview.

consideration of requirements for all five IS components, not just for software and data. Regarding hardware, the team might ask: Are there special needs or restrictions on hardware? Is there an organizational standard governing what kinds of hardware may or may not be used? Must the new system use existing hardware? What requirements are there for communications and network hardware or cloud services?

Similarly, the team should consider requirements for procedures and personnel: Do accounting controls require procedures that separate duties and authorities? Are there restrictions that some actions can be taken only by certain departments or specific personnel? Are there policy requirements or union rules that restrict activities to certain categories of employees? Will the system need to interface with information systems from other companies and organizations? In short, requirements need to be considered for all of the components of the new information system.

These questions are examples of the kinds of questions that must be asked and answered during requirements analysis.

APPROVE REQUIREMENTS

Once the requirements have been specified, the users must review and approve them before the project continues. The easiest and cheapest time to alter the information system is in the requirements phase. Changing a requirement at this stage is simply a matter of changing a description. Changing a requirement in the implementation phase may require weeks of reworking applications components and the database structure.

ROLE OF A PROTOTYPE

Because requirements are difficult to specify, building a working prototype, as was done for the PRIDE system, can be quite beneficial. Whereas future systems users often struggle to understand and relate to requirements expressed as word descriptions and sketches, working with a prototype provides direct experience. As they work with a prototype, users will assess usability and remember features and functions they have forgotten to mention. Additionally, prototypes provide evidence to assess the system's technical and organizational feasibility. Further, prototypes create data that can be used to estimate both development and operational costs.

To be useful, a prototype needs to work; mock-ups of forms and reports, while helpful, will not generate the benefits just described. The prototype needs to put the user into the experience of employing the system to do his or her tasks.

Prototypes can be expensive to create; however, this expense is often justified not only for the greater clarity and completeness of requirements, but also because parts of the prototype can often be re-used in the operational system. Much of the PRIDE code that generated the smartphone display at the start of Chapter 9 (page 221) will be re-used in the operational system.

Unfortunately, systems developers face a dilemma when funding prototypes; the cost of the prototype occurs early in the process, sometimes well before full project funding is available. "We need the prototype to get the funds, and we need the funds to get the prototype." Unfortunately, no uniform solution to this dilemma exists, except the application of experience guided by intuition. Once again we see the need for nonroutine problem-solving skills.

Q6 HOW ARE THE FIVE COMPONENTS DESIGNED?

Each of the five components is designed in this next stage. Typically, the team designs each component by developing alternatives, evaluating each of those alternatives against the requirements, and then selecting among those alternatives. Accurate requirements are critical here; if they are incomplete or wrong, then they will be poor guides for evaluation. Figure 10-6 shows that design tasks pertain to each of the five IS components.

HARDWARE DESIGN

For hardware, the team determines specifications for the hardware they need and the source of that hardware. They can purchase the hardware, lease it, or lease time from a hosting service in the cloud. (The team is not designing hardware in the sense of building a CPU or a disk drive.)

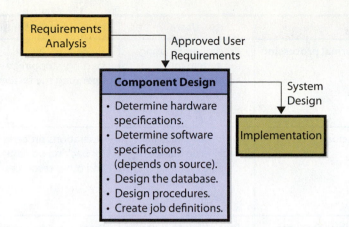

Figure 10-6
SDLC: Component Design Phase

For PRIDE, the data will be stored in the cloud and perhaps some of the application processing will be done there as well. In this sense, hardware design is a matter of what cloud resources are needed. However, PRIDE users also need to decide which mobile devices they intend to support. This decision involves interaction with software design; if PRIDE uses a thin-client application, the project can afford to support more devices than if they must create native applications for iOS, Android, and Windows RT.

SOFTWARE DESIGN

Software design depends on the source of the programs. For off-the-shelf software, the team must determine candidate products and evaluate them against the requirements. For off-the-shelf-with-alteration software, the team identifies products to be acquired off-the-shelf and then determines the alterations required. For custom-developed programs, the team produces design documentation for writing program code.

For a cloud-based system like PRIDE, one important design decision is where application processing will occur. All can occur on mobile devices, all can occur on cloud-servers, or a mixture can be used. Furthermore, for mobile systems projects, like PRIDE, at this stage the team will decide whether they are building a thin-client or native application.

DATABASE DESIGN

If developers are constructing a database, then during this phase they convert the data model to a database design using techniques such as those described in Chapter 5. If developers are using off-the-shelf programs, then little database design needs to be done; the programs will handle their own database processing.

PROCEDURE DESIGN

For a business information system, the system developers and the organization must also design procedures for both users and operations personnel. Procedures need to be developed for normal, backup, and failure recovery operations, as summarized in Figure 10-7. Usually, teams of systems analysts and key users design the procedures.

DESIGN OF JOB DESCRIPTIONS

With regard to people, design involves developing job descriptions for both users and operations personnel. Sometimes new information systems require new jobs. If so, the duties and responsibilities for these jobs need to be defined in accordance with the organization's human

Figure 10-7
Procedures to be Designed

	Users	**Operations Personnel**
Normal processing	• Procedures for using the system to accomplish business tasks.	• Procedures for starting, stopping, and operating the system.
Backup	• User procedures for backing up data and other resources.	• Operations procedures for backing up data and other resources.
Failure recovery	• Procedures to continue operations when the system fails. • Procedures to convert back to the system after recovery.	• Procedures to identify the source of failure and get it fixed. • Procedures to recover and restart the system.

resources policies. More often, organizations add new duties and responsibilities to existing jobs. In this case, developers define these new tasks and responsibilities in this phase. Sometimes, the personnel design task is as simple as statements such as, "Jason will be in charge of managing passwords." As with procedures, teams of systems analysts and users determine job descriptions and functions.

Q7 HOW IS AN INFORMATION SYSTEM IMPLEMENTED?

Once the design is complete, the next phase in the SDLC is implementation. Tasks in this phase are to build, test, and convert the users to the new system (see Figure 10-8). Developers construct each of the components independently. They obtain, install, and test hardware. They license and install off-the-shelf programs; they write adaptations and custom programs, as necessary. They construct a database and fill it with data. They document, review, and test procedures, and they create training programs. Finally, the organization hires and trains needed personnel.

Figure 10-8
SDLC: Implementation Phase

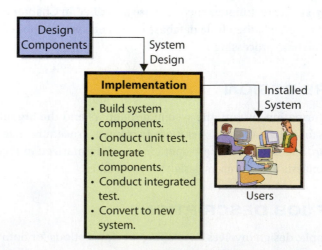

SYSTEM TESTING

Once developers have constructed and tested all of the components, they integrate the individual components and test the system. So far, we have glossed over testing as if there is nothing to it. In fact, software and system testing are difficult, time-consuming, and complex tasks. Developers need to design and develop test plans and record the results of tests. They need to devise a system to assign fixes to people and to verify that the fixes are correct and complete.

A **test plan** consists of sequences of actions that users will take when using the new system. Test plans include not only the normal actions that users will take, but also incorrect actions. A comprehensive test plan should cause every line of program code to be executed. The test plan should cause every error message to be displayed. Testing, retesting, and re-retesting consume huge amounts of labor. Often, developers can reduce the labor cost of testing by writing programs that invoke system features automatically.

Today, many IT professionals work as testing specialists. Testing, or **product quality assurance (PQA)**, as it is often called, is an important career. PQA personnel usually construct the test plan with the advice and assistance of users. PQA test engineers perform testing, and they also supervise user test activity. Many PQA professionals are programmers who write automated test programs.

In addition to IT professionals, users should be involved in system testing. Users participate in the development of test plans and test cases. They also can be part of the test team, usually working under the direction of PQA personnel. Users have the final say on whether the system is ready for use. If you are invited to participate as a user tester, take that responsibility seriously. It will become much more difficult to fix problems after you have begun to use the system in production. *For any system on which you will rely, it is important (and wise) to become involved in the development of test cases as well as testing itself.* It is unprofessional, unwise, and unfair to the development team to sit on the sidelines until the system is finished and then complain about missing or misguided features!

Beta testing is the process of allowing future system users to try out the new system on their own. Software vendors, such as Microsoft, often release beta versions of their products for users to try and to test. Such users report problems back to the vendor. Beta testing is the last stage of testing. Normally, products in the beta test phase are complete and fully functioning; they typically have few serious errors. Organizations that are developing large new information systems sometimes use a beta-testing process just as software vendors do.

SYSTEM CONVERSION

Once the system has passed integrated testing, the organization installs the new system. The term **system conversion** is often used for this activity because it implies the process of *converting* business activity from the old system to the new.

Organizations can implement a system conversion in one of four ways:

- Pilot
- Phased
- Parallel
- Plunge

IS professionals recommend any of the first three, depending on the circumstances. In most cases, companies should avoid "taking the plunge!"

With **pilot installation**, the organization implements the entire system on a limited portion of the business. Dr. Flores is doing pilot with the PRIDE system when he chooses to use it for just a few of the patients that could benefit from it. The advantage of pilot implementation is that if the system fails, the failure is contained within a limited boundary. This reduces exposure of the business and also protects the new system from developing a negative reputation throughout the organization.

As the name implies, with **phased installation** the new system is installed in phases across the organization. Once a given piece works, then the organization installs and tests another piece of the system, until the entire system has been installed. Some systems are so tightly integrated that they cannot be set up in phased pieces. Such systems must be installed using one of the other techniques.

With **parallel installation**, the new system runs in parallel with the old one until the new system is tested and fully operational. Parallel installation is expensive, because the organization incurs the costs of running both systems. Users must work double time, if you will, to run both systems. Then, considerable work is needed to determine if the results of the new system are consistent with those of the old system.

However, some organizations consider the costs of parallel installation to be a form of insurance. It is the slowest and most expensive style of installation, but it does provide an easy fallback position if the new system fails.

The final style of conversion is **plunge installation** (sometimes called *direct installation*). With it, the organization shuts off the old system and starts the new system. If the new system fails, the organization is in trouble: Nothing can be done until either the new system is fixed or the old one is reinstalled. Because of the risk, organizations should avoid this conversion style, if possible. The one exception is if the new system is providing a new capability that is not vital to the operation of the organization.

Figure 10-9 summarizes the tasks for each of the five components during the design and implementation phases. Use this figure to test your knowledge of the tasks in each phase.

Figure 10-9
Design and Implementation for the Five Components

	Hardware	Software	Data	Procedures	People
Design	Determine hardware specifications.	Select off-the-shelf programs. Design alterations and custom programs as necessary.	Design database and related structures.	Design user and operations procedures.	Develop user and operations job descriptions.
Implementation	Obtain, install, and test hardware.	License and install off-the-shelf programs. Write alterations and custom programs. Test programs.	Create database. Fill with data. Test data.	Document procedures. Create training programs. Review and test procedures.	Hire and train personnel.
	Integrated Test and Conversion				

Unit test each component

WHAT ARE THE TASKS FOR SYSTEM MAINTENANCE?

The last phase of the SDLC is maintenance. Maintenance is a misnomer; the work done during this phase is either to *fix* the system so that it works correctly or to *adapt* it to changes in requirements.

Figure 10-10 shows tasks during the maintenance phase. First, there needs to be a means for tracking both failures[2] and requests for enhancements to meet new requirements. For small systems, organizations can track failures and enhancements using word-processing documents. As systems become larger, however, and as the number of failure and enhancement requests increases, many organizations find it necessary to develop a failure-tracking database. Such a database contains a description of each failure or enhancement. It also records who reported the problem, who will make the fix or enhancement, what the status of that work is, and whether the fix or enhancement has been tested and verified by the originator.

Typically, IS personnel prioritize system problems according to their severity. They fix high-priority items as soon as possible, and they fix low-priority items as time and resources become available.

With regard to the software component, software developers group fixes for high-priority failures into a **patch** that can be applied to all copies of a given product. Software vendors supply patches to fix security and other critical problems. They usually bundle fixes of low-priority problems into larger groups called **service packs**. Users apply service packs in much the same way that they apply patches, except that service packs typically involve fixes to hundreds or thousands of problems.

By the way, you may be surprised to learn this, but all commercial software products are shipped with known failures. Usually vendors test their products and remove the most serious

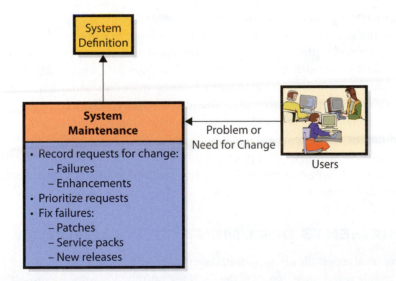

Figure 10-10
SDLC System Maintenance Phase

---

[2]A *failure* is a difference between what the system does and what it is supposed to do. Sometimes, you will hear the term *bug* used instead of *failure*. As a future user, call failures *failures*, because that's what they are. Don't have a *bugs list*; have a *failures list*. Don't have an *unresolved bug*; have an *unresolved failure*. A few months of managing an organization that is coping with a serious failure will show you the importance of this difference in terms.

problems, but they seldom, if ever, remove all of the defects they know about. Shipping with defects is an industry practice; Microsoft, Adobe, Oracle, IBM, and many others ship products with known problems.

Because an enhancement is an adaptation to new requirements, developers usually prioritize enhancement requests separate from failures. The decision to make an enhancement includes a business decision that the enhancement will generate an acceptable rate of return. Although minor enhancements are made using service packs, major enhancement requests usually result in a new release of a product.

As you read this, keep in mind that although we usually think of failures and enhancements as applying to software, they can apply to the other components as well. There can be hardware or database failures or enhancements. There can also be failures and enhancements in procedures and people, though the latter is usually expressed in more humane terms than *failure* or *enhancement*. The underlying idea is the same, however.

As stated earlier, note that the maintenance phase starts another cycle of the SDLC process. The decision to enhance a system is a decision to restart the systems development process. Even a simple failure fix goes through all of the phases of the SDLC; if it is a small fix, a single person may work through those phases in an abbreviated form. But each of those phases is repeated, nonetheless.

WHAT ARE SOME OF THE PROBLEMS WITH THE SDLC?

Although the industry has experienced notable successes with the SDLC process, there have also been many problems with it, as discussed in this section.

THE SDLC WATERFALL

The Guide on pages 274–275 states the challenges and difficulties with project estimation in the real world.

One of the reasons for SDLC problems is due to the **waterfall** nature of the SDLC. Like a series of waterfalls, the process is supposed to operate in a sequence of nonrepetitive phases. For example, the team completes the requirements phase and goes over the waterfall into the design phase, and on through the process (look back to Figure 10-3, page 259).

Unfortunately, systems development seldom works so smoothly. Often, there is a need to crawl back up the waterfall, if you will, and repeat work in a prior phase. Most commonly, when design work begins and the team evaluates alternatives, they learn that some requirements statements are incomplete or missing. At that point, the team needs to do more requirements work, yet that phase is supposedly finished. On some projects, the team goes back and forth between requirements and design so many times that the project seems to be out of control.

REQUIREMENTS DOCUMENTATION DIFFICULTY

Another problem, especially on complicated systems, is the difficulty of documenting requirements in a usable way. I once managed the database portion of a software project at Boeing in which we invested more than 70 labor-years into a requirements statement. When printed, the requirements document consisted of 20-some volumes that stood 7 feet tall when stacked on top of one another.

When we entered the design phase, no one really knew all the requirements that concerned a particular feature. We would begin to design a feature only to find that we had not considered a requirement buried somewhere in the documentation. In short, the requirements were so unwieldy as to be nearly useless. Additionally, during the requirements analysis interval, the airplane business moved on. By the time we entered the design phase, many requirements were incomplete, and some were obsolete. Projects that spend so much time documenting requirements are sometimes said to be in **analysis paralysis.**

SCHEDULING AND BUDGETING DIFFICULTIES

For a new, large-scale system, schedule and budgeting estimates are so approximate as to become nearly laughable. Management attempts to put a serious face on the need for a schedule and a budget, but when you are developing a large, multiyear, multimillion-dollar project, estimates of labor hours and completion dates are approximate and fuzzy. The employees on the project, who are the source for the estimates, know little about how long something will take and about how much they had actually guessed. They know that the total budget and timeline is a summation of everyone's similar guesses. Many large projects live in a fantasy world of budgets and timelines.

In truth, the software community has done much work to improve software development forecasting. But for large projects with large SDLC phases, just too much is unknown for any technique to work well. So, development methodologies other than the SDLC have emerged for developing systems through a series of small, manageable chunks. Rapid application development, object-oriented development, and extreme programming are three such methodologies.

How does the knowledge in this chapter help you?

Kelly, Emily, Addison, and Drew at GearUp all need the knowledge of this chapter. If they had it, they would know to specify the scope of their project and determine requirements well before they think about creating an iOS or any other mobile application. Similarly, Flores, his partners, and potential investors need to know the basics of the development process as well if for no other reason than to understand the difficulties and risks of developing new information systems, particularly inter-enterprise systems, such as PRIDE.

At some point in your career, you will need this knowledge. You will be running a business unit or a department or a project that needs an information system. You will need to know how to proceed, and the knowledge of this chapter will get you started on the right path and help you manage your way through the process.

Ethics Guide

Estimation Ethics

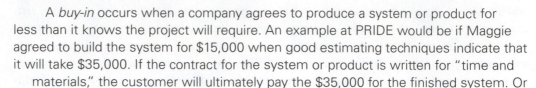

A *buy-in* occurs when a company agrees to produce a system or product for less than it knows the project will require. An example at PRIDE would be if Maggie agreed to build the system for $15,000 when good estimating techniques indicate that it will take $35,000. If the contract for the system or product is written for "time and materials," the customer will ultimately pay the $35,000 for the finished system. Or the customer will cancel the project once the true cost is known. If the contract for the system or product is written for a fixed cost, then the developer will absorb the extra costs. The latter strategy is used if the contract opens up other business opportunities that are worth the $20,000 loss.

Buy-ins always involve deceit. Most would agree that buying in on a time-and-materials project, planning to stick the customer with the full cost later, is unethical and wrong. Opinions vary on buying-in on a fixed-price contract. Some would say buying-in is always deceitful and should be avoided. Others say that it is just one of many different business strategies.

What about in-house projects? Do the ethics change if an in-house development team is building a system for use in-house? If team members know there is only $50,000 in the budget for some new system, should they start the project if they believe its true cost is $75,000? If they do start, at some point senior management will either have to admit a mistake and cancel the project or find the additional $25,000. Project sponsors can make all sorts of excuses for such a buy-in. For example, "I know the company needs this system. If management doesn't realize it and fund it appropriately, then we'll just force their hand."

These issues become even stickier if team members disagree about how much the project will cost. Suppose one faction of the team believes the new system will cost $35,000, another faction estimates $50,000, and a third thinks $65,000. Can the project sponsors justify taking the average? Or, should they describe the range of estimates?

Other buy-ins are more subtle. Suppose you are a project manager of an exciting new project that is possibly a career-maker for you. You are incredibly busy, working 6 days a week and long hours each day. Your team has developed an estimate for $50,000 for your project. A little voice in the back of your mind says that maybe not all costs for every aspect of the project are included in that estimate. You mean to follow up on that thought, but more pressing matters in your schedule take precedence. Soon you find yourself in front of management, presenting the $50,000 estimate. You probably should have found the time to investigate the estimate, but you didn't. Is your behavior unethical?

Or suppose you approach a more senior manager with your dilemma. You tell the senior manager, "I think there may be other costs, but I know that $50,000 is all we've got. What should I do?" Suppose the senior manager says something like, "Well, let's go forward. You don't know of anything else, and we can always find more budget elsewhere if we have to." How do you respond?

You can buy-in on schedule as well as cost. If the marketing department says, "We have to have the new product for the trade show," do you agree, even if you know it's highly unlikely? What if marketing says, "If we don't have it by then, we should just cancel the project"? Suppose it's not impossible to make that schedule, it's just highly unlikely. How do you respond?

DISCUSSION QUESTIONS

1. Do you agree that buying-in on a time-and-materials project is always unethical? Explain your reasoning. Are there circumstances in which it could be illegal?

2. Suppose you learn through the grapevine that your opponents in a competitive bid are buying-in on a time-and-materials contract. Does this change your answer to question 1?

3. Suppose you are a project manager who is preparing a request for proposal on a time-and-materials systems development project. What can you do to prevent buy-ins?

4. Under what circumstances do you think buying-in on a fixed-price contract is ethical? What are the dangers of this strategy?

5. Explain why in-house development projects are always time-and-materials projects.

6. Given your answer to question 5, is buying-in on an in-house project always unethical? Under what circumstances do you think it is ethical? Under what circumstances do you think it is justifiable, even if it is unethical?

7. Suppose you ask a senior manager for advice, as described in the Ethics Guide. Does the manager's response absolve you of guilt? Suppose you ask the manager and then do not follow her guidance. What problems result?

8. Explain how you can buy-in on schedule as well as costs.

9. For an in-house project, how do you respond to the marketing manager who says that the project should be cancelled if it will not be ready for the trade show? In your answer, suppose that you disagree with this opinion—suppose you know the system has value regardless of whether it is done by the trade show.

Source: apops/Fotolia

Guide

The Real Estimation Process

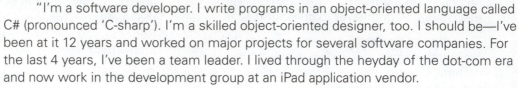

"I'm a software developer. I write programs in an object-oriented language called C# (pronounced 'C-sharp'). I'm a skilled object-oriented designer, too. I should be—I've been at it 12 years and worked on major projects for several software companies. For the last 4 years, I've been a team leader. I lived through the heyday of the dot-com era and now work in the development group at an iPad application vendor.

"All of this estimating theory is just that—theory. It's not really the way things work. Sure, I've been on projects in which we tried different estimation techniques. But here's what really happens: You develop an estimate using whatever technique you want. Your estimate goes in with the estimates of all the other team leaders. The project manager sums all those estimates together and produces an overall estimate for the project.

"By the way, in my projects, time has been a much bigger factor than money. At one software company I worked for, you could be 300 percent over your dollar budget and get no more than a slap on the wrist. Be 2 weeks late, however, and you were finished.

"Anyway, the project managers take the project schedule to senior management for approval, and what happens? Senior management thinks they are negotiating. 'Oh, no,' they say, 'that's way too long. You can surely take a month off that schedule. We'll approve the project, but we want it done by February 1 instead of March 1.'

"Now, what's their justification? They think that tight schedules make for efficient work. You know that everyone will work extra hard to meet the tighter timeframe. They know Parkinson's Law—'Work expands so as to fill the time available for its completion.' So, fearing the possibility of wasting time because of too-lenient schedules, they lop a month off our estimate.

"Estimates are what they are; you can't knock off a month or two without some problem, somewhere. What does happen is that projects get behind, and then management expects us to work longer and longer hours. Like they said in the early years at Microsoft, 'We have flexible working hours. You can work any 65 hours per week you want.'

"Not that our estimation techniques are all that great, either. Most software developers are optimists. They schedule things as if everything will go as planned, and things seldom do. Also, schedulers usually don't allow for vacations, sick days, trips to the dentist, training on new technology, peer reviews, and all the other things we do in addition to writing software.

"So we start with optimistic schedules on our end; then management negotiates a month or two off, and voilà, we have a late project. After a while, management has been burned by late projects so much that they mentally add the month or even more back onto the official schedule. Then both sides work in a fantasy world, where no one believes the schedule, but everyone pretends they do.

"I like my job. I like software development. Management here is no better or worse than in other places. As long as I have interesting work to do, I'll stay here. But I'm not working myself silly to meet these fantasy deadlines."

DISCUSSION QUESTIONS

1. What do you think of this developer's attitude? Do you think he's unduly pessimistic, or do you think there's merit to what he says?

2. What do you think of his idea that management thinks they're negotiating? Should management negotiate schedules? Why or why not?

3. Suppose a project actually requires 12 months to complete. Which do you think is likely to cost more: (a) having an official schedule of 11 months with at least a 1-month overrun or (b) having an official schedule of 13 months and, following Parkinson's Law, having the project take 13 months?

4. Suppose you are a business manager, and an information system is being developed for your use. You review the scheduling documents and see that little time has been allowed for vacations, sick leave, miscellaneous other work, and so forth. What do you do?

5. Describe the intangible costs of having an organizational belief that schedules are always unreasonable.

6. If this developer worked for you, how would you deal with his attitude about scheduling?

7. Do you think there is something different when scheduling information systems development projects than when scheduling other types of projects? What characteristics might make such projects unique? In what ways are they the same as other projects?

8. What do you think managers should do in light of your answer to question 7?

ACTIVE REVIEW

Use this Active Review to verify that you understand the ideas and concepts that answer this chapter's study questions.

Q1 WHAT IS SYSTEMS DEVELOPMENT?

Define *systems development*. Explain how systems development differs from program development. Describe the types of expertise needed for systems development projects. Explain why Dr. Flores needs the knowledge in this chapter.

Q2 WHY IS SYSTEMS DEVELOPMENT DIFFICULT AND RISKY?

Describe the risk in systems development. Summarize the difficulties posed by the following: requirements definition, requirements changes, scheduling and budgeting, changing technology, and diseconomies of scale.

Q3 WHAT ARE THE FIVE PHASES OF THE SDLC?

Name the five phases in the systems development life cycle, and briefly describe each.

Q4 HOW IS SYSTEM DEFINITION ACCOMPLISHED?

Using Figure 10-4 as a guide, explain how you would describe the systems definition task. Name and describe four elements of feasibility. (*Hint:* The four types of feasibility can be arranged Cost, Operational, Schedule, Technical; arranged this way, the first letter of each makes the acronym *COST*.)

Q5 WHAT IS THE USERS' ROLE IN THE REQUIREMENTS PHASE?

Summarize the tasks in the requirements phase. Describe the role for users in this phase. Discuss what you believe will happen if users are not involved or if users do not take this work seriously. Describe the role users play in requirements approval.

Q6 HOW ARE THE FIVE COMPONENTS DESIGNED?

Summarize design activities for each of the five components of an information system. Explain six categories of procedure that need to be designed.

Q7 HOW IS AN INFORMATION SYSTEM IMPLEMENTED?

Name the two major tasks in systems implementation. Summarize the system testing process. Describe the difference between system and software testing. Explain testing tasks for each of the five components. Name four types of system conversion. Describe each way, and give an example of when each would be effective.

Q8 WHAT ARE THE TASKS FOR SYSTEM MAINTENANCE?

Explain why the term *maintenance* is a misnomer. Summarize tasks in the maintenance phase.

Q9 WHAT ARE SOME OF THE PROBLEMS WITH THE SDLC?

Explain why the SDLC is considered a waterfall process, and describe why this characteristic can be a problem. Describe problems that occur when attempting to develop requirements using the SDLC. Summarize scheduling and budgeting difficulties that the SDLC presents.

How does the knowledge in this chapter help you?

Summarize how Kelly, Emily, Addison, and Drew could use the knowledge of this chapter. Summarize how Flores, his partners, and potential PRIDE investors could. State two ways in which you might need this knowledge in the future.

KEY TERMS AND CONCEPTS

Analysis paralysis 271
Beta testing 267
Brooks' Law 258
Business analyst 261
Component design 259
Cost feasibility 260
Implementation 259
Maintenance 259
Organizational feasibility 261
Parallel installation 268

Patch 269
Phased installation 268
Pilot installation 267
Plunge installation 268
Product quality assurance
    (PQA) 267
Requirements analysis 259
Schedule feasibility 261
Service packs 269

System conversion 267
System definition 259
Systems analyst 261
Systems development 255
Systems development life cycle
    (SDLC) 258
Technical feasibility 261
Test plan 267
Waterfall 270

USING YOUR KNOWLEDGE

1. Assume that you are an intern working with Maggie and that you are present at the initial conversations she has with Dr. Flores. Assume that Maggie asks you to help her investigate this opportunity.

   a. Develop a plan for this project using the SDLC. Describe, in general terms, the work to be done in each phase.

   b. Specify in detail the tasks that must be accomplished during the system definition phase.

   c. Write a memo to Maggie explaining how you think she should investigate all four types of feasibility.

2. Answer question 1. Assume that Dr. Flores pushes back because he thinks that Maggie is making the project overly complicated, possibly to increase the size of her consulting engagement. Write a one-page memo explaining to Dr. Flores why it is important to follow the SDLC or some similar process.

3. Use Google or Bing to search for the phrase "what is a business analyst?" Investigate several of the links that you find and answer the following questions:

   a. What are the primary job responsibilities of a business analyst?

   b. What knowledge do business analysts need?

   c. What skills and personal traits do successful business analysts need?

   d. Would a career as a business analyst be interesting to you? Explain why or why not.

COLLABORATION EXERCISE 10

Before you start this exercise, read Chapter Extensions 1 and 2, which describe collaboration techniques as well as tools for managing collaboration tasks. In particular, consider using Google Drive, Google+, Windows Live SkyDrive, Microsoft SharePoint, or some other collaboration tool.

Wilma Baker, Jerry Barker, and Chris Bickel met in June 2013 at a convention of resort owners and tourism operators. They sat next to each other by chance while waiting for a presentation; after introducing themselves and laughing at the odd sound of their three names, they were surprised to learn that they managed similar businesses. Wilma Baker lives in Santa Fe, New Mexico, and specializes in renting homes and apartments to visitors to Santa Fe. Jerry Barker lives in Whistler Village, British Columbia, and specializes in renting condos to skiers and other visitors to the Whistler/Blackcomb Resort. Chris Bickel lives in Chatham, Massachusetts, and specializes in renting homes and condos to vacationers to Cape Cod.

The three agreed to have lunch after the presentation. During lunch, they shared frustrations about the difficulty of obtaining new customers, especially in the current economic downturn. Barker was especially concerned about finding customers to fill the facilities that had been constructed to host the Olympics several years prior.

As the conversation developed, they began to wonder if there was some way to combine forces (i.e., they were seeking a competitive advantage from an alliance). So, they decided to skip one of the next day's presentations and meet to discuss ways to form an alliance. Ideas they wanted to discuss further were sharing customer data, developing a joint reservation service, and exchanging property listings.

As they talked, it became clear they had no interest in merging their businesses; each wanted to stay independent. They also discovered that each was very concerned, even paranoid, about protecting their existing customer base from poaching. Still, the conflict was not as bad as it first seemed. Barker's business was primarily the ski trade, and winter was his busiest season; Bickel's business was mostly Cape Cod vacations, and she was busiest during the summer. Baker's high season was the summer and fall. So, it seemed there was enough difference in their high seasons that they would not necessarily cannibalize their businesses by selling the others' offerings to their own customers.

The question then became how to proceed. Given their desire to protect their own customers, they did not want to develop a common customer database. The best idea seemed to be to share data about properties. That way they could keep control of their customers but still have an opportunity to sell time at the others' properties.

They discussed several alternatives. Each could develop her or his own property database, and the three could then share those databases over the Internet. Or, they could develop a centralized property database that they would all use. Or, they could find some other way to share property listings.

Because we do not know Baker, Barker, and Bickel's detailed requirements, you cannot develop a plan for a specific system. In general, however, they first need to decide how elaborate an information system they want to construct. Consider the following two alternatives:

a. They could build a simple system centered on email. With it, each company sends property descriptions to the others via email. Each independent company then forwards these descriptions to its own customers, also using email. When a customer makes a reservation for a property, that request is then forwarded back to the property manager via email.

b. They could construct a more complex system using a cloud-based, shared database that contains data on all their properties and reservations. Because reservations tracking is a common business task, it is likely that they can license an existing application with this capability.

1. From the description given, define the scope of the project.

2. Consider technical feasibility of the two alternatives:
   a. Name and describe criteria you would use for alternative a.
   b. Name and describe criteria you would use for alternative b.
   c. Is it possible to know, without further investigation, whether either alternative is technically feasible? Why or why not?

3. Consider organizational feasibility:
   a. Explain what organizational feasibility means in the context of an inter-enterprise system.
   b. List criteria you would use for assessing organizational feasibility for these alternatives. Differentiate criteria between the two alternatives if you think it is important to do so.
   c. Is either alternative a or b more likely to be organizationally feasible than the other? Explain your answer.

4. Consider schedule feasibility:
   a. List criteria you would use for schedule feasibility for these alternatives. Differentiate criteria between the two alternatives if you think it is important to do so.
   b. Is either alternative a or b more likely to be schedule feasible than the other? Explain your answer.

5. Consider cost feasibility:
   a. List sources of the major development costs for alternative a.
   b. List sources of the major operational costs for alternative a.
   c. List sources of the major development costs for alternative b.
   d. List sources of the major operational costs for alternative b.
   e. Which alternative is likely to be cheaper to develop?
   f. List and describe factors that may make alternative a cheaper to operate.
   g. List and describe factors that may make alternative b cheaper to operate.

6. Given your answers to questions 2 through 5, which of the alternatives do you believe is likely to be feasible? It could be both, just one, or neither. Justify your answer.

7. What would you say if one of the three principals were to ask you at this point, "Is it worthwhile for me to even consider this idea anymore?" Justify your answer. Without more data, you cannot make a true assessment, but apply your knowledge, experience, and intuition to formulate a response to that question.

CASE STUDY 10

The Cost of PRIDE?

If Dr. Flores, his partners, and outside investors are to continue the PRIDE project, they need to assess its investment potential. Flores might be willing to take some loss for the sake of professional service to his patients, but from the dialog in the opening of this chapter, it doesn't sound likely that his partners would. And, no successful investor would consider putting money into a losing proposition.

To assess PRIDE's investment potential, we need to know both the revenue potential as well as the costs of developing and operating it. We don't know the PRIDE business model and so we cannot assess the revenue aspect of this investment. Such an assessment belongs in your entrepreneurship text and not in an MIS text, in any case.

However, it is appropriate for us to discuss what a system like PRIDE will cost. By now, you should have sufficient knowledge to at least be able to determine the important cost factors, even though you don't know the particular values.

Figure 10-11 lists potential development and operational cost sources for each of the five components of the PRIDE system. Most of these cost sources are obvious from the discussion of the SDLC in this chapter. A few, however, may be unexpected. For one, notice the hardware and software developer infrastructure costs. Developers need computers on which to write and test code, and they need development software such as Microsoft Visual Studio. There are likely network, server, and cloud-services costs for developers as well. Finally, developers will need mobile devices of the type for which they are developing. A full panoply of iOS devices, Android devices, and Windows RT devices will be needed if all of those operations systems are to be supported.

In the case of PRIDE, software is all custom-developed, so appreciable software development costs should be anticipated. Estimating those costs will be difficult. We will discuss PRIDE security in Chapter 12; for now, realize that applications will need to be developed to enable users to enter and update their security settings. All software will need to be designed to limit access to that prescribed by users' security settings.

Sources of data development costs are self-explanatory. As stated in the chapter, there is normally considerable uncertainty about the time required for data modeling and database design. Because of the PRIDE prototype, this uncertainty will be less.

Procedures for all users must be designed and documented. These tasks are often more expensive than anticipated because those who develop the system often believe it will be easier to use than it is. Procedures need to be more detailed and better documented than they believe. Finally, operational jobs need to be defined, job descriptions written for operations and support personnel, and possibly for development

	Hardware	Software	Data	Procedures	People

Development	• Developer hardware infrastructure
	• Development cloud-servers
		• Developer software infrastructure
		• Prescription entry application
		• Exercise equipment application
		• Performance reporting application for:
		  Healthcare providers
		  Patients
		  Health clubs
		• Security/privacy applications
			• Data modeling
			• Database design
			• Test data entry
			• Setup data for operational
			• Development cloud storage costs
				• Design and document procedures for:
				  Healthcare providers
				  Patients
				  Health clubs
					• Create staff job descriptions
					• Hire operations and support personnel
					• Train personnel

	Integration and Testing Costs				
Operational	• PRIDE servers • Maintenance developer hardware • Maintenance & testing cloud-servers	• Software maintenance expenses	• Operational cloud storage costs • Backup and recovery costs	• Customer support expense	• Salaries • Contractor fees • New employee training • Ongoing training

Figure 10-11
Sources of PRIDE Costs

personnel if ongoing development is anticipated. Personnel need to be hired and trained.

As you learned in this chapter, test plans need to be written and integrated system testing conducted. This activity may necessitate full-time product quality assurance (PQA) personnel as well.

The major sources of non-maintenance, operational expense will be cloud hardware, staff salaries, and contractor fees. Depending on how popular and how difficult PRIDE is to use, there may be considerable customer support expense as well. Of course, operational expenses depend upon the number of users and the frequency of their use. The staff will need to estimate usage data and, if possible, develop an operational cost model that is driven by the number of active users.

Maintenance costs are an unknown. They depend upon the quality of the initial software and how much rework needs to be done once the system becomes operational. They also depend upon how much the PRIDE environment changes. Competitors may force the development of new features and functions, and changes in medical practice payment, insurance policies, and governmental regulations may force changes that will not be known until they occur.

QUESTIONS

Suppose that you have been hired by a potential investor to assess the adequacy of the cost forecasts that the PRIDE team developed. Assume the team has used a model of cost sources like that in Figure 10-11.

The potential investor has asked you to address the following questions, in particular:

1. Which development expenses are likely to be:
   a. The largest
   b. The most difficult to estimate
   c. Not included in Figure 10-11

2. Which operational expenses are likely to be:
   a. The largest
   b. The most difficult to estimate
   c. Not included in Figure 10-11

3. Considering operational expenses,
   a. Which operational costs depend upon the number of doctors and the frequency of their use, and which do not?
   b. Which operational costs depend upon the number of patients and the frequency of their use, and which do not?
   c. Which operational costs depend upon the number of health club users and the frequency of their use, and which do not?
   d. How would a potential investor use answers to questions 3a-c for assessing the long-run costs if PRIDE is successful?

4. Suppose Dr. Flores has told your investor that he is willing to hire Maggie and other experts as needed to fully investigate any two sources of costs.
   a. Of the cost sources in Figure 10-11, which two would you choose? Justify your choice.
   b. List and describe criteria you would use for assessing the completeness and accuracy of the response.

5. Suppose you decide, using data that we do not yet have, that the PRIDE upside potential is large enough to justify the investment risk, if the cost estimates are accurate. They might be quite accurate, but then again, they could be low by a factor of 3 or even 5. How would you advise the investor who hired you?

6. Suppose the investor who hired you tells you that you haven't done your job if you can't get closer than a factor of 3 to 5 in your assessment of their cost assessment. How do you respond?

7. Assume that some of the costs are simply not knowable, by anyone, however skilled they are, at the time of the analysis. A good example is the cost of adapting PRIDE software to changes in healthcare law. Did you include any such costs in your answer to question 4? If so, are you wasting Maggie's time and Flores' money by asking them? How would you advise your investor to consider such costs?

Information Systems Management

"I've worked with him before, but not on an HTML5 project." Maggie Jensen is standing at a whiteboard in Dr. Romero Flores' conference room. They're discussing the pros and cons of outsourcing PRIDE development to India.

"But it was a phone application?" Flores has just finished a three-hour heart surgery, and he's struggling to move from the world of surgery to that of high tech.

"Yes, but native iOS —" Maggie can't tell if he knows what iOS means. "It's an iPad/iPhone application."

"Well, why don't we do that?" Flores is still distracted.

"We can. But then when we have to develop native applications for the Android, and Windows 8 phones, if we go there. So, we have to do a lot of rewriting."

"And we don't have to do that if we use HTML5?" Flores is getting into the flow of the conversation.

"Nope."

"Why doesn't everyone do that?" he asks.

"Well, it's newer and today's browsers implement HTML5 differently, so we still have to do a bit of customizing." Maggie is hoping this isn't too much geek speak.

"You mean it's different with IE than with Chrome?" Flores shows he's following her.

"Yes, and different from Safari and Opera, and different on different phones . . ."

"Why don't they all do it the same way?"

"Wish I knew. It's frustrating to all of us. Actually, the problem is the way they implement CSS3 more than it is HTML5 . . ." As she says this, she realizes she's gone too far . . .

"Stop! That's enough! I thought heart surgery was complicated. . . . So tell me about this guy."

STUDY QUESTIONS

Q1 WHAT ARE THE FUNCTIONS AND ORGANIZATION OF THE IS DEPARTMENT?

Q2 HOW DO ORGANIZATIONS PLAN THE USE OF IS?

Q3 WHAT ARE THE ADVANTAGES AND DISADVANTAGES OF OUTSOURCING?

Q4 WHAT ARE YOUR USER RIGHTS AND RESPONSIBILITIES?

How does the **knowledge** in this chapter help **you?**

"I don't know anything about doing business in India."

"His name is Ajit Barid. At least that's the name of his company." Maggie looks a little sheepish.

"That's not his name?"

"I don't know. Maybe. You know what Ajit Barid means?" She starts to smile . . .

"No. What?"

"Invincible cloud."

"Ummm . . . probably not the name his mother gave him . . . Or she was prophetic. Maggie, this makes me nervous. I don't know anything about doing business in India. The guy takes our money and runs, what do we do? " Flores is down to business now.

"Well, we don't pay him till he delivers . . . or at least not much. But, I've had positive experience with him and his references are good."

"What if he gives our code to somebody else? Or our ideas? What if we find some horrible bug in his code and we can't find him to fix it? What if he just disappears? What if he gets two-thirds done and then loses interest . . . or goes to work on someone else's project?" Flores is on a roll.

"All are risks, I agree. But it will cost you four to six times as much to develop over here." She starts to list risks on the whiteboard.

"Well, it's been my experience that you get what you pay for in this life . . ."

"You want me to find you some local developers?" Maggie thinks local development is a poor choice, but she wants him to feel comfortable with the decision.

"Yes, no, I mean no. I don't think so. How'd you meet him?"

"At a conference when he was working for Microsoft in their Hyderabad facility. He was programming SharePoint cloud features. When the iPad took off, he left Microsoft and started his own company. That's when I hired him to build the iOS app."

"That worked out OK?" Flores wants to be convinced.

"Yes, but it was one of his first jobs . . . he had to get it right for us."

"What do you think? What would you do?"

Maggie is taken aback by the question . . . not what she expects from a successful heart surgeon. "Well, I think the biggest risk is his success. You know, the restaurant that gets the great reviews and then is buried in new customers, and the kitchen falls apart."

"Doesn't he have more employees now?"

"Yes, he does, and I know he's a good developer, but I don't know whether he's a good manager."

"OK, what else?" Flores is all business.

 **Optional Extension for this chapter is • CE17: Business Process Management 582**

"Well, HTML5 and CSS3 are newer than Objective-C, which is what he used for the iPad. But, they're easier, too. On the other hand, CSS can be tricky. I guess I'd say inexperience with this dev environment would be another risk factor."

"What about money?"

"Well, like I said, we structure the agreement so we don't pay much until we know it all works."

"So what else do you worry about?" Again, he's appealing to her expertise.

"Loss of time. Maybe he gets distracted, doesn't finish the app, or hires someone else to do it, and they can't. And September rolls around and we find that, while we're not out any real money, we've lost most of a year of time."

"I don't like the sound of that."

"Neither do I," Maggie responds while she adds schedule risk to her list.

"You think maybe we should bite the bullet and hire our own programmers?"

"Good heavens, no! No way! That would be incredibly expensive, we couldn't keep them busy, and you don't know anything about managing software people. That would be a disaster." Maggie is certain here, and she tries to make that obvious as she speaks.

"But, what about long term?"

"Long term, we'll need a small operations staff. One that keeps everything running, answers customer questions, deals with security problems, and so forth. But I think you'll be outsourcing development for a very long time." Again, she speaks with an authoritative tone.

"So?" Flores' tone shows he wants to wrap up this conversation.

Maggie summarizes, "Let me finish the requirements document and then get a proposal and bid from Ajit as well as a local, domestic developer. We'll look at the proposals and bids and then make a decision. One problem, though. . ."

"What's that?"

"The local developer may outsource it anyway."

"You mean we pay the local developer to hire Ajit or his cousin?" Flores shakes his head.

"Something like that."

Flores gets up from the table. "That's crazy."

"Maybe not. Let's see what we get."

 ## Q1 WHAT ARE THE FUNCTIONS AND ORGANIZATION OF THE IS DEPARTMENT?

The major functions of the information systems department[1] are as follows:

- Plan the use of IS to accomplish organizational goals and strategy.
- Manage outsourcing relationships.
- Protect information assets.
- Develop, operate, and maintain the organization's computing infrastructure.
- Develop, operate, and maintain applications.

We will consider the first two functions in questions Q2 and Q3 of this chapter. The protection function is the topic of Chapter 12. The last two functions are important for IS majors, but less so for other business professionals, and we will not consider them in this text. To set the stage, consider the organization of the IS department.

---

[1]Often, the department we are calling the *IS department* is known in organizations as the *IT department*. That name is a misnomer however, because the IT department manages systems as well as technology. If you hear the term *IT department* in industry, don't assume that the scope of that department is limited to technology.

Figure 11-1
Typical Senior-Level
Reporting Relationships

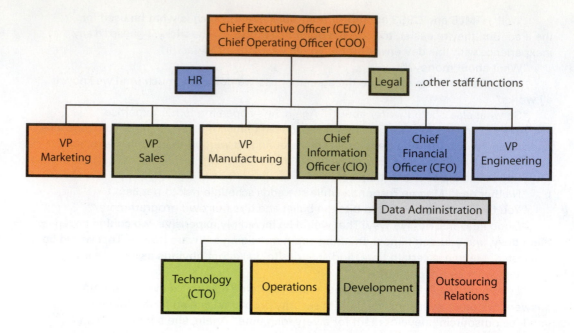

HOW IS THE IS DEPARTMENT ORGANIZED?

Figure 11-1 shows typical top-level reporting relationships. As you will learn in your management classes, organizational structure varies depending on the organization's size, culture, competitive environment, industry, and other factors. Larger organizations with independent divisions will have a group of senior executives like those shown here for each division. Smaller companies may combine some of these departments. Consider the structure in Figure 11-1 as typical.

The title of the principal manager of the IS department varies from organization to organization. A common title is **chief information officer**, or **CIO**. Other common titles are *vice president of information services, director of information services*, and, less commonly, *director of computer services*.

In Figure 11-1, the CIO, like other senior executives, reports to the *chief executive officer* (CEO), though sometimes these executives report to the *chief operating officer* (COO), who, in turn, reports to the CEO. In some companies, the CIO reports to the *chief financial officer* (CFO). That reporting arrangement might make sense if the primary information systems support only accounting and finance activities. In organizations such as manufacturers that operate significant nonaccounting information systems, the arrangement shown in Figure 11-1 is more common and effective.

The structure of the IS department also varies among organizations. Figure 11-1 shows a typical IS department with four groups and a data administration staff function.

Most IS departments include a *technology* office that investigates new information systems technologies and determines how the organization can benefit from them. For example, today many organizations are investigating social media and elastic cloud opportunities and planning how they can use those capabilities to better accomplish their goals and objectives. An individual called the **chief technology officer**, or **CTO**, often heads the technology group. The CTO evaluates new technologies, new ideas, and new capabilities and identifies those that are most relevant to the organization. The CTO's job requires deep knowledge of information technology and the ability to envision and innovate applications for the organization.

The next group in Figure 11-1, *Operations,* manages the computing infrastructure, including individual computers, in-house server farms, networks, and communications media. This group includes system and network administrators. As you will learn, an important function for this group is to monitor the user experience and respond to user problems.

The third group in the IS department in Figure 11-1 is *Development*. This group manages the process of creating new information systems as well as maintaining existing information systems. (Recall from Chapter 10 that in the context of information systems *maintenance* means either fixing problems or adapting existing information systems to support new features and functions.)

The size and structure of the development group depends on whether programs are developed in-house. If not, this department will be staffed primarily by business and systems analysts who work with users, operations, and vendors to acquire and install licensed software and to set up the system components around that software. If the organization develops programs in-house, then this department will include programmers, test engineers, technical writers, and other development personnel.

The last IS department group in Figure 11-1 is *Outsourcing Relations*. This group exists in organizations that have negotiated outsourcing agreements with other companies to provide equipment, applications, or other services. You will learn more about outsourcing later in this chapter.

Figure 11-1 also includes a *Data Administration* staff function. The purpose of this group is to protect data and information assets by establishing data standards and data management practices and policies.

There are many variations on the structure of the IS department shown in Figure 11-1. In larger organizations, the operations group may itself consist of several different departments. Sometimes, there is a separate group for data warehousing and data marts.

As you examine Figure 11-1, keep the distinction between IS and IT in mind. *Information systems (IS)* exist to help the organization achieve its goals and objectives. Information systems have the five components we have discussed throughout this text. *Information technology (IT)* is simply technology. It concerns the products, techniques, procedures, and designs of computer-based technology. IT must be placed into the structure of an IS before an organization can use it.

WHAT IS-RELATED JOB POSITIONS EXIST?

IS departments provide a wide range of interesting and well-paying jobs. Many students enter the MIS class thinking that the IS departments consist only of programmers and computer technicians. If you reflect on the five components of an information system, you can understand why this cannot be true. The data, procedures, and people components of an information system require professionals with highly developed interpersonal communications skills.

Figure 11-2 summarizes the major job positions in the IS industry. With the exception of computer technician and possibly of PQA test engineer, all of these positions require a 4-year degree. Furthermore, with the exception of programmer and PQA test engineer, all of these positions require business knowledge. In most cases, successful professionals have a degree in business. Note, too, that most positions require good verbal and written communications skills. Business, including information systems, is a social activity.

Many of the positions in Figure 11-2 have a wide salary range. Lower salaries are for professionals with limited experience or for those who work in smaller companies or work on small projects. The larger salaries are for those with deep knowledge and experience who work for large companies on large projects. Do not expect to begin your career at the high end of these ranges. As noted, all salaries are for positions in the United States and are shown in U.S. dollars.

Figure 11-2
Job Positions in the Information Systems Industry

Title	Responsibilities	Knowledge, Skill, and Characteristics Requirements	United States 2012 Salary Range (USD)
Business analyst	Work with business leaders and planners to develop processes and systems that implement business strategy and goals.	Knowledge of business planning, strategy, process management, and technology. Can deal with complexity. See big picture but work with details. Strong interpersonal and communications skills needed.	$75,000–$125,000
System analyst	Work with users to determine system requirements, design and develop job descriptions and procedures, help determine system test plans.	Strong interpersonal and communications skills. Knowledge of both business and technology. Adaptable.	$65,000–$125,000
Programmer	Design and write computer programs.	Logical thinking and design skills, knowledge of one or more programming languages.	$50,000–$150,000
PQA test engineer	Develop test plans, design and write automated test scripts, perform testing.	Logical thinking, basic programming, superb organizational skills, eye for detail.	$40,000–$95,000
Technical writer	Write program documentation, help-text, procedures, job descriptions, training materials.	Quick learner, clear writing skills, high verbal communications skills.	$40,000–$95,000
User support representative	Help users solve problems, provide training.	Communications and people skills. Product knowledge. Patience.	$40,000–$65,000
Computer technician	Install software, repair computer equipment and networks.	Associate degree, diagnostic skills.	$30,000–$65,000
Network administrator	Monitor, maintain, fix, and tune computer networks.	Diagnostic skills, in-depth knowledge of communications technologies and products.	$75,000–$200,000+
Consultant	Wide range of activities: programming, testing, database design, communications and networks, project management, security and risk management, social media, strategic planning.	Quick learner, entrepreneurial attitude, communications and people skills. Respond well to pressure. Particular knowledge depends on work.	From $35 per hour for a contract tester to more than $500 per hour for strategic consulting to executive group.
Salesperson	Sell software, network, communications, and consulting services.	Quick learner, knowledge of product, superb professional sales skills.	$65,000–$200,000+
Small-scale project manager	Initiate, plan, manage, monitor, and close down projects.	Management and people skills, technology knowledge. Highly organized.	$75,000–$150,000
Large-scale project manager	Initiate, plan, monitor, and close down complex projects.	Executive and management skills. Deep project management knowledge.	$150,000–$250,000+
Database administrator	Manage and protect database.	Diplomatic skills, database technology knowledge.	$75,000–$250,000
Chief technology officer (CTO)	Advise CIO, executive group, and project managers on emerging technologies.	Quick learner, good communications skills, business background, deep knowledge of IT.	$125,000–$300,000+
Chief information officer (CIO)	Manage IT department, communicate with executive staff on IT- and IS-related matters. Member of the executive group.	Superb management skills, deep knowledge of business and technology, and good business judgment. Good communicator. Balanced and unflappable.	$150,000–$500,000, plus executive benefits and privileges.

(By the way, for all but the most technical positions, knowledge of a business specialty can add to your marketability. If you have the time, a dual major can be an excellent choice. Popular and successful dual majors are accounting and information systems, marketing and information systems, and management and information systems.)

 ## HOW DO ORGANIZATIONS PLAN THE USE OF IS?

We begin our discussion of IS functions with planning. Figure 11-3 lists the major IS planning functions.

ALIGN INFORMATION SYSTEMS WITH ORGANIZATIONAL STRATEGY

The purpose of an information system is to help the organization accomplish its goals and objectives. In order to do so, all information systems must be aligned with the organization's competitive strategy.

Recall the four competitive strategies from Chapter 3. The first two strategies are an organization can be a cost leader either across an industry or within an industry segment. Alternatively, for the second two strategies, an organization can differentiate its products or services either across the industry or within a segment. Whatever the organizational strategy, the CIO and the IS department must constantly be vigilant to align IS with it.

Maintaining alignment between IS direction and organizational strategy is a continuing process. As strategies change, as the organization merges with other organizations, as divisions are sold, IS must evolve along with the organization.

Unfortunately, however, IS infrastructure is not malleable. Changing a network requires time and resources. Integrating disparate information systems applications is even slower and more expensive. This fact often is not appreciated in the executive suite. Without a persuasive CIO, IS can be perceived as a drag on the organization's opportunities.

COMMUNICATE IS ISSUES TO THE EXECUTIVE GROUP

This last observation leads to the second IS planning function in Figure 11-3. The CIO is the representative for IS and IT issues within the executive staff. The CIO provides the IS perspective during discussions of problem solutions, proposals, and new initiatives.

For example, when considering a merger, it is important that the company consider integration of information systems in the merged entities. This consideration needs to be addressed during the evaluation of the merger opportunity. Too often, such issues are not considered until after the deal has been signed. Such delayed consideration is a mistake; the costs of the integration need to be factored into the economics of the purchase. Involving the CIO in high-level discussions is the best way to avoid such problems.

- Align information systems with organizational strategy; maintain alignment as organization changes.
- Communicate IS/IT issues to executive group.
- Develop/enforce IS priorities within the IS department.
- Sponsor steering committee.

Figure 11-3
Planning the Use of IS/IT

DEVELOP PRIORITIES AND ENFORCE THEM WITHIN THE IS DEPARTMENT

The next IS planning function in Figure 11-3 concerns priorities. The CIO must ensure that priorities consistent with the overall organizational strategy are developed and then communicated to the IS department. At the same time, the CIO must also ensure that the department evaluates proposals and projects for using new technology in light of those communicated priorities.

Technology is seductive, particularly to IS professionals. The CTO may enthusiastically claim, "By moving all our reporting services to the cloud, we can do this and this and this . . ." Although true, the question that the CIO must continually ask is whether those new possibilities are consistent with the organization's strategy and direction.

Thus, the CIO must not only establish and communicate such priorities, but enforce them as well. The department must evaluate every proposal, at the earliest stage possible, as to whether it is consistent with the organization's goals and aligned with its strategy.

Furthermore, no organization can afford to implement every good idea. Even projects that are aligned with the organization's strategy must be prioritized. The objective of everyone in the IS department must be to develop the most appropriate systems possible, given constraints on time and money. Well-thought-out and clearly communicated priorities are essential.

SPONSOR THE STEERING COMMITTEE

To learn more about business process management, see Chapter Extension 17.

The final planning function in Figure 11-3 is to sponsor the steering committee. A **steering committee** is a group of senior managers from the major business functions that works with the CIO to set the IS priorities and decide among major IS projects and alternatives.

The steering committee serves an important communication function between IS and the users. In the steering committee, information systems personnel can discuss potential IS initiatives and directions with the user community. At the same time, the steering committee provides a forum for users to express their needs, frustrations, and other issues they have with the IS department.

Typically, the IS department sets up the steering committee's schedule and agenda and conducts the meetings. The CEO and other members of the executive staff determine the membership of the steering committee.

One other task related to planning the use of IT is to establish the organization's computer-use policy. For more on computer-use issues, read the Ethics Guide on pages 298–299.

 WHAT ARE THE ADVANTAGES AND DISADVANTAGES OF OUTSOURCING?

Outsourcing is the process of hiring another organization to perform a service. Outsourcing is done to save costs, to gain expertise, and to free management time.

The father of modern management, Peter Drucker, is reputed to have said, "Your back room is someone else's front room." For instance, in most companies, running the cafeteria is not an essential function for business success; thus, the employee cafeteria is a "back room." Google wants to be the worldwide leader in search and mobile computing hardware and applications, all supported by ever-increasing ad revenue. It does not want to be known for how well it runs its cafeterias. Using Drucker's sentiment, Google is better off hiring another company, one that specializes in food services, to run its cafeterias.

Because food service is some company's "front room," that company will be better able to provide a quality product at a fair price. Outsourcing to a food vendor will also free Google's management from attention on the cafeteria. Food quality, chef scheduling, plastic fork acquisition, waste disposal, and so on, will all be another company's concern. Google can focus on search, mobile computing, and advertising-revenue growth.

Experiencing MIS   INCLASS EXERCISE 11

Setting up the PRIDE Systems IS Department

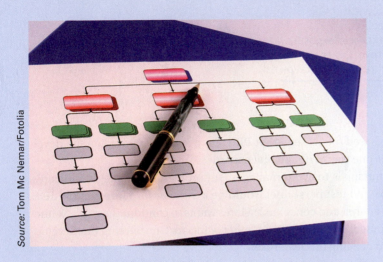

Source: Tom Mc Nemar/Fotolia

Let's suppose that Dr. Flores was able to attain investment funds sufficient to implement PRIDE for medical practices, patients, and health clubs. Assume that he and his investors elected to wait until they had that portion of the business operating before they included insurance companies and employers.

Clearly, it makes no sense to attempt to integrate the new operation with his surgical practice. Assume that, instead, the investment group formed a new company entitled PRIDE Systems. PRIDE Systems will employ managers, sales and marketing, and customer support personnel. Additionally, through a combination of in-house personnel and outsourcing, they will also staff an IS department.

Suppose you are asked to help plan that new department. Form a group, as instructed by your professor, and answer the following questions:

1. State the major functions of this new IS department. Explain how each of the functions defined in this chapter pertain to PRIDE.

2. Assume that the experience of hiring Ajit Barid worked well and that they plan to continue application development with him. Describe factors that may make the investors nervous about this decision. Explain how you would respond to each of those factors.

3. Assume that PRIDE Systems will hire a cloud vendor to provide PaaS functionality. Explain what this means in general, and what it means in particular for PRIDE.

4. Given your answers to questions 2 and 3,
   a. What will be the function and goals of the Operations group (see Figure 11-1)?
   b. What will be the function and goals of the Development group? What job descriptions will this group need to staff?
   c. What will be the function and goals of the Outsourcing Relations group?
   d. Will PRIDE Systems need a CTO? Justify your answer.

5. Understanding that PRIDE Systems is a small startup company that needs to conserve its investment dollars, would you recommend outsourcing any of the following functions? If so, explain the risks of doing so. If not, explain how you would justify the costs associated with staffing that function with employees.
   a. CTO
   b. Operations
   c. Outsourcing relations

6. Using Drucker's analogy, is IS Management in the front room or the back room for PRIDE Systems?

7. Summarize what you have learned in this exercise in a one-minute statement that you could use in a job interview with a small company.

OUTSOURCING INFORMATION SYSTEMS

Many companies today have chosen to outsource portions of their information systems activities. Figure 11-4 lists popular reasons for doing so. Consider each major group of reasons.

Management Advantages

First, outsourcing can be an easy way to gain expertise. Neither Maggie nor Dr. Flores knows how to build an iOS or an HTML5 application. Maggie could learn to do so, but it is not the direction in which she wants to go with her business and her career. Similarly, neither know how

Figure 11-4
Popular Reasons for
Outsourcing IS Services

- Management advantages
  - Obtain expertise.
  - Avoid management problems.
  - Free management time.

- Cost reduction
  - Obtain part-time services.
  - Gain economies of scale.

- Risk reduction
  - Cap financial exposure.
  - Improve quality.
  - Reduce implementation risk.

to create and manage a cloud-based report server for PRIDE reporting. Outsourcing the development of these applications is one way to obtain that expertise.

Another reason for outsourcing is to avoid management problems. As Maggie indicates, hiring their own programmers and test personnel would be a disaster for Flores and PRIDE. Maggie wants to be a business analyst and consultant; Flores wants to continue surgery. Neither knows how to manage development personnel, and neither wants to. Outsourcing the development function saves them from needing this expertise.

Similarly, some companies choose to outsource to save management time and attention. Lucas at GearUp has the skills to manage a new software development project, but he may choose not to invest the time.

Note, too, that it's not just Lucas' time. It is also time taken from more senior managers who approve the purchase and hiring requisitions for that activity. And, those senior managers, like Kelly, will need to devote the time necessary to learn enough about Web farms to approve or reject the requisitions. Outsourcing saves both direct and indirect management time.

Cost Reduction

Other common reasons for choosing to outsource concern cost reductions. With outsourcing, organizations can obtain part-time services. Another benefit of outsourcing is to gain economies of scale. If 25 organizations develop their own payroll applications in-house, then when the tax law changes, 25 different groups will have to learn the new law, change their software to meet the law, test the changes, and write the documentation explaining the changes. However, if those same 25 organizations outsource to the same payroll vendor, then that vendor can make all of the adjustments once, and the cost of the change can be amortized over all of them (thus lowering the cost that the vendor must charge).

Risk Reduction

Another reason for outsourcing is to reduce risk. First, outsourcing can cap financial risk. In a typical outsourcing contract, the outsource vendor will agree to a fixed price contract for services. This occurs, for example, when companies outsource their hardware to cloud vendors. Another way to cap financial is as Maggie recommends: delay paying the bulk of the fee until the work is completed and the software (or other component) is working. In the first case, outsourcing reduces risk by capping the total due; in the second, it ensures that little money is spent until the job is done.

Second, outsourcing can reduce risk by ensuring a certain level of quality, or avoiding the risk of having substandard quality. A company that specializes in food service knows what to do to provide a certain level of quality. It has the expertise to ensure, for example, that only healthy food is served. So, too, a company that specializes in, say, cloud-server hosting, knows what to do to provide a certain level of reliability for a given workload.

Note that there is no guarantee that outsourcing will provide a certain level of quality or higher quality than could be achieved in-house. If it doesn't outsource the cafeteria, Google might get lucky and hire only great chefs. Maggie might get lucky and hire the world's best software developer. But, in general, a professional outsourcing firm knows how to avoid giving everyone food poisoning or how to develop new mobile applications. And, if that minimum level of quality is not provided, it is easier to hire another vendor than it is to fire and rehire internal staff.

Finally, organizations choose to outsource IS in order to reduce implementation risk. Hiring an outside cloud vendor reduces the risk of picking the wrong brand of hardware or the wrong virtualization software, or implementing tax law changes incorrectly. Outsourcing gathers all of these risks into the one risk of choosing the right vendor. Once the company has chosen the vendor, further risk management is up to that vendor.

INTERNATIONAL OUTSOURCING

Choosing to use an outsourcing developer in India is not unique to PRIDE. Many firms head-quartered in the United States have chosen to outsource overseas. Microsoft and Dell, for example, have outsourced major portions of their customer support activities to companies outside the United States. India is a popular choice because it has a large, well-educated, English-speaking population that will work for 20 to 30 percent of the labor cost in the United States. China and other countries are used as well. In fact, with modern telephone technology and Internet-enabled service databases, a single service call can be initiated in the United States, partially processed in India, then Singapore, and finalized by an employee in England. The customer knows only that he has been put on hold for brief periods of time.

International outsourcing is particularly advantageous for customer support and other functions that must be operational 24/7. Amazon.com, for example, operates customer service centers in the United States, India, and Ireland. During the evening hours in the United States, customer service reps in India, where it is daytime, handle the calls. When night falls in India, customer service reps in Ireland handle the early morning calls from the east coast of the United States. In this way, companies can provide 24/7 service without requiring employees to work night shifts.

By the way, as you learned in Chapter 1, the key protection for your job is to become someone who excels at nonroutine symbolic analysis. Someone with the ability to find innovative applications of new technology also is unlikely to lose his or her job to overseas workers.

WHAT ARE THE OUTSOURCING ALTERNATIVES?

Organizations have found hundreds of different ways to outsource information systems and portions of information systems. Figure 11-5 organizes the major categories of alternatives according to information systems components.

Some organizations outsource the acquisition and operation of computer hardware. Electronic Data Systems (EDS) has been successful for more than 30 years as an outsource vendor of hardware infrastructure. Figure 11-5 shows another alternative, outsourcing the computers in the cloud via IaaS.

Acquiring licensed software, as discussed in Chapters 4 and 10, is a form of outsourcing. Rather than develop the software in-house, an organization licenses it from another vendor. Such licensing allows the software vendor to amortize the cost of software maintenance over all

Figure 11-5
IS/IT Outsourcing
Alternatives

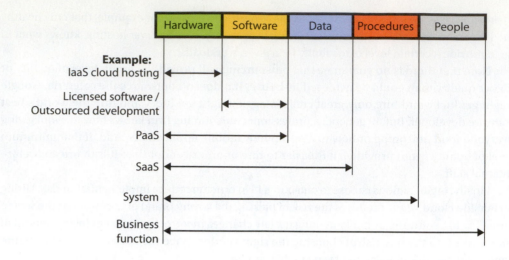

of the users, thus reducing that cost for all users. Another option is Platform as a Service (PaaS), which is the leasing of hardware pre-installed operating systems as well as possibly DBMS systems. Microsoft's Azure is one such PaaS offering.

Some organizations choose to outsource the development of software. Such outsourcing might be for an entire application, as with PRIDE, or it could also be for making customizations to licensed software, as is frequently done with ERP implementations.

Yet another alternative is Software as a Service (SaaS), in which hardware and both operating system and application software is leased. Salesforce.com is a typical example of a company that offers SaaS.

It is also possible to outsource an entire system. PeopleSoft (now owned by Oracle) attained prominence by providing the entire payroll function as an outsourced service. In such a solution, as the arrow in Figure 11-5 implies, the vendor provides hardware, software, data, and some procedures. The company need provide only employee and work information; the payroll outsource vendor does the rest.

Finally, some organizations choose to outsource an entire business function. For years, many companies have outsourced to travel agencies the function of arranging for employee travel. Some of these outsource vendors even operate offices within the company facilities. Such agreements are much broader than outsourcing IS, but information systems are key components of the applications that are outsourced.

WHAT ARE THE RISKS OF OUTSOURCING?

Not everyone agrees on the desirability of outsourcing. For potential pitfalls, read the example in the Guide on pages 300–301.

With so many advantages and with so many different outsourcing alternatives, you might wonder why any company has any in-house IS/IT functions. In fact, outsourcing presents significant risks, as listed in Figure 11-6.

Loss of Control

The first risk of outsourcing is a loss of control. For PRIDE, once Dr. Flores contracts with Ajit, Ajit is in control. At least for several weeks or months. If he makes PRIDE a priority project and devotes his attention and the attention of his employees as needed, all can work out well. On the other hand, if he obtains a larger, more lucrative contract soon after he starts PRIDE, schedule and quality problems can develop. Neither Flores nor Maggie have any control over this eventuality. If they pay at the end, they may not lose money, but they can lose time.

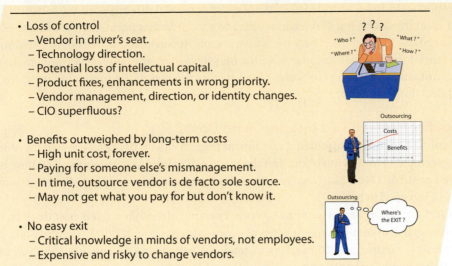

Figure 11-6
Outsourcing Risks

- Loss of control
  - Vendor in driver's seat.
  - Technology direction.
  - Potential loss of intellectual capital.
  - Product fixes, enhancements in wrong priority.
  - Vendor management, direction, or identity changes.
  - CIO superfluous?

- Benefits outweighed by long-term costs
  - High unit cost, forever.
  - Paying for someone else's mismanagement.
  - In time, outsource vendor is de facto sole source.
  - May not get what you pay for but don't know it.

- No easy exit
  - Critical knowledge in minds of vendors, not employees.
  - Expensive and risky to change vendors.

For service-oriented outsourcing, say the outsourcing of IT infrastructure, the vendor is in the driver's seat. Each outsource vendor has methods and procedures for its service. The organization and its employees will have to conform to those procedures. For example, a hardware infrastructure vendor will have standard forms and procedures for requesting a computer, for recording and processing a computer problem, or for providing routine maintenance on computers. Once the vendor is in charge, employees must conform.

When outsourcing the cafeteria, employees have only those food choices that the vendor provides. Similarly, when obtaining computer hardware and services, the employees will need to take what the vendor supports. Employees who want equipment that is not on the vendor's list will be out of luck.

Unless the contract requires otherwise, the outsource vendor can choose the technology that it wants to implement. If the vendor, for some reason, is slow to pick up on a significant new technology, then the hiring organization will be slow to attain benefits from that technology. An organization can find itself at a competitive disadvantage because it cannot offer the same IS services as its competitors.

Another concern is a potential loss of intellectual capital. The company may need to reveal proprietary trade secrets, methods, or procedures to the outsource vendor's employees. As part of its normal operations, that vendor may move employees to competing organizations, and the company may lose intellectual capital as that happens. The loss need not be intellectual theft; it could simply be that the vendor's employees learned to work in a new and better way at your company, and then they take that learning to your competitor.

Similarly, all software has failures and problems. Quality vendors track those shortcomings and fix them according to a set of priorities. When a company outsources a system, it no longer has control over prioritizing those fixes. Such control belongs to the vendor. A fix that might be critical to your organization might be of low priority to the outsource vendor.

Other problems are that the outsource vendor may change management, adopt a different strategic direction, or be acquired. When any of those changes occur, priorities may change, and an outsource vendor that was a good choice at one time might be a bad fit after it changes direction. It can be difficult and expensive to change an outsource vendor when this occurs.

The final loss-of-control risk is that the company's CIO can become superfluous. When users need a critical service that is outsourced, the CIO must turn to the vendor for a response. In time, users learn that it is quicker to deal directly with the outsource vendor, and soon the CIO is out of the communication loop. At that point, the vendor has essentially replaced the CIO, who has become a figurehead. However, employees of the outsource vendor work for a different company, with a bias toward their employer. Critical managers will thus not share the same goals and objectives as the rest of the management team. Biased, bad decisions can result.

Benefits Outweighed by Long-Term Costs

The initial benefits of outsourcing can appear huge. A cap on financial exposure, a reduction of management time and attention, and the release of many management and staffing problems are all possible. (Most likely, outsource vendors promise these very benefits.) Outsourcing can appear too good to be true.

In fact, it *can be* too good to be true. For one, although a fixed cost does indeed cap exposure, it also removes the benefits of economies of scale. If PRIDE demand takes off, and suddenly GearUp needs 200 servers instead of 20, the using organization will pay 200 times the fixed cost of supporting one server. It is likely, however, that because of economies of scale, the costs of supporting 200 servers are far less than 10 times the costs of supporting 20 servers. If they were hosting those servers in-house, they, rather than the vendor, would be the beneficiary.

Also, the outsource vendor may change its pricing strategy over time. Initially, an organization obtains a competitive bid from several outsource vendors. However, as the winning vendor learns more about the business and as relationships develop between the organization's employees and those of the vendor, it becomes difficult for other firms to compete for subsequent contracts. The vendor becomes the *de facto* sole source and, with little competitive pressure, might increase its prices.

Another problem is that an organization can find itself paying for another organization's mismanagement, with little knowledge that that is the case. If PRIDE outsources its servers, it is difficult for it to know if the vendor is well managed. The PRIDE investors may be paying for poor management; even worse, it may suffer the consequences of poor management, such as lost data. It will be very difficult for PRIDE to learn about such mismanagement.

No Easy Exit

The final category of outsourcing risk concerns ending the agreement. There is no easy exit. For one, the outsource vendor's employees have gained significant knowledge of the company. They know the server requirements in customer support, they know the patterns of usage, and they know the best procedures for downloading operational data into the data warehouse. Consequently, lack of knowledge will make it difficult to bring the outsourced service back in-house.

Also, because the vendor has become so tightly integrated into the business, parting company can be exceedingly risky. Closing down the employee cafeteria for a few weeks while finding another food vendor would be unpopular, but employees would survive. Shutting down the enterprise network for a few weeks would be impossible; the business would not survive. Because of such risk, the company must invest considerable work, duplication of effort, management time, and expense to change to another vendor. In truth, choosing an outsource vendor can be a one-way street.

At PRIDE, if, after the initial application development, the team decides to change development vendors, it may be very difficult to do. The new vendor will not know the application code as well as the current one who created it. It may become cost infeasible to consider moving to another better, lower-cost vendor.

Choosing to outsource is a difficult decision. In fact, the correct decision might not be clear, but time and events could force the company to decide.

You have a right to:
– Computer hardware and programs that allow you to perform your job proficiently
– Reliable network and Internet connections
– A secure computing environment
– Protection from viruses, worms, and other threats
– Contribute to requirements for new system features and functions
– Reliable systems development and maintenance
– Prompt attention to problems, concerns, and complaints
– Properly prioritized problem fixes and resolutions
– Effective training

You have a responsibility to:
– Learn basic computer skills
– Learn standard techniques and procedures for the applications you use
– Follow security and backup procedures
– Protect your password(s)
– Use computers and mobile devices . . . according to your employer's computer use policy
– Make no unauthorized hardware modifications
– Install only authorized programs
– Apply software patches and fixes when directed to do so
– When asked, devote the time required to respond carefully and completely to requests for requirements for new system features and functions
– Avoid reporting trivial problems

Figure 11-7
User Information Systems Rights and Responsibilities

Q4 WHAT ARE YOUR USER RIGHTS AND RESPONSIBILITIES?

As a future user of information systems, you have both rights and responsibilities in your relationship with the IS department. The items in Figure 11-7 list what you are entitled to receive and indicate what you are expected to contribute.

YOUR USER RIGHTS

You have a right to have the computing resources you need to perform your work as proficiently as you want. You have a right to the computer hardware and programs that you need. If you process huge files for data-mining applications, you have a right to the huge disks and the fast processor that you need. However, if you merely receive email and consult the corporate Web portal, then your right is for more modest requirements (leaving the more powerful resources for those in the organization who need them).

You have a right to reliable network and Internet services. *Reliable* means that you can process without problems almost all of the time. It means that you never go to work wondering, "Will the network be available today?" Network problems should be rare.

You also have a right to a secure computing environment. The organization should protect your computer and its files, and you should not normally even need to think about security. From time to time, the organization might ask you to take particular actions to protect your computer and files, and you should take those actions. But such requests should be rare and related to specific outside threats.

You have a right to participate in requirements meetings for new applications that you will use and for major changes to applications that you currently use. You may choose to delegate this right to others, or your department may delegate that right for you, but if so, you have a right to contribute your thoughts through that representative.

You have a right to reliable systems development and maintenance. Although schedule slippages of a month or two are common in many development projects, you should not have to endure schedule slippages of six months or more. Such slippages are evidence of incompetent systems development.

Additionally, you have a right to receive prompt attention to your problems, concerns, and complaints about information services. You have a right to have a means to report problems, and you have a right to know that your problem has been received and at least registered with the IS department. You have a right to have your problem resolved, consistent with established priorities. This means that an annoying problem that allows you to conduct your work will be prioritized below another's problem that interferes with his ability to do his job.

Finally, you have a right to effective training. It should be training that you can understand and that enables you to use systems to perform your particular job. The organization should provide training in a format and on a schedule that is convenient to you.

YOUR USER RESPONSIBILITIES

You also have responsibilities toward the IS department and your organization. Specifically, you have a responsibility to learn basic computer skills and to learn the techniques and procedures for the applications you use. You should not expect hand-holding for basic operations. Nor should you expect to receive repetitive training and support for the same issue.

You have a responsibility to follow security and backup procedures. This is especially important because actions that you fail to take might cause problems for your fellow employees and your organization as well as for you. In particular, you are responsible for protecting your password(s). In the next chapter, you will learn that this is important not only to protect your computer, but, because of intersystem authentication, it is important to protect your organization's networks and databases as well.

You have a responsibility for using your computer resources in a manner that is consistent with your employer's policy. Many employers allow limited email for critical family matters while at work, but discourage frequent and long casual email. You have a responsibility to know your employer's policy and to follow it. Further, if your employer has policy concerning use of personal mobile devices at work, you have a responsibility to follow it.

You also have a responsibility to make no unauthorized hardware modifications to your computer and to install only authorized programs. One reason for this policy is that your IS department constructs automated maintenance programs for upgrading your computer. Unauthorized hardware and programs might interfere with these programs. Additionally, the installation of unauthorized hardware or programs can cause you problems that the IS department will have to fix.

You have a responsibility to install computer updates and fixes when asked to do so. This is particularly important for patches that concern security, backup, and recovery. When asked for input to requirements for new and adapted systems, you have a responsibility to take the time necessary to provide thoughtful and complete responses. If you do not have that time, you should delegate your input to someone else.

Finally, you have a responsibility to treat information systems professionals professionally. Everyone works for the same company, everyone wants to succeed, and professionalism and courtesy will go a long way on all sides. One form of professional behavior is to learn basic computer skills so that you avoid reporting trivial problems.

How does the **knowledge** in this chapter help **you?**

You now know the primary responsibilities of that department and can understand why the IS department may implement standards and policies that it does. You know the planning functions of IS and how they relate to the rest of your organization. You also know the reasons for outsourcing IS services, the most common and popular outsource alternatives, and the outsourcing risks. Finally, you know your rights and responsibilities with regard to services provided by your IS department.

All of this knowledge will help you be a better consumer of the services of your IS department. If you work in a small company, with little or no IS support, you know the kinds of work that must be done and the advantages, disadvantages, and choices for outsourcing that work. If you find yourself in Flores' position, you know the advantages and disadvantages of outsourcing software development. Finally, knowledge of your rights and responsibilities will enable you to be a more effective business professional by setting reasonable expectations as to what you can expect from the IS department, while at the same time knowing what the IS department expects of you.

Ethics Guide

Using the Corporate Computer

Suppose you work at a company that has the following computer use policy:

Computers, email, social networking, and the Internet are to be used primarily for official company business. Small amounts of personal email can be exchanged with friends and family, and occasional usage of the Internet is permitted, but such usage should be limited and never interfere with your work.

Suppose you are a manager, and you learn that one of your employees has been engaged in the following activities:

1. Playing computer games during work hours
2. Playing computer games on the company computer before and after work hours
3. Responding to emails from an ill parent
4. Watching DVDs during lunch and other breaks
5. Sending emails to plan a party that involves mostly people from work
6. Sending emails to plan a party that involves no one from work
7. Searching the Web for a new car
8. Reading the news on CNN.com
9. Checking the stock market over the Internet
10. Bidding on items for personal use on eBay
11. Selling personal items on eBay
12. Paying personal bills online
13. Paying personal bills online when traveling on company business
14. Buying an airplane ticket for an ill parent over the Internet
15. Changing the content of a personal Facebook page
16. Changing the content of a personal business Web site
17. Buying an airplane ticket for a personal vacation over the Internet
18. Responding to personal Twitter messages

DISCUSSION QUESTIONS

1. Explain how you would respond to each situation.

2. Suppose someone from the IS department notifies you that one of your employees is spending 3 hours a day writing Twitter messages. How do you respond?

3. For question 2, suppose you ask how the IS department knows about your employee and you are told, "We secretly monitor computer usage." Do you object to such monitoring? Why or why not?

4. Suppose someone from the IS department notifies you that one of your employees is sending many personal emails. When you ask how they know the emails are personal, you are told that IS measures account activity and when suspicious email usage is suspected the IS department reads employees' email. Do you think such reading is legal? Is it ethical? How do you respond?

5. As an employee, if you know that your company occasionally reads employees' email, does that change your behavior? If so, does that justify the company reading your email? Does this situation differ from having someone read your personal postal mail that happens to be delivered to you at work? Why or why not?

6. Write what you think is the best corporate policy for personal computer usage at work. Specifically address Facebook, Pinterest, Twitter, and other personal social networking activity.

Source: Blue Jean Images/SuperStock

Guide

Is Outsourcing Fool's Gold?

"People are kidding themselves. It sounds so good—just pay a fixed, known amount to some vendor for your computer infrastructure, and all your problems go away. Everyone has the computers they need, the network never goes down, and you never have to endure another horrible meeting about network protocols, HTTPs, and the latest worm. You're off into information systems nirvana. . . .

"Except it doesn't work that way. You trade one set of problems for another. Consider the outsourcing of computer infrastructure. What's the first thing the outsource vendor does? It hires all of the employees who were doing the work for you. Remember that lazy, incompetent network administrator that the company had—the one who never seemed to get anything done? Well, he's baaaaack, as an employee of your outsource company. Only this time he has an excuse, 'Company policy won't allow me to do it that way.'

"So the outsourcers get their first-level employees by hiring the ones you had. Of course, the outsourcer says it will provide management oversight, and if the employees don't work out, they'll be gone. What you're really outsourcing is middle-level management of the same IT personnel you had. But there's no way of knowing whether the managers they supply are any better than the ones you had.

"Also, you think you had bureaucratic problems before? Every vendor has a set of forms, procedures, committees, reports, and other management 'tools.' They will tell you that you have to do things according to the standard blueprint. They have to say that because if they allowed every company to be different, they'd never be able to gain any leverage themselves, and they'd never be profitable.

"So now you're paying a premium for the services of your former employees, who are now managed by strangers who are paid by the outsource vendor, who evaluates those managers on how well they follow the outsource vendor's profit-generating procedures. How quickly can they turn your operation into a clone of all their other clients? Do you really want to do that?

"Suppose you figure all this out and decide to get out of it. Now what? How do you undo an outsource agreement? All the critical knowledge is in the minds of the outsource vendor's employees, who have no incentive to work for you. In fact, their employment contract probably prohibits it. So now you have to take an existing operation within your own company, hire employees to staff that function, and relearn everything you ought to have learned in the first place.

"Gimme a break. Outsourcing is fool's gold, an expensive leap away from responsibility. It's like saying, 'We can't figure out how to manage an important function in our company, so you do it!' You can't get away from IS problems by hiring someone else to manage them for you. At least you care about *your* bottom line."

DISCUSSION QUESTIONS

1. Hiring an organization's existing IS staff is common practice when starting a new outsourcing arrangement. What are the advantages of this practice to the outsource vendor? What are the advantages to the organization?

2. Suppose you work for an outsource vendor. How do you respond to the charge that your managers care only about how they appear to their employer (the outsource vendor), not how they actually perform for the organization?

3. Consider the statement, "We can't figure out how to manage an important function in our company, so you do it!" Do you agree with the sentiment of this statement? If this is true, is it necessarily bad? Why or why not?

4. Explain how it is possible for an outsource vendor to achieve economies of scale that are not possible for the hiring organization. Does this phenomenon justify outsourcing? Why or why not?

5. In what ways is outsourcing IS infrastructure like outsourcing the company cafeteria? In what ways is it different? What general conclusions can you make about infrastructure outsourcing?

6. This guide assumes that the outsourcing agreement is for the organization's computing infrastructure. Outsourcing for software development, as PRIDE is doing, involves less direct involvement with the contractor. Explain how your answers to questions 2–5 would be different for software outsourcing.

7. How do your answers to questions 2–5 differ if the outsourcing agreement is just for PaaS resources?

Source: goldenangel/Fotolia

ACTIVE REVIEW

Use this Active Review to verify that you understand the ideas and concepts that answer the chapter's study questions.

Q1 WHAT ARE THE FUNCTIONS AND ORGANIZATION OF THE IS DEPARTMENT?

List the five primary functions of the IS department. Define *CIO* and explain the CIO's typical reporting relationships. Name the four groups found in a typical IS department, and explain the major responsibilities of each. Define *CTO,* and explain typical CTO responsibilities. Explain the purpose of the data administration function.

Q2 HOW DO ORGANIZATIONS PLAN THE USE OF IS?

Explain the importance of strategic alignment as it pertains to IS planning. Explain why maintaining alignment can be difficult. Describe the CIO's relationship to the rest of the executive staff. Describe the CIO's responsibilities with regard to priorities. Explain challenges to this task. Define *steering committee* and explain the CIO's role with regard to it.

Q3 WHAT ARE THE ADVANTAGES AND DISADVANTAGES OF OUTSOURCING?

Define *outsourcing.* Explain how Drucker's statement, "Your back room is someone else's front room" pertains to outsourcing. Summarize the management advantages, cost advantages, and risks of outsourcing. Differentiate among IaaS, PaaS, and SaaS and give an example of each. Explain why international outsourcing can be particularly advantageous. Describe skills you can develop that will protect you from having your job outsourced. Summarize the outsourcing risks concerning control, long-term costs, and exit strategy.

Q4 WHAT ARE YOUR USER RIGHTS AND RESPONSIBILITIES?

Explain in your own words the meaning of each of your user rights as listed in Figure 11-7. Explain in your own words the meaning of each of your user responsibilities in Figure 11-7.

How does the **knowledge** in this chapter help **you?**

State how the knowledge of this chapter will help you as an employee of a large company. State how it will help you if you work for a small company. Explain how this knowledge will help you should you find yourself in Flores' position. Explain how this knowledge will enable you to be a more effective business professional.

KEY TERMS AND CONCEPTS

Chief information officer (CIO) 284
Chief technology officer (CTO) 284

Green computing 303
Outsourcing 288

Steering committee 288

USING YOUR KNOWLEDGE

1. According to this chapter, information systems, products, and technology are not malleable; they are difficult to change, alter, or bend. How do you think senior executives other than the CIO view this lack of malleability? For example, how do you think IS appears during a corporate merger?

2. Suppose you represent an investor group that is acquiring hospitals across the nation and integrating them into a unified system. List five potential problems and risks concerning information systems. How do you think IS-related risks compare to other risks in such an acquisition program?

3. What happens to IS when corporate direction changes rapidly? How will IS appear to other departments? What happens to IS when the corporate strategy changes frequently? Do you think such frequent changes are a greater problem to IS than to other business functions? Why or why not?

4. Consider the following statement: "In many ways, choosing an outsource vendor is a one-way street." Explain what this statement means. Do you agree with it? Why or why not? Does your answer change depending on what systems components are being outsourced? Why or why not?

5. Using the dialog that opened this chapter, as well as Figures 11-4 and 11-6, list the advantages and disadvantages of outsourcing PRIDE application development. Briefly describe each.

COLLABORATION EXERCISE 11

Before you start this exercise, read Chapter Extensions 1 and 2, which describe collaboration techniques as well as tools for managing collaboration tasks. In particular, consider using Google Drive, Google+, Windows Live SkyDrive, Microsoft SharePoint, or some other collaboration tool.

Green computing is environmentally conscious computing consisting of three major components: power management, virtualization, and e-waste management. In this exercise, we focus on power.

You know, of course, that computers (and related equipment, such as printers) consume electricity. That burden is light for any single computer or printer. But consider all of the computers and printers in the United States that will be running tonight, with no one in the office. Proponents of green computing encourage companies and employees to reduce power and water consumption by turning off devices when not in use.

Is this issue important? Is it just a concession to environmentalists to make computing professionals appear virtuous? Form a team and develop your own, informed opinion by considering computer use at your campus.

1. Search the Internet to determine the power requirements for typical computing and office equipment. Consider laptop computers, desktop computers, CRT monitors, LCD monitors, and printers. For this exercise, ignore server computers. As you search, be aware that a *watt* is a measure of electrical power. It is *watts* that the green computing movement wants to reduce.

2. Estimate the number of each type of device in use on your campus. Use your university's Web site to determine the number of colleges, departments, faculty, staff, and students. Make assumptions about the number of computers, copiers, and other types of equipment used by each.

3. Using the data from items 1 and 2, estimate the total power used by computing and related devices on your campus.

4. A computer that is in screensaver mode uses the same amount of power as one in regular mode. Computers that are in sleep mode, however, use much less power, say 6 watts per hour. Reflect on computer use on your campus and estimate the amount of time that computing devices are in sleep versus screensaver or use mode. Compute the savings in power that result from sleep mode.

5. Computers that are automatically updated by the IS department with software upgrades and patches cannot be allowed to go into sleep mode because if they are sleeping they will not be able to receive the upgrade. Hence, some universities prohibit sleep mode on university computers (sleep mode is never used on servers, by the way). Determine the cost, in watts, of such a policy.

6. Calculate the monthly cost, in watts, if:
   a. All user computers run full time night and day.
   b. All user computers run full time during work hours and in sleep mode during off-hours.
   c. All user computers are shut off during nonwork hours.

7. Given your answers to items 1–6, is computer power management during off-hours a significant concern? In comparison to the other costs of running a university, does this issue really matter? Discuss this question among your group and explain your answer.

CASE STUDY 11

iApp$$$$ 4 U

Let's suppose that you have a great idea for an iOS application. It doesn't matter what it is; it could be something to make life easier for college students or your parents, or something to track healthcare expenses and payments for your grandparents. Whatever it is, let's assume that the idea is a great one.

First, what is the value of that idea? According to Raven Zachary, writing on the O'Reilly blog, it is zero.

[1]*Nada*. According to Zachary, no professional iPhone developer (he wrote this in 2008 about iPhone apps) will take equity or the promise of future revenue sharing in exchange for cash. There is too much cash-paying work. And, ideas are only as good as their implementation, a fact that is true for every business project, not just iOS applications.

So, how can you go about getting your iOS application developed? According to *OS X Daily*, in 2010 iOS developers in the United States and countries in the European Union were charging $50 to $250 per hour, and a typical, smaller application required 4 to 6 weeks to create.[2] Tech-Crunch polled 124 developers and found that the average cost of creating an iPhone app was $6,453,[3] but that number included projects that were programmed using cheaper, offshore developers.

These costs are incomplete. They include programming time, but not time to specify requirements nor to design the user interface, both of which are time-consuming tasks. Also, it is not clear that these costs include testing time nor the time needed to marshal the app through the Apple review process before it can appear in the App Store.

So, what are your options? First, do as much work as you can. Reread the stages in the systems development life cycle in Chapter 10 (pages 258–259). Determine how many of those stages you can do yourself. Unless you are already a skilled object-oriented programmer and comfortable writing in Objective-C, you cannot do the coding yourself. You might, however, be able to reduce development costs if you design the user interface and specify the ways that your users will employ it. You can also develop at least the skeleton of a test plan. You might also perform some of the testing tasks yourself.

If you have, let's round up, say $10,000 that you're willing to invest, then you could outsource the development to a developer in the United States. If not, you have two other possible choices: outsource offshore or hire a computer science student. Elance is a clearinghouse for iOS development experts; it lists developers, their locations, typical costs, and ratings provided by previous customers.[4] As you can see, you can hire developers in India, Russian, the Ukraine, Romania, and other countries. Costs tend to be in the $2,000 range for a simple app, but again, that estimate probably does not include all the costs you will incur getting your application into the App Store.

What about hiring a local computer science student? The price might be right, certainly far less than a professional developer, but this alternative is fraught with problems. First, good students are in high demand, and, second, good students are still, well, students. They need to study and don't have as much time to devote to your app. And, hard as it is to believe, some students are flakes. However, if you have a friend whom you trust, you might make this option work.

One other option is to divide and conquer. Break your really great idea up into smaller apps. Pick one that is sure to be a hit, and sell it cheaply, say for $.99. Use the money that you earn from that application to fund the next application, one that you might sell for more.

QUESTIONS

1. What characteristics make a mobile application great? Describe at least five characteristics that compel you to buy applications. What characteristics would make an application easy and cheap to develop? Difficult and expensive?

2. Visit *http://techcrunch.com/2010/05/16/iphone-app-sales-exposed*. Summarize the returns earned by both the top and more typical applications.

3. Reread pages 258–259 of Chapter 10 about the SDLC process. List tasks to perform and assess whether you could perform each task. If you cannot perform that task, describe how you could outsource that task and estimate how much you think it would cost for a simple application.

---

[1]http://blogs.oreilly.com/iphone/2008/11/turning-ideas-into-application.html, accessed August 2011.
[2]http://osxdaily.com/2010/09/07/iphone-development-costs/, accessed August 2011.
[3]http://techcrunch.com/2010/05/16/iphone-app-sales-exposed/, accessed August 2011.
[4]http://www.elance.com/groups/iPhone_Development_Experts, accessed August 2011.

4. Visit *www.elance.com* and identify five potential outsource vendors that you could use to develop your app. Describe criteria you would use for selecting one of these vendors.

5. Explain how you think Google's purchase of Motorola Mobility changes the opportunity for iOS apps. In theory, does this purchase cause you to believe it would be wiser for you to develop on the Android or on the Windows 7 phone?

6. Search the Web for "Android developers" and related terms. Does it appear that the process of creating an Android app is easier, cheaper, or more desirable than creating an iOS app?

7. This case assumes that you have made the decision to develop an iOS application. Take an opposing view that developing a thin-client browser application would be a better decision. Explain how you would justify a thin-client app as a better decision.

8. Prepare a 1-minute summary of your experience with this exercise that you could use in a job interview to demonstrate innovative thinking. Give your summary to the rest of your class.

chapter

12

Information Security Management

"We have to *design* it for privacy . . . and security." Ajit Barid is videoconferencing with Dr. Romero Flores and Maggie Jensen. Ajit is in his company offices in Hyderabad, India; Flores is in his office in Austin, Texas; and Maggie is in her office in Denver, Colorado.

"That sounds expensive. What do you mean, Ajit?" Flores is still getting comfortable with his outsourcing vendor.

"Well, to do this right, we need to design it so that the patient has control over the dissemination of the data." Ajit's voice comes in clearly, even though he is 11,000 miles away.

"Yes, I think we had that in our requirements statement."

"Dr. Flores," Maggie jumps into the conversation, "because we'll have, we hope, thousands and thousands of users, we need to store their privacy settings in a database."

"OK. I get that."

"That's the way to do it, but it also means that we need to have proper security over that database." Ajit continues.

"All right. I get that, too. So we just have people sign into the privacy database with their name as password?"

"Yes, we do, but we have to be careful to avoid problems like SQL injection attacks," Ajit doesn't know how much to explain.

"*Injection*? Now we're speaking my language. But what is SQL?"

Maggie doesn't want the conversation to get technical. She knows they're going to get bogged down as Flores tries to understand. He's a very bright man, and he won't be able to let anything go. She doesn't want to use their time tutoring him on SQL.

STUDY QUESTIONS

Q1 WHAT IS THE GOAL OF INFORMATION SYSTEMS SECURITY?

Q2 HOW BIG IS THE COMPUTER SECURITY PROBLEM?

Q3 HOW SHOULD YOU RESPOND TO SECURITY THREATS?

Q4 HOW SHOULD ORGANIZATIONS RESPOND TO SECURITY THREATS?

Q5 HOW CAN TECHNICAL SAFEGUARDS PROTECT AGAINST SECURITY THREATS?

Q6 HOW CAN DATA SAFEGUARDS PROTECT AGAINST SECURITY THREATS?

Q7 HOW CAN HUMAN SAFEGUARDS PROTECT AGAINST SECURITY THREATS?

Q8 HOW SHOULD ORGANIZATIONS RESPOND TO SECURITY INCIDENTS?

How does the **knowledge** in this chapter help **you?**

"We have to design it for privacy and security."

"How about this, Dr. Flores . . ." Maggie says cautiously, "rather than use your time for these details, why don't you let us work through the issues? There are a number of well-known attacks and issues that we need to design for, and we'll do that."

"OK, but I was starting to enjoy this. Injections. You guys have sutures, too?"

"No, but we talk about Band-Aids over bugs . . ."

"Ajit!" Maggie interrupts, "Let's let Dr. Flores get back to his practice. You and I can talk about this off-line." Maggie is determined to cut this conversation off before it's out of control.

Ajit and Maggie are videoconferencing an hour later:

"OK, Maggie, I'm sorry. I just couldn't resist. I wanted to get his reaction to *viruses* and *worms*, too . . ."

"I'm so glad you didn't." Maggie is relieved he sees her point. "What have you got?"

"The relationships among people and healthcare professionals, employers, insurance companies, and health clubs are all many-to-many."

"Right. I understand that, Ajit, but what does it have to do with privacy?"

"Well, we can use the intersection table for each to store the patient's privacy settings. And we only let the patients have access to forms having this data." (See figure on the next page.)

"Makes sense. I like it . . . a clean design."

"Privacy settings are carried in the PersonalPolicyStatement attribute. Possible values are 'No access,' 'Non-identifying,' 'Summary,' and 'Full Access.' The last two include patient identity."

"OK, but don't hard-code them. We may have others."

"Would I do that? If we showed this to Flores, he'd see what we mean by *design for security*."

"Ajit, don't go there."

"OK."

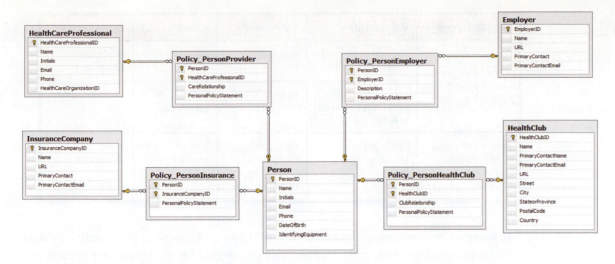

 ## WHAT IS THE GOAL OF INFORMATION SYSTEMS SECURITY?

Information systems security involves a trade-off between cost and risk. To understand the nature of this trade-off, we begin with a description of the security threat/loss scenario and then discuss the sources of security threats. Following that, we'll state the goal of information systems security.

THE IS SECURITY THREAT/LOSS SCENARIO

Figure 12-1 illustrates the major elements of the security problem that individuals and organizations confront today. A **threat** is a person or organization that seeks to obtain or alter data or other assets illegally, without the owner's permission and often without the owner's knowledge. A **vulnerability** is an opportunity for threats to gain access to individual or organizational assets. For example, when you buy something online, you provide your credit card data; when that data is transmitted over the Internet, it is vulnerable to threats. A **safeguard** is some measure that individuals or organizations take to block the threat from obtaining the asset. Notice in Figure 12-1 that safeguards are not always effective; some threats achieve their goal despite safeguards. Finally, the **target** is the asset that is desired by the threat.

Figure 12-2 shows examples of threats/targets, vulnerabilities, safeguards, and results. In the first two rows, an Xbox gamer (the threat) wants your credit card data (the target) to buy more games using your account. As stated previously, when you provide your credit card data for an online transaction, that data is vulnerable to the threat as it travels over the Internet. However, if, as shown in the first row of Figure 12-2, you conduct your transaction using HTTPS rather than HTTP (discussed in Q5), you will be using an effective safeguard, and you will successfully counter the threat.

Figure 12-1
Threat/Loss Scenario

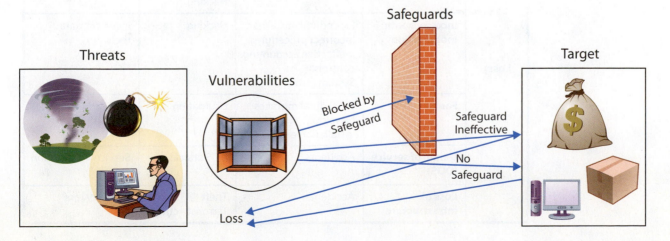

Figure 12-2
Examples of Threat/Loss

Threat/Target	Vulnerability	Safeguard	Result	Explanation
Xbox Live gamer wants your credit card data	You use your credit card to buy online	Buy only using https	No loss	Effective safeguard
	You send credit card data to friend in email	None	Loss of credit card data	No safeguard
Employee posts sensitive data to public Google+ group	Public access to not-secure group	Passwords Procedures Employee training	Loss of sensitive data	Ineffective safeguard

If, however, as described in the second row of Figure 12-2, you send your credit card data to a friend via email, you will, in most cases, have no safeguard at all. That data is open to any threat that happens to sniff your traffic on the Internet. In this case, you may soon be paying for hours and hours of Xbox games for a person whom you do not even know.

The bottom row of Figure 12-2 shows another situation. Here, an employee at work obtains sensitive data and posts it on what he thinks is a work-only Google+ group. However, the employee errs and instead posts it to a public group. The target is the sensitive data, and the vulnerability is public access to the group. In this case, there are several safeguards that should have prevented this loss; the employee needed passwords to obtain the sensitive data and to join the private, work-only group. The employer has procedures that state employees are not to post confidential data to any public site, such as Google+, but these procedures were either unknown or ignored. A third safeguard is the training that all employees are given. Because the employee ignores the procedures, though, all of those safeguards are ineffective and the data is exposed to the public.

WHAT ARE THE SOURCES OF THREATS?

Figure 12-3 summarizes the sources of security threats. The type of threat is shown in the columns, and the type of loss is shown in the rows.

Figure 12-3
Security Problems and Sources

		Threat		
		Human Error	**Computer Crime**	**Natural Disasters**
Loss	**Unauthorized data disclosure**	Procedural mistakes	Pretexting Phishing Spoofing Sniffing Hacking	Disclosure during recovery
	Incorrect data modification	Procedural mistakes Incorrect procedures Ineffective accounting controls System errors	Hacking	Incorrect data recovery
	Faulty service	Procedural mistakes Development and installation errors	Usurpation	Service improperly restored
	Denial of service (DOS)	Accidents	DOS attacks	Service interruption
	Loss of infrastructure	Accidents	Theft Terrorist activity	Property loss

Human Error

Human errors and mistakes include accidental problems caused by both employees and nonemployees. An example is an employee who misunderstands operating procedures and accidentally deletes customer records. Another example is an employee who, in the course of backing up a database, inadvertently installs an old database on top of the current one. This category also includes poorly written application programs and poorly designed procedures. Finally, human errors and mistakes include physical accidents, such as driving a forklift through the wall of a computer room.

Computer Crime

The second threat type is *computer crime*. This threat type includes employees and former employees who intentionally destroy data or other system components. It also includes hackers who break into a system and virus and worm writers who infect computer systems. Computer crime also includes terrorists and those who break into a system to steal for financial gain.

Natural Events and Disasters

Natural events and disasters are the third type of security threat. This category includes fires, floods, hurricanes, earthquakes, tsunamis, avalanches, and other acts of nature. Problems in this category include not only the initial loss of capability and service, but also losses stemming from actions to recover from the initial problem.

WHAT TYPES OF SECURITY LOSS EXIST?

Five types of security loss exist: unauthorized data disclosure, incorrect data modification, faulty service, denial of service, and loss of infrastructure. Consider each.

Unauthorized Data Disclosure

Unauthorized data disclosure occurs when a threat obtains data that is supposed to be protected. It can occur by human error when someone inadvertently releases data in violation of policy. An example at a university is a department administrator who posts student names, identification numbers, and grades in a public place, when the releasing of names and grades violates state law. Other examples are employees who unknowingly or carelessly release proprietary data to competitors or to the media and WikiLeaks, which is famous for leaking data, as is the third example in Figure 12-2.

The popularity and efficacy of search engines has created another source of inadvertent disclosure. Employees who place restricted data on Web sites that can be reached by search engines might mistakenly publish proprietary or restricted data over the Web.

Of course, proprietary and personal data can also be released and obtained maliciously. **Pretexting** occurs when someone deceives by pretending to be someone else. A common scam involves a telephone caller who pretends to be from a credit card company and claims to be checking the validity of credit card numbers: "I'm checking your MasterCard number; it begins with 5491. Can you verify the rest of the number?" Thousands of MasterCard numbers start with 5491; the caller is attempting to steal a valid number.

Phishing is a similar technique for obtaining unauthorized data that uses pretexting via email. The **phisher** pretends to be a legitimate company and sends an email requesting confidential data, such as account numbers, Social Security numbers, account passwords, and so forth. Phishing compromises legitimate brands and trademarks.

Spoofing is another term for someone pretending to be someone else. If you pretend to be your professor, you are spoofing your professor. **IP spoofing** occurs when an intruder uses another site's IP address to masquerade as that other site. **Email spoofing** is a synonym for phishing.

Sniffing is a technique for intercepting computer communications. With wired networks, sniffing requires a physical connection to the network. With wireless networks, no such connection is required: **Drive-by sniffers** simply take computers with wireless connections through an area and search for unprotected wireless networks. They can monitor and intercept wireless traffic at will. Even protected wireless networks are vulnerable, as you will learn. Spyware and adware are two other sniffing techniques discussed later in this chapter.

Other forms of computer crime include **hacking**, which is breaking into computers, servers, or networks to steal data such as customer lists, product inventory data, employee data, and other proprietary and confidential data.

Finally, people might inadvertently disclose data during recovery from a natural disaster. During a recovery, everyone is so focused on restoring system capability that they might ignore normal security safeguards. A request like "I need a copy of the customer database backup" will receive far less scrutiny during disaster recovery than at other times.

Incorrect Data Modification

The second type of security loss in Figure 12-3 is *incorrect data modification*. Examples include incorrectly increasing a customer's discount or incorrectly modifying an employee's salary, earned days of vacation, or annual bonus. Other examples include placing incorrect information, such as incorrect price changes, on a company's Web site or company portal.

Incorrect data modification can occur through human error when employees follow procedures incorrectly or when procedures have been designed incorrectly. For proper internal control on systems that process financial data or control inventories of assets, such as products and equipment, companies should ensure separation of duties and authorities and have multiple checks and balances in place.

A final type of incorrect data modification caused by human error includes *system errors*. An example is the lost-update problem discussed in Chapter 5 (page 117).

Computer criminals can make unauthorized data modifications by hacking into a computer system. For example, hackers could hack into a system and transfer people's account balances or place orders to ship goods to unauthorized locations and customers.

Finally, faulty recovery actions after a disaster can result in incorrect data changes. The faulty actions can be unintentional or malicious.

Faulty Service

The third type of security loss, *faulty service*, includes problems that result because of incorrect system operation. Faulty service could include incorrect data modification, as just described. It also could include systems that work incorrectly by sending the wrong goods to a customer or the ordered goods to the wrong customer, incorrectly billing customers, or sending the wrong information to employees. Humans can inadvertently cause faulty service by making procedural mistakes. System developers can write programs incorrectly or make errors during the installation of hardware, software programs, and data.

Usurpation occurs when computer criminals invade a computer system and replace legitimate programs with their own unauthorized ones that shut down legitimate applications and substitute their own processing to spy, steal and manipulate data, or other purposes. Faulty service can also result when service is improperly restored during recovery from natural disasters.

Denial of Service

Human error in following procedures or a lack of procedures can result in **denial of service (DOS)**, the fourth type of loss. For example, humans can inadvertently shut down a Web server or corporate gateway router by starting a computationally intensive application. An OLAP application that uses the operational DBMS can consume so many DBMS resources that order-entry transactions cannot get through.

Computer criminals can launch denial-of-service attacks in which a malicious hacker floods a Web server, for example, with millions of bogus service requests that so occupy the server that it cannot service legitimate requests. Also, computer worms can infiltrate a network with so much artificial traffic that legitimate traffic cannot get through. Finally, natural disasters may cause systems to fail, resulting in denial of service.

Loss of Infrastructure

Many times, human accidents cause loss of infrastructure, the last loss type. Examples are a bulldozer cutting a conduit of fiber-optic cables and the floor buffer crashing into a rack of Web servers.

Theft and terrorist events also cause loss of infrastructure. For instance, a disgruntled, terminated employee might walk off with corporate data servers, routers, or other crucial equipment. Terrorist events also can cause the loss of physical plants and equipment.

Natural disasters present the largest risk for infrastructure loss. A fire, flood, earthquake, or similar event can destroy data centers and all they contain.

You may be wondering why Figure 12-3 does not include viruses, worms, and Trojan horses. The answer is that viruses, worms, and Trojan horses are techniques for causing some of the problems in the figure. They can cause a denial-of-service attack, or they can be used to cause malicious, unauthorized data access or data loss.

Finally, a new threat term has come into recent use. An **Advanced Persistent Threat (APT)** is a sophisticated, possibly long-running, computer hack that is perpetrated by large, well-funded organizations like governments. APTs are a means to engage in cyberwarefare. Examples of APT are *Stuxnet* and *Flame*. Stuxnet is reputed to have been used to set back the Iranian nuclear program by causing Iranian centrifuges to malfunction. Flame is a large and complex computer program that is reputed to have hacked into computers and to operate as a cyber spy, capturing screen images, email and text messages, and even searching nearby smartphones using Bluetooth communication. Search the Internet for these terms to learn more. If you work in the military or for intelligence agencies, you will certainly be concerned, if not involved, with APTs. Further discussion of APTs is beyond the scope of this text.

GOAL OF INFORMATION SYSTEMS SECURITY

As shown in Figure 12-1, threats can be stopped, or if not stopped, the costs of loss can be reduced by creating appropriate safeguards. However, safeguards are expensive to create and maintain. They also reduce work efficiency by making common tasks more difficult, adding additional labor expense. The goal of information security is to find an appropriate trade-off between the risk of loss and the cost of implementing safeguards.

Business professionals need to consider that trade-off carefully. In your personal life, you should certainly employ antivirus software. You should probably implement other safeguards that you'll learn about in the next question. Some safeguards, like deleting browser cookies, will make using your computer more difficult. Are such safeguards worth it? You need to assess the risks and benefits for yourself.

Similar comments pertain to organizations, though they need to go about it more systematically. The bottom line is, don't just let whatever happens, happen. Get in front of the security problem by making the appropriate trade-off for your life and your business.

 ## HOW BIG IS THE COMPUTER SECURITY PROBLEM?

We do not know the full extent of the data and financial losses due to computer security threats. Certainly, the losses due to human error are enormous, but few organizations compute those losses and even fewer publish them. Losses due to natural disasters are also enormous and impossible to compute. The earthquake in Japan shut down Japanese manufacturing, and losses rippled through the supply chain from the Far East to Europe and the United States. One can only imagine the enormous expense for Japanese companies as they restored their information systems.

Figure 12-4

Sample Arrests and Convictions Reported by the U.S. Department of Justice

Source: U.S. Justice Department CSI Computer Crime & Security Survey

Date	Event	Loss
8/10/11	Credit card theft using credit card data purchased from Russian individuals	$770,000
7/19/11	Denial of service attack on PayPal by disgruntled customers	Unknown
7/13/11	Former employee stole former co-workers' email credentials and hacked their email accounts to obtain customer and sales data	Unknown
6/29/11	Fraudulent sale of nonexistent items on eBay, Craigslist, and AutoTrader.com	Unknown
6/22/11	Spoofing IRS tax preparation services	$209,000
6/22/11	Two individuals from Latvia phished antivirus software to obtain credit card data and payments for nonexistent software from more than one million users	$74 million
5/19/11	Former Bank of America computer programmer altered cash machine code to dispense money without a transaction record	$419,000

With regard to computer crime losses, in 2011, the U.S. Justice Department published a list of computer crime news on its site at *www.justice.gov/criminal/cybercrime.*[1] Some of the major arrests, charges, and convictions for a 3-month period in 2011 are shown in Figure 12-4. By no means is this a comprehensive list of computer crime during those months in the United States. Take it as anecdotal evidence of the kinds of crimes that are being committed. For every one crime that results in an arrest, there are likely 10, or even hundreds or thousands, that go unreported or unsolved.

Each year, Verizon investigates computer crime cases, in some years in conjunction with the U.S. Secret Service. In 2011, they reported that the number of data-loss security incidents reached an all-time high, but the number of data records lost fell dramatically for the second year in a row. The authors conclude that large data sites have implemented effective controls but that smaller ones have not. Thus, data theft was most successful at small and medium-sized businesses.

According to the cases they investigated, the four most frequent computer crimes involved criminal activity against servers. The next two were code insertion, including viruses, and data loss from users' computers.

One of the oldest and most respected surveys of computer crimes is conducted by the Computer Security Institute (CSI; previously known as the FBI/CSI survey). This survey has been conducted since 1995, and the organizations involved in the survey are balanced among for-profit and nonprofit organizations and government agencies. The respondents are also balanced for size of organization, from small to very large. You can obtain a copy of the most recent survey at *http://gocsi.com* (registration is required).

In the most recent 2011 report, CSI stated that too few respondents had provided financial loss data for it to be able to report any estimate of the total cost of losses. However, the CSI survey does provide useful data about the percentage of different types of attacks. Figure 12-5 shows the trend in computer crime incidents over the past 10 years. As shown, two-thirds of the respondents reported malware infections, up substantially in the last 2 years. Abuse of servers and emails by employees and others inside the organization has been declining steadily since 2007. We don't know if that is the result of better employee training, or the fact that employees value their jobs more since the recession began. Laptop and mobile device theft is down, but still over one-third of the respondents reported such loss.

Organizations that have been phished (where their identity had been spoofed by others) have increased to 40 percent. This means that nearly half of the respondents have been phished! (See Experiencing MIS InClass on page 318.)

---

[1] Unfortunately, the Justice Department no longer publishes that list.

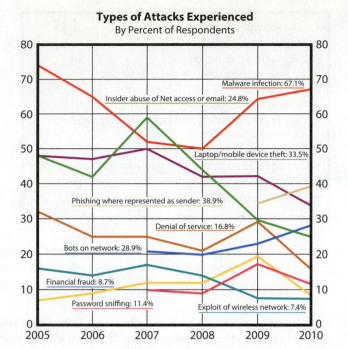

Types of Attacks Experienced
By Percent of Respondents

Malware infection: 67.1%
Insider abuse of Net access or email: 24.8%
Laptop/mobile device theft: 33.5%
Phishing where represented as sender: 38.9%
Denial of service: 16.8%
Bots on network: 28.9%
Financial fraud: 8.7%
Password sniffing: 11.4%
Exploit of wireless network: 7.4%

Figure 12-5
Types of Attacks Experienced

Source: 2010 CSI Computer Crime and Security Survey

Regarding the cost of data computer crime, in September 2011, Norton, a maker of antivirus software licensed by Symantec, claimed that total computer crime losses in 24 countries during the prior 12 months exceeded $388 billion. They estimated that $114 billion of that were direct cash losses and that the remainder, $274 billion, were costs associated with time that victims invested in recovering from crime incidents. According to this report, in those same countries, over one million people per day were victims of a computer crime. Not surprisingly, heavy users of the Internet (more than 49 hours per week) were the most common victims.[2]

These surveys and studies are helpful, but unfortunately, it is impossible to assess the accuracy of the Norton or any other estimate of the cost of computer crime. Many incidents, possibly most, go unreported. As CSI has learned, organizations are, understandably, reluctant to release news of monetary and data losses due to computer crime. However, based on the plethora of ill-gotten products that can be purchased for less than $1,000, including credit card details, fake credit cards, bank credentials, online pay service credentials, and so on, we know that the losses must be substantial.

One of the most sobering facts, however, was observed by Professor Randy Boyle of Longwood University, author of *Applied Information Security* and *Corporate Computer and Network Security.* Dr. Boyle writes about intrusion detection systems. An **intrusion detection system (IDS)** is a computer program that senses when another computer is attempting to scan the disk or otherwise access a computer. According to Boyle, "When I run an IDS on a computer on the public Internet, some nights I get more than 1,000 attempts, mostly from foreign countries. There is nothing you can do about it except use reasonable safeguards."[3]

HOW SHOULD YOU RESPOND TO SECURITY THREATS?

As stated at the end of Q1, your personal IS security goal should be to find an effective trade-off between the risk of loss and the cost of safeguards. However, few individuals take security as seriously as they should, and most fail to implement even low-cost safeguards.

Figure 12-6 lists recommended personal security safeguards. The first safeguard is to take security seriously. You cannot see the attempts that are being made, right now, to compromise

To learn more about safeguards, read the Ethics Guide on pages 332–333

[2]http://us.norton.com/content/en/us/home_homeoffice/html/cybercrimereport, accessed September 2011.
[3]Private correspondence with the author, August 20, 2011.

Figure 12-6
Personal Security Safeguards

- Take security seriously
- Create strong passwords
- Use multiple passwords
- Send no valuable data via email or IM
- Use https at trusted, reputable vendors
- Remove high-value assets from computers
- Clear browsing history, temporary files, and cookies (CCleaner or equivalent)
- Update antivirus software
- Demonstrate security concern to your fellow workers
- Follow organizational security directives and guidelines
- Consider security for all business initiatives

your computer. Even though you are unaware of these threats, they are present, as you just learned. When your security is compromised, the first indication you will receive will be bogus charges on your credit card or messages from friends complaining about the disgusting email they just received from your email account.

If you decide to take computer security seriously, the single most important safeguard you can implement is to create and use strong passwords. We discussed ways of doing this in Chapter 1 (page 14). To summarize, do not use any word, in any language, as part of your password. Use passwords with a mixture of upper- and lowercase letters and numbers.

Such nonword passwords are still vulnerable to a **brute force attack** in which the password cracker tries every possible combination of characters. John Pozadzides estimates that a brute force attack can crack a six-character password of either upper- or lowercase letters in about 5 minutes. However, brute force requires 8.5 days to crack a password having a mixture of upper- and lowercase letters, numbers, and special characters. A 10-digit password of only upper- and lowercase letters takes 4.5 years to crack, but one using a mix of letters, numbers, and special characters requires nearly 2 million years. A 12-digit, letter-only password requires 3 million years, and a 12-digit mixed password will take many, many millions of years.[4] All of these estimates assume, of course, that the password contains no word in any language. The bottom line is this: Use long passwords with no words, at least 10 characters, and a mix of letters, numbers, and special characters.

In addition to using long, complex passwords, you should also use different passwords for different sites. That way, if one of your passwords is compromised, you do not lose control of all of your accounts.

Never send passwords, credit card data, or any other data in email or IM. Most email and IM is not protected by encryption (see Q5), and you should assume that anything you write in email or IM could find its way to the front page of the *New York Times* tomorrow.

Buy only from reputable vendors, and when buying online, use only HTTPS. If the vendor does not support HTTPS in its transactions (look for *https://* in the address line of your browser), do not buy from that vendor.

You can reduce your vulnerability to loss by removing high-value assets from your computers. Now, and especially later as a business professional, make it your practice not to travel out of your office with a laptop or other device that contains any data that you do not need. In general, store proprietary data on servers or removable devices that do not travel with you. (Office 365, by the way, uses HTTPS to transfer data to and from SharePoint. You can use it or a similar application for processing documents from public locations like airports while you are traveling.)

Your browser automatically stores a history of your browsing activities and temporary files that contain sensitive data about where you've visited, what you've purchased, what your

---

[4]John Pozadzides, "How I'd Hack Your Weak Passwords." One Man's Blog, March 26, 2007. http://onemansblog .com/2007/03/26/how-id-hack-your-weak-passwords/, accessed August 2011. When Pozadzides wrote this in 2007, it was for a personal computer. Using 2012 technology, these times would be half or less. Using a cloud-based network of servers for password cracking would cut these times by 90 percent or more.

account names and passwords are, and so forth. It also creates **cookies**, which are small files that your browser stores on your computer when you visit Web sites (see Case 9, pages 248–250). Cookies enable you to access Web sites without having to sign in every time, and they speed up processing of some sites. Unfortunately, some cookies also contain sensitive security data. The best safeguard is to remove your browsing history, temporary files, and cookies from your computer and to set your browser to disable history and cookies.

CCleaner is a free, open source product that will do a more thorough job of removing all such data (*http://download.cnet.com/ccleaner/*) than browsers do. You should make a backup of your computer before using CCleaner, however.

Removing and disabling cookies presents an excellent example of the trade-off between improved security and cost. Your security will be substantially improved, but your computer will be more difficult to use. You decide, but make a conscious decision; do not let ignorance of the vulnerability of such data make the decision for you.

We will address the use of antivirus software in Q5. The last three items in Figure 12-6 apply once you become a business professional. With your coworkers, and especially with those whom you manage, you should demonstrate a concern and respect for security. You should also follow all organizational security directives and guidelines. Finally, like Maggie and Ajit at the start of this chapter, consider security in all of your business initiatives.

HOW SHOULD ORGANIZATIONS RESPOND TO SECURITY THREATS?

Q3 discussed ways that you as an individual should respond to security threats. In the case of organizations, a broader and more systematic approach needs to be taken. To begin, senior management needs to address two critical security functions: security policy and risk management.

Considering the first, senior management must establish a company-wide security policy that states the organization's posture regarding data that it gathers about its customers, suppliers, partners, and employees. At a minimum, the policy should stipulate:

- What sensitive data the organization will store
- How it will process that data
- Whether data will be shared with other organizations
- How employees and others can obtain copies of data stored about them
- How employees and others can request changes to inaccurate data
- What employees can do with their own mobile devices at work
- What nonorganizational activities employees can take with employee-owned equipment

Specific policy depends on whether the organization is governmental or nongovernmental, on whether it is publically held or private, on the organization's industry, on the relationship of management to employees, and other factors. As a new hire, seek out your employer's security policy if it is not discussed with you in new-employee training.

The second senior management security function is to manage risk. Risk cannot be eliminated, so *manage risk* means to proactively balance the trade-off between risk and cost. This trade-off varies from industry to industry and from organization to organization. Financial institutions are obvious targets for theft and must invest heavily in security safeguards. On the other hand, a bowling alley is unlikely to be much of a target, unless of course, it stores credit card data on computers or mobile devices! (A decision that would be part of its security policy, and which would seem to be unwise, not only for a bowling alley but also for most small businesses.)

To make trade-off decisions, organizations need to create an inventory of the data that they store and the threats to which that data is subject. Figure 12-5 is a good source for understanding categories and frequencies of threat. Given this inventory, the organization needs to decide how much risk it wishes to take, or, stated differently, which security safeguards it wishes to implement.

Experiencing MIS

INCLASS EXERCISE 12

Phishing for Credit Cards, Identifying Numbers, Bank Accounts

Source: PC-PROD/Fotolia

A phisher is an individual or organization that spoofs legitimate companies in an attempt to illegally capture personal data such as credit card numbers, email accounts, and driver's license numbers. Some phishers install malicious program code on users' computers as well.

Phishing is usually initiated via email. Phishers steal legitimate logos and trademarks and use official-sounding words in an attempt to fool users into revealing personal data or clicking a link. Phishers do not bother with laws about trademark use. They place names and logos like Visa, MasterCard, Discover, and American Express on their Web pages and use them as bait. In some cases, phishers copy the entire look and feel of a legitimate company's Web site.

In this exercise, you and a group of your fellow students will be asked to investigate phishing attacks. If you search the Web for *phishing*, be aware that your search may bring the attention of an active phisher. Therefore, do not give any data to any site that you visit as part of this exercise!

1. To learn the fundamentals of phishing, visit the following site: *www.microsoft.com/protect/fraud/phishing /symptoms.aspx*. To see recent examples of phishing attacks, visit *www.fraudwatchinternational.com /phishing/*.
   a. Using examples from these Web sites, describe how phishing works.
   b. Explain why a link that appears to be legitimate, such as *www.microsoft.mysite.com* may, in fact, be a link to a phisher's site.
   c. List five indicators of a phishing attack.
   d. Write an email that you could send to a friend or relative who is not well versed in technical matters that explains what phishing is and how your friend or relative can avoid it.

2. Suppose you received the email in Figure 1 and mistakenly clicked *See more details here*. When you did so, you were taken to the Web page shown in Figure 2. List every phishing symptom that you find in these two figures and explain why it is a symptom.

3. Suppose you work for an organization that is being phished.
   a. How would you learn that your organization is being attacked?
   b. What steps should your organization take in response to the attack?
   c. What liability, if any, do you think your organization has for damages to customers that result from a phishing attack that carries your brand and trademarks?

4. Summarize why phishing is a serious problem to commerce today.

5. Describe actions that industry organizations, companies, governments, or individuals can take to help to reduce phishing.

Your Order ID: "17152492"

Order Date: "09/07/12"

Product Purchased: "Two First Class Tickets to Cozumel"

Your card type: "CREDIT"

Total Price: "$349.00"

Hello, when you purchased your tickets you provided an incorrect mailing address.

See more details here

Please follow the link and modify your mailing address or cancel your order. If you have questions, feel free to contact us account@usefulbill.com

Figure 1
Fake Phishing Email

Figure 2
Fake Phishing Screen

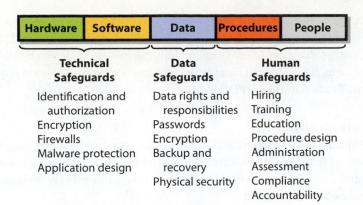

Figure 12-7
Security Safeguards as
They Relate to the Five
Components

An easy way to remember information systems safeguards is to arrange them according to the five components of an information system, as shown in Figure 12-7. Some of the safeguards involve computer hardware and software. Some involve data; others involve procedures and people. We will consider technical, data, and human safeguards in the next three questions.

 HOW CAN TECHNICAL SAFEGUARDS PROTECT AGAINST SECURITY THREATS?

Technical safeguards involve the hardware and software components of an information system. Figure 12-8 lists primary technical safeguards. Consider each.

IDENTIFICATION AND AUTHENTICATION

Every information system today should require users to sign on with a user name and password. The user name *identifies* the user (the process of **identification**), and the password *authenticates* that user (the process of **authentication**).

Passwords have important weaknesses. In spite of repeated warnings, users often share their passwords; and many people choose ineffective, simple passwords. In fact, the 2011 Verizon report cited earlier states, "Absent, weak, and stolen credentials are careening out of control.[5]" Because of these problems, some organizations choose to use smart cards and biometric authentication in addition to passwords.

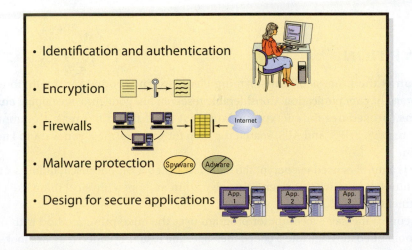

Figure 12-8
Technical Safeguards

[5] *Verizon 2011 Data Breach Investigations Report*, p. 3. http://www.verizonbusiness.com/resources/reports /rp_data-breach-investigations-report-2011_en_xg.pdf, accessed June 2012.

Smart Cards

A **smart card** is a plastic card similar to a credit card. Unlike credit, debit, and ATM cards, which have a magnetic strip, smart cards have a microchip. The microchip, which holds far more data than a magnetic strip, is loaded with identifying data. Users of smart cards are required to enter a **personal identification number (PIN)** to be authenticated.

Biometric Authentication

Biometric authentication uses personal physical characteristics such as fingerprints, facial features, and retinal scans to authenticate users. Biometric authentication provides strong authentication, but the required equipment is expensive. Often, too, users resist biometric identification because they feel it is invasive.

Biometric authentication is in the early stages of adoption. Because of its strength, it likely will see increased usage in the future. It is also likely that legislators will pass laws governing the use, storage, and protection requirements for biometric data. For more on biometrics, search for *biometrics* at *http://searchsecurity.techtarget.com.*

Note that authentication methods fall into three categories: what you know (password or PIN), what you have (smart card), and what you are (biometric).

SINGLE SIGN-ON FOR MULTIPLE SYSTEMS

Information systems often require multiple sources of authentication. For example, when you sign on to your personal computer, you need to be authenticated. When you access the LAN in your department, you need to be authenticated again. When you traverse your organization's WAN, you will need to be authenticated to even more networks. Also, if your request requires database data, the DBMS server that manages that database will authenticate you yet again.

It would be annoying to enter a name and password for every one of these resources. You might have to use and remember five or six different passwords just to access the data you need to perform your job. It would be equally undesirable to send your password across all of these networks. The further your password travels, the greater the risk it can be compromised.

Instead, today's operating systems have the capability to authenticate you to networks and other servers. You sign on to your local computer and provide authentication data; from that point on your operating system authenticates you to another network or server, which can authenticate you to yet another network and server, and so forth. Because this is so, your identity and passwords open many doors beyond those on your local computer; remember this when you choose your passwords!

ENCRYPTION

Encryption is the process of transforming clear text into coded, unintelligible text for secure storage or communication. Considerable research has gone into developing **encryption algorithms** (procedures for encrypting data) that are difficult to break. Commonly used methods are DES, 3DES, and AES; search the Web for these terms if you want to know more about them.

A **key** is a number used to encrypt the data. It is called a *key* because it unlocks a message, but it is a number used with an encryption algorithm and not a physical thing like the key to your apartment.

To encode a message, a computer program uses the encryption method with the key to convert a noncoded message into a coded message. The resulting coded message looks like gibberish. Decoding (decrypting) a message is similar; a key is applied to the coded message to recover the original text. With **symmetric encryption**, the same key (again, a number) is used to encode and to decode. With **asymmetric encryption**, two keys are used; one key encodes the message, and the other key decodes the message. Symmetric encryption is simpler and much faster than asymmetric encryption.

A special version of asymmetric encryption, **public key/private key**, is used on the Internet. With this method, each site has a public key for encoding messages and a private key for decoding them. Before we explain how that works, consider the following analogy.

Suppose you send a friend an open combination lock (like you have on your gym locker). Suppose you are the only one who knows the combination to that lock. Now, suppose your friend puts something in a box and locks the lock. Now, neither your friend nor anyone else can open that box. They send the locked box to you, and you apply the combination to open the box.

A public key is like the combination lock, and the private key is like the combination. Your friend uses the public key to code the message (lock the box), and you use the private key to decode the message (use the combination to open the lock).

Now, suppose we have two generic computers, A and B. Suppose A wants to send an encrypted message to B. To do so, A sends B its public key (in our analogy, A sends B an open combination lock). Now B applies A's public key to the message and sends the resulting coded message back to A. At that point, neither B nor anyone other than A can decode that message. It is like the box with a locked combination lock. When A receives the coded message, A applies its private key (the combination in our analogy) to unlock or decrypt the message.

Again, public keys are like open combination locks. Computer A will send a lock to anyone who asks for one. But A never sends its private key (the combination) to anyone. Private keys stay private.

Most secure communication over the Internet uses a protocol called **HTTPS**. With HTTPS, data are encrypted using a protocol called the **Secure Socket Layer (SSL)**, which is also known as **Transport Layer Security (TLS)**. SSL/TLS uses a combination of public key/private key and symmetric encryption.

The basic idea is this: Symmetric encryption is fast and is preferred. But, the two parties (say you and a Web site) don't share a symmetric key. So, the two of you use public/private encryption to share the same symmetric key. Once you both have that key, you use symmetric encryption.

Figure 12-9 summarizes how SSL/TLS works when you communicate securely with a Web site:

1. Your computer obtains the public key of the Web site to which it will connect.
2. Your computer generates a key for symmetric encryption.

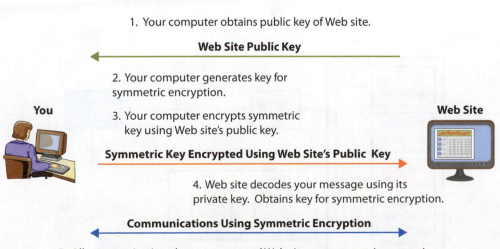

1. Your computer obtains public key of Web site.

Web Site Public Key

2. Your computer generates key for symmetric encryption.

3. Your computer encrypts symmetric key using Web site's public key.

Symmetric Key Encrypted Using Web Site's Public Key

4. Web site decodes your message using its private key. Obtains key for symmetric encryption.

Communications Using Symmetric Encryption

5. All communications between you and Web site use symmetric encryption.

You / Web Site

Figure 12-9
The Essence of HTTPS (SSL or TLS)

3. Your computer encodes that key using the Web site's public key. It sends the encrypted symmetric key to the Web site.

4. The Web site then decodes the symmetric key using its private key.

5. From that point forward, your computer and the Web site communicate using symmetric encryption.

At the end of the session, your computer and the secure site discard the keys. Using this strategy, the bulk of the secure communication occurs using the faster symmetric encryption. Also, because keys are used for short intervals, there is less likelihood they can be discovered.

Use of SSL/TLS makes it safe to send sensitive data such as credit card numbers and bank balances. Just be certain that you see *https://* in your browser and not just *http://*.

FIREWALLS

A **firewall** is a computing device that prevents unauthorized network access. A firewall can be a special-purpose computer or it can be a program on a general-purpose computer or on a router.

Organizations normally use multiple firewalls. A **perimeter firewall** sits outside the organizational network; it is the first device that Internet traffic encounters. In addition to perimeter firewalls, some organizations employ **internal firewalls** inside the organizational network. Figure 12-10 shows the use of a perimeter firewall that protects all of an organization's computers and a second internal firewall that protects a LAN.

A **packet-filtering firewall** examines each part of a message and determines whether to let that part pass. To make this decision, it examines the source address, the destination address(es), and other data.

Packet-filtering firewalls can prohibit outsiders from starting a session with any user behind the firewall. They can also disallow traffic from particular sites, such as known hacker addresses. They can prohibit traffic from legitimate, but unwanted, addresses, such as competitors' computers, and filter outbound traffic as well. They can keep employees from accessing specific sites, such as those of competitors, ones with pornographic material, or popular news sources. As a future manager, if you have particular sites which you do not want your employees to access, you can ask your IS department to enforce that limit via the firewall.

Packet-filtering firewalls are the simplest type of firewall. Other firewalls filter on a more sophisticated basis. If you take a data communications class, you will learn about them. For now, just understand that firewalls help to protect organizational computers from unauthorized network access.

Figure 12-10
Use of Multiple Firewalls

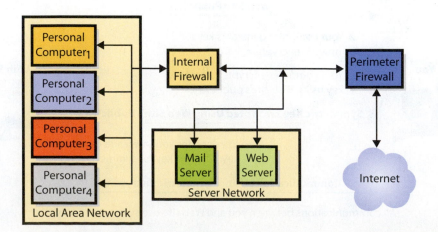

No computer should connect to the Internet without firewall protection. Many ISPs provide firewalls for their customers. By nature, these firewalls are generic. Large organizations supplement such generic firewalls with their own. Most home routers include firewalls, and Microsoft Windows has a built-in firewall as well. Third parties also license firewall products.

MALWARE PROTECTION

The next technical safeguard in our list in Figure 12-8 concerns malware. We defined the important terms in Chapter 4. To review:

- **Malware** is viruses, worms, Trojan horses, spyware, and adware.
  - A **virus** is a computer program that replicates itself. The program code that causes unwanted or harmful activity is called the **payload.**
  - **Trojan horses** are viruses that masquerade as useful programs or files.
  - A **worm** is a virus that propagates using the Internet or other computer network.
- **Spyware** programs are installed on the user's computer without the user's knowledge or permission.
- **Adware** is similar to spyware but it watches user activity and produce pop-up ads.

Figure 12-11 lists some of the symptoms of adware and spyware. Sometimes these symptoms develop slowly over time as more malware components are installed. Should these symptoms occur on your computer, remove the spyware or adware using antimalware programs.

Malware Safeguards

Fortunately, it is possible to avoid most malware using the following malware safeguards:

1. *Install antivirus and antispyware programs on your computer.* Your IT department will have a list of recommended (perhaps required) programs for this purpose. If you choose a program for yourself, choose one from a reputable vendor. Check reviews of antimalware software on the Web before purchasing.

2. *Set up your antimalware programs to scan your computer frequently.* You should scan your computer at least once a week and possibly more often. When you detect malware code, use the antimalware software to remove it. If the code cannot be removed, contact your IT department or antimalware vendor.

3. *Update malware definitions.* **Malware definitions**—patterns that exist in malware code—should be downloaded frequently. Antimalware vendors update these definitions continuously, and you should install these updates as they become available.

4. *Open email attachments only from known sources.* Also, even when opening attachments from known sources, do so with great care. According to professor and security

- Slow system startup
- Sluggish system performance
- Many pop-up advertisements
- Suspicious browser homepage changes
- Suspicious changes to the taskbar and other system interfaces
- Unusual hard-disk activity

Figure 12-11
Spyware and Adware Symptoms

---

[6]Ray Panko, *Corporate Computer and Network Security* (Upper Saddle River, NJ: Prentice Hall, 2004), p. 165.

expert Ray Panko, about 90 percent of all viruses are spread by email attachments.[6] This statistic is not surprising, because most organizations are protected by firewalls. With a properly configured firewall, email is the only outside-initiated traffic that can reach user computers.

Most antimalware programs check email attachments for malware code. However, all users should form the habit of *never* opening an email attachment from an unknown source. Also, if you receive an unexpected email from a known source or an email from a known source that has a suspicious subject (or no subject), odd spelling, or poor grammar, do not open the attachment without first verifying with the known source that the attachment is legitimate.

5. *Promptly install software updates from legitimate sources.* Unfortunately, all programs are chock full of security holes; vendors are fixing them as rapidly as they are discovered, but the practice is inexact. Install patches to the operating system and application programs promptly.

6. *Browse only in reputable Internet neighborhoods.* It is possible for some malware to install itself when you do nothing more than open a Web page. Don't go there!

DESIGN FOR SECURE APPLICATIONS

The final technical safeguard in Figure 12-8 concerns the design of applications. As you learned in the opening vignette, Ajit and Maggie are designing PRIDE with security in mind; PRIDE will store users' privacy setting in a database, and they will develop all applications to first read the privacy settings before revealing any data in exercise reports. Most likely, they will design their programs so that privacy data is processed by programs on servers; that design means that such data need be transmitted over the Internet only when it is created or modified.

As mentioned in the opening vignette, the term **SQL injection attack**, occurs when a user enters a SQL statement into a form in which they are supposed to enter a name or other data. If the program is improperly designed, it will accept this code and make it part of a database command that it issues. Improper data disclosure and data damage and loss are possible consequences. A well-designed application will make such injections ineffective.

As a future IS user, you will not design programs yourself. However, you should ensure that any information system developed for you and your department includes security as one of the application requirements.

 HOW CAN DATA SAFEGUARDS PROTECT AGAINST SECURITY THREATS?

Data safeguards protect databases and other organizational data. Two organizational units are responsible for data safeguards. **Data administration** refers to an organization-wide function that is in charge of developing data policies and enforcing data standards. Data administration is a staff function to the CIO, as discussed in Chapter 11.

Database administration refers to a function that pertains to a particular database. ERP, CRM, and MRP databases each have a database administration function. Database administration develops procedures and practices to ensure efficient and orderly multiuser processing of the database, to control changes to the database structure, and to protect the database. Database administration was summarized in Chapter 5.

Both data and database administration are involved in establishing the data safeguards in Figure 12-12. First, data administration should define data policies such as "We will not share identifying customer data with any other organization" and the like. Then, data administration and database

Figure 12-12
Data Safeguards

- Define data policies
- Data rights and responsibilities
- Rights enforced by user accounts authenticated by passwords
- Data encryption
- Backup and recovery procedures
- Physical security

administration(s) work together to specify user data rights and responsibilities. Third, those rights should be enforced by user accounts that are authenticated, at least by passwords.

The organization should protect sensitive data by storing it in encrypted form. Such encryption uses one or more keys in ways similar to that described for data communication encryption. One potential problem with stored data, however, is that the key might be lost or that disgruntled or terminated employees might destroy it. Because of this possibility, when data are encrypted, a trusted party should have a copy of the encryption key. This safety procedure is sometimes called **key escrow**.

Another data safeguard is to periodically create backup copies of database contents. The organization should store at least some of these backups off premises, possibly in a remote location. Additionally, IT personnel should periodically practice recovery to ensure that the backups are valid and that effective recovery procedures exist. Do not assume that just because a backup is made that the database is protected.

Physical security is another data safeguard. The computers that run the DBMS and all devices that store database data should reside in locked, controlled-access facilities. If not, they are subject not only to theft, but also to damage. For better security, the organization should keep a log showing who entered the facility, when, and for what purpose.

When organizations store databases in the cloud, all of the safeguards in Figure 12-12 should be part of the service contract.

Q7 HOW CAN HUMAN SAFEGUARDS PROTECT AGAINST SECURITY THREATS?

Human safeguards involve the people and procedure components of information systems. In general, human safeguards result when authorized users follow appropriate procedures for system use and recovery. Restricting access to authorized users requires effective authentication methods and careful user account management. In addition, appropriate security procedures must be designed as part of every information system, and users should be trained on the importance and use of those procedures. In this section, we will consider the development of human safeguards for employees.

HUMAN SAFEGUARDS FOR EMPLOYEES

Figure 12-13 lists security considerations for employees. The first is position definitions.

Position Definitions

Effective human safeguards begin with definitions of job tasks and responsibilities. In general, job descriptions should provide a separation of duties and authorities. For example, no single individual should be allowed to both approve expenses and write checks. Instead, one person should approve expenses, another pay them, and a third should account for the payment.

Figure 12-13
Security Policy for In-house Staff

- Position definition
  - Separate duties and authorities
  - Determine least privilege
  - Document position sensitivity

"OK to pay this."

- Hiring and screening

"Where did you last work?"

- Dissemination and enforcement
  - responsibility
  - accountability
  - compliance

"Let's talk security..."

- Termination
  - Friendly

"Congratulations on your new job."

- Unfriendly

"We've closed your accounts. Good-bye."

Similarly, in inventory, no single person should be allowed to authorize an inventory withdrawal and also to remove the items from inventory.

Given appropriate job descriptions, user accounts should be defined to give users the *least possible privilege* needed to perform their jobs. For example, users whose job description does not include modifying data should be given accounts with read-only privilege. Similarly, user accounts should prohibit users from accessing data their job description does not require. Because of the problem of semantic security, access to even seemingly innocuous data may need to be limited.

Finally, the security sensitivity should be documented for each position. Some jobs involve highly sensitive data (e.g., employee compensation, salesperson quotas, and proprietary marketing or technical data). Other positions involve no sensitive data. Documenting *position sensitivity* enables security personnel to prioritize their activities in accordance with the possible risk and loss.

Hiring and Screening

Security considerations should be part of the hiring process. Of course, if the position involves no sensitive data and no access to information systems, then screening for information systems security purposes will be minimal. When hiring for high-sensitivity positions, however, extensive interviews, references, and background investigations are appropriate. Note, too, that security screening applies not only to new employees, but also to employees who are promoted into sensitive positions.

Dissemination and Enforcement

Employees cannot be expected to follow security policies and procedures that they do not know about. Therefore, employees need to be made aware of the security policies, procedures, and responsibilities they will have.

Employee security training begins during new-employee training, with the explanation of general security policies and procedures. That general training must be amplified in accordance with the position's sensitivity and responsibilities. Promoted employees should receive security training that is appropriate to their new positions. The company should not provide user accounts and passwords until employees have completed required security training.

Enforcement consists of three interdependent factors: responsibility, accountability, and compliance. First, the company should clearly define the security *responsibilities* of each position. The design of the security program should be such that employees can be held *accountable* for security violations. Procedures should exist so that when critical data are lost, it is possible to determine how the loss occurred and who is accountable. Finally, the security program should encourage security *compliance*. Employee activities should regularly be monitored for compliance, and management should specify disciplinary action to be taken in light of noncompliance.

Management attitude is crucial: Employee compliance is greater when management demonstrates, both in word and deed, a serious concern for security. If managers write passwords on staff bulletin boards, shout passwords down hallways, or ignore physical security procedures, then employee security attitudes and employee security compliance will suffer. Note, too, that effective security is a continuing management responsibility. Regular reminders about security are essential.

Termination

Companies also must establish security policies and procedures for the termination of employees. Many employee terminations are friendly and occur as the result of promotion, retirement, or when the employee resigns to take another position. Standard human resources policies should ensure that system administrators receive notification in advance of the employee's last day, so that they can remove accounts and passwords. The need to recover keys for encrypted data and any other special security requirements should be part of the employee's out-processing.

Unfriendly termination is more difficult, because employees may be tempted to take malicious or harmful actions. In such a case, system administrators may need to remove user accounts and passwords prior to notifying the employee of his or her termination. Other actions may be needed to protect the company's information assets. A terminated sales employee, for example, may attempt to take the company's confidential customer and sales-prospect data for future use at another company. The terminating employer should take steps to protect those data prior to the termination.

The human resources department should be aware of the importance of giving IS administrators early notification of employee termination. No blanket policy exists; the information systems department must assess each case on an individual basis.

ACCOUNT ADMINISTRATION

The administration of user accounts, passwords, and help-desk policies and procedures is another important human safeguard.

Account Management

Account management concerns the creation of new user accounts, the modification of existing account permissions, and the removal of unneeded accounts. Information system administrators perform all of these tasks, but account users have the responsibility to notify the administrators of the need for these actions. The IT department should create standard procedures for this purpose. As a future user, you can improve your relationship with IS personnel by providing early and timely notification of the need for account changes.

The existence of accounts that are no longer necessary is a serious security threat. IS administrators cannot know when an account should be removed; it is up to users and managers to give such notification.

Password Management

Passwords are the primary means of authentication. They are important not just for access to the user's computer, but also for authentication to other networks and servers to which the user may have access. Because of the importance of passwords, the National Institute of Standards and Technology (NIST) recommends that employees be required to sign statements similar to that shown in Figure 12-14.

When an account is created, users should immediately change the password they are given to a password of their own. In fact, well-constructed systems require the user to change the password on first use.

Additionally, users should change passwords frequently thereafter. Some systems will require a password change every 3 months or perhaps more frequently. Users grumble at the nuisance of making such changes, but frequent password changes reduce the risk of password loss, as well as the extent of damage if an existing password is compromised.

Some users create two passwords and switch back and forth between those two. This strategy results in poor security, and some password systems do not allow the user to reuse recently used passwords. Again, users may view this policy as a nuisance, but it is important.

Help-Desk Policies

In the past, help desks have been a serious security risk. A user who had forgotten his password would call the help desk and plead for the help-desk representative to tell him his password or to reset the password to something else. "I can't get this report out without it!" was (and is) a common lament.

The problem for help-desk representatives is, of course, that they have no way of determining that they are talking with the true user and not someone spoofing a true user. But, they are in a bind: If they do not help in some way, the help desk is perceived to be the "unhelpful desk."

To resolve such problems, many systems give the help-desk representative a means of authenticating the user. Typically, the help-desk information system has answers to questions that only the true user would know, such as the user's birthplace, mother's maiden name, or last four digits of an important account number. Usually, when a password is changed, notification of that change is sent to the user in an email. Email, as you learned, is sent as plaintext, however, so the new password itself ought not to be emailed. If you ever receive notification that your password was reset when you did not request such a reset, immediately contact IT security. Someone has compromised your account.

Figure 12-14
Sample Account
Acknowledgment Form

I hereby acknowledge personal receipt of the system password(s) associated with the user IDs listed below. I understand that I am responsible for protecting the password(s), will comply with all applicable system security standards, and will not divulge my password(s) to any person. I further understand that I must report to the Information Systems Security Officer any problem I encounter in the use of the password(s) or when I have reason to believe that the private nature of my password(s) has been compromised.

All such help-desk measures reduce the strength of the security system, and, if the employee's position is sufficiently sensitive, they may create too large a vulnerability. In such a case, the user may just be out of luck. The account will be deleted, and the user must repeat the account-application process.

SYSTEMS PROCEDURES

Figure 12-15 shows a grid of procedure types—normal operation, backup, and recovery. Procedures of each type should exist for each information system. For example, the order-entry system will have procedures of each of these types, as will the Web storefront, the inventory system, and so forth. The definition and use of standardized procedures reduces the likelihood of computer crime and other malicious activity by insiders. It also ensures that the system's security policy is enforced.

Procedures exist for both users and operations personnel. For each type of user, the company should develop procedures for normal, backup, and recovery operations. As a future user, you will be primarily concerned with user procedures. Normal-use procedures should provide safeguards appropriate to the sensitivity of the information system.

Backup procedures concern the creation of backup data to be used in the event of failure. Whereas operations personnel have the responsibility for backing up system databases and other systems data, departmental personnel have the need to back up data on their own computers. Good questions to ponder are, "What would happen if I lost my computer or mobile device tomorrow?" "What would happen if someone dropped my computer during an airport security inspection?" "What would happen if my computer were stolen?" Employees should ensure that they back up critical business data on their computers. The IT department may help in this effort by designing backup procedures and making backup facilities available.

Finally, systems analysts should develop procedures for system recovery. First, how will the department manage its affairs when a critical system is unavailable? Customers will want to order and manufacturing will want to remove items from inventory even though a critical information system is unavailable. How will the department respond? Once the system is returned to service, how will records of business activities during the outage be entered into the system? How will service be resumed? The system developers should ask and answer these questions and others like them and develop procedures accordingly.

SECURITY MONITORING

Security monitoring is the last of the human safeguards we will consider. Important monitoring functions are activity log analyses, security testing, and investigating and learning from security incidents.

Figure 12-15
Systems Procedures

	System Users	**Operations Personnel**
Normal operation	Use the system to perform job tasks, with security appropriate to sensitivity.	Operate data center equipment, manage networks, run Web servers, and do related operational tasks.
Backup	Prepare for loss of system functionality.	Back up Web site resources, databases, administrative data, account and password data, and other data.
Recovery	Accomplish job tasks during failure. Know tasks to do during system recovery.	Recover systems from backed up data. Perform role of help desk during recovery.

Many information system programs produce *activity logs*. Firewalls produce logs of their activities, including lists of all dropped packets, infiltration attempts, and unauthorized access attempts from within the firewall. DBMS products produce logs of successful and failed log-ins. Web servers produce voluminous logs of Web activities. The operating systems in personal computers can produce logs of log-ins and firewall activities.

None of these logs adds any value to an organization unless someone looks at them. Accordingly, an important security function is to analyze these logs for threat patterns, successful and unsuccessful attacks, and evidence of security vulnerabilities.

Additionally, companies should test their security programs. Both in-house personnel and outside security consultants should conduct such testing.

Another important monitoring function is to investigate security incidents. How did the problem occur? Have safeguards been created to prevent a recurrence of such problems? Does the incident indicate vulnerabilities in other portions of the security system? What else can be learned from the incident?

Security systems reside in a dynamic environment. Organization structures change. Companies are acquired or sold; mergers occur. New systems require new security measures. New technology changes the security landscape, and new threats arise. Security personnel must constantly monitor the situation and determine if the existing security policy and safeguards are adequate. If changes are needed, security personnel need to take appropriate action.

Security, like quality, is an ongoing process. There is no final state that represents a secure system or company. Instead, companies must monitor security on a continuing basis.

 ## HOW SHOULD ORGANIZATIONS RESPOND TO SECURITY INCIDENTS?

The last component of a security plan that we will consider is incident response. Figure 12-16 lists the major factors. First, every organization should have an incident-response plan as part of the security program. No organization should wait until some asset has been lost or compromised before deciding what to do. The plan should include how employees are to respond to security problems, whom they should contact, the reports they should make, and steps they can take to reduce further loss.

Consider, for example, a virus. An incident-response plan will stipulate what an employee should do when he or she notices the virus. It should specify whom to contact and what to do. It may stipulate that the employee should turn off the computer and physically disconnect from the network. The plan should also indicate what users with wireless computers should do.

The plan should provide centralized reporting of all security incidents. Such reporting will enable an organization to determine if it is under systematic attack or an incident is isolated. Centralized reporting also allows the organization to learn about security threats, take consistent actions in response, and apply specialized expertise to all security problems.

Figure 12-16
Factors in Incident Response

- Have plan in place
- Centralized reporting
- Specific responses
  - Speed
  - Preparation pays
  - Don't make problem worse
- Practice

When an incident does occur, speed is of the essence. Viruses and worms can spread very quickly across an organization's networks, and a fast response will help to mitigate the consequences. Because of the need for speed, preparation pays. The incident-response plan should identify critical personnel and their off-hours contact information. These personnel should be trained on where to go and what to do when they get there. Without adequate preparation, there is substantial risk that the actions of well-meaning people will make the problem worse. Also, the rumor mill will be alive with all sorts of nutty ideas about what to do. A cadre of well-informed, trained personnel will serve to dampen such rumors.

Finally, organizations should periodically practice incident response. Without such practice, personnel will be poorly informed on the response plan, and the plan itself may have flaws that only become apparent during a drill.

To learn more about International MIS, see Chapter Extension 18.

How does the **knowledge** in this chapter help **you?**

The knowledge in this chapter helps you by making you aware of the threats to computer security both for you as an individual, business professional, as well as for any organization in which you work. You know that both you and your organization must trade off the risk of loss against the cost of safeguards. You have learned techniques that you can and should employ to protect your own computing devices and your data. You know how organizations should respond to security threats. This chapter introduced you to technical, data, and human safeguards and summarized how organizations should respond to security incidents.

One more time: above all, create and use strong passwords!

Congratulations! You've reached the end of the chapters. Take a moment to consider how you will use what you've learned, as described in the Guide on pages 334–335.

Ethics Guide

Metasecurity

Recall from Chapter 5 that metadata is data about data. In a similar vein, metasecurity is security about security. In other words, it asks the question, "How do we secure the security system?"

Consider an obvious problem: What is a secure way to store a file of accounts and passwords? Such files must exist; otherwise, operating systems would be unable to authenticate users. But, how should one store such a file? It cannot be stored as plain text, because anyone who reads the file gains unlimited access to the computer, the network, and other assets. So, it must be stored in encrypted form, but how? And who should know the encryption key?

Consider another problem. Suppose you work at the help desk at Vanguard Funds, and part of your job is to reset user passwords when users forget them. Clearly, this is an essential job that needs to be done, but what keeps you from resetting the passwords of accounts held by elderly people who never look at their statements? What keeps you from accessing those accounts with your reset password and moving funds to the accounts of your friends?

The accounting profession has dealt with some of these problems for decades and has developed a set of procedures and standards known as *accounting controls*. In general, these controls involve procedures that provide checks and balances, independent reviews of activity logs, control of critical assets, and so forth. Properly designed and implemented, such controls will catch the help-desk representative performing unauthorized account transfers. But many computer network threats are new, proper safeguards are under development, and some threats are not yet known.

The safeguards for some problems have unexpected consequences. For example, suppose you give one of your employees the task of finding security flaws in your network and financial applications (an activity called *white-hat hcking*). Assume that your employee finds ways to crack into your system and, say, schedule undetectable, unauthorized shipments of goods from inventory to any address she wants. Your employee reports the flaws, and you fix them. Except, how do you know she reported all the flaws she found?

Further, when she's finished, what do you do with your white-hat hacker? You are afraid to fire her, because you have no idea what she'll do with the knowledge she has. But what job can she safely perform now that she knows the holes in your security system? Do you want her, ever again, to have an account and password in your corporate computer network? Even if you fix all the problems she reports, which is doubtful, you suspect that she can always find more.

Or consider Microsoft's problem. If you were a computer criminal, where is the ultimate place to lodge a Trojan horse or trapdoor? In Windows code. Microsoft hires hundreds of people to write its operating system—people who work all over the world.

Of course, Microsoft performs background screening on everyone it can, but did it get a complete and accurate background report on every Windows programmer in India, France, Ireland, China, and so on? Microsoft uses careful procedures for controlling what code gets into its products, but even still, somebody at Microsoft must lose sleep over the possibilities.

Ironically, the answers for many metasecurity problems lie in openness. Encryption experts generally agree that any encryption algorithm that relies on secrecy is ultimately doomed, because the secret will get out. Secrecy with encryption must lie only with the (temporary) keys that are used, and not with a secret method. Thus, encryption algorithms are published openly, and anyone with a mathematical bent is encouraged to find (and report) flaws. An algorithm is safe to deploy only when thousands of people have tested and retested it. One very common wireless security protocol, Wired Equivalency Protocol, or WEP, was unwisely deployed before it was tested, and thousands upon thousands of wireless networks were vulnerable as a result; some still are.

Clearly, hardware and software are only part of the problem. Metasecurity extends to the data, procedures, and people components as well. It's a fascinating field, one that is continually developing, and one of great importance. It would make an interesting career choice—but be careful what you learn!

Source: Piotr Marcinski/Shutterstock

DISCUSSION QUESTIONS

1. Explain the term *metasecurity*. Describe two metasecurity problems not mentioned in this guide.

2. Explain the control problem that exists when personnel can reset customer passwords. Describe a way to reduce this threat using an audit log and at least two independent employees.

3. Describe the dilemma posed by an in-house hacker. Describe the problem of using an outside company for white-hat hacking. If you were asked to manage a project to test your computer network security, would you use in-house or outsourced personnel? Why?

4. A typical corporate computer has software from Microsoft, SAP, Siebel, Oracle, and possibly dozens of smaller vendors. How do users know that none of the software from these companies contains a Trojan horse?

5. Explain why part of the security solution lies in openness. Describe how openness applies to accounting controls like the one you designed in your answer to question 2. Explain the danger of procedural controls that rely on secrecy.

Source: Sergey Sukhorukov/ Shutterstock

Guide

The Final, Final Word

Congratulations! You've made it through the entire book. With this knowledge you are well prepared to be an effective user of information systems. And with work and imagination, you can be much more than that. Many interesting opportunities are available to those who can apply information in innovative ways. Your professor has done what she can do, and the rest, as they say, is up to you.

So what's next? Back in Chapter 1 we claimed that Introduction to MIS is the most important course in the business curriculum today. That claim was based on the availability of nearly free data communications and data storage and the need for skills as a nonroutine problem solver.

By now, you've learned many of the ways that businesses and organizations use these resources and information systems based upon those resources. You've also seen how GearUp and PRIDE use information systems to solve problems and to further competitive strategies.

How can you use this knowledge? Chapter 1 claimed that future business professionals must be able "to assess, evaluate, and apply emerging information technology to business." Have you learned how to do that? Has your experience thinking about the PRIDE system helped prepare you to do that? You probably know the meaning of many more terms than you did when you started this class, and such knowledge is important. But, even more important is the ability to use that knowledge to apply MIS to your business interests.

Chapter 1 also reviewed the work of the RAND Corporation and that of Robert Reich on what professional workers in the 21st century need to know. Those sources state that such workers need to know how to innovate the use of technology and how to "collaborate, reason abstractly, think in terms of systems, and experiment." Have you learned those behaviors? Or, at least, are you better at them than when you started this course?

As of August 2012, the unemployment rate among people under 25 was in the neighborhood of 20 percent. Under these circumstances, good jobs will be difficult to obtain. You need to apply every asset you have. One of those assets is the knowledge you've gained in this class. Take the time to do the exercises at the end of this guide, and then use those answers in your job interviews!

Look for the job you truly want to do, get that job, and work hard. In the movie *Glass: A Portrait of Philp in Twelve Parts*, the composer Philip Glass claimed he knew the secret to success. It was, he said, "Get up early and work hard all day." That quotation seems obvious and hardly worth stating. Except that it has the ring of truth. And, if you can find a job you truly love, it isn't even hard. Actually, it's fun, most of the time. So, use what you've learned in this class to obtain the job you truly want!

DISCUSSION QUESTIONS

1. Reflect on what you have learned from this course. Write two paragraphs on how the knowledge you have gained will help you to "assess, evaluate, and apply emerging information technology to business." Shape your writing around the kind of job that you want to obtain upon graduation.

2. Write two paragraphs on how the knowledge and experiences you've had in this class will help you to "collaborate, reason abstractly, think in terms of systems, and experiment." Again, shape your writing around the kind of job you wish to obtain.

3. Using your answer to question 1, extract three or four sentences about yourself that you could use in a job interview.

4. Using your answer to question 2, extract three or four sentences about yourself that you could use in a job interview.

5. Practice using your answers to questions 3 and 4 in a job interview with a classmate, roommate, or friend.

Source: wavebreakmedia ltd /Shutterstock

ACTIVE REVIEW

Use this Active Review to verify that you understand the ideas and concepts that answer the chapter's study questions.

Q1 WHAT IS THE GOAL OF INFORMATION SYSTEMS SECURITY?

Define *threat, vulnerability, safeguard,* and *target.* Give an example of each. List three types of threats and five types of security losses. Give different examples for the three rows of Figure 12-2. Summarize each of the elements in the cells of Figure 12-3. Explain why it is difficult to know the true cost of computer crime. Explain the goal of IS security.

Q2 HOW BIG IS THE COMPUTER SECURITY PROBLEM?

Explain why it is difficult to know the true size of the computer security problem. Interpret the Verizon study results that showed the number of records lost has declined substantially while the number of incidents has increased. Explain important trends in Figure 12-5. Summarize the Norton survey results. Define *IDS* and explain why the use of an IDS program is sobering, to say the least.

Q3 HOW SHOULD YOU RESPOND TO SECURITY THREATS?

Explain each of the elements in Figure 12-6. Define *brute force attack.* Summarize the characteristics of a strong password. Explain how your identity and password do more than just open doors on your computer. Define *cookie* and explain why using a program like CCleaner is a good example of the computer security trade-off.

Q4 HOW SHOULD ORGANIZATIONS RESPOND TO SECURITY THREATS?

Name and describe two security functions that senior management should address. Summarize the contents of a security policy. Explain what it means to manage risk. Summarize the steps that organizations should take when balancing risk and cost.

Q5 HOW CAN TECHNICAL SAFEGUARDS PROTECT AGAINST SECURITY THREATS?

List five technical safeguards. Define *identification* and *authentication.* Describe three types of authentication. Explain how SSL/TLS works. Define *firewall,* and explain its purpose. Define *malware,* and name five types of malware. Describe six ways to protect against malware. Summarize why malware is a serious problem. Explain how PRIDE is designed for security.

Q6 HOW CAN DATA SAFEGUARDS PROTECT AGAINST SECURITY THREATS?

Define *data administration* and *database administration,* and explain their difference. List data safeguards.

Q7 HOW CAN HUMAN SAFEGUARDS PROTECT AGAINST SECURITY THREATS?

Summarize human safeguards for each activity in Figure 12-12. Summarize safeguards that pertain to nonemployee personnel. Describe three dimensions of safeguards for account administration. Explain how system procedures can serve as human safeguards. Describe security monitoring techniques.

Q8 HOW SHOULD ORGANIZATIONS RESPOND TO SECURITY INCIDENTS?

Summarize the actions that an organization should take when dealing with a security incident.

How does the **knowledge** in this chapter help **you?**

Summarize the knowledge you have learned from this chapter and explain how it helps you be a both a better business professional and a better employee. State the one behavior you should choose, above all. Do it!

KEY TERMS AND CONCEPTS

USING YOUR KNOWLEDGE

1. Credit reporting agencies are required to provide you with a free credit report each year. Most such reports do not include your credit score, but they do provide the details on which your credit score is based. Use one of the following companies to obtain your free report: *www.equifax.com, www.experion.com,* and *www.transunion.com.*

   a. You should review your credit report for obvious errors. However, other checks are appropriate. Search the Web for guidance on how best to review your credit records. Summarize what you learn.

   b. What actions can you take if you find errors in your credit report?

   c. Define *identity theft.* Search the Web and determine the best course of action if someone thinks he has been the victim of identity theft.

2. Suppose you lose your company laptop at an airport. What should you do? Does it matter what data are stored on your disk drive? If the computer contained sensitive or proprietary data, are you necessarily in trouble? Under what circumstances should you now focus on updating your resume for your new employer?

3. Suppose you alert your boss to the security threats in Figure 12-3 and to the safeguards in Figure 12-7. Suppose he says, "Very interesting. Tell me more." In preparing for the meeting, you decide to create a list of talking points.

   a. Write a brief explanation of each threat in Figure 12-3.

   b. Explain how the five components relate to safeguards.

   c. Describe two to three technical, two to three data, and two to three human safeguards.

   d. Write a brief description about the safeguards in Figure 12-12.

   e. List security procedures that pertain to you, a temporary employee.

   f. List procedures that your department should have with regard to disaster planning.

4. Suppose you need to terminate an employee who works in your department. Summarize security protections you must take. How would you behave differently if this termination were a friendly one?

5. Read about MapReduce and Hadoop in Q4 of Chapter 9 if you have not already done so. Is MapReduce suitable for password cracking? Explain your answer. Assume that it is. If it takes 4.5 years for one computer to crack a password, how long will it take 10,000 computers to crack one using Hadoop? If it takes 2 million years to crack a password, how long will it take 10,000 computers to crack one? What does this tell you about password construction?

COLLABORATION EXERCISE 12

Before you start this exercise, read Chapter Extensions 1 and 2, which describe collaboration techniques as well as tools for managing collaboration tasks. In particular, consider using Google Drive, Google+, Windows Live SkyDrive, Microsoft Office 365, or some other collaboration toolset.

Opinions vary on whether the cloud databases are more or less secure than in-house hosted databases. Some experts claim that cloud databases from reputable vendors such as Microsoft, Amazon, and Oracle are far more secure than in-house hosted ones. Others claim that the risk of mismanagement by a cloud vendor is too high; organizations should store critical and confidential data only in-house.

Working with your team, take a position on this issue by answering the following questions:

1. Search the Internet for *ISO 27001*. Explain the purpose of this standard.

2. Does compliance with ISO 27001 mean that a data center is secure? Does it mean that no security threat against compliant data centers will be successful? What does it mean?

3. Search the Internet for evidence that Microsoft Azure complies with ISO 27001. Summarize your findings.

4. Search the Internet for evidence that Amazon's EC2 complies with ISO 27001. Summarize your findings.

   SAS 70 is an auditing standard that provides guidance for an auditor issuing a report about internal controls implemented by a cloud services provider. However, to assess the adequacy of a data center's controls, it is necessary to read and analyze the report that was prepared in accordance with SAS 70.

5. Search the Internet for evidence that Microsoft's auditors have issued a report in accordance with SAS 70. Summarize your findings.

6. Search the Internet for evidence that Amazon's auditors have issued a report in accordance with SAS 70. Summarize your findings.

7. Compare and contrast your answers to questions 3/4 and 5/6. Does your comparison cause you to believe that there are significant differences with regard to security and control between Azure and EC2?

8. Many small businesses operate with local servers running in broom closets or the like. Explain what using a cloud vendor that is compliant with these standards and statements means to such companies.

9. Suppose a publicly traded large organization operates its own Web farm and has certifications indicating that it has complied with ISO 27001 and has issued a statement of controls in accordance with SAS 70 that shows controls are at least adequate. Is there any reason to believe that the organization's data assets on that Web farm are more or less secure than they would be if stored in Azure or EC2? Explain your answer.

10. Based on your answers to these questions, create a general statement as to the desirability, considering only data security, of storing data on Azure and EC2 as compared to storing it on servers managed in-house.

CASE STUDY 12

Moore's Law, One More Time . . .

According to Stewart Baker, former counsel for the National Security Agency, "What we've been seeing, over the last decade or so, is that Moore's Law is working more for the bad guys than the good guys."[1] Should we agree?

If you are in the business of cracking passwords using brute force techniques, then doubling the speed of a CPU will halve the time needed to crack a password. That seems like a real benefit to the criminal, but for a reasonably strong password—one that takes, say, 200 years to crack—halving that time is still 100 years, which is too long for computer crime. But, if the infiltrator uses Hadoop on 1,000 computers, then 100 years becomes 36 days, which may or may not be timely for the criminal's purposes. Certainly, then, faster CPUs benefit password cracking, at least.

Also, the availability of cheap, large, fast disks, and hence cheap storage, enables criminals to inexpensively store millions of common passwords, all the words in all the world's languages, and other useful password-cracking data. Furthermore, cheap storage enables criminals to store the gigabytes of data they reap from snooping; data that can be mined at leisure for user identities, passwords, birth dates, Social Security numbers, credit card accounts, and so forth. Certainly, nearly free data storage benefits computer crime as well.

But maybe we're missing the greatest benefit. Thirty minutes of searching the terms *data breach* and *data loss* with Google in August 2011 netted the following seven events, all of which occurred in 2011:

1. In June, 1.3 million Sega game players lost birth date, email, and encrypted password data due to a security breach.[2]

2. In April, 70 million Sony game players had their credit card data stolen.[3]

3. A flaw in iOS 3.0 enabled criminals to invade the email accounts of 144,000 people, including former White House Chief of Staff Rahm Emanuel. In fairness to Apple, the problem seemed to lie more with AT&T than Apple.[4]

4. A flaw in iOS, up to version 4.3, enabled hackers to obtain administration account privileges from users who downloaded Acrobat PDF files. The problem was Apple's, not Adobe's.[5] It has since been fixed.

5. Friendly neighbor Ian Wood stole $57,000 from his neighbors by using personal data he obtained on Facebook to access their online accounts. He followed the "forget your password" instructions and responded to questions using the Facebook data. When he gained access to the accounts, he requested new credit cards, which he then stole from his neighbors' mailboxes.[6]

6. Phishers spoofing Twitter obtained Twitter account data by claiming that Twitter was about to start charging for its services. To object, all the user had to do was to register his or her Twitter ID and password at a fake Twitter account. The phisher took the objectors' data.[7]

7. In the too-ironic-to-believe category, a Chinese television program promoting the Chinese military showed a screenshot of an attempt to hack into the IP address 138.26.72.17. At the time, that address belonged to a university in the United States. Apparently the editor of the program didn't know what an IP address was.[8]

This 30-minute search actually yielded many more examples than listed here; try it yourself.

What can we learn from these seven scenarios? What technology do they share? Data communications. Recall from Chapter 1 that Moore's Law makes data communications essentially free. These seven events are some of the consequences of that fact.

Now consider that millions of mobile devices will further increase data communications, and you can see that the opportunities for computer criminals will only increase—exponentially, in fact.

[1]David Talbot, "Moore's Outlaws," *MIT Technology Review*, Vol. 113, No. 4, August 2010.
[2]http://www.reuters.com/article/2011/06/19/us-sega-hackers-idUSL3E7HJ01520110619, accessed August 2011
[3]http://www.bostonherald.com/business/technology/general/view.bg?articleid=1333548, accessed August 2011
[4]http://ismashphone.com/2010/11/5-of-the-most-notable-ios-security-holes-weve-seen.html, accessed August 2011
[5]http://www.mobiledia.com/news/97150.html, accessed August 2011
[6]http://technolog.msnbc.msn.com/_news/2011/08/16/7387638-man-steals-57k-from-neighbors-using-their-facebook-info?GT1=43001, accessed August 2011
[7]http://digitallife.today.com/_news/2011/08/19/7416549-no-you-wont-have-to-pay-to-use-twitter-in-october?GT1=43001, accessed August 2011.
[8]http://www.v3.co.uk/v3-uk/security-watchdog-blog/2103749/chinese-government-caught-tv-film-hacking-west, accessed August 2011

QUESTIONS

1. Query the Internet for the terms *data breach* and *data loss*. Find seven interesting examples of your own.
   a. Briefly describe the example and the loss.
   b. As best you can from the available description, name one safeguard that would have prevented the loss, or at least would have limited the loss.
   c. In what ways does it appear from this brief sample that data losses have changed since August 2011?

2. Explain why Moore's Law makes it increasingly more important to create strong passwords.

3. Use one or more of the crime scenarios listed in this case study to explain why it is important to use different passwords for different accounts.

4. Explain how data communications played an important role in each of the crime scenarios listed in this case study.

5. Do you agree that Moore's Law is helping the "bad guys" more than the "good guys"? Why or why not? Use evidence in this case, knowledge from this chapter, and your own experience in your answer.

6. Suppose you had a disk full of a day's Internet traffic into your university's primary router. Explain how you could mine this data. Name at least seven different types of data you are likely to find and explain how you would go about finding it.

7. Describe, in your own words, why increased use of mobile devices is likely to create even greater opportunities for computer criminals.

8. Review Figure 12-6 and explain how the measures recommended in the figure would have helped anyone who had the misfortune to be a victim in any of the seven scenarios presented in the case study.

chapter extension 1

Chapter 1 provides the background for this Extension.

Collaboration Information Systems for Decision Making, Problem Solving, and Project Management

Q1

WHAT ARE THE TWO KEY CHARACTERISTICS OF COLLABORATION?

To answer this question, we must first distinguish between the terms *cooperation* and *collaboration*. **Cooperation** is a group of people working together, all doing essentially the same type of work, to accomplish a job. A group of four painters, each painting a different wall in the same room, are working cooperatively. Similarly, a group of checkers at the grocery store or clerks at the post office are working cooperatively to service customers. A cooperative group can accomplish a given task faster than an individual working alone can, but the cooperative result is usually not better in quality than the result of someone working alone.

In this text, we define **collaboration** as a group of people working together to achieve a common goal *via a process of feedback and iteration*. Using feedback and iteration, one person will produce something, say the draft of a document, and a second person will review that draft and provide critical feedback. Given the feedback, the original author or someone else will then revise the first draft to produce a second. The work proceeds in a series of stages, or *iterations*, in which something is produced, members criticize it, and then another version is produced. Using iteration and feedback, the group's result can be better than what any single individual can produce alone. This is possible because different group members provide different perspectives. "Oh, I never thought of it that way," is a typical signal of collaboration success.

Many, perhaps most, student groups incorrectly use cooperation rather than collaboration. Given an assignment, a group of five students will break it up into five pieces, work to accomplish their piece independently, and then merge their independent work for grading by the professor. Such a process will enable the project to be completed more quickly, with less work by any single individual, but it will not be better than the result obtained if the students were to work alone.

In contrast, when students work collaboratively, they set forth an initial idea or work product, provide feedback to one another on those ideas or products, and then revise in accordance with feedback. Such a process can produce a result far superior to that produced by any student working alone.

STUDY QUESTIONS

Q1 WHAT ARE THE TWO KEY CHARACTERISTICS OF COLLABORATION?

Q2 WHAT ARE THREE CRITERIA FOR SUCCESSFUL COLLABORATION?

Q3 WHAT ARE THE FOUR PRIMARY PURPOSES OF COLLABORATION?

Q4 WHAT ARE THE COMPONENTS AND FUNCTIONS OF A COLLABORATION INFORMATION SYSTEM?

CE1

IMPORTANCE OF EFFECTIVE CRITICAL FEEDBACK

Given this definition, for collaboration to be successful members must provide and receive *critical* feedback. A group in which everyone is too polite to say anything critical cannot collaborate. As Darwin John, the world's first chief information officer (CIO), once said, "If two of you have the exact same idea, then we have no need for one of you." On the other hand, a group that is so critical and negative that members come to distrust, even hate, one another cannot effectively collaborate either. For most groups, success is achieved between these extremes.

To underline this point, consider the research of Ditkoff, Allen, Moore, and Pollard. They surveyed 108 business professionals to determine the qualities, attitudes, and skills that make a good collaborator.[1] Figure CE1-1 lists the most and least important characteristics reported in the survey. Most students are surprised to learn that five of the top 12 characteristics involve disagreement (highlighted in red in Figure CE1-1). Most students believe that "we should all get along"

Figure CE1-1
Important and Not Important Characteristics of a Collaborator

---

Twelve Most Important Characteristics for an Effective Collaborator

1. Is enthusiastic about the subject of our collaboration.

2. Is open-minded and curious.

3. Speaks their mind even if it's an unpopular viewpoint.

4. Gets back to me and others in a timely way.

5. Is willing to enter into difficult conversations.

6. Is a perceptive listener.

7. Is skillful at giving/receiving negative feedback.

8. Is willing to put forward unpopular ideas.

9. Is self-managing and requires "low maintenance."

10. Is known for following through on commitments.

11. Is willing to dig into the topic with zeal.

12. Thinks differently than I do/brings different perspectives.

Nine Least Important Characteristics for an Effective Collaborator

31. Is well organized.

32. Is someone I immediately liked. The chemistry is good.

33. Has already earned my trust.

34. Has experience as a collaborator.

35. Is a skilled and persuasive presenter.

36. Is gregarious and dynamic.

37. Is someone I knew beforehand.

38. Has an established reputation in field of our collaboration.

39. Is an experienced businessperson.

---

[1] Dave Pollard, "The Ideal Collaborative Team." Available at: http://www.ideachampions.com/downloads/collaborationresults.pdf (accessed June 2012).

and more or less have the same idea and opinions about team matters. Although it is important for the team to be sociable enough to work together, this research indicates that it is also important for team members to have different ideas and opinions and to express them to each other.

When we think about collaboration as an iterative process in which team members give and receive feedback, these results are not surprising. During collaboration, team members learn from each other, and it will be difficult to learn if no one is willing to express different, or even unpopular, ideas. The respondents also seem to be saying, "You can be negative, as long as you care about what we're doing." These collaboration skills do not come naturally to people who have been taught to "play well with others," but that may be why they were so highly ranked in the survey.

The characteristics rated *not relevant* are also revealing. Experience as a collaborator or in business does not seem to matter. Being popular also is not important. A big surprise, however, is that being well organized was rated 31st out of 39 characteristics. Perhaps collaboration itself is not a very well organized process?

GUIDELINES FOR GIVING AND RECEIVING CRITICAL FEEDBACK

Giving and receiving critical feedback is the single most important collaboration skill. So, before we discuss the role that information systems can play for improving collaboration, study the guidelines for giving and receiving critical feedback shown in Figure CE1-2.

Many students have found that when they first form a collaborative group, it's useful to begin with a discussion of critical feedback guidelines such as those in Figure CE1-2. Begin with this list, and then, using feedback and iteration, develop your own list. Of course, if a group member does not follow the agreed-upon guidelines, someone will have to provide critical feedback to that effect as well.

WARNING!

If you are like most undergraduate business students, especially freshmen or sophomores, your life experience is keeping you from understanding the need for collaboration. So far, almost everyone you know has the same experiences as you and, more or less, thinks like you. Your

Figure CE1-2
Guidelines for Providing and Receiving Critical Feedback

Guideline	Example
Be specific.	"I was confused until I got to Section 2" rather than "The whole thing is a disorganized mess."
Offer suggestions.	"Consider moving Section 2 to the beginning of the document."
Avoid personal comments.	Never: "Only an idiot would miss that point … or write that document."
Strive for balance.	"I thought Section 2 was particularly good. What do you think about moving it to the start of the document?"
Question your emotions.	"Why do I feel so angry about the comment he just made? What's going on? Is my anger helping me?"
Do not dominate.	If there are five members of the group, unless you have special expertise, you are entitled to just 20 percent of the words/time.
Demonstrate a commitment to the group.	"I know this is painful, but if we can make these changes our result will be so much better." or "Ouch. I really didn't want to have to redo that section, but if you all think it's important, I'll do it."

friends and associates have the same educational background, scored more or less the same on standardized tests, and have the same orientation toward success. So, why collaborate? Most of you think the same way, anyway: "What does the professor want and what's the easiest, fastest way to get it to her?"

So, consider this thought experiment. Your company is planning to build a new facility that is critical for the success of a new product line and will create 300 new jobs. The county government won't issue a building permit because the site is prone to landslides. Your engineers believe your design overcomes that hazard, but your CFO is concerned about possible litigation in the event there is a problem. Your corporate counsel is investigating the best way to overcome the county's objections while limiting liability. Meanwhile, a local environmental group is protesting your site because they believe it is too close to an eagle's nest. Your public relations director is meeting with those local groups every week.

Do you proceed with the project?

To decide, you create a working team of the chief engineer, the chief financial officer (CFO), your legal counsel, and the PR director. Each of those people has different education and expertise, different life experience, and different values. In fact, the only thing they have in common is that they are paid by your company. That team will participate collaboratively in ways that are far different from your experience so far. Keep this example in mind as you continue to read.

Bottom line: The two key characteristics of collaboration are iteration and feedback.

WHAT ARE THREE CRITERIA FOR SUCCESSFUL COLLABORATION?

J. Richard Hackman studied teamwork for many years, and his book *Leading Teams* contains many useful concepts and tips for future managers.[2] According to Hackman, there are three primary criteria for judging team success:

- Successful outcome
- Growth in team capability
- Meaningful and satisfying experience

SUCCESSFUL OUTCOME

Most students are primarily concerned with the first criterion. They want to achieve a good outcome, measured by their grade, or they want to get the project done with an acceptable grade while minimizing the effort required. For business professionals, teams need to accomplish their goals: make a decision, solve a problem, or manage a project. Whatever the objective is, the first success criterion is, "Did we do it?"

Although not as apparent in student teams, most business teams also need to ask, "Did we do it within the time and budget allowed?" Teams that produce a work product too late or far over budget are not successful, even if they did achieve their goal.

GROWTH IN TEAM CAPABILITY

The other two criteria are surprising to most students, probably because most student teams are short-lived. But, in business, where teams often last months or years, it makes sense to ask, "Did the team get better?" If you're a football fan, you've undoubtedly heard your college's coach

---

[2] J. Richard Hackman, *Leading Teams: Setting the Stage for Great Performances* (Boston: Harvard Business Press, 2002).

say, "We really improved as the season progressed." (Of course, for the team with 2 wins and 12 losses, you didn't hear that.) Football teams last only a season. If the team is permanent, say a team of customer support personnel, the benefits of team growth are even greater. Over time, the team's process quality increases. It becomes more efficient because it can provide more service for a given cost or the same service for less cost.

With experience, teams can become more effective as well. Activities are combined or eliminated. Linkages are established so that "the left hand knows what the right hand is doing," or needs, or can provide. Teams also get better as individuals improve at their tasks. Part of that improvement is the learning curve; as someone does something over and over, he or she gets better at it. But team members also teach task skills and give knowledge to one another. Team members also provide perspectives that other team members need. We will investigate several of these possibilities in Chapters 7 and 8.

MEANINGFUL AND SATISFYING EXPERIENCE

The third element of Hackman's definition of team success is that team members have a meaningful and satisfying experience. Of course, the nature of team goals is a major factor in making work meaningful. But few of us have the opportunity to develop a life-saving cancer vaccine or safely land a stricken airliner in the middle of the Hudson River in winter. For most of us, it's a matter of making the product, or creating the shipment, or accounting for the payment, or finding the prospects, and so on.

So, in the more mundane world of most business professionals, what makes work meaningful? Hackman cites numerous studies in his book, and one common thread is that the work is perceived as meaningful *by the team*. Keeping prices up to date in the product database may not be the most exciting work, but if that task is perceived by the team as important, it will become meaningful.

Furthermore, if an individual's work is not only perceived as important, but the person doing that work is also given credit for it, then the experience will be perceived as meaningful. So, recognition for work well done is vitally important for a meaningful work experience.

Another aspect of team satisfaction is camaraderie. Business professionals, just like students, are energized when they have the feeling that they are part of a group, each person doing his or her own job, and combining efforts to achieve something worthwhile that is better than any could have done alone.

WHAT ARE THE FOUR PRIMARY PURPOSES OF COLLABORATION?

Collaborative teams accomplish four primary purposes:

- Become informed
- Make decisions
- Solve problems
- Manage projects

These four purposes build on each other. For example, making a decision requires that team members be informed. In turn, to solve a problem, the team must have the ability to make decisions (and become informed). Finally, to conduct a project, the team must be able to solve problems (and make decisions and become informed).

Before we continue, understand you can use the hierarchy of these four purposes to build your professional skills. You cannot make good decisions if you do not have the skills to inform yourself. You cannot solve problems if you are unable to make good decisions. And you cannot manage projects if you don't know how to solve problems!

In this question, we will consider the collaborative nature of these four purposes and describe requirements for information systems that support them, starting with the most basic, becoming informed.

BECOMING INFORMED

Informing is the first and most fundamental collaboration purpose. Two individuals can receive the same data but construct different interpretations or, as stated in the terms of Chapter 2, conceive different information. The goal of the informing is to ensure, as much as possible, that team members are conceiving information in the same way.

For example, the team at GearUp has been assigned the task of reducing operational expenses. One of the team's first tasks is to ensure that everyone understands that goal and, further, understands what constitutes an operational expense.

Informing, and hence all of the purposes of collaboration, presents several requirements for collaborative information systems. As you would expect, team members need to be able to share data and to communicate with one another to share interpretations. Furthermore, because memories are faulty and team membership can change, it is also necessary to document the team's understanding of the information conceived. To avoid having to go "over and over and over" a topic, a repository of information, such as a wiki, is needed.

DECISION MAKING

Collaboration is used for some types of decision making, but not all. Consequently, to understand the role for collaboration we must begin with an analysis of decision making. Decisions are made at three levels: *operational, managerial,* and *strategic*.

Operational Decisions

Operational decisions are those that support operational, day-to-day activities. Typical operational decisions are: How many widgets should we order from vendor A? Should we extend credit to vendor B? Which invoices should we pay today? In almost all cases, operational decisions need not involve collaboration.

Managerial Decisions

Managerial decisions are decisions about the allocation and utilization of resources. Typical decisions are: How much should we budget for computer hardware and programs for department A next year? How many engineers should we assign to project B? How many square feet of warehouse space do we need for the coming year?

In general, if a managerial decision requires consideration of different perspectives, then it will benefit from collaboration. For example, consider the decision of whether to increase employee pay in the coming year. No single individual has the answer. The decision depends on an analysis of inflation, industry trends, the organization's profitability, the influence of unions, and other factors. Senior managers, accountants, human resources personnel, labor relationships managers, and others will each bring a different perspective to the decision. They will produce a work product for the decision, evaluate that product, and make revisions in an iterative fashion—the essence of collaboration.

Strategic Decisions

Strategic decisions are those that support broad-scope, organizational issues. Typical decisions at the strategic level are: Should we start a new product line? Should we open a centralized warehouse in Tennessee? Should we acquire company A?

Strategic decisions are almost always collaborative. Consider a decision about whether to move manufacturing operations to China. This decision affects every employee in the organization, the organization's suppliers, its customers, and its shareholders. Many factors and many perspectives on each of those factors must be considered.

The Decision Process

Information systems can be classified based on whether their decision processes are *structured* or *unstructured*. These terms refer to the method or process by which the decision is to be made, not to the nature of the underlying problem. A **structured decision** process is one for which there is an understood and accepted method for making the decision. A formula for computing the reorder quantity of an item in inventory is an example of a structured decision process. A standard method for allocating furniture and equipment to employees is another structured decision process. Structured decisions seldom require collaboration.

An **unstructured decision** process is one for which there is no agreed-on decision-making method. Predicting the future direction of the economy or the stock market is a classic example. The prediction method varies from person to person; it is neither standardized nor broadly accepted. Another example of an unstructured decision process is assessing how well suited an employee is for performing a particular job. Managers vary in the manner in which they make such assessments. Unstructured decisions are often collaborative.

The Relationship Between Decision Type and Decision Process

The decision type and decision process are loosely related. Decisions at the operational level tend to be structured, and decisions at the strategic level tend to be unstructured. Managerial decisions tend to be both structured and unstructured.

We use the words *tend to be* because there are exceptions to the relationship. Some operational decisions are unstructured (e.g., "How many taxicab drivers do we need on the night before the homecoming game?"), and some strategic decisions can be structured (e.g., "How should we assign sales quotas for a new product?"). In general, however, the relationship holds.

Decision Making and Collaboration Systems

As stated, few structured decisions involve collaboration. Deciding, for example, how much of product A to order from vendor B does not require the feedback and iteration among members that typify collaboration. Although the process of generating the order might require the coordinated work of people in purchasing, accounting, and manufacturing, there is seldom a need for one person to comment on someone else's work. In fact, involving collaboration in routine, structured decisions is expensive, wasteful, and frustrating. "Do we have to have a meeting about everything?" is a common lament.

The situation is different for unstructured decisions, because feedback and iteration are crucial. Members bring different ideas and perspectives about what is to be decided, how the decision will be reached, what criteria are important, and how decision alternatives score against those criteria. The group may make tentative conclusions or discuss potential outcomes of those conclusions, and members will often revise their positions. Figure CE1-3 illustrates the change in the need for collaboration as decision processes become less structured.

PROBLEM SOLVING

Problem solving is the third primary reason for collaborating. A **problem** is a perceived difference between what is and what ought to be. Because it is a perception, different people can have different problem definitions.

Therefore, the first and arguably the most important task for a problem-solving collaborative group is defining the problem. For example, the GearUp team has been assigned the problem of finding ways of reducing operational expenses. As stated as part of the informing purpose, the group needs first to ensure that the team members understand this goal and have a common definition of what an operational expense is.

Figure CE1-3
Collaboration Needs for
Decision Making

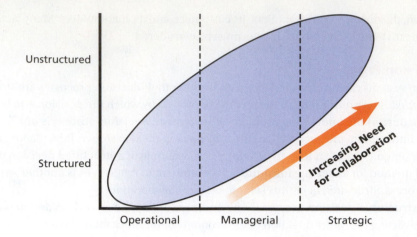

However, because a problem is a difference between what is and what ought to be, the statement, "reduce operational expenses" does not go far enough. Is saving one dollar enough of a reduction? Is saving $100,000 enough? Does it take $1,000,000 for the reduction to be enough? A better problem definition would be to reduce operational expenses by 10 percent or by $100,000 or some other more specific statement of what is desired.

Figure CE1-4 lists the principal problem-solving tasks. Because this text is about information systems and not about problem solving *per se*, we will not delve into those tasks here. Just note the work that needs to be done, and consider the role of feedback and iteration for each of these tasks.

PROJECT MANAGEMENT

Project management is a rich and complicated subject, with many theories and methods and techniques.

Projects are formed to create or produce something. The end goal might be a marketing plan, the design of a new factory, or a new product, or it could be performing the annual audit. Because projects vary so much in nature and size, we will summarize generic project phases here. Figure CE1-5 shows project management with four phases, the major tasks of each, and the kinds of data that collaborative teams need to share.

Starting Phase

The fundamental purpose of the starting phase is to set the ground rules for the project and the team. In industry, teams need to determine or understand what authority they have. Is the project given to the team? Or, is a part of the team's task to identify what the project is? Is the team free to determine team membership, or is membership given? Can the team devise its own methods for accomplishing the project, or is a particular method required? Student teams differ from those in industry because the team's authority and membership are set by the instructor. However, although student teams do not have the authority to define the project, they do have the authority to determine how that project will be accomplished.

Figure CE1-4
Problem-Solving Tasks

- Define the problem.
- Identify alternative solutions.
- Specify evaluation criteria.
- Evaluate alternatives.
- Select an alternative.
- Implement solution.

Phase	Tasks	Shared Data
Starting	Set team authority. Set project scope and initial budget. Form team. Establish team roles, responsibilities, and authorities. Establish team rules.	Team member personal data Start-up documents
Planning	Determine tasks and dependencies. Assign tasks. Determine schedule. Revise budget.	Project plan, budget, and other documents
Doing	Perform project tasks. Manage tasks and budget. Solve problems. Reschedule tasks, as necessary. Document and report progress.	Work in process Updated tasks Updated project schedule Updated project budget Project status documents
Finalizing	Determine completion. Prepare archival documents. Disband team.	Archival documents

Other tasks during the starting phase are to set the scope of the project and to establish an initial budget. Often this budget is preliminary and is revised after the project has been planned. An initial team is formed during this phase with the understanding that team membership may change as the project progresses. It is important to set team member expectations at the outset. What role will each team member play, and what responsibilities and authority will he or she have? Team rules are also established as discussed under decision making.

Planning Phase

The purpose of the planning phase is to determine "who will do what and by when." Work activities are defined, and resources such as personnel, budget, and equipment are assigned to them. Tasks often depend on one other. For example, you cannot evaluate alternatives until you have created a list of alternatives to evaluate. In this case, we say that there is a *task dependency* between the task *Evaluate alternatives* and the task *Create a list of alternatives*. The *Evaluate alternatives* task cannot begin until the completion of the *Create a list of alternatives* task.

Once tasks and resources have been assigned, it is possible to determine the project schedule. If the schedule is unacceptable, more resources can be added to the project, or the project scope can be reduced. Assessing trade-offs among schedule, cost, and scope is one of the most important tasks not only during the planning phase, but throughout the project. The project budget is usually revised during the planning phase as well.

Doing Phase

Project tasks are accomplished during the doing phase. The key management challenge here is to ensure that tasks are accomplished on time, and, if not, to identify schedule problems as early as possible. As work progresses, additional trade-offs must be made, and often it is necessary to add or delete tasks, change task assignments, add or remove task labor or other resources, and so forth. Another important task is to document and report project progress.

Finalizing Phase

Are we done? This question is an important and sometimes difficult one to answer. If work is not finished, the team needs to define more tasks and continue the doing phase. If the answer is yes, then the team needs to document its results, document information for future teams, close down the project, and disband the team.

Review the third column of Figure CE1-5. All of this project data needs to be stored in a location accessible to the team. Furthermore, all the data is subject to feedback and iteration. That means that there will be hundreds, perhaps thousands, of versions of data items to be managed. We will consider ways that collaborative information systems can facilitate the management of such data in Chapter Extension 2.

WHAT ARE THE COMPONENTS AND FUNCTIONS OF A COLLABORATION INFORMATION SYSTEM?

As you would expect, a **collaboration information system** or, more simply, a **collaboration system**, is an information system that supports collaboration. Given our discussion in Q1, this means that the system needs to support iteration and feedback among team members. We will discuss specific system features in Chapter Extension 2. For now, consider the components of a collaboration system as well as its basic functions.

THE FIVE COLLABORATION SYSTEM COMPONENTS

As information systems, collaboration systems have the five components of every information system: hardware, software, data, procedures, and people. Concerning hardware, most collaboration systems are hosted on organizational servers or in what is called *the cloud*, which you will learn about in Chapters 4 and 5. We will ignore that component in the discussion in this chapter extension. Just know that the tools you're using and the data you're sharing are supported by computer hardware, somewhere. Collaboration programs are applications like email or text messaging that support collaborative work; we will discuss many such programs in the next chapter extension.

Collaboration involves two types of data. **Project data** is data that is part of the collaboration's work product. For example, for a team that is designing a new product, design documents are examples of project data. A document that describes a recommended solution is project data for a problem-solving project. **Project metadata** is data that is used to manage the project. Schedules, tasks, budgets, and other managerial data are examples of project metadata. Both types of data, by the way, are subject to iteration and feedback.

Collaboration information systems procedures specify standards, policies, and techniques for conducting the team's work. An example is procedures for reviewing documents or other work products. To reduce confusion and increase control, the team might establish a procedure that specifies who will review documents and in what sequence. Rules about who can do what to which data are also codified in procedures.

The final component of a collaboration system is, of course, people. We discussed the importance of the ability to give and receive critical feedback in Q1. In addition, team members know how and when to use collaboration applications.

PRIMARY FUNCTIONS: COMMUNICATION AND CONTENT SHARING

Figure CE1-6 lists the five important collaboration activities discussed in Q1 and Q2 and summarizes the requirements those activities pose for collaboration systems. Notice these requirements fall into two categories: communication and the sharing of content. The second, fourth, and last of these activities concern communication, and the first and third concern tracking and require the storage and sharing of content. We will consider communication and content storage in the next two questions.

Figure CE1-6
Collaboration System
Requirements

Collaborative Activity	Information Systems Requirements
Iteration.	Track many versions of many documents and other work product.
Feedback.	Provide easy-to-use and readily available multiparty communication.
Accomplish task within time and budget.	Track tasks, schedules, budgets, and other project metadata. Account for and report progress and status.
Promote team growth.	Provide for intrateam teaching.
Increase team satisfaction.	Provide for team and member recognition.

Figure CE1-7 lists the four purposes of collaboration activities discussed in Q3 and summarizes IS requirements for collaboration systems for each purpose. Again, notice that these requirements fall into communication and content-sharing categories. As you think about your own collaboration projects in school, use Figures CE1-6 and CE1-7 as a guide for determining the tools you need for your own collaboration system.

Note the difference between the terms *collaboration system* and *collaboration tool*. A **collaboration tool** is the program component of a collaboration system. For the tool to be useful, it must be surrounded by the other four components of an information system.

Figure CE1-7
IS Requirements for Different
Collaboration Purposes

Purpose	IS Requirements
Become informed.	Share data. Support group communication. Store history.
Make decisions.	Share decision criteria, alternative descriptions, evaluation tools, evaluation results, and implementation plan. Support group communication during decision-making process. Publish decision, as needed. Store records of process and results.
Solve problems.	Share problem definitions, solution alternatives, costs and benefits, alternative evaluations, and solution implementation plan. Support group communication. Publish problem and solution, as needed. Store problem definition, alternatives, analysis, and plan.
Conduct projects.	Support starting, planning, doing, and finalizing project phases.

ACTIVE REVIEW

Use this Active Review to verify that you understand the ideas and concepts that answer the chapter extension's study questions.

Q1 WHAT ARE TWO KEY CHARACTERISTICS OF COLLABORATION?

In your own words, explain the difference between cooperation and collaboration. Name the two key characteristics of collaboration and explain how they improve group work. Summarize important skills for collaborators and list what you believe are the best ways to give and receive critical feedback.

Q2 WHAT ARE THREE CRITERIA FOR SUCCESSFUL COLLABORATION?

Name and describe three criteria for collaboration success. Summarize how these criteria differ between student and professional teams.

Q3 WHAT ARE THE FOUR PRIMARY PURPOSES OF COLLABORATION?

Name and describe four primary purposes of collaboration. Explain their relationship. Describe ways that collaboration systems can contribute to each purpose.

Q4 WHAT ARE THE COMPONENTS AND FUNCTIONS OF A COLLABORATION INFORMATION SYSTEM?

Name and describe the five components of a collaboration information system. Name and describe two key collaboration IS functions.

KEY TERMS AND CONCEPTS

USING YOUR KNOWLEDGE

1. Give an example of a cooperative team and a collaborative team. Use examples other than those in this book. Explain why iteration and feedback is more important for collaboration than for cooperation. Summarize factors that cause most student teams to be cooperative and not collaborative. What is the disadvantage when student teams are not collaborative? How can information systems be used to make it easier for students to truly collaborate?

2. Suppose you are the manager of a campaign to elect one of your friends as university student body president.
   a. Describe why this campaign will be more successful if managed collaboratively than cooperatively.
   b. Explain how each of the criteria for team success pertains to this campaign. Are the second and third criteria important? Explain your answer.
   c. Describe how each of the four primary purposes of collaboration pertains to this campaign. Explain the hierarchical nature of these four factors.
   d. Suppose that one of the tasks for the campaign team is to decide how to allocate scarce labor. Where in Figure CE1-3 does this decision lie? Explain your answer.

3. Consider the use of information technology to run this campaign. Using the four rows in Figure CE1-7, answer the following questions:
   a. Suppose that you attempt to use nothing other than face-to-face meetings, email and texting for communication during this campaign. For each purpose, what problems can you expect if you use only these two?
   b. For which purpose(s) might you use Microsoft PowerPoint? For which purpose(s) might you use Microsoft Excel?
   c. Assuming you are using only face-to-face meetings, email, texting, PowerPoint, and Excel, how will you share documents? What problems might you expect?
   d. Describe what you think would be the single most important additional collaboration tool that you could add to your team.

(This exercise is continued at the end of Chapter Extension 2, when you will be asked to consider other collaboration tools.)

Collaborative Information Systems for Student Projects

 Q1 WHAT ARE THE IS REQUIREMENTS FOR STUDENT PROJECT COLLABORATIONS?

Your MIS class will help you gain knowledge and skills that you'll use throughout your business career. But, why wait? You can benefit from this knowledge right now and put it to use tonight. Most business courses involve a team project—why not use what you're learning to construct a collaboration IS that will make teamwork easier and can help your team achieve a better product? You can use it for projects not only in this class, but also, with some leadership on your part, for teams in other classes as well.

To begin, read Chapter Extension 1, if you have not already done so. Ensure that you understand the difference between *cooperation* and *collaboration*. Also ensure that any team that will use the system you're building wants to *collaborate*. If they just want to cooperate, you won't need this system. Finally, make sure you understand the need for and relationship of informing, deciding, solving problems, and managing projects.

Figure CE2-1 summarizes requirements for an IS that supports collaborative student teams. The requirements are divided into three categories as shown.

REQUIRED FEATURES

A collaborative information system must support the following three categories of requirements:

- Communication
- Content sharing
- Project planning and management

Regarding team communication, if you meet face-to-face, you most likely will need some medium for sharing ideas. You can use a whiteboard or similar device, but that means in order to have a minutes or other record of the team's work, someone needs to copy the results to paper or a file. Another approach is to use PowerPoint or OneNote and a projector during the meeting. At the end, those files can be shared with all team members to serve as minutes. You'll see other ways of using collaborative tools during meetings later in this extension.

By default, most student teams attempt to meet face-to-face. But why? Such meetings are difficult to schedule and invariably someone can't be on campus, is stuck in traffic, misses the bus, or whatever. In the next question, you'll see tools for online meetings that make face-to-face meetings less important.

CE2

- **Required Features**
  - Communication
  - Content sharing
  - Project planning and management

- **Nice-to-Have Features**
  - Discussion forums
  - Surveys
  - Wikis
  - Blogs
  - Photo/Video Sharing

- **Collaboration Tool Characteristics**
  - Free/cheap
  - Easy to learn/use
  - Integrated features
  - Provides evidence of versions
  - Used in business

If your team is going to practice feedback and iteration, it needs some way to share content and to track different versions of content items. When team members work on documents at the same time, the system should provide a means to ensure that one user's changes don't override another's. Some tools do that automatically; however if your team does not use such a tool, you must develop procedures to avoid lost work.

As discussed in Chapter Extension 1, project planning and management necessitates the creation of tasks and assigning those tasks to individuals. The fundamental goal is to "decide who's going to do what, and by when." When those decisions have been made, the task, person, and date due need to be recorded somewhere so that all team members can follow progress (or lack thereof) and so that team members can be held accountable for their tasks. Of course, nothing goes as planned, and so this capability needs to allow tasks to be altered when necessary. Teams also need the ability to keep track of events such as intermediate meetings, or final reviews, etc.

NICE-TO-HAVE FEATURES

The features in the next category are not essential, but they can make teamwork easier and more effective. Also, some of these features might be required for certain types of projects.

Discussion forums are useful when the team needs to meet on some topic, but everyone cannot meet at the same time. Surveys obtain team members' opinions outside of team meetings as well. Wikis are useful for documenting team knowledge; blogs enable team members to publish their ideas. Sharing photos and videos can be a great way of building team cohesion.

COLLABORATION TOOL CHARACTERISTICS

The last category of requirements concerns characteristics of the collaboration tool (the computer program part of the IS). It needs to be free, or at least cheap. It should be easy to learn and use, though the discussion of Figure CE2-18 may have a surprise for you in that regard. Feature integration is very useful, but rare. An example of such integration occurs when someone changes a task and the collaboration tool automatically sends an email change notification to the person who has that task.

If your professor wants to evaluate your collaboration, you will want to submit evidence of many versions and contributions from team members as part of your project deliverable. Some collaboration tools automatically generate such data, as you will see. Finally, you will benefit if the tool you use is one that you will likely employ in your professional career. Blackboard and

Moodle (course management software) have support for collaboration, but they are nearly unknown in business. Google Drive and SharePoint, on the other hand, are well known. SharePoint skills, in particular, are in great demand in industry and knowing how to use it gives you a competitive advantage.

Q2 HOW CAN YOU USE COLLABORATION TOOLS TO IMPROVE TEAM COMMUNICATION?

Team communication is one of the three mandatory requirements for student team collaborations. The particular tools used depend on the ways that the team communicates, as summarized in Figure CE2-2. **Synchronous communication** occurs when all team members meet at the same time, such as with conference calls or face-to-face meetings. **Asynchronous communication** occurs when team members do not meet at the same time. Employees who work different shifts at the same location, or team members who work in different time zones around the world, must meet asynchronously. Most student teams can meet at the same time.

As stated in Q1, for most face-to-face meetings, you need little software support; you may want to use PowerPoint, OneNote, or another application and a projector for team discussions. However, *given today's communication technology, most students should forgo face-to-face meetings.* As stated in Q1, they are too difficult to arrange and seldom worth the trouble. Instead, learn to use **virtual meetings** in which participants do not meet in the same place, and possibly not at the same time.

If your virtual meeting is synchronous (all meet at the same time), you can use conference calls, multiparty text chat, screen sharing, webinars, or videoconferencing. Some students find it weird to use text chat for school projects, but why not? You can attend meetings wherever you are, without using your voice. Google Text supports multiparty text chat, as does Microsoft Lync. Google or Bing "multiparty text chat" to find other, similar products.

Screen-sharing applications enable users to view the same whiteboard, application, or other display. Figure CE2-3 shows an example whiteboard for a GearUp meeting. This whiteboard, which is part of Office 365 Lync (we will discuss Lync further in Q5), allows multiple people to contribute simultaneously. To organize the simultaneous conversation, the whiteboard real estate is divided among the members of the group, as shown. Some groups save their whiteboards as minutes of the meeting.

A **webinar** is a virtual meeting in which attendees view one of the attendees' computer screens for a more formal and organized presentation. WebEx (*www.webex.com*) is a popular commercial webinar application used in virtual sales presentations.

Figure CE2-2
Collaboration Tools for Communication

Synchronous		Asynchronous
Shared calendars Invitation and attendance		
Single location	Multiple locations	Single or multiple locations
Office applications such as Word and PowerPoint Shared whiteboards	Conference calls Multiparty text chat Screen sharing Webinars Videoconferencing	Email Discussion forums Team surveys

Virtual meetings

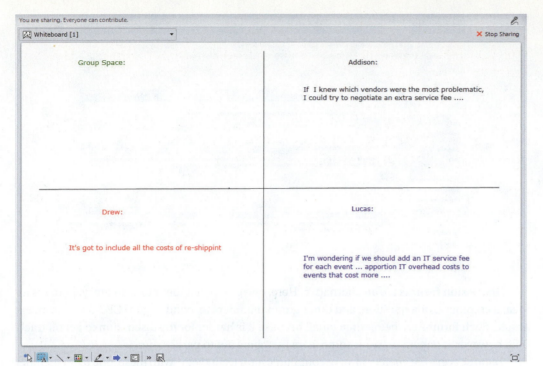

Figure CE2-3
Office 365 Lync Whiteboard
Showing Simultaneous
Contributions

If everyone on your team has a camera on his or her computer, you can also do **videoconferencing**, like that shown in Figure CE2-4. Skype is a common choice for student videoconferencing, but you can also Microsoft Lync and others as well. Search the Internet for *videoconferencing tools*. Videoconferencing is more intrusive than text chat (you have to comb your hair), but it does have a more personal touch.

In some classes and situations, synchronous meetings, even virtual ones, are impossible to arrange. You just cannot get everyone together at the same time. In this circumstance, when the team must meet asynchronously, most students try to communicate via **email**. The problem with email is that there is too much freedom. Not everyone will participate, because it is easy to hide from email. Discussion threads become disorganized and disconnected. After the fact, it is difficult to find particular emails, comments, or attachments.

Figure CE2-4
Videoconferencing Example

Source: © Corbis Bridge/Alamy

Figure CE2-5
Example Discussion Forum

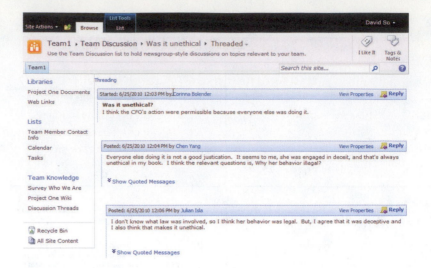

Discussion forums are an alternative. Here, one group member posts an entry, perhaps an idea, a comment, or a question, and other group members respond. Figure CE2-5 shows an example. Such forums are better than email because it is harder for the discussion to get off track. Still, however, it remains easy for some team members not to participate.

Team surveys are another form of communication technology. With these, one team member creates a list of questions and other team members respond. Surveys are an effective way to obtain team opinions; they are generally easy to complete, so most team members will participate. Also, it is easy to determine who has not yet responded. Figure CE2-6 shows the results of one team survey. SurveyMonkey (www.surveymonkey.com) is one common survey application program. You can find others on the Internet. Microsoft SharePoint has a built-in survey capability, as we discuss in Q5.

Video and audio recordings are also useful for asynchronous communication. Key presentations or discussions can be recorded and played back for team members at their convenience. Such recordings are also useful for training new employees.

Figure CE2-6
Example Survey Report

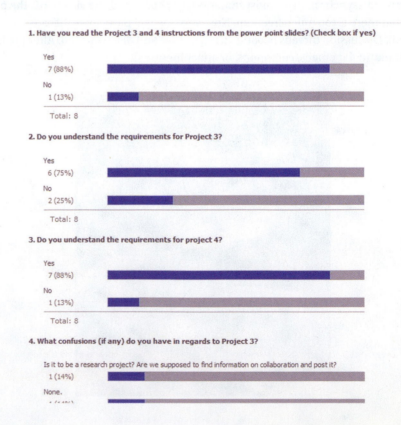

HOW CAN YOU USE COLLABORATION TOOLS TO SHARE CONTENT?

Content sharing is the second required function for student collaboration systems. To enable iteration and feedback, team members need to share both project data, such as documents, illustrations, spreadsheets, and other data, as well as project metadata, such as tasks, schedules, and budgets. The collaboration tool you use for sharing content depends on the degree of control that you want. Figure CE2-7 lists collaboration tools for three categories of content: no control, version management, and version control.

SHARED CONTENT WITH NO CONTROL

The most primitive way to share content is via email attachments. However, email attachments have numerous problems. For one, there is always the danger that someone does not receive an email, does not notice it in his or her inbox, or does not bother to save the attachments. Then, too, if three users obtain the same document as an email attachment, each changes it, and each sends back the changed document via email, then different, incompatible versions of that document will be floating around. So, although email is simple, easy, and readily available, it will not suffice for collaborations in which there are many document versions or for which there is a desire for content control.

Another way to share content is to place it on a shared **file server**, which is simply a computer that stores files . . . just like the disk in your local computer. If your team has access to a file server, you can put documents on the server and others can download them, make changes, and upload them back onto the server. Often a technology called **FTP** is used to get and put documents (discussed in Chapter 6).

Storing documents on servers is better than using email attachments because documents have a single storage location. They are not scattered in different team members' email boxes, and team members have a known location for finding documents.

However, without any additional control, it is possible for team members to interfere with one another's work. For example, suppose team members A and B download a document and edit it, but without knowing about the other's edits. Person A stores his version back on the server and then person B stores her version back on the server. In this scenario, person A's changes will be lost.

Furthermore, without any version management, it will be impossible to know who changed the document and when. Neither person A nor person B will know whose version of the document is on the server. To avoid such problems, the team will need to develop manual procedures to prevent two people from working on the same document at the same time, or they will need to use a tool that supports version management.

Alternatives for Sharing Content		
No Control	Version Management	Version Control
Email with attachments Shared files on a server	Wikis Google Drive Windows Live SkyDrive	Microsoft SharePoint

Increasing degree of content control

Figure CE2-7
Collaboration Tools for Sharing Content

SHARED CONTENT WITH VERSION MANAGEMENT

Systems that provide **version management** track changes to documents and provide features and functions to accommodate concurrent work. How this is done depends on the particular system used. In this section, we consider two free and readily available tools: Google Drive and Windows Live SkyDrive.

Google Drive

Google Drive is a free service that provides a virtual drive in the cloud into which you can create folders and store files, including documents, spreadsheets, presentations, drawings, and other types of data, as shown in Figure CE2-8. (Google Drive is evolving; by the time you read this, Google may have added additional file types or changed the system from what is described here. Google the name "Google Drive" to obtain the latest data.)

With Google Drive, anyone who edits a document must have a Google account, which is not the same as a Gmail account. You can establish a Google account using an email address from Hotmail, a university, or any other email service. Your Google account will be affiliated with whatever email account you enter.

To create a Google document, go to *http://drive.google.com* (note that there is no *www* in this address). Sign in with (or create) your Google account. From that point on, you can create, upload, process, save, and download documents. You can also save most of those documents to PDF and Microsoft Office formats, such as Word, Excel, and PowerPoint.

With Google Drive, you can make documents available to others by entering their email addresses or Google accounts. Those users are notified that the document exists and are given a link by which they can access it. If they have a Google account, they can edit the document; otherwise they can just view the document.

Documents are stored on a Google server. Users can access the documents from Google and simultaneously see and edit documents. In the background, Google merges the users' activities into a single document. You are notified that another user is editing a document at the same time as you are, and you can refresh the document to see their latest changes. Google tracks document revisions, with brief summaries of changes made. Figure CE2-9 shows a sample revision for a document that has been shared among three users. You can improve your collaboration activity even more by combining Google Drive with Google+.

Figure CE2-8
Google Drive Creation Options

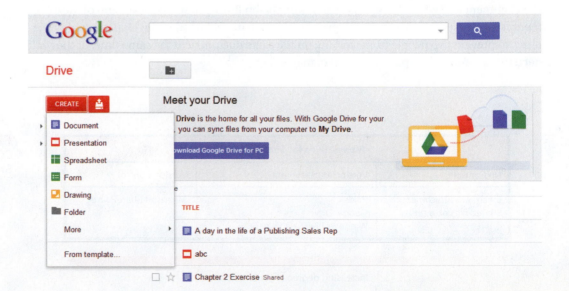

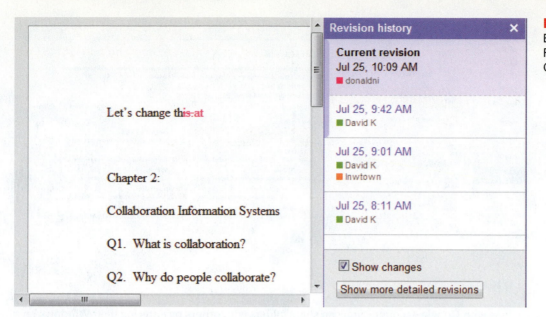

Figure CE2-9
Example of Sharing a
Revised Document on
Google Drive

Windows Live SkyDrive

Windows Live SkyDrive is Microsoft's response to Google Drive. It provides the ability to store and share Office documents and other files and offers free storage. Additionally, SkyDrive includes license-free Web application versions of Word, Excel, PowerPoint, and OneNote called **Office Web Apps**. These applications run in the browser and are quite easy to use. Figure CE2-10 shows an instance of the Word Web App. These programs have less functionality than desktop Office programs, but they are free and readily accessed on the Web.

In addition to Office Web Apps, the desktop Office 2010 applications are tightly integrated with SkyDrive. You can open and save documents directly from and to SkyDrive from inside Microsoft Office products, as illustrated in Figure CE2-11.

To set up a SkyDrive account, you need a Windows Live ID. If you have either a Hotmail or an MSN email account, that account is your Windows Live ID. If you do not have a Hotmail or an MSN email account, you can create a Windows Live ID with some other email account, or you can create a new Hotmail account, which is free.

Once you have a Windows Live ID, go to *www.skydrive.com* and sign in. You will be given 25 GB of storage. You can create file folders and files and use either Office or other Office Web Apps as well.

Notation such as 25 GB refers to the amount of data you can store. See Chapter 4.

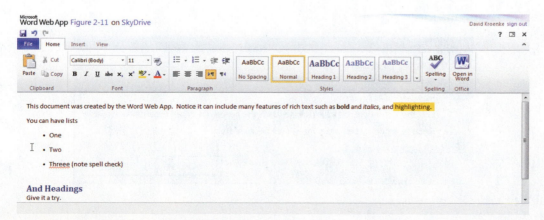

Figure CE2-10
Example Use of Word
Web App

Figure CE2-11

Saving a Word 2010 Document in a SkyDrive Account

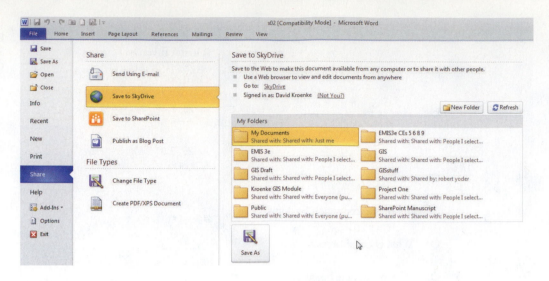

As with Google accounts, you can share folders with others by entering their Windows Live IDs or their email accounts. Users who have a Windows Live ID can view and edit documents; users who do not have a Windows Live ID can only view documents.

Only one user at a time can open SkyDrive documents for editing. If you attempt to open a document that someone else is editing, you'll receive the message shown in Figure CE2-12. As shown, you can open the document in read-only mode, you can have your changes merged with the document when it is available, or you can simply be notified when the document is available.

Both Google Drive and Windows Live SkyDrive are free and very easy to use. They are both far superior to exchanging documents via email or via a file server. If you are not using one of these two products, you should.

SHARED CONTENT WITH VERSION CONTROL

Version management systems improve the tracking of shared content and potentially eliminate problems caused by concurrent document access. They do not, however, provide **version control**, the process that occurs when the collaboration tool limits, and sometimes even directs, user activity. Version control involves one or more of the following capabilities:

- User activity limited by permissions
- Document checkout
- Workflow control

Figure CE2-12

Opening a Document Locked by Another User in Word Web App

Permission-Limited Activity

With most version control tools, each team member is given an account with a set of permissions. Then, shared documents are placed into shared directories, sometimes called **libraries**. For example, on a shared site with four libraries, a particular user might be given read-only permission for library 1; read and edit permission for library 2; read, edit, and delete permission for library 3; and no permission even to see library 4.

Document Checkout

With version control applications, document directories can be set up so that users are required to check out documents before they can modify them. When a document is checked out, no other user can obtain it for the purpose of editing it. Once the document has been checked in, other users can obtain it for editing.

Figure CE2-13 shows a screen for a user of Microsoft SharePoint 2010. The user, Allison Brown (shown in the upper right-hand corner of the screen), is checking out a document named Project One Assignment. Once she has it checked out, she can edit it and return it to this library. While she has the document checked out, no other user will be able to edit it, and her changes will not be visible to others.

Workflow Control

Collaboration tools that provide **workflow control** manage activities in a pre-defined process. If, for example, a group wants documents to be reviewed and approved by team members in a particular sequence, the group would define that workflow to the tool. Then, the workflow is started, and the emails to manage the process are sent as defined. For example, Figure CE2-14 shows a SharePoint workflow in which the group defined a document review process that involves a sequence of reviews by three people. Given this definition, when a document is submitted to a library, SharePoint assigns a task to the first person, Joseph Schumpeter, to approve the document and sends an email to him to that effect. Once he has completed his review (the green checkmark means that he has already done so), SharePoint assigns a task for and sends an email to Adam Smith to approve the document. When all three reviewers have completed their review, SharePoint marks the document as approved. If any disapprove, the document is marked accordingly and the workflow is terminated.

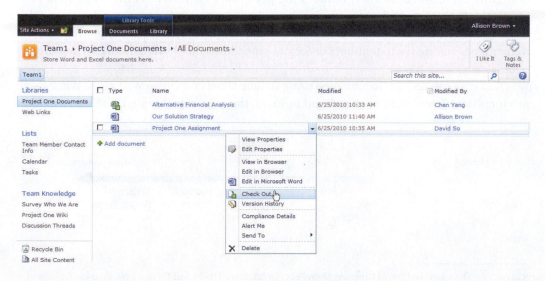

Figure CE2-13
Checking Out a Document

Figure CE2-14
Example Workflow

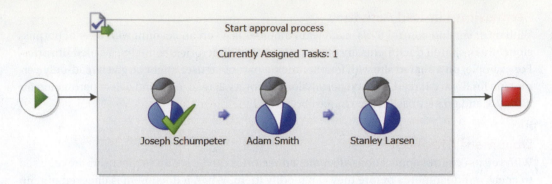

Workflows can be defined for complicated, multistage business processes. See *SharePoint for Students*[1] for more on how to create them.

Numerous version control applications exist. For general business use, Share-Point is the most popular. Other document control systems include MasterControl (*www.mastercontrol .com*) and Document Locator (*www.documentlocator.com*). Software development teams use applications such as CVS (*www.nongnu.org/cvs*) or Subversion (*http://subversion.tigris.org*) to control versions of software code, test plans, and product documentation.

HOW CAN YOU USE COLLABORATION TOOLS FOR PROJECT PLANNING AND MANAGEMENT?

Project management is a deep and rich topic for which many books have been written and many products developed. Here, we will touch on the essentials.

Fundamentally, when planning a project, you need to decide *who will do what work and by what date.* To hold team members accountable for their assignments, the team needs some way of documenting and sharing tasks, assignments, and due dates.

Figure CE2-15 shows a continuum of task and project management products. The most primitive alternative is to make a task list in either Microsoft Word or Excel. Excel is slightly preferred because it reduces the keystrokes required to enter repetitive data like dates. Both of these desktop products provide no support for concurrent access. Files must be shared via email or a file server, and the loss of concurrent changes is possible. Agreements among team members or formal procedures that limit concurrent activity are necessary.

Task data can also be documented using Google Drive and Office Web Apps. While these products have fewer features than Word or Excel, they are free. Google Drive also supports

Figure CE2-15
Continuum of Task Tracking/
Project Management Tools

[1]Carey Cole, Steve Fox, and David Kroenke, *SharePoint for Students* (Upper Saddle River, NJ: Pearson Education, 2012), pp. 116–129.

concurrent access and update. Another possibility is to place task descriptions, including the name of the person assigned the task, on the due date of a shared Google calendar.

The next product in Figure CE2-15, Microsoft SharePoint, includes more robust task management capability. With it, you can create a special type of list, called a **task list**, that is preconfigured to store data such as task title, description, assigned to, due date, status, predecessor tasks and other useful task data. Users can also add their own data to the default format of the task list.

With SharePoint, it is possible to filter task lists to show only noncompleted tasks, or only tasks that are overdue, or tasks that are due within the next few days, or all of these as different reports on the team's site. SharePoint includes the option of showing task lists as daily, weekly, or monthly calendars. With Office 365, team members can set alerts on task lists so that when tasks change, Office 365 will automatically send emails about those changes to team members.

Many other task management products are available from smaller vendors. Basecamp is one popular product (see *http://basecamp.com*). You can find others on the Web.

Microsoft Project and Microsoft Project Server are the two most robust task management tools shown in Figure CE2-15. With them, project managers can specify task dependencies, which are constraints on tasks such as Task A cannot begin before Task B, or both Tasks A and B must start (or end) together. Both products will enforce such dependencies and produce schedules and identify critical, blocking tasks in special-purpose graphical displays. Project is a desktop program that generates files that can be accessed only by one user at a time; Project Server allows many people to access shared project data via a Web browser.

 ## WHICH COLLABORATION INFORMATION SYSTEM IS RIGHT FOR YOUR TEAM?

So far, we have addressed the base requirements of a collaboration IS for a student team and we've looked at a variety of collaboration tools that support communication, content sharing, and task management. What can you do with this knowledge? What system is right for you and your teams? In this question we will define and set up your evaluation of three sets of collaboration tools. Figure CE2-16 summarizes three different sets of collaboration tools that you might use.

THE MINIMAL COLLABORATION TOOL SET

The first, the Minimal set, is shown in the second column of Figure CE2-16. With this set, you will be able to collaborate with your team, though you will get little support from the software. In particular, you will need to manage concurrent access by setting up procedures and agreements to ensure that one user's work doesn't conflict with another's. Your collaboration will be with text only; you will not have access to audio or video so you cannot hear or see your collaborators. You also will not be able to view documents or whiteboards during your meeting. This set is probably close to what you're already doing.

THE GOOD COLLABORATION TOOL SET

The third column of Figure CE2-16 shows a more sophisticated set of collaboration tools. With it, you will have the ability to conduct multiparty audio and video virtual meetings, and you will also have support for concurrent access to document, spreadsheet, and

Three Collaboration Tool Sets

	Minimal	Good	Comprehensive
Communication	Email; multiparty text chat	Skype	Microsoft Lync
Content Sharing	Email or file server	Google Drive	SharePoint
Task Management	Word or Excel files	Google Calendar	SharePoint lists integrated with email
Nice-to-Have Features		Discussion boards, surveys, Wikis, blogs, share pictures/videos from third-party tools	Built-in discussion boards, surveys, Wikis, blogs, picture/video sharing
Cost	Free	Free	$10/month per user or Free
Ease of Use (time to learn)	None	1 hour	3 hours
Value to Future Business Professional	None	Limited	Great
Limitations	All text, no voice or video; no tool integration	Tools not integrated, must learn to use several products. Cannot share live documents	Cost, learning curve required

Figure CE2-16
Three Collaboration Tool Sets

presentation files. Without work on your part, however, you will not have any of the nice-to-have feature requirements discussed in Q1. If you want any of them, you will need to search the Internet to find products that support surveys, Wikis, blogs, and share pictures and videos.

THE COMPREHENSIVE COLLABORATION TOOL SET

The third set of collaboration tools is shown in the last column of Figure CE2-16. This tool set is provided by Microsoft's product Office 365. Office 365 is delivered as a cloud-based service over the Internet. (See Chapter 6 for the meaning of the term *cloud-based.*) Figure CE2-17 summarizes Office 365 features.

This set is the best of these three because it includes content management and control, workflow control, online meetings in which participants can view shared whiteboards, applications, and monitors. Furthermore, this set is integrated; SharePoint alerts can send emails via the Microsoft email server Exchange when tasks or other lists and libraries change. You can click on users' names in emails or in SharePoint, and Office 365 will automatically start a Lync text, audio, or video conversation with that user if he or she is currently available. All text messages that you send via Lync are automatically recorded and stored in your email folder.

CHOOSING THE SET FOR YOUR TEAM

Which set should you choose for your team? Unless your university has already implemented Office 365 university-wide, you will have to pay for it. You can obtain a 30-day free trial, and if

Component	Features
Lync	Multiparty text chat Audio- and videoconferencing Online content sharing Webinars with PowerPoint
SharePoint Online	Content management and control using libraries and lists Discussion forums Surveys Wikis Blogs
Exchange	Email integrated with Lync and SharePoint Online
Office 2010	Concurrent editing for Word, Excel, PowerPoint, and OneNote
Hosted integration	Infrastructure built, managed, and operated by Microsoft

your team can finish its work in that amount of time, you might choose to do so. Otherwise, your team will need to pay a minimum of $10 per month per user. So, if cost is the only factor, you can rule out Office 365.[2]

But, even if you can afford the most comprehensive, you may not want to use it. As noted in Figure CE2-16, team members need to be willing to invest something on the order of three hours to begin to use the basic Office 365 features. Less time, on the order of an hour, will be required to learn to use the Good tool set, and you most likely already know how to use the Minimal set.

When evaluating learning time consider Figure CE2-18. This diagram is a product **power curve**, which is a graph that shows the relationship of the **power** (the utility that one gains from a software product) as a function of the time using that product. A flat line means you are investing time without any increase in power. The ideal power curve starts at a positive value at time zero and has no flat spots.

The Minimal product set gives you some power at time zero because you already know how to use it. However, as you use it over time, your project will gain complexity, and the problems of controlling concurrent access will actually cause power to decrease. The Good set has a short

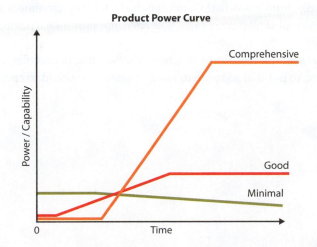

Product Power Curve

Power / Capability vs. Time

Comprehensive

Good

Minimal

0 — Time

[2]To sign up for Office 365, go to http://www.microsoft.com/en-us/office365/free-office365-trial.aspx

flat spot as you get to know it. However, your power then increases over time until you reach the most capability your team can do with it. The Comprehensive set has a longer flat spot in the beginning because it will take longer to learn. However, because it has such a rich collaboration feature set, you will be able to gain considerable collaborative power, much more so than with the Good set, and the maximum capability is much greater than the Good set's.

Finally, consider the next-to-last row in Figure CE2-16. The Minimal set has no value to you as a future professional and contributes nothing to your professional competitive advantage. The Good set has some limited value; there are organizations that use Google Drive and Skype. The Comprehensive set has the potential to give you a considerable competitive advantage, particularly because SharePoint skills are highly valued in industry. You can use knowledge of Office 365 to demonstrate the currency of your knowledge in job interviews.

So, which is the right set for your team? It's up to you. See Exercise 3 on page 370.

DON'T FORGET PROCEDURES AND PEOPLE!

One last and very important point: Most of this chapter extension focuses on collaboration tools, the software component of an information system. Regarding the other four components, you need not worry about hardware, at least not for the Good or Comprehensive sets because those tools are hosted on hardware in the cloud. The data component is up to you; it will be your content as well as your metadata for project management and for demonstrating that your team practiced iteration and feedback.

As you evaluate alternatives, however, you need to think seriously about the procedure and people components. How are team members going to use these tools? Your team needs to have agreement on tools usage, even if you do not formally document procedures. As noted, such procedures are especially necessary for controlling concurrent access in the Minimal system. You need to have agreement not only on how to use these tools, but also on what happens when teammates don't use these tools. What will you do, for example, if teammates persist in emailing documents instead of using Google Drive or SharePoint?

Additionally, how will your team train their members in the use of these tools? Will you divvy up responsibility for learning features and then teach the skills to one another? You will find a plethora of training materials on the Web.[3] But, who will find them, learn them, and then teach the others?

Finally, does your team need to create any special job or roles? Do you want to identify, for example, someone to monitor your shared documents to ensure that deliverables are stored appropriately? Do you want someone identified to store minutes of meetings? Or to remove completed tasks from a task list? Or to keep the task list in agreement with current planning? Consider these and similar needs and, if needed, appoint such a person before problems develop.

Remember this example as a future business professional: In commerce, we are never selecting just software; to put that software to use as a system, we need to create all five of the IS components!

---

[3]See also David Kroenke and Donald Nilson. *Office 365 in Business.* John Wiley, 2011.

ACTIVE REVIEW

Use this Active Review to verify that you understand the ideas and concepts that answer the chapter extension's study questions.

Q1 WHAT ARE THE IS REQUIREMENTS FOR STUDENT PROJECT COLLABORATIONS?

Summarize why you should learn about collaboration IS for today as well as later. Name the three categories of requirements discussed in this chapter extension. Name and describe the three required sets of features. Summarize the other two sets of features.

Q2 HOW CAN YOU USE COLLABORATION TOOLS TO IMPROVE TEAM COMMUNICATION?

Explain why communication is important to collaboration. Define *synchronous* and *asynchronous communication* and explain when each is used. Name two collaboration tools that can be used to help set up synchronous meetings. Describe collaboration tools that can be used for face-to-face meetings. Describe tools that can be used for virtual, synchronous meetings. Describe tools that can be used for virtual, asynchronous meetings.

Q3 HOW CAN YOU USE COLLABORATION TOOLS TO SHARE CONTENT?

Describe two ways that content is shared with no control and explain the problems that can occur. Explain how control is provided by Google Drive and Windows Live SkyDrive. Explain the difference between version management and version control. Describe how user accounts, passwords, and libraries are used to control user activity. Explain how check in/check out works. Describe workflows and give an example.

Q4 HOW CAN YOU USE COLLABORATION TOOLS FOR PROJECT PLANNING AND MANAGEMENT?

State the fundamental decision that needs to be made when planning a project and explain why these decisions must be documented for the team. Summarize the ways that each of the products in Figure CE2-15 are used to create such documentation.

Q5 WHICH COLLABORATION INFORMATION SYSTEM IS RIGHT FOR YOUR TEAM?

Describe the three collaboration tool sets described and indicate how each meets the minimum requirements for collaboration. Explain the differences among them. Summarize the criteria for choosing the right set for your team. Explain the meaning of the power curve and discuss the power curve for each of the three alternatives described.

KEY TERMS AND CONCEPTS

USING YOUR KNOWLEDGE

1. Evaluate Q1. Based on your experience as a team member, do you agree that the three requirements are mandatory for a collaborative team? Justify your answer. Modify those requirements in any way you see fit to better describe your own collaborative team experience. Do you find any of the nice-to-have requirements unnecessary? Would you add any others? Do you think any of the collaboration tool characteristics requirements are unnecessary? Would you add any?

2. Based on your answers to question 1, revise the list in Figure CE2-1 so that it is appropriate for your team experience. Discuss your revised list with others and describe any changes they would make to it.

3. Choose one of the three alternatives described in Q5 for use by your collaborative team. To do so, answer the following questions (if possible, answer these questions with your team):

   a. Using your and your teammates' answers to question 2, create your team's list of requirements.

   b. Create a list of criteria for selecting collaboration tools and creating a collaboration IS. Start with the items in the first column of Figure CE2-16, but add, modify, or delete items depending on your answer to question 3a.

   c. Score the three alternatives in Q5 against your requirements and your criteria. If you wish, change any of the elements of those three alternatives to create a fourth alternative. Score it as well.

   d. Based on your answer to question 3c, select a collaboration tool set. Explain your selection.

   e. Given your answer to question 3d, how will you construct your collaboration IS? Specifically, what procedures will you need to develop and how will your team members obtain training? Will you need to have any special jobs or roles for your team members? If so, describe them.

chapter extension **3**

Chapter 4 provides the background for this Extension.

Introduction to Microsoft Excel 2010

This chapter extension teaches basic skills with Microsoft Excel, a product for creating and processing spreadsheets. If you already know how to use Excel, use this chapter extension for review. Otherwise, use this chapter extension to gain essential knowledge, which every businessperson needs today.

 ## WHAT IS A SPREADSHEET?

A **spreadsheet** is a table of data having rows and columns. Long before the advent of the computer, accountants and financial planners used paper spreadsheets to make financial calculations. Today, the term *spreadsheet* almost always refers to an *electronic* spreadsheet, and most frequently to a spreadsheet that is processed by Microsoft Excel. Electronic spreadsheets provide incredible labor savings over paper spreadsheets and were a major factor in the early adoption of personal computers.

As shown in Figure CE3-1, Excel spreadsheets have rows and columns. The rows are identified by numbers, and the columns are identified by letters. Because there are only 26 letters in the alphabet, the following scheme is used to label columns: The letters A through Z identify the first 26 columns; the letters AA through AZ identify the next 26; BA through BZ the next 26; and so forth.

In Excel, the term **worksheet** refers to a spreadsheet. One or more worksheets are combined to form a **workbook**. In the lower left-hand corner of Figure CE3-1, notice three tabs.

 **STUDY QUESTIONS**

Q1 WHAT IS A SPREADSHEET?

Q2 HOW DO YOU GET STARTED WITH EXCEL?

Q3 HOW CAN YOU ENTER DATA?

Q4 HOW CAN YOU INSERT AND DELETE ROWS AND COLUMNS AND CHANGE THEIR SIZE?

Q5 HOW CAN YOU FORMAT DATA?

Q6 HOW CAN YOU CREATE A (SIMPLE) FORMULA?

Q7 HOW CAN YOU PRINT RESULTS?

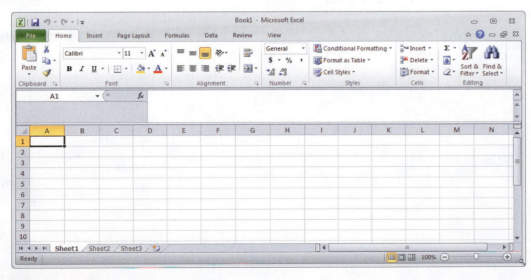

Figure CE3-1
Excel Spreadsheet Showing Rows and Columns
Source: Microsoft Excel 2010

The current tab is named *Sheet1*; two other tabs are named *Sheet2* and *Sheet3*. Each sheet is a separate spreadsheet (or equivalently, worksheet), and the collection of the three sheets comprises the workbook.

Figure CE3-1 shows a spreadsheet processed by Excel 2010, the current version of Excel. You can process spreadsheets in earlier versions of Excel, but the structure of commands and menu items will be different from that described here. If you are just starting to learn Excel, learn Excel 2010 rather than an earlier version.

The intersection of a row and a column is called a **cell**. Each cell is identified by the name of its row and column. In Figure CE3-1, the cell named A1 is highlighted. The cell K5 is the cell in the K column, row number 5. The cell AB1207 (not visible in Figure CE3-1) is the cell located in column AB and row 1207.

You may be asking, "Row 1207? How many rows and columns can I have?" Don't bother asking . . . you can have more than you will ever need or want. And, if you should ever run out of rows and columns, you're using the wrong tool. In that case, you probably should be using Microsoft Access or another DBMS (see Chapter 5) instead.

HOW DO YOU GET STARTED WITH EXCEL?

When you first start Excel 2010, it will create a workbook exactly like that in Figure CE3-1. Even though you haven't done anything yet, your first task should be to save your workbook under an appropriate name. Life is uncertain; you never know when a computer might fail or power might be cut off or some other unplanned event might occur. Get in the habit of saving your work initially and then frequently after that.

To save your workbook, click *File* with your left mouse button (in the following text, unless otherwise specified, the term *click* means to click with the left mouse button), ignore the big green banner that says Info, and click *Save*, as shown in Figure CE3-2. The display in Figure CE3-3 will appear. In the lower center, find the label *File name:* and to the right of that label enter a

Figure CE3-2
Saving Your Workbook in Excel

Source: Microsoft Excel 2010

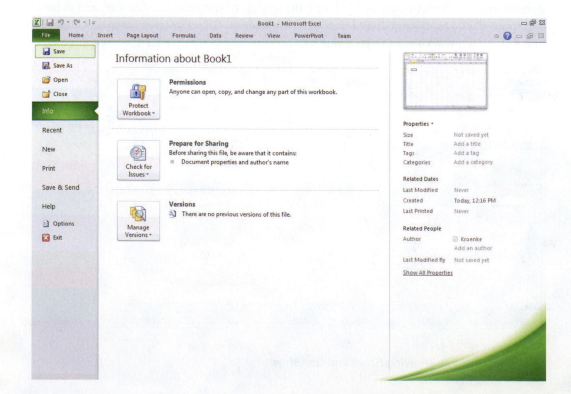

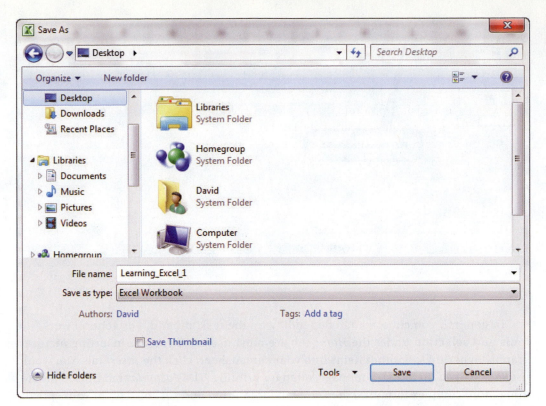

Figure CE3-3
Entering a File Name in Excel
Source: Microsoft Excel 2010

name for this file. In Figure CE3-3, I have entered the file name *Learning_Excel_1*. Your instructor may have given you instructions for creating file names; if so, follow them. Otherwise, follow this example or use some other scheme. Click the *Save* button to save your workbook. Once you have saved your workbook, you can perform subsequent saves by clicking the small disk icon located next to the Excel icon at the top left.

Figure CE3-4 shows the workbook. A sequence of tabs appears in a horizontal line, just below the Excel icon. These tabs control the contents of the **ribbon**, which is the wide bar of tools and selections that appears just under the tabs. In Figure CE3-4, the *Home* tab has been selected, and the contents of the ribbon concern fonts, alignment, and so forth. Figure CE3-5 shows the appearance of the ribbon when the *Page Layout* tab is selected.

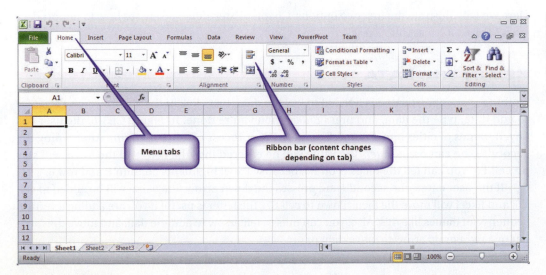

Figure CE3-4
Excel Menu Tabs and Ribbon Bar
Source: Microsoft Excel 2010

Figure CE3-5
Ribbon with Page Layout
Tab Selected

Source: Microsoft Excel 2010

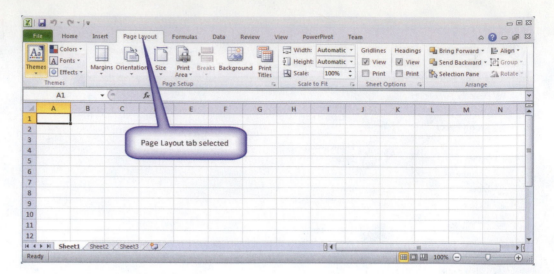

In general, you choose a tab depending on the task at hand. For general work, the tools and selection under the *Home* tab are most useful. If you are inserting pictures, graphs, hyperlinks, or other items into your spreadsheet, click the *Insert* tab. You would use *Page Layout* to format your page, often for printing. The *Formulas* tab is used for creating more complex formulas, the *Data* tab for filtering and sorting data in your spreadsheet, the *Review* tab for tracking changes and making comments, the *View* tab for configuring the appearance of Excel, and the *Add-Ins* tab for using nonstandard features that have been added to Excel.

At this point, don't worry about which tab to choose; just click around to see the tools and selections available. If in doubt, click on the *Home* tab, because it holds the most frequently used tools and selections.

 HOW CAN YOU ENTER DATA?

Data can be entered into an Excel worksheet in three ways:

- Key in the data.
- Let Excel add data based on a pattern.
- Import data from another program.

Here we will illustrate the first two options. Chapter Extension 6 discusses how to import data from Microsoft Access into Excel.

KEY IN THE DATA

Nothing very sophisticated is needed to key the data. Just click in the cell in which you want to add data, type the data, and press *Enter* when you're done. In Figure CE3-6, the user has keyed names of cities into column E and is in the process of adding *Miami.* After typing the second *i,* she can press *Enter.* The value will be entered into the cell, and the focus will stay on cell E6. You can tell the focus is on E6, because Excel highlights column E and row 6.

If the user enters the second *i* and presses the down arrow, the value will be added to cell E6, and Excel will move the focus down to cell E7. The latter is useful if you are adding a vertical sequence of names like this. Also, you can press a left arrow to add the data and move the focus left or a right or up arrow to move right or up.

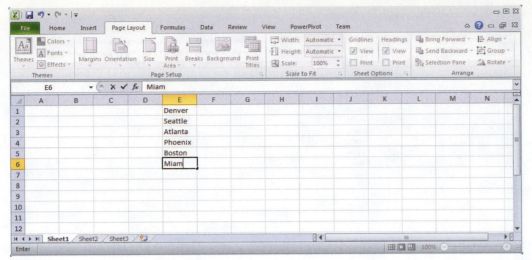

Figure CE3-6
Entering City Names
in Column E

Source: Microsoft Excel 2010

In Figure CE3-6, notice the row just above the spreadsheet, immediately above the names of the columns. In that row, the value E6 indicates that cell E6 has the focus and further to the right the letters *Miam* indicate the current value of that cell.

Figure CE3-7 shows a sequence of seven city names. But, notice that the user never entered the second *i* in Miami. To correct this, she can go back to that cell and retype the entire word *Miami* or she can go to the cell and press the <F2> function key. In the latter case, she can just add the missing *i* to the word and press Enter (or down or up, etc.). Using the F2 key is recommended when you have a long value in a cell and you just want to fix a letter or two without retyping the whole entry. (If nothing happens when you press F2, press the F Lock key on your keyboard. Then press F2 again.)

LET EXCEL ADD THE DATA USING A PATTERN

Suppose that for some reason for each of the cities we want to have the number 100 in column G of the spreadsheet in Figure CE3-7. Another way of saying this is that we want the value 100 to be entered into cells G1 through G7. One way of proceeding is to type the value 100 in each of the seven rows. There's a better way, however.

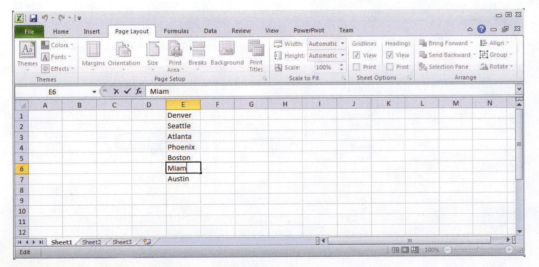

Figure CE3-7
Using a Function Key to
Make Entry Corrections

Source: Microsoft Excel 2010

Figure CE3-8

Entering Identical Data in Multiple Cells, Step 1

Source: Microsoft Excel 2010

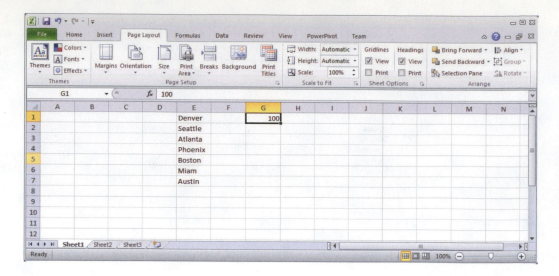

If our user types the value 100 into cell G1, presses Enter, and then clicks cell G1, a rectangle will be drawn around the cell with a little black box in the lower right-hand corner, as shown in Figure CE3-8. Now if the user drags (left-click and hold the mouse button down as you move the mouse) that little black box down to cell G7, Excel will fill in the value 100 into all of those cells. Figure CE3-9 shows the user dragging the cells, and Figure CE3-10 shows the result.

But it gets much better! Suppose we want the numbers in column G to identify the cities. Say we want the first city, Denver, to have the number 100, the second city, Seattle, to have the number 200, the third city, Atlanta, to have the number 300, and so forth.

Excel will fill in the values we want if we give it an indication of the pattern to follow. So, if our user types 100 in cell G1, 200 in cell G2, and then *selects both cells G1 and G2*, Excel will draw a rectangle around the two cells, and again show the small black box, as shown in Figure CE3-11. If the user drags the small black box, Excel will fill in the numbers in a sequence, as shown in Figure CE3-12.

Excel is sophisticated in its interpretation of the patterns. If you key *January* and *February* into cells C1 and C2 and then select both cells and drag down, Excel will fill in with March, April, May, and so on. Or, if in column A you key in the sequence *Q1, Q2, Q3,* and *Q4* and then select all four values and drag the small black box, Excel will repeat the sequence Q1 through Q4. Figure CE3-13 shows the results of these last two operations.

Figure CE3-9

Entering Identical Data in Multiple Cells, Step 2

Source: Microsoft Excel 2010

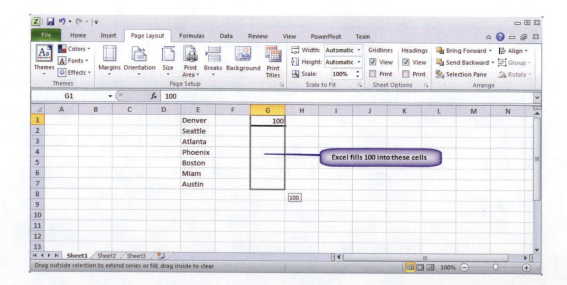

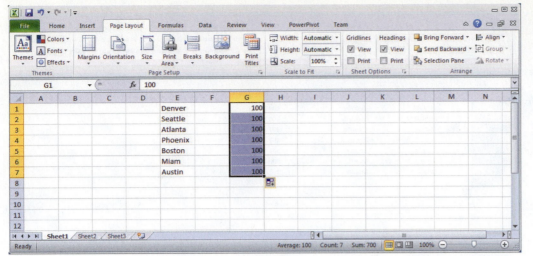

Figure CE3-10
Identical Data Entered
in Multiple Cells

Source: Microsoft Excel 2010

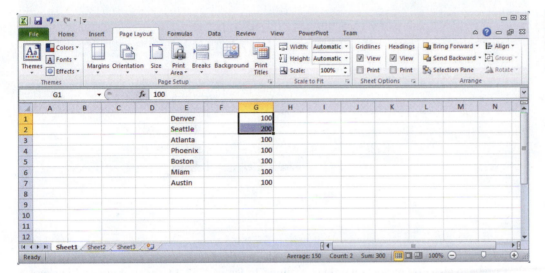

Figure CE3-11
Entering Patterned Data
in Multiple Cells

Source: Microsoft Excel 2010

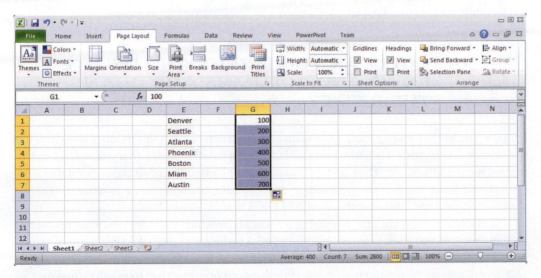

Figure CE3-12
Patterned Data Entered
in Multiple Cells

Source: Microsoft Excel 2010

Figure CE3-13
Sophisticated Entry of Patterned Data in Multiple Cells

Source: Microsoft Excel 2010

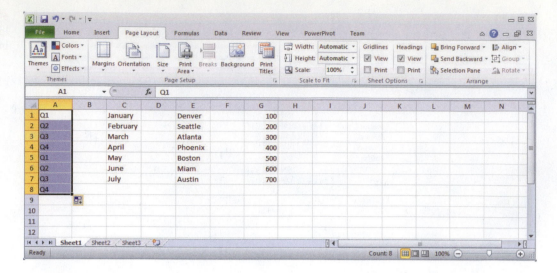

Figure CE3-14
Patterned Data Within Text Values

Source: Microsoft Excel 2010

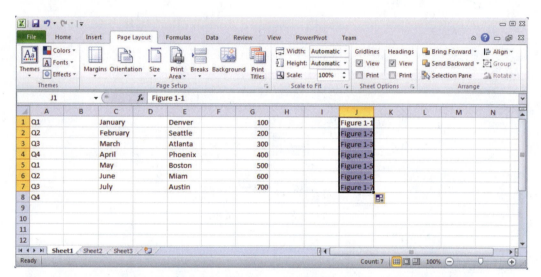

Excel will also find patterns within text values. In Figure CE3-14, the user entered *Figure 1-1* into cell J1, and *Figure 1-2* into cell J2. Selecting and dragging cells J1 and J2 produced the sequence shown in Figure CE3-14.

HOW CAN YOU INSERT AND DELETE ROWS AND COLUMNS AND CHANGE THEIR SIZE?

Suppose you are the manager of a sales team and you are recording this month's sales into the spreadsheet in Figure CE3-15. You enter the data shown but then realize that you've forgotten to add column headings. You'd like column A to have the heading *Sales Rep* and column B to have the heading *Sales*. You don't want to retype all of the data; instead, you want to insert two new rows so that you can add the labels as well as a blank line.

To insert new rows, click the number of the row above which you want new rows, and select as many rows as you want to insert. In Figure CE3-16, the user has clicked row 1 and selected two rows. Now, using the right mouse button, click the selection. The menu shown in Figure CE3-16 will appear. Using your mouse, left-click the word *Insert* and two rows will be inserted, as shown in Figure CE3-17. If you had selected only one row, then only one row would be added. If you had selected five rows, then five rows would be added.

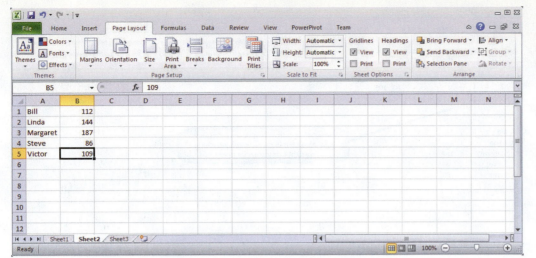

Figure CE3-15
Spreadsheet to Which User
Wants to Add New Rows for
Column Headings

Source: Microsoft Excel 2010

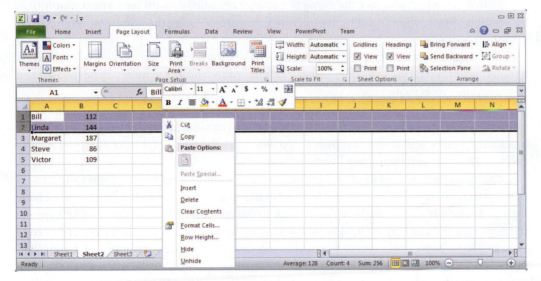

Figure CE3-16
Menu for Adding Inserts
Such as New Rows

Source: Microsoft Excel 2010

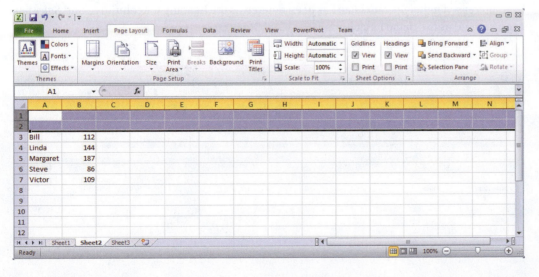

Figure CE3-17
Spreadsheet to Which User
Has Added New Rows for
Column Headings

Source: Microsoft Excel 2010

Figure CE3-18

Changing Cursor to a Vertical Bar to Change Column Widths

Source: Microsoft Excel 2010

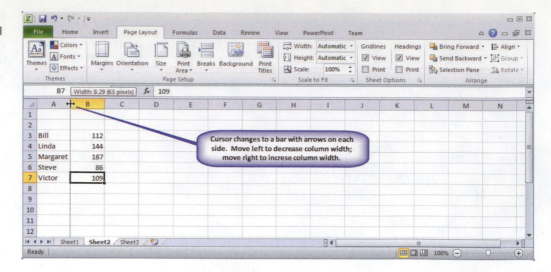

Notice that when you click the name of a row (or column) you are selecting the *entire* row (or column). Thus, when you click the 1 of row 1, you are selecting the entire row, even if it has 1,000 or more columns.

You can use a similar approach to delete rows. Click the name of the row (or rows) you want to delete and then right-click. Then, left-click the word *Delete*. Those rows will be deleted and any remaining rows moved up.

Adding and deleting columns is similar. To add a column, click the name of the column before which you want to insert columns, select as many columns to the right of that as you want to add, right-click, and then select *Insert*. To delete, click the name of the columns you want to delete, right-click, and then select *Delete*.

Changing the width of a column or the height of a row is easy. Suppose in Figure CE3-17 that you want to include both first and last names in column A. At present, column A is not large enough to show both names. To make it larger, in the column headings click the line between the A and the B. Your cursor changes to a vertical bar with an arrow on each side, as shown in Figure CE3-18. Move the cursor to the right to increase the size of the column and to the left to decrease it. Similarly, to increase or decrease the height of a row, click the line between the line numbers and drag up to decrease the row height and down to increase it.

Figure CE3-19 shows the spreadsheet after column A has been made wider and row 1 has been increased in height. *Sales Rep* has been entered as the heading for column A, and *Sales* has been entered as the name for column B.

Figure CE3-19

Spreadsheet with Rows Added and Sizes of Columns Changed

Source: Microsoft Excel 2010

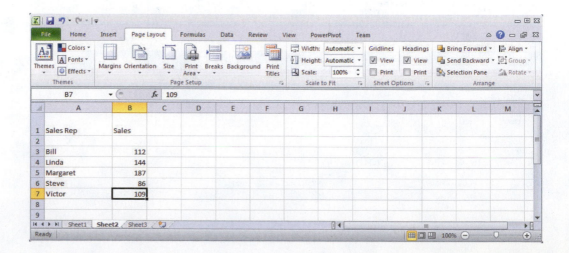

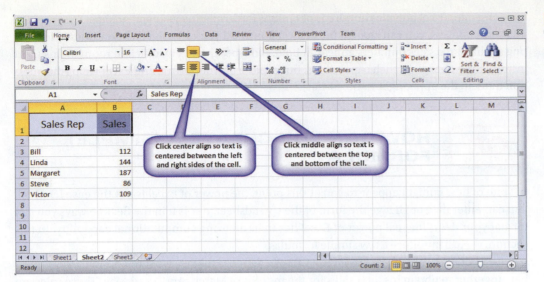

Figure CE3-20
Centering Labels in Cells
Source: Microsoft Excel 2010

 HOW CAN YOU FORMAT DATA?

Excel has a powerful and complicated set of tools for formatting spreadsheets. Here we will just scratch the surface with a few of the hundreds of possibilities.

The spreadsheet in Figure CE3-19 is boring and misleading. It would be better if the headings were centered over the columns and if they looked like headings. Also, are the sales in dollars or some other currency? If in dollars, they should have a dollar sign and maybe two decimal points.

To make the headings more interesting, highlight cells A1 and B1 (to do this, click A1 and hold the mouse button down as you move the mouse pointer to B1) and in the *Font* section of the ribbon select 16 rather than 11. This action increases the font size of the labels. In the same *Font* section of the ribbon, with A1 and B1 selected, click the bucket of paint. Select a medium blue. Now, still with cells A1 and B1 selected, in the *Alignment* section of the ribbon click the center icons, as shown in Figure CE3-20. Your labels will appear centered both horizontally and vertically in the cell.

The sales figures are actually in dollars, but they are formatted incorrectly. To place dollar signs in front of them, select cells B3 to B7 and in the *Number* section of the ribbon click the down arrow next to the dollar sign. Select $ English (United States), and your spreadsheet will be formatted like that in Figure CE3-21.

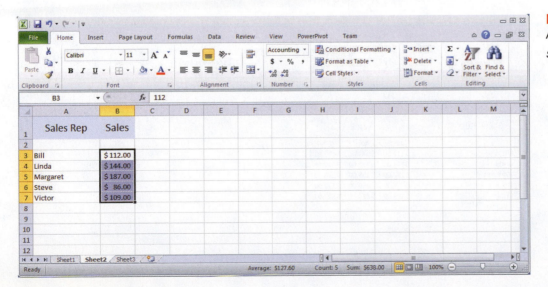

Figure CE3-21
Adding Dollar Signs in Cells
Source: Microsoft Excel 2010

As stated, Excel provides hundreds of options for formatting your spreadsheet. You can add lines and borders, you can change the color of font, and you can even add conditional formatting so that large sales numbers appear in bold, red type. There is insufficient room in this short introduction to explain such capabilities, but explore on your own using Excel Help (the question mark in the upper right-hand corner).

Q6 HOW CAN YOU CREATE A (SIMPLE) FORMULA?

In spite of how it might appear to you at this point, the power of Excel is not the ease by which you can enter data or change the form of the spreadsheet, nor is it in the flexible ways you can format your data. The real power of Excel lies in its amazing computational capability. In this section, we will introduce a few simple formulas.

Consider the spreadsheet in Figure CE3-22. Suppose that we want to add Bill's sales numbers together to obtain his total sales for the months of March, April, and May. Those sales are located in cells C3, D3, and E3, respectively. A logical way to add the three together is with the following formula: *C3+D3+E3*.

To enter this formula in Excel, first choose the cell into which you want to place the total. For the spreadsheet in Figure CE3-22, suppose that is cell G3. Click that cell and enter the expression *=C3+D3+E3* and then press *Enter*. The result will appear as shown in Figure CE3-23. (Be sure to start with an equal sign. If you omit the equal sign, Excel will think you're attempting to enter label or text value and will just show the letters *C3+D3+E3* in the cell.)

Before you go on, select cell G3 and press the F2 function key, as shown in Figure CE3-24. Notice the color coding that Excel presents. The term *C3* is shown in blue ink, and the C3 cell is outlined in blue; *D3* and *E3* are shown in other colors. Whenever you have a problem with a calculation, press F2 to have Excel highlight the cells involved in that calculation.

The next operation is actually quite amazing. Suppose that you want to add the 3 months' sales data for all of the salespeople. To do that, right-click cell G3 and select *Copy*. Next, highlight cells G4 through G7, right-click, and select *Paste*. The formula will be copied into each of the cells. The correct totals will appear in each row.

Here's the amazing part: When Excel copied the formula, it did not do so blindly. Instead, it adjusted the terms of the formula so that each would refer to cells in the row to which it was copied. To verify this, highlight cell G5, for example, and press F2, as shown in Figure CE3-25.

Figure CE3-22
Selecting Cells to Be Summed

Source: Microsoft Excel 2010

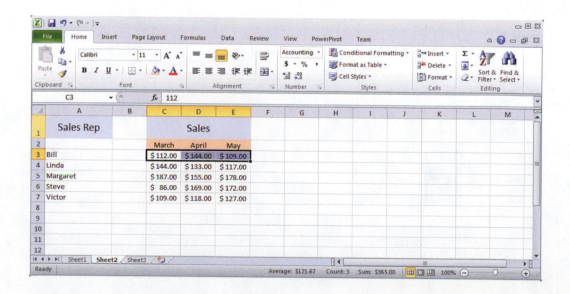

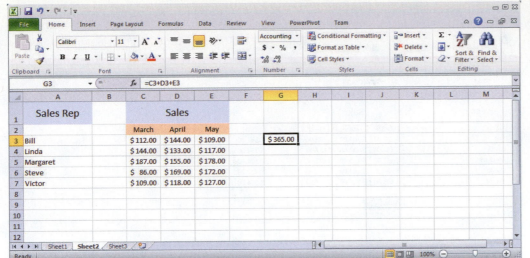

Figure CE3-23
The Result of Applying a Formula That Summed Cells C3, D3, and E3

Source: Microsoft Excel 2010

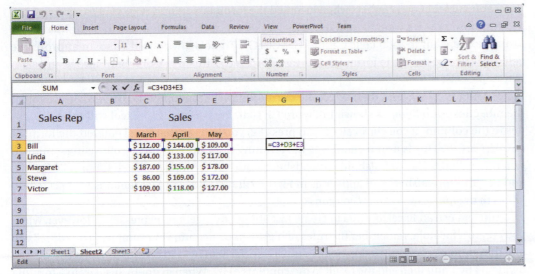

Figure CE3-24
Using the F2 Function Key to Show Color Coding of Cells Involved in a Calculation

Source: Microsoft Excel 2010

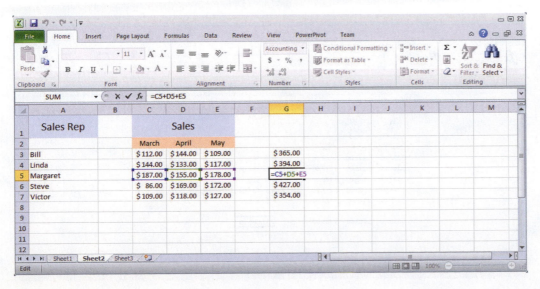

Figure CE3-25
Using the F2 Function Key to Confirm That a Formula Was Correctly Copied into Multiple Cells

Source: Microsoft Excel 2010

Figure CE3-26
Auto Sum Function

Source: Microsoft Excel 2010

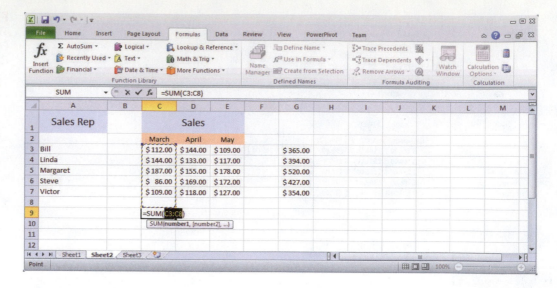

Notice that the formula in this cell is *=C5+D5+E5*. The formula you copied was *=C3+D3+E3*. Excel adjusted the row numbers when it copied the formula!

Suppose now we want to total the sales for each month. To obtain the total for March, for example, we want to total cells C3+C4+C5+C6+C7. To do so, we could go to an appropriate cell, say C9, and enter the formula *=C3+C4+C5+C6+C7*. This will work, but there is an easier way to proceed.

Highlight cell C9 and then select the *Formulas* tab at the top of the ribbon. At the top of the tab, click *Auto Sum,* as shown in Figure CE3-26. Press *Enter,* and Excel will total the values in the column. If you click cell C9 and press F2, you will see that Excel entered the formula *=SUM(C3:C8)*. This is a shorthand way of summing the values in those cells using a built-in function called **SUM**. To finish this spreadsheet, copy the formula from cell C9 to cells D9, E9, and G9. The spreadsheet will appear as in Figure CE3-27. Now all that remains to do is to add labels to the *total* row and *total* column.

You can use an Excel formula to create just about any algebraic expression. However, when you create a formula, remember the rules of high school algebra. For example, *=(B2+B3)/7* will add the contents of cell B2 to those of B3 and divide the sum by 7. In contrast, *=B2+B3/7* will first divide B3 by 7 and then add the result to the contents of B2. When in doubt, just key in a formula you think might work and experiment until you get the results you want.

Figure CE3-27
Summing Sales by Month

Source: Microsoft Excel 2010

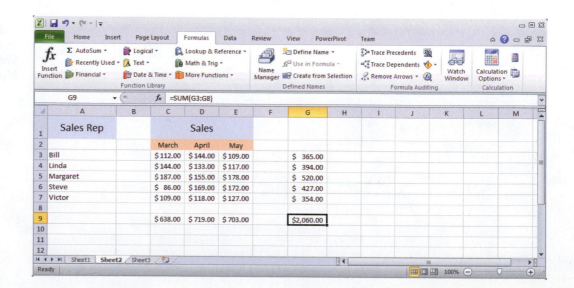

Q7 HOW CAN YOU PRINT RESULTS?

Excel provides a wide variety of tools and settings for printing worksheets. Here we will illustrate several features that will give you an idea of the possibilities. After you have read this section, you can experiment on your own.

Before you start printing, you can save paper and ink if you make use of Excel's Print Preview feature. To do so, click *File* and then *Print,* as shown in Figure CE3-28. Before you click the large Print button (next to Copies), examine the Print Preview thumbnail of your printout to see if you like it. If you do, press *Print,* and Excel will print your document. For now, however, select the *Page Layout* tab in the Excel ribbon.

The tools and selections in the Page Layout ribbon determine how the document will be arranged as a printed document. In this ribbon, the next to last group is *Sheet Options;* in that group, notice that you have the option of viewing and printing gridlines as well as column and row headings.

If you now select *Print* under *Gridlines* and *Headings,* and then select *Print Preview,* you can see that your worksheet will be printed with guidelines and headings, as shown in Figure CE3-29. Most people prefer to see gridlines and headings in the screen display but not see them, or at least not see the headings, in the printed display. Click *Close Print Preview* to return to the spreadsheet view. For now, check *View* and *Print Guidelines,* but under *Headings* check only *View.*

As you can see, you have many other options in the *Page Layout* ribbon. Use *Margins* to set the size of the page margins. *Orientation* refers to whether the worksheet is printed normally (upright) on the page (called *Portrait*) or sideways on the page (called *Landscape*). Try each and preview your print to see the impact they have.

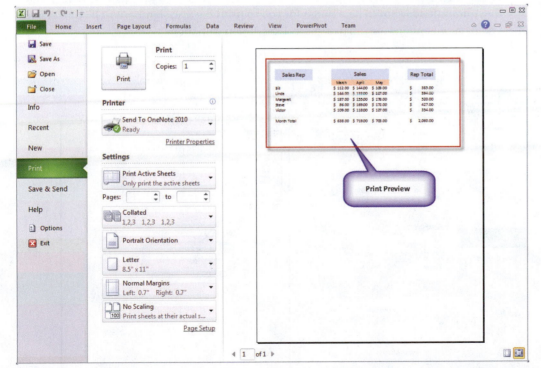

Figure CE3-28
The Print Preview Screen in Excel

Source: Microsoft Excel 2010

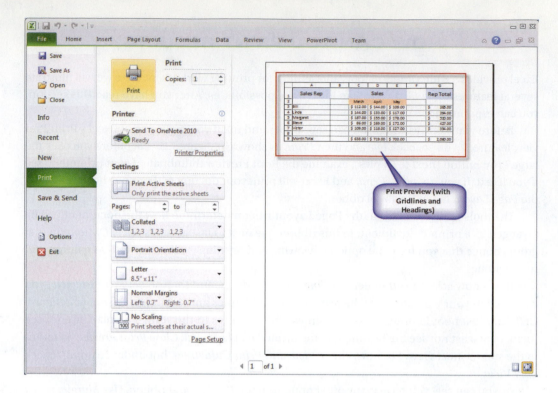

You can use print area to specify the portion of the spreadsheet that you want to print. If for some reason you want to list only the name of the sales reps, you can highlight cells A1 through A7 and then click *Print Area* and then click *Set Print Area*. If you do this, your print preview will appear as in Figure CE3-30.

These commands should be enough for you to print basic assignments. Of course, Excel offers many more options for you to explore. Experiment with them!

Figure CE3-30
Using Print Preview to
Select Only a Portion of the
Spreadsheet

Source: Microsoft Excel 2010

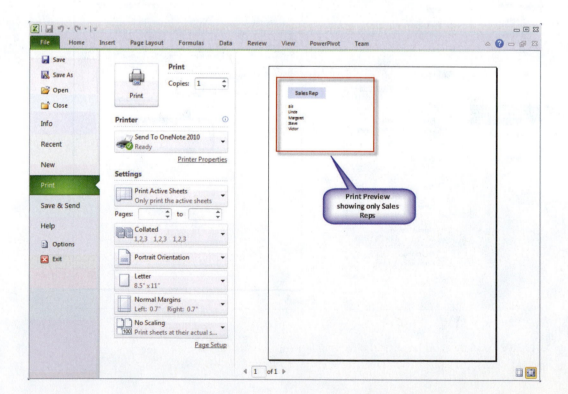

ACTIVE REVIEW

Use this Active Review to verify that you understand the ideas and concepts that answer this chapter extension's study questions.

Q1 WHAT IS A SPREADSHEET?

Explain how the following terms are related: *spreadsheet, electronic spreadsheet, Microsoft Excel, worksheet,* and *workbook.* Explain how spreadsheet cells are addressed. Where would you find cell Q54?

Q2 HOW DO YOU GET STARTED WITH EXCEL?

Describe the first task you should do when creating a spreadsheet. Open a new workbook and give it the name *My_Sample_WB.* Explain the relationship of tabs and tools and selections. Which tab is the most likely one to have the tools and selections you need?

Q3 HOW CAN YOU ENTER DATA?

List three ways of entering data into Excel. Describe the advantage of using the F2 key to edit data. Explain two ways that Excel uses a pattern to enter data.

Q4 HOW CAN YOU INSERT AND DELETE ROWS AND COLUMNS AND CHANGE THEIR SIZE?

Describe how to insert and delete rows. Describe a circumstance in which you would need to insert rows. Describe how to make a row taller or shorter. Describe how to change the width of a column.

Q5 HOW CAN YOU FORMAT DATA?

Open Excel and explain the purpose of each of the icons in the *Font* section of the *Home* tab of the ribbon. Explain the purpose of the *Alignment* and *Number* sections.

Q6 HOW CAN YOU CREATE A (SIMPLE) FORMULA?

Write the expression you would need to add the content of cell B2 to the content of cell B7. Write the expression to multiply the content of cell C4 by 7.3. Write the expression to find the average of the values in cells D7, D8, and D9. Use a built-in formula to total the values in cells E2, E3, E4, E5, E6, and E7.

Q7 HOW CAN YOU PRINT RESULTS?

Explain the purpose and use of *Print Preview.* Open Excel, go to the *Page Layout* tab, and explain the purpose of the *Margins, Orientation,* and *Print Area* tools in the *Page Setup* section. Also, explain the function of the *View* and *Print* checkboxes in the *Gridlines* and *Headings* portion of the *Sheet Options* section.

KEY TERMS AND CONCEPTS

Cell 372
Ribbon 373

Spreadsheet 371
SUM 384

Workbook 371
Worksheet 371

USING YOUR KNOWLEDGE

1. Open Excel and duplicate each of the actions in this chapter extension.

2. Create a new workbook and take the following actions:
   a. Name and save your workbook using a name of your own choosing.
   b. Enter the value *This is the content of cell C7* into cell C7.
   c. Use F2 to change the value in cell C7 to *This is part of the content of cell C7.*
   d. Add the value *January* to cells B2 through B14. Key the data just once.

e. Add the value *January* to cell C2 and the value *February* to cell C3. Highlight both cells C2 and C3 and drag the small black box down to cell C14. Explain what happens.

f. Create a list of odd numbers from 1 to 11 in cells C3 through C8. Key only the values 1 and 3.

g. Enter the value *MIS-1* in cell D2 and the value *MIS-2* in cell D3. Highlight cells D2 and D3 and drag the small black box down to cell D14. Explain what happens.

3. Click the tab named *Sheet2* in the workbook you used for question 2.

a. Place the labels *Part Description, Quantity on Hand, Cost,* and *Total Value* in cells A2, A3, A4, and A5, respectively. Center each label in its cell and make the labels bold. (Do this by highlighting the labels and clicking the bold **B** in the *Font* section of the *Home* tab.) Make each column large enough to show the entire label after formatting.

b. In cells B3, B4, B5, B6, and B7, respectively, enter the following values:

This is where one would type the description of Part 1

This is where one would type the description of Part 2

This is where one would type the description of Part 3

This is where one would type the description of Part 4

This is where one would type the description of Part 5

Enter these values using the fewest possible keystrokes.

c. Enter the quantity-on-hand values *100, 150, 100, 175,* and *200* in cells C3 through C7, respectively. Enter these values using the fewest possible keystrokes.

d. Enter the values *$100, $178, $87, $195,* and *$117* in cells D3 through D7, respectively. Do not enter the dollar signs. Instead, enter only the numbers and then reformat the cells so that Excel will place them.

e. In cell E3, enter a formula that will multiply the quantity on hand (C3) by the cost (D3).

f. Create the same formula in cells E4 through E7. Use select and copy operations.

g. Explain what is magic about the operation in part f.

h. Print the result of your activities in parts a–f. Print your document in landscape mode, showing cell boundaries and row and column names.

Chapter 5 provides the background for this Extension.

Database Design

In this chapter extension, you will learn about data modeling and how data models are transformed into database designs. You'll also learn the important role that business professionals have in the development of a database application system.

 WHO WILL VOLUNTEER?

Suppose you are the manager of fund-raising for a local public television station. Twice a year you conduct fund drives during which the station runs commercials that ask viewers to donate. These drives are important; they provide nearly 40 percent of the station's operating budget.

One of your job functions is to find volunteers to staff the phones during these drives. You need 10 volunteers per night for six nights, or 60 people, twice per year. The volunteers' job is exhausting, and normally a volunteer will work only one night during a drive.

Finding volunteers for each drive is a perpetual headache. Two months before a drive begins, you and your staff start calling potential volunteers. You first call volunteers from prior drives, using a roster that your administrative assistant prepares for each drive. Some volunteers have been helping for years; you'd like to know that information before you call them so that you can tell them how much you appreciate their continuing support. Unfortunately, the roster does not have that data.

Additionally, some volunteers are more effective than others. Some have a particular knack for increasing the callers' donations. Although those data are available, the information is not in a format that you can use when calling for volunteers. You think you could better staff the fund-raising drives if you had that missing information.

You know that you can use a computer database to keep better track of prior volunteers' service and performance, but you are not sure how to proceed. By the end of this chapter extension, when we return to this fund-raising situation, you will know what to do.

 HOW ARE DATABASE APPLICATION SYSTEMS DEVELOPED?

You learned in Chapter 5 that a database application system consists of a database, a DBMS, and one or more database applications. A database application, in turn, consists of forms, reports, queries, and possibly application programs. The question then becomes: How are such systems developed? And, even more important to you, what is the users' role? We will address these questions in this chapter extension.

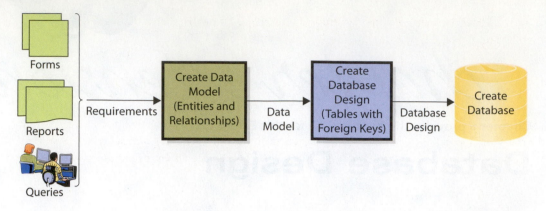

Figure CE4-1 summarizes the database application system development process. First, the developers interview users and develop the requirements for the new system. During this process, the developers analyze existing forms, reports, queries, and other user activities. They also determine the need for new forms, reports, and queries. The requirements for the database are then summarized in something called a **data model**, which is a logical representation of the structure of the data. The data model contains a description of both the data and the relationships among the data. It is akin to a blueprint. Just as building architects create a blueprint before they start construction, so, too, database developers create a data model before they start designing the database.

Once the users have validated and approved the data model, it is transformed into a database design. After that, the design is implemented in a database, and that database is then filled with user data.

You will learn much more about systems development in Chapter 10 and its related extensions. We discuss data modeling here because users have a crucial role in the success of any database development: They must validate and approve the data model. Only the users know what should be in the database.

Consider, for example, a database of students that an adviser uses for his or her advisees. What should be in it? Students? Classes? Records of emails from students? Records of meetings with students? Majors? Student Organizations? Even when we know what themes should be in the database, we must ask, how detailed should the records be? Should the database include campus addresses? Home addresses? Billing addresses?

In fact, there are many possibilities, and the database developers do not and cannot know what to include. They do know, however, that a database must include all the data necessary for the users to perform their jobs. Ideally, it contains that amount of data and no more. So during database development, the developers must rely on the users to tell them what they need in the database. They will rely on the users to check the data model and to verify it for correctness, completeness, and appropriate level of detail. That verification will be your job. We begin with a discussion of the entity-relationship data model—the most common tool to use to construct data models.

Q3   WHAT ARE THE COMPONENTS OF THE ENTITY-RELATIONSHIP DATA MODEL?

The most popular technique for creating a data model is the **entity-relationship (E-R) data model**. With it, developers describe the content of a database by defining the things (*entities*) that will be stored in the database and the *relationships* among those entities. A second, less popular, tool for data modeling is the **Unified Modeling Language (UML)**. We will not describe that tool here. However, if you learn how to interpret E-R models, with a bit of study you will be able to understand UML models as well.

ENTITIES

An **entity** is some thing that the users want to track. Examples of entities are *Order, Customer, Salesperson,* and *Item.* Some entities represent a physical object, such as *Item* or *Salesperson;* others represent a logical construct or transaction, such as *Order* or *Contract.* For reasons beyond this discussion, entity names are always singular. We use *Order,* not *Orders; Salesperson,* not *Salespersons.*

Entities have **attributes** that describe characteristics of the entity. Example attributes of *Order* are *OrderNumber, OrderDate, SubTotal, Tax, Total,* and so forth. Example attributes of *Salesperson* are *SalespersonName, Email, Phone,* and so forth.

Entities have an **identifier**, which is an attribute (or group of attributes) whose value is associated with one and only one entity instance. For example, *OrderNumber* is an identifier of *Order,* because only one *Order* instance has a given value of *OrderNumber.* For the same reason, *CustomerNumber* is an identifier of *Customer.* If each member of the sales staff has a unique name, then *SalespersonName* is an identifier of *Salesperson.*

Before we continue, consider that last sentence. Is the salesperson's name unique among the sales staff? Both now and in the future? Who decides the answer to such a question? Only the users know whether this is true; the database developers cannot know. This example underlines why it is important for you to be able to interpret data models, because only users like yourself will know for sure.

Figure CE4-2 shows examples of entities for the Student database. Each entity is shown in a rectangle. The name of the entity is just above the rectangle, and the identifier is shown in a section at the top of the entity. Entity attributes are shown in the remainder of the rectangle. In Figure CE4-2, the *Adviser* entity has an identifier called *AdviserName* and the attributes *Phone, CampusAddress,* and *EmailAddress.*

Observe that the entities *Email* and *Office_Visit* do not have an identifier. Unlike *Student* or *Adviser,* the users do not have an attribute that identifies a particular email. In fact, *Email* and *Office_Visit* are identified, in part, by their relationship to Student. For now, we need not worry about that. The data model needs only to show how users view their world. When it comes to database design, the designer will deal with the missing identifiers by adding columns, possibly using hidden identifiers, to implement the users' view. You can learn about the modeling and representation of such entities if you enroll in a database class.

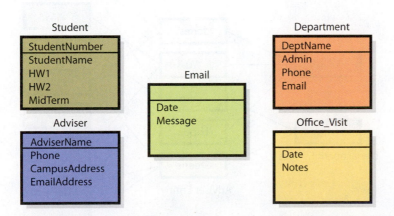

Figure CE4-2
Student Data Model Entities

RELATIONSHIPS

Entities have **relationships** to each other. An *Order*, for example, has a relationship to a *Customer* entity and also to a *Salesperson* entity. In the Student database, a *Student* has a relationship to an *Adviser*, and an *Adviser* has a relationship to a *Department*.

Figure CE4-3 shows sample *Department*, *Adviser*, and *Student* entities and their relationships. For simplicity, this figure shows just the identifier of the entities and not the other attributes. For this sample data, *Accounting* has three professors, Jones, Wu, and Lopez, and *Finance* has two professors, Smith and Greene.

The relationship between *Advisers* and *Students* is a bit more complicated, because in this example an adviser is allowed to advise many students and a student is allowed to have many advisers. Perhaps this happens because students can have multiple majors. In any case, note that Professor Jones advises students 100 and 400 and that student 100 is advised by both Professors Jones and Smith.

Diagrams like the one in Figure CE4-3 are too cumbersome for use in database design discussions. Instead, database designers use diagrams called **entity-relationship (E-R) diagrams**. Figure CE4-4 shows an E-R diagram for the data in Figure CE4-3. In this figure, all of the entities of one type are represented by a single rectangle. Thus, there are rectangles for the *Department*, *Adviser*, and *Student* entities. Attributes are shown as before in Figure CE4-2.

Additionally, a line is used to represent a relationship between two entities. Notice the line between *Department* and *Adviser*, for example. The forked lines on the right side of that line signify that a department may have more than one adviser. The little lines, which are referred to as a **crow's foot**, are shorthand for the multiple lines between *Department* and *Adviser* in Figure CE4-3. Relationships like this one are called **one-to-many (1:N) relationships** because one department can have many advisers.

Now examine the line between *Adviser* and *Student*. Here, a crow's foot appears at each end of the line. This notation signifies that an adviser can be related to many students and that a student can be related to many advisers, which is the situation in Figure CE4-3. Relationships like this one are called **many-to-many (N:M) relationships**, because one adviser can have many students and one student can have many advisers.

Students sometimes find the notation N:M confusing. Interpret the *N* and *M* to mean that a variable number, greater than one, is allowed on each side of the relationship. Such a relationship is not written *N:N*, because that notation would imply that there are the same number of entities on each side of the relationship, which is not necessarily true. *N:M* means that more

Figure CE4-3

Example of *Department*, *Adviser*, and *Student* Entities and Relationships

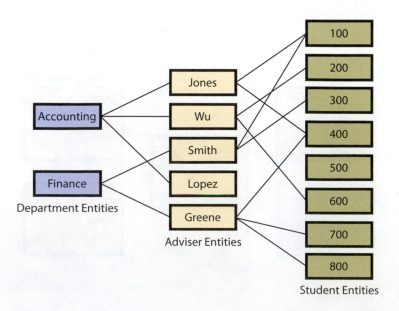

Department Entities

Adviser Entities

Student Entities

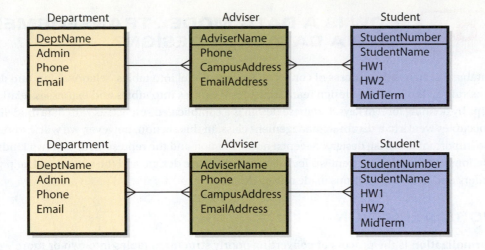

Figure CE4-4
Example Relationships—
Version 1

Figure CE4-5
Example Relationships—
Version 2

than one entity is allowed on each side of the relationship and that the number of entities on each side can be different.

Figure CE4-4 is an example of an entity-relationship diagram. Unfortunately, there are several different styles of entity-relationship diagrams. This one is called, not surprisingly, a **crow's-foot diagram** version. You may learn other versions if you take a database management class.

Figure CE4-5 shows the same entities with different assumptions. Here, advisers may advise in more than one department, but a student may have only one adviser, representing a policy that students may not have multiple majors.

Which, if either of these versions—Figure CE4-4 or Figure CE4-5—is correct? Only the users know. These alternatives illustrate the kinds of questions you will need to answer when a database designer asks you to check a data model for correctness.

The crow's-foot notation shows the maximum number of entities that can be involved in a relationship. Accordingly, they are called the relationship's **maximum cardinality**. Common examples of maximum cardinality are 1:N, N:M, and 1:1 (not shown).

Another important question is, "What is the minimum number of entities required in the relationship?" Must an adviser have a student to advise, and must a student have an adviser? Constraints on minimum requirements are called **minimum cardinalities**.

Figure CE4-6 presents a third version of this E-R diagram that shows both maximum and minimum cardinalities. The vertical bar on a line means that at least one entity of that type is required. The small oval means that the entity is optional; the relationship need not have an entity of that type.

Thus, in Figure CE4-6, a department is not required to have a relationship to any adviser, but an adviser is required to belong to a department. Similarly, an adviser is not required to have a relationship to a student, but a student is required to have a relationship to an adviser. Note, also, that the maximum cardinalities in Figure CE4-6 have been changed so that both are 1:N.

Is the model in Figure CE4-6 a good one? It depends on the rules of the university. Again, only the users know for sure.

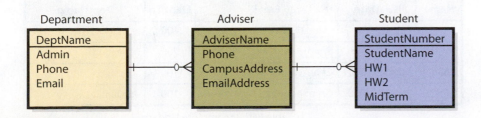

HOW IS A DATA MODEL TRANSFORMED INTO A DATABASE DESIGN?

Database design is the process of converting a data model into tables, relationships, and data constraints. The database design team transforms entities into tables and expresses relationships by defining foreign keys. Database design is a complicated subject; as with data modeling, it occupies weeks in a database management class. In this section, however, we will introduce two important database design concepts: normalization and the representation of two kinds of relationships. The first concept is a foundation of database design, and the second will help you understand key considerations made during design.

NORMALIZATION

Normalization is the process of converting poorly structured tables into two or more well-structured tables. A table is such a simple construct that you may wonder how one could possibly be poorly structured. In truth, there are many ways that tables can be malformed—so many, in fact, that researchers have published hundreds of papers on this topic alone.

Consider the *Employee* table in Figure CE4-7. It lists employee names, hire dates, email addresses, and the name and number of the department in which the employee works. This table seems innocent enough. But consider what happens when the Accounting department changes its name to Accounting and Finance. Because department names are duplicated in this table, every row that has a value of "Accounting" must be changed to "Accounting and Finance."

Data Integrity Problems

Suppose the Accounting name change is correctly made in two rows, but not in the third. The result is shown in Figure CE4-7. This table has what is called a **data integrity problem**: Some rows indicate that the name of Department 100 is Accounting and Finance, and another row indicates that the name of Department 100 is Accounting.

This problem is easy to spot in this small table. But consider a table in a large database that has over 300,000 rows. Once a table that large develops serious data integrity problems, months of labor will be required to remove them.

Figure CE4-7
A Poorly Designed
Employee Table

Employee

Name	HireDate	Email	DeptNo	DeptName
Jones	Feb 1, 2010	Jones@ourcompany.com	100	Accounting
Smith	Dec 3, 2007	Smith@ourcompany.com	200	Marketing
Chau	March 7, 2007	Chau@ourcompany.com	100	Accounting
Greene	July 17, 2010	Greene@ourcompany.com	100	Accounting

a. Table Before Update

Employee

Name	HireDate	Email	DeptNo	DeptName
Jones	Feb 1, 2010	Jones@ourcompany.com	100	Accounting and Finance
Smith	Dec 3, 2007	Smith@ourcompany.com	200	Marketing
Chau	March 7, 2007	Chau@ourcompany.com	100	Accounting and Finance
Greene	July 17, 2010	Greene@ourcompany.com	100	Accounting

b. Table with Incomplete Update

Data integrity problems are serious. A table that has data integrity problems will produce incorrect and inconsistent information. Users will lose confidence in the information, and the system will develop a poor reputation. Information systems with poor reputations become heavy burdens to the organizations that use them.

Normalizing for Data Integrity

The data integrity problem can occur only if data are duplicated. Because of this, one easy way to eliminate the problem is to eliminate the duplicated data. We can do this by transforming the table design in Figure CE4-7a into two tables, as shown in Figure CE4-8. Here, the name of the department is stored just once, therefore no data inconsistencies can occur.

Of course, to produce an employee report that includes the department name, the two tables in Figure CE4-8 will need to be joined back together. Because such joining of tables is common, DBMS products have been programmed to perform it efficiently, but it still requires work. From this example, you can see a trade-off in database design: Normalized tables eliminate data duplication, but they can be slower to process. Dealing with such trade-offs is an important consideration in database design.

The general goal of normalization is to construct tables such that every table has a *single* topic or theme. In good writing, every paragraph should have a single theme. This is true of databases as well; every table should have a single theme. The problem with the table design in Figure CE4-7 is that it has two independent themes: employees and departments. The way to correct the problem is to split the table into two tables, each with its own theme. In this case, we create an *Employee* table and a *Department* table, as shown in Figure CE4-8.

As mentioned, there are dozens of ways that tables can be poorly formed. Database practitioners classify tables into various **normal forms** according to the kinds of problems they have. Transforming a table into a normal form to remove duplicated data and other problems is called *normalizing* the table.[1] Thus, when you hear a database designer say, "Those tables are not normalized," she does not mean that the tables have irregular, not-normal data. Instead, she means that the tables have a format that could cause data integrity problems.

Employee

Name	HireDate	Email	DeptNo
Jones	Feb 1, 2010	Jones@ourcompany.com	100
Smith	Dec 3, 2011	Smith@ourcompany.com	200
Chau	March 7, 2007	Chau@ourcompany.com	100
Greene	July 17, 2010	Greene@ourcompany.com	100

Department

DeptNo	DeptName
100	Accounting
200	Marketing
300	Information Systems

Figure CE4-8
Two Normalized Tables

---

[1] See David Kroenke and David Auer, *Database Processing*, 12th ed. (Upper Saddle River, NJ: Prentice Hall, 2012) for more information.

Summary of Normalization

As a future user of databases, you do not need to know the details of normalization. Instead, understand the general principle that every normalized (well-formed) table has one and only one theme. Further, tables that are not normalized are subject to data integrity problems.

Be aware, too, that normalization is just one criterion for evaluating database designs. Because normalized designs can be slower to process, database designers sometimes choose to accept non-normalized tables. The best design depends on the users' requirements.

REPRESENTING RELATIONSHIPS

Figure CE4-9 shows the steps involved in transforming a data model into a relational database design. First, the database designer creates a table for each entity. The identifier of the entity becomes the key of the table. Each attribute of the entity becomes a column of the table. Next, the resulting tables are normalized so that each table has a single theme. Once that has been done, the next step is to represent the relationship among those tables.

For example, consider the E-R diagram in Figure CE4-10a. The *Adviser* entity has a 1:N relationship to the *Student* entity. To create the database design, we construct a table for *Adviser* and a second table for *Student*, as shown in Figure CE4-10b. The key of the *Adviser* table is *AdviserName*, and the key of the *Student* table is *StudentNumber*.

Further, the *EmailAddress* attribute of the *Adviser* entity becomes the *EmailAddress* column of the *Adviser* table, and the *StudentName* and *MidTerm* attributes of the *Student* entity become the *StudentName* and *MidTerm* columns of the *Student* table.

The next task is to represent the relationship. Because we are using the relational model, we know that we must add a foreign key to one of the two tables. The possibilities are: (1) place the foreign key *StudentNumber* in the *Adviser* table or (2) place the foreign key *AdviserName* in the *Student* table.

The correct choice is to place *AdviserName* in the *Student* table, as shown in Figure CE4-10c. To determine a student's adviser, we just look into the *AdviserName* column of that student's row. To determine the adviser's students, we search the *AdviserName* column in the *Student* table to determine which rows have that adviser's name. If a student changes advisers, we simply change the value in the *AdviserName* column. Changing *Jackson* to *Jones* in the first row, for example, will assign student 100 to Professor Jones.

For this data model, placing *StudentNumber* in *Adviser* would be incorrect. If we were to do that, we could assign only one student to an adviser. There is no place to assign a second adviser.

This strategy for placing foreign keys will not work for N:M relationships, however. Consider the data model in Figure CE4-11a (page 398); here, there is an N:M relationship between advisers and students. An adviser may have many students, and a student may have multiple advisers

Figure CE4-9
Transforming a Data Model into a Database Design

- Represent each entity with a table
  - Entity identifier becomes table key
  - Entity attributes become table columns
- Normalize tables as necessary
- Represent relationships
  - Use foreign keys
  - Add additional tables for N:M relationships

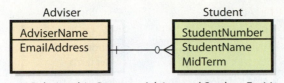

a. 1: N Relationship Between Adviser and Student Entities

Adviser Table—Key is AdviserName

AdviserName	EmailAddress
Jones	Jones@myuniv.edu
Choi	Choi@myuniv.edu
Jackson	Jackson@myuniv.edu

Student Table—Key is StudentNumber

StudentNumber	StudentName	MidTerm
100	Lisa	90
200	Jennie	85
300	Jason	82
400	Terry	95

b. Creating a Table for Each Entity

Adviser Table—Key is AdviserName

AdviserName	EmailAddress
Jones	Jones@myuniv.edu
Choi	Choi@myuniv.edu
Jackson	Jackson@myuniv.edu

Foreign Key
Column
Represents
Relationship

Student—Key is StudentNumber

StudentNumber	StudentName	MidTerm	AdviserName
100	Lisa	90	Jackson
200	Jennie	85	Jackson
300	Jason	82	Choi
400	Terry	95	Jackson

c. Using the AdviserName Foreign Key to Represent the 1:N Relationship

(for multiple majors). The strategy we used for the 1:N data model will not work here. To see why, examine Figure CE4-11b. If student 100 has more than one adviser, there is no place to record second or subsequent advisers.

It turns out that to represent an N:M relationship, we need to create a third table, as shown in Figure CE4-11c. The third table has two columns, *AdviserName* and *Student-Number*. Each row of the table means that the given adviser advises the student with the given number.

As you can imagine, there is a great deal more to database design than we have presented here. Still, this section should give you an idea of the tasks that need to be accomplished to create a database. You should also realize that the database design is a direct consequence of decisions made in the data model. If the data model is wrong, the database design will be wrong as well.

Figure CE4-11
Representing an N:M
Relationship

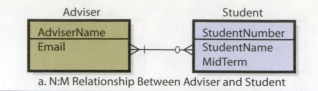

a. N:M Relationship Between Adviser and Student

Adviser—Key is AdviserName

AdviserName	Email
Jones	Jones@myuniv.edu
Choi	Choi@myuniv.edu
Jackson	Jackson@myuniv.edu

No room to place second or third AdviserName

Student—Key is StudentNumber

StudentNumber	StudentName	MidTerm	AdviserName
100	Lisa	90	Jackson
200	Jennie	85	Jackson
300	Jason	82	Choi
400	Terry	95	Jackson

b. Incorrect Representation of N:M Relationship

Adviser—Key is AdviserName

AdviserName	Email
Jones	Jones@myuniv.edu
Choi	Choi@myuniv.edu
Jackson	Jackson@myuniv.edu

Student—Key is StudentNumber

StudentNumber	StudentName	MidTerm
100	Lisa	90
200	Jennie	85
300	Jason	82
400	Terry	95

Adviser_Student_Intersection

AdviserName	StudentNumber
Jackson	100
Jackson	200
Choi	300
Jackson	400
Choi	100
Jones	100

Student 100 has three advisers.

c. Adviser_Student_Intersection Table Represents the N:M Relationship

WHAT IS THE USERS' ROLE?

As stated, a database is a model of how the users view their business world. This means that the users are the final judges as to what data the database should contain and how the records in that database should be related to one another.

The easiest time to change the database structure is during the data modeling stage. Changing a relationship from 1:N to N:M in a data model is simply a matter of changing the 1:N notation to N:M. However, once the database has been constructed, loaded with data, and application forms, reports, queries, and application programs created, changing a 1:N relationship to N:M means weeks of work.

You can glean some idea of why this might be true by contrasting Figure CE4-10c with Figure CE4-11c. Suppose that instead of having just a few rows, each table has thousands of rows; in that case, transforming the database from one format to the other involves considerable work. Even worse, however, is that application components will need to be changed as well. For example, if students have at most one adviser, then a single text box can be used to enter *AdviserName*. If students can have multiple advisers, then a multiple-row table will need to be used to enter *AdviserName*, and a program will need to be written to store the values of *AdviserName* into the *Adviser_Student_ Intersection* table. There are dozens of other consequences as well, consequences that will translate into wasted labor and wasted expense.

The conclusion from this discussion is that user review of a data model is crucial. When a database is developed for your use, you must carefully review the data model. If you do not understand any aspect of it, you should ask for clarification until you do. The data model must accurately reflect your view of the business. If it does not, the database will be designed incorrectly, and the applications will be difficult to use, if not worthless. Do not proceed unless the data model is accurate.

As a corollary, when asked to review a data model, take that review seriously. Devote the time necessary to perform a thorough review. Any mistakes you miss will come back to haunt you, and by then the cost of correction may be very high with regard to both time and expense. This brief introduction to data modeling shows why databases can be more difficult to develop than spreadsheets.

WHO WILL VOLUNTEER? (CONTINUED)

Knowing what you know now, if you were the manager of fund-raising at the TV station, you would hire a consultant and expect the consultant to interview all of the key users. From those interviews, the consultant would then construct a data model.

You now know that the structure of the database must reflect the way the users think about their activities. If the consultant did not take the time to interview you and your staff or did not construct a data model and ask you to review it, you would know that you are not receiving good service and would take corrective action.

Suppose you found a consultant who interviewed your staff for several hours and then constructed the data model shown in Figure CE4-12. This data model has an entity for *Prospect*, an entity for *Employee*, and three additional entities for *Contact*, *Phone*, and *Work*. The *Contact*

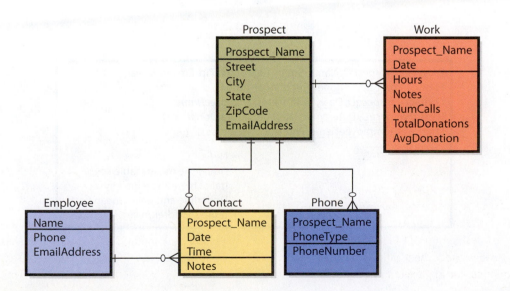

Figure CE4-12
Data Model for Volunteer Database

Figure CE4-13
First Table Design for
Volunteer Database

Prospect (<u>Name</u>, Street, City, State, Zip, EmailAddress)
Phone (<u>*Name*</u>, <u>PhoneType</u>, PhoneNumber)
Contact (<u>*Name*</u>, <u>Date</u>, <u>Time</u>, Notes, *EmployeeName*)
Work (<u>*Name*</u>, <u>Date</u>, Notes, NumCalls, TotalDonations)
Employee (<u>EmployeeName</u>, Phone, EmailAddress)

Note:
Underline means table key.
Italics means foreign key.
Underline and italics mean both
table and foreign key.

entity records contacts that you or other employees have made with the prospective volunteer. This record is necessary so that you know what has been said to whom. The *Phone* entity is used to record multiple phone numbers for each prospective volunteer, and the *Work* entity records work that the prospect has performed for the station.

After you reviewed and approved this data model, the consultant constructed the database design shown in Figure CE4-13. In this design, table keys are underlined, foreign keys are shown in italics, and columns that are both table and foreign keys are underlined and italicized. Observe that the *Name* column is the table key of *Prospect*, and it is both part of the table key and a foreign key in *Phone, Contact*, and *Work*.

The consultant did not like having the *Name* column used as a key or as part of a key in so many tables. Based on her interviews, she suspected that prospect names are fluid—and that sometimes the same prospect name is recorded in different ways (e.g., sometimes with a middle initial and sometimes without). If that were to happen, phone, contact, and work data could be misallocated to prospect names. Accordingly, the consultant added a new column, *ProspectID* to the prospect table and created the design shown in Figure CE4-14. Values of this ID will have no meaning to the users, but the ID will be used to ensure that each prospect obtains a unique record in the Volunteer database. Because this ID has no meaning to the users, the consultant will hide it on forms and reports that users see.

There is one difference between the data model and the table designs. In the data model, the *Work* entity has an attribute, *AvgDonation*, but there is no corresponding *AvgDonation* column in the *Work* table. The consultant decided that there was no need to store this value in the database because it could readily be computed on forms and reports using the values in the *NumCalls* and *TotalDonations* columns.

Figure CE4-14
Second Table Design for
Volunteer Database

Prospect (<u>*ProspectID*</u>, Name, Street, City, State, Zip, EmailAddress)
Phone (<u>*ProspectID*</u>, <u>PhoneType</u>, PhoneNumber)
Contact (<u>*ProspectID*</u>, <u>Date</u>, <u>Time</u>, Notes, *EmployeeName*)
Work (<u>*ProspectID*</u>, <u>Date</u>, Notes, NumCalls, TotalDonations)
Employee (<u>EmployeeName</u>, Phone, EmailAddress)

Note:
Underline means table key.
Italics means foreign key.
Underline and italics mean both
table and foreign key.

Figure CE4-15
Volunteer Prospect Data Entry Form

Source: Microsoft Access 2010

Once the tables had been designed, the consultant created a Microsoft Access 2007 database. She defined the tables in Access, created relationships among the tables, and constructed forms and reports. Figure CE4-15 shows the primary data entry form used for the Volunteer database. The top portion of the form has contact data, including multiple phone numbers. It is important to know the type of the phone number so that you and your staff know if you're calling someone at work or another setting. The middle and bottom sections of this form have contact and prior work data. Observe that *AvgDonation* has been computed from the *NumCalls* and *Total Donations* columns.

You were quite pleased with this database application, and you're certain that it helped you to improve the volunteer staffing at the station. Of course, over time, you thought of several new requirements, and you already have changes in mind for next year.

ACTIVE REVIEW

Use this Active Review to verify that you understand the ideas and concepts in this chapter extension's study questions.

Q1 WHO WILL VOLUNTEER?

Summarize the problem that the fund-raising manager must solve. Explain how a database can help solve this problem. Describe the missing information. In your own words, what data must be available to construct the missing information?

Q2 HOW ARE DATABASE APPLICATION SYSTEMS DEVELOPED?

Name and briefly describe the components of a database application system. Explain the difference between a database application system and a database application program. Using Figure CE4-1 as a guide, describe the major steps in the process of developing a database application system. Explain what role is crucial for users and why that role is so important.

Q3 WHAT ARE THE COMPONENTS OF THE ENTITY-RELATIONSHIP DATA MODEL?

Define the terms *entity*, *attributes*, and *relationship*. Give an example of two entities (other than those in this book) that have a 1:N relationship. Give an example of two entities that have an N:M relationship. Explain the difference between maximum and minimum cardinality. Show two entities having a 1:N relationship in which one is required and one is optional.

Q4 HOW IS A DATA MODEL TRANSFORMED INTO A DATABASE DESIGN?

Give an example of a data integrity problem. Describe, in general terms, the process of normalization. Explain how normalizing data prevents data integrity problems. Explain the disadvantage of normalized data. Using your examples from Q3, show how 1:N relationships are expressed in relational database designs. Show how N:M relationships are expressed in relational database designs.

Q5 WHAT IS THE USERS' ROLE?

Describe the major role for users in the development of a database application system. Explain what is required to change a 1:N relationship to an N:M relationship during the data modeling stage. Explain what is required to make that same change after the database application systems has been constructed. Describe how this knowledge impacts your behavior when a database application system is being constructed for your use.

Q6 WHO WILL VOLUNTEER? (CONTINUED)

Examine Figure CE4-12. Describe the maximum and minimum cardinality for each relationship. Justify these cardinalities. Change the relationship between *Prospect* and *Phone* to N:M, and explain what this means. Change the relationship between *Prospect* and *Work* to 1:1, and explain what this means. Explain how each relationship is represented in the design in Figure CE4-14. Show examples of both primary keys and foreign keys in this figure. In *Contact*, determine whether *EmployeeName* is part of a primary key or part of a foreign key.

Explain what problem the consultant foresaw in the use of the *Name* attribute. Explain how that problem was avoided. The consultant added an attribute to the data model that was not part of the users' world. Explain why that attribute will not add unnecessary complication to the users' work experiences.

KEY TERMS AND CONCEPTS

Attribute 391
Crow's foot 392
Crow's foot diagram 393
Data integrity problem 394
Data model 390
Entity 391

Entity-relationship (E-R) diagram 392
Entity-relationship (E-R) data
  model 390
Identifier 391
Many-to-many (N:M) relationship 392
Maximum cardinality 393

Minimum cardinality 393
Normal form 395
Normalization 394
One-to-many (1:N) relationship 392
Relationship 392
Unified Modeling Language (UML) 390

USING YOUR KNOWLEDGE

1. Explain how you could use a spreadsheet to solve the volunteer problem at the television station. What data would you place in each column and row of your spreadsheet? Name each column and row of your spreadsheet. What advantages does a database have over a spreadsheet for this problem? Compare and contrast your spreadsheet solution to the database solution shown in the design in Figure CE4-14 and the data entry form in Figure CE4-15.

2. Suppose you are asked to build a database application for a sports league. Assume that your application is to keep track of teams and equipment that is checked out to teams. Explain the steps that need to be taken to develop this application. Specify entities and their relationships. Build an E-R diagram. Ensure your diagram shows both minimum and maximum cardinalities. Transform your E-R diagram into a relational design.

3. Suppose you are asked to build a database application for a bicycle rental shop. Assume your database is to track customers, bicycles, and rentals. Explain the steps that need to be taken to develop this application. Specify entities and their relationships. Build an E-R diagram. Ensure your diagram shows both minimum and maximum cardinalities. Transform your E-R diagram into a relational design.

4. Assume you work at the television station and are asked to evaluate the data model in Figure CE4-12. Suppose that you want to differentiate between prospects who have worked in the past and those who have never worked, but who are prospects for future work. Say that one of the data modelers tells you, "No problem. We'll know that because any *Prospect* entity that has no relationship to a *Work* entity is a prospect who has never worked." Restate the data modeler's response in your own words. Does this seem like a satisfactory solution? What if you want to keep *Prospect* data that pertains only to prospects who have worked? (No such attributes are shown in *Prospect* in Figure CE4-12, but say there is an attribute such as *YearFirstVolunteered* or some other attribute that pertains to prospects who have worked in the past.) Show an alternative E-R diagram that would differentiate between prospects who have worked in the past and those who have not. Compare and contrast your alternative to the one shown in Figure CE4-12.

5. Suppose you manage a department that is developing a database application. The IT professionals who are developing the system ask you to identify two employees to evaluate data models. What criteria would you use in selecting those employees? What instructions would you give them? Suppose one of the employees says to you, "I go to those meetings, but I just don't understand what they're talking about." How would you respond? Suppose that you go to one of those meetings and don't understand what they're talking about. What would you do? Describe a role for a prototype in this situation. How would you justify the request for a prototype?

Using Microsoft Access 2010

In this chapter extension, you will learn fundamental techniques for creating a database and a database application with Microsoft Access.

 HOW DO YOU CREATE TABLES?

Before using Access or any other DBMS, you should have created a data model from the users' requirements, and you must transform that data model into a database design. For the purpose of this chapter extension, we will use a portion of the database design created in Chapter Extension 4. Specifically, we will create a database with the following two tables:

> PROSPECT (<u>ProspectID</u>, Name, Street, City, State, Zip, Email Address)

and

> WORK (*<u>ProspectID</u>*, <u>Date</u>, <u>Hour</u>, NumCalls, TotalDonations)

As in Chapter Extension 4, an underlined attribute is the primary key and an italicized attribute is a foreign key. Thus, <u>ProspectID</u> is the primary key of PROSPECT, and the combination (<u>ProspectID</u>, <u>Date</u>, <u>Hour</u>) is the primary key of WORK. *ProspectID* is also a foreign key in WORK, hence it is shown both underlined and in italics. The data model and database design in Chapter Extension 4 specified that the key of WORK is the combination (<u>ProspectID</u>, <u>Date</u>). Upon review, the users stated that prospects will sometimes work more than one time during the day. For scheduling and other purposes, the users want to record both the date and the hour that someone worked. Accordingly, the database designer added the Hour attribute and made it part of the key of WORK.

The assumption in this design is that each row of WORK represents an hour's work. If a prospect works for consecutive hours, say from 7 to 9 PM, then he or she would have two rows, one with an Hour value of 1900 and a second with an Hour value of 2000. Figure CE5-1 further documents the attributes of the design. Sample data for this table are shown in Figure CE5-2 on page 406.

Note the ambiguity in the name *PROSPECT*. Before someone has become a volunteer, he is a prospect, and the term is fine. However, once that person has actually done work, he is no longer merely a prospect. This ambiguity occurs because the database is used both for finding volunteers and for recording their experiences once they have joined. We could rename PROSPECT as VOLUNTEER, but then we'd still have a problem. The person is not a volunteer until he has actually agreed to become one. So, for now, just assume that a PROSPECT who has one or more WORK records is no longer a prospect but has become a volunteer.

Table	Attribute (Column)	Remarks	Data Type	Example Value
PROSPECT	ProspectID	An identifying number provided by Access when a row is created. The value has no meaning to the user.	AutoNumber	55
PROSPECT	Name	A prospect's name.	Text (50)	Emily Jones
PROSPECT	Street	Prospect's contact street address.	Text (50)	123 West Elm
PROSPECT	City	Prospect's contact city.	Text (40)	Miami
PROSPECT	State	Prospect's contact state.	Text (2)	FL
PROSPECT	Zip	Prospect's contact zip code.	Text (10)	30210-4567 or 30210
PROSPECT	EmailAddress	Prospect's contact email address.	Text (65)	ExamplePerson@somewhere.com
WORK	ProspectID	Foreign key to PROSPECT. Value provided when relationship is created.	Number (Long Integer)	55
WORK	Date	The date of work.	Date	9/15/2012
WORK	Hour	The hour at which work is started.	Number (Integer)	0800 or 1900 (7 PM)
WORK	NumCalls	The number of calls taken.	Number (Integer)	25
WORK	TotalDonations	The total of donations generated.	Currency	$10,575
WORK	AvgDonations	The average donation.	Currency	To be computed in queries and reports

Figure CE5-1
Attributes of the Database

STARTING ACCESS

Figure CE5-3 shows the opening screen for Microsoft Access 2010. (If you use another version of Access, your screen will appear differently, but the essentials will be the same.) To create a new database, select Blank database under *Available Templates* in the center of the screen. Then, type the name of your new database under *File Name* (here we use *Volunteer*). Access will suggest a directory; change it if you want to use another one, and then click *Create*. You will see the screen shown in Figure CE5-4 on page 407.

CREATING TABLES

Access opens the new database by creating a default table named Table 1. We want to modify the design of this table, so in the upper left-hand corner, where you see a pencil and a right angle square, click *View* and select *Design View*. Access will ask you to name your table. Enter *PROSPECT* and click *OK*. Your screen will appear as in Figure CE5-5 on page 408.

The screen shown in Figure CE5-5 has three parts. The left-hand pane lists all of the tables in your database. At this point, you should see only the PROSPECT table in this list. We will use the upper part of the right-hand pane to enter the name of each attribute (which Access calls *Fields*) and its *Data Type*. We can optionally enter a *Description* of that field.

Example of PROSPECT Data

Prospect ID	Name	Street	City	State	Zip	EmailAddress
1	Carson Wu	123 Elm	Los Angeles	CA	98007	Carson@somewhere.com
2	Emily Jackson	2234 17th	Pasadena	CA	97005	JacksonE@elsewhere.com
3	Peter Lopez	331 Moses Drive	Fullerton	CA	97330	PeterL@ourcompany.com
4	Lynda Dennison	54 Strand	Manhattan Beach	CA	97881	Lynda@somewhere.com
5	Carter Fillmore III	Restricted	Brentwood	CA	98220	Carter@BigBucks.com
6	CJ Greene	77 Sunset Strip	Hollywood	CA	97330	CJ@HollywoodProducers.com
7	Jolisa Jackson	2234 17th	Pasadena	CA	97005	JacksonJ@elsewhere.com

Example of WORK Data

ProspectID	Date	Hour	NumCalls	TotalDonations
3	9/15/2011	1600	17	8755
3	9/15/2011	1700	28	11578
5	9/15/2011	1700	25	15588
5	9/20/2011	1800	37	29887
5	9/10/2012	1700	30	21440
5	9/10/2012	1800	39	37050
6	9/15/2011	1700	33	21445
6	9/16/2011	1700	27	17558
6	9/10/2012	1700	31	22550
6	9/10/2012	1800	37	36700

Figure CE5-2
Sample Data

The Description is used for documentation; as you will see, Access displays any text you enter as help text on forms. In the bottom part of the screen, we set the properties of each field (or attribute, using our term). To start designing the table, replace the *Field Name* ID with *ProspectID.* Access has already set its type to *AutoNumber,* so you can leave that alone.

To create the rest of the table, enter the *Field Names* and *Data Types* according to our design.[1] Figure CE5-6 shows how to set the length of a Text Data Type. In this figure, the user has set City to *Text* and then has moved down into the bottom part of this form and entered 40 under *Field Size.* You will do the same thing to set the length of all of the Text Field Names. The complete table is shown in Figure CE5-7.

---

[1]When you enter the Name field, Access will give you an error message. Ignore the message and click OK. The fact that you are using a reserved word for this example will not be a problem. If you want to be safe, you could enter *PName* or *ProspectName* (rather than *Name*) and avoid this issue. Many people, including me, believe that Access 2010 is poorly designed. This restriction is a case in point; you ought to be able to enter any value for Field Name the way you want. Access 2010 should stay out of your way; you shouldn't have to stay out of its way!

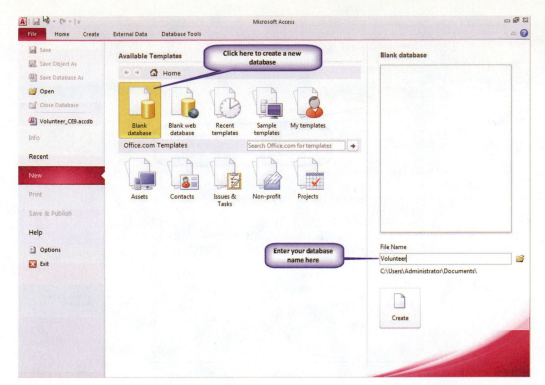

Figure CE5-3
Opening Screen for
Microsoft Access 2010

Source: Microsoft Access 2010

ProspectID is the primary key of this table, and the little key icon next to the ProspectID *Field Name* means Access has already made it so. If we wanted to make another field the primary key, we would highlight that field and then click the *Primary Key* icon in the left-hand portion of the *Design* ribbon.

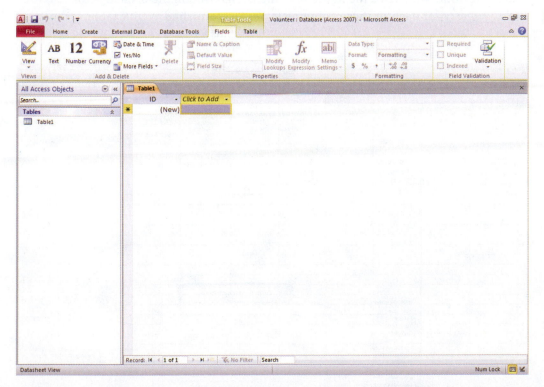

Figure CE5-4
Access Opens with a Start
on a Table Definition[2]

Source: Microsoft Access 2010

[2]Midway during the Office 2010 release cycle, Microsoft changed the banner at the top of Access windows. The banner in early versions read (Access 2007) as in Figures CE5-4–CE5-12a. Later versions read (Access 2007–2010) as in Figure CE5-12b. Depending on which Access release you have, you will see one title version or the other, and for all practical purposes, this difference is unimportant. We will show both title versions in this extension.

Figure CE5-5
Creating Tables in Access,
Step 1

Source: Microsoft Access 2010

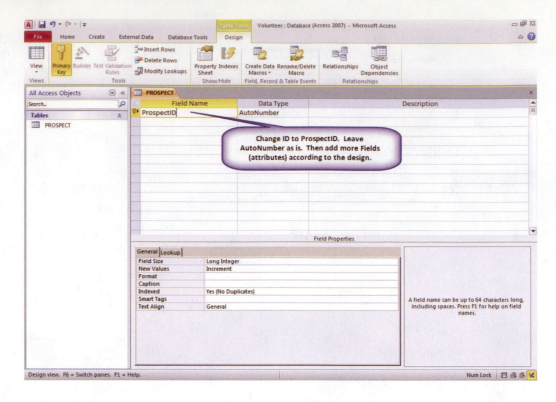

Follow similar steps to create the WORK table. The only difference is that you will need to create a key of the three columns (ProspectID, Date, Hour). To create that key, highlight all three rows by dragging over the three squares to the left of the names of ProspectID, Date, and Hour. Then click the *Key* icon in the *Design* ribbon. Also, change the *Required Field Property* for each of these columns to *Yes.* The finished WORK table is shown in

Figure CE5-6
Creating Tables in Access,
Step 2

Source: Microsoft Access 2010

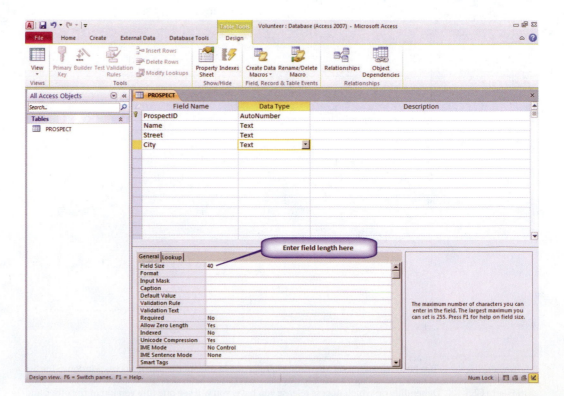

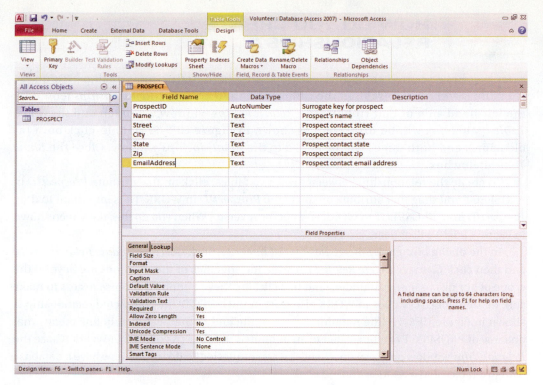

Figure CE5-7
Complete Sample
PROSPECT Table

Source: Microsoft Access 2010

Figure CE5-8. This figure also shows that the user selected *Number* for the *Data Type* of *NumCalls* and then set its *Field Size* (lower pane) to *Integer*. This same technique was used to set the *Data Type* of ProspectID (in WORK) to *Number* (*Field Size* of *Long Integer*) and that of *Hour* to *Number* (*Field Size* of *Integer*).

At this point, close both tables and save your work. You have created your first database!

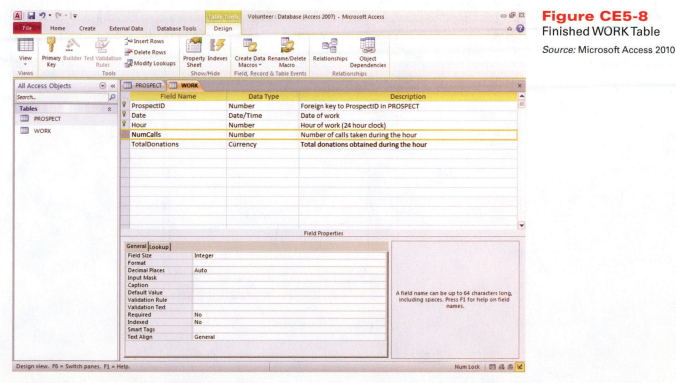

Figure CE5-8
Finished WORK Table

Source: Microsoft Access 2010

HOW DO YOU CREATE RELATIONSHIPS?

After you have created the tables, the next step is to define relationships. To do so, click the *Database Tools* tab in the ribbon and then click the *Relationships* icon near the left-hand side of that ribbon. The *Relationships* window will open and the *Show Table* dialog box will be displayed, as shown in Figure CE5-9. Double-click both table names and both tables will be added to the *Relationships* window. Close the *Show Table* dialog box.

To create the relationship between these two tables, click on the attribute *ProspectID* in PROSPECT and drag that attribute on top of the *ProspectID* in WORK. (It is important to drag *ProspectID* from PROSPECT to WORK and not the reverse.) When you do this, the screen shown in Figure CE5-10 will appear.

In the dialog box, click *Enforce Referential Integrity*, click *Cascade Update Related Fields*, and then click *Cascade Delete Related Records.* The specifics of these actions are beyond the scope of our discussion. Just understand that clicking these options will cause Access to make sure that ProspectID values in WORK also exist in PROSPECT. The completed relationship is shown in Figure CE5-11. The notation *1 . . . ∞* at the end of the relationship line means that one row of PROSPECT can be related to an unlimited number (*N*) of rows in WORK. Close the *Relationships* window and save the changes when requested to do so. You now have a database with two tables and a relationship.

The next step is to enter data. To enter data, double-click the table name in the *All Tables* pane. The table will appear, and you can enter values into each cell. You cannot and need not enter values for the *ProspectID* field. Access will create those values for you.

Enter the data in Figure CE5-2 for both PROSPECT and WORK, and you will see a display like that in Figures CE5-12a and CE5-12b (page 412). Examine the lower left-hand corner of Figure CE5-12b. The text *Total donations obtained during the hour* is the Description that

Figure CE5-9
The Show Table Dialog Box in Access
Source: Microsoft Access 2010

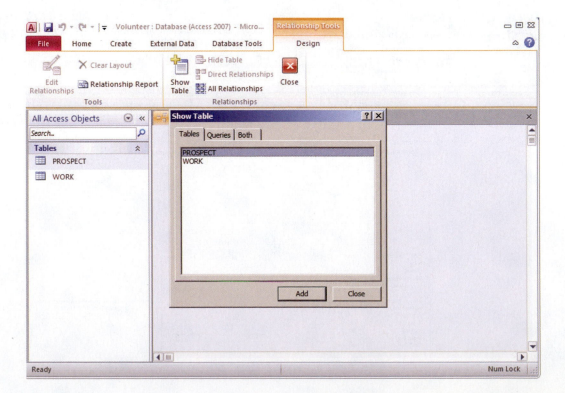

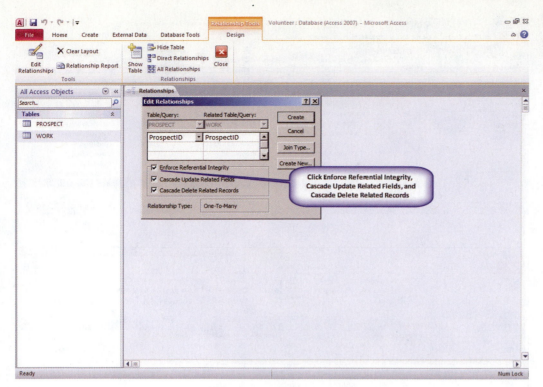

Figure CE5-10
Creating a Relationship
Between Two Tables

Source: Microsoft Access 2010

you provided when you defined the TotalDonations column when the WORK table was created. (You can see this in the TotalDonations column in Figure CE5-8.) Access displays this text because the focus is on the TotalDonations column in the active table window (WORK). Move your cursor from field to field and watch this text change.

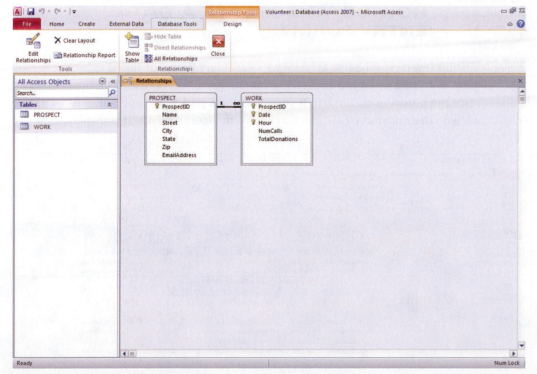

Figure CE5-11
Completed Relationship
Between PROSPECT and
WORK Tables

Source: Microsoft Access 2010

Figure CE5-12a
Tables with Data Entered
for PROSPECT

Source: Microsoft Access 2010

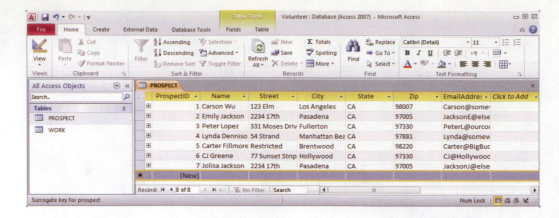

Figure CE5-12b
Tables with Data Entered
for WORK

Source: Microsoft Access 2010

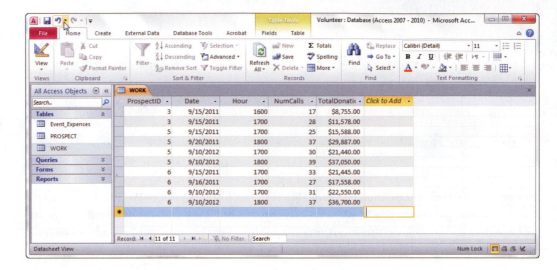

Q3 HOW DO YOU CREATE A DATA ENTRY FORM?

Access provides several alternatives for creating a data entry form. The first is to use the default table display, as you did when you entered the data shown in Figure CE5-12. In the PROSPECT table, notice the plus sign on the left. If you click those plus signs, you will see the PROSPECT rows with their related WORK rows, as shown in Figure CE5-13. This display, although

Figure CE5-13
Default Table Display

Source: Microsoft Access 2010

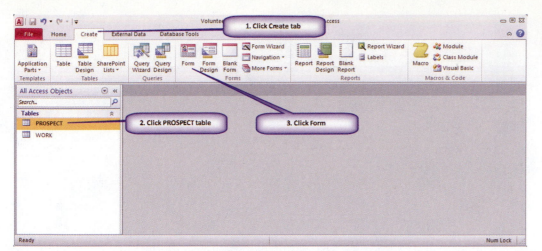

Figure CE5-14
Starting the Form Generator
Source: Microsoft Access 2010

convenient, is limited in its capability. It also does not provide a very pleasing user interface. For more generality and better design, you can use the Access form generator.

Access can generate a data entry form that is more pleasing to view and easier to use than that in Figure CE5-13. The process is shown in Figure CE5-14. First, click the *Create tab* to open the *Create ribbon.* Next, click the PROSPECT table (this causes Access to create a form for PROS-PECT). Finally, click *Form.* Access uses metadata about the tables and their relationship to create the data entry form in Figure CE5-15.

You can use this form to modify data; just type over any data that you wish to change. You can also add data. To add work data, just click in the last row of the work grid; in this case that would be the third row of this grid. To delete a record, click the *Home* tab, and then in the *Records* section click the down arrow next to *Delete* and select *Delete Record.* This action will delete the prospect data and all related work data (not shown in Figure CE5-15).

This form is fine, but we can make it better. For one, ProspectID is a surrogate key and has no meaning to the user. Access uses that key to keep track of each PROSPECT row. Because it has no meaning to the user (in fact, the user cannot change or otherwise modify its value), we should remove it from the form. Also, we might like to reduce the size of the fields as well as reduce the size of the work area and center it on the form. Figure CE5-16 shows the form after these changes. It is smaller and cleaner, and it will be easier to use.

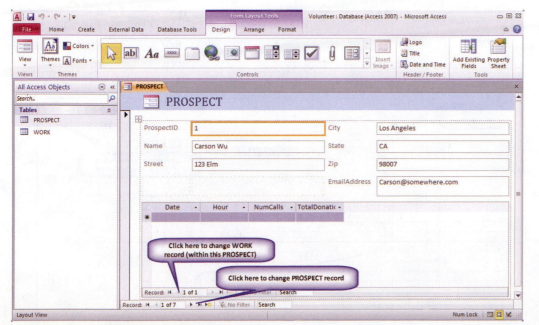

Figure CE5-15
Resulting Data Entry Form
Source: Microsoft Access 2010

Figure CE5-16
Reformatted Data Entry Form

Source: Microsoft Access 2010

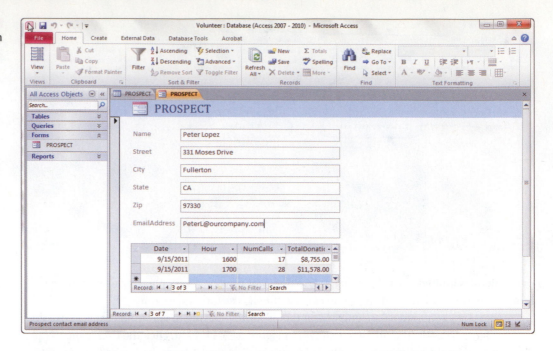

The data about a prospect is shown in the top portion of this form, and data about that person's work sessions is shown in the bottom portion. The user of this form has clicked the arrow at the bottom of the form to bring up the third Prospect record, the one for Peter Lopez. Notice that he has two work sessions. If you click the arrow in the next-to-last row of this form, you will change the focus of the work record. To make the changes shown, see the steps illustrated in Figure CE5-17. First, click the *View* button in the ribbon and then select *Design View.* The form will open in Design mode; click the right edge of the rightmost rectangle and, holding your mouse down, drag to the left. Access will reduce the width of each of these fields.

Third, to resize the work subform, click within the area labeled *Table.WORK.* Next, click that table area's right edge and drag to the left. Access will reduce the size of this subform. Lift up on your mouse and then click again and you can move the area to center it under the PROSPECT fields.

Figure CE5-17
Process for Reformatting
Data Entry Form

Source: Microsoft Access 2010

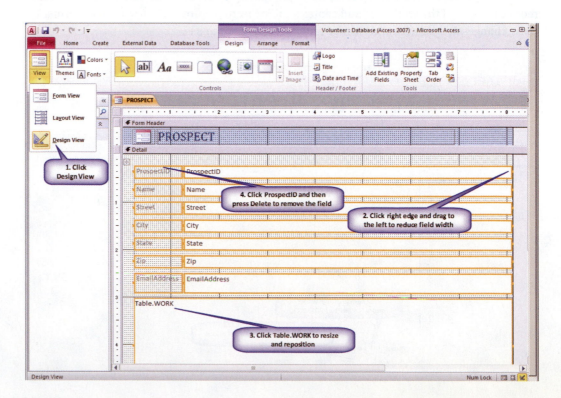

Finally, click *ProspectID*, as shown in step 4. Press the *Delete* key, and the ProspectID field will be removed from the form. Click *View/Form View*, and your form should look like that in Figure CE5-16. You can go back to *Design View* to make more adjustments, if necessary.

To save your form, either close it and Access will give you the chance to save it or click the *Office* button and select *Save*. Save with an informative file name, such as PROSPECT Data Entry Form.

There are many options for customizing Access forms. You can learn about them if you take a database processing class after you complete this MIS class.

HOW DO YOU CREATE QUERIES USING THE QUERY DESIGN TOOL?

Like all modern DBMS products, Access can process the SQL query language. Learning that language, however, is beyond the scope of this textbook. However, Access does provide a graphical interface that we can use to create and process queries, and that graphical interface will generate SQL statements for us.

To begin, first clean up your screen by closing the PROSPECT Data Entry Form. Click the *Create* tab in the ribbon, and in the *Queries* section click the *Query Design* button. You should see the display shown in Figure CE5-18. Double-click the names of both the PROSPECT and WORK tables, and close the *Show Table* window. Access will have placed both tables into the query design form, as shown in Figure CE5-19. Notice that Access remembers the relationship between the two tables (shown by the line connecting ProspectID in PROSPECT to the same attribute in WORK).

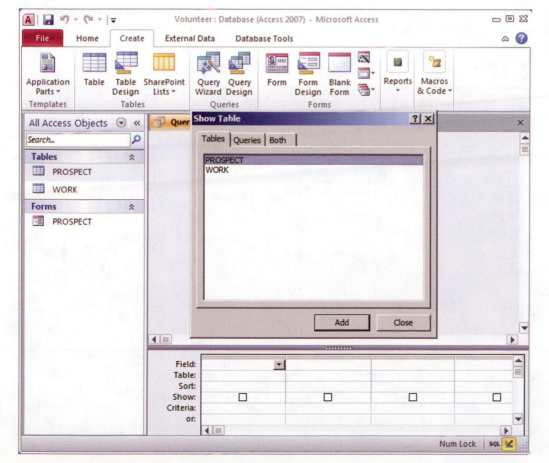

Figure CE5-18
Creating a Query, Step 1

Source: Microsoft Access 2010

Figure CE5-19
Creating a Query, Step 2

Source: Microsoft Access 2010

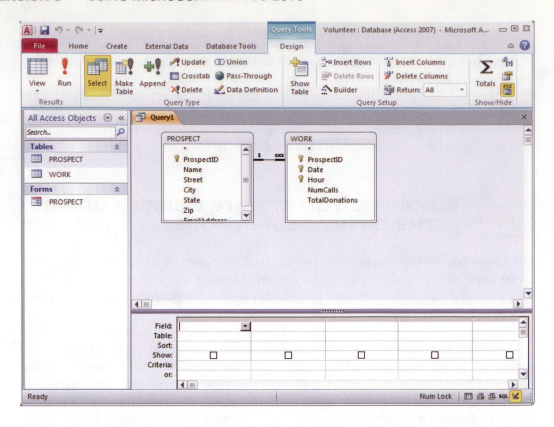

To create a query, drag columns out of the PROSPECT and WORK tables into the grid in the lower part of the query definition form. In Figure CE5-20, the *Name, EmailAddress, NumCalls,* and *TotalDonations* columns have been placed into that grid. Note, too, that the *Ascending* keyword has been selected for the *Name* column. That selection tells Access to present the data in alphabetical order by name.

Figure CE5-20
Creating a Query, Step 3

Source: Microsoft Access 2010

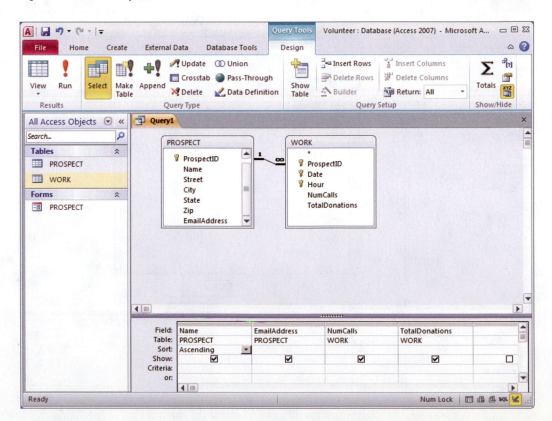

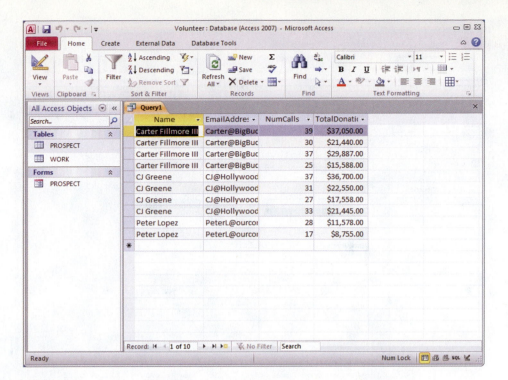

Figure CE5-21
Results of *TotalDonations* Query

Source: Microsoft Access 2010

If you now click the red exclamation point labeled *Run* in the *Results* section of the ribbon, the result shown in Figure CE5-21 will appear. Notice that only PROSPECT rows that have at least one WORK row are shown. By default, for queries of two or more tables Access (and SQL) shows only those rows that have value matches in both tables. Save the query under the name *NameAndDonationQuery*.

Queries have many useful purposes. For example, suppose we want to see the average dollar value of donation generated per hour of work. This query, which is just slightly beyond the scope of this chapter extension, can readily be created using either the Access graphical tool or SQL. The results of such a query are shown in Figure CE5-22. This query processes the *NameAndDonationQuery* query just created. Again, if you take a database class, you will learn how to create queries like this and others of even greater complexity (and utility).

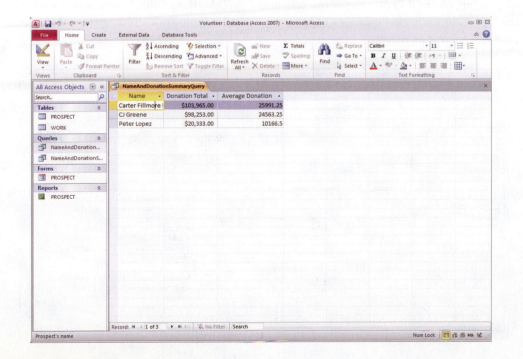

Figure CE5-22
Result of More Advanced Query

Source: Microsoft Access 2010

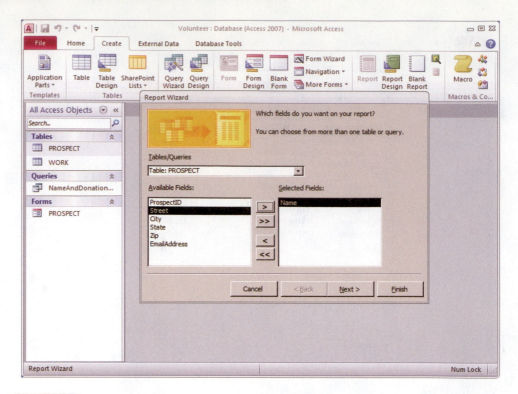

HOW DO YOU CREATE A REPORT?

You can create a report using a process similar to that for forms, but the report won't include the WORK data. To create a report with data from two or more tables, we must use the Report Wizard. Click the *Create* tab, and then in the Reports section click *Report Wizard*.

Now, click *Table:PROSPECT* in the *Table/Queries* combo box, highlight *Name* in the *Available Fields* list, and click the single chevron (>) to add Name to the report. You will see the display shown in Figure CE5-23.

Using a similar process, add *EmailAddress*. Then select *Table:WORK* in the *Table/Queries* combo box and add *Date, Hour, NumCalls*, and *TotalDonations*. Click *Finish*, and you will see the report shown in Figure CE5-24. (By the way, we are skipping numerous options that Access provides in creating reports.)

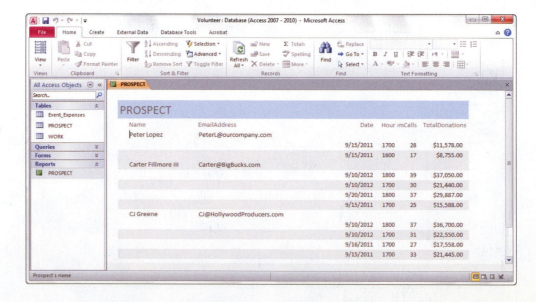

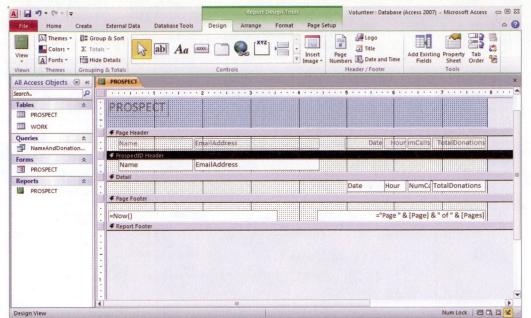

Figure CE5-25
Report Design View

Source: Microsoft Access 2010

We will consider just one of those options now. Suppose we want to show the total donations that a prospect has obtained, for all hours of his or her work. To do that, first click *Close Print Preview* in the right-hand corner of the ribbon. Your report will appear as shown in Figure CE5-25. (If it does not appear like this, click *View, Design View* in the ribbon.)

In the ribbon, click *Group and Sort* in the *Grouping & Totals* section. In the bottom of the form, click *More,* and then click the down arrow next to the phrase *with no totals.* Next, select *TotalDonations* from the *TotalOn* box, and then check *Show Grand Total* and *Show subtotal in group footer,* as illustrated in Figure CE5-26.

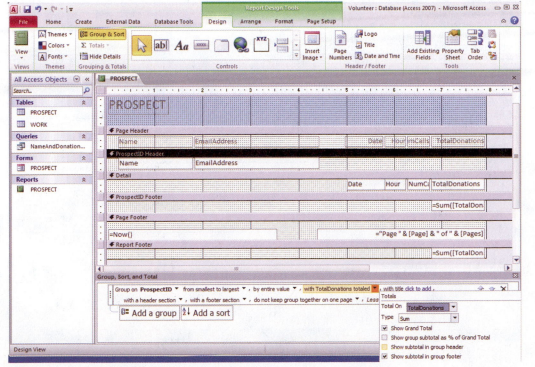

Figure CE5-26
Creating a Sum of *TotalDonations* for Each Prospect

Source: Microsoft Access 2010

Figure CE5-27
Report with Sum of
TotalDonations

Source: Microsoft Access 2010

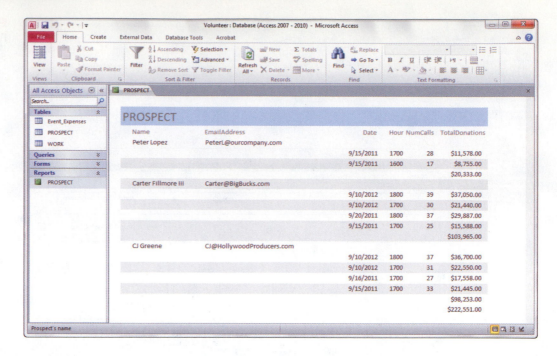

Click the *Report* icon in the *View* section of the ribbon, and you will see the report shown in Figure CE5-27. The only remaining problem is that the label NumCalls is cut off. We need to expand the box that contains this value. To do so, select *Layout View* from *View* in the ribbon, click *Date,* and then slide it slightly to the left. Do the same with Hour. Then expand NumCalls until you can see all of the label, as shown in Figure CE5-28. Click *Report View* in *View*, and your report should appear as shown in Figure CE5-29.

Figure CE5-28
Increasing the Size of the
NumCalls Field

Source: Microsoft Access 2010

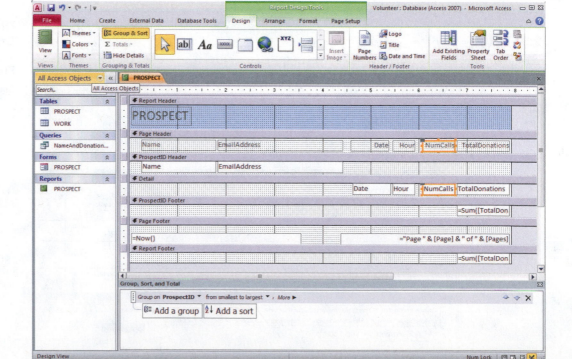

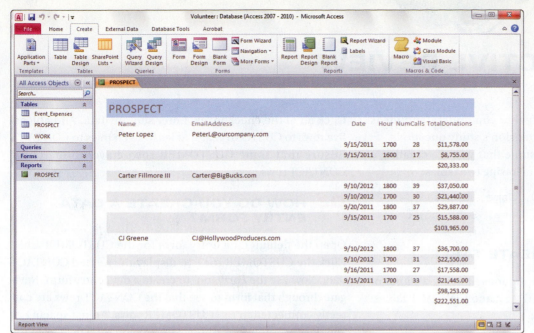

Figure CE5-29
Final Version of Report

Source: Microsoft Access 2010

ACTIVE REVIEW

Use this Active Review to verify that you understand ideas and concepts in this chapter extension's study questions.

For this Active Review, assume that you are creating a database application having the following two tables:

CUSTOMER (<u>CustomerID</u>, Name, Email)
CONTACT (<u>CustomerID</u>, <u>Date</u>, Subject)

Q1 HOW DO YOU CREATE TABLES?

Open Access and create a new database having a name of your choosing. Create the CUSTOMER and CONTACT tables. Assume the following data types:

Attribute (Field)	Data Type
CustomerID (in CUSTOMER)	AutoNumber
Name	Text (50)
Email	Text (75)
CustomerID (in CONTACT)	Number (long integer)
Date	Date
Subject	Text (200)

Add Description entries to the Field definitions that you think are appropriate.

Q2 HOW DO YOU CREATE RELATIONSHIPS?

Open the *Relationships* window and create a relationship from CUSTOMER to CONTACT using the CustomerID attribute.

Click all of the checkboxes. Enter sample data. Add at least five rows to CUSTOMER and at least seven rows to CONTACT. Ensure that some CUSTOMER rows have no matching CONTACT rows.

Q3 HOW DO YOU CREATE A DATA ENTRY FORM?

Open the default data entry form for the CUSTOMER table. Click the CUSTOMER rows to display the related CONTACT data. Now use the *Form* tool to create a data entry form. Navigate through that form to see that the CONTACT rows are correctly connected to the CUSTOMER rows. Adjust spacing as you deem appropriate; remove the CustomerID field from the CUSTOMER section.

Q4 HOW DO YOU CREATE QUERIES USING THE QUERY DESIGN TOOL?

Create a query that displays Name, Email, Date, and Subject. Sort the results of Name in alphabetical order.

Q5 HOW DO YOU CREATE A REPORT?

Use the Report Wizard to create a report that has Name, Email, Date, and Subject. View that report. Add a group total for each CUSTOMER that counts the number of contacts for each customer. Follow the procedure shown, except instead of selecting Sum for Type choose *Count Records* instead.

USING YOUR KNOWLEDGE

1. Answer question 2 at the end of Chapter Extension 4 (page 403). Use Access to implement your database design. Create the tables and add sample data. Create a data entry form that shows teams and the equipment they have checked out. Verify that the form correctly processes new checkouts, changes to checkouts, and equipment returns. Create a report that shows each team, the items they have checked out, and the number of items they have checked out. (Use *Count Records* as explained in Active Review Q5.)

2. Answer question 3 at the end of Chapter Extension 4 (page 403). Create an Access database for the CUSTOMER and RENTAL tables only. Create the tables and add sample data. Create a data entry form that shows customers and all of their rentals (assume customers rent bicycles more than once). Verify that the form correctly processes new rentals, changes to rentals, and rental returns. Create a report that shows each customer, the rentals they have made, and the total rental fee for all of their rentals.

Chapter 5 provides the background for this Extension.

Using Excel and Access Together

Excel and Access are two different products with two different purposes. In this chapter extension, you will learn how to use them together to analyze data in ways that neither can do alone. You will also learn how to create graphs in Excel and group totals in Access queries.

WHY USE EXCEL AND ACCESS TOGETHER?

As you learned in Chapter Extension 3, Excel is superb at processing interrelated formulas. Because of this strength, business users often select Excel for processing financial statements, creating budgets, and performing financial analyses. As you will learn in this chapter extension, you can use Excel to create sophisticated and stylish graphics with very little work on your part. (Excel has a lot of work to do, though!)

Access is a DBMS, and as you learned in Chapter 5 the primary purpose of a DBMS is to keep track of things. Access is superior for tracking orders, inventory, equipment, people, and so forth. As you learned in Chapter Extension 5, you can readily create data entry forms, queries, and sophisticated and professional reports with Access. In this chapter extension, you will learn how to create more sophisticated queries.

But, what if you want to use Excel to process data stored in Access? What if you want, for example, to create graphs of Access data? Or what if you want to include Access data in a financial analysis? You could rekey all of the Access data into Excel, but that process is not only labor-intensive (and therefore expensive), but also error-prone. Similarly, what if you want to use Access to summarize Excel data and produce sophisticated reports? Again, you could rekey the data into Access, but with the same disadvantages.

In both cases, a better approach than rekeying is to import or export the data to or from Excel or Access. We begin with a discussion of import/export in the next question.

WHAT IS IMPORT/EXPORT?

Import/export is the process of transferring data from one computer system to another. We can say that system A imports data from system B or, equivalently, that system B exports data to system A.

In almost all cases, including Excel and Access, import/export does not maintain an active connection to the source of the data. For example, when you import Access data into Excel, the data are current at the time of the import. If users subsequently change the Access data, the

STUDY QUESTIONS

Q1 WHY USE EXCEL AND ACCESS TOGETHER?

Q2 WHAT IS IMPORT/EXPORT?

Q3 HOW CAN YOU CREATE CHARTS WITH EXCEL?

Q4 HOW CAN YOU CREATE GROUP TOTALS IN ACCESS?

Q5 HOW CAN YOU USE EXCEL TO GRAPH ACCESS DATA?

Q6 HOW CAN YOU USE ACCESS TO REPORT EXCEL DATA?

Q7 HOW CAN YOU COMBINE EXCEL AND ACCESS TO ANALYZE DATA?

Figure CE6-1

Example of Data Exported from University Enrollment System

Source: Microsoft Access 2010

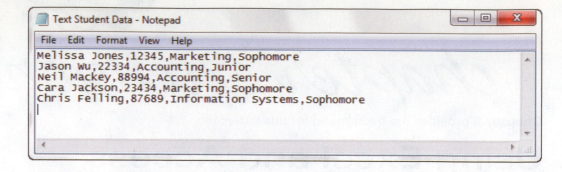

imported data in Excel will be out-of-date until you re-import it. Because imported data can become out-of-date, you should develop procedures (either manual or automated) to ensure that data are refreshed on a timely basis.

IMPORT/EXPORT OF TEXT DATA

A common way for systems to exchange data is to create files of text. One system will export text data, and another will import it. Consider, for example, a professor who wants to track students' in-class comments using Microsoft Access. Most university enrollment systems can export class enrollment data into text files. Figure CE6-1 shows a typical export.

This file contains students' names, numbers, majors, and grade levels. Notice that the field values are separated by commas. Accordingly, such a file is called a **comma-delimited file**. Sometimes, however, the data itself contains commas, and so commas cannot be used to separate field data. In that case, some other character is used to delimit the fields. The tab character is frequently used, in which case the export file is called a **tab-delimited file**.

Delimited text files are easy to import into either Excel or Access. In Access, just create (or open a database) and click the *External Data* tab, as shown in Figure CE6-2. Next, as shown in Figure CE6-3, select the file that contains the data, and check *Import the source data into a new table in the current database,* (Ignore the other option, it's not very useful and is beyond the scope of our discussion.) When you click *OK*, a multiple-panel wizard opens.

Figure CE6-2

External Data Menu Choice

Source: Microsoft Access 2010

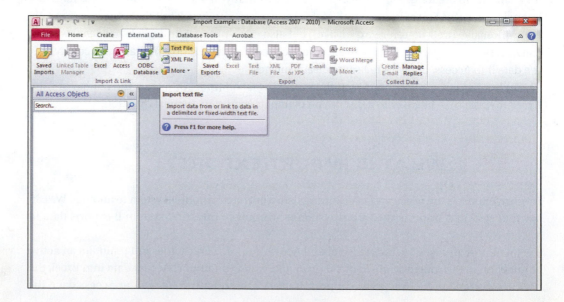

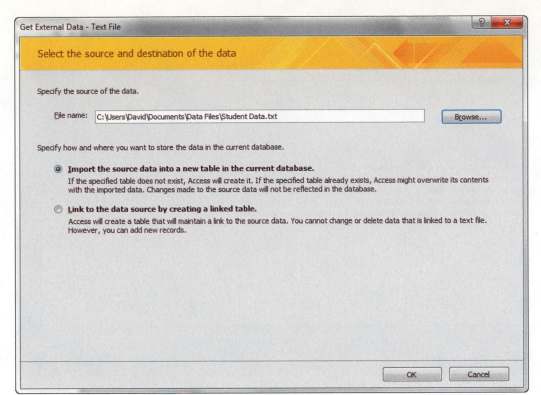

Figure CE6-3
Specifying the Source File
and Destination

Source: Microsoft Access 2010

In Figure CE6-4a, you specify that your file is delimited. To assist you, Access shows the first rows of the file. Click *Next* to specify the delimiter; here we are using the comma, as shown in Figure CE6-4b. Click *Next* again and you will be given a chance to name the fields as well as to specify their data type. Ignore Indexed. In Figure CE6-4c, we have renamed the first three columns and are about to rename the fourth. In the next screen (not shown), you have

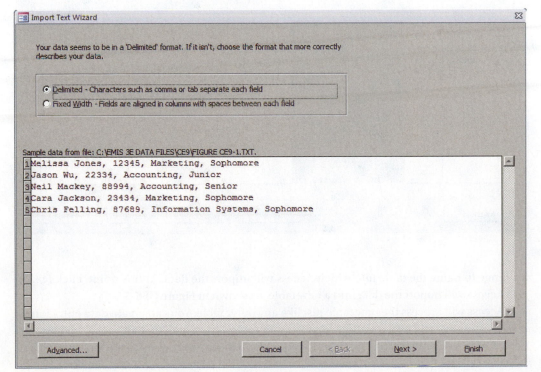

Figure CE6-4a
Importing Text Data into
Access: Specifying a
Delimited File

Source: Microsoft Access 2010

Figure CE6-4b

Importing Text Data into Access: Specifying a Comma-Delimited File

Source: Microsoft Access 2010

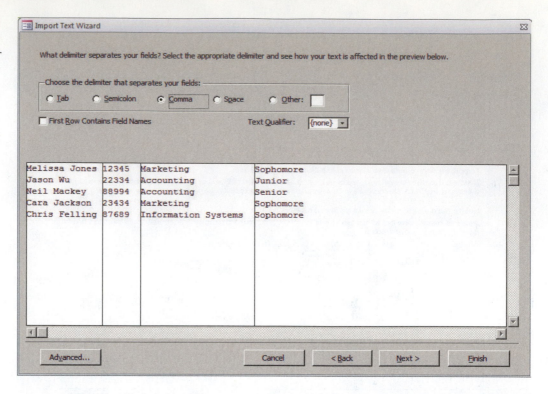

Figure CE6-4c

Importing Text Data into Access: Naming and Describing Columns During Import

Source: Microsoft Access 2010

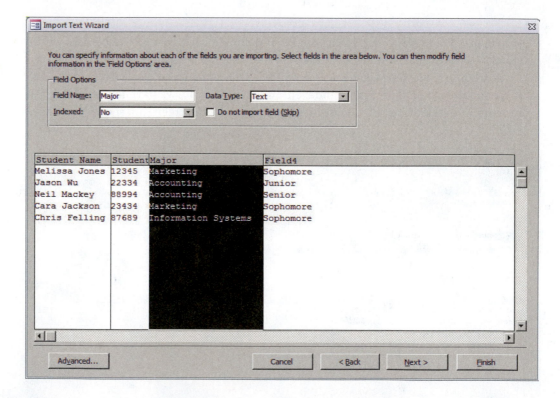

a chance to name the table into which Access will import the data. At this point, click *Finish*, and Access will import the data into a new table, as shown in Figure CE6-5.

Access will process the new table just like any other table. You can create data entry forms, reports, queries, and even relationships to other tables. Note, too, that although we have imported only five rows in this example, it would be no more work for us to import 50, 5,000, or 50,000 rows.

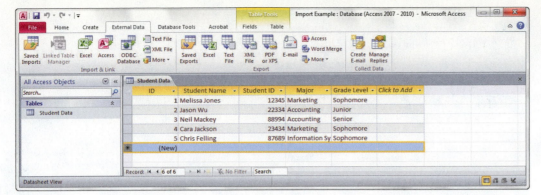

Figure CE6-5
Data After Import
Source: Microsoft Access 2010

You can follow an almost identical process to import data into Excel. (Memo to Microsoft: Why isn't it *exactly* the same process?) Open Excel, click the *Data* tab, and in the *Get External Data* section of that ribbon click *From Text*. You will need to specify a comma delimiter and indicate where in the worksheet you want the data placed. This process is easy, as you will see when you do question 1 of Using Your Knowledge at the end of this extension.

IMPORT/EXPORT OF EXCEL AND ACCESS DATA

One way you could exchange data between Excel and Access would be to export the data into a text file and then import that text data. However, because many users want to transfer data between Excel and Access, Microsoft has created special tools for that purpose. You can use Access to both export and import data. You can use Excel to import data from Access. You will see examples of the use of the specialized import/export tools in sections Q5 and Q6. Before we turn to these tools, we will first consider additional features of Excel and Access.

 HOW CAN YOU CREATE CHARTS WITH EXCEL?

Microsoft Excel includes comprehensive tools for graphing data. You can use it to construct column and bar charts, pie charts, line and scatter plots, and other graphs. Here you will learn how to construct pie and column charts. Follow the discussion in this section to learn the gist of the process, and then learn more by experimenting with Excel. You can make custom charts quite easily; like the rest of Office 2010, however, it's a matter of finding the ribbon that has the tool you want.

In this section, we will construct charts for donations obtained by three volunteers. We won't import this data from Access yet, but instead will assume that the names and donations values have been keyed in by hand.

CREATING A PIE CHART

Figure CE6-6 shows a pie chart of Total Donations for three volunteers. This chart, which is very easy to create, is one example of the kind of graph that Excel can produce. To create this pie chart, we highlight cells D4 through E7, click the *Insert* tab in the ribbon, and in the *Charts* section of that ribbon select the *Pie* icon (shown in Figure CE6-7). As you can see, Excel can create several different versions of pie charts; here, we have selected the first choice.

Figure CE6-6
Pie Chart

Source: Microsoft Access 2010

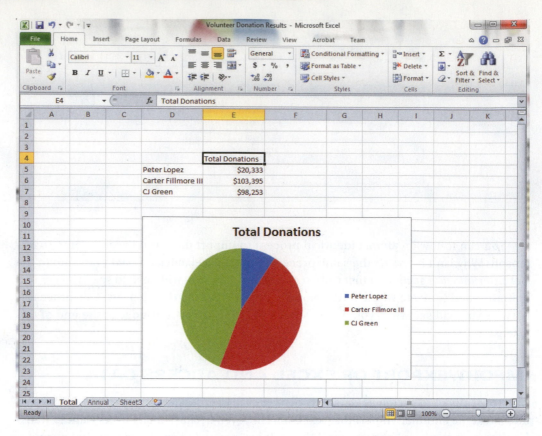

Figure CE6-7
Creating the Pie Chart

Source: Microsoft Access 2010

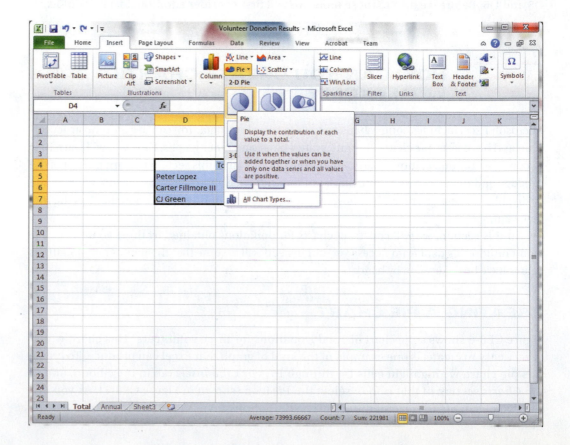

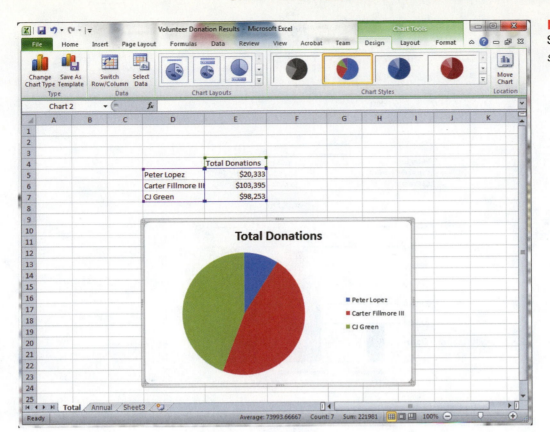

Figure CE6-8
Selecting the Chart Tools
Source: Microsoft Access 2010

Excel provides many different tools to customize a graph. To access them, click the graph you want to change. Excel will show a special tab called *Chart Tools* at the top of the window. Click *Chart Tools* to make them available, as shown in Figure CE6-8. The discussion of these tools is beyond the scope of this chapter extension. But, they are intuitive, and you can learn much about their use by experimenting with them.

CREATING A COLUMN CHART

The pie chart in Figure CE6-6 shows only the total data for each volunteer. If we want to compare results for two years, we can do so with a column or bar chart. Figure CE6-9 shows a column chart.

To create the column chart, we highlighted the data and selected *Column* in the *Charts* section of the *Insert* tab, as shown in Figure CE6-10. With one exception, Excel created the chart shown in Figure CE6-9 with no further work on our part.

The exception concerns the title. Notice that the data on which the graph is based do not include any text that would make a suitable title. Hence, when Excel first produced the graph shown in Figure CE6-9, the graph had no title. To insert a title, we click the column chart, select *Chart Tools*, click the *Layout* tab, click *Chart Title*, and select *Center Overlay Title*. Excel has placed a textbox for the title on the graph, and we enter *Total Donations by Year* into that textbox, as shown in Figure CE6-11 (page 431).

As you can imagine, Excel has many, many options for creating interesting and informative graphs. As stated, one good way to learn more is to create some data and experiment. You can also find many resources for learning Excel on the Web.

Figure CE6-9
Sample Column Chart

Source: Microsoft Access 2010

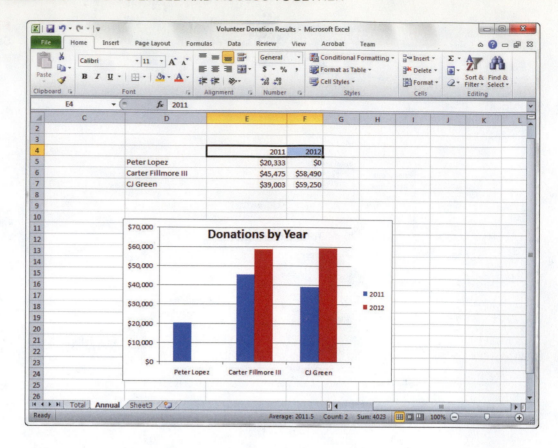

Figure CE6-10
Creating the Column Chart

Source: Microsoft Access 2010

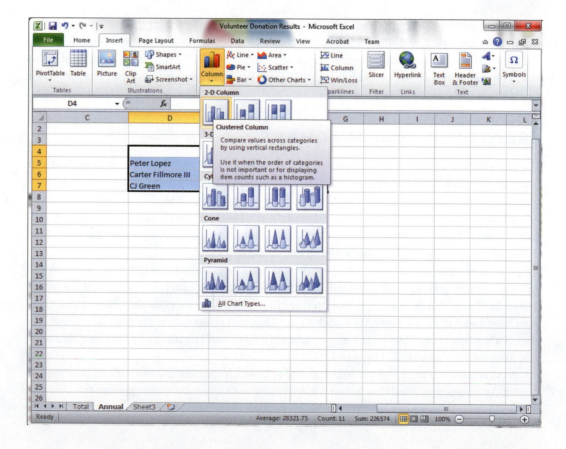

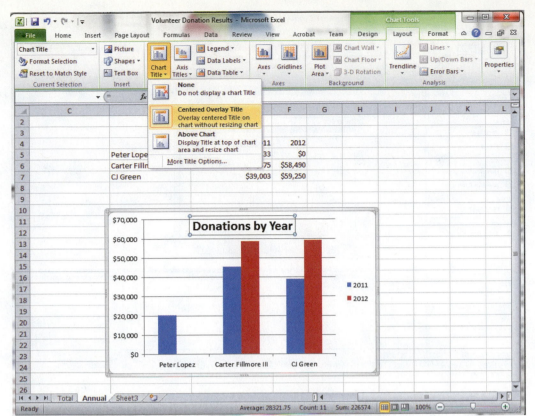

Figure CE6-11
Creating the Chart Title
Source: Microsoft Access 2010

HOW CAN YOU CREATE GROUP TOTALS IN ACCESS?

In Chapter Extension 5, you learned how to create basic queries in Access. With more advanced queries, you can create considerably more information from the same amount of data. To learn some of the possibilities, consider the Volunteer database that we created in Chapter Extension 5.

Suppose a manager of the station wants to know the total of TotalDonations[1] for each date of fundraising effort. Maybe she thinks that certain dates are more advantageous than others. To create this information, we can query the WORK table, group all donations for a given date, and then sum the TotalDonations for each group.

To do that, we need to open the Volunteer database, click the *Create* tab, click *Query Design*, and then, as shown in Figure CE6-12, select the WORK table for the query. After adding that table, click *Close*.[2]

Now, to add Date and TotalDonations to the query output, double-click *Date* and *TotalDonations* in the WORK table diagram. Access adds them to the query contents table at the bottom of the query, as shown in Figure CE6-13. To group the WORK rows according to date, we click the *Totals* button in the *Show/Hide* section of the *Design* tab. When we do this, Access adds a row labeled *Total* to the query contents table, as shown in Figure CE6-14.

---

[1]The terminology may be confusing. The value in TotalDonations is the total of all donations received by a particular volunteer in a particular hour on a particular date. Here, the manager wants to know the total of all donations for all volunteers for all hours on a given date.

[2]Midway during the Office 2010 release cycle, Microsoft changed the banner at the top of Access windows. The banner in early versions read (Access 2007). Later versions read (Access 2007-2010). Depending on which Access release you have, you will see one title version or the other, and for all practical purposes, this difference is unimportant. We will show both title versions in this extension.

Figure CE6-12
Selecting the WORK Table for
the Query
Source: Microsoft Access 2010

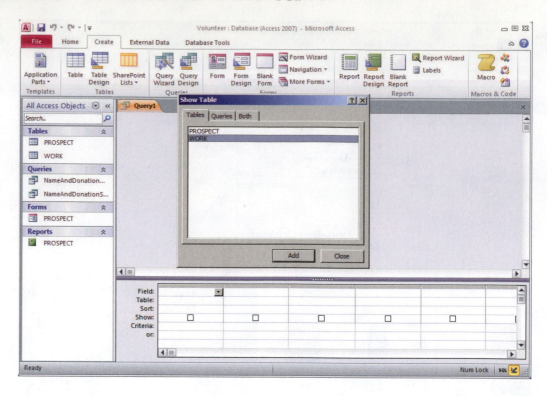

To group the rows by date, we need to select the keyword *Group By* in the Total row under *Date*. To sum TotalDonations for each group, we need to select the keyword *Sum* under the TotalDonations column, in that same Total row. Figure CE6-14 shows this last action.

We run the query by clicking the large exclamation point in the *Results* section of the *Design* ribbon, and the results shown in Figure CE6-15 are generated. Access has summed TotalDonations for each Date. We save this query using the name *EventDateTotals*.

Figure CE6-13
Adding Data and
TotalDonations to the Query
Source: Microsoft Access 2010

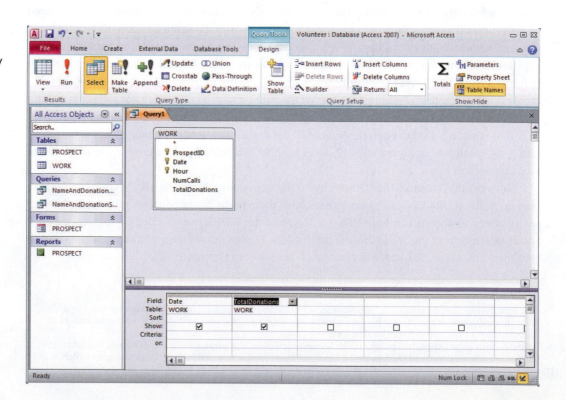

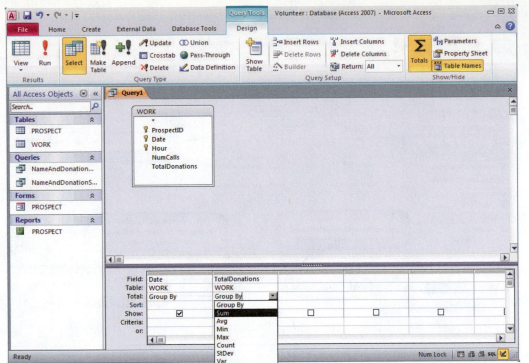

Figure CE6-14
Selecting Sum in the Total Row for TotalDonations

Source: Microsoft Access 2010

Suppose we want to perform another, similar query, but for a more complicated example. Say we want to show the name of each volunteer (called PROSPECT in this database), the total number of hours each has worked, and the total donations obtained. Recall that each row of WORK details the results from one hour's activity. Therefore, we can compute the total number of hours a prospect worked by counting the number of rows for that prospect's ID.

The process is summarized in Figure CE6-16. To begin, we open *Query Design* and add both the PROSPECT and WORK tables. Now, we just need to complete the following seven steps:

1. In the PROSPECT table, double-click *Name* to insert it into the query results.
2. In the WORK table, double-click *ProspectID* and *TotalDonations* to insert them into the query.

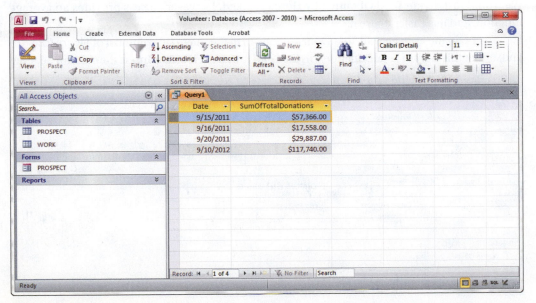

Figure CE6-15
Results of Query with Group by Date

Source: Microsoft Access 2010

Figure CE6-16
Process for Creating a Query
to Compute Total Hours and
Donations for Each Prospect

Source: Microsoft Access 2010

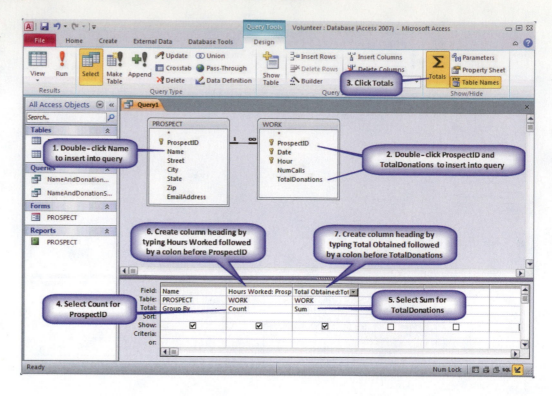

Figure CE6-16
Process for Creating a Query
to Compute Total Hours and
Donations for Each Prospect

Source: Microsoft Access 2010

3. In the ribbon, click the *Totals* icon to cause Access to insert the Total row into the query contents table.

4. In the *Total* row under ProspectID, select *Count.* This informs Access to count the number of times each value of ProspectID occurred in the table.

5. In the *Total* row under TotalDonations, select *Sum.*

6. Create a column heading for the ProspectID column by typing the heading *Hours Worked,* followed by a colon in front of ProspectID.

7. Create a column heading for the TotalDonations column by typing the heading *Total Obtained,* followed by a colon in front of TotalDonations.

Running the query produces the results shown in Figure CE6-17.

We could use this query to compute the average donation total per hour for each worker. We would just divide Total Obtained by Hours Worked. However, Access provides an average function, and it is easier to use it.

To obtain the average, add TotalDonations again to the query (in column 4 of Figure CE6-18) and, under this copy of TotalDonations, in the *Total* row, we select *Avg.* Insert the column heading

Figure CE6-17
Results of the Query in
Figure CE6-16

Source: Microsoft Access 2010

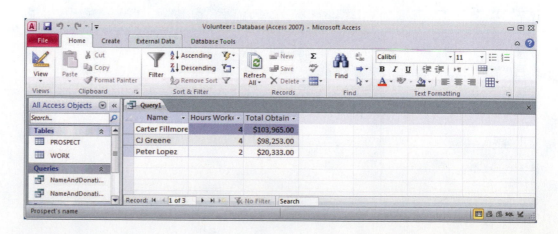

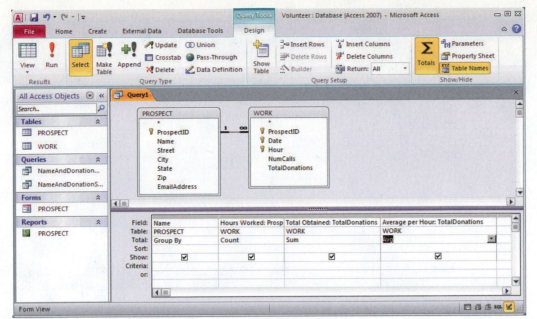

Figure CE6-18
Adding Average Donations
per Hour
Source: Microsoft Access 2010

Average per Hour. Running this query generates the results in Figure CE6-19. Use a calculator to verify the averages are what you would expect. Save this query using the name *AvgDonationQuery.*

Again, to learn more about queries and Access create a table, enter some data, and experiment!

 HOW CAN YOU USE EXCEL TO GRAPH ACCESS DATA?

We can produce interesting data presentations by combining the results of the discussions in the last two sections. In particular, we can import the Access query created in Q4 into Excel and then use Excel's graphing capability to display the results.

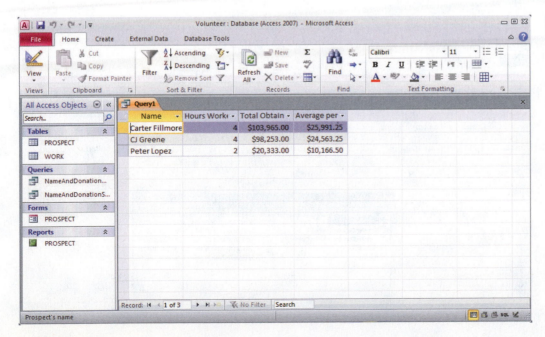

Figure CE6-19
Results of the Query
in Figure CE6-17
Source: Microsoft Access 2010

Figure CE6-20
Menu to Import Data from
Access into Excel

Source: Microsoft Access 2010

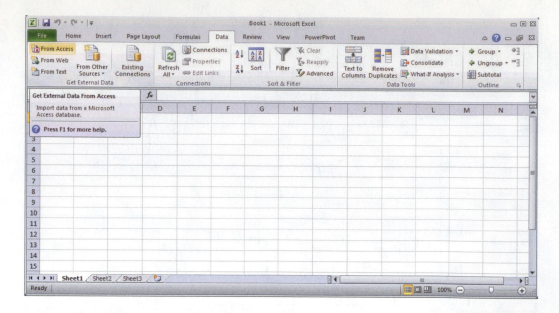

To import data into Excel, open Excel, click the *Data* tab in the ribbon and then, in the *Get External Data* section, select *From Access*, as shown in Figure CE6-20. After you select the Volunteer database (not shown), Excel will query Access to determine the tables and queries that exist in that database. Excel will display the results, as shown in Figure CE6-21. Select *AvgDonationQuery* and click *OK*.

Next, Excel will ask how you want the data displayed. Choose *Table* and *Existing worksheet*, and enter an absolute address for the top, left-hand corner of the table. In Figure CE6-22, cell C3 (*C3*) was chosen. Click *OK*.

Excel will cause Access to run this query and will place the results into the worksheet in the location you specified. The results are shown in Figure CE6-23. Notice that Excel does not format the currency values as currency. To overcome this deficiency, highlight the cells containing the currency amounts and click *Currency* in the *Number* section of the *Home* ribbon. Next, click the *small arrow* in the bottom-right corner of the *Number* section, and select *zero decimal points*. The spreadsheet will appear as in Figure CE6-24.

Figure CE6-21
Selecting the Query to Import

Source: Microsoft Access 2010

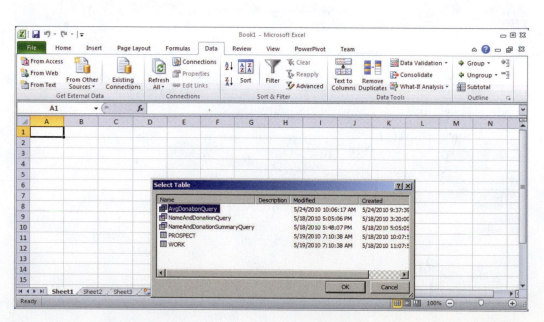

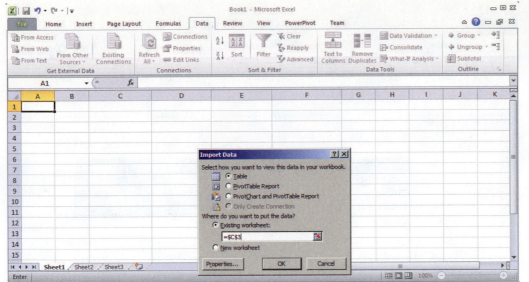

Figure CE6-22

Placing the Imported Data in the Spreadsheet

Source: Microsoft Access 2010

To create the bar chart, follow the procedure explained in the discussion of Q3. To simplify the chart, delete the Hours Worked column. To do so, right-click the *D* in the Hours Worked column heading and then select Delete.

Now, to make the chart, highlight cells C3 through E6, click the *Insert* tab, and select *bar chart.* Next, to insert a title, click *Chart Tools, Layout, Chart Title,* and then *Centered Overlay Title.* Then type the chart's title. In Figure CE6-25, we entered Donations Collected by Volunteer as the title and reduced the font size (in the Home ribbon) to 14.

Reflect a moment on what we have done. We used Access to keep track of volunteers and their received donations and to query and group data, all tasks for which Access is ideally suited. However, we then imported that data into Excel and used Excel's easy graphing capability to create the bar chart. Cool!

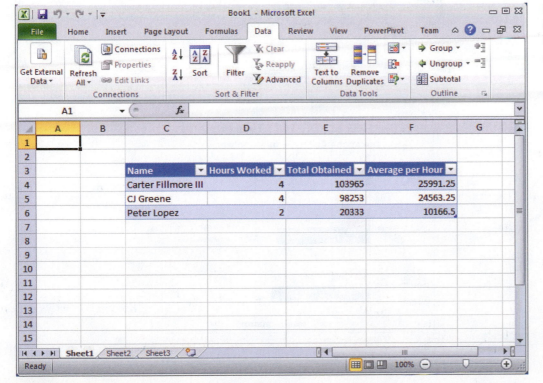

Figure CE6-23

Spreadsheet with Imported Data

Source: Microsoft Access 2010

Figure CE6-24
Formatted Imported Data

Source: Microsoft Access 2010

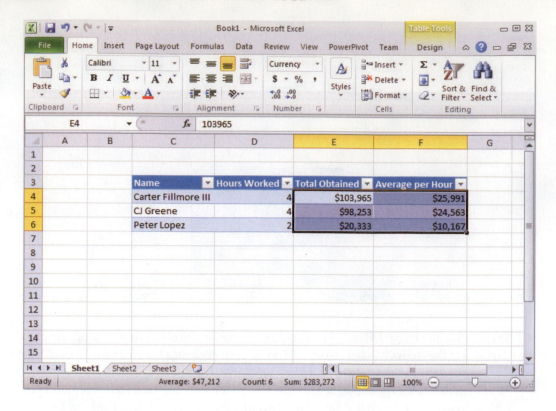

Figure CE6-25
A Bar Chart of the
Imported Data

Source: Microsoft Access 2010

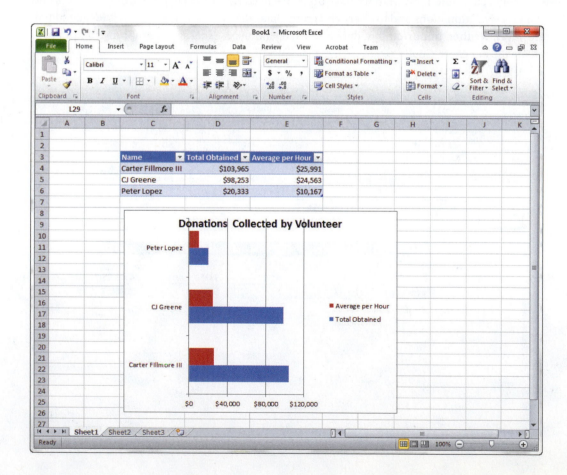

Q6   HOW CAN YOU USE ACCESS TO REPORT EXCEL DATA?

In Chapter Extension 5, you learned how easy it is to create professional-looking reports in Access. You can sort, group, and format data to present the data in context, creating information. But what if your data doesn't reside in Access? What if it is stored in an Excel worksheet, instead?

You learned in Q2 how to import text data into Access. Here, you will learn how to use a similar process to import data from Excel.

Consider the event expense data in the Excel worksheet in Figure CE6-26. Suppose that you want to produce two different reports from this data. In one, you want to group all expenses for a given expense category and produce an expense total for that category. In the second, you want to group all the expenses for particular dates and produce an expense total for each date. You can do both of these by importing this Excel data into Access and using the Access report generator.

To begin, you need to identify the data that you want to transfer. An easy way to do this is to create a **named range**, which is a subset of the cells in a worksheet that has a unique name. To create a named range for the expense data, first highlight all of the data (including the column headings) and then click the *Formulas* tab. In the *Defined Names* section, click *Define Name* and then enter a suitable name. In Figure CE6-27, we use the name *Event_Expenses*. (Range names cannot contain any spaces, so the underscore character is used to connect the words *Event* and *Expense*.)

To import the data into Access we will use a process similar to that for importing text data. First, close the workbook that has the data. Then, open the Access database into which you want to import the data, click the *External Data* tab, and, in the *Import* section, click

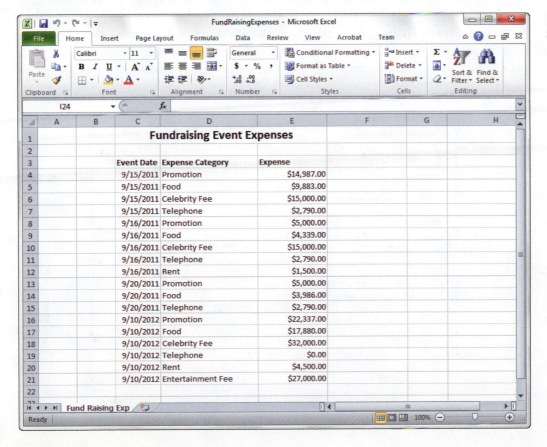

Figure CE6-26
Sample Expense Data

Source: Microsoft Access 2010

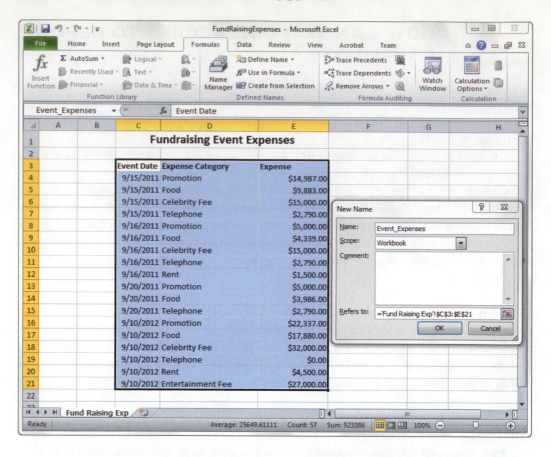

Excel. In the screen that appears, select the spreadsheet that has the data and click *Import the source data into a new table in the current database,* as shown in Figure CE6-28. Click *OK* to continue.

In the next form that appears, click *Show Name Ranges* and select the *Event_Expenses* range, as shown in Figure CE6-29a. Click *Next.* Check *First Row Contains Column Names* if it is not already checked. Your screen should look like that in Figure CE6-29b. At this point, Access

Figure CE6-28
Importing an Excel File
Source: Microsoft Access 2010

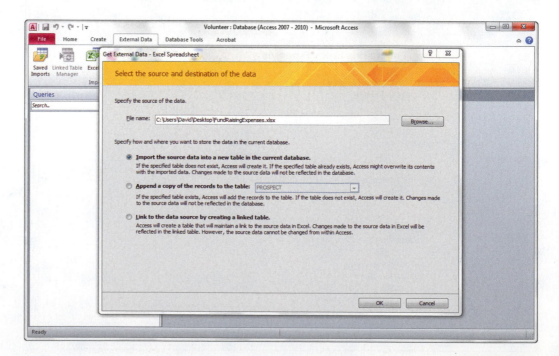

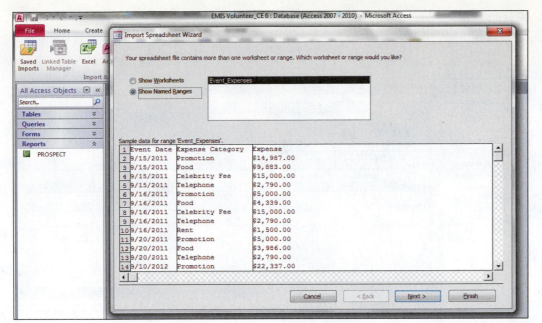

Figure CE6-29a
Importing Excel Data into
Access: Importing the Data in
the Named Range

Source: Microsoft Access 2010

has enough metadata to perform the import correctly, so you can click *Finish*. If you're curious, just click *Next* to see the default import values that Access will use. When asked if you want to save the import steps, ignore the instructions and just click *Close*.

At this point, Access has imported the data and placed it into a table named Event_Expenses. Open that table to ensure that the data has been imported as you would expect. Observe that Access added a surrogate key named ID. We will ignore this field in this example.

With the Event_Expenses table highlighted, click *Create* and, in the *Reports* section of the ribbon, click *Report*. Access creates a report that we will modify to obtain the format we want.

First, in the *View* section, click the down arrow and select *Design View*. Click in an unused part of this screen to deselect all of the columns (those outlined in a heavy yellow/brown line). Once everything has been deselected, click *ID* in the *Page Header* to give it the focus and then press *Delete*. Do the same for ID in the Detail section. The ID column will be removed from the

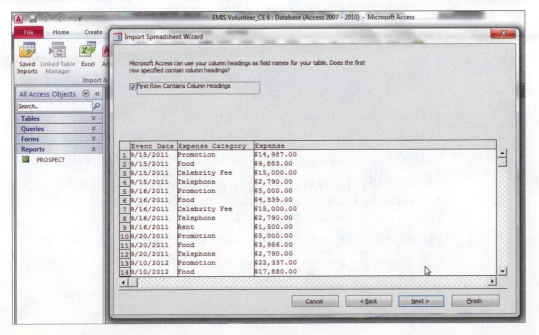

Figure CE6-29b
Importing Excel Data into
Access: Access Has Metadata
to Guide Import

Source: Microsoft Access 2010

Figure CE6-30
Grouping Report Data by
Expense Category

Source: Microsoft Access 2010

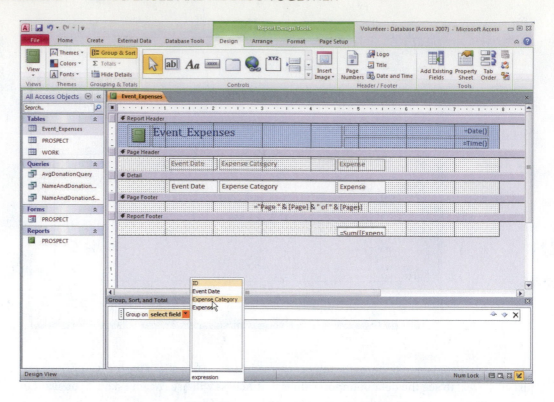

report. (If you don't deselect everything before you press delete, you will delete all of the report's contents. If you do this, just close the report without saving it and start over.)

In the *Grouping & Totals* section of the *Design* ribbon, click *Group & Sort*, if it is not already clicked. Then, at the bottom of the report design window, click *Add a group*. Then click *Expense Category*, as shown in Figure CE6-30. At the bottom of the design window, click *More* and then click *with Expense totaled*. As shown in Figure CE6-31, select *Expense* for *Total On* and click

Figure CE6-31
Creating Group Totals

Source: Microsoft Access 2010

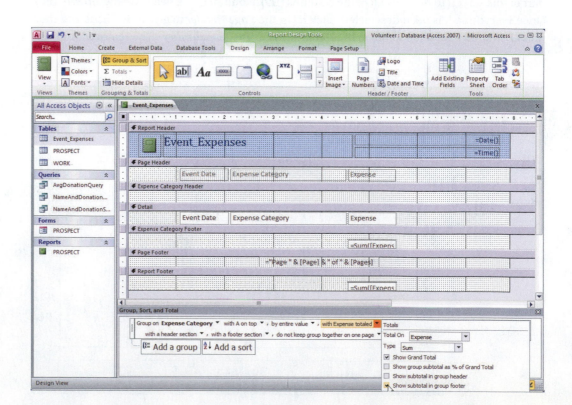

Figure CE6-32
Resulting Report
Source: Microsoft Access 2010

Event_Expenses

Friday, June 01, 2012
7:10:22 AM

Event Date	Expense Category	Expense
9/15/2011	Celebrity Fee	$15,000.00
9/10/2012	Celebrity Fee	$32,000.00
9/16/2011	Celebrity Fee	$15,000.00
		$62,000.00
9/10/2012	Entertainment Fee	$27,000.00
		$27,000.00
9/15/2011	Food	$9,883.00
9/10/2012	Food	$17,880.00
9/20/2011	Food	$3,986.00
9/16/2011	Food	$4,339.00
		$36,088.00
9/20/2011	Promotion	$5,000.00
9/10/2012	Promotion	$22,337.00
9/16/2011	Promotion	$5,000.00
9/15/2011	Promotion	$14,987.00
		$47,324.00
9/16/2011	Rent	$1,500.00
9/10/2012	Rent	$4,500.00
		$6,000.00
9/20/2011	Telephone	$2,790.00
9/15/2011	Telephone	$2,790.00
9/10/2012	Telephone	$0.00

Show Grand Total and *Show subtotal in group footer.* At this point your report is finished. In Views, click the report icon and you will see a report like that in Figure CE6-32.

You can perform a similar series of steps to create a report that is grouped by Event Date rather than Expense Category.

Q7   HOW CAN YOU COMBINE EXCEL AND ACCESS TO ANALYZE DATA?

In Q5, you learned how to use Excel to graph Access data. In this section, you will learn how to use Excel to perform calculations on data imported from Access. We will use the Event_Expense data imported from Excel in the last section.

We begin by creating a query to sum all of the expenses for a given date. As shown in Figure CE6-33, open the database with the Event_Expense data and click *Create/Query Design* in the *Queries.* Next, click *Event_Expenses* and then *Close.* Now add Event Date and Expense to the query, click *Totals* to create the Total row in the query contents grid, and select *Group By* under *Event Date* and *Sum* under *Expense.* The heading *Total Event Expense* is also shown in Figure CE6-33. Save this query with the name *EventExpenseTotals.*

Figure CE6-33
Creating a Query to Sum
Expenses by Date

Source: Microsoft Access 2010

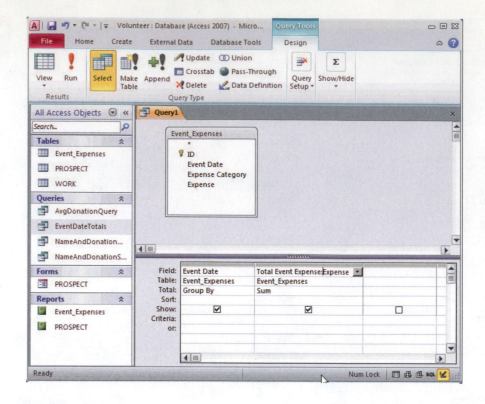

Now we are going to create a query that combines the results of two other queries. Specifically, we are going to merge EventExpenseTotals (the query we just created) with the EventDateTotals query we created in Q4. To do this, click *Create/Query Design*, but this time click the *Queries* tab in the *Show Table* window, as shown in Figure CE6-34. Now add both EventDateTotals and EventExpenseTotals to the query.

Figure CE6-34
Combining the Results
of Two Queries

Source: Microsoft Access 2010

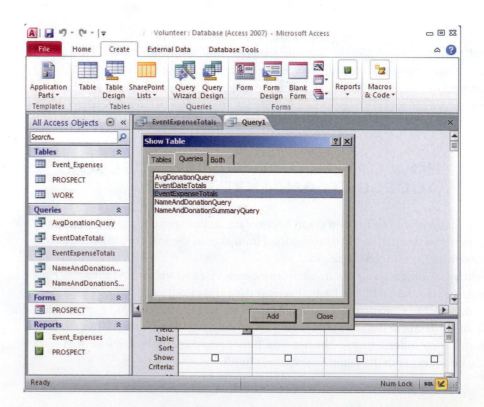

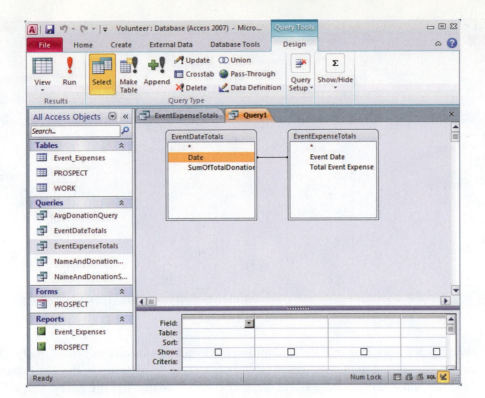

Figure CE6-35
Matching Date Values in
the Two Queries
Source: Microsoft Access 2010

We need to inform Access that the Date values in the two queries are the same. To do so, drag the Date field in EventDateTotals and drop it on top of Event Date in the EventExpense-Totals query. The result is shown in Figure CE6-35. Now add Date, SumOfTotalDonation, and Total Event Expense to the query, as shown in Figure CE6-36. Run the query, and you will see the result, as shown in Figure CE6-37. Save your query with the name *Event Results and Expenses.*

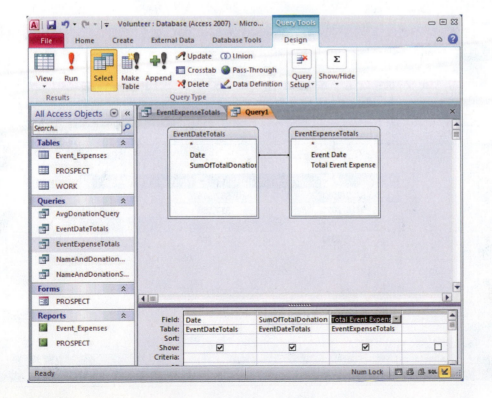

Figure CE6-36
Query with Columns Added
Source: Microsoft Access 2010

Figure CE6-37
Result of Query in
Figure CE6-36

Source: Microsoft Access 2010

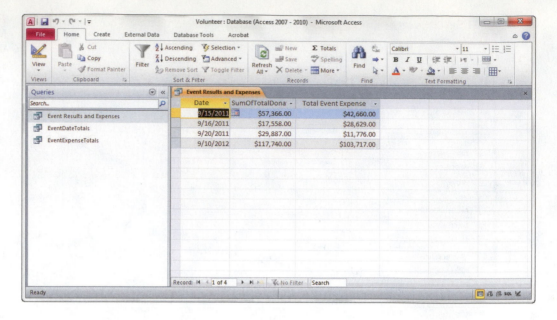

Now, open a workbook in Excel and import the Event Results and Expenses query. Use the same process used in the discussion of Q5. Click *Data From Access* in the *Get External Data* section of the ribbon. Then select the Access database that has the query, and select *Event Results and Expenses.* In Figure CE6-38, we have placed the upper left-hand corner of the data in cell B2.

Now, we can operate on this data just as if we had entered it via the keyboard. We can graph it as described in Q5. Or, we can analyze it as shown in Figure CE6-39. Here, the user is computing the Net Gain, Net Gain as a Percent of Expense, and Totals for donations and expenses. The focus is on cell F3; notice that this cell contains the formula = *C3–D3* which computes the difference between two imported numbers.

Figure CE6-38
Query in Figure CE6-36
Imported to Excel

Source: Microsoft Access 2010

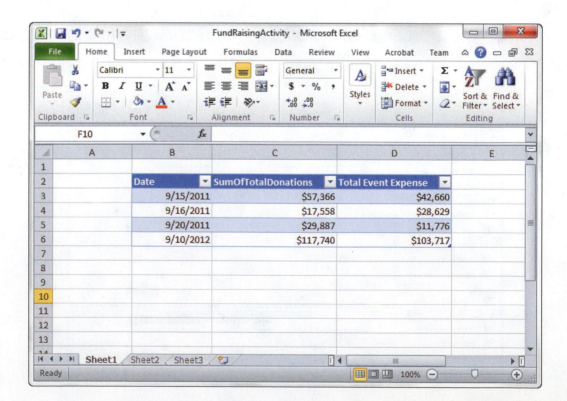

Figure CE6-39
Imported to Excel

Source: Microsoft Access 2010

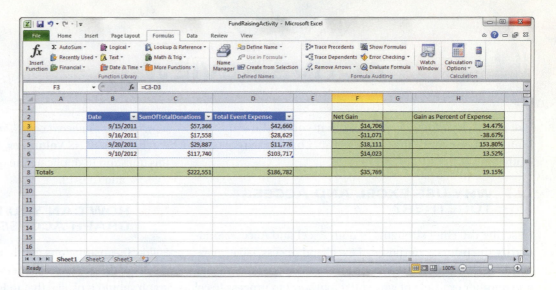

Reflect for a moment on the history of this data. The Total Donation data originated in Access and was summed using an Access query. The expense data began as Excel data in the FundRaising Exp worksheet and was imported into Access, where it was summed. The results of the Total Event Expense query were then imported back to Excel, where it was analyzed as shown in Figure CE6-39!

ACTIVE REVIEW

Use this Active Review to verify that you understand the ideas and concepts that answer this chapter extension's study questions.

Q1 WHY USE EXCEL AND ACCESS TOGETHER?

Describe the chief strengths of both Excel and Access. Summarize the primary purposes of Excel and Access. Give an example of why you might want to process Access data in Excel and another example of why you might want to process Excel data in Access.

Q2 WHAT IS IMPORT/EXPORT?

Define *import/export*. Explain how data can become out-of-date when using import/export and describe a solution to this problem. Explain the difference between comma-delimited and tab-delimited data. Go to the text's Web site at *www.pearsonhighered.com/kroenke* and obtain the text file **EMIS CE6 Student Data.txt** Follow the process described in Q2 to import the data into Access. Explain how you could use a text file to transfer data from Access to Excel. Describe tools that Microsoft provides that make this unnecessary.

Q3 HOW CAN YOU CREATE CHARTS WITH EXCEL?

Follow the steps explained in Q3 to create the graphics shown in Figures CE6-6 and CE6-9. Enter data manually as described in Q3.

Q4 HOW CAN YOU CREATE GROUP TOTALS IN ACCESS?

Explain the term *day's total of TotalDonations*. Explain what the *Group By* function does. Go to the text's Web site at *www.pearsonhighered.com/kroenke* and download the Access database file **EMIS Volunteer_CE6**. Follow the instructions in this question to duplicate the query shown in Figures CE6-15, CE6-17, and CE6-19.

Q5 HOW CAN YOU USE EXCEL TO GRAPH ACCESS DATA?

Follow the instructions in this section to use Excel to graph the results of the query you generated in your review for Q4. Your graph should look like that in Figure CE6-25. Explain how this exercise takes advantage of some of the relative strengths of these two products.

Q6 HOW CAN YOU USE ACCESS TO REPORT EXCEL DATA?

Explain why you might want to use Access to create reports on Excel data. Go to the text's Web site at *www.pearsonhighered.com/kroenke* and download the Excel file **EMIS CE6 FundRaisingExpenses.xslx**. Follow the instructions in discussion of this question to create a report like that in Figure CE6-32. Use the same Access database that you used for your review of Q4.

Q7 HOW CAN YOU COMBINE EXCEL AND ACCESS TO ANALYZE DATA?

Open the database with the Event_Expense query that you created in your review of Q6. Follow the procedures described in this section to create an Excel worksheet that looks like that shown in Figure CE6-39. Explain how some of this data made a roundtrip from Excel to Access and back to Excel. Does this make sense? Why or why not?

KEY TERMS AND CONCEPTS

Comma-delimited file 424   Named range 439   Tab-delimited file 424
Import/export 423

USING YOUR KNOWLEDGE

1. Create a spreadsheet of sample college expenses. Place a grid in your spreadsheet that has three rows—*Rent, Food, Entertainment*—and three columns—*2010, 2011, 2012.* Enter realistic, but hypothetical, data. Create a pie chart showing the expenses for 2010. Create a column chart for expenses for all 3 years. Create a bar chart for expenses for all 3 years. Do you prefer the column chart or the bar chart? Explain.

2. Create an Access database with a table called *My_ Expenses* that has the fields Date, Expense Category, and Amount. Fill the table with 12 rows of hypothetical student expense data. Ensure that you have several expenses for each date and for each expense category. Create a query that shows the total expenses for each date. Create a query that shows the total and average expenses for each category.

3. Export the data that you created in question 2 to an Excel spreadsheet. Create a pie chart of the data for expenses by category. Create a bar chart for expenses by category and date (one bar of each date within a category).

4. Open the database you created in question 2. Import the data from Excel that you created for question 3 into this database. (Yes, you are re-importing the same data from Excel that you previously exported to Excel. You should have the original copy of the data as well.) Compare the values for the original data to the values of the export/import data. They should be the same. Using the imported data, construct a report similar to that in Figure CE6-32.

5. Using the workbook that you created in your answer to question 3, add a budgeted amount column for each expense category. Enter values for each budgeted amount. Add a column showing the difference between the budgeted amount and the actual amount. Generalize this example. Describe a business scenario in which a financial analyst would obtain data from a database and compare it to data in a spreadsheet.

chapter extension 7

Chapters 4 and 6 provide the background for this extension.

Mobile Systems

Q1   WHAT ARE MOBILE SYSTEMS?

Mobile systems are information systems that support users in motion. Mobile systems users access the system from *any place*—at home, at work, in the car, on the bus, or at the beach—using any smart device, such as smartphone, tablet, or PC. The possibilities are endless.

Mobile systems users move not only geographically, they also move from device to device. The user who starts reading a book on an iPad on a bus, continues reading that book on a PC at work, and finishes it on a Kindle Fire at home, is mobile both geographically and across devices.

As shown in Figure CE7-1, the major elements in a mobile system are *users in motion*, *mobile devices*, *wireless connectivity*, and *cloud-based resources*.[1] A **mobile device** is a small, lightweight, power-conserving, computing device that is capable of wireless connectivity. Almost all mobile devices have a display and some means for data entry. Mobile devices include smartphones, tablets, personal digital assistants, and smaller, lighter laptops. Desktop computers, Xboxes, and large, heavy, power-hungry laptops are not mobile devices.

You learned about wireless connectivity and the cloud in Chapter 6. In this extension, we'll extend that cloud discussion to address mobile systems in Q4.

Q2   WHY ARE MOBILE SYSTEMS IMPORTANT?

The major reason for the importance of mobile systems is the size of their market. As of 2012, there are 5.9 billion wireless subscriptions. One-third of those subscriptions involve smartphones or other mobile devices, meaning there are already 1.9 billion mobile system

Figure CE7-1
Elements of a Mobile Information System

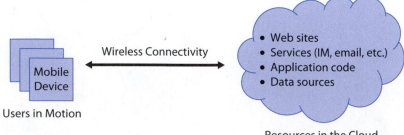

---

[1]Some mobile applications access organizational assets via VPNs and are not, strictly speaking, accessing cloud-based assets. We'll ignore that possibility here.

subscriptions, worldwide![2] Even more impressive, the remaining two-thirds of those subscriptions, or 3.9 billion, provide an enormous opportunity of future mobile system users, ready to purchase these devices.

According to a May 2012 issue of the *MIT Technology Review*, smartphones have achieved mainstream use by 40 percent of the U.S. market in four years. That's faster than any other technology except television in the early 1950s, which tied the smartphone adoption rate.[3]

Additionally, mobile use is favored by the young. According to Nielsen's measures of mobile device use, the younger the age group, the greater the percentage of people with mobile devices. Further, younger people have more devices per capita than older groups.[4] These young cohorts will further increase mobile systems use in the years to come.

Because of this vast and growing market, mobile systems are having a major impact on business and society today—impact that is forcing industry change while creating new career opportunities for mobile-IS-savvy professionals as well as large numbers of new, interesting mobile-IS-related jobs.

Figure CE7-2 summarizes the mobile-system impact for each of the five components of an information system. We will discuss this figure for each of the components, starting with hardware.

HARDWARE

Clearly, increasing demand for mobile systems means the sales of many more mobile devices, often at the expense of PC sales. Hewlett-Packard, a large PC manufacturer, learned this fact when it didn't respond quickly enough to the onslaught of mobile devices and was forced to

Figure CE7-2
Five Components of Mobile Change and Opportunity

	Hardware	Software	Data	Procedures	People
Impact of mobile systems growth	Many, many more mobile devices will be sold.	Compact interfaces; new technology for active users; application scaling.	More data, but more information? Less device real estate means fewer ads possible.	Always on, always at work. Employee lifestyle becomes hybrid of personal and professional.	Ability to thrive in a dynamic environment more important.
Industry changes	PCs less important; high demand (and requirement) for innovative devices as well as cheap copycats.	HTML5 and CSS3 increase capability of thin-clients.	Loss of control. Less room for advertisement.	Personal mobile devices at work policy.	More part-time employees and independent contractors.
Career opportunities	Jobs for mobile device sales, marketing, support.	New technology levels the playing field for HTML5, graphics skills. Business expertise needed for mobile requirements. New companies!	Reporting, data mining even more important. Design of effective mobile reports.	Innovative use of just-in-time data. Need for adjusting business processes gives another premium to non-routine problem solvers.	Independent contractors (and some employees) work where and when they want. What is this new social organism?

[2]http://mobithinking.com/mobile-marketing-tools/latest-mobile-stats, accessed May 2012.
[3]Michael Degusta. "Are Smart Phones Spreading Faster than Any Other Technology in Human History?" *MIT Technology Review*, May 9, 2012. Accessed online at http://www.technologyreview.com/business/40321/, May 2012.
[4]http://blog.nielsen.com/nielsenwire/online_mobile/survey-new-u-s-smartphone-growth-by-age-and-income, accessed May 2012.

eliminate 27,000 jobs in 2012. In the future, there will be high demand for innovative mobile devices as well as cheap copycats.

If you're reading this book, you're unlikely to be a hardware engineer, and if you're not living in Asia, you're also unlikely to be involved in hardware manufacturing. However, any market having 3.9 billion prospects is a market ripe with opportunities in marketing, sales, logistics, customer support, and related activities.

SOFTWARE

The reduced size of mobile devices requires the invention of new, innovative interfaces, as we will discuss in Q4. The mobile user is an active user and expects an active screen experience. The premium will be for moving graphics, changing Web pages, and animation. Applications will need to scale from the very smallest to the very largest, while providing a user experience appropriate to the device's size.

Rapid technology change in mobile software continually levels the playing field. Today, for example, expert programmers in Objective-C (the language used to create native iOS applications, see Q3), better not rest on their laurels. HTML5 and CSS3 are gaining popularity, and they will reduce the need for Objective-C expertise. Further, while languages like Objective-C are difficult and time-consuming to learn, HTML5 and CSS3 are less so. With the reduced barrier to entry, hoards of less experienced and less educated new entrants will appear as competitors. You might be one of them.

Not a computer programmer? Are you a business analyst? Do you want to be Drew, at GearUp? If so, Kelly, Emily, and Jason will rely on you to provide requirements for GearUp's mobile applications. The capabilities of mobile software in two years will be drastically different from those today. How do you, as Drew, respond? Maybe GearUp doesn't need an iOS application after all. Maybe it's too late. Instead, maybe GearUp needs a thin-client HTML5 application. GearUp and many other organizations will need employees with the skills and abilities to assess the contribution that mobile technology can make to their strategies.

Additionally, continually evolving software means new and exciting entrepreneurial opportunities. Are you sorry that you missed the early days working at Facebook? Right now, somewhere, there is another Mark Zuckerberg starting . . . well, what? Because of the continually changing software environment, new opportunities abound and will continue to do so for decades.

DATA

Many more mobile systems mean an incredible amount of new data, data that professionals can use to create much more information. But, as you learned in Chapter 1, more data doesn't necessarily mean more information. In fact, many business professionals believe they're drowning in data while starving for information. What can be done with all of this mobile-systems data to enable humans to conceive information of greater value to them? Smaller screens mean less room for advertising, a factor that limited the success of the Facebook public offering in May 2012.

On the other hand, not all the news is good, at least not for many organizations. Mobile systems can cause organizations to lose control over their data. In the past, employees used only computer equipment provided by the employer and connected only via employer-managed networks. In that situation, it is possible for the organization to control who does what with which data and where. No longer. Employees come to work with their own mobile devices. Data leakage is inevitable.

With more people using mobile devices, and with less room for ads, online advertising revenue may be sharply reduced, possibly endangering the revenue model that supports most of the Web's free content. If this happens, dramatic change is just around the corner!

Data mining and reporting, described in Chapter 8 and Chapter Extensions 12 and 13, become more important for addressing this need. The design of better, mobile-systems reporting is another. Again, opportunities abound.

PROCEDURES

Mobile systems are always on. They have no business hours. And people who use mobile systems are equally always on. In the mobile world, we're always open for business. It is impossible to be out of the office.

One consequence of always-on is the blending of our personal and the professional. Such blending means, in part, that business will intrude on your personal life, and your personal life will intrude on your business. This intrusion can be distracting and stressful; it can also lead to richer, more complex relationships. For example, with mobility, Addison may find herself discussing a problem with her daughter while talking at home to a seller at General Sports. Their business relationship can become more personal and hence stronger; it can also become awkward and weird.

As stated, employees will expect to use their mobile devices at work. But because of the loss of control, should they? In truth, who can keep them from it? If the organization blocks them from connecting to the work-related networks, they can connect over the wireless networks that they pay for themselves. In this case, the organization is entirely out of the loop. We will discuss these issues in more detail in Q5.

Mobile systems' functionality, just-in-time data, changing relationships, and other consequences of mobility will alter business processes.

Mobile systems offer **just-in-time data**, which is data delivered to the user at the precise time it is needed. A pharmaceutical salesperson uses just-in-time data when she accesses a mobile system to obtain the latest literature on a new drug while waiting for the doctor to whom she will pitch it. She needn't remember the drug's characteristics any longer than it takes her to walk down the hallway and make the sale.

Furthermore, some organizations will passively wait for change to happen, while others will proactively re-engineer their processes to incorporate mobile systems for higher process quality. Either way, the need for business process change creates opportunity for creative, nonroutine business problems solvers.

PEOPLE

Mobile systems change the value of our thinking. For example, just-in-time data removes the premium on the ability to memorize vast quantities of product data, but creates a premium for the ability to access, query, and present that data. Mobile systems increase the speed of business, giving an advantage to those who can nimbly respond to changing conditions and succeed with the unexpected.

With the ability to be connected and always on, organizations may find they can be just as effective with part-time employees and independent contractors. The increasing regulatory complexity and cost of full-time employees will create an incentive for organizations to do just that.

As that occurs, professionals who can thrive in a dynamic environment with little need for direct supervision will find that they can work both where and when they want—at least a good part of the time. Once you're always on and remote, it doesn't matter if you're always-on in New Jersey or always-on in Vermont. New lifestyle choices become possible for such workers. Beyond individuals, what entity are we creating with this new always-on, always connected society? Biologists say that multicellular organisms such as amoeba arose when individual cells bonded together for mutual benefit. Are mobile systems the analog of the nervous system? Is a group of continually connected people, working together in the context of inter-related jobs and personal lives, something new? Is a new, always-on, part business, part personal, multi-person organism being born before our eyes? And, if so, what does that mean for commerce? What an incredible time to be starting a business career!

 ## HOW DO NATIVE AND BROWSER-BASED MOBILE APPLICATIONS COMPARE?

Drew embarrassed himself with his lack of knowledge in the dialog at the start of Chapter 6. Even worse, he's fixated on an iOS application, which could have been a great decision last year, but may not be now. Or, perhaps iOS is correct, as long as they also build an Android application. And does he know whether one version can work for both iOS and Android? Or, because GearUp already has a browser application, why don't they re-engineer it with the latest browser technology? Wouldn't that be just as good?

Drew, Emily, and Kelly are business professionals, not technologists, yet they will be called upon to answer questions and make decisions like these. You might be as well, so you need to understand the alternatives and how they compare.

To begin, there are two primary ways for developing mobile applications. On the one hand, organizations can develop a **native application**, which is a thick-client application that is designed to work with a particular operating system, and sometimes even designed to work only with a particular mobile device that runs that operating system. On the other hand, they can develop a thin-client application that runs within a browser. In this case, the browser provides a more-or-less consistent environment for the application; the peculiarities of operating systems and hardware are handled by the browser's code and hidden from the thin-client application.

Figure CE7-3 contrasts native and thin-client mobile applications on their important characteristics. Consider the Native Application column first.

DEVELOPING NATIVE MOBILE APPLICATIONS

Native mobile applications are developed using serious, heavy-duty, professional programming languages. iOS applications are constructed using Objective-C, Android applications are constructed using Java, and Windows applications are constructed using C#, VB.Net, and others. All of these languages are **object-oriented**, which means they can be used to create difficult, complex applications, and, if used properly, will result in high-performance code that is easy to alter when requirements change. The particular characteristics of object-oriented languages are beyond the scope of this text.

Object-oriented languages can only be used by professional programmers who have devoted years to learning object-oriented design and coding skills. Typically such developers were computer science majors in college.

The benefit of such languages is that they give programmers close control over the assets of the mobile device and enable the creation of sophisticated and complex user interfaces. They also can be very efficient and fast-performing. The limits on native applications are usually budget and not technological. You can get just about any application you can afford.

The downside of native applications is that they are, well, native. They only run on the operating system for which they are programmed. An iOS mobile application must be completely recoded in order to run on Android, and re-coded again to run on Windows.[5] Thus, to reach all mobile users, an organization will need to support and maintain three separate versions of the

---

[5]Not quite true. Much of the design and possibly some of the code can be re-used between native applications. But, for your planning, assume that it all must be redone. Not enough will carry over to make it worth considering.

	Native Mobile Applications	Thin-client Mobile Applications
Development Languages	Objective-C Java C#, VB.net (object-oriented languages)	HTML5 CSS3 JavaScript (scripting languages)
Developed by	Professional programmers, only	Professional programmers and technically oriented Web developers and business professionals
Skill level required	High	Low to high
Difficulty	High	Easy to hard, depending on application requirements
Developer's Degree	Computer science	Computer science, Information systems, Graphic design
User Experience	Can be superb, depending on programming quality	Simple to sophisticated, depending on program quality
Possible applications	Whatever you can pay for …	Some limits prohibit very sophisticated applications
Dependency	iOS, Android, Windows	Browser differences, only
Cost	High. Difficult work by highly paid employees; multiple versions required	Low to medium … easier work by lesser paid employees, only multiple browser files necessary. Sophisticated applications may require high-skill and pay.
Application distribution	Via application stores (e.g., Apple Store)	Via Web sites
Example	Vanguard iPad application (free in Apple Store)	Seafood Web site: www.wildrhodyseafood.com Picozu editor: www.picozu.com/editor

Figure CE7-3
Characteristics of Native and Thin-client Applications

same application. They will also have to staff and manage three different development teams, with three different skill sets.

As a general rule, the cost of native applications is high. Many organizations reduce that cost by outsourcing development to India and other countries (see the introduction to Chapter 11), but native applications are still expensive relative to thin-client applications. The standard way for distributing native applications is via a company store, such as iTunes, owned by Apple. An excellent example of a native application is Vanguard's iPad application. It is easy to use, has complex functionality, and is highly secure, as you would expect. Companies such as Vanguard must and can afford to pay for exceedingly high quality applications.

DEVELOPING THIN-CLIENT MOBILE APPLICATIONS

The third column in Figure CE7-3 summarizes thin-client application characteristics. Such applications run inside a browser such as Firefox, Chrome, Opera, or Internet Explorer (IE). The browser handles the idiosyncrasies of the operating system and underlying hardware. In theory, an organization should be able to develop a single application and have it run flawlessly on all browsers on all mobile devices. Unfortunately, there are some differences in the way that browsers implement the thin-client code. The announcement in Figure CE7-4 exhibits the

THIS APPLICATION WILL RUN ON ALL MODERN BROWSERS EXCEPT INTERNET EXPLORER. IF YOU ARE SEEING THIS MESSAGE, THEN YOU ARE USING SOME VERSION OF IE. PLEASE DOWNLOAD AND INSTAL ANY OF THE FOLLOWING MODERN BROWSERS TO RUN THIS APPLICATION:
1. GOOGLE CHROME
2. MOZILLA FIREFOX
3. OPERA

Figure CE7-4
One Consequence of Browser Differences for Thin-client Applications
Source: http://www.gethugames.in/spirocanvas/ Reprinted by permission.

frustration of GetHuGames' developers when trying to make their thin-client application Spiro-Canvas run on Internet Explorer 9[6] (*www.GetHuGames.in/SpiroCanvas*).

As shown in the first row of Figure CE7-3, thin-client development languages are HTML5, CSS3, and Javascript. These are not object-oriented languages and hence are much easier to learn to use. HTML5 is the latest version of HTML, which you learned about in Chapter 6. The advantages of this version are the support for graphics, animation, 3D drawing, and other sophisticated user experiences. CSS3 is used with HTML5 to specify the appearance of content coded in HTML. Javascript is a scripting programming language that is much easier to learn than object-oriented languages. It is used to provide the underlying logic of the application.

Thin-client applications can be written by professional programmers, and, indeed, most are. However, it is possible for technically oriented Web developers and business professionals to develop them as well. The entry-level technical skill level required is low, and simple applications are relatively easy to develop. Sophisticated user experiences, like that in SpiroCanvas, are difficult. Thin-client application developers may have degrees in computer science, information systems, or graphic design.

The user experience provided by a thin-client application varies considerably. Some are simply fancy Web-based brochures (*www.wildrhodyseafood.com*), others are quite sophisticated, such as SpiroCanvas in Figure CE7-5 (*http://GetHuGames.in/*), or even more impressive, *www.biodigitalhuman.com* in Figure CE7-6 (runs in Opera; may not yet work in other browsers).

Thin-client applications are limited by the capabilities of the browser. While browsers are becoming increasingly sophisticated, they cannot offer the full capabilities of the underlying operating system and hardware. Thus, thin-browser applications are unable to support very specialized and complex applications.

As stated, the major advantage of thin-clients over native applications is that they will run on any operating system and mobile device. As demonstrated in Figure CE7-3, there are some browser differences, but these differences are very minor when compared with the differences between iOS, Android, and Windows. In general, unlike native applications, you can assume that a thin-client application has one code base and one development team.

---

[6]As of May 2012, IE implemented CSS3 differently than other browsers. This difference has probably been fixed by the time you read this, but some other difference in IE or other browsers may very well exist. The warning of browser differences is still applicable.

Figure CE7-5
GetHuGames
SpiroCanvas

*Source: http://www
.gethugames.in/
spirocanvas/* Reprinted by
permission.

Because thin-client applications can be developed by less skilled, lesser paid employees, and because only one code base and one development team is necessary, they are considerably cheaper to develop than native applications. However, this statement assumes applications of equivalent complexity. A simple native application can be cheaper to develop than a complex thin-client application.

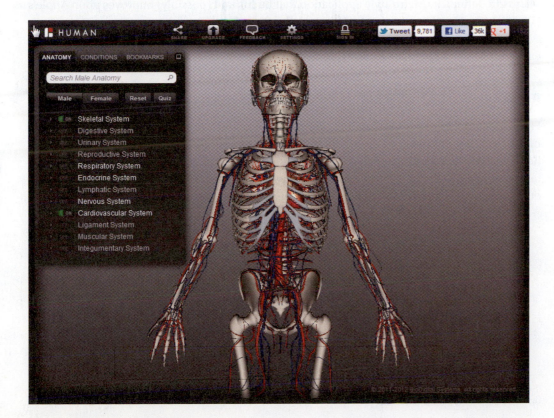

Figure CE7-6
Sophisticated HTML5
Application

Source: Image created using
the BioDigital Human
(*www.biodigitalhuman.com*)

Users obtain thin-client applications via the Web. When you go to www.picozu.com/editor, the required HTML5, CSS3, and JavaScript files are downloaded automatically over the Web. Updates to the application are automatic and seamless. You need not install (or re-install) anything. This difference is an advantage to the user; it makes it more difficult, however, to earn money from your application. Apple, for example, will sell your application and pay you a royalty. However, unless you require users to buy your thin-client application (which is possible, but rare), you'll have to give it away. To companies like GearUp, application revenue is not important. To you, it might be.

WHICH IS BETTER?

You know the answer to that question. If it were clear-cut, we'd only be discussing one alternative. It's not. The choice depends on your strategy, your particular goals, the requirements for your application, your budget, your schedule, your tolerance for managing technical projects, your need for application revenue, and other factors. In general, thin-client applications are cheaper to develop and maintain, but they may lack the Wow factor. You and your organization have to decide for yourselves!

WHAT CHARACTERIZES QUALITY MOBILE USER EXPERIENCES?

A **user interface (UI)** is the presentation format of an application. It consists of windows, menus, icons, dialog boxes, toolbars, etc., as well as user content. A **user experience (UX)** is a newer term that refers not only to the UI, but also to the way that the application behaves within that UI.

Apple redefined the UX for mobile applications when it introduced the iPhone with touch, gravity sensing portrait / landscape orientation, and other innovative UX behavior. Since then Microsoft defined its Metro style application that builds and (possibly) improves upon Apple's UX. Apple may be about to advance UX again. Stay tuned.

Figure CE7-7 lists the primary characteristics of a quality mobile application.[7] Consider each.

FEATURE CONTENT

First, quality mobile user interfaces should place the primary emphasis on users' content, giving such content as much of the display as possible. Rather than show menus, toolbars, and heavy window borders, the content should be shown cleanly and in center stage. **Chrome** is a term that refers to the visual overhead in a computer display. It is the windows, the menus, and other apparatus that drive the application. Because mobile screen size is often limited, modern

Figure CE7-7
Characteristics of a Quality
Mobile UX

- Feature content and support direct interaction
- Use context-sensitive chrome when needed
- Provide animation and lively behavior
- Design to scale and share (display and data)
- Use the cloud

[7]See http://msdn.microsoft.com/en-us/library/windows/apps/hh464920.aspx for the source of much of this figure, as well as for an extended discussion of Metro style UX. Accessed May, 2012.

Figure CE7-8
Chrome-less Interface

Source: Microsoft:
http://blogs.msdn
.com/b/windowsstore/
archive/2012/01/20/
designing-the-windows-
store-user-experience.aspx

Windows Store landing page

mobile applications eliminate it as much as possible. (By the way, do not confuse this use of *chrome* with Google Chrome, the popular browser.)

Figure CE7-8 shows the chrome-less mobile Windows Store application. The user doesn't need a toolbar (chrome) for learning more about a product; the user intuitively knows to click the image to see more.

Using content to drive application behavior is called **direct interaction.** For another example, when you see blue, underlined type, you know to tap on it to navigate to that Web site. Similarly, if users want to highlight a word, they know to touch it to see what will happen.

USE CONTEXT-SENSITIVE CHROME

Designing for direct action reduces the need for chrome, but not entirely. In an online store application, once you select the application, say a game, you'll need controls to play it. For such cases, mobile applications do provide chrome, but it is **context-sensitive chrome**, meaning it pops up in the display when appropriate. Ideally, no button or command name is ever shown in a disabled (grayed-out) state. Instead, if it's disabled, the application doesn't show it, thus simplifying the UI and reserving more of the display for the users' content.

PROVIDE ANIMATION AND LIVELY BEHAVIOR

Great mobile applications are lively. They capture your attention with motion and sound. If you are not doing something, they are. For example, an icon to play a movie has the movie's preview playing inside it. An unused game displays a sample game underway. When you do act, something happens immediately. The touched word or image changes color, pops up, or does something to give you active feedback that the application is alive and running.

All of this is easy to comprehend for games and entertainment applications. How these ideas pertain to commercial applications is on the leading edge of commercial UX design. Everyone wants activity, but when you access your mobile Vanguard application, do you

Figure CE7-9
Example of Application
Scaling

Source: Maxx-Studio/Shutterstock.

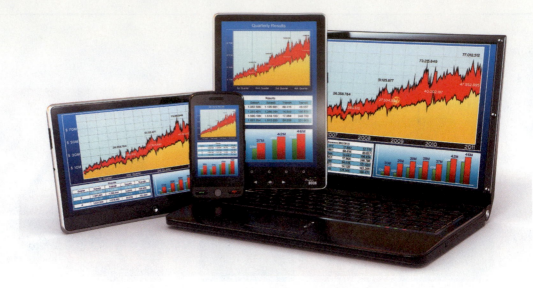

really want to watch the application shrink if your portfolio value has diminished? Or watch it crash to the bottom of your display if the market is down substantially? Or hear *Money, Money, Money* every time the market is up? Probably not. What is appropriate is being determined today; there is lots of opportunity for techno-savvy, marketing-oriented, graphics designers here.

DESIGN TO SCALE AND SHARE

Mobile applications appear on phones, tablets, PCs, and even large displays. Applications must be designed so that they can scale up and down without appearing awkward or taking over the device. Note the slightly different appearances of the application in the displays in Figure CE7-9.

Modern operating systems (native applications) and browsers (thin-client applications) are designed to support such scaling. IE10, for example, allows applications to provide three sizes and versions of graphics; IE will choose the version that is appropriate for the size of the device on which it is running.

Mobile applications share their device with other mobile applications. They need to be designed to share the display effectively; applications that aggressively take over the screen are unappreciated by users and other application developers.

Mobile applications also need to be designed to share data. For example, Windows 8 introduces a feature called **charms**, which are icons that slide in from the right of the display. One of the default charms is Share, and it is used to share data from one mobile application to another. IE10 allows Web pages to share thumbnails, descriptions, and links with other applications. If a user wants to email a page, IE10 will provide the shared thumbnail, description, and link to the mail application, as shown in Figure CE7-10.

Understand the power of this functionality; the thin-client application in the Web page has declared the data it will share; here it has provided the thumbnail picture, the description, and the link, as shown in the right hand side of Figure CE7-10. Any program can receive that data. The Web page programmer has no idea where that data may go or be displayed. It could be emailed, as shown here, but it could equally go to a graphics application, or travel planning applications, or a social networking application, or an event planning application, etc.

This example focuses on Windows 8 and IE10, but the concepts pertain equally to iOS, Android, and other browsers as well.

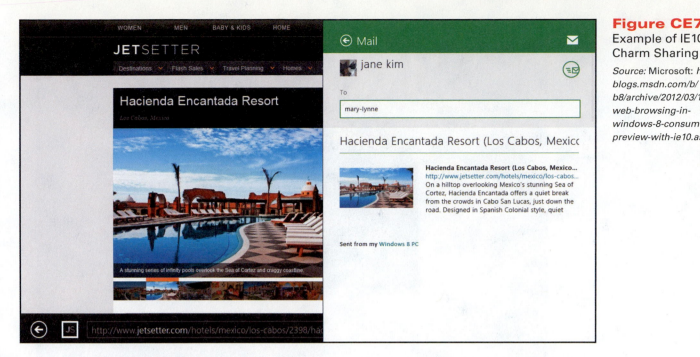

Figure CE7-10
Example of IE10
Charm Sharing

Source: Microsoft: *http://
blogs.msdn.com/b/
b8/archive/2012/03/13/
web-browsing-in-
windows-8-consumer-
preview-with-ie10.aspx*

USE THE CLOUD

Figure CE7-11 lists the primary cloud assets that mobile applications use. Web sites and services like IM and email are obvious. Less obvious are the use of services such as Fulfillment by Amazon (see Case 2). By using that service, the developers of the mobile application can harness the power of Amazon's inventory and process management software with very little development work on their own.

Another use of the cloud is to extend the application itself. Mobile devices are frequently (almost always?) running on battery power and minimizing power use is important. Consequently, some applications move complex code that requires substantial processing onto powered and powerful cloud servers. Doing so also improves security because data that is used for intermediate calculations need not be transmitted over the Internet.

Roaming occurs when users move their activities, especially long-running transactions (reading a book, for example) across devices. The best mobile applications do this transparently; the user need take no action. Figure CE7-12 shows a message created by a Kindle app when a book was opened on an iPad that had previously been read on an iPhone. This tracking and informing was entirely automatic.

Figure CE7-11
Mobile Systems Cloud Use

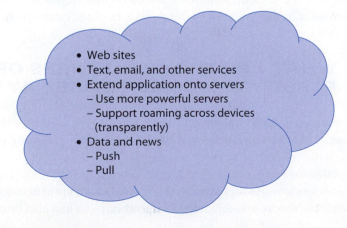

- Web sites
- Text, email, and other services
- Extend application onto servers
  - Use more powerful servers
  - Support roaming across devices
    (transparently)
- Data and news
  - Push
  - Pull

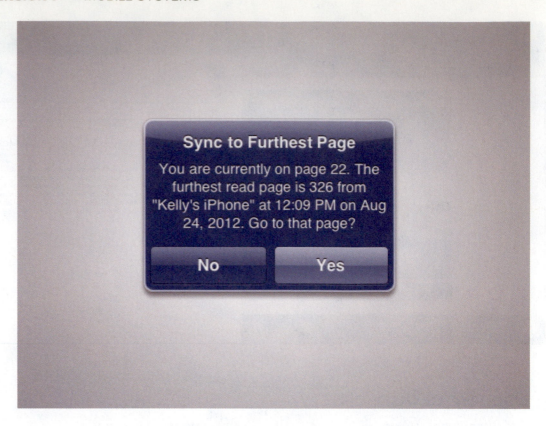

Roaming on reading devices is interesting, but even greater power will be achieved when mobile applications allow roaming for other long-running transactions as well; editing a document, spreadsheet, or other Office document are examples. At some point (not yet), applications like CRM and ERP may support roaming as well.

The last cloud use in Figure CE7-11 concerns data. Live, active mobile applications are designed to receive the latest application data and automatically show it to the user, perhaps in a graphically exciting *breaking news* type banner. Such data includes industry or employee news, but it could also be SharePoint alerts, updates to orders, changes in credit ratings or banking accounts, and so forth. **Push data** is data that the server sends to or pushes onto the device. **Pull data** is data that the device requests from the server. (Notice that those terms use the server's perspective.) Of the two types, push data is more impressive to users because they need do nothing to receive it. On the other hand, excessive pushing is annoying.

Drew and the others at GearUp should use the knowledge in this section and the list in Figure CE7-7 when defining the requirements for their mobile application. So should you!

WHAT ARE THE CHALLENGES OF PERSONAL MOBILE DEVICES AT WORK?

So far, we've focused on mobile applications that organizations create for their customers and others to use. In this last question we will address the use of mobile systems *within* organizations.

In truth, organizations today have a love/hate relationship with their employees' use of their own mobile devices at work. They love the cost-saving possibility of having employees buy their own hardware, but they hate the increased vulnerability and loss of control. The result, at

Advantages	Disadvantages
Cost savings	Data loss or damage
Greater employee satisfaction	Loss of control
Reduced need for training	Compatibility problems
Higher productivity	Risk of infection
Reduced support costs	Greater support costs

Figure CE7-13
Advantages and Disadvantages of Employee Use of Mobile Systems at Work

least today, is a wide array of organizational attitudes. In fact, as of 2012, the majority of organizations are waffling; only 43 percent of all organizations have created an official mobile-use policy at all.[8]

ADVANTAGES AND DISADVANTAGES OF EMPLOYEE USE OF MOBILE SYSTEMS AT WORK

Figure CE7-13 summarizes the advantages and disadvantages of employee use of mobile systems at work. Advantages include the cost savings just mentioned as well as greater employee satisfaction of using devices that the employees chose according to their own preferences rather than organization-supplied PCs. Because employees are already using these devices for their own purposes, they need less training and can be more productive. All of this means reduced support costs.

On the other hand, employee use of mobile devices has significant disadvantages. First, there is the real danger of lost or damaged data. When data is brought into employee-owned computing devices, the organization loses control over where it goes or what happens to it. In May 2012, IBM disallowed the use Apple's voice searching application, Siri, on employees' mobile devices for just that reason.[9] If an employee loses his or her device, the data goes with it. Further, when employees leave the organization, the data on their personal devices needs to be deleted, somehow.

Organizations also lose control over the updating of software and the applications that users employ. This control loss leads to compatibility problems as well; users can process data, for example, edit documents, with software that is incompatible with the organization's standard software. The result to the organization is a mess of inconsistent documents.

Possibly the greatest disadvantage of employee use of their own devices is the risk of infection. The organization cannot know where the users have been with their devices or what they've done when they've been there. The possibility of severe viruses infecting the organization's networks is both frightening and real. Finally, all of these disadvantages can also lead, ironically, to greater support costs.

Given all that, organizations cannot avoid the issue. Whatever the costs and risks, employees are bringing their own devices to work. Ignoring the issue will simply make matters worse.

SURVEY OF ORGANIZATIONAL BYOD POLICY

A **BYOD (bring your own device) policy** is a statement concerning employees' permissions and responsibilities when they use their own device for organizational business. Figure CE7-14 arranges

---

[8]http://www.cdh.com/
[9]http://www.cnn.com/2012/05/23/tech/mobile/ibm-siri-ban/index.html?iphoneemail, accessed May 2012.

		Control				
		Low ←				→ High
High	Full VPN Access to Organizational Systems			You're responsible for damage	We'll check it out, reload software and data, and manage it remotely	If you connect it, we own it
Functionality	Organizational Services on Public Internet		We'll offer limited systems you can access from any device			
	Access to Internet	We'll be a coffee shop				
Low	None	They don't exist				

BYOD policies according to functionality and control. Starting in the lower left-hand corner, the most primitive policy is to ignore mobile use. That posture, which provides neither functionality to the employee nor control to the organization, has no advantages and—as just stated—cannot last.

The next step up in functionality is for the organization to offer its wireless network to mobile, as if it were a coffee shop. The advantage to the organization of this policy is that the organization can sniff employees' mobile traffic, thus learning how employees are using their devices (and time) during work.

The next policy provides more functionality and somewhat more control. Here, the organization creates secure application services using https that require employee sign-on and can be accessed from any device, mobile or not. Such applications can be used when employees are at work or elsewhere. These services provide controlled access to some organizations' assets.

A fourth policy is more of a gambit than a policy. The organization tells employees that they can sign on to the organization's network with their mobile devices, but the employee is financially responsible for any damage they do. The hope is that few employees know what their exposure is and hence decide not to do so.

A more enlightened policy is to manage the users' devices as if they were owned by the organization. With this policy, employees turn over their mobile devices to the IS Department, which cleanses and re-loads software, and installs programs that enable the IS Department to manage the device remotely. Numerous vendors license products called **mobile device management (MDM) software** to assist this process. These products install and update software, backup and restore mobile devices, wipe software and data from devices in the event the device is lost or the employee leaves the company, report usage, and provide other mobile device management data.

This policy benefits the organization, but some employees resist turning over the management of their own hardware to the organization. This resistance can be softened if the organization pays at least a portion of the hardware expense.

The most controlling policy is for the organization to declare that it owns any mobile device that employees connect to its network. To be enforceable, this policy must be part of the employee's contract. It is taken by organizations that manage very secure operations and environments. In some military / intelligence organizations, the policy is that any smart device that ever enters the workplace may never leave it. The advantages of these six policies are summarized in Figure CE7-15.

BYOD Policy	Description	Advantage to Organization
They don't exist	Organization looks the other way when employees bring mobile devices to work.	None.
We'll be a coffee shop	You'll be able to sign in to our wireless network using your mobile device.	Packet sniffing of employee mobile device use at work.
We'll offer limited systems you can access from any device	Organization creates https:// applications with sign-in and offers access to noncritical business systems.	Employees gain public access from any device, not just mobile devices, without having to use VPN accounts.
You're responsible for damage	Threatening posture to discourage employee use of mobile devices at work.	Appear to be permissive without actually being so.
We'll check it out, reload software, then manage remotely	Employees can use their mobile devices just as if they were computers provided by the corporate IS Department.	Employee buys the hardware.
If you connect it, we own it	Employees are not to use mobile devices at work. If they do, they lose them. Part of employment agreement.	Ultimate in control for highly secure work situations (intelligence, military).

BYOD policies are rapidly evolving and many organizations have not yet determined what is best for them. If your employer has a committee to develop such policies, join it if you can. Doing so will provide a great way to gain exposure to the leading technology thinkers at your organization.

ACTIVE REVIEW

Use this Active Review to verify that you understand the ideas and concepts that answer this chapter extension's study questions.

Q1 WHAT ARE MOBILE SYSTEMS?

Define mobile systems. Name and describe the four elements of a mobile system.

Q2 WHY ARE MOBILE SYSTEMS IMPORTANT?

Describe the size of the mobile market and explain why there are 3.9 billion mobile prospects. Explain why the mobile market will become stronger in the future. Explain why a problem for one organization is an opportunity for another. Using the five component model, describe particular opportunities for each component. Define *just-in-time data* and explain how it changes the value of human thinking.

Q3 HOW DO NATIVE AND BROWSER-BASED MOBILE APPLICATIONS COMPARE?

In your own words, summarize the differences between native applications and thin-client applications. In high-level terms, explain the difference between object-oriented languages and scripting languages. Explain each cell of Figure CE7-3. State which is better: native or thin-client applications.

Q4 WHAT CHARACTERIZES QUALITY MOBILE USER EXPERIENCES?

Explain the difference between the terms *UI* and *UX*. Describe how each of the following can affect the UX of a mobile application: user content, context-sensitive chrome, animation and lively behavior, scaling and sharing, the cloud. Define *chrome*, *charms, roaming, push,* and *pull*.

Q5 WHAT ARE THE CHALLENGES OF PERSONAL MOBILE DEVICES AT WORK?

Summarize the advantages and disadvantages of employees' use of mobile systems at work. Define *BYOD* and *BYOD policy*. Name six possible policies and compare them in terms of functionality and organizational control. Summarize the advantage of each to employers.

KEY TERMS AND CONCEPTS

Bring Your Own Device (BYOD) policy 463
Charms 460
Chrome 458
Context-sensitive chrome 459
Direct interaction 459

Just-in-time data 453
Mobile device 450
Mobile device management (MDM) software 464
Mobile systems 450
Native application 454

Object-oriented 454
Pull data 462
Push data 462
Roaming 461
User experience (UX) 458
User interface (UI) 458

USING YOUR KNOWLEDGE

Examine Figure CE7-2 and reflect on each component. Select the component of greatest interest to you. Reread the section of Q2 that relates to that component. Describe what you think will be the business consequences of the changes brought about by mobile computing related to that component.

1. Examine Figure CE7-2 and reflect on each component.
   a. Describe a job that you would like to have upon graduation.
   b. Describe how changes in mobile hardware will impact that job.
   c. Explain how you can use your knowledge of the differences between native and thin-client mobile application development to help you in that job.
   d. Explain two ways that just-in-time data will impact that job.
   e. Describe two ways that mobile systems will change business processes in that job.
   f. Explain ways that mobile systems will change the premium on the skills necessary for that job.
   g. Summarize your answers to questions b-f in a two-paragraph statement that you could use in a job interview.

2. Suppose that you are Drew at GearUp. List five criteria you would use in helping GearUp decide whether it should develop a native or a thin-client mobile application.

3. Choose a mobile application that you frequently use. It could be Facebook, Twitter, or some other more vertical application. Evaluate that application according to the principles in Figure CE7-7.

4. Describe how the class enrollment application at your university could benefit from a mobile application that uses the cloud.

5. Judging from your personal experience, describe the BYOD policy that appears to be in place at your university. Explain the advantages and disadvantages of the policy to you as a student and to the organization as a whole. How do you think that BYOD policy will change in the next five years? Explain your answer.

Functional Applications

Q1 WHAT IS THE DIFFERENCE BETWEEN A FUNCTIONAL IS AND A FUNCTIONAL APPLICATION?

Functional systems are information systems that support a single enterprise function, within a single department or other workgroup. Examples are the accounts payable IS, the sales lead-tracking IS, and the customer support IS. As stated in Chapter 7, management of functional IS is easier than for cross-functional or inter-enterprise systems, because the procedures and people involved fall under the direction of a single functional manager. Functional IS do not cross departmental or organizational boundaries.

Functional application is the computer program component within a functional IS. Few organizations develop their own functional applications. Instead, most license functional application software from a vendor and then adapt. Adaptation is necessary because organizations differ in the procedures they have; almost never does an off-the-shelf functional application provide a perfect fit.

CREATING FUNCTIONAL INFORMATION SYSTEMS

To create functional information systems, organizations first determine the requirements of the business function (see Chapter 10 for more on this important topic). They then evaluate functional applications and select one that provides the closest fit. Next, the organization implements the functional application in the context of its particular needs. During implementation, either the business activities are altered to match the software or the software is altered to meet the organization's activities. For many reasons, most organizations choose to adapt their procedures to match the software.

During implementation, the functional application is transformed into an information system. As licensed, the functional application will have software, a database design, and some default procedures. During implementation, the organization will build the remaining components of an information system. It will acquire and install hardware, fill the database with data, adapt standard procedures, and train staff. Thus, the organization acquires the functional application software and creates components around it to form the functional IS.

AN EXAMPLE OF A FUNCTIONAL APPLICATION

Medical partnerships such as the one to which Dr. Flores belongs use numerous functional applications. An application for managing patient appointments is a typical example. Many vendors offer appointment applications for professional offices, and some even offer

applications especially for medical offices. When opening their office, Flores, his partners and staff are unlikely to employ full-time IT personnel, so they would probably hire a consultant to help them select the appropriate appointment application and construct the IS around it.

As just described, the consultant would meet with staff to determine the partnership's requirements, especially any that are unique to this group. Most surgical practices schedule office visits around surgeries. However, the need for cardiac surgery can arise unexpectedly, and surgeries can take longer than anticipated. Therefore, Flores's office needs an appointment system that allows for rapid and easy re-juggling of the schedule. This requirement would differ, for example, from that of, say, a hand surgeon, where emergency procedures are rare.

(Obviously, the more experience the consultant has with cardiac surgeries, the better the job he or she can do. Keep this example in mind if you find yourself needing to hire a consultant for a similar purpose.)

Once the package is selected, the consultant will guide the creation and implementation of the other components of the IS as described in Chapter 10. When implementing procedures, the project needs to allow time for employee training on the new system. Surprisingly, this need is sometimes forgotten. In the following sections, we will describe features and functions of functional applications that organizations can license. From this example, be aware that acquiring such applications is just the tip of the iceberg. Once organizations have licensed the software, they need to create information systems around that software in such a way that they implement their own, unique functional systems. As a future manager, understand that the bulk of the work for you and your organization occurs *after* the software acquisition.

WHAT ARE THE FUNCTIONS OF SALES AND MARKETING APPLICATIONS?

The primary purpose of the sales function is to find prospects and transform them into customers by selling them something. Sales departments also *manage customers*, which is a euphemism for selling existing customers more products. Other functional sales activities forecast future sales.

In marketing, systems exist to manage products and brands. Companies use such systems to assess the effectiveness of marketing messages, advertising, and promotions and to determine product demand among various market segments. Figure CE8-1 shows specific functions for sales and marketing applications. **Lead-generation applications** (also called *prospect-generation* applications) include those used to send both postal mail and email. Web sites are commonly used to generate leads as well. Some Web sites feature just product information; other sites offer to send the prospect white papers or other documents of value in exchange for the prospect's contact information.

Lead-tracking applications record lead data and product interests and keep records of customer contacts. Figure CE8-2 shows a form used by a small company that sells classic 1960s muscle cars (fast cars with large engines and underdesigned brakes). The company uses this form for both lead tracking and customer management. (Note that the company uses the term *customer* rather than *lead* or *prospect*.) As you can see, the application maintains customer name and contact data, the customer's product interests, past purchases, and a history of all contacts with the customer.

It is not clear from this form whether *Autos Currently Owned* represents autos purchased just from Bainbridge or autos the customer has purchased from any source. This ambiguity illustrates the need for procedures and employee training. If Bainbridge has five salespeople, and if two of them record only autos purchased from Bainbridge while the other three record autos

Figure CE8-1
Functions of Sales
and Marketing
Applications

- **Prospect (or lead) generation**
  - Mailings
  - Emailings
  - Web site

- **Lead tracking**
  - Record leads
  - Track product interests
  - Maintain history of contacts

- **Customer management**
  - Maintain customer contact and order history
  - Maintain and report credit status
  - Track product interests

- **Sales forecasting**
  - Record individual sales projections
  - Roll up sales projections into district, region, national, and international
  - Track variances over time

- **Product and brand management**
  - Obtain sales results from order processing or receivables applications
  - Compare results to projections
  - Assess promotions, advertising, and sales channels
  - Assess product success in market segments
  - Manage product life cycle

Figure CE8-2
Form Used for Lead Tracking
and Customer Management

Source: Microsoft Access 2010

Bainbridge Limited Auto Sales
Customer Data Form

First Name	Donald
Last Name	Nielstrom
Occupation	Software Engineer
Cell Phone	206.444.1234
Work Phone	425.009.1234
Home Phone	
Email	DN@Nielstrom.com
Salesperson	Johnson

Auto Interests
1960 Chev 409
1965 Mustang

Autos Currently Owned
1957 Chev 2dr Bellaire
1962 Corvette
1966 Cadillac Convertible

Contacts

Contact Date	Type	Remarks
9/19/2011	Phone	Customer called to ask about green 409. Already sold!
11/17/2011	Email	Emailed him regarding potential sale of his Corvette
11/20/2011	Email	Done responded "Absolutely not."
2/27/2012	Phone	Called to check in with him. His first priority is to find the 409. Call immediately when h

Record: 1 of 4   No Filter   Search

Record: 1 of 1   No Filter   Search

purchased from any source, the data will be inconsistent. Subsequent reports or analyses based on this data will be hampered by this discrepancy. Again, applications (programs) are not information systems!

Companies use **customer management applications** to obtain additional sales from existing customers. As Figure CE8-1 shows, such applications maintain customer contact and order-history data and track product interests, and some maintain information about the customer's credit status with the organization. The latter data are used to prevent salespeople from generating orders that the accounts receivable department will later refuse due to poor customer credit.

The most common functional applications in marketing are **product and brand management applications**. With these, records of past sales are imported from order processing or accounts receivable systems and compared to projections and other sales estimates. The company uses the comparisons to assess the effectiveness of promotions and advertising as well as sales channels. It also can use such systems to assess the desirability of the product to different market segments. Finally, the company uses such applications to manage the product through its life cycle. Sales trends may indicate the need for new versions of the product or may help to determine when it is time to remove a product from the market.

In truth, it is impossible to manage a product or a brand without these kinds of information. Without the data, there is no feedback, and anyone's guess is as good as any other's with regard to the effectiveness of the marketing messaging, promotions, advertising, and other marketing activities.

WHAT ARE THE FUNCTIONS OF OPERATIONS APPLICATIONS?

Operations activities concern the management of finished-goods inventory and the movement of goods from that inventory to the customer. **Operations applications** are especially prominent for nonmanufacturers, such as distributors, wholesalers, and retailers. For manufacturing companies, many, if not all, of the operations functions are merged into manufacturing systems.

Figure CE8-3 lists the principal operations applications. Order entry applications record customer purchases. Typically, an order entry application obtains customer contact and shipping data, verifies customer credit, validates payment method, and enters the order into a queue for processing. Order management applications track the order through the fulfillment process, arrange for and schedule shipping, and process exceptions (such as out-of-stock products). Order management applications inform customers of order status and scheduled delivery dates.

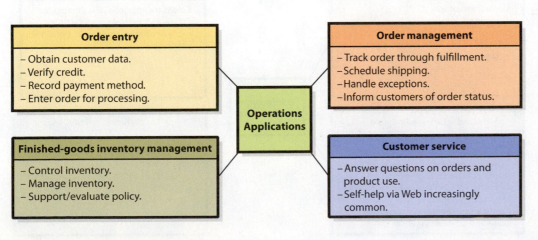

Figure CE8-3
Functions of Operations Applications

In nonmanufacturing organizations, operations applications include features to manage finished-goods inventory. We will not address those applications here; see the discussion of inventory applications in the next section. As you read that discussion, just realize that non-manufacturers do not have raw materials or goods-in-process inventories. They have only finished-goods inventories.

Customer service is the last operations application in Figure CE8-3. Customers call customer service to ask questions about products, order status, and problems and to make complaints. Today, many organizations are placing as much of the customer service function on Web pages as they can. Many organizations allow customers direct access to order status and delivery information. Also, organizations are increasingly providing product-use support using Enterprise 2.0 techniques.

WHAT ARE THE FUNCTIONS OF MANUFACTURING APPLICATIONS?

Manufacturing applications facilitate the production of goods. As shown in Figure CE8-4, manufacturing applications include inventory, planning, scheduling, and operations. We begin with inventory.

INVENTORY APPLICATIONS

Inventory applications support inventory control, management, and policy. In terms of inventory control, inventory applications track goods and materials into, out of, and between inventories. Inventory tracking requires that items be identified by a number. In the least sophisticated systems, employees must enter inventory numbers manually. Today, however, most applications use UPC bar codes (the familiar bar code you find on items at the grocery store) or RFIDs (radio frequency identification tags) to track items as they move in, around, and out of inventories.

Inventory management applications use past data to compute stocking levels, reorder levels, and reorder quantities in accordance with inventory policy. They also have features for assisting inventory counts and for computing inventory losses from those counts and from inventory-processing data.

With regard to inventory policy, there are two schools of thought in modern operations management. Some companies view inventories primarily as assets. In this view, large inventories are beneficial. Their cost is justified, because large inventories minimize disruptions in operations or sales due to outages. Large finished-goods inventories increase sales by offering greater product selection and availability to the customer.

Figure CE8-4
Functions of Manufacturing Applications

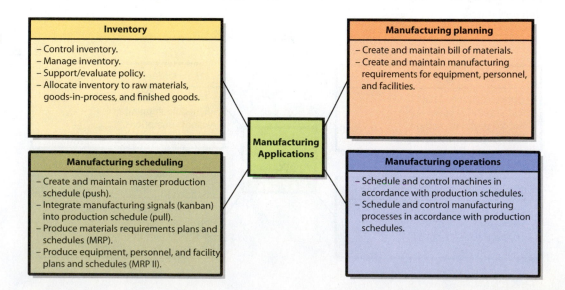

Other companies, such as Dell, view inventories primarily as liabilities. In this view, companies seek to keep inventories as small as possible and to eliminate them completely if possible. The ultimate expression of this view is demonstrated in the **just-in-time (JIT) inventory policy**. This policy seeks to have production inputs (both raw materials and work-in-process) delivered to the manufacturing site just as they are needed. By scheduling delivery of inputs in this way, companies are able to reduce inventories to a minimum.

Still others use both philosophies: Walmart, for example, has large inventories in its stores, but minimizes all other inventories in its warehouses and distribution centers.

Inventory applications help an organization implement its particular philosophy and determine the appropriate balance between inventory cost and item availability, given that philosophy. Features include computing the inventory's return on investment (ROI), reports on the effectiveness of current inventory policy, and some means of evaluating alternative inventory policies by performing what-if analyses.

MANUFACTURING PLANNING APPLICATIONS

In order to plan materials for manufacturing, it is first necessary to record the components of the manufactured items. A **bill of materials (BOM)** is a list of the materials that comprise a product. This list is more complicated than it might sound, because the materials that comprise a product can be subassemblies that need to be manufactured. Thus, the BOM is a list of materials, and materials within materials, and materials within materials within materials, and so forth.

In addition to the BOM, if the manufacturing application schedules equipment, people, and facilities, then a record of those resources for each manufactured product is required as well. The company may augment the BOM to show labor and equipment requirements or it may create a separate nonmaterial requirements file.

Figure CE8-5 shows a sample BOM for a child's red wagon having four components: handle bar, wagon body, front-wheel assembly, and rear-wheel assembly. Three of these have the subcomponent parts shown. Of course, each of these subcomponents could have sub-subcomponents, and so forth, but these are not shown. Altogether, the BOM shows all of the parts needed to make the wagon and the relationships of those parts to each other.

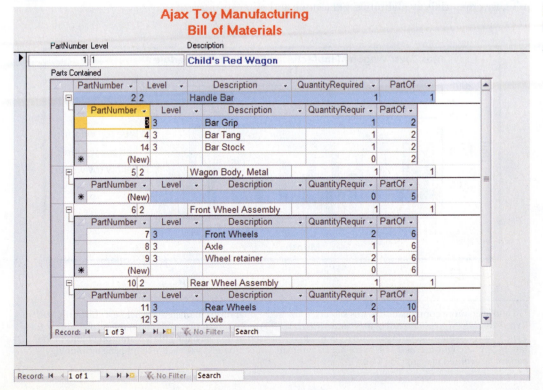

Figure CE8-5
Bill of Materials Example

Source: Microsoft Access 2010

MANUFACTURING SCHEDULING APPLICATIONS

Companies use three philosophies to create a manufacturing schedule. One is to generate a **master production schedule (MPS)** which is a plan for producing products. To create the MPS, the company analyzes past sales levels and makes estimates of future sales. This process is called a **push manufacturing process** because the company pushes the products into sales (and customers) according to the MPS.

Figure CE8-6 shows a manufacturing schedule for wagon production at a toy company. This plan includes three colors of wagons and shows subtle production increases prior to the summer months and prior to the holiday season. Again, the company obtains these production levels by analyzing past sales. The MPS for an actual manufacturer would, of course, be more complicated.

A second philosophy is not to use a preplanned, forecasted schedule, but rather to plan manufacturing in response to signals from customers or downstream production processes that products or components are currently needed. The Japanese word *kanban*, which means "card," is sometimes used to refer to the signal to build something. Manufacturing processes that respond to kanbans must be more flexible than those that are MPS-based. A process based on such signals is sometimes called a **pull manufacturing process**, because the products are pulled through manufacturing by demand.

Finally, a third philosophy is a combination of the two. The company creates an MPS and plans manufacturing according to the MPS, but it uses kanban-like signals to modify the schedule. For example, if the company receives signals that indicate increased customer demand, it might add an extra production shift for a while in order to build inventory to meet the increased demand. This combination approach requires sophisticated information systems for implementation.

Two acronyms are common in the manufacturing domain: **Materials requirements planning (MRP)** is an application that plans the need for materials and inventories of materials used in the manufacturing process. MRP does not include the planning of personnel, equipment, or facilities requirements.

Manufacturing resource planning (MRP II) is a follow-up to MRP that includes the planning of materials, personnel, and machinery. MRP II supports many linkages across the organization, including linkages with sales and marketing via the development of a master production schedule. MRP II also includes the capability to perform what-if analyses on variances in schedules, raw materials availabilities, personnel, and other resources.[1]

Figure CE8-6
Sample Manufacturing Plan

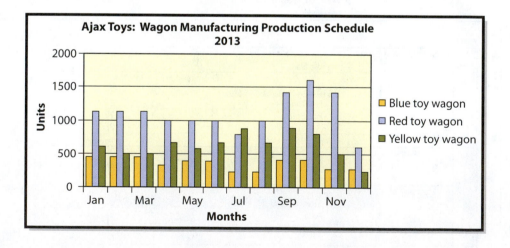

---

[1]To add even more complication to this subject, some in the operations management field use the terms *MRP Type I* and *MRP Type II* instead of *MRP* and *MRP II*. *MRP Type I* refers to material requirements planning; *MRP Type II* refers to manufacturing resource planning. When used in this way, the different interpretations of the letters *MRP* are ignored, as if *MRP* were not an acronym. Unfortunately, such sets of confusing terminology cannot be avoided in a growing field.

MANUFACTURING OPERATIONS

A fourth category of IS in manufacturing is the control of machinery and production processes. Computer programs operate lathes, mills, and robots, and even entire production lines. In a modern facility, these programs have linkages to the manufacturing-scheduling applications. Because they run machines rather than directly support business activities, we will not consider them further.

 WHAT ARE THE FUNCTIONS OF HUMAN RESOURCES APPLICATIONS?

Human resources applications support recruitment, compensation, assessment, development and training, and planning. The first-era human resources (HR) applications did little more than compute payroll. Modern HR applications concern all dimensions of HR activity, as listed in Figure CE8-7.

Depending on the size and sophistication of the company, recruiting methods may be simple or very complex. In a small company, posting a job may be a simple task requiring one or two approvals. In a larger, more formal organization, posting a new job may involve multiple levels of approval requiring use of tightly controlled and standardized procedures.

Compensation includes payroll for both salaried employees and hourly employees. It may also include pay to consultants and permanent, but nonemployee, workers, such as contractors and consultants. Compensation refers not only to pay, but also to the processing and tracking of vacation, sick leave, and health care and other benefits. Compensation activities also support retirement plans, company stock purchases, and stock options and grants. They can also include transferring employee contribution payments to charitable organizations such as the United Way and others.

Employee assessment includes the publication of standard job and skill descriptions as well as support for employee performance evaluations. Such support may include applications that allow employees to create self-evaluations and to evaluate peers and subordinates. Employee assessment is used for the basis of compensation increases as well as promotion.

Development and training activities vary widely from firm to firm. Some organizations define career paths formally, with specific jobs, skills, experience, and training requirements. HR applications have features and functions to support the publication of these paths. Some HR applications track training classes, instructors, and students.

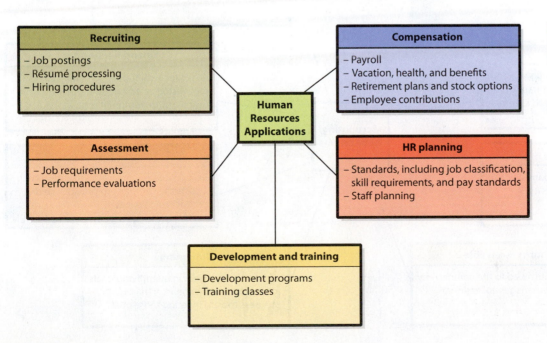

Figure CE8-7
Functions of Human Resources Applications

Finally, HR applications must support planning functions. These include the creation and publication of organizational standards, job classifications, and compensation ranges for those classifications. Planning also includes determining future requirements for employees by level, experience, skill, and other factors.

Q6 WHAT ARE THE FUNCTIONS OF ACCOUNTING APPLICATIONS?

Typical **accounting applications** are listed in Figure CE8-8. You know what a general ledger is from your accounting classes. Financial reporting applications use the general ledger data to produce financial statements and other reports for management, investors, and federal reporting agencies such as the Securities and Exchange Commission (SEC).

Cost-accounting applications determine the marginal cost and relative profitability of products and product families. Budgeting applications allocate and schedule revenues and expenses and compare actual financial results to the plan.

Accounts receivable includes not just recording receivables and the payments against receivables, but also account aging and collections management. Accounts payable applications include features to reconcile payments against purchases and to schedule payments according to the organization's payment policy.

Cash management is the process of scheduling payments and receivables and planning the use of cash so as to balance the organization's cash needs against cash availability. Other financial management applications concern checking account reconciliation, as well as managing electronic funds transfer throughout the organization. Finally, treasury applications concern the management and investment of the organization's cash and payment of cash dividends.

Figure CE8-8
Functions of Accounting
Applications

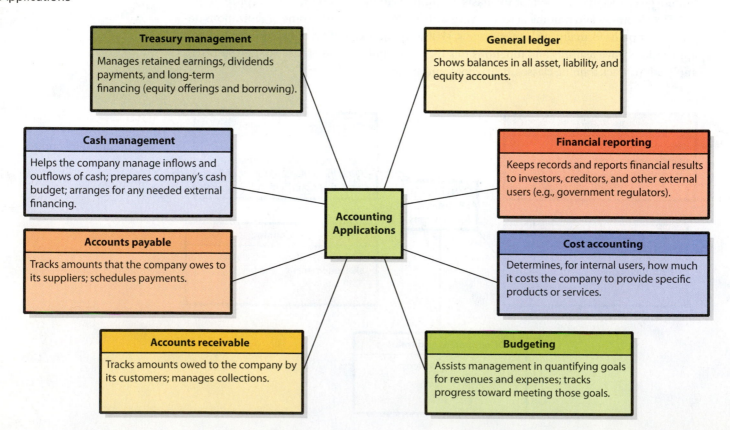

ACTIVE REVIEW

Use this Active Review to verify that you understand the ideas and concepts that answer this chapter extension's study questions.

Q1 WHAT IS THE DIFFERENCE BETWEEN A FUNCTIONAL IS AND A FUNCTIONAL APPLICATION?

Define *functional system* and *functional application,* and distinguish between them. Explain why adaptation is usually required when licensing functional applications. Differentiate functional applications from functional information systems. Explain the statement, "To support business processes, functional applications must be converted to information systems." Explain why acquiring a functional application is just the tip of the iceberg.

Q2 WHAT ARE THE FUNCTIONS OF SALES AND MARKETING APPLICATIONS?

List the functional categories of sales and marketing applications and describe the primary functions of each.

Q3 WHAT ARE THE FUNCTIONS OF OPERATIONS APPLICATIONS?

List the functional categories of operations applications and describe the primary functions of each.

Q4 WHAT ARE THE FUNCTIONS OF MANUFACTURING APPLICATIONS?

List the functional categories of manufacturing applications and describe the primary functions of each. Explain just-in-time inventory policy. Describe a bill of materials and give a brief example. Describe push manufacturing and explain the role of the MPS. Describe pull manufacturing systems and explain the term *kanban.* Decode the acronyms *MRP* and *MRP II,* and explain the functions of each.

Q5 WHAT ARE THE FUNCTIONS OF HUMAN RESOURCES APPLICATIONS?

List the functional categories of human resource applications and describe the primary functions of each.

Q6 WHAT ARE THE FUNCTIONS OF ACCOUNTING APPLICATIONS?

List the functional categories of accounting applications and describe the primary functions of each.

KEY TERMS AND CONCEPTS

Accounting applications 476
Customer management
   applications 471
Bill of materials (BOM) 473
Functional application 468
Functional systems 468
Human resources applications 475
Inventory applications 472

Just-in-time (JIT) inventory policy 473
Lead-generation applications 469
Lead-tracking applications 469
Manufacturing applications 472
Manufacturing resource planning
   (MRP II) 474
Master production schedule
   (MPS) 474

Materials requirements planning
   (MRP) 474
Operations applications 471
Product and brand management
   applications 471
Pull manufacturing process 474
Push manufacturing process 474

USING YOUR KNOWLEDGE

1. The text uses the example of an appointment schedule system as a functional application. Give three examples of other functional systems that the Flores' group will need. Briefly describe each.

2. In your own words, explain the differences between functional applications and functional information systems. Suppose you manage the office staff at Flores' medical practice, and you've just been informed that they are going to implement a new appointment system. Write a one-page memo to the practice partners explaining the role that you think you should have in this process. Justify your statements.

3. The text indicates that when a new customer-facing application is implemented, both employees and customers need to be trained. It is easy to envision employee training, but how do you train your customers? Identify three techniques that you could use to train customers. Employees are paid for training; to customers, it's a nuisance. Describe techniques you could use to incentivize your customers to use the three customer training techniques you identified.

4. Based on this chapter extension, choose the category of functional application that is closest to your major. Select one application from the list of applications described for that category. For that application:
   a. Google or Bing your application and identify five possible off-the-shelf applications.
   b. Characterize the differences among those five applications.
   c. Describe, in general terms, how you would go about evaluating those five applications.
   d. List criteria you would use to select one of those applications.
   e. Summarize the risks of choosing the wrong application.

Enterprise Resource Planning (ERP) Systems

Q1 — WHAT IS THE PURPOSE OF ERP SYSTEMS?

As stated in Chapter 7, **enterprise resource planning (ERP)** is a suite of applications, called **modules**; a database; and a set of inherent processes for consolidating business operations into a single, consistent, computing platform. An **ERP system** is an information system based on ERP technology. ERP systems integrate all of an organization's purchasing, human resources, production, sales, and accounting data into a single system.

The primary purpose of an ERP system is integration; an ERP system allows the left hand of the organization to know what the right hand is doing. This integration allows real-time updates, globally, whenever and wherever a transaction takes place. Critical business decisions can then be made on a timely basis using the latest data.

To understand the utility of this integration, consider the pre-ERP systems shown in Figure CE9-1. This diagram of the processes used by a bicycle manufacturer includes five different databases, one each for vendors, raw materials, finished goods, manufacturing plan, and CRM. Consider the problems that appear with such separated data when the sales department closes a large order, say for 1,000 bicycles.

First, should the company take the order? Can it meet the schedule requirements for such a large order? Suppose one of the primary parts vendors recently lost capacity due to an earthquake, and the manufacturer cannot obtain parts for the order in time. If so, the order schedule ought not to be approved. However, with such separated systems, this situation is unknown.

Even if parts can be obtained, until the order is entered into the finished-goods database, purchasing is unaware of the need to buy new parts. The same comment applies to manufacturing. Until the new order is entered into the manufacturing plan, the production department doesn't know that it needs to increase manufacturing. And, as with parts, does the company have sufficient machine and floor capacity to fill the order on a timely basis? Does it have sufficient personnel with the correct skill sets? Should it be hiring? Can production meet the order schedule? No one knows before the order is approved.

Figure CE9-1 does not show accounting. We can assume, however, that the company has a separate accounting system that is similarly isolated. Eventually, records of business activity find their way to the accounting department and will be posted into the general ledger. With such a pre-ERP system, financial statements are always dated, becoming available several weeks after the close of the quarter or other accounting period.

Contrast this situation with the ERP system in Figure CE9-2. Here, all activity is processed by ERP application programs and consolidated data are stored in a centralized ERP database. When sales is confronted with the opportunity to sell 1,000 bicycles, the information that it needs to confirm that the order, schedule, and terms are feasible can be obtained from the ERP

CE9

Figure CE9-1
Pre-ERP Information Systems

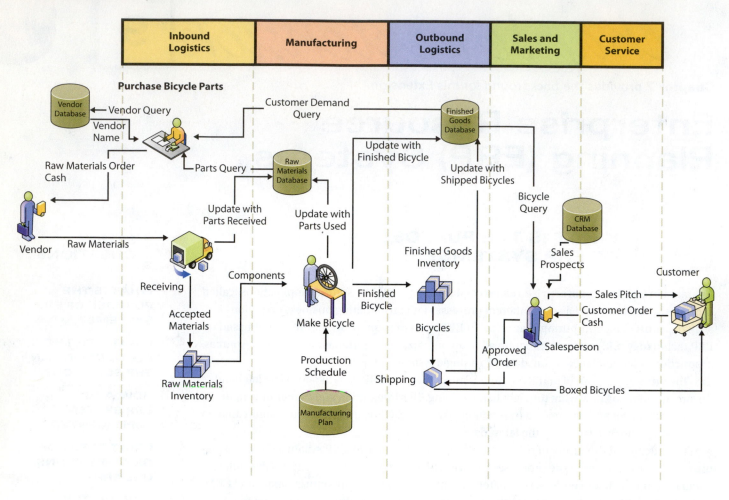

system immediately. Once the order is accepted, all departments, including purchasing, manu-facturing, human resources, and accounting, are notified. Further, transactions are posted to the ERP database as they occur; the result is that financial statements are available quickly, and in most cases correct financial statements can be produced in real time. With such integration, ERP systems can display the current status of critical business factors to managers and executives, as shown in the sales dashboard in Figure CE9-3.

Of course, the devil is in the details. It's one thing to draw a rectangle on a chart, label it "ERP application programs," and then assume that data integration takes all the problems away. It is far more difficult to write those application programs and to design the database to store that inte-grated data. Even more problematic, what procedures should employees and others use to process those application programs? Specifically, what actions should salespeople take before they approve a large order? The following are some of the questions that procedures need to answer or resolve:

- How does the sales department determine that an order is large? By dollars? By volume?
- Who approves customer credit (and how)?
- Who approves production capacity (and how)?
- Who approves schedule and terms (and how)?
- What actions need to be taken if the customer modifies the order?
- How does management obtain oversight on sales activity?

As you can imagine, many other questions must be answered as well.

Figure CE9-2
ERP Information Systems

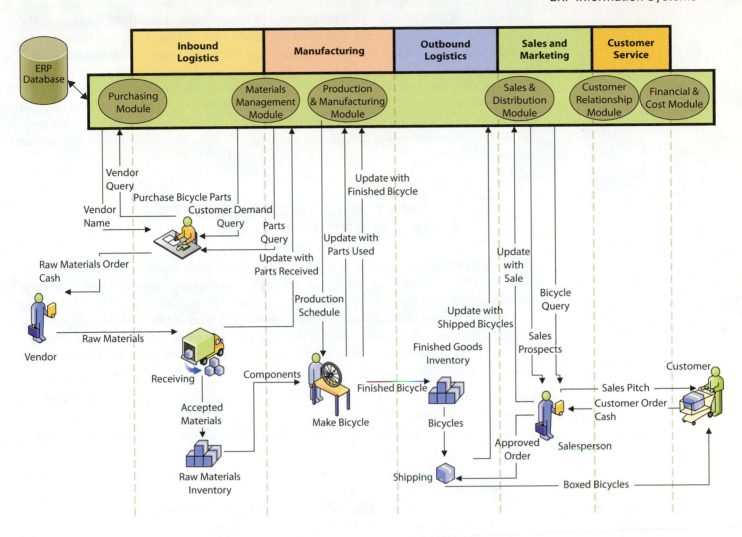

Figure CE9-3
Sales Dashboard

Source: Microsoft Corporation.

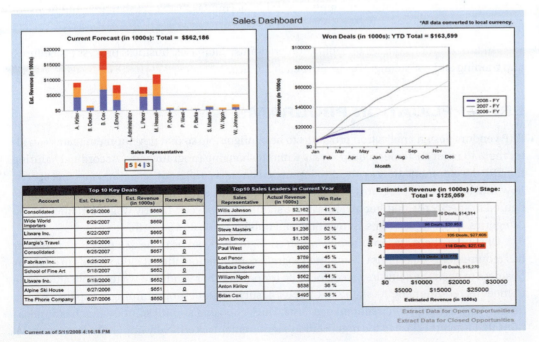

In the late 1980s and early 1990s, some organizations attempted to develop their own ERP applications and procedures. The process was too difficult and expensive for most to succeed. During that era, ERP software vendors developed ERP applications that included program code, databases, and inherent processes that addressed issues such as those just listed. Today, almost no organization develops its own ERP software; such systems are licensed from vendors such as those described in Q4.

Even with solutions provided by ERP vendors, however, the process of converting an organization from systems such as those in Figure CE9-1 to an ERP system such as the one that in Figure CE9-2 is daunting and expensive. For most organizations, it is a multiyear project that involves millions of dollars and hundreds of employees, consultants, and vendor personnel.

WHAT ARE THE ELEMENTS OF AN ERP SOLUTION?

The term *ERP* has been applied to a wide array of application solutions. Some vendors attempted to catch the buzz for ERP by misapplying the term to applications that were nothing more than one or two integrated functional applications.

The organization ERPSoftware360 publishes a wealth of information about ERP vendors, products, solutions, and applications. According to its Web site (*www.erpsoftware360.com/erp-101.htm*), for a product to be considered a true ERP product, it must include applications that integrate the following:

- Supply chain (procurement, sales order processing, inventory management, supplier management, and related activities)
- Manufacturing (scheduling, capacity planning, quality control, bill of materials, and related activities)
- CRM (sales prospecting, customer management, marketing, customer support, call center support)
- Human resources (payroll, time and attendance, HR management, commission calculations, benefits administration, and related activities)
- Accounting (general ledger, accounts receivable, accounts payable, cash management, fixed-asset accounting)

An ERP solution consists of application programs, databases, business process procedures, and training and consulting. We consider each, in turn.

ERP APPLICATION PROGRAMS

ERP vendors design application programs to be configurable so that development teams can alter them to meet customer requirements without changing program code. Accordingly, during the ERP development process, the development team sets configuration parameters that specify how ERP application programs will operate. For example, an hourly payroll application is configured to specify the number of hours in the standard workweek, hourly wages for different job categories, wage adjustments for overtime and holiday work, and so forth.

Of course, there are limits to how much configuration can be done. If a new ERP customer has requirements that cannot be met via program configuration, then it either needs to adapt its business to what the software can do or write (or pay another vendor to write) application code to meet its requirement. As stated in Chapter 4, such custom programming is expensive both initially and in long-term maintenance costs. Thus, choosing an ERP solution that has applications that function close to the organization's requirements is critically important to success.

ERP DATABASES

An ERP solution includes a database design as well as initial configuration data. It does not, of course, contain the company's operational data. During development, the team must enter the initial values for that data as part of the development effort.

If your only experience with databases is creating a few tables in Microsoft Access, then you probably underestimate the value and importance of ERP database designs. SAP, the leading vendor of ERP solutions, provides ERP databases that contain over 15,000 tables. The design includes the metadata for those tables, as well as their relationships to each other and rules and constraints about how the data in some tables must relate to data in other tables. As stated, the ERP solution also contains tables filled with initial configuration data.

Furthermore, although we did not discuss this database feature in Chapter 5, large organizational databases contain two types of program code. The first, called a **trigger**, is a computer program stored within the database that runs to keep the database consistent when certain conditions arise. The second, called a **stored procedure**, is a computer program stored in the database that is used to enforce business rules. An example of such a rule would be never to sell certain items at a discount. Triggers and stored procedures are also part of the ERP solution.

Reflect on the difficulty of creating and validating data models and you will have some idea of the amount of intellectual capital invested in a database design of 15,000 tables. Also, consider the magnitude of the task of filling such a database with users' data!

BUSINESS PROCESS PROCEDURES

The third component of an ERP solution is a set of inherent procedures that implement standard business processes. ERP vendors develop hundreds, or even thousands, of procedures that enable the ERP customer organization to accomplish its work using the applications provided by the vendor. Figure CE9-4 shows a part of the SAP ordering business process; this process implements a portion of the activities shown on the left-hand side of Figure CE9-2. Some ERP vendors call the inherent processes that are defined in the ERP solution **process blueprints**.

Without delving into the details, you should be able to understand the flow of work outlined in this process. Every function (rounded rectangle) consists of a set of procedures for accomplishing that function. Typically, these procedures require an ERP user to use application menus, screens, and reports to accomplish the activity.

As with application programs, ERP users must either adapt to the predefined, inherent processes and procedures or design new ones. In the latter case, the design of new procedures may necessitate changes to application programs and to database structures as well. Perhaps you can begin to understand why organizations attempt to conform to vendor standards.

TRAINING AND CONSULTING

Because of the complexity and difficulty of implementing and using ERP solutions, ERP vendors have developed training curricula and classes. SAP operates universities, in which customers and potential customers receive training both before and after the ERP implementation. In addition, ERP vendors typically conduct classes on site. To reduce expenses, the vendors sometimes train some of the organization's employees, called Super Users, to become in-house trainers, in training sessions called **train the trainer**.

ERP training falls into two broad categories. The first category is training about how to implement the ERP solution. This training includes topics such as obtaining top-level management support, preparing the organization for change, and dealing with the inevitable resistance that develops when people are asked to perform work in new ways. The second category is training on how to use the ERP application software; this training includes specific steps for using the ERP applications to accomplish the activities in processes such as that in Figure CE9-4.

Figure CE9-4

Example of SAP Ordering
Process

Source: Thomas A. Curran, Andrew
Ladd, Dennis Ladd, *SAP/R/3 Reporting
and E-Business Intelligence,* 1st ed.
Copyright 2000.

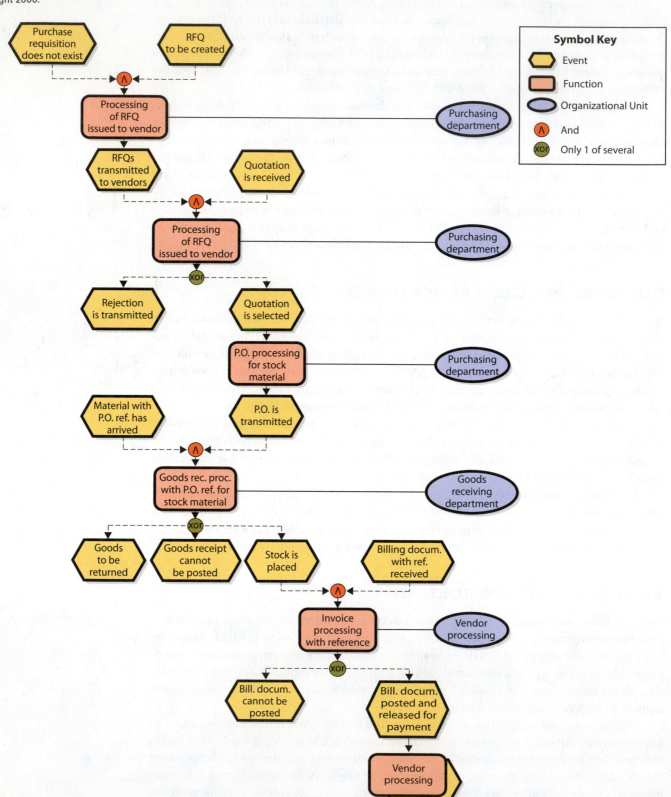

ERP vendors also provide on-site consulting for implementing and using the ERP system. Additionally, an industry of ERP third-party consultants has developed to support new ERP customers and implementations. These consultants provide knowledge gained through numerous ERP implementations. Such knowledge is valued because most organizations only go through an ERP conversion once. Ironically, having done so, they now know how to do it. Consequently, some employees, seasoned by an ERP conversion with their employer, leave that company to become ERP consultants.

HOW ARE ERP SYSTEMS IMPLEMENTED?

Figure CE9-5 summarizes the major tasks in the implementation of an ERP application. The first task is to create a model of current business procedures and practices, which is called the **as-is model**. Managers and analysts then compare those as-is processes to the ERP process blueprints and note differences. The company then must find ways to eliminate the differences, either by changing the existing business process to match the ERP process or by altering the ERP system.

To appreciate the magnitude of these tasks, consider that the SAP blueprint contains over a thousand process models. Organizations that are adopting ERP must review those models and determine which ones are appropriate to them. Then, they compare the ERP models to the models developed based on their current practices. Inevitably, some current-practice models are incomplete, vague, or inaccurate, so the team must repeat the existing process models. In some cases, it is impossible to reconcile any existing system against the blueprint model. If so, the team must adapt, cope, and define new procedures, often to the confusion of current employees.

Once the differences between as-is processes and the blueprint have been reconciled, the next step is to implement the system. Before implementation starts, however, users must be trained on the new processes, procedures, and use of the ERP system's features and function. Additionally, the company needs to conduct a simulation test of the new system to identify problems. Then, the organization must convert its data, procedures, and personnel to the new ERP system. All of this happens while the business continues to run on the old system.

As you'll learn in Chapter 10, plunging the organization into the new system is an invitation to disaster. Instead, a thorough and well-planned test of the new system is necessary, followed by a careful rollout of the new system in stages. Realize, too, that while the new ERP system is being installed normal business activity continues. Somehow the employees of the organization

Figure CE9-5
ERP Implementation

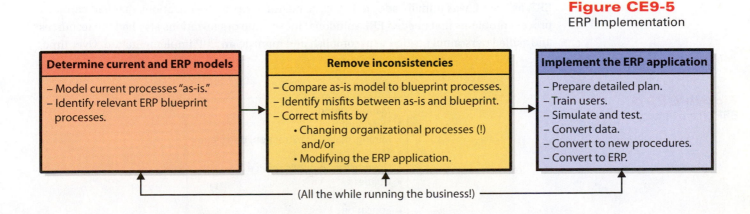

Determine current and ERP models	Remove inconsistencies	Implement the ERP application

– Model current processes "as-is."
– Identify relevant ERP blueprint processes.
	– Compare as-is model to blueprint processes.
	– Identify misfits between as-is and blueprint.
	– Correct misfits by
	  • Changing organizational processes (!) and/or
	  • Modifying the ERP application.
		– Prepare detailed plan.
		– Train users.
		– Simulate and test.
		– Convert data.
		– Convert to new procedures.
		– Convert to ERP.

(All the while running the business!)

must continue to run the company while the rollout is underway. It is a difficult and challenging time for any organization that undergoes this process.

Implementing an ERP system is not for the faint of heart. Because so much organizational change is required, all ERP projects must have the full support of the CEO and executive staff. Like all cross-functional processes, ERP crosses departmental boundaries, and no single departmental manager has the authority to force an ERP implementation. Instead, full support for the task must come from the top of the organization. Even with such support there is bound to be concern and second-guessing.

 WHAT TYPES OF ORGANIZATIONS USE ERP?

ERP originated as an outgrowth of MRP II manufacturing functional applications (see Chapter Extension 8). ERP extended MRP II from just the planning and scheduling of manufacturing to include the planning and use of facilities, people, equipment, materials flow, orders, customers, and accounting, encompassing the scope described in Q2.

ERP BY INDUSTRY TYPE

Because of its origins, the first major ERP customers were large manufacturers. Manufacturers in the aerospace, automotive, and industrial equipment industries led the way. SAP, currently the market leader, spurred ERP growth by providing industry-specific implementations. For example, as SAP assisted one auto manufacturer in using its product, it learned process patterns that were typical of auto manufacturers. Over time, it constructed an auto–manufacturing-specific ERP solution as a product offering. These **industry-specific solutions** became popular, and today SAP and other ERP vendors offer dozens of them. SAP, for example, has 24 industry-specific versions of its ERP products.

Given their success with manufacturers, it was natural for ERP vendors to go up the supply chain and sell ERP solutions to distributors, raw materials extractors and processors, and the petroleum industry. At the same time, health care was becoming more complex, and hospitals were changing from a service to a profit orientation. As you learned in Chapter 7, hospital systems are incredibly complex, and they were ripe candidates for ERP sales and solutions. Over time, ERP use spread to companies and organizations in other industries, as shown in Figure CE9-6.

ERP BY ORGANIZATION SIZE

ERP, as stated, was initially adopted by large manufacturing organizations that had complex process problems that needed ERP solutions. Those large organizations also had the resources and skilled personnel needed to accomplish and manage an ERP implementation. Over time,

Figure CE9-6
ERP Use by Industry

- Manufacturing
- Distribution
- Mining, materials extraction, petroleum
- Medical care
- Government & public service
- Utilities
- Retail
- Education

ERP use spread downward from large companies with billions of dollars in sales to midsized companies with $100 million in sales. Today, ERP is used in small organizations with $5 million to $100 million in sales.

The value chains and basic business processes are similar for small and large organizations. The steps required to check credit, verify product availability, and approve terms are no different for order processing at Amazon.com than they are at Phil's muffler shop. They differ in scale, but not in character.

However, companies of different sizes have one very important difference that has a major impact on ERP: the availability of skilled IT personnel. Small organizations employ only one or two IT specialists who not only manage the ERP system, but the entire IS department as well (see Chapter 11 for a discussion of these responsibilities). They are spread very thin and often are in over their heads during an ERP implementation. Smaller, simpler ERP solutions are common among these companies, as discussed in Q5.

Midsized organizations expand IT from one person to a small staff, but frequently this staff is isolated from senior management. Such isolation creates misunderstanding and distrust. As stated in Q3, because of the expense, organizational disruption, and length of ERP projects, senior management must be committed to the ERP solution. When IT management is isolated, such commitment is difficult to obtain and may not be strong. This issue is so prevalent that many ERP consultants say the first step in moving toward ERP is to obtain deep senior-level management commitment to the project.

Large organizations have a full IT staff that is headed by the chief information officer (CIO), who is a business and IT professional who sits on the executive board and is an active participant in organizational strategic planning. ERP implementation will be part of that strategic process and, once begun, will have the full backing of the entire executive group. See *www.erpsoftware360.com/software-markets.htm* for more information about the role and use of ERP by size of business.

INTERNATIONAL ERP

Another way that the ERP needs of large organizations differ from those of small organizations is international presence. Most billion-dollar companies operate in multiple countries, and the ERP application programs must be available in several languages. Inherent ERP procedures must be adaptable to different cultures. Some companies can declare a single "company language" and force all company business to be transacted in that language (usually English). Other companies must accommodate multiple languages in their ERP solution. We discuss IS internationalization in Chapter Extension 18.

Once implemented, ERP brings huge benefits to multinational organizations. International ERP solutions are designed to support multiple currencies and languages, manage international transfers of goods in inventories, and work effectively with international supply chains. Even more important, ERP solutions provide a worldwide consolidation of financial statements on a timely basis. See *http://advice.cio.com/puneesh/deploy_erp_to_improve_globalization_efficiency_of_your_organization* for more details on the advantages of ERP to international organizations.

Q5 HOW DO THE MAJOR ERP VENDORS COMPARE?

Although more than 100 different companies advertise ERP products, not all of those products meet the minimal ERP criteria listed in Q2. Even of those that do, the bulk of the market is held by the five vendors described in Figure CE9-7.

Figure CE9-7
Characteristics of Top
ERP Vendors

Company	ERP Market Rank	Remarks	Future
Epicor	5	Strong, industry-specific solutions, especially retail.	Epicor 9 designed for flexibility (SOA). Highly configurable ERP. Lower cost.
Microsoft Dynamics	4	Four products acquired AX, Nav, GP, and Solomon. AX and Nav more comprehensive. Solomon on the way out? Large VAR channel.	Products not well integrated with Office. Not integrated at all with Microsoft development languages. Product direction uncertain. Watch for Microsoft ERP announcement on the cloud (Azure).
Infor	3	Privately held corporation that has acquired an ERP product named Baan, along with more than 20 others.	Spans larger small companies to smaller large companies. Offers many solutions.
Oracle	2	Combination of in-house and acquired (PeopleSoft, Siebel) products.	Intensely competitive company with strong technology base. Large customer base. Flexible SOA architecture. Expensive. Oracle CEO Ellison owns 70% of NetSuite.
SAP	1	Led ERP success. Largest vendor, most comprehensive solution. Largest customers.	Technology older. Expensive and seriously challenged by less expensive alternatives. Huge customer base. Future growth uncertain.

ERP VENDOR MARKET RANKING

Figure CE9-7 presents the ERP vendors by market rank rather than by market share because it is difficult to obtain comparable revenue numbers. Infor is owned by private-equity investors and does not publish financial data. Microsoft's ERP revenue is combined with its CRM revenue; thus its true ERP revenue is unknown. Similarly, Oracle and SAP combine ERP revenue with revenue generated by other products.

The rankings were obtained as follows:

- Epicor, which was acquired by the private equity firm Apax partners in 2011, is estimated to have revenues in the $800 million range, but only half, or $400 million, is thought to be ERP system revenue.

- Microsoft Dynamics' revenue is reported to be in the range of $1.3 billion, but that revenue includes general ledger accounting system sales. Still, even though Dynamics' ERP-only revenue is uncertain, it is most likely greater than Epicor's $400 million.

- Industry estimates for Infor's revenue are in the range of $1.8 billion.

- Oracle's ERP revenue is known to be more than Infor's $1.8 billion. Judging by the number of installations and the size of the company's customers, Oracle's ERP revenue is considerably less than SAP's.

In 2005,[1] AMR Research reported that SAP had 42 percent of the market, Oracle 20 percent, Microsoft 4 percent, Infor 2 percent, and Epicor 1 percent. However, Infor has substantially increased its market position since 2005, and its revenues have surpassed Microsoft's.

---

[1]Marianne Bradford, *Modern ERP* (Lulu.com, 2008), p. 11.

ERP PRODUCTS

Figure CE9-8 shows how the ERP products from each of these companies relate to the size of their customers. Both Epicor and Microsoft Dynamics address the needs of small and midsized organizations. Infor has a product for almost everyone, as you'll see. Oracle and SAP serve the largest organizations. Specific product details follow.

Epicor

Epicor is known primarily for its retail-oriented ERP software, although it is broadening its penetration in other industry segments. Its lead ERP product, Epicor 9, is based on a modern software development design pattern called *service-oriented architecture (SOA)*. This design pattern enables cost-effective application flexibility and allows organizations to connect their application programs with Epicor 9 in highly customizable ways. Epicor's products are lower in cost than those from other companies.

Microsoft Dynamics

Microsoft offers five ERP products, all obtained via acquisition: AX (pronounced "A and X," not "axe"), Nav, GP, Solomon, and Dynamics CRM. AX and Nav have the most capabilities; GP is more limited and easier to use. The future of Solomon is cloudy; supposedly Microsoft outsources the maintenance of the code to provide continuing support to existing customers. To add to the confusion, although Dynamics CRM is primarily a CRM product, it is extensible in ways that enable customers to use it for ERP as well as CRM.

Microsoft is in the process of consolidating its offerings. Most likely AX will continue going forward as a true ERP product for larger organizations. Dynamics CRM will serve as a CRM product as well as a platform for custom ERP solutions. Dynamics GP, which is the easiest of the products to install, will continue as a general-ledger program that can also be used as a platform for simpler ERP solutions.

Microsoft relies heavily on its network of independent software vendors to create customer solutions using the Dynamics platform. These vendors take off-the-shelf Dynamics products and adapt and customize them for particular situations. Further developments in

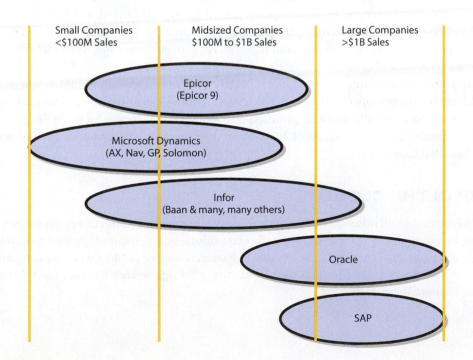

Figure CE9-8
Top ERP Vendors and Customer Size

the Dynamics product line are likely. Search *www.microsoft.com* for the keyword *dynamics* to learn more.

Infor

Infor was purchased in 2002 by private-equity investors, primarily Golden Gate Partners. The company then went on an acquisition binge to consolidate multiple product offerings under one sales and marketing organization. It purchased Baan, a well-known and successful ERP company, along with more than 20 other companies. Today, Infor sells many ERP products for many different industries.

As you might imagine, the products vary in purpose, scope, and quality. They span the mid-range, serving higher-end small companies and lower-end large companies. The Infor story is still being written; the company remains little known, despite its sizable revenue and expansive product portfolio.

Oracle

Oracle is an intensely competitive company with a deep base of technology and high-quality technical staff. Oracle developed some of its ERP products in-house, and complemented those products with the acquisition of PeopleSoft (high-quality HR products) and Siebel (high-quality CRM products).

Oracle's ERP products are designed according to SOA principles and hence are adaptable and customizable. Beginning with its first DMBS product release, Oracle has never been known to create easy-to-use products. It is known, however, for producing fully featured products with superior performance. They are also expensive.

Oracle CEO Larry Ellison owns 70 percent of NetSuite, a company that offers a cloud-based solution for integrated financial reporting for large, international organizations. It would not be unexpected for Oracle to acquire that company as the part of a future ERP product in the cloud.

SAP

SAP is the gold standard of ERP products. It led the direction of the ERP industry in the 1990s and the first decade of the 21st century. SAP sells to the largest companies and offers the most expensive of the ERP products.

Ironically, SAP's past success creates a problem today. SAP uses classic, thick-client, client-server architecture. Because of its installed base, SAP cannot make a rapid move to cloud-based solutions. Instead, it must focus resources and attention on the needs of its current customers (and the attendant, large revenue stream from their maintenance contracts).

In 2003, SAP announced Netweaver, which is an SOA-based system that serves as the backbone for integrating existing SAP applications. Netweaver is believed to be the way in which SAP will gradually move its products and installed base toward a more flexible and modern product architecture. As of 2010, Netweaver has not achieved prominence in the SAP installed base.

ERP IN THE CLOUD

ERP vendors, like all other software vendors today, are engaged in the development of new cloud-based products. You can expect many acquisitions by the major players such as Oracle and SAP. In fact, as of early 2012, Oracle and SAP seem to be in a bidding war over companies that can add cloud-based products to their existing offerings. Search the Web for *Ariba and Vitrue acquisitions* to learn more.

The problem for all ERP vendors, but particularly for Oracle and SAP, is their past success. They have licensed and installed billions of dollars of client-server ERP software, and they cannot walk away from those products or the revenue of lucrative support contracts that they entail. Further, their customers face similar challenges. They want to move to the lower costs of the cloud, but they cannot plunge into new cloud-based solutions without causing considerable organizational turmoil, if not failure.

Thus, both ERP vendors and their customers seek application and systems migration strategies that will enable them to maintain quality service, while at the same time using the cloud as much as they can.

Mobile systems further complicate this situation. Not only do companies need to move their applications to the cloud, they also need to provide both thin-client and native mobile applications. However, ERP systems contain business critical and exceedingly confidential data; allowing access via mobile devices is potentially a serious security threat. See also the BYOD policy in Chapter Extension 7.

As of 2012, the story is just starting to be told. You can expect that it will continue to evolve over the early years of your career. If you are interested in operations and information systems, this is a great opportunity for employment.

ACTIVE REVIEW

Use this Active Review to verify that you understand ideas and concepts that answer this chapter extension's study questions.

Q1 WHAT IS THE PURPOSE OF ERP SYSTEMS?

Define *ERP* and *ERP system*. Identify the primary purpose of an ERP system. Summarize the problems that the bicycle manufacturer in Figure CE9-1 has. Explain how the ERP system in Figure CE9-2 overcomes those problems. Explain why "the devil is in the details." Describe the reasons that organizations find it next to impossible to create their own ERP solutions.

Q2 WHAT ARE THE ELEMENTS OF AN ERP SOLUTION?

List the requirements that a system must meet to be considered a legitimate ERP solution. Name four components of an ERP solution. Explain how and why ERP applications are configurable. Describe the components of an ERP database design. Define *trigger* and *stored procedure*. How do such designs differ from the design of the typical Access database? Explain the importance of *process blueprints*. Interpret Figure CE9-4. Explain the term *train the trainer,* and summarize two categories of training. Explain the role of consultants in ERP implementations.

Q3 HOW ARE ERP SYSTEMS IMPLEMENTED?

Summarize the process shown in Figure CE9-5. Explain why it is expensive and time consuming. Explain why it is necessary for the project to have the full support of senior management.

Q4 WHAT TYPES OF ORGANIZATIONS USE ERP?

Describe the origins of ERP, and explain how those origins led to the initial ERP implementations in industry. Define *industry-specific solution.* Summarize the three categories of business size defined in this chapter extension. Explain how the fundamental ERP processes are the same for different sized organizations and how the IT departments differ. Describe the value of ERP systems for international organizations.

Q5 HOW DO THE MAJOR ERP VENDORS COMPARE?

Name the five primary ERP vendors and rank them according to market size. Name and describe the primary product(s) of each of those five vendors. Explain how the vendors' products relate to customer size. Describe the status of ERP in the cloud, and summarize the opportunities and challenges of cloud-based ERP to both vendors and customers.

KEY TERMS AND CONCEPTS

As-is model 485
Enterprise resource planning (ERP) 479
ERP system 479

Industry-specific solution 486
Modules 479
Process blueprint 483

Stored procedure 483
Train the trainer 483
Trigger 483

USING YOUR KNOWLEDGE

1. Using the patient discharge process in Figure 7-5 (page 170), explain how the hospital benefits from an ERP solution. Describe why integration of patient records in one system is better than spreading patient records across separated databases. Explain the value of an industry-specific ERP solution to the hospital.

2. In your own words, restate how ERP systems eliminate the problems of departmental information silos.

   Reread GearUp's process problem in Chapter 2. How would an ERP system make it possible for buyers to have access to operations' experience with vendors? If GearUp wanted to implement, which of the vendors in Figure CE9-7 would likely have a suitable product. Would you recommend ERP to GearUp? Why or why not?

3. Google or Bing each of the five vendors in Figure CE9-7. In what ways have their product offerings changed since this edition was written? Do those vendors have new products? Have they made important acquisitions? Have they been acquired? Have any new companies made important inroads into their market share? Update Figure CE9-7 with any important late-breaking news.

4. Search the Web for the phrase *ERP in the Cloud*. Summarize major cloud-based ERP products that are available at the time of your search. Search for *SAP acquisitions* as well as *Oracle acquisitions*. Summarize recent acquisition activity. Summarize what you think appear to be SAP and Oracle cloud-based ERP strategies.

5. Go to *www.microsoft.com* and search for "Microsoft Dynamics." Ignore Dynamics CRM. Have any important changes occurred in Microsoft's ERP product offerings since this edition was written? Has Microsoft brought a cloud-based ERP solution to market? Have any of the four ERP systems described in the chapter extension been better integrated with Office or the Microsoft Developer's platform? Using your knowledge guided by experience, what do you think are Microsoft's intentions with regard to ERP?

Supply Chain Management

 WHAT ARE TYPICAL INTER-ENTERPRISE PROCESSES?

As stated in Chapter 7, an inter-enterprise is an information system that is shared by two or more independent organizations. The PRIDE system is an inter-enterprise system. Inter-enterprise system management is more difficult than management for other types of processes, because cooperation is governed by negotiation and contract, and conflict resolution is done by negotiation, arbitration, and litigation.

Inter-enterprise IS vary in scope and complexity. An example of a simple inter-enterprise IS is a sales process at a small retailer in which the retailer processes customers' credit card transactions. The retailer, customer, and credit card company (and possibly the bank that issued the card) are all part of the business process that processes the payment. Such a process is common, standardized, and relatively simple; few businesses give it much thought. Processing of checks using the **Automated Clearing House (ACH)** system among banks is another example of a standardized inter-enterprise system though one that is more complicated than that for processing credit card transactions.

At the other end of the spectrum are customized inter-enterprise systems among large companies. Consider, for example, the inter-enterprise IS that exists among Boeing, General Electric, and other companies for supplying engines to the 787 aircraft, whose production Boeing has largely outsourced. The complexity of the interactions among the supplying organizations, as well as the number of supplying organizations, meant that new, customized inter-enterprise processes had to be designed and agreed upon.

This chapter extension considers a sample inter-enterprise IS of supply chain management among distributors and retailers. We will consider supply chain management from a generic standpoint using examples that are much simpler than the Boeing/GE process. Understanding the principles in this chapter extension will serve as a good basis if you work in more complicated supply chain situations during your career.

Q2 **WHAT IS A SUPPLY CHAIN?**

A **supply chain** is a network of organizations and facilities that transforms raw materials into products delivered to customers. Figure CE10-1 shows a generic supply chain. Customers order from retailers, who, in turn, order from distributors, who, in turn, order from manufacturers, who, in turn, order from suppliers. In addition to the organizations shown here, the supply chain also includes transportation companies, warehouses, and inventories and some means for transmitting messages and information among the organizations involved.

Figure CE10-1
Supply Chain Relationships

Because of disintermediation, not every supply chain has all of these organizations. Dell, for example, sells directly to the customer. Both the distributor and retailer organizations are omitted from its supply chain. In other supply chains, manufacturers sell directly to retailers and omit the distribution level.

The term *chain* is misleading. *Chain* implies that each organization is connected to just one company up (toward the supplier) and down (toward the customer) the chain. That is not the case. Instead, at each level, an organization can work with many organizations both up and down the supply chain. Thus, a supply chain and the processes that support it are networks.

To understand the operation of a supply chain, consider Figure CE10-2. Suppose you decide to take up cross-country skiing. You go to a recreation vendor such as REI (either by visiting one of its stores or its Web site) and purchase skis, bindings, boots, and poles. To fill your order, REI removes those items from its inventory of goods. Those goods have been purchased, in turn, from distributors. According to Figure CE10-2, REI purchases the skis, bindings, and poles from one distributor and boots from a second. The distributors, in turn, purchase the required items from the manufacturers, which, in turn, buy raw materials from their suppliers.

The only source of revenue in a supply chain is the customer. In the REI example, you spend your money on the ski equipment. From that point all the way back up the supply chain to the raw material suppliers, there is no further injection of cash. The money you spend on the ski equipment is passed back up the supply chain as payments for goods or raw materials. Again, the customer is the only source of revenue.

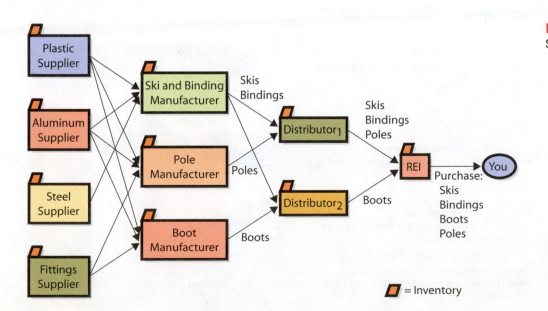

Figure CE10-2
Supply Chain Example

WHAT FACTORS AFFECT SUPPLY CHAIN PERFORMANCE?

Four major factors, or *drivers*, affect supply chain performance: facilities, inventory, transportation, and information.[1] Figure CE10-3 lists these drivers of supply chain performance. We will summarize the first three factors in this text and focus our attention on the fourth factor, information. (You can learn in detail about the first three factors in operations management classes.)

As Figure CE10-3 indicates, *facilities* concern the location, size, and operations methodology of the places where products are fabricated, assembled, or stored. The optimal design of facilities is a complicated subject. For example, given all of REI's stores and its e-commerce site, where should it locate its warehouses? How large should they be? How should items be stored and retrieved from the inventories? If one considers facilities for the entire supply chain, these decisions become even more complicated.

Inventory includes all of the materials in the supply chain, including raw materials, in-process work, and finished goods. Each company in Figure CE10-2 maintains one or more inventories. When you and others purchase items from REI, its inventory is reduced, and at some point REI reorders from its distributors. The distributors, in turn, maintain their inventories, and at some point they reorder from the manufacturers, and so forth.

Managing an inventory requires balancing between availability and cost. Inventory managers can increase product availability by increasing inventory size. Doing so, however, increases the cost of the inventory and, thus, reduces the company's profitability. However, decreasing the size of the inventory increases the odds that an item will be unavailable for purchase. If that happens, the customer may order from a different source, which will reduce the company's revenue and profit. Inventory management is always a balance between availability and cost.

Inventory management decisions include not only the size of the inventory, but also the frequency with which items are reordered and the size of reorders. For example, assume that REI determines that it needs an inventory of 1,000 boots per month. It can order

Figure CE10-3
Drivers of Supply Chain
Performance

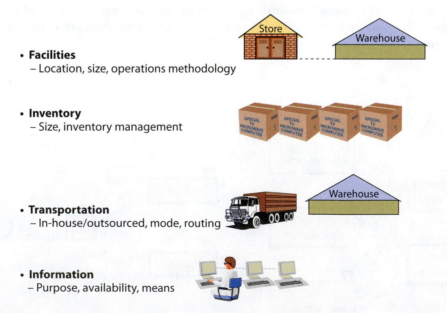

- **Facilities**
  – Location, size, operations methodology

- **Inventory**
  – Size, inventory management

- **Transportation**
  – In-house/outsourced, mode, routing

- **Information**
  – Purpose, availability, means

[1]Sunil Chopra and Peter Meindl, *Supply Chain Management,* 4th ed. (Upper Saddle River, NJ: Prentice Hall, 2004), pp. 41–43.

the full 1,000 at the start of the month or it can order 250 four times per month. Decisions like this and other inventory management decisions have a major impact on supply chain performance.

Transportation, the third driver in Figure CE10-3, concerns the movement of materials in the supply chain. Some organizations have their own transportation facilities; others use outsourced vendors such as Roadway, UPS, and FedEx; still others use a combination. The transportation mode (such as surface versus air) influences both speed and cost. Routing decisions affect how goods are moved from stage to stage throughout the supply chain.

The fourth driver, *information*, is the factor that most concerns us. Information influences supply chain performance by affecting the ways that organizations in the supply chain request, respond, and inform one another. Figure CE10-3 lists three factors of information: purpose, availability, and means. The *purpose* of the information can be transactional, such as orders and order returns, or it can be informational, such as the sharing of inventory and customer order data. *Availability* refers to the ways in which organizations share their information; that is, which organizations have access to which information and when. Finally, *means* refers to the methods by which the information is transmitted. Modern organizations use some version of the SOA standards for exchanging information.

We will expand on the role of information in the supply chain throughout this chapter extension. For now, however, we consider two of the ways that information can affect supply chain performance: supply chain profitability and the bullwhip effect.

Q4 HOW DOES SUPPLY CHAIN PROFITABILITY DIFFER FROM ORGANIZATIONAL PROFITABILITY?

Each of the organizations in Figures CE10-1 and CE10-2 is an independent company, with its own goals and objectives. Each has a competitive strategy that may differ from the competitive strategies of the other organizations in the supply chain. Left alone, each organization will maximize its own profit, regardless of the consequences of its actions on the profitability of the others.

Supply chain profitability is the difference between the sum of the revenue generated by the supply chain and the sum of the costs that all organizations in the supply chain incur to obtain that revenue. In general, the maximum profit to the supply chain *will not* occur if each organization in the supply chain maximizes its own profits in isolation. Usually, the profitability of the supply chain increases if one or more of the organizations operates at less than its own maximum profitability.

To see why this is so, consider your purchase of the ski equipment from REI. Assume that you purchase either the complete package of skis, bindings, boots, and poles or you purchase nothing. If you cannot obtain boots, for example, the utility of skis, bindings, and poles is nil. In this situation, an outage of boots causes a loss of revenue not just for the boots, but also for the entire ski package.

According to Figure CE10-2, REI buys boots from distributor 2 and the rest of the package from distributor 1. If boots are unavailable, distributor 2 loses the revenue of selling boots, but does not suffer any of the revenue loss from the nonsale of skis, bindings, and poles. Thus, distributor 2 will carry an inventory of boots that is optimized considering only the loss of boot revenue—not considering the loss of revenue for the entire package. In this case, the profitability to the supply chain will increase if distributor 2 carries an inventory of boots that is larger than optimal for it.

In theory, the way to solve this problem is to use some form of transfer payment to induce distributor 2 to carry a larger boot inventory. For example, REI could pay distributor 2 a premium for the sale of boots in packages and recover a portion of this premium from distributor 1, who would recover a portion of it from the manufacturers, and so forth, up the supply chain. In truth, such a solution is difficult to implement. For higher-priced items or for items with very high volume, there can be an economic benefit for creating an information system to identify such a situation. If the dynamic is long-lasting, it will be worthwhile to negotiate the transfer-payment agreements. All of this requires a comprehensive supply-chain-wide information system, as you will see.

Q5   WHAT IS THE BULLWHIP EFFECT?

The **bullwhip effect** is a phenomenon in which the variability in the size and timing of orders increases at each stage up the supply chain, from customer to supplier (in Figure CE10-2, from *You* all the way back to the suppliers). Figure CE10-4 summarizes the situation. In a famous study,[2] the bullwhip effect was observed in Procter & Gamble's supply chain for diapers.

As you can imagine, except for random variation, diaper demand is constant. Diaper use is not seasonal; the requirement for diapers doesn't change with fashion or anything else. The number of babies determines diaper demand, and that number is constant or possibly slowly changing.

Retailers do not order from the distributor with the sale of every diaper package. The retailer waits until the diaper inventory falls below a certain level, called the *reorder quantity*. Then the retailer orders a supply of diapers, perhaps ordering a few more than it expects to sell to ensure that it does not have an outage.

The distributor receives the retailer's orders and follows the same process. It waits until its supply falls below the reorder quantity, and then it reorders from the manufacturer, with

The Ethics Guide on pages 500–501 discusses some of the ethical issues that occur in supply chain information sharing.

Figure CE10-4
The Bullwhip Effect

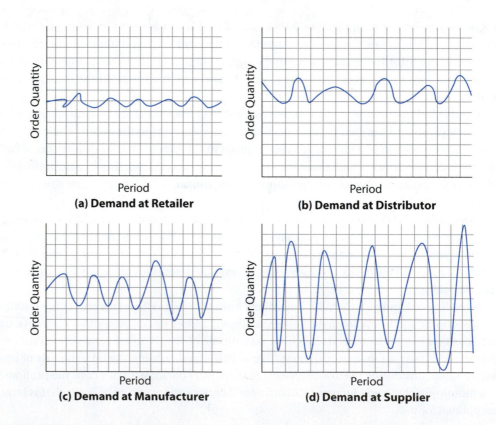

(a) Demand at Retailer

(b) Demand at Distributor

(c) Demand at Manufacturer

(d) Demand at Supplier

[2]Hau L. Lee, V. Padmanabhan, and S. Whang, "The Bullwhip Effect in Supply Chains," *Sloan Management Review,* Spring 1997, pp. 93–102.

perhaps an increased amount to prevent outages. The manufacturer, in turn, uses a similar process with the raw-materials suppliers.

Because of the nature of this process, small changes in demand at the retailer are amplified at each stage of the supply chain. As shown in Figure CE10-4, those small changes become quite large variations on the supplier end.

The bullwhip effect is a natural dynamic that occurs because of the multistage nature of the supply chain. It is not related to erratic consumer demand, as the study of diapers indicated. You may have seen a similar effect while driving on the freeway. One car slows down, the car just behind it slows down a bit more abruptly, which causes the third car in line to slow down even more abruptly, and so forth, until the thirtieth car or so is slamming on its brakes.

The large fluctuations of the bullwhip effect force distributors, manufacturers, and suppliers to carry larger inventories than should be necessary to meet the real consumer demand. Thus, the bullwhip effect reduces the overall profitability of the supply chain.

One way to eliminate the bullwhip effect is to give all participants in the supply chain access to consumer-demand information from the retailer. Each organization can plan its inventory or manufacturing based on the true demand (the demand from the only party that introduces money into the system) and not on the observed demand from the next organization up the supply chain. Of course, an *inter-enterprise information system* is necessary to share such data.

Q6 HOW DO INFORMATION SYSTEMS AFFECT SUPPLY CHAIN PERFORMANCE?

Information systems have had an exceedingly positive impact on supply chain performance. CRM and less-integrated functional systems, such as e-commerce sales systems, have dramatically reduced the costs of buying and selling. Sourcing, buying, and selling have all become faster, easier, more effective, and less costly. Distributed systems in the cloud have enabled businesses to integrate their information systems with less cost and greater speed and agility than ever before.

The presence of information systems has expanded supply chain **speed**, which is the dollar value of goods exchanged in a given period of time. Without information systems, Amazon.com would not have been able to process an average of 158 items per second for 24 hours on November 29, 2010. And, without information systems, it would not have been able to deliver 99 percent of those items on time.

As shown in Figure CE10-5, a third factor is that information systems have enabled both suppliers and customers to reduce the size of their inventories and, thus, reduce their inventory costs. This reduction is possible because the speed and efficiency provided by information systems enables the processing of small orders, quickly.

Information systems also improve delivery scheduling. Using information systems, suppliers can deliver materials and components at the time and in the sequence needed. Such delivery enables just-in-time inventory, and it allows manufacturers to reduce raw materials inventory size as well as the handling of raw materials.

> • Reduce costs of buying and selling.
> • Increase supply chain speed.
> • Reduce size and cost of inventories.
> • Improve delivery scheduling—enable JIT.
> • Fix bullwhip effect.
> • Do not optimize supply chain profitability.

Figure CE10-5
Benefits of Information Systems on Supply Chain Performance

Ethics Guide

The Ethics of Supply Chain Information Sharing

Suppose that you work for a distributor that has developed information systems to read inventory data both up and down the supply chain. You can query the finished goods inventories of your manufacturers and the store inventories of your retailers. These systems were developed to increase supply chain efficiency and profitability. Consider the following situations:

Situation A: You notice that the store inventories of all retailers are running low on items in a particular product family. You know the retailers will soon send rush orders for some of those items, and, in anticipation, you accumulate an oversupply of those items. You query the manufacturers' inventory data, and you find that the manufacturers' finished goods inventories are low. Because you believe you have the only supply of those items, you increase their price by 15 percent. When the retailers ask why, you claim extra transportation costs. In fact, all of the increase is going straight to your bottom line.

Situation B: Unknown to you, one of your competitors has also accumulated a large inventory of those same items. Your competitor does not increase prices on those items, and consequently you sell none at your increased price. You decide you need to keep better track of your competitors' inventories in the future.

You have no direct way to read your competitors' inventories, but you can infer their inventories by watching the decrease of inventory levels on the manufacturer side and comparing that decrease to the sales on the retail side. You know what's been produced, and you know what's been sold. You also know how much resides in your inventory. The difference must be held in your competitor's inventories. Using that process, you now can estimate your competitors' inventories.

Situation C: Assume that the agreement that you have with the retailers is that you are able to query all of their current inventory levels but only the orders they have with you. You are not supposed to be able to query orders they have with your competitors. However, the information system contains a flaw, and by mistake you are able to query everyone's orders, your own as well as your competitors'.

Situation D: Assume the same agreement with your retailers as in situation C. One of your developers, however, notices a hole in the retailer's security system and writes a program to exploit that hole. You now have access to all of the retailer's sales, inventory, and order data.

1. Is the price increase in situation A legal? Is it ethical? Is it smart? Why or why not? Is it ethical to claim transportation costs have caused the increase? What are some of the long-term consequences of this action?

2. In situation B, is it legal for you to query and analyze the data to estimate your competitors' inventory levels? Is it ethical? Would you recommend this kind of analysis?

3. Do you have a responsibility to reveal the hole in the information system in situation C? What are the consequences if you do not reveal this problem? Is it illegal or unethical for you to benefit from this mistake?

4. Do you have a responsibility to reveal the hole in the information system in situation D? What are the consequences if you do not reveal this problem? Is it illegal or ethical or unethical? for you to benefit from this mistake? Is your response different between situations C and D? Why or why not?

5. In a supply chain, it is likely that other organizations can query your data as well as you querying theirs. What steps do you think you need to take to ensure that your own systems are not being misused and do not have errors or security holes?

Source: JanMika/Fotilia

Information systems have the capability to eliminate the bullwhip effect, though doing so requires retailers to be willing to share sales data with the entire supply chain. Such sharing entails some risk, and many retailers refuse to release such data. Part of the problem is that the benefit of releasing such data accrues to the supply chain and not to the retailer. Although there is some possibility that eliminating the bullwhip effect will reduce prices, many retailers view it only as a *potential* possibility. In their view, it is more likely that the savings will be kept by upstream companies.

This doubt brings us to the last factor in Figure CE10-5. Information systems do not optimize supply chain profitability. They benefit the companies that actively participate in a particular information system. However, as noted, maximizing individual company profitability does not necessarily maximize supply chain profitability. Perhaps some system of transfer payments will someday be worked out, but not during my career, and I doubt during yours either.

ACTIVE REVIEW

Use this Active Review to verify that you understand the ideas and concepts that answer this chapter extension's study questions.

Q1 WHAT ARE TYPICAL INTER-ENTERPRISE PROCESSES?

Define inter-enterprise system, and explain why system management is more difficult for such processes than for functional or cross-functional processes. Give examples, other than ones in this book, of simple, standardized inter-enterprise processes and of complex, customized inter-enterprise processes.

Q2 WHAT IS A SUPPLY CHAIN?

Define *supply chain.* Explain how disintermediation affects supply chain structure. Explain why the term *chain* is misleading. Give an example of a supply chain different from the one in Figure CE10-2.

Q3 WHAT FACTORS AFFECT SUPPLY CHAIN PERFORMANCE?

Name the four factors that influence supply chain performance. Briefly explain each.

Q4 HOW DOES SUPPLY CHAIN PROFITABILITY DIFFER FROM ORGANIZATIONAL PROFITABILITY?

Explain the difference between supply chain profitability and organizational profitability. Give an example that demonstrates why maximizing organizational profitability does not necessarily lead to the maximization of supply chain profitability. Explain how, in theory, these two can be made the same.

Q5 WHAT IS THE BULLWHIP EFFECT?

Define the *bullwhip effect*, and explain how it occurs. Describe why the bullwhip effect is undesirable. Explain how information systems can eliminate this effect.

Q6 HOW DO INFORMATION SYSTEMS AFFECT SUPPLY CHAIN PERFORMANCE?

List the ways in which inter-enterprise information systems affect supply chain performance. Define *speed* as it pertains to supply chains. Explain why information systems cannot, today, maximize supply chain profit.

KEY TERMS AND CONCEPTS

Automated Clearing House (ACH) 494
Bullwhip effect 498

Speed 499
Supply chain 494

Supply chain profitability 497

USING YOUR KNOWLEDGE

1. Create a process diagram for the inter-enterprise process that exists to process debit card payments at a grocery store. Create separate swim lanes for the customer, the store, and the customer's bank. Make necessary assumptions and state them. Include sufficient detail so that your process includes the processing of a PIN.

2. Consider the supply chain for Amazon.com. Assume that Amazon.com buys books directly from publishers and also buys from book distributors. Ignore used book sales.
   a. Diagram this supply chain. Use Figure CE10-2 as an example. Because shippers are so important to Amazon.com, include them in your diagram.

b. Explain how the four factors described in Q3 affect this supply chain's performance. Describe how these factors affect Amazon.com's profitability.

c. Do you think the bullwhip effect is a problem for this supply chain? Why or why not?

d. Explain how Amazon.com could use inter-enterprise information systems to obtain time and cost savings for Amazon.com.

3. Search the Internet for the term *supply chain management in the cloud.* Look for at least one vendor that has a cloud-based software offering (IBM is one, but use another if you find it more interesting). Summarize the product offering. In what ways is it cloud based? In what ways will this offering appeal to multiple companies involved in a supply chain inter-enterprise IS.

4. Search the Internet for the term *supply chain management in the cloud.* Look for a case study about a company that has implemented a cloud-based supply chain system. From the case, summarize the ways that the system has resulted in the benefits listed in Figure CE10-5. Summarize benefits in that figure that have not been realized.

chapter extension 11

Chapter 8 provides the background for this Extension.

Hyper-Social Organizations and Knowledge Management

 Q1 **WHAT ARE THE CHARACTERISTICS OF A HYPER-SOCIAL ORGANIZATION?**

As you learned in Chapter 8, the theory of social capital provides an economic perspective on social media. Another perspective is the sociological one developed by Gossieaux and Moran[1] in a model they call the *hyper-social organization*. According to this model, using social media (SM) in an old-style, organization-centric manner is ineffective. The true value of social media can only be achieved when organizations use social media to interact with customers, employees, and partners in a more humane, relationship-oriented way. Rather than sending *messages* that attempt to manage, influence, and control, hyper-social organizations create *relationships* in which both parties perceive and gain value.

Thus, a **hyper-social organization** is an organization that uses social media to transform its interactions with customers, employees, and partners into mutually satisfying relationships with them and their communities. In particular, a hyper-social organization is one that has made the four transitions, called *pillars,* shown in Figure CE11-1. The concepts and language of this model are marketing-oriented, but in this model, marketing is broadly conceived to pertain to employees and partners as well as customers. Consider each of the transitions in Figure CE11-1.

STUDY QUESTIONS

Q1 WHAT ARE THE CHARACTERISTICS OF A HYPER-SOCIAL ORGANIZATION?

Q2 WHAT ARE THE BENEFITS OF KNOWLEDGE MANAGEMENT?

Q3 WHAT ARE EXPERT SYSTEMS?

Q4 WHAT ARE CONTENT MANAGEMENT SYSTEMS?

Q5 HOW DO HYPER-SOCIAL ORGANIZATIONS MANAGE KNOWLEDGE?

Consumers → Humans
Market Segments → Tribes
Channels → Networks
Structure & Control → Messiness

Figure CE11-1
Four Pillars of the Hyper-Social Organization

[1]Francois Gossieaux and Edward K. Moran, *The Hyper-Social Organization* (New York: McGraw-Hill), 2010.
[2]David Court, Dave Elzinga, Susan Mulder, and Ole Jorgen Vetvik, "The Consumer Decision Journey," *McKinsey Quarterly*, June 2009, www.mckinseyquarterly.com/The_consumer_decision_journey_2373, accessed August 2011.

CONSUMERS BECOME HUMANS

According to recent studies, consumers are skeptical of organizational messages and no longer listen. A McKinsey study found that two-thirds of purchase-decision touch points involve SM-based reviews and recommendations outside the realm of organizational messaging.[2] Such skepticism may not be new; it could be that consumers have always held it, but until now social media, advertising and PR were the consumers' only data source. New or not, that skepticism gives a competitive advantage to hyper-social organizations.

Today, customers want informed, useful interactions that help them solve particular problems and satisfy unique needs. Customers increasingly ignore prepackaged organizational messages that tout product benefits. An example of this new style is the sales force in Apple stores that has been trained to act as customer problem-solving consultants and not as sellers of products. Organizations' SM sites need to mirror this behavior; otherwise, social media is nothing more than another channel for classic advertising.

Consider the social media groups that PRIDE will create to encourage patient exercise. Sending emails to members of those groups to promote exercise, or even sending emails to the tribes of those members, is using social media in a pre-hyper-social way. Patients, friends, and families are treated as entities to be influenced, and while such an email campaign is cheaper than printing and mailing instructions, it isn't more effective. However, if PRIDE creates an SM environment in which group members and families can share their successes and failures in an open and honest way, then PRIDE will be relating to the patients and their families as humans with complex personalities and difficult issues.

MARKET SEGMENTS BECOME TRIBES

The second pillar of the hyper-social organization is the transformation of thinking from market segments to tribes. Market segments have key traits and characteristics; tribes, as discussed in Chapter 8, have relationships for defending beliefs or seeking the truth.

Using traditional market-segment thinking, GearUp, the company discussed in the first part of this book, would promote an upcoming soccer event to a market segment of, say, 20- to 25-year-old women who work in retail and live in certain zip codes. Using tribal thinking, GearUp would market to communities that defend the belief that soccer is a great game or to communities that grieved over the last game of the 2011 Women's World Soccer Cup. Such tribal marketing would enable GearUp to follow relationships beyond 25-year-old women to customers and markets that are ripe for sales, but of which GearUp is ignorant. It might be, for example, that the community that is grieving that World Cup game includes 65-year-old grandfathers who are predisposed to buy soccer balls for their granddaughters. Relating to the community will bring those customers into GearUp's network.

A similar transformation is important within organizations. A company with an employee morale problem would, using market-segment thinking, find the categories of employees who are most discontented using the "market segment" of, say, job titles. They might find a major source of discontent among customer support representatives who are working with customers frustrated by failures in a defective product. The traditional management response would be something like, "That's always a problem in customer support; give 'em a bonus." If, instead, the organization were to focus on the seeker-of-the-truth community inside the organization that wants the defective product fixed, it would engage engineers, parts purchasing agents, manufacturing quality assurance employees, as well as customer support. By relating to and supporting a solution by that internal tribe, the company will not only improve morale but also solve the problem and increase internal social capital.

Activity	SMIS
Sense	Reputation management services (e.g., www.reputation.com); Twitter, Facebook, LinkedIn, blogs, other
Engage	Social media; Twitter, Facebook, LinkedIn, blogs, other
Activate	Integrate SM presence with CRM, ERP, other operational systems
Measure	Social monitoring services (e.g., WebiMax); in-house metrics
Story tell	Blogs, videos, YouTube, white papers for benefit of SM communities

easy to order your product, if sales are your goal, but not the obvious nor the immediate purpose of your relationship. Publish the successes of community members in ways that favor your organization but that take a back seat to the community.

HOW CAN SOCIAL MEDIA INFORMATION SYSTEMS (SMIS) FOSTER HYPER-SOCIAL ORGANIZATIONS?

SMIS play a key role for implementing the SEAMS process. Figure CE11-3 summarizes important systems for each of the activities in Figure CE11-2. Before discussing that figure, however, realize that all of these activities require the involvement of personnel in the hyper-social organization. Organizations need to staff and manage this activity, just as they formerly did for their media-buying activity.

Sense Activities

Sensing involves two functions: (1) determining what the communities you care about are saying about you and (2) identifying the structure, goals, and dynamic of communities with which you want to relate. For the first, many organizations hire reputation management services like those provided by Reputation.com and others. These services can be expensive because they must be staffed by human beings who read, comprehend, filter, and synthesize SM conversations about your organization. Of course, an organization can also do its own reputation management as well.

The second function is to identify communities with which you wish to engage and determine their type (defender of belief or seeker of truth), their structure, their key contributors, their goals and objectives, and their willingness to engage with organizations like yours. Given that data, you can then craft the best way of engaging those communities.

Engage

Once you have identified your important communities and have a plan, the next activity is to engage with those communities by creating relationships. Today, organizations use Facebook, Twitter, LinkedIn, and others for this purpose. They also support employee and partner **blogs** and other social media.

Personnel who perform these functions need to be trained in organizational policy and know the strategy and tactics to be used for the engagement. Many organizations have a few **key users** who are personnel trained to perform SM engagement tasks. Nonkey users submit ideas and responses to key users for publication in communities. In this way, the key users serve as a buffer and a filter for possible inappropriate content.

Activate

Although it is important that organizations engage in authentic relationships with the community and not attempt to use the community as a pure advertising and sales channel, it is

CHANNELS BECOME NETWORKS

According to the third pillar of the hyper-social organization, channels become networks. Prior to 1980, organizational communication was highly restricted to a few channels. The United States had three major national TV networks and no more than a half-dozen major national newspapers. Consumers got their news twice a day: in the morning in the paper and in the evening on the 6 o'clock nightly news.

In that highly constrained environment, organizations could control messaging via paid advertising and public relations efforts to manipulate editors and writers. It was easy to get the consumers' attention because there were no alternatives. The Internet, Web sites, broadcast email, cable TV, and smartphones have blown those existing channels apart. Only those over 60 watch the evening news, and they are notoriously poor consumers. With the myriad of communications channels available today, there is so much traffic that organizations find it nearly impossible to obtain attention in these channels.

As stated earlier, social media enables people to form communities based on common interests, and to obtain any of the consumers' attention today organizations must engage with networks in those communities, based on those interests. And, the communities are bored with, even disdainful of, traditional product data.

According to Gossieaux and Moran, another key difference is that channels transmit *data*, whereas networks transmit *knowledge*. Actually, many consumers would disagree that ads, at least, carry data. They carry the subliminal message that if you, too, buy that car, or paint, or soap, you too will be handsome, admired, or loved and happy. In any case, that kind of "data" has no power in today's networks. Instead, hyper-social organizations use channels to transmit messages valued by recipients. For example, doctors and staff can use PRIDE to transmit new techniques for increasing patient exercise, recent research on the relationship of exercise and post-operation health, the latest developments in post-operative cardiac care, and so forth.

STRUCTURE AND CONTROL BECOME MESSY

The final pillar of the hyper-social organization is a transition from established, structured messaging processes to fluid, dynamic ones. Organizations and executives no longer plan and control organizational messaging. Such messaging emerges via a dynamic, SM-based process. That concept is anathema to traditional organizations and managers, and in the early years of your career, you are likely to be part of helping your organization overcome resistance to it.

To facilitate that transition, the hyper-social organization model defines a dynamic process, called **SEAMS**, with the five major activities shown in Figure CE11-2. The theme that runs through all five of these activities is to engage with communities with authentic relationships that are important to the community. Having done so, in the activate activity, connect your efforts to whatever value chain and process will achieve your organization's strategies. Make it

Activity	Description
Sense	Important communities. What they do, where they hang out, what they care about, how your organization can relate to them.
Engage	In relationships. Talk *with*, not to, community members (customers, employees, partners).
Activate	Connect communities to your internal value chains and processes (Figure 8-6).
Measure	Success in terms of social capital.
Story tell	Publicize community successes. Take a backseat role to the community.

Figure CE11-2
SEAMS Dynamic Process Activities

also important that the organization make it easy for community members to obtain sales-oriented materials and to purchase when they want to. Thus, hooks into the organization's CRM, ERP, and other operational systems need to be provided in a discreet and appropriate manner. By the way, designing applications according to SOA principles greatly facilitates this task.

Measure

As with the sensing activity, many organizations use outside social monitoring services such as WebiMax to assess the effectiveness of the organization's SM efforts. In addition, organizations also staff in-house measuring activities.

Measurements include not only the number of mentions in the target communities, but also the response to the organization's own SM presence. These measurements answer questions such as: How many commenters? How many reviewers? What is the traffic rate on the organization's SM sites, and how is it changing?

Gossieaux and Moran caution that such measurements are likely to overlook the **active lurker**, someone who reads, consumes, and observes activity in one social medium and then broadcasts it in some other medium. An example is someone who sees an interesting feature in GearUp's SM presence and sends a link to that feature to his or her friends. GearUp will be able to measure the traffic generated from the shared link, but they are unable to determine which traffic is due to the active lurker.

Story Telling

Given relationships to important communities, the organization should then develop stories about their interaction with the community and publish those stories back to the community. Dr. Flores and his staff might, for example, commission a video crew to "tell the story" of someone's surgery and follow-up using the PRIDE system and SM site. YouTube is, of course, a common site for such videos. For more technical products, white papers on the appropriate use or solution to problems are also popular.

Storytelling must observe one limit, however. Stories must be authentic accounts of interactions that are important to the SM community. Thinly disguised advertisements will be ignored at best and ridiculed at worst. You can find a story example that Microsoft did of an early user of Office 365 at *www.youtube.com/watch?v=2O4Uc5mUSLA*.

WHAT ARE THE BENEFITS OF KNOWLEDGE MANAGEMENT?

Nothing is more frustrating for a manager to contemplate than the situation in which one employee struggles with a problem that another employee knows how to solve easily. Or, to learn of a customer who returns a large order because the customer could not perform a basic operation with the product that many employees (and other customers) can readily perform. Even worse, someone in the customer's organization may know how to use the product, but the people who bought it didn't know that.

Knowledge management (KM) is the process of creating value from intellectual capital and sharing that knowledge with employees, managers, suppliers, customers, and others who need that capital. The goal of knowledge management is to prevent the kinds of problems just described.

Knowledge management was done before social media, and we discuss two such KM systems in Q3 and Q4. However, notice in the first sentence of this paragraph that the scope of KM (employees, managers, suppliers, customer, and others . . .) is the same scope as that of the use of SM in hyper-social organizations. In fact, modern knowledge management ascribes to hyper-social organization theory, as we will discuss in Q5.

Before we turn to those specific technologies, however, consider the overall goals and benefits of KM. KM benefits organizations in two fundamental ways:

- Improve Process Quality
- Increase team strength

As you know, process quality is measured by effectiveness and efficiency, and knowledge management can improve both. KM enables employees to share knowledge with each other and with customers and other partners. By doing so, it enables the employees in the organization to better achieve the organization's strategy. At the same time, sharing knowledge enables employees to solve problems more quickly and to otherwise accomplish work with less time and other resources, hence improving process efficiency.

Additionally, recall from Chapter Extension 2 that successful teams not only accomplish their assigned tasks, they also grow in capability, both as a team and as individuals. By sharing knowledge, team members learn from one another, avoid making repetitive mistakes, and grow as business professionals.

For example, consider the help desk at any organization, say, one that provides support for electronic components like iPhones. When a user has a problem with an iPhone, he or she might contact Apple support for help. The customer service department has, collectively, seen just about any problem that can ever occur with an iPhone. The organization, as a whole, knows how to solve the user's problem. However, that is no guarantee that a particular support representative knows how to solve that problem. The goal of KM is to enable employees to be able to use knowledge possessed collectively by people in the organization. By doing so, both process quality and team capability improve.

Q3 WHAT ARE EXPERT SYSTEMS?

Organizations are inanimate; they themselves are not knowledgeable. Rather, it is the employees of organizations who possess knowledge. The earliest KM systems, called expert systems, attempted to directly capture employee expertise. They existed long before social media, and in fact were in use long before the Internet.

Expert systems are rule-based systems that encode human knowledge in the form of **If/ Then rules.** Such rules are statements that specify if a particular condition exists, then to take some action. Figure CE11-4 shows an example of a few rules that could be part of a medical expert system for diagnosing heart disease. In this set of rules, the system examines various factors for heart disease and computes a *CardiacRiskFactor*. Depending on the value of that risk factor, other variables are given values.

Figure CE11-4
Example of If/Then Rules

Other rules here...

IF CardiacRiskFactor = 'Null' THEN Set CardiacRiskFactor = 0
IF PatientSex = 'Male' THEN Add 3 to CardiacRiskFactor
IF PatientAge >55 THEN Add 2 to CardiacRiskFactor
IF FamilyHeartHistory = 'True' THEN Add 5 to CardiacRiskFactor
IF CholesterolScore = 'Problematic' THEN Add 4 to CardiacRiskFactor
IF BloodPressure = 'Problematic' THEN Add 3 to CardiacRiskFactor
IF CardiacRiskFactor >15 THEN Set EchoCardiagramTest = 'Schedule'
...
Other rules here...

The set of rules shown here may need to be processed many times because it is possible that *CardiacRiskFactor* is used on the If side of a rule occurring before these rules. Unlike this example, an operational expert system may consist of hundreds, if not thousands, of rules.

The programs that process a set of rules are called **expert systems shells**. Typically, the shell processes rules until no value changes. At that point, the values of all the variables are reported as results.

To create the system of rules, the expert system development team interviews human experts in the domain of interest. The rules in Figure CE11-4 would have been obtained by interviewing cardiologists who are known to be particularly adept at diagnosing cardiac disease. Such a system encodes the knowledge of those highly skilled experts and makes it available to less-skilled or less-knowledgeable professionals.

Many expert systems were created in the late 1980s and early 1990s, but only a few have enjoyed success. They suffer from three major disadvantages. First, they are difficult and expensive to develop. They require many labor hours from both experts in the domain under study and designers of expert systems. This expense is compounded by the high opportunity cost of tying up domain experts. Such experts are normally some of the most sought-after employees in an organization.

Second, expert systems are difficult to maintain. Because of the nature of rule-based systems, the introduction of a new rule in the middle of hundreds of others can have unexpected consequences. A small change can cause very different outcomes. Unfortunately, such side effects cannot be predicted or eliminated. They are the nature of complex rule-based systems.

Third, expert systems were unable to live up to the high expectations set by their name. Initially, proponents of expert systems hoped to be able to duplicate the performance of highly trained experts, like doctors. It turned out, however, that no expert system has the same diagnostic ability as knowledgeable, skilled, and experienced doctors. Even when expert systems were developed that came close in ability, changes in medical technology required constant changing of the expert system, and the problems caused by unexpected consequences made such changes very expensive.

The few expert systems that have been successful have addressed more restricted problems than duplicating a doctor's diagnostic ability. They address problems such as checking for harmful prescription drug interactions and configuring products to meet customer specifications. These systems require many fewer rules and are therefore more manageable to maintain. However, unless expert systems technology gets a boost from massively parallel computing (think MapReduce and Hadoop in Chapter 9), their problems will cause them to fade from use.

 ## WHAT ARE CONTENT MANAGEMENT SYSTEMS?

Content management systems (CMS) are information systems that support the management and delivery of documents and other expressions of employee knowledge. Typical users of content management systems are companies that sell complicated products and want to share their knowledge of those products with employees and customers. Someone at Toyota, for example, knows how to change the timing belt on the four-cylinder 2013 Toyota Camry. Toyota wants to share that knowledge with car owners, mechanics, and Toyota employees.

Similarly, Cisco wants to share with network administrators its knowledge about how to determine if a Cisco router is malfunctioning. Microsoft wants to share with the data miners of the world its knowledge about how to use its Data Transformation Services product to move data from an Oracle database into Excel.

Figure CE11-5
Document Management
at Microsoft.com

Source: http://microsoft.com/backstage/
inside.htm, accessed February 2004.

- 110GB of content
- 3.2 million files
- Content created/changed 24/7 at a rate of 5GB per day
- 1,100 databases
- Multiple languages
- 125 million unique users per month
- 999 million page views per month

WHAT ARE THE CHALLENGES OF CONTENT MANAGEMENT?

Content management systems face serious challenges. First, most content databases are huge; some have thousands of individual documents, pages, and graphics. Figure CE11-5 shows the scale of the content management problem at Microsoft.com (*www.microsoft.com*) back in 2003. (Microsoft no longer publishes this data. We can assume that it is at least an order of magnitude larger today.)

A second challenge is that CMS content is dynamic. The size of the content store in Figure CE11-5 is impressive, but the more critical number is the amount of new or changed content per day: 5GB. This means that roughly 5 percent of the content of Microsoft.com changes *every day*. Clearly, managing content versions is crucial to the success of CMS.

Another complication for content management systems is that documents do not exist in isolation from each other. Documents refer to one another, and multiple documents may refer to the same product or procedure. When one of them changes, others must change as well. To manage these connections, content management systems must maintain linkages among documents so that content dependencies are known and used to maintain document consistency.

A fourth complication is that document contents are perishable. Documents become obsolete and need to be altered, removed, or replaced. Consider, for example, what happens when a new product is announced. As of this writing, Microsoft is promoting Windows RT as a future product. The day Windows RT ships, however, all of this content will need to be altered or removed to reflect that the product has shipped.

Finally, consider the content management problem for multinational companies. Figure CE11-6 shows the many languages for which 3M needs to provide Web content. 3M has tens of thousands of products, some of which are harmful when used improperly. 3M must publish product safety data for all such products in all the languages shown. Every document, in whatever language it was authored, must be translated into all languages before it can be published on 3M's site. And when one of them changes, all of the translated versions must change as well.

WHAT ARE CONTENT MANAGEMENT APPLICATION ALTERNATIVES?

Three common alternatives for content management applications are:

- In-house custom
- Off-the-shelf
- Public search engine

In-house Custom

In the past, organizations developed their own in-house content management applications. A customer support department, for example, might develop in-house database applications to track customer problems and their resolution. Operations might develop an in-house system

Figure CE11-6
Need for Multilanguage
Content

Source: Reproduced with
permission of 3M

to track machine maintenance procedures. Like all custom applications, however, custom content management applications are expensive to develop and maintain. Unless the domain of the content management is crucial to the organization's strategy and no off-the-shelf solution is available, most organizations today choose not to support a custom CMS application.

Off-the-Shelf

Because of the expense of custom applications, many organizations today use off-the-shelf software. Horizontal market products like Microsoft SharePoint provide generalized facilities to manage documents and other content types. As you learned in CE 1, SharePoint supports document libraries and can track and manage document versions. Additionally, SharePoint provides workflows for automated document processing and also supports document search. Office 365 provides SharePoint document processing and access in the cloud, using mobile devices when needed.

Some organizations choose vertical market off-the-shelf applications. An accounting firm, for example, may license a vertical market application to manage document flow for the processing of tax returns or the management of audit documents. Another example is law firms that use vertical applications to manage documents for court cases and other work.

Such off-the-shelf products have considerably more functionality than most in-house systems and they are far less expensive to maintain. Keep in mind, however, that the software is just one component of a content management system. Organizations need to develop data structures and procedures for managing their content; they also need to train users.

Public Search Engines

The largest collection of documents ever assembled exists on the Internet, and the world's best-known document search engine is Google. When you Google a term, you are tapping into the world's largest content management system. This system, however, was not designed for a particular KM purpose; it just emerged.

Because Google searches through all public sites of all organizations, Google is usually the fastest and easiest way to find a public document. This often is true even within an organization. It may be easier, for example, for a General Motors employee to find a General Motors document using Google than using an in-house search engine. Google will have crawled through the General Motors site and will have indexed all documents using its superior technology.

This is content management on the cheap. Just put documents on a public server and let Google or Bing do the rest! However, documents that reside behind a corporate firewall are not publicly accessible and will not be reachable by Google or other search engines. Organizations must index their own proprietary documents and provide their own search capability for them.

Q5 HOW DO HYPER-SOCIAL ORGANIZATIONS MANAGE KNOWLEDGE?

In recent years, social media has changed the orientation of knowledge management. In the past, the focus was on structured systems like expert systems and content management systems. These KM techniques relied on planned and prestructured content management and delivery methods. As you learned in the SLATES model in Chapter 8, social media fosters emergence. In the KM context, employees and others express their knowledge in a variety of modes and media, and the mechanisms for managing and delivering that knowledge emerge from usage.

We define **hyper-social knowledge management** as the application of social media and related applications for the management and delivery of organizational knowledge resources. Progressive organizations encourage their employees to Tweet, post on Facebook or other social media sites, write blogs, and post videos on YouTube and any of the other sites. Of course, as discussed in Chapter 8, such organizations need to develop and publish employee social media policy as well.

Hyper-organization theory provides a framework for understanding this new direction in KM. In this frame, the focus moves from the knowledge and content *per se* to the fostering of authentic relationships among the creators and the users of that knowledge. (As you learned, fostering authentic relationships is the characteristic of hyper-social organizations.)

Blogs provide an obvious example. An employee in customer support who writes a daily blog on current, common customer problems is expressing authentic opinions on the company's products, positive and possibly negative. If the blogs are perceived as authentic, customers will comment upon blog entries and, in the process, teach others how they solved those problems themselves. The open airing of product use issues may make traditional marketing personnel uncomfortable, but this KM technique does insert the company in the middle of customer conversations about possible product problems, and, while it does lose control, the organization is at least a party to those conversations. As stated in Q1, hyper-social organizations move from controlled processes to messy ones.

HYPER-SOCIAL KM ALTERNATIVE MEDIA

Figure CE11-7 lists common hyper-social KM alternative media, whether each medium is used for public, private, or either, and the best group type. Except for rich directories, you know what each of these is already, so we need not define them. As you look through this list, however, consider how they can be used with the particular goal of sharing knowledge. Blogs are well suited for sharing of opinions and reactions.

Wikis can be either public or private. Private wikis are particularly useful for technical teams, such as engineering teams, who need to share common definitions for terms and principles. Surveys are well suited to problem solving along the direction guided by the survey questions.

A **rich directory**, in the next row of Figure CE11-7, is an employee directory that includes not only the standard name, email, phone, and address, but also organizational structure and expertise. With a rich directory, it is possible to determine where in the organization someone works, who is the first common manager between two people, and what past projects

Figure CE11-7
Hyper-Social KM Media

Media	Public or Private	Best for :
Blogs	Either	Defender of belief
Discussion groups (including FAQ)	Either	Problem solving
Wikis	Either	Either
Surveys	Either	Problem solving
Rich directories, e.g. Active Directory	Private	Problem solving
Standard SM: Facebook, Twitter, etc.	Public	Defender of belief
YouTube	Public	Either

and expertise an individual has. For international organizations, such directories also include languages spoken. Microsoft's product Active Directory is the most popular rich directory.

Rich directories are particularly useful in large organizations where people with particular expertise are unknown. For example, who at 3M knows which 3M product is the best to use to glue teak to fiberglass? Probably dozens, but who are they and who is the closest to a factory in Brazil? If no one is near Brazil, does anyone of them speak Portuguese?

Most organizations find standard social media like Facebook and Twitter best used for defender of belief groups. Finally, YouTube can be used for either; videos of employees showing how to solve problems are particularly useful. Go to *www.lie-nielsen.com* and click YouTube to see examples.

RESISTANCE TO HYPER-SOCIAL KNOWLEDGE SHARING

Two human factors inhibit knowledge sharing in hyper-social organizations. The first is that employees can be reluctant to exhibit their ignorance. Out of fear of appearing incompetent, employees may not submit entries to blogs or discussion groups. Such reluctance can sometimes be reduced by the attitude and posture of managers. One strategy for employees in this situation is to provide private media that can only be accessed by a smaller group of people who have an interest in a specific problem. Members of that smaller group can then discuss the issue in a less-inhibiting forum.

The other inhibiting human factor is employee competition. "Look," says the top salesperson. "I earn a substantial bonus from being the top salesperson. Why would I want to share my sales techniques with others? I'd just be strengthening the competition." This understandable perspective may not be changeable. A hyper-social KM application may be ill-suited to a competitive group. Or, the company may be able to restructure rewards and incentives to foster sharing of ideas among employees (e.g., giving a bonus to the group that develops the best idea).

Even in situations where there is no direct competition, employees may be reluctant to share ideas out of shyness, fear of ridicule, or inertia. In these cases, a strong management endorsement for knowledge sharing can be effective, especially if that endorsement is followed by strong, positive feedback. As one senior manager said, "There is nothing wrong with praise or cash, and especially cash."

ACTIVE REVIEW

Use this Active Review to verify that you understand the ideas and concepts that answer this chapter extension's study questions.

Q1 WHAT ARE THE CHARACTERISTICS OF A HYPER-SOCIAL ORGANIZATION?

Define hyper-social organization. Name the four pillars of hyper-social organization, explain each, and give an example of differences of each state in each transition. Explain how the term *messy* pertains to process types. Explain the nature of each SEAMS activity and give an example of the user of SMIS for each.

Q2 WHAT ARE THE BENEFITS OF KNOWLEDGE MANAGEMENT?

Define *knowledge management*. Explain five key benefits of KM. Briefly describe three types of KM systems.

Q3 WHAT ARE EXPERT SYSTEMS?

Define *expert systems, If/Then rules,* and *expert systems shell.* Explain how expert system rules are created. Summarize the three major disadvantages of expert systems and assess their future.

Q4 WHAT ARE CONTENT MANAGEMENT SYSTEMS?

Define *content management system (CMS).* Give two examples, other than those in this text, of the use of a CMS. Describe five challenges organizations face for managing content. Name three CMS application alternatives and explain the use of each.

Q5 HOW DO HYPER-SOCIAL ORGANIZATIONS MANAGE KNOWLEDGE?

Explain how social media has changed the orientation of knowledge management. Define *hyper-social knowledge management*. Explain the focus of hyper-social KM. Explain how a blog written by a customer support representative is an example of hyper-social KM. Explain the hyper-social KM use of each medium in Figure CE11-7. Explain the entries in the second and third columns of this table. Define *rich directory* and explain three uses for it. Summarize possible employee resistance to hyper-social knowledge sharing, and name two management techniques for reducing it.

KEY TERMS AND CONCEPTS

USING YOUR KNOWLEDGE

1. Visit your university's public Web site. Describe characteristics of this Web site that indicate your university is a hyper-social organization. Describe characteristics that indicate it is not hyper-social. How could your university use the SEAMS principles to become more hyper-social?

2. Develop the If/Then rules for an expert system that determines whether a particular student can enroll in a class. For your system, is there a need for multiple passes through the rule set? How accurate do you think your system would be? Which of the disadvantages of expert systems described in the text apply to this system?

3. Consider the test bank that students in a fraternity, sorority, or other organization maintain. Is such a test bank an example of a content management system? Is it a computer-based system? Does it need to be computer-based to be considered a content management system? If it is not computer-based, describe advantages of having it be computer-based. What features and functions would you want in such a system? How could such a test bank be indexed? By professor? By class? What other dimensions might be used for indexing?

4. Assume you developed the system in question 3. Is it legal to use such a system? Is it ethical? Assume that your system is unavailable to all students. Is it unfair? How could you apply the skills and knowledge you obtained in developing such a system to your future career?

5. Explain how the challenges for content management systems described in this chapter extension would apply to the test bank system in your answer to question 3.

6. Explain how you could use hyper-social KM for improving your experience in your MIS class. Identify which media in Figure CE11-7 are applicable to improving class experience. For those that are applicable, give an example of their use. Is this idea worth trying? Why or why not?

chapter extension 12

Chapter 9 provides the background for this Extension.

Database Marketing

Q1 WHAT IS A DATABASE MARKETING OPPORTUNITY?

Database marketing is the application of business intelligence systems to the planning and execution of marketing programs. The term is broader than it sounds. Databases are a key component of database marketing, but, as you'll see, data mining techniques are also very important. To understand the need for database marketing, consider the following scenario:

Mary Keeling owns and operates Carbon Creek Gardens, a retailer of trees, garden plants, perennial and annual flowers, and bulbs. "The Gardens," as her customers call it, also sells bags of soil, fertilizer, small garden tools, and garden sculptures. Mary started the business 10 years ago when she bought a section of land that, because of water drainage, was unsuited for residential development. With hard work and perseverance, Mary has created a warm and inviting environment with a unique and carefully selected inventory of plants. The Gardens has become a favorite nursery for serious gardeners in her community.

"The problem," she says, "is that I've grown so large, I've lost track of my customers. The other day, I ran into Tootsie Swan at the grocery store, and I realized I hadn't seen her in ages. I said something like, 'Hi, Tootsie, I haven't seen you for a while,' and that statement unleashed an angry torrent from her. It turns out that she'd been in over a year ago and wanted to return a plant. One of my part-time employees waited on her and had apparently insulted her or at least didn't give her the service she wanted. So she decided not to come back to The Gardens.

"Tootsie was one of my best customers. I'd lost her, and I didn't even know it! That really frustrates me. Is it inevitable that as I get bigger, I lose track of my customers? I don't think so. Somehow, I have to find out when regular customers aren't coming around. Had I known Tootsie had stopped shopping with us, I'd have called her to see what was going on. I need customers like her.

"I've got all sorts of data in my sales database. It seems like the information I need is in there, but how do I get it out?"

Mary needs database marketing.

Q2 HOW DOES RFM ANALYSIS CLASSIFY CUSTOMERS?

RFM analysis is a way of analyzing and ranking customers according to their purchasing patterns.[1] It is a simple technique that considers how *recently* (R) a customer has ordered, how *frequently* (F) a customer orders, and how much *money* (M) the customer spends per order. We consider this technique here because it is a useful analysis that can be easily implemented.

---

[1]Arthur Middleton Hughes, "Boosting Response with RFM," *Marketing Tools*, May 1996. See also *www.dbmarketing.com*.

Customer	RFM Score		
Ajax	1	1	3
Bloominghams	5	1	1
Caruthers	5	4	5
Davidson	3	3	3

To produce an RFM score, the program first sorts customer purchase records by the date of most recent (R) purchase. In a common form of this analysis, the program then divides the customers into five groups and gives customers in each group a score of 1 to 5. Thus, the 20 percent of the customers having the most recent orders are given an **R score** of 1, the 20 percent of the customers having the next most recent orders are given an R score of 2, and so forth, down to the last 20 percent, who are given an R score of 5.

The program then re-sorts the customers on the basis of how frequently they order. The 20 percent of the customers who order most frequently are given an **F score** of 1, the next 20 percent of most frequently ordering customers are given a score of 2, and so forth, down to the least frequently ordering customers, who are given an F score of 5.

Finally, the program sorts the customers again according to the amount spent on their orders. The 20 percent who have ordered the most expensive items are given an **M score** of 1, the next 20 percent are given an M score of 2, and so forth, down to the 20 percent who spend the least, who are given an M score of 5.

Figure CE12-1 shows sample RFM data. The first customer, Ajax, has ordered recently and orders frequently. The company's M score of 3 indicates, however, that it does not order the most expensive goods. From these scores, the sales team members can surmise that Ajax is a good and regular customer but that they should attempt to up-sell more expensive goods to Ajax.

The second customer in Figure CE12-1 could be a problem. Bloominghams has not ordered in some time, but when it did order in the past, it ordered frequently, and its orders were of the highest monetary value. This data suggests that Bloominghams may have taken its business to another vendor. Someone from the sales team should contact this customer immediately.

No one on the sales team should be talking to the third customer, Caruthers. This company has not ordered for some time; it did not order frequently; and, when it did order, it bought the least-expensive items, and not many of them. The sales team should not waste any time on this customer; if Caruthers goes to the competition, the loss would be minimal.

The last customer, Davidson, is right in the middle. Davidson is an OK customer, but probably no one in sales should spend much time with it. Perhaps sales can set up an automated contact system or use the Davidson account as a training exercise for an eager departmental assistant or intern.

A reporting system can generate the RFM data and deliver it in many ways. For example, a report of RFM scores for all customers can be pushed to the vice president of sales; reports with scores for particular regions can be pushed to regional sales managers; and reports of scores for particular accounts can be pushed to the account salespeople. All of this reporting can be automated.

Q3 HOW DOES MARKET-BASKET ANALYSIS IDENTIFY CROSS-SELLING OPPORTUNITIES?

Suppose you run a dive shop, and one day you realize that one of your salespeople is much better at up-selling to your customers. Any of your sales associates can fill a customer's order, but this one salesperson is especially good at selling customers items *in addition to* those for which they ask. One day, you ask him how he does it.

"It's simple," he says. "I just ask myself what is the next product they would want to buy. If someone buys a dive computer, I don't try to sell her fins. If she's buying a dive computer, she's already a diver and she already has fins. But, these dive computer displays are hard to read. A better mask makes it easier to read the display and get the full benefit from the dive computer."

A **market-basket analysis** is a data mining technique for determining sales patterns. A market-basket analysis shows the products that customers tend to buy together. In marketing transactions, the fact that customers who buy product *X* also buy product *Y* creates a **cross-selling** opportunity; that is, "If they're buying *X*, sell them *Y*" or "If they're buying *Y*, sell them *X*."

Figure CE12-2 shows hypothetical sales data from 400 sales transactions at a dive shop. The first row of numbers under each column is the total number of times an item was sold. For example, the 270 in the first row of *Mask* means that 270 of the 400 transactions included masks. The 90 under *Dive Computer* means that 90 of the 400 transactions included dive computers.

We can use the numbers in the first row to estimate the probability that a customer will purchase an item. Because 270 of the 400 transactions were masks, we can estimate the probability that a customer will buy a mask to be 270/400, or .675.

In market-basket terminology, **support** is the probability that two items will be purchased together. To estimate that probability, we examine sales transactions and count the number of times that two items occurred in the same transaction. For the data in Figure CE12-2, fins and masks appeared together 250 times, and thus the support for fins and a mask is 250/400, or .625. Similarly, the support for fins and weights is 20/400, or .05.

These data are interesting by themselves, but we can refine the analysis by taking another step and considering additional probabilities. For example, what proportion of the customers who bought a mask also bought fins? Masks were purchased 270 times, and of those individuals who bought masks, 250 also bought fins. Thus, given that a customer bought a mask, we can

Figure CE12-2
Market-Basket Example

	Mask	Tank	Fins	Weights	Dive Computer
Mask	270	10	250	10	90
Tank	10	200	40	130	30
Fins	250	40	280	20	20
Weights	10	130	20	130	10
Dive Computer	90	30	20	10	120

	Support				
Num Trans	400				
Mask	0.675	0.025	0.625	0.025	0.225
Tank	0.025	0.5	0.1	0.325	0.075
Fins	0.625	0.1	0.7	0.05	0.05
Weights	0.025	0.325	0.05	0.325	0.025
Dive Computer	0.225	0.075	0.05	0.025	0.3

	Confidence				
Mask	1	0.05	0.892857143	0.076923077	0.75
Tank	0.037037037	1	0.142857143	1	0.25
Fins	0.925925926	0.2	1	0.153846154	0.166666667
Weights	0.037037037	0.65	0.071428571	1	0.083333333
Dive Computer	0.333333333	0.15	0.071428571	0.076923077	1

	Lift (Improvement)				
Mask		0.074074074	1.322751323	0.113960114	1.111111111
Tank	0.074074074		0.285714286	2	0.5
Fins	1.322751323	0.285714286		0.21978022	0.238095238
Weights	0.113960114	2	0.21978022		0.256410256
Dive Computer	1.111111111	0.5	0.238095238	0.256410256	

estimate the probability that he or she will buy fins to be 250/270, or .926. In market-basket terminology, such a conditional probability estimate is called the **confidence**.

Reflect on the meaning of this confidence value. The likelihood of someone walking in the door and buying fins is 250/400, or .625. But the likelihood of someone buying fins, given that he or she bought a mask, is .926. Thus, if someone buys a mask, the likelihood that he or she will also buy fins increases substantially, from .625 to .926. Thus, all sales personnel should be trained to try to sell fins to anyone buying a mask.

Now consider dive computers and fins. Of the 400 transactions, fins were sold 250 times, so the probability that someone walks into the store and buys fins is .625. But of the 90 purchases of dive computers, only 20 appeared with fins. So the likelihood of someone buying fins, given he or she bought a dive computer, is 20/90 or .1666. Thus, when someone buys a dive computer, the likelihood that she will also buy fins falls from .625 to .1666.

The ratio of confidence to the base probability of buying an item is called **lift**. Lift shows how much the base probability increases or decreases when other products are purchased. The lift of fins and a mask is the confidence of fins given a mask, divided by the base probability of fins. In Figure CE12-2, the lift of fins and a mask is .926/.625, or 1.32. Thus, the likelihood that people buy fins when they buy a mask increases by 32 percent. Surprisingly, it turns out that the lift of fins and a mask is the same as the lift of a mask and fins. Both are 1.32.

We need to be careful here, though, because this analysis only shows shopping carts with two items. We cannot say from this data what the likelihood is that customers, given that they bought a mask, will buy both weights and fins. To assess that probability, we need to analyze shopping carts with three items. This statement illustrates, once again, that we need to know what problem we're solving before we start to build the information system to mine the data. The problem definition will help us decide if we need to analyze three-item, four-item, or some other sized shopping cart.

Many organizations are benefiting from market-basket analysis today. You can expect that this technique will become a standard CRM analysis during your career.

By the way, one famous market-basket analysis shows a high correlation of the purchase of beer and diapers.[2] That correlation was strongest on Thursdays. Interviews indicated that customers were buying goods for the weekend, goods which included both beer and diapers.

HOW DO DECISION TREES IDENTIFY MARKET SEGMENTS?

A **decision tree** is a hierarchical arrangement of criteria that predict a classification or a value. Here, we will consider decision trees that predict classifications. Decision tree analyses are an unsupervised data mining technique: The analyst sets up the computer program and provides the data to analyze, and the decision tree program produces the tree.

A DECISION TREE FOR STUDENT PERFORMANCE

The basic idea of a decision tree is to select attributes that are most useful for classifying entities on some criterion. Suppose, for example, that we want to classify students according to the grades they earn in the MIS class. To create a decision tree, we first gather data about grades and attributes of students in past classes.

We then input that data into the decision tree program. The program analyzes all of the attributes and selects an attribute that creates the most disparate groups. The logic is that the

[2]Michael J. A. Berry and Gordon Linoff, *Data Mining Techniques for Marketing, Sales, and Customer Support* (New York: John Wiley, 1997).

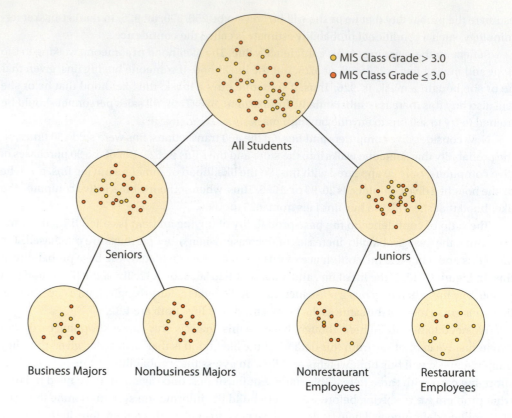

more different the groups, the better the classification will be. For example, if every student who lived off campus earned a grade higher than 3.0 and if every student who lived on campus earned a grade lower than 3.0, then the program would use the variable *live-off-campus* or *live-on-campus* to classify students. In this unrealistic example, the program would be a perfect classifier, because each group is pure, with no misclassifications.

More realistically, consider Figure CE12-3, which shows a hypothetical decision tree analysis of MIS class grades. Again, assume we are classifying students depending on whether their GPA was greater than 3.0 or less than or equal to 3.0.

The decision tree tool that created this tree examined students' characteristics, such as their class (junior or senior), their major, their employment, their age, their club affiliations, and other student characteristics. It then used values of those characteristics to create groups that were as different as possible on the classification GPA above or below 3.0.

For the results shown here, the decision tree program determined that the best first criterion is whether the students are juniors or seniors. In this case, the classification was imperfect, as shown by the fact that neither the senior nor the junior groups consisted only of students with GPAs above or below 3.0. Still, it did create groups that were less mixed than in the *All Students* group.

Next, the program examined other criteria to further subdivide *Seniors* and *Juniors* so as to create even more pure groups. The program divided the senior group into subgroups: those who are business majors and those who are not. The program's analysis of the junior data, however, determined that the difference between majors is not significant. Instead, the best classifier (the one that generated the most different groups) is whether the junior worked in a restaurant.

Examining this data, we see that junior restaurant employees do well in the class, but junior nonrestaurant employees and senior nonbusiness majors do poorly. Performance in the other senior group is mixed. (Remember, these data are hypothetical.)

Many problems exist with classification schemes, especially those that classify people. The Ethics Guide on page 524–525 examines some of them.

A decision tree like the one in Figure CE12-3 can be transformed into a set of decision rules having the format, If/Then. Decision rules for this example are:

- If student is a junior and works in a restaurant, then predict grade > 3.0.
- If student is a senior and is a nonbusiness major, then predict grade < 3.0.
- If student is a junior and does not work in a restaurant, then predict grade < 3.0.
- If student is a senior and is a business major, then make no prediction.[3]

As stated, decision tree algorithms create groups that are as pure as possible, or stated otherwise, as different from each other as possible. The algorithms use several metrics for measuring difference among groups. Further explanation of those techniques is beyond the scope of this textbook. For now, just be sure to understand that maximum difference among groups is used as the criterion for constructing the decision tree.

Let's now apply the decision tree technique to a business situation.

A DECISION TREE FOR LOAN EVALUATION

A common business application of decision trees is to classify loans by likelihood of default. Organizations analyze data from past loans to produce a decision tree that can be converted to loan-decision rules. A financial institution could use such a tree to assess the default risk on a new loan. Sometimes, too, financial institutions sell a group of loans (called a *loan portfolio*) to one another. The results of a decision tree program can be used to evaluate the risk in a given portfolio.

Figure CE12-4 shows an example provided by Insightful Corporation, a vendor of business intelligence tools. This example was generated using its Insightful Miner product. This tool examined data from 3,485 loans. Of those loans, 72 percent had no default and 28 percent did default. To perform the analysis, the decision tree tool examined values of six different loan characteristics.

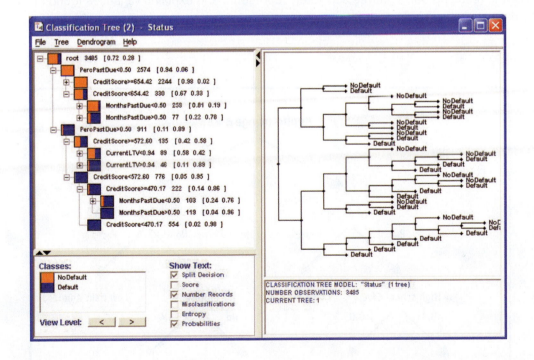

Figure CE12-4
Credit Score Decision Tree

Source: Used with permission of Insightful Corporation. Copyright © 1999–2005 Insightful Corporation. All Rights Reserved.

---

[3]Do not confuse these If/Then rules with those in expert systems. These rules are developed as a result of data mining via decision tree analysis. Typically, there are 10 or 12 such rules. Expert system rules are created by interviewing human experts. Typically, there are hundreds, or even thousands, of such rules.

Ethics Guide

The Ethics of Classification

Classification is a useful human skill. Imagine walking into your favorite clothing store and seeing all of the clothes piled together on a center table. T-shirts, pants, and socks intermingle, with the sizes mixed up. Retail stores organized like this would not survive, nor would distributors or manufacturers who managed their inventories this way. Sorting and classifying are necessary, important, and essential activities. But those activities can also be dangerous.

Serious ethical issues arise when we classify people. What makes someone a good or bad "prospect"? If we're talking about classifying customers in order to prioritize our sales calls, then the ethical issue may not be too serious. What about classifying applicants for college? As long as there are more applicants than positions, some sort of classification and selection process must be done. But what kind?

Suppose a university collects data on the demographics and the performance of all of its students. The admissions committee then processes these data using a decision tree data mining program. Assume the analysis is conducted properly and the tool uses statistically valid measures to obtain statistically valid results. Thus, the following resulting decision tree accurately represents and explains variances found in the data; no human judgment (or prejudice) was involved.

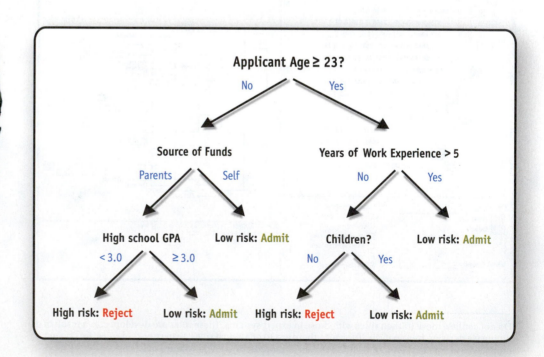

DISCUSSION QUESTIONS

1. Explain what conditions in the data could have caused this particular structure to emerge. For example, what conditions may have existed for self-funding students under the age of 23 to be classified as low risk? Explain how you think the three other branches in this tree may have come about.

2. Consider this tree from the standpoint of:

a. A 23-year-old woman whose job experience is 3 years as a successful Wall Street financial analyst.

b. A 28-year-old gay male with 4 years' job experience who has no children and pays for [or funds] his own college education.

c. The university fund-raising committee that wants to raise money from parent donations.

d. A student who was seriously ill while attending a top-notch high school but managed to graduate with a GPA of 2.9 by working independently on her classes from her hospital room.

3. Suppose you work in admissions and your university's public relations department asks you to meet with the local press for an article it is preparing regarding your admittance policy. How do you prepare for the press meeting?

4. Would your answer to question 3 change if you work at a private rather than a public institution? Would it change if you work at a small liberal arts college rather than a large engineering-oriented university?

5. What conclusions do you make regarding the use of decision trees for categorizing student applicants?

6. What conclusions do you make regarding the use of decision trees for categorizing prospects in general?

In this example, the decision tree program determined that the percentage of the loan that is past due (*PercPastDue*) is the best first criterion. Reading Figure CE12-4, you can see that of the 2,574 loans with a *PercPastDue* value of .5 or less (more than half paid off), 94 percent were not in default. Hence, any loan that is more than half paid off has little risk of default.

Reading down several lines in this tree, 911 loans had a value of *PercPastDue* greater than .5; of those loans, 89 percent were in default.

These two major categories are then further subdivided into three classifications: *CreditScore* is a creditworthiness score obtained from a credit agency; *MonthsPastDue* is the number of months since a payment; and *CurrentLTV* is the current ratio of outstanding balance of the loan to the value of the loan's collateral.

With a decision tree like this, the financial institution can structure a marketing program for "instant approval" refinancing. For example, from Figure CE12-4, the bank can deduce the following rules:

- If the loan is more than half paid, then accept the loan.
- If the loan is less than half paid and
  - If *CreditScore* is greater than 572.6 and
  - If *CurrentLTV* is less than .94, then accept the loan.
- Otherwise, reject the loan.

These rules identify loans the bank will approve, and they also specify characteristics that identify a particular market segment. On the basis of this analysis, the bank can structure a marketing campaign to appeal to that segment.

We have shown here how decision trees can identify a market segment, but realize that they can be used for numerous other classification and prediction problems as well. They are easy to understand and—even better—easy to implement using decision rules. They also can work with many types of variables, and they deal well with missing values. Organizations can use decision trees by themselves or combine them with other techniques. In some cases, organizations use decision trees to select variables that are then used by other types of data mining tools.

ACTIVE REVIEW

Use this Active Review to verify that you understand the ideas and concepts that answer this chapter extension's study questions.

Q1 WHAT IS A DATABASE MARKETING OPPORTUNITY?

Define *database marketing*. Explain why the term is a misnomer. Give an example of the need for database marketing other than ones described in this chapter extension.

Q2 HOW DOES RFM ANALYSIS CLASSIFY CUSTOMERS?

Explain the meaning of *R*, *F*, and *M scores*. Describe how each score is computed. State the action(s) that should be taken for customers having the following RFM scores: [1, 1, 3], [5, 4, 5], [2, 2, 2], [3, 1, 1], [1, 3, 1], and [1, 1, 1].

Q3 HOW DOES MARKET-BASKET ANALYSIS IDENTIFY CROSS-SELLING OPPORTUNITIES?

Define *cross-selling*. Define *support, confidence*, and *lift*. In Figure CE12-2, state the probability that someone walks into the store and buys fins. Compute the support for fins and a dive computer. Explain what it means if the value of lift is greater than 1. Explain what it means if the value of lift is less than 1. Compute the lift for fins and a dive computer.

Q4 HOW DO DECISION TREES IDENTIFY MARKET SEGMENTS?

Define *decision tree*, and explain the basic idea of decision trees. For the hypothetical data in Figure CE12-3, state the grade you would predict for senior nonbusiness students. State the grade you would predict for junior restaurant employees. State the grade you would predict for senior business majors. Explain how a decision tree could be used to identify a desirable market segment for loan refinancing.

KEY TERMS AND CONCEPTS

Confidence 521
Cross-selling 520
Database marketing 518
Decision tree 521

F score 519
Lift 521
M score 519
Market-basket analysis 520

R score 519
RFM analysis 518
Support 520

USING YOUR KNOWLEDGE

1. Of the three database marketing techniques described in this chapter extension, which best solves the problem at Carbon Creek Gardens? Explain how Mary could have used that technique to identify Tootsie as a lost customer.

2. Describe a use for RFM analysis at GearUp. Explain what you would do for customers that have the following scores: [1, 1, 1], [3,1,1], [1, 4, 1], [3, 3, 1], and [1, 1, 3].

3. Describe an application for market-basket analysis other than for a dive shop. Explain how you would use the knowledge that two products have a lift of 7. Explain how you would use the knowledge that two products have a lift of .003. If they have a lift of 1.03? If they have a lift of 2.1?

4. Describe an application for decision tree analysis for customer service and support at a computer vendor like Dell. Assume your decision tree analysis considered customer name, company, number of employees at that company, job title, and number and type of computer systems purchased. How could you use the results of your analysis to classify the knowledge and experience of your customers? How could you use those results to structure the buying experience for each of those customers? What other uses can you think of for the results of this decision tree analysis?

chapter extension 13

Chapter 9 provides the background for this Extension.

Reporting Systems and OLAP

 STUDY QUESTIONS

Q1 **HOW DO REPORTING SYSTEMS ENABLE PEOPLE TO CREATE INFORMATION?**

Q2 **WHAT ARE THE COMPONENTS AND CHARACTERISTICS OF REPORTING SYSTEMS?**

Q3 **HOW ARE REPORTS AUTHORED, MANAGED, AND DELIVERED?**

Q4 **HOW ARE OLAP REPORTS DYNAMIC?**

 HOW DO REPORTING SYSTEMS ENABLE PEOPLE TO CREATE INFORMATION?

A **reporting system** is an information system that enables people to create information by processing data from disparate sources and delivering that information to the proper users on a timely basis. Chapter 1 discussed the difference between data and information. There we said that people conceive information from data. We also said that they do so by seeing data presented in a meaningful context. Reporting systems manipulate data into that meaningful context using four fundamental operations:

1. Filtering data
2. Sorting data
3. Grouping data
4. Making simple calculations on the data

Consider the sales data shown in Figure CE13-1. This list of raw data is hardly a meaningful context. It is just a list of data. We can create a meaningful context for this data by *sorting* by customer name, as shown in Figure CE13-2. In this format, we can see that some customers have ordered more than once, and we can readily find their orders.

This is a step forward, but we can produce by *grouping* the orders, as shown in Figure CE13-3 on page 530. Notice that the reporting tool not only grouped the orders, but it also *computed* the number of orders for each customer and the total purchase amount per customer.

Suppose we are interested in repeat customers. If so, we can *filter* the groups of orders to select only those customers that have two or more orders. The results of these operations are shown in Figure CE13-4 on page 530. The report in this figure not only has filtered the results, but it also has *formatted* them for easier understanding. Compare Figure CE13-4 to Figure CE13-1. If your goal is to identify your best customers, the report in Figure CE13-4 shows data in a far more useful context and will save you considerable work.

In the remainder of this chapter extension, we will consider the components and functions of these reporting systems, as well as some examples.

CE13

Figure CE13-1
Raw Sales Data

ID	CustomerName	CustomerEmail	DateOfSale	Amount
1	Ashley, Jane	JA@somewhere.com	5/5/2012	$110.00
2	Corning,Sandra	KD@somewhereelse.com	7/7/2012	$375.00
3	Ching, Kam Hoong	KHC@somewhere.com	5/17/2012	$55.00
4	Rikki, Nicole	GC@righthere.com	6/19/2011	$155.00
5	Corning,Sandra	SC@somewhereelse.com	2/4/2012	$195.00
6	Scott, Rex	RS@somewhere.com	7/15/2012	$56.00
7	Corovic,Jose	JC@somewhere.com	11/12/2012	$55.00
8	McGovern, Adrian	BL@righthere.com	11/12/2011	$47.00
9	Wei, Guang	GW@ourcompany.com	11/28/2012	$385.00
10	Dixon,Eleonor	ED@somewhere.com	5/17/2012	$108.00
11	Lee,Brandon	BL@somewhereelse.com	5/5/2011	$74.00
12	Duong,Linda	LD@righthere.com	5/17/2012	$485.00
13	Dixon, James T	JTD@somewhere.com	4/3/2012	$285.00
14	La Pierre,Anna	SG@righthere.com	9/22/2012	$120.00
15	La Pierre,Anna	WS@somewhere.com	3/14/2012	$47.50
16	La Pierre,Anna	TR@righthere.com	9/22/2012	$580.00
17	Ryan, Mark	MR@somewhereelse.com	11/3/2012	$42.00
18	Rikki, Nicole	MR@righthere.com	3/14/2012	$175.00
19	Scott, Bryan	BS@somewhere.com	3/17/2012	$145.00
20	Warrem, Jason	JW@ourcompany.com	5/12/2012	$160.00
21	La Pierre,Anna	ALP@somewhereelse.com	3/15/2012	$52.00
22	Angel, Kathy	KA@righthere.com	9/15/2012	$195.00
23	La Pierre,Anna	JQ@somewhere.com	4/12/2012	$44.00
24	Casimiro, Amanda	AC@somewhere.com	12/7/2012	$52.00
25	McGovern, Adrian	AM@ourcompany.com	3/17/2012	$52.00
26	Menstell,Lori Lee	LLM@ourcompany.com	10/18/2012	$72.00
27	La Pierre,Anna	DJ@righthere.com	12/7/2012	$175.00
28	Nurul,Nicole	NN@somewhere.com	10/12/2012	$84.00
29	Menstell,Lori Lee	VB@ourcompany.com	9/24/2012	$120.00
30	Pham,Mary	MP@somewhere.com	3/14/2012	$38.00
31	Redmond, Louise	LR@ourcompany.com	1/3/2012	$140.00
32	Jordan, Matthew	MJ@righthere.com	3/14/2012	$645.00
33	Drew, Richard	RD@righthere.com	10/3/2012	$42.00
34	Adams, James	JA3@somewhere.com	1/15/2012	$145.00
35	Garrett, James	JG@ourcompany.com	3/14/2012	$38.00
36	Lunden,Haley	HL@somewhere.com	11/17/2010	$52.00
37	UTran,Diem Thi	DTU@righthere.com	5/3/2011	$275.00
38	Austin, James	JA7@somewhere.com	1/15/2012	$55.00
39	Bernard, Steven	SB@ourcompany.com	9/17/2012	$78.00
40	Daniel, James	JD@somewhere.com	1/18/2012	$52.00

Figure CE13-2
Sales Data Sorted by
Customer Name

ID	CustomerName	CustomerEmail	DateOfSale	Amount
34	Adams, James	JA3@somewhere.com	1/15/2012	$145.00
22	Angel, Kathy	KA@righthere.com	9/15/2012	$195.00
1	Ashley, Jane	JA@somewhere.com	5/5/2012	$110.00
38	Austin, James	JA7@somewhere.com	1/15/2012	$55.00
39	Bernard, Steven	SB@ourcompany.com	9/17/2012	$78.00
24	Casimiro, Amanda	AC@somewhere.com	12/7/2012	$52.00
3	Ching, Kam Hoong	KHC@somewhere.com	5/17/2012	$55.00
2	Corning,Sandra	KD@somewhereelse.com	7/7/2012	$375.00
5	Corning,Sandra	SC@somewhereelse.com	2/4/2012	$195.00
7	Corovic,Jose	JC@somewhere.com	11/12/2012	$55.00
40	Daniel, James	JD@somewhere.com	1/18/2012	$52.00
13	Dixon, James T	JTD@somewhere.com	4/3/2012	$285.00
10	Dixon,Eleonor	ED@somewhere.com	5/17/2012	$108.00
33	Drew, Richard	RD@righthere.com	10/3/2012	$42.00
12	Duong,Linda	LD@righthere.com	5/17/2012	$485.00
35	Garrett, James	JG@ourcompany.com	3/14/2012	$38.00
32	Jordan, Matthew	MJ@righthere.com	3/14/2012	$645.00
27	La Pierre,Anna	DJ@righthere.com	12/7/2012	$175.00
14	La Pierre,Anna	SG@righthere.com	9/22/2012	$120.00
16	La Pierre,Anna	TR@righthere.com	9/22/2012	$580.00
21	La Pierre,Anna	ALP@somewhereelse.com	3/15/2012	$52.00
23	La Pierre,Anna	JQ@somewhere.com	4/12/2012	$44.00
15	La Pierre,Anna	WS@somewhere.com	3/14/2012	$47.50
11	Lee,Brandon	BL@somewhereelse.com	5/5/2011	$74.00
36	Lunden,Haley	HL@somewhere.com	11/17/2010	$52.00
8	McGovern, Adrian	BL@righthere.com	11/12/2011	$47.00
25	McGovern, Adrian	AM@ourcompany.com	3/17/2012	$52.00
26	Menstell,Lori Lee	LLM@ourcompany.com	10/18/2012	$72.00
29	Menstell,Lori Lee	VB@ourcompany.com	9/24/2012	$120.00
28	Nurul,Nicole	NN@somewhere.com	10/12/2012	$84.00
30	Pham,Mary	MP@somewhere.com	3/14/2012	$38.00
31	Redmond, Louise	LR@ourcompany.com	1/3/2012	$140.00
4	Rikki, Nicole	GC@righthere.com	6/19/2011	$155.00
18	Rikki, Nicole	MR@righthere.com	3/14/2012	$175.00
17	Ryan, Mark	MR@somewhereelse.com	11/3/2012	$42.00
19	Scott, Bryan	BS@somewhere.com	3/17/2012	$145.00
6	Scott, Rex	RS@somewhere.com	7/15/2012	$56.00
37	UTran,Diem Thi	DTU@righthere.com	5/3/2011	$275.00
20	Warrem, Jason	JW@ourcompany.com	5/12/2012	$160.00
9	Wei, Guang	GW@ourcompany.com	11/28/2012	$385.00

Figure CE13-3
Sales Data Sorted by
Customer Name and
Grouped by Number of
Orders and Purchase Amount

CustomerName ▾	NumOrders ▾	TotalPurchas ▾
Adams, James	1	$145.00
Angel, Kathy	1	$195.00
Ashley, Jane	1	$110.00
Austin, James	1	$55.00
Bernard, Steven	1	$78.00
Casimiro, Amanda	1	$52.00
Ching, Kam Hoong	1	$55.00
Corning,Sandra	2	$570.00
Corovic,Jose	1	$55.00
Daniel, James	1	$52.00
Dixon, James T	1	$285.00
Dixon,Eleonor	1	$108.00
Drew, Richard	1	$42.00
Duong,Linda	1	$485.00
Garrett, James	1	$38.00
Jordan, Matthew	1	$645.00
La Pierre,Anna	6	$1,018.50
Lee,Brandon	1	$74.00
Lunden,Haley	1	$52.00
McGovern, Adrian	2	$99.00
Menstell,Lori Lee	2	$192.00
Nurul,Nicole	1	$84.00
Pham,Mary	1	$38.00
Redmond, Louise	1	$140.00
Rikki, Nicole	2	$330.00
Ryan, Mark	1	$42.00
Scott, Bryan	1	$145.00
Scott, Rex	1	$56.00
UTran,Diem Thi	1	$275.00
Warrem, Jason	1	$160.00

Figure CE13-4
Sales Data Filtered to Show
Repeat Customers

Repeat Customers

NumOrders	CustomerName	TotalPurchases
6	La Pierre,Anna	$1,018.50
2	Corning,Sandra	$570.00
2	Rikki, Nicole	$330.00
2	Menstell,Lori Lee	$192.00
2	McGovern, Adrian	$99.00

Q2   WHAT ARE THE COMPONENTS AND CHARACTERISTICS OF REPORTING SYSTEMS?

Figure CE13-5 shows the major components of a reporting system. Data from disparate data sources are read and combined, using filtering, sorting, grouping, and simple calculating, to produce meaningful contexts. Figure CE13-5 combines data from an Oracle database, a SQL Server database, and other nondatabase data. Some data are generated within the organization, other data are obtained from public sources, and still other data may be purchased from data utilities.

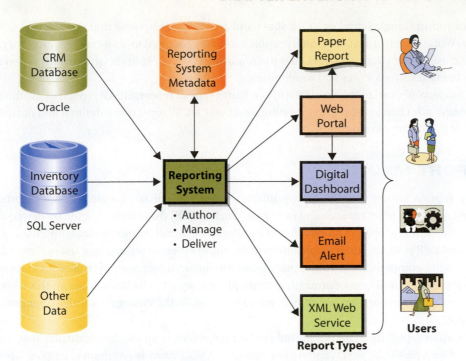

Figure CE13-5
Components of a Reporting System

A reporting system maintains a database of reporting metadata. The metadata describe reports, users, groups, roles, events, and other entities involved in the reporting activity. The reporting system uses the metadata to prepare and deliver reports to the proper users on a timely basis.

As shown in Figure CE13-5, organizations can prepare reports in a variety of formats. Figure CE13-6 lists report characteristics by type, media, and mode, which we discuss next.

REPORT TYPE

In terms of **report type**, reports can be *static* or *dynamic*. **Static reports** are prepared once from the underlying data, and they do not change. A report of past year's sales, for example, is a static report. Other reports are dynamic; at the time of creation, the reporting system reads the most current data and generates the report using that fresh data. A report on sales today and a report on current stock prices are both **dynamic reports**.

Query reports are prepared in response to data entered by users. Google provides a handy example of a query report: You enter the keywords you want to search on, and the reporting

Type	Media	Mode
Static	Paper and PDF file	Push
Dynamic	Computer screen via application	Pull
Query	Web site	
Online analytical processing (OLAP)	Digital dashboard	
	Alerts via email or cell phone	
	Export to Excel, Quicken, TurboTax, QuickBooks, or other application	
	XML Web service	

Figure CE13-6
Summary of Report Characteristics

system within Google searches its database and generates a response that is particular to your query. Within an organization, a query report could be generated to show current inventory levels. The user enters item numbers, and the reporting system responds with inventory levels of those items at various stores and warehouses.

Online analytical processing (*OLAP*) is a fourth type of report. OLAP reports allow the user to dynamically change the report grouping structures. OLAP reports are defined and illustrated in Q4 of this chapter extension.

REPORT MEDIA

Today, reports are delivered via many different **report media**, or channels. Some reports are printed on paper; others are created in formats, such as PDF, that can be printed or viewed electronically. Other reports are delivered to computer screens and mobile devices. Applications for CRM and ERP systems, for example, include dozens of different reports that users view online. Additionally, companies sometimes place reports on internal corporate Web sites for employees to access. For example, an organization might place a report of its latest sales on the sales department's Web site or a report on customers serviced on the customer service department's Web site.

Another report medium is a **digital dashboard**, which is an electronic display that is customized for a particular user. Vendors like Yahoo! and MSN provide common examples. Users of these services can define content they want—say, a local weather forecast, a list of stock prices, or a list of news sources—and the vendor constructs the display customized for each user. Figure CE13-7 shows an example.

Other dashboards are particular to an organization. Executives at a manufacturing organization, for example, might have a dashboard that shows up-to-the-minute production and sales activities.

Alerts are another form of report. Users can declare that they wish to receive notification of events, say, via email or on their cell phones. Of course, some cell phones are capable of displaying Web pages, and digital dashboards can be delivered to them as well.

Some reports are exported from the report generator to another program, such as Excel, Quicken, QuickBooks, and so forth. For example, application programs at many banks can export customer checking account transactions into Excel, Quicken, or Money.

Finally, reports can be published via a Web service. The Web service produces the report in response to requests from the service-consuming application. This style of reporting is particularly useful for inter-enterprise information systems like supply chain management.

Figure CE13-7
Digital Dashboard Example

Source: Microsoft Corporation

REPORT MODE

The final report characteristic in Figure CE13-6 is the **report mode**, a term which refers to the way a report is initiated. Organizations send a **push report** to users according to a pre-set schedule. Users receive the report without any activity on their part. In contrast, users must request a **pull report**. To obtain a pull report, a user goes to a Web portal or digital dashboard and clicks a link or button to cause the reporting system to produce and deliver the report.

HOW ARE REPORTS AUTHORED, MANAGED, AND DELIVERED?

In the middle of Figure CE13-5, under the drawing of the reporting system, three functions of a reporting system are listed: author, manage, and deliver. Consider each.

REPORT AUTHORING

Report authoring involves connecting to data sources, creating the report structure, and formatting the report. You can learn how to create a report for Microsoft Access in Chapter Extension 5, question 5 (starting on page 418).

Of course, much organizational data resides in databases other than Access. One common way that developers author reports is to use tools such as Microsoft's Visual Studio that can connect to many different data sources. For example, in Figure CE13-8, a report author is using Visual Studio to connect to a database that contains source data and has just entered a SQL statement, shown in the lower-center portion of this display, to generate a report. Visual Studio can be used to format the report as well.

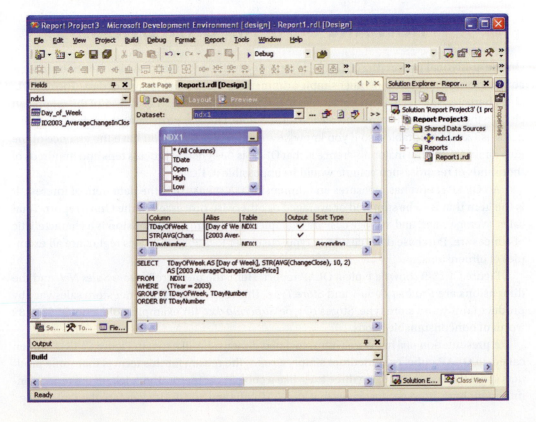

Figure CE13-8
Connecting to a Report Data Source Using Visual Studio

Source: Microsoft product screenshot reprinted with permission from Microsoft Corporation.

REPORT MANAGEMENT

The purpose of **report management** is to define who receives what reports, when, and by what means. Most report management systems allow the report administrator to define user accounts and user groups and to assign particular users to particular groups. For example, all of the salespeople would be assigned to the sales group, all of the executives assigned to the executive group, and so forth. All of these data are stored in the reporting system's metadata shown in Figure CE13-5 (page 531).

Reports that have been created using the report authoring system are assigned to groups and users. Assigning reports to groups saves the administrator work: When a report is created, changed, or removed, the administrator need only change the report assignments to the group. All of the users in the group will inherit the changes.

As stated, the report management metadata indicate which format of this report is to be sent to which user. The metadata also indicate what channel is to be used and whether the report is to be pushed or pulled. If the report is to be pushed, the administrator declares whether the report is to be generated on a regular schedule or as an alert.

REPORT DELIVERY

The **report delivery** function of a reporting system pushes reports or allows them to be pulled according to report management metadata. Reports can be delivered via an email server, via a Web site, via SOA services, or by other program-specific means. The report delivery system uses the operating system and other program security components to ensure that only authorized users receive authorized reports. It also ensures that push reports are produced at appropriate times.

For query reports, the report delivery system serves as an intermediary between the user and the report generator. It receives user query data, such as the item numbers in an inventory query, passes the query data to the report generator, receives the resulting report, and delivers the report to the user.

HOW ARE OLAP REPORTS DYNAMIC?

Online analytical processing (OLAP) is a reporting technology that provides the ability to sum, count, average, and perform other simple arithmetic operations on groups of data. The remarkable characteristic of OLAP reports is that their format is dynamic. The viewer of the report can change the report's structure—hence the term *online*. OLAP reports have the same characteristics as Excel Pivot tables, so if you know how such tables work, you have the essence of the idea about OLAP. The major difference is that OLAP is designed to process tens and hundreds of thousands of records; such volume would be impossible in Excel.

An OLAP report has measures and dimensions. A **measure** is the data item of interest. It is the item that is to be summed or averaged or otherwise processed in the OLAP report. Total sales, average sales, and average cost are examples of measures. A **dimension** is a characteristic of a measure. Purchase date, customer type, customer location, and sales region are all examples of dimensions.

Figure CE13-9 shows a typical OLAP report. Here, the measure is *Store Sales Net*, and the dimensions are *Product Family* and *Store Type*. This report shows how net store sales vary by product family and store type. Stores of type *Supermarket*, for example, sold a net of $36,189 worth of nonconsumable goods.

A presentation of a measure with associated dimensions like that in Figure CE13-9 is often called an **OLAP cube**, or sometimes simply a *cube*. The reason for this term is that some products show these displays using three axes, like a cube in geometry. The origin of the term is unimportant here, however. Just know that an *OLAP cube* and an *OLAP report* are the same thing.

	A	B	C	D	E	F	G
1							
2							
3	Store Sales Net	Store Type					
4	Product Family	Deluxe Supermarket	Gourmet Supermarket	Mid-Size Grocery	Small Grocery	Supermarket	Grand Total
5	Drink	$8,119.05	$2,392.83	$1,409.50	$685.89	$16,751.71	$29,358.98
6	Food	$70,276.11	$20,026.18	$10,392.19	$6,109.72	$138,960.67	$245,764.87
7	Nonconsumable	$18,884.24	$5,064.79	$2,813.73	$1,534.90	$36,189.40	$64,487.05
8	Grand Total	$97,279.40	$27,483.80	$14,615.42	$8,330.51	$191,901.77	$339,610.90

Figure CE13-9
OLAP Product Family by Store Type

The OLAP report in Figure CE13-9 was generated by SQL Server Analysis Services and is displayed in an Excel Pivot table. The data were taken from a sample instructional database, called Food Mart, that is provided with SQL Server. It is possible to display OLAP cubes in many ways besides with Excel. Some third-party vendors provide more extensive graphical displays. Possibly the easiest to use OLAP/graphical display product available is Tableau from Tableau Software. Visit *www.TableauSoftware.com* to see useful demos and tutorials. You can also find excellent examples at *www.TableauServer.com*.

As stated earlier, the distinguishing characteristic of an OLAP report is that the user can alter the format of the report. Figure CE13-10 shows such an alteration. Here, the user added another dimension, *Store Country and State*, to the horizontal display. Product-family sales are now broken out by the location of the stores. Observe that the sample data include only stores in the United States and only in the western states of California, Oregon, and Washington.

With an OLAP report, it is possible to **drill down** into the data. This term means to further divide the data into more detail. In Figure CE13-11, for example, the user has drilled down into the stores located in California; the OLAP report now shows sales data for the four cities in California that have stores.

	A	B	C	D	E	F	G	H	I
1									
2									
3	Store Sales Net			Store Type					
4	Product Family	Store Country	Store State	Deluxe Supermarket	Gourmet Supermarket	Mid-Size Grocery	Small Grocery	Supermarket	Grand Total
5	Drink	USA	CA		$2,392.83		$227.38	$5,920.76	$8,540.97
6			OR	$4,438.49				$2,862.45	$7,300.94
7			WA	$3,680.56		$1,409.50	$458.51	$7,968.50	$13,517.07
8		USA Total		$8,119.05	$2,392.83	$1,409.50	$685.89	$16,751.71	$29,358.98
9	Drink Total			$8,119.05	$2,392.83	$1,409.50	$685.89	$16,751.71	$29,358.98
10	Food	USA	CA		$20,026.18		$1,960.53	$47,226.11	$69,212.82
11			OR	$37,778.35				$23,818.87	$61,597.22
12			WA	$32,497.76		$10,392.19	$4,149.19	$67,915.69	$114,954.83
13		USA Total		$70,276.11	$20,026.18	$10,392.19	$6,109.72	$138,960.67	$245,764.87
14	Food Total			$70,276.11	$20,026.18	$10,392.19	$6,109.72	$138,960.67	$245,764.87
15	Nonconsumable	USA	CA		$5,064.79		$474.35	$12,344.49	$17,883.63
16			OR	$10,177.89				$6,428.53	$16,606.41
17			WA	$8,706.36		$2,813.73	$1,060.54	$17,416.38	$29,997.01
18		USA Total		$18,884.24	$5,064.79	$2,813.73	$1,534.90	$36,189.40	$64,487.05
19	Nonconsumable Total			$18,884.24	$5,064.79	$2,813.73	$1,534.90	$36,189.40	$64,487.05
20	Grand Total			$97,279.40	$27,483.80	$14,615.42	$8,330.51	$191,901.77	$339,610.90

Figure CE13-10
OLAP Product Family and Store Location by Store Type

	A	B	C	D	E	F	G	H	I	J
3	Store Sales Net				Store Type ▼					
4	Store Country ▼	Store Sta	Store City	Product Family ▼	Deluxe Super	Gourmet Supermarket	Mid-Size Grocery	Small Grocery	Supermarket	Grand Total
5	USA	CA	Beverly Hills	Drink		$2,392.83				$2,392.83
6				Food		$20,026.18				$20,026.18
7				Nonconsumable		$5,064.79				$5,064.79
8			Beverly Hills Total			$27,483.80				$27,483.80
9			Los Angeles	Drink					$2,870.33	$2,870.33
10				Food					$23,598.28	$23,598.28
11				Nonconsumable					$6,305.14	$6,305.14
12			Los Angeles Total						$32,773.74	$32,773.74
13			San Diego	Drink					$3,050.43	$3,050.43
14				Food					$23,627.83	$23,627.83
15				Nonconsumable					$6,039.34	$6,039.34
16			San Diego Total						$32,717.61	$32,717.61
17			San Francisco	Drink				$227.38		$227.38
18				Food				$1,960.53		$1,960.53
19				Nonconsumable				$474.35		$474.35
20			San Francisco Total					$2,662.26		$2,662.26
21		CA Total				$27,483.80		$2,662.26	$65,491.35	$95,637.41
22		OR		Drink	$4,438.49				$2,862.45	$7,300.94
23				Food	$37,778.35				$23,818.87	$61,597.22
24				Nonconsumable	$10,177.89				$6,428.53	$16,606.41
25		OR Total			$52,394.72				$33,109.85	$85,504.57
26		WA		Drink	$3,680.56		$1,409.50	$458.51	$7,968.50	$13,517.07
27				Food	$32,497.76		$10,392.19	$4,149.19	$67,915.69	$114,954.83
28				Nonconsumable	$8,706.36		$2,813.73	$1,060.54	$17,416.38	$29,997.01
29		WA Total			$44,884.68		$14,615.42	$5,668.24	$93,300.57	$158,468.91
30	USA Total				$97,279.40	$27,483.80	$14,615.42	$8,330.51	$191,901.77	$339,610.90
31	Grand Total				$97,279.40	$27,483.80	$14,615.42	$8,330.51	$191,901.77	$339,610.90

Figure CE13-11
OLAP Product Family and Store Location by Store Type, Showing Sales Data for Four Cities

Notice another difference between Figures CE13-10 and CE13-11. The user has not only drilled down, but she has also changed the order of the dimensions. Figure CE13-10 shows *Product Family* and then store location within *Product Family*. Figure CE13-11 shows store location and then *Product Family* within store location.

Both displays are valid and useful, depending on the user's perspective. A product manager might like to see product families first and then store location data. A sales manager might like to see store locations first and then product data. OLAP reports provide both perspectives, and the user can switch between them while viewing the report.

Unfortunately, all of this flexibility comes at a cost. If the database is large, doing the necessary calculating, grouping, and sorting for such dynamic displays will require substantial computing power. Although standard, commercial DBMS products do have the features and functions required to create OLAP reports, they are not designed for such work. They are designed, instead, to provide rapid response to transaction processing applications, such as order entry or manufacturing operations.

Accordingly, special-purpose products called **OLAP servers** have been developed to perform OLAP analysis. As shown in Figure CE13-12, an OLAP server reads data from an operational database, performs preliminary calculations, and stores the results of those calculations in an OLAP database. (Databases that are structured to support OLAP processing are called **dimensional databases**.) Several different schemes are used for this storage, but the particulars of those schemes are beyond this discussion. Normally, for performance and security reasons the OLAP server and the DBMS run on separate computers.

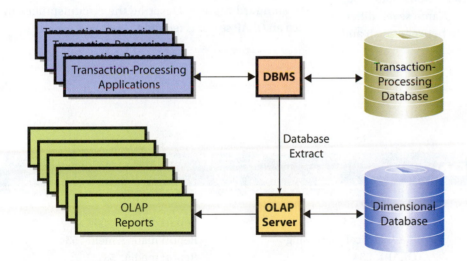

Figure CE13-12
Role of OLAP Server and
Dimensional Database

ACTIVE REVIEW

Use this Active Review to verify that you understand the ideas and concepts that answer the chapters extension's study questions.

Q1 HOW DO REPORTING SYSTEMS ENABLE PEOPLE TO CREATE INFORMATION?

Describe the purpose of a reporting system. Explain how reporting systems enable people to create information. List four basic reporting operations. Using Figures CE13-1 and CE13-4, explain how each context enables the creation of more information.

Q2 WHAT ARE THE COMPONENTS AND CHARACTERISTICS OF REPORTING SYSTEMS?

Describe the role of each of the components in Figure CE13-5. Explain what reporting metadata describes. Name four types of reports, and give an example of each. Name seven different report media. Explain the difference between push and pull reports.

Q3 HOW ARE REPORTS AUTHORED, MANAGED, AND DELIVERED?

Name the three functions of report authoring. Explain the purpose of report management. Describe the role of metadata for report management. Describe the report delivery function. Explain the role of report delivery for security and for query reports.

Q4 HOW ARE OLAP REPORTS DYNAMIC?

Describe the basic operation of an OLAP report. Define *measure*, and give an example. Define *dimension*, and give at least two examples. Using hypothetical data and Figure CE13-9 as a guide, show how your measure and dimensions would appear in an OLAP report. Show how the structure of the report changes if you switch the two dimensions. Using your sample data, explain why OLAP reports are considered more dynamic than standard reports. Describe the circumstances under which an OLAP server is required.

KEY TERMS AND CONCEPTS

Alert 532
Digital dashboard 532
Dimension 534
Dimensional databases 537
Drill down 535
Dynamic report 531
Measure 534
OLAP cube 534

OLAP servers 537
Online analytical processing (OLAP) 534
Pull report 533
Push report 533
Query report 531
Report authoring 533

Report delivery 534
Report management 534
Report media 532
Report mode 533
Report type 531
Reporting system 528
Static reports 531

USING YOUR KNOWLEDGE

1. Explain the difference in the following two expressions:
   a. Reporting systems create information.
   b. Reporting systems enable the creation of information.

2. In your own words, explain the phrase *meaningful context*.

3. Assume that you are a buyer at GearUp and you are asked to describe the kind of report you want to help you negotiate with problematic vendors. Describe (or sketch the outline of) a report that would give you a meaningful context about:
   a. Damaged goods
   b. Short shipments (shipments when vendors didn't ship the full amount they'd agreed to ship)

4. Same scenario as question 3, except assume that you anticipate that vendors will respond by saying, "Ah, we're no different from any of your other vendors." Answer questions 3a and 3b for this situation.

5. Assume you have data like that shown in the opening vignette of Chapter 8 (page 191). Describe (or sketch the format of) a report that would help you understand how frequently each patient uses PRIDE. Assume that you want to rank patients on frequency of use for all patients and for each doctor's patients.

6. Describe (or sketch the format of) a report that would help each doctor understand the degree of exercise compliance (how well each patient conforms to his or her exercise prescription) for each of his or her patients. Assume you have data for the data items shown in Figure 7-17 (page 190).

7. Explain how the cell phone display shown in the opening vignette of Chapter 9 is a report. From this example, describe how you think reporting will change as mobile systems become common.

Chapter 9 provides the background for this Extension.

Geographic Information Systems (GIS)

Q1 WHAT ARE THE COMPONENTS OF A GEOGRAPHIC INFORMATION SYSTEM?

A **geographic information system (GIS)** is an information system that captures, stores, analyzes, and displays geospatial data. As an information system, a GIS has the five components that all such systems have. It is the term *geospatial data* that makes GIS unique among IS. The root *geo* refers to the earth, and *spatial data* are data that can be ordered in some space. Thus, **geospatial data** means that data that can be ordered in reference to the earth. GIS are sometimes used for mapping the Moon, Mars, and other planets, but, in general, when people say GIS, they are referring to a system for processing earth's geographic data.

Of the four definitions of information discussed in Chapter 1, the one that best fits GIS is *data presented in a meaningful context.* Consider Figure CE14-1, which shows census tracts that have primary care physician shortages in the state of Indiana. Because few of us keep the boundaries of census tracts in our minds, data in this format are not informative. However, consider that same data as presented in Figure CE14-2. Healthcare planners who are familiar with the geography of Indiana will find this map, along with a key to the meanings of the color-coded census tracts, to be much more informative than the list in Figure CE14-1. Hence, GIS create information by manipulating and displaying data in a geospatial context.

Figure CE14-1
Listing of Geographic Data

Source: U.S. Department of Health and Human Services, Health Resources and Services Administration.

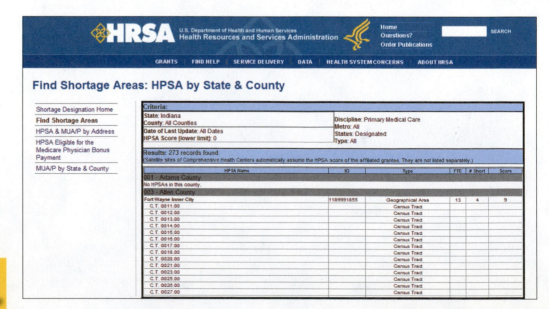

CE14

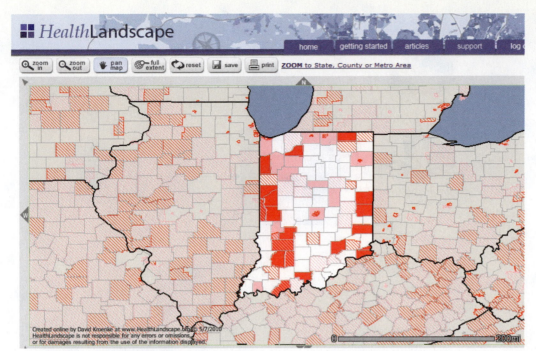

Figure CE14-2
Map of Data in Figure CE14-1

Source: Used with permission
of HealthLandscape, LLC.
www.healthlandscape.org

GIS are subject to the same trends as other information systems. As of 1990, most GIS were stand-alone desktop applications. Throughout the 1990s, some of this capability was moved to thick-client, client-server applications, and in the first part of this century some GIS applications, notably graphical viewers such as Google Maps and Bing Maps, moved to cloud-based, thin-client applications. Undoubtedly, GIS applications that use HTML5 are in development now. Today, we see GIS operating on all of these platforms, from stand-alone computers to thin clients accessing data in the cloud.

Let's consider each of the five components of a GIS.

HARDWARE

Like all IS, GIS hardware includes client and server computers and network equipment. As stated, GIS run the gamut of hardware, from stand-alone applications, to classic client-server applications, to the three-tier architecture described in Chapter 6. However, GIS also employ special-purpose hardware for capturing geospatial data. Such hardware includes surveying equipment, cameras, satellite devices, GPS devices, map scanners, and additional specialized input hardware. That specialized equipment is outside the scope of this discussion.

SOFTWARE

In addition to operating systems, GIS software includes application-specific programs, a GIS, and a DBMS. Figure CE14-3 shows the relationship of these programs. Notice the ambiguity in use of the term *GIS*. We have defined a GIS as an information system with all five components. However, and unfortunately, the term *GIS* is also used to refer to a computer program, the **GIS application**, that manages geospatial data.

Application-specific programs are akin to application programs for database systems. They are created to add special-purpose features and functions on top of the raw GIS mapping capability. The map in Figure CE14-2 was produced using a medical-specific application developed by HealthLandscape, a corporation that provides GIS solutions for healthcare and other

Figure CE14-3
Structure of GIS Application
Components

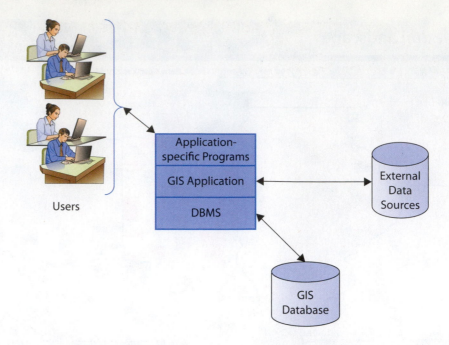

industries. The application uses ArcGIS, a generic GIS, which is a program that provides tools for importing and exporting, storing, analyzing, and displaying geospatial data. ArcGIS, in turn, calls upon a DBMS for the storage and retrieval of data.

In addition to ArcGIS, other popular commercial GIS programs include Autodesk, MapInfo, Bentley GIS, and many others. Open-source GIS include GRASS and uDig. Search the Web to learn more about any of these products.

A common scenario for business use of GIS is for the GIS application to obtain base geospatial data from a service like Google Earth or Bing Maps, add organizational-specific data from its own database, and display that data to clients in browsers. In Q3, you'll see an example of how Harley-Davidson implements this scenario.

GIS applications vary in their ease of use. Some GIS viewer applications like Google Earth are intended for the public user, and its intuitive interface is easy to employ. However, tools for inputting, manipulating, and structuring GIS outputs can be complicated and difficult to use. Most GIS provide a set of tools and expect the geospatial analyst to know how to use those tools to accomplish particular tasks.

DATA

GIS consist of a blend of external geospatial and relational database data. Some of the data in the map in Figure CE14-2 came from external government data sources. Some of it is geospatial data stored in the GIS database, and some of it is relational (table) data concerning physicians, population characteristics, community medical needs, and so forth.

The database design techniques you learned in Chapter 5 and Chapter Extension 4, work well for relational data, but not so well for geospatial data. How can you represent the shape of a census tract in rows of a table? Even more problematic, how can the application use traditional database tables to rapidly perform queries like "List the census tracts that contain more than three hospitals"?

Or, for even more complexity, suppose you want to obtain the names of restaurants within a 10-minute drive of a movie theater. The GIS must be able to determine the optimal route to each restaurant, and the design of data storage for the computation of such routes is challenging. To add another layer of complexity, suppose you want to know the names of restaurants within a 10-minute drive of that theater *for the current traffic conditions*. The storage of geospatial data must be designed to readily integrate external data from traffic sources.

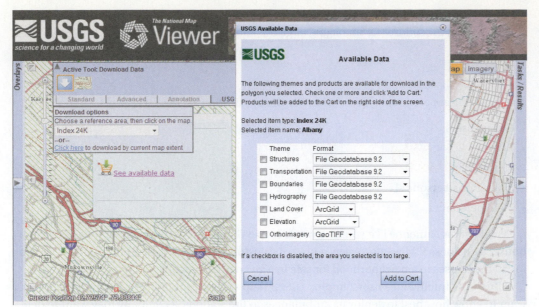

Figure CE14-4
Example Geospatial Data
Available from the U.S.
Government

Source: The National Map Viewer,
USGS, *http://viewer.nationalmap.gov/
viewer.*

Because of these special requirements, most GIS applications extend the base capabilities of the DBMS with data structures and tools that provide unique functions for processing geospatial data. Because of the importance of GIS today, DBMS vendors such as Oracle, Microsoft, and others have augmented their standard DBMS products to provide geospatial database capabilities.

Like the map in Figure CE14-2, GIS frequently combine data from several sources. Some is purchased from Google, Microsoft, or other sources, and much is available for free from national and local governments. The U.S. Government provides hundreds of different types of free geospatial data; Figure CE14-4 shows a few examples. Go to *http://viewer.nationalmap .gov/viewer* to learn more. (Don't be misled by the Add to Cart button. The data are free; you add what you want to your cart, input your email address, and the site mails you the data for you to input to your GIS application. That data will be useless to you, however, unless you have a GIS program and know how to use it.)

PROCEDURES

Figure CE14-5 shows procedures necessary for using a GIS. For sites like Google Maps/Earth and Bing Maps, the user interface is designed to be intuitive and easy to use. For more complicated sites with more domain-specific capabilities, procedures are needed to help users obtain and process the data they need. We will discuss this further in Q4, when we discuss GIS for business intelligence.

Procedures are also needed for importing and exporting bulk data. This task can be complex and is important, especially for GIS sites that have multiple users whose analyses can be invalidated by incorrect or unexpected data imports. Finally, many, perhaps hundreds, of maps

- Find a map
- Search (point, near, include) features
- Zoom in/out
- Navigate the map
- Change the views
- Add, edit, and delete user data
- Import/export bulk data
- Manage map libraries

Figure CE14-5
Typical Procedures for
GIS Use

are produced for various purposes and studies, and these maps are often shared among a group. Consequently, procedures for managing large map libraries are important.

PEOPLE

The following are common types of users for GIS applications:

- Casual users
- BI users
- Developers
- Operations personnel
- Field personnel

A casual user is someone like you who wants to use Google Maps to find directions to a friend's house, a business that wants to view a map of a customer's location, or a house hunter looking for all the houses in a neighborhood for sale in a given price range.

Business intelligence users employ GIS to help solve a problem. For example, a city may want to know how best to deploy its ambulances to fire stations, a company may want to determine how best to locate retail stores, or a police department may want to know if the locations of particular crimes in a city are changing. Such users need to know how best to employ the GIS to solve their problem.

By the way, do not be misled by one of the terms in the definition of GIS. We said that a GIS is an IS for capturing, storing, analyzing, and displaying geospatial data. GIS application programs can capture, store, and display geospatial data in an automated fashion. However, few GIS applications *analyze* data. Few GIS programs are sophisticated enough to state where the city should put its ambulances, for example. Instead, people, working with the GIS application's tools, analyze the geospatial data. Thus, it is the IS, including people, that analyze geospatial data. The GIS system augments human intuition for solving unstructured problems.

Developers create GIS systems in response to requirements, as described in Chapter 10. Operations personnel run and maintain the system; a major responsibility for GIS operations personnel is maintaining the currency of database data. Field personnel are involved in the capture of geospatial data.

Before we turn to examples of the use of GIS in business, you need to understand the composition of computer-based maps and a few related issues and problems.

 HOW ARE GIS MAPS CONSTRUCTED?

A GIS map typically consists of layers of individual maps that are placed over one another. One layer might, for example, portray the terrain such as mountains and valleys and slopes. Another layer might portray vegetation, another layer portray streets and highways, another layer buildings, and so forth. Each layer is placed on top of the others. The map that is shown to the user is a composite of several maps. The GIS display manager can add, remove, or reorder layers according to the users' needs.

The construction and management of these layers, although easy to describe, is filled with challenges. To understand some of those challenges, you need to know basic map characteristics.

RASTER VERSUS VECTOR MAPS

Each map layer is constructed in one of two formats: raster or vector. A **raster map** consists of pixels, each of which has some value; often that value is a color, but it could also be a

Figure CE14-6
Raster Versus Vector Format

a. Two Shapes in Raster Format   b. Two Shapes in Vector Format

data value, such as elevation or temperature. Pictures that you take with your camera are recorded in color raster format. Figure CE14-6(a) shows the outline of two shapes in raster format.

A **vector map** consists of points, lines, and shapes. Figure CE14-6(b) shows the outline of the same two shapes in vector format. Here, each shape is an ordered list of points and, because these shapes are closed, the first and last points are the same.

Each format has strengths and weaknesses and both are used in GIS. Raster maps are easy to create from pictures and scanners and, at the scale in which they were created, they show details well. However, raster maps become blurry when enlarged, as you have probably noticed when you zoom too far into a photo. Also, when raster maps are shrunk, features disappear. For example, the small triangular shape will disappear if that raster image is reduced beyond a certain point.

Because raster maps are made of pixels, straight lines can appear irregular, like the right edge of the triangle in Figure CE14-6(a). Finally, GIS applications cannot readily identify features on a raster map. You can look at a raster map of the United States and find the Mississippi River, but a computer program cannot.

Vector maps overcome the deficiencies of raster maps, but are difficult to create. In most cases, some human involvement is required to construct a vector map. Programs for converting raster maps to vector maps exist, but the results are seldom satisfying.

Once created, however, vector maps scale perfectly. You can double or halve the size of a vector map as many times as you want without loss of fidelity. Straight lines are always straight lines. (By the way, although not shown in Figure CE14-6(b), vector maps include many types of curved lines and shapes; with enough points, any curved shape can be represented in a vector map.) Because vector features are named, they are readily identifiable by programs. A user who searched the vector map in Figure CE14-6(b) for "Shape One" will readily find it, and a user who searches for "Shape Three" will know for certain that it does not exist on the map.

The layers in most GIS maps are a combination of raster and vector layers. In Google Maps and Bing Maps, you can turn layers on and off. In Bing, if you select *Aerial*, you'll see a raster map; if you select *Road,* you'll see a vector map. If you select both, you'll see a raster map with a vector map on top of it. In Figure CE14-7, the left-hand section of the map is in vector format and the right-hand section is a raster image with vector features added on top of it.

When combining layers of different types, map alignment is important. If the alignment is poor, you'll see roads in places where they are not, for example. Techniques for aligning layers exist but are beyond the scope of our discussion.

Figure CE14-7
Vector and Raster Image Examples

Source: The National Map Viewer, USGS, *http://viewer.nationalmap .gov/viewer.*

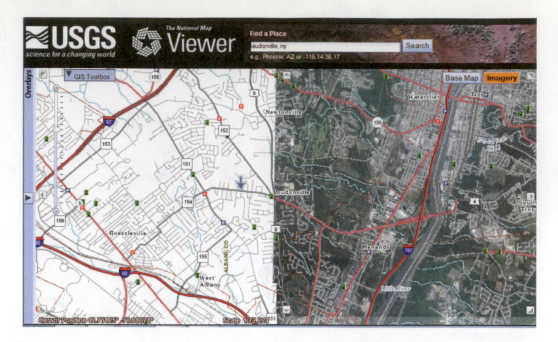

MAPPING THE EARTH

Constructing a map of the earth requires answers to three difficult questions:

- How big is the earth?
- What is the shape of the earth?
- How can the curved surface of the earth be shown flat?

How Big Is the Earth?

In order to compute map elevations, we need to know what sea level is. But, because of tides, the sea level constantly changes. At what point, worldwide, are all the tides at sea level? This question has no satisfying answer, and so cartographers (map makers) ask another question. What is the radius of the earth? An answer to that question determines a sensible value for sea level, worldwide. However, to use that approach for computing elevations, we must answer the second question.

What Is the Shape of the Earth?

The earth is not a perfect sphere; in fact, it is not a sphere at all. The best geometric model for the surface of the earth is an ellipsoid, which is a three-dimensional ellipse. Think of the earth as having the shape of an orange that you are squeezing on the top and bottom so that is it fatter than it is tall.

Because the earth is an ellipsoid, the question of how big the earth is requires not just a single radius, as for a sphere, but two radii. One radius is needed for the vertical dimension and one for the horizontal dimension. See Figure CE14-8.

Given values for these radii, elevations for points on the earth can be determined. A **datum** is a set of elevations based on particular values of the earth's radii. Over the years, different radii values have been used, and the result is numerous datums. WGS84 is a worldwide datum; NAD83 is a datum for North America, GRS80 is yet a third worldwide datum. The differences (and the explanation of the names) of these datums are unimportant to us, except that when importing data from different sources the data must arise from the same datum or the data must be converted to a single datum. Most GIS applications include tools for such conversions.

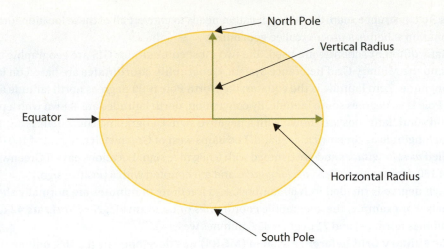

Figure CE14-8
Earth Modeled as an
Ellipsoid

How Can the Curved Surface of the Earth Be Shown Flat?

It can't, at least not without error. You cannot accurately portray the surface of an ellipsoid on a flat piece of paper or flat computer screen. Every flat map of the earth has significant distortions; the trick with GIS is to choose a mapping technique with distortions that are the least important for the application.

A **map projection** is a technique for placing locations on the surface of the earth onto a flat surface. Over the centuries, cartographers have devised numerous map projections that result in different types of distortion. Some of these projections are accurate in the way they portray area; they are said to preserve area. Others, which are used for local navigation, preserve angles between map features. Other projections show the shortest distance between two points on the surface of the earth as a straight line on the map. And some projections are compromises of all of these. Figure CE14-9 shows two common map projections: a Mercator projection, which is good for navigation but distorts areas, and a Peters projection, which preserves areas but distorts angles and cannot be used for navigation.

When composing layered maps, it is important that the maps be based on the same map projection. Combining layers that use different projections produces nonsense. Most GIS applications have tools for converting commonly used projections.

WHERE IS IT?

A GIS application needs a means for placing features on maps. Buildings are identified by addresses and legal descriptions, natural features are identified by latitude and longitude, population characteristics are identified by census tract, and physical features are identified by other

Figure CE14-9
Mercator and Peters Map
Projections

Source: © 2009, Akademische
Verlagsanstalt. www.ODTmaps.com.
Reprinted by permission.

means. To construct a map, the GIS application needs to convert all of these location identifiers to a common scheme, a process called **geocoding**.

Many different schemes are used. The two most common for GIS are geographic coordinates and the Military Grid Reference System. **Geographic coordinates** are based on latitude and longitude. Zero latitude is the equator; the North Pole is 90 degrees north latitude and the South Pole is 90 degrees south latitude. By convention, north latitudes are shown with a positive sign and south latitudes are shown with a negative sign. Geographic coordinates (arbitrarily) set zero longitude at Greenwich, England. Locations west of Greenwich and east of 180 degrees are called *west longitudes* and are denoted with a negative sign. Locations east of Greenwich but west of 180 degrees are called *east longitudes* and are denoted with a positive sign.

Each degree is divided into 60 minutes, and fractions of minutes are normally shown as decimals. For example, the geographic coordinates of Loudonville, New York, are 42 degrees 42.6 minutes north (+) and 71 degrees 45.6 minutes west (−).

The **Military Grid Reference System (MGRS)** was developed by the U.S. military in 1947 and is used in GIS applications, worldwide. It was created before GPS, when longitudes were difficult to determine and always suspect. It divides the earth into 60 north-south segments, like segments in an orange. The segments are called **zones**. Zones are divided into squares that are 6 degrees east/west and 8 degrees north/south. Each square has a two-letter identifier. Within a square, distances are measured in meters from the east boundary and from the north boundary. In MGRS, the coordinates of Loudonville, New York, are 18T XN 01957 28809. Thus, it is located in the zone 18T block XN of that zone and is 1,957 meters east of the right-hand border of that block and 28,809 meters north of the southern border of that block. (Well, not quite. This location identifies a 1-meter square. The entire town of Loudonville is not located in that square!)

Numerous additional coordinate systems based upon the MGRS are in use today. In fact, if you go to the USGS National Map Viewer, you'll be offered a choice of four different coordinate systems.

The bottom line is that many alternatives exist for creating maps and for expressing locations on maps. When combining data from different sources, the GIS application must convert that data into consistent formats.

HOW DO ORGANIZATIONS USE GIS?

Organizations use GIS for the same reasons they do any information system; namely, to achieve their goals and objectives, which for competitive organizations means to obtain a competitive advantage. The ways in which GIS are used are as varied as there are different competitive strategies. In this section, we will examine GIS use on Web sites, for asset tracking, and as a BI tool.

HOW DO ORGANIZATIONS USE GIS ON THEIR WEB SITES?

The motorcycle manufacturer Harley-Davidson provides an excellent example of GIS use in its Ride Planner application. Figure CE14-10 shows the introductory screen. This display shows a vector-based map of the United States as well as public user procedures (and the location of the Harley-Davidson museum!). Suppose a rider wants to plan a motorcycle trip through the Capitol Reef National Park in Utah. To do so, the user would zoom into Utah by clicking repeatedly until he or she obtained a map with a scale that is useful for planning that trip. This site uses Microsoft Bing to provide zooming and map display, so the map quality is high and the user interface is already familiar to many users.

Harley-Davidson adds its own GIS data on top of the Bing-provided maps, as shown in Figure CE14-11. This map shows the location of the nearest Harley-Davidson franchise (dealer)

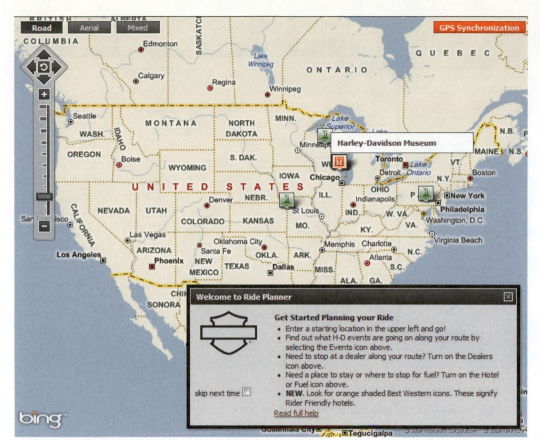

Figure CE14-10

Harley-Davidson Ride Planner

Source: http://rideplanner.harley-davidson.com/rideplanner/ridePlanner.jsp?locale=en_US&bmLocale=en_US. Courtesy of Harley-Davidson Motor Company.

in St. George, Utah. If the user clicks that symbol, the GIS will display additional data about the dealership: its facilities, hours, phone number, location, and so forth. Further, by clicking *Hotels*, the ride planner learns locations of Best Western Hotels that have agreed to provide discounts to Harley-Davidson riders.

Figure CE14-11

Planning a Capitol Reef Ride: Roads

Source: http://rideplanner.harley-davidson.com/rideplanner/ridePlanner.jsp?locale=en_US&bmLocale=en_US. Courtesy of Harley-Davidson Motor Company.

Figure CE14-12
User-Generated Content
via GIS

Source: http://rideplanner.harley-davidson.com/rideplanner/ridePlanner.jsp?locale=en_US&bmLocale=en_US. Courtesy of Harley-Davidson Motor Company.

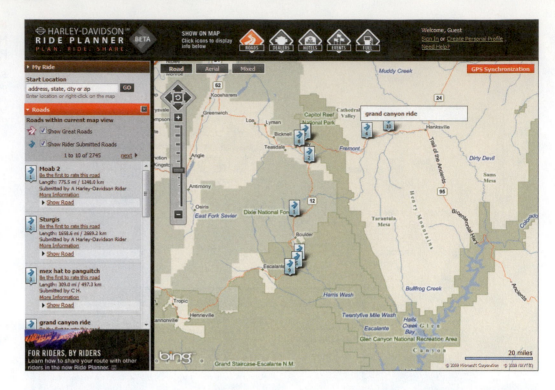

Figure CE14-12 shows another option. When the user clicked *Roads,* the GIS displayed trip reports that had been submitted by Harley-Davidson riders. When the user clicked *Grand Canyon ride,* the data in Figure CE14-13 was displayed. The site has many additional features, which you can explore by visiting *www.harley-davidson.com*. Under the *Experience* menu, click *Ride Planner.*

Reflect for a moment on how this site contributes to Harley-Davidson's competitive strengths. It promotes its museum. It raises the barrier to entry for other motorcycle manufacturers and creates brand loyalty among customers. It reinforces alliances between the manufacturer and its franchises. It also reinforces alliances with cooperating hotels. Finally, it provides users an opportunity to contribute content and to form social networks with each other.

Because these tools are built on Microsoft Bing, Harley-Davidson was able to bring it to market much faster and at far less expense than if it had developed the base mapping capability itself.

Figure CE14-13
User Contributed Data

Source: http://rideplanner.harley-davidson.com/rideplanner/ridePlanner.jsp?locale=en_US&bmLocale=en_US. Courtesy of Harley-Davidson Motor Company.

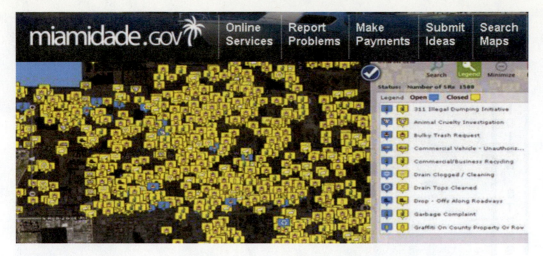

Figure CE14-14
Miami-Dade 311 Service
Request Call patterns

Source: *http://miamidade.gov/wps/
portal/main/311trends*

GIS are used on the Web sites of nonprofit organizations as well as government agencies. Figure CE14-14 shows a Web-based GIS application that displays 311-call (government services) data. Miami-Dade County created this application in-house.

USING GIS FOR ASSET TRACKING

Asset tracking is another organizational use of GIS. One common example is to track the movement of goods in the supply chain using a GPS device and a GIS. An onboard GPS and transmitter reports the location of the asset, say a pallet of goods, a truck, a container, or even a single item within a container. The reported locations are input to a GIS, and the locations of all such assets can be plotted on a GIS display.

A **geofence** is a geographic boundary set up within a GIS. One application for such boundaries is to notify personnel when trucks or other containers are nearing their destination. In this way, organizations can assemble the crew necessary to deal with the arrival of goods on a just-in-time basis.

One intriguing use of a geofence is to protect company personnel when they operate in politically dangerous locations. A geofence is established for safe zones. Any time an employee moves into an unsafe zone, as would happen in a kidnapping, the GIS notifies security personnel. Blue CRM is a risk management firm that provides just this capability. Visit *www.bluecrm.co.uk* to learn more.

USING GIS FOR BUSINESS INTELLIGENCE

GIS have become important for BI systems that involve geospatial data. A common application for GIS is to inform decisions about the location of resources and facilities. In this section, we will consider a typical example.

Community Health Network is a nonprofit organization that employs more than 10,000 people in the greater Indianapolis, Indiana, metropolitan area. It owns and operates four hospitals, many clinics, and a behavioral care pavilion. Community Health's primary charter is to provide access to health care services to a broad spectrum of people, particularly those who live in medically underserved neighborhoods.

Community Health Network endeavors to place facilities and medical professionals close to the point of need. As you can see in Figure CE14-15, it has placed its Health Centers in locations (census tracts) that have professional shortages or that are underserved in some other way.

Figure CE14-15
Community Health Network
Facilities

Source: Used with permission
of HealthLandscape, LLC.
www.healthlandscape.org

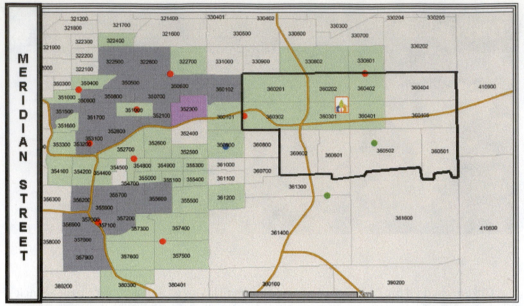

Legend:

🏠 Jane Pauley Community Health Center
🟪 Tracts with Health Profession Shortage Areas
🟩 Tracts with Medically Underserved Area / Population
🔴 Community Health Centers
🔵 Hospitals
🟢 School Based Health Clinics

Because populations are dynamic, the client needs of the Community Health Network change over time. Economic conditions change the number of people who need assistance, and people move in, out, and within the areas served by Community Health Network. For example, in recent years the Fall Creek Place neighborhood, which had been economically blighted, has become gentrified as part of Indianapolis' urban renewal. With this gentrification, many of the poor who had lived in that neighborhood were displaced. Those who moved still need medical services, however, and Community Health Services needs to know how this displacement impacted needs at other locations.

Community Health uses GIS to investigate such changes in population and economic conditions. The number of vacant residences in a neighborhood is correlated with poverty, and so changes in medical needs are correlated with changes in number of vacant residences. Figure CE14-16 shows maps of vacant residences for the first and last quarters of 2008. By comparing these maps, Community Health gains visibility on how medical needs may have changed during this year. Its analysis include not only maps, but other data sources as well. For example, if the map analysis indicates a possible increase in the number of disadvantaged people, analysts check for other evidence of poverty, such as an increase in free/reduced lunch requirements in schools. Combining maps and other data helps Community Health to decide when and where to open new community health clinics. Such information also helps them to obtain funding for those clinics.

Community Health Network specializes in providing access to healthcare services; they do not specialize in GIS. Consequently, they contract with HealthLandscape, a for-profit organization that operates specialized GIS for medical applications, worldwide. HealthLandscape uses ArcGIS as its GIS application and adds data about medical needs that it obtains from a variety of sources, chiefly government agencies. Go to *www.healthlandscape.org* to learn about HealthLandscape's products. Also, see Using Your Knowledge, Exercise 5, on page 559.

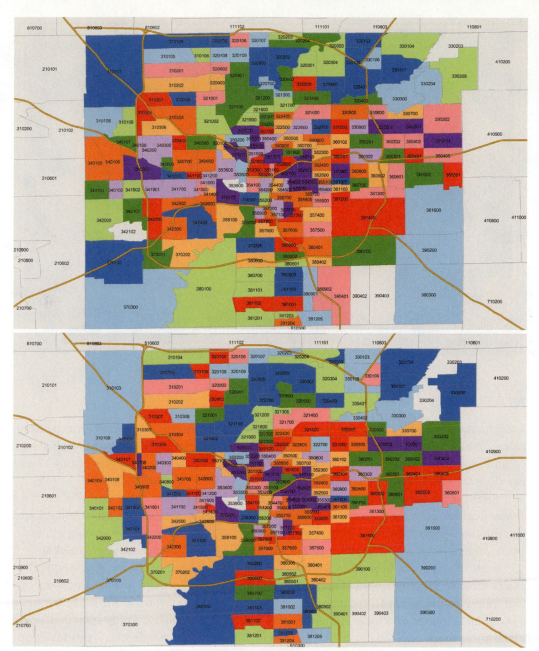

Figure CE14-16
Maps Used to Assess Change
in Need for Medical Access

Source: Used with permission
of HealthLandscape, LLC.
www.healthlandscape.org

a. Total Vacant Residences,
Q1 2008

b. Total Vacant Residences,
Q4 2008

HOW DO MAPS DECEIVE?

As you have learned, GIS maps create information by placing geospatial data into a meaningful context. Unfortunately, maps are also effective at deception. For some reason, perhaps the way humans process visual data, we tend to be less critical of maps and other graphic displays than we are of prose. Perhaps signals in the visual cortex bypass our critical apparatus.

Recall that all flat maps require distortion of some type. The judicious use of this distortion can lead map viewers into unwarranted conclusions. Accordingly, maps are used for propaganda, for advertising, and for biased reporting and analysis. In this question, we will discuss how maps are biased, how they seem to communicate more than they do, and how they can be structured to deceive.

Figure CE14-17

A Proper (or Improper?) Map of the World

Source: McArthur's Universal Corrective Map of the World. © 1979 McArthur. Available world-wide from ODT, Inc. (1-800-736-1293; *www .ODTmaps.com*; Fax: 413-549-3503; E-mail: *odtstore@odt.org*). Also available in Australia from McArthur Maps, 208 Queens Parade, North Fitzroy, 3068, Australia. ODTmaps. com publishes a variety of alternative world maps including other south-on-top maps, equal area maps, and world population maps.

MAP BIAS

Every human being is embedded in a culture and holds unconscious, or at least unrecognized, cultural biases. Like fish that are unaware of water, we swim in our culture and seldom challenge cultural values, including those embedded in maps. For example, examine Figure CE14-17 and pay close attention to your thinking as you do so.

There is no reason that south cannot be up, nor is there any reason that Australia and New Zealand cannot be in the top or center of a map. Doing so places Mexico above the United States and the United States above Canada. If you live in any of these countries, something will seem wrong with the implications of this map, but only your cultural biases cause you to think so.

Some direction has to be up, and other than the fact that North is *always* up, cartographers can be forgiven for standard world maps. However, because all flat maps involve distortion, cartographers (or today, any GIS user) can create maps that use distortion to artificially reinforce a position. Someone who wants to emphasize world hunger could use a projection that would make Africa much larger in proportion to other continents. Or, someone who wants to de-emphasize world hunger could use a projection that would make Africa much smaller. Similarly, maps can be constructed that show two features much closer together than they are in proportion to the distances of other features. And, with modern GIS, it is possible for the untrained person to unknowingly create a great looking map that is full of distortions that appear to be meaningful. So, the first guide to map use is to pay attention to map orientation, projection, scale, and source.

PROBLEMS WITH CHOROPLETH MAPS

The map in Figure CE14-18 is an instance of a **thematic map**, or a map that shows themes about geographic locations. It is also an instance of a **choropleth map**, which is a map that displays colors, shades, or patterns in accordance with category values of underlying data.

Choropleth maps have numerous problems (or opportunities if you're looking for deception possibilities). First, they convey homogeneity that seldom exists. The map in Figure CE14-18 makes it appear that everyone who lives in the Midwest voted Republican in 2004. If you are a Democrat, you can use this map to reconfirm whatever bias you have about people who live in the Midwest. If you are a Republican, you can use it to reconfirm whatever bias you have about people on the West Coast, etc.

2004 U.S. Presidential Election Results

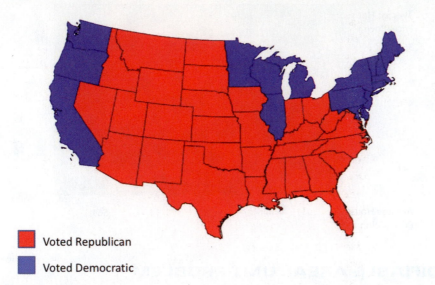

■ Voted Republican

■ Voted Democratic

Figure CE14-18
Thematic, Choropleth Map
Example

Source: Bob Yoder.

Reality is, of course, much more complicated. In the state of Washington, for example, the eastern half of the state voted heavily Republican in the 2004 election; but this fact is not visible in this map. Furthermore, the election was close in some states and not at all close in others. It is impossible to discern these differences on a choropleth map.

Figure CE14-19 demonstrates other interpretation problems of choropleth maps. A first look at this map would cause you to conclude that Africanized honey bees (so-called killer bees) are a growing menace. Perhaps such bees are a menace, but we can't conclude that from this map.

What, actually, does this map communicate? The large county in Nevada apparently had one or more Africanized bees in 1999. But because the entire county is colored, the map visually implies that the bees visited every part of that county. Furthermore, was the county visited by one bee or thousands? And, are the bees still there? Or did they move on? In fact, in spite of appearances, this map only communicates that at least one bee was found somewhere in a county in the year indicated. The results in the entire map could have been created by one very busy bee. But, by its structure, it seems to communicate more. It is also poorly designed; it has too many colors that are difficult to interpret.

It's unfair to criticize this map without reading the article that goes with it. But, use it as a caution to think carefully before unconsciously accepting what maps seem to say to our visual cortex.

Figure CE14-19
What Is the Information
in This Map?

*Source: http://www.ars.
usda.gov/Research/docs.
htm?docid=11059&page=6.*

First found in southern Texas in 1990, Africanized honey bees are now found in much of the South.

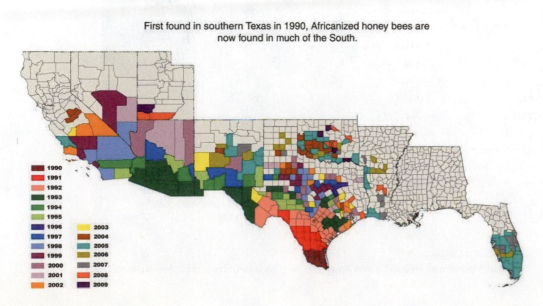

1990	
1991	
1992	
1993	
1994	
1995	
1996	2003
1997	2004
1998	2005
1999	2006
2000	2007
2001	2008
2002	2009

Figure CE14-20
Average Housing Prices by
City Block

Cells contain the average house price on each city block.

Average House
Price (Rows):

366

456

821

300	350	375	375	300	350
400	425	350	380	400	390
500	425	375	400	450	400
625	400	485	395	550	475
700	800	835	825	850	875
900	550	875	950	800	900

Average House
Price (Columns):   531   551   561

MODIFIABLE AREAL UNIT PROBLEM

The **modifiable areal unit problem (MAUP)** is a condition that occurs when point-based spatial data are aggregated into regions and the results depend on how the regions are defined.[1]

For GIS, it occurs when geospatial point data are grouped into geographic regions. It is a problem because the results obtained depend on the definition of the regions, and thus different region definitions can give very different results.

Consider the housing price data in Figure CE14-20. Suppose that each square represents a city block, and the number represents the average price of houses on that block. Notice that if we group the data into three vertical columns, the average house prices are 531, 551, and 561; all values are about the same. However, if we group the data into three horizontal columns, the average values are 366, 456, and 821. In this form, it is not too difficult to see that these differences are due only to grouping.

However, suppose we want to show that our city is a homogenous, middle-class one, so we construct the choropleth map shown in Figure CE14-21. We can use soft shades of a neutral color like green to reinforce our position.

Figure CE14-21
First Grouping of Data in
Figure CE14-20

Average House
Price: 531   551   561

Three Equal Middle-Class Neighborhoods,
Slightly Nicer Homes in the East

---

[1]See Mark Monmonier, *How to Lie with Maps,* 2nd ed. (Chicago: University of Chicago Press, 1996).

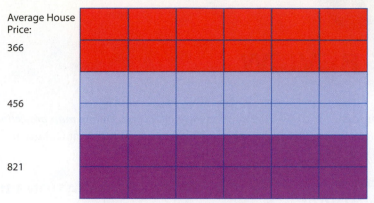

Figure CE14-22
Second Grouping of Data in
Figure CE14-20

Average House
Price:

366

456

821

Neighborhood Segregated by Strong Economic Boundaries:
Poor in the North, Rich in the South

But, grouping the same data in rows, as in Figure CE14-22, we can also show that this city (no longer ours!) is highly segregated. The poor live in the north and the rich in the south. We can also use emotional colors like red for poor and the princely purple for the rich.

Which is it? Is it a homogenous or segregated neighborhood? The only difference between Figures CE14-21 and CE14-22 is MAUP. By the way, in politics, they call MAUP *gerrymandering*.

The bottom line: Don't jump to conclusions when viewing maps, especially choropleth maps. Take the time to understand the bias of the map, the required distortion, the false homogeneity of choropleth maps, the use of emotional colors, and MAUP.

ACTIVE REVIEW

Use this Active Review to verify that you understand the ideas and concepts that answer the chapter extension's study questions.

Q1 WHAT ARE THE COMPONENTS OF A GEOGRAPHIC INFORMATION SYSTEM?

Define *GIS* and *geospatial data*. Identify the type of information that is most appropriate for GIS, and explain why it is most appropriate. Summarize each of the five components of a GIS. Explain the role of application-specific programs and a GIS application. Name two GIS applications. Describe challenges for storing geospatial data. List three types of geospatial data available from the U.S. government. Name and describe the five types of GIS users.

Q2 HOW ARE GIS MAPS CONSTRUCTED?

Explain how maps are layered. Define *raster* and *vector maps,* and compare and contrast their advantages and disadvantages. Explain how sea level is determined, and describe the shape of the earth. Define *datum*. Explain why all flat maps of the earth involve distortion. Define *map projection*. Name and briefly describe two techniques that GIS use for locating features on maps.

Q3 HOW DO ORGANIZATIONS USE GIS?

Summarize features of the Harley-Davidson Ride Planner application. Explain how this application contributes to Harley-Davidson's competitive strength. Summarize the ways organizations use GIS for asset tracking. Describe the challenges faced by Community Health Network when it tries to use GIS to determine where to place its clinics. Summarize the role of GIS in making location decisions.

Q4 HOW DO MAPS DECEIVE?

Explain why maps are good candidates for creating deception. Describe the bias in maps and summarize your reaction to the map in Figure CE14-17. Describe thematic and choropleth maps. Summarize interpretation problems for the maps in Figures CE14-18 and CE14-19. What does the map in Figure CE14-19 actually convey? What does it appear to convey? Define *MAUP*, and explain how it is illustrated in Figures CE14-21 and CE14-22.

KEY TERMS AND CONCEPTS

Choropleth map 554
Datum 546
Geocoding 548
Geofence 551
Geographic coordinates 548
Geographic information system
  (GIS) 540

Geospatial data 540
GIS application 541
Map projection 547
Military Grid Reference System
  (MGRS) 548
Modifiable areal unit problem
  (MAUP) 556

Raster map 544
Thematic map 554
Vector map 545
Zone 548

USING YOUR KNOWLEDGE

1. Visit *www.harley-davidson.com* and plan a trip. Explain the roles played by the software components in Figure CE14-3 as you do so. Keep in mind that the base map data are coming from Microsoft Bing.

2. Use the Harley-Davidson Ride Planner to find a dealer in Grand Junction, Colorado. Use either Google Maps or Microsoft Bing to locate a nearby Mexican restaurant. Summarize the geospatial and structured database data that are required to produce these results. Is the phone number of the restaurant you found data or information to you? Explain.

3. Compare and contrast Google Maps and Google Earth. Summarize the disadvantages of a thick client to both you and Google. Install Google Earth. Find the restaurant you identified in your answer to question 2 in both Google Maps and Google Earth. Do you think Google Earth is worth installing? Why or why not?

4. Visit *http://udig.refractions.net*. Summarize the capability of the products offered at this site. Find and describe two interesting maps in the uDig gallery. Visit *http://grass.osgeo.org*. Summarize the capability of the products offered at this site. Go to the GRASS gallery and find and describe one interesting vector map and one interesting raster map. (Look in the Screenshots category in the left-hand menu on the homepage.) Summarize the process you would use to choose one of these products if you were looking for an open-source GIS product.

5. Visit *www.healthlandscape.org* and navigate to *My HealthLandscape*. Summarize the capability and benefits of this site. Create an account as a public user. Zoom to the county of your home town. Using the menu on the right, go to *Health Workforce Data*. Produce a map of Health Center Locations in your home county.

6. Use the knowledge you gained from Q4 of this chapter extension to construct a personal guide to map interpretation. List rules and reminders that you should use when interpreting maps, especially choropleth maps.

chapter extension 15

Chapter 10 provides the background for this Extension.

Systems Development Project Management

Q1 WHY IS FORMALIZED PROJECT MANAGEMENT NECESSARY?

GearUp is a small company and it might be possible for it to apply the systems development life cycle (SDLC) without formalized project management. Small companies can sometimes get along by implementing small IS projects on an informal, catch-as-catch-can basis. Of course, good project management would be beneficial, but it might not be required. The situation is different for PRIDE, however, because the system development, even though relatively simple, involves several different organizations. PRIDE development will benefit from formal project management.

The situation is similar for projects at medium-sized and large companies. Here, IS projects are large and complex, and strong, formalized project management is mandatory. Information systems at such companies have many features and functions. They require substantial computer resources and necessitate the creation of multifaceted, complicated computer programs. They process databases with hundreds of tables; dozens, possibly hundreds, of relationships; and terabytes of data. Such large-scale systems affect many business processes and support hundreds, possibly thousands, of concurrent users.

Because of their size, such systems require a large development team, often comprising 50 to 100 or more business and systems analysts, programmers, PQA engineers, and managers. To add further complexity, large-scale systems are often simultaneously developed at multiple sites. A project might involve teams in the United States, India, China, and other countries. Additionally, the development of large-scale systems can involve integrating products and services from different companies, as is done with PRIDE. In these larger development projects, some companies provide licensed software; others provide particular expertise, such as database design; and others provide development labor. Large-scale systems are frequently localized for different languages. Finally, large-scale systems development requires extended development intervals, sometimes as long as 5 or 6 years. Figure CE15-1 summarizes the characteristics of large-scale systems.

The Internal Revenue Service provides a good example of a large-scale IS project. The IRS employs more than 100,000 people in 1,000 different sites and processes over 200 million tax returns a year. Starting in 1995, it set out to modernize the information systems for processing tax returns. Today, more than 18 years and several billion dollars later, it has not completed that project.

Formalized project management is a necessity for such large-scale projects. Without it, millions, even billions, of dollars will be wasted, projects will run late, and team morale will be low. In this chapter extension, we will consider the major components of IS project management. We begin the discussion of IS project management by discussing project trade-offs.

CE15

- Many features and functions
- Large, complex computer programs
- Databases with hundreds of tables, dozens to hundreds of relationships, and terabytes of data
- Affect many business processes
- Support hundreds or thousands of concurrent users
- Large development team
- Multiple sites
- International development
- Integration of work from several companies
- Localization necessary
- Extended development intervals

Figure CE15-1
Characteristics of Large-Scale Systems Development Projects

Q2   WHAT ARE THE TRADE-OFFS IN REQUIREMENTS, COST, AND TIME?

Systems development projects require the balancing of three critical drivers: **requirements** (scope)[1], **cost**, and **time**. To understand this balancing challenge, consider the construction of something relatively simple—say, a piece of jewelry, like a necklace, or the deck on the side of a house. The more elaborate the necklace or the deck, the more time it will take. The less elaborate, the less time it will take. Further, if we embellish the necklace with diamonds and precious gems, it will cost more. Similarly, if we construct the deck from old crates it will be cheaper than if we construct it of clear-grained, prime Port Orford cedar.

We can summarize this situation as shown in Figure CE15-2. We can *trade off* requirements against time and against cost. If we make the necklace simpler, it will take less time. If we eliminate the diamonds and gems, it will be cheaper. The same **trade-offs** exist in the construction of anything: houses, airplanes, buildings, ships, furniture, *and* information systems.

The relationship between time and cost is more complicated. Normally, we can reduce time by increasing cost, but *only to a point*. For example, we can reduce the time it takes to produce a deck by hiring more laborers. At some point, however, there will be so many laborers working on the deck that they will get in one another's way, and the time to finish the deck will actually increase. Thus, at some point, adding more people creates **diseconomies of scale** (recall Brooks' Law in Chapter 10).

In some projects, we can reduce costs by increasing time. If, for example, we are required to pay laborers time-and-a-half for overtime, we can reduce costs by eliminating overtime. If finishing the deck—by, say, Friday—requires overtime, then it may be cheaper to avoid overtime by completing the deck sometime the next week. This trade-off is not always true, however. By extending the project interval, we will need to pay labor and overhead for a longer period of time. Adding more time can increase cost.

Consider how these trade-offs pertain to information systems. We specify a set of requirements for the new information system, and we schedule labor over a period of time. Suppose the initial schedule indicates the system will be finished in 2 years. If business requirements necessitate the project be finished in 1 year, we must shorten the schedule. We can proceed in two ways: reduce the requirements or add labor. For the former, we eliminate functions and features. For the latter, we hire more staff or contract with other vendors for development services. Deciding which course to take will be difficult and risky.

---

[1]When we speak of information systems, we usually refer to the characteristics of the system to be constructed as *requirements*. The discipline of project management refers to those characteristics as project *scope*. If you read literature from the Project Management Institute, for example, it will use the term *scope* in the same sense that we use requirements. For the purposes of this chapter extension, consider scope and *requirements* to be the same.

Figure CE15-2
Primary Drivers of Systems
Development

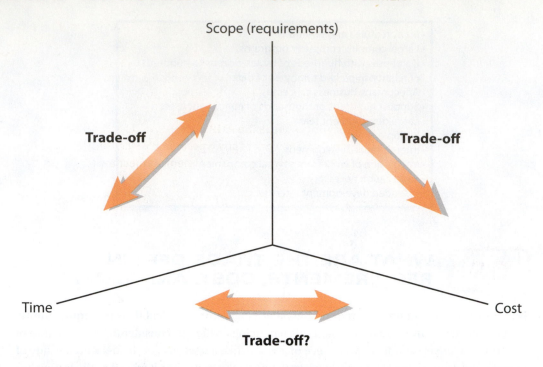

Furthermore, in most projects, we cannot make these decisions once and for all. We begin with a plan, called the **baseline**. It stipulates the tasks to be accomplished, the labor and other resources assigned to those tasks, and the schedule for completion. However, nothing ever goes according to plan, and the larger the project and the longer the development interval, the more things will violate the plan. Critical people may leave the company; a hurricane may destroy an office; the company may have a bad quarter and freeze hiring just as the project is staffing up; technology will change; competitors may do something that makes the project more (or less) important; or the company may be sold and new management may change requirements and priorities. When these events occur, project managers must reassess the trade-offs between requirements, cost, and time. It is a balancing act undertaken in the presence of continual change and substantial risk and uncertainty.

Q3 WHAT ARE THE DIMENSIONS OF PROJECT MANAGEMENT?

Many methods exist for developing information systems. Chapter 10 described the SDLC, the workhorse of the industry for years. This technique stipulates phases and processes for constructing information systems, but it does not address the management of projects, particularly large-scale projects. The systems definition phase of the SDLC, for example, stipulates that the project should be planned, but it does not indicate how. It stipulates that components need to be designed, but it does not address the management of the design activity, nor the communications among employees, groups, and sites. And so forth.

Large-scale projects require formalized project management. Although Kelly, the general manager at GearUp, can get by with informal meetings with Lucas and her employees, Alaska Airlines cannot deliver mobile applications for reservations that way. A formalized project management process is needed.

Over the years, people have proposed dozens of different project management methodologies and processes. In recent years, the process promulgated by the **Project Management Institute (PMI)** has achieved prominence. PMI is an international organization focused on disseminating best practices in project management. Both the American National Standards Institute (ANSI) and International Standards Organization (ISO) have endorsed PMI's work.

PMI publishes project management documents and offers project management training. It also offers the **Project Management Professional (PMP)** certification. Professionals who have 4,500 hours of project work experience can earn the certification by passing PMI's examination. Once you have the required work experience, the PMP is a worthwhile certification for any professional involved in project management work of any type. (The PMP certification pertains to project management in general, not only to information systems project management. See *www.pmi.org* for more information.)

Since its origin in 1969, PMI has evaluated many project management concepts and techniques and brought the best of them together under the umbrella of a document titled the *Project Management Body of Knowledge (PMBOK®) Guide.* This document contains what many believe are the best project management processes, practices, and techniques. The document does not describe the details of each practice or technique, but instead identifies those practices that are known to be effective for different situations and briefly describes their use. Versions of this document are denoted by the year in which they are published. As of 2012, the current version is *A Guide to the Project Management Body of Knowledge* (*PMBOK® Guide*), Fourth Edition.

The *PMBOK® Guide* is organized according to the grid in Figure CE15-3, which shows five *process groups* and nine *knowledge areas.* The process groups refer to different stages in the life of a project; the nine knowledge areas refer to factors to be managed throughout the life of the project.

You can surmise the meanings of the process groups from their titles. The knowledge areas provide an excellent summary of project management dimensions. *Project integration* refers to the management of the overall project and the construction of the final product. We have already discussed the trade-offs among *scope* (*requirements*), *time,* and *cost. Quality* management refers to quality assurance; for an IS project, it concerns planning and managing the product quality-assurance function.

Project Management Processes

Knowledge Areas	Initiating	Planning	Executing	Monitoring and Controlling	Closing
Project integration					
Scope (requirements)					
Time					
Cost					
Quality					
Human resources					
Communications					
Risk					
Procurement					

Figure CE15-3
Dimensions of Project Management

The nature of *human resources* management is clear from its name. *Communications* management concerns the methods, media, and schedules for communicating with the project's sponsors, within the team itself, and with others having an interest in the progress of the project. The decision to use a team SharePoint site, for example, would be part of communications management. Risk is inherent in all projects, and especially so for projects that involve new technology or the innovative application of existing technology. The purpose of *risk* management is to ensure that managers understand project risks and balance risk factors—or that they take other appropriate action to mitigate unwanted outcomes. Finally, *procurement* management concerns contracts with outside vendors for services, materials, and outsourcing of functions.

The *PMBOK® Guide* specifies practices, documents, techniques, and methods to be used for most of the cells of the grid in Figure CE15-3. For specific guidance on particular practices for process groups or knowledge areas, see the *PMBOK® Guide*. The particular contents of each cell are beyond the scope of this text; to learn more, take a project management class. However, you can consider the elements in Figure CE15-3 as a summary of the dimensions or factors that large-scale information systems development projects must address.

HOW DOES A WORK BREAKDOWN STRUCTURE DRIVE PROJECT MANAGEMENT?

The key strategy for large-scale systems development—and, indeed, the key strategy for any project—is to divide and conquer. Break up large tasks into smaller tasks and continue breaking up the tasks until they are small enough to manage, thus enabling you to estimate time and costs. Each task should culminate in one or more **deliverables** Examples of deliverables are documents, designs, prototypes, data models, database designs, working data-entry screens, and the like. Without a deliverable, it is impossible to know if the task was accomplished.

A **work breakdown structure (WBS)** is a hierarchy of the tasks required to complete a project. The WBS for a large project is huge; it might entail hundreds or even thousands of tasks. Figure CE15-4 shows the WBS for the system definition phase of the operational PRIDE system. The overall task, *System definition,* is divided into *Define goals and scope, Assess feasibility, Plan project,* and *Form project team.* Each of those tasks is broken into smaller tasks, until the work has been divided into a number of small tasks that can be managed and estimated.

Note, by the way, that the term **scope** is being used here in two different ways. As used in this WBS example, *scope* means to define the system boundaries, which is the sense in which it is used in the SDLC. As noted in Q3, scope for the *PMBOK® Guide* means to define the requirements. That use of scope does not appear in Figure CE15-4.

Once the project is deconstructed into small tasks, the next step is to define task dependencies and to estimate task durations. Regarding dependencies, some tasks must begin at the same time, some tasks must end at the same time, and some tasks cannot start until other tasks have finished. Task dependencies are normally input to planning software such as Microsoft Project. Figure CE15-5 shows the WBS as input to Microsoft Project, with task dependencies and durations defined. The display on the right, called a **Gantt chart**, shows tasks, dates, and dependencies.

All of the tasks from the WBS have been entered, and each task has been assigned a duration. Task dependencies have also been specified, although the means used to do so is beyond our discussion. The two red arrows emerging from task 4, *Define system boundaries,* indicate that neither the *Review results* task nor the *Assess feasibility* task can begin until *Define system*

System definition		
1.1	Define goals and scope	
	1.1.1	Define goals
	1.1.2	Define system boundaries
	1.1.3	Review results
	1.1.4	Document results
1.2	Assess feasibility	
	1.2.1	Cost
	1.2.2	Schedule
	1.2.3	Technical
	1.2.4	Organizational
	1.2.5	Document feasibility
	1.2.6	Management review and go/no go decision
1.3	Plan project	
	1.3.1	Establish milestones
	1.3.2	Create WBS
		1.3.2.1 Levels 1 and 2
		1.3.2.2 Levels 3+
	1.3.3	Document WBS
		1.3.3.1 Create WBS baseline
		1.3.3.2 Input to Project
	1.3.4	Determine resource requirements
		1.3.4.1 Personnel
		1.3.4.2 Computing
		1.3.4.3 Office space
		1.3.4.4 Travel and Meeting Expense
	1.3.5	Management review
		1.3.5.1 Prepare presentation
		1.3.5.2 Prepare background documents
		1.3.5.3 Give presentation
		1.3.5.4 Incorporate feedback into plan
		1.3.5.5 Approve project
1.4	Form project team	
	1.4.1	Meet with HR
	1.4.2	Meet with IT Director
	1.4.3	Develop job descriptions
	1.4.4	Meet with available personnel
	1.4.5	Hire personnel

Figure CE15-4

Sample Work Breakdown Structure for the Definition Phase of a Thin-Client Order-Entry System

boundaries is completed. Other task dependencies are also shown; you can learn about them in a project management class.

The **critical path** is the sequence of activities that determine the earliest date by which the project can be completed. Reflect for a moment on that statement: The earliest date is the date determined by considering the *longest path* through the network of activities. Paying attention to task dependencies, the planner will compress the tasks as much as possible. Those tasks

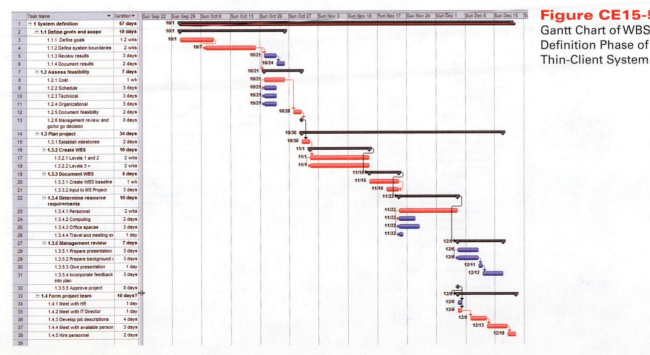

Figure CE15-5

Gantt Chart of WBS for Definition Phase of a Thin-Client System that cannot be further compressed lie on the critical path. Microsoft Project and other project-planning applications can readily identify critical path tasks.

Figure CE15-5 shows the tasks on the critical path in red. Consider the first part of the WBS. The project planner specified that task 4 cannot begin until 2 days before task 3 starts. (That's the meaning of the red arrow emerging from task 3.) Neither task 5 nor task 8 can begin until task 4 is completed. Task 8 will take longer than tasks 5 and 6, and so task 8—not tasks 5 or 6—is on the critical path. Thus, the critical path to this point is tasks 3, 4, and 8. You can trace the critical path through the rest of the WBS by following the tasks shown in red, though the entire WBS and critical path are not shown.

Using Microsoft Project or a similar product, it is possible to assign personnel to tasks and to stipulate the percentage of time that each person devotes to a task. Figure CE15-6 shows a Gantt chart for which this has been done. The notation means that Eleanore works only 25 percent of the time on task 3; Lynda and Richard work full time. Additionally, one can assign costs to personnel and compute a labor budget for each task and for the WBS overall. One can assign resources to tasks and use Microsoft Project to detect and prevent two tasks from using the same resources. Resource costs can be assigned and summed as well.

Managers can use the critical path to perform **critical path analysis**. First, note that if a task is on the critical path, and if that task runs late, the project will be late. Hence, tasks on the critical path cannot be allowed to run late if the project is to be delivered on time. Second, tasks not on the critical path can run late to the point at which they would become part of the critical path. Hence, up to a point, resources can be taken from noncritical path tasks to shorten tasks on the critical path. Using critical path analysis, managers can move resources among tasks so as to compress the schedule.

So far, we have discussed the role of the WBS for planning. It can be used for monitoring as well. The final WBS plan is denoted the **baseline WBS**. This baseline shows the planned tasks, dependencies, durations, and resource assignments. As the project proceeds, project managers

Figure CE15-6
Gantt Chart with Resources Assigned

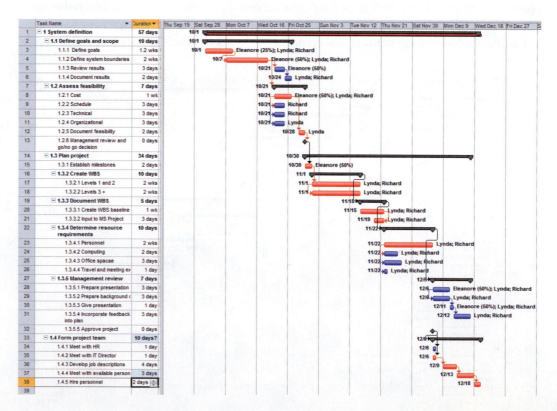

can input actual dates, labor hours, and resource costs. At any point in time, Microsoft Project can report whether the project is ahead or behind schedule and how the actual project costs compare to baseline costs.

As you can see, the WBS provides invaluable project management information. In fact, it is the single most important management tool for large-scale projects.

Q5 WHAT IS THE BIGGEST CHALLENGE FOR PLANNING A SYSTEMS DEVELOPMENT PROJECT?

As noted in Chapter 10, the biggest challenge in planning systems development is scheduling. How long does it take to develop a large data model? How long does it take to adapt that data model to the users' satisfaction? How long does it take to develop a computer program to process PRIDE privacy data on a cloud server if no one on the team has ever developed a cloud-based server application before?

Fred Brooks defined software as "logical poetry." It is pure thought-stuff. Some years ago, when I pressed a seasoned software developer for a schedule, he responded by asking me, "What would Shakespeare have said if someone asked him how long it would take him to write *Hamlet*?" Another common rejoinder is, "What would a fisherman say if you ask him how long will it take to catch three fish? He doesn't know, and neither do I."

No company should know better how to estimate software schedules than Microsoft. It has more experience developing software than any other company; it is loaded with smart, even brilliant, developers; it can draw from enormous financial resources, and it has strong incentives to schedule projects accurately. However, Microsoft Vista was delivered 2 years late. It was supposed to take 3 years, and it took 5. That's a 67 percent schedule overrun from the largest software developer in the world on what is arguably the world's most important computer program.

Part of the problem is that errors accumulate. If scheduling a single task is difficult, then scheduling a large-scale project becomes a nightmare. Suppose you have a WBS with thousands of tasks, and any one of those tasks can be 67 percent over schedule. It is impossible to do any credible planning. The term *critical path* loses meaning when there is that much doubt about task duration. In that setting, every task has some chance of being on the critical path.

Organizations take three approaches to this challenge. The first is to avoid the major schedule risks and never develop software in-house. Instead, they license software from vendors. For example, few companies choose to develop their own ERP or CRM software. ERP or CRM systems still have the substantial schedule risks of adapting procedures and training personnel, but those risks are much smaller than the schedule risks of developing complex software and databases.

But what if no suitable software exists? In that case, companies take one of two remaining approaches. They can admit the impossibility of systems development scheduling and plan accordingly. They abandon the SDLC and decide to invest a certain level of resources into a project, manage it as best they can, and take the schedule that results.

Project sponsors dislike such approaches because they feel they are signing a blank check. But sometimes it is just a matter of admitting the reality that exists: "We don't know, and it's worse to pretend that we do."

The third approach is to attempt to schedule the development project in spite of all the difficulties. Several different estimation techniques can be used. If the project is similar to a past project, the schedule data from that past project can be used for planning. When such similar past projects exist, this technique can produce quality schedule estimates. If there is no such

To learn of an innovative way of scheduling projects, see Chapter Extension 16, Agile Development.

past project, managers can estimate the number of **lines of code** that will need to be written. Then they can use industry or company averages to estimate the time required. Another technique is to estimate the **function points** in a program, use each function point to determine the number of lines of code, and use that number to estimate schedules. A function point is simply a feature or function of the new program. Updating a customer record is an example. For more information on the use of lines of code and function points for software scheduling, visit *www.codeproject.com/Articles/9266/Software-Project-Cost-Estimates-Using-COCOMO-II-Mo*. Of course, lines of code and function point techniques estimate schedules only for software components. The schedules for creating databases and the other system components must be estimated using other techniques.

Chapter Extension 16 describes development techniques other than the SDLC. Scrum, in particular, is good for schedule uncertainties because requirements are managed so as to fit within the time available. The result of a scrum project is a finished product that can be used; if there is insufficient time for complete development, some of the requirements will be unmet. But, the final system will be a working version of at least some portion of the requirements.

During your career, be aware of the challenges and difficulties of scheduling large-scale information systems development. As a user or manager, do not take schedules as guarantees. Plan for schedule slippage, and if it does *not* occur, be pleasantly surprised.

WHAT ARE THE BIGGEST CHALLENGES FOR MANAGING A SYSTEMS DEVELOPMENT PROJECT?

The challenges of managing large-scale systems development projects arise from four different factors:

- Coordination
- Diseconomies of scale
- Configuration control
- Unexpected events

Larger IS development projects are usually organized into a variety of development groups that work independently. Coordinating the work of these independent groups can be difficult, particularly if the groups reside in different geographic locations or different countries. An accurate and complete WBS facilitates coordination, but no project ever proceeds exactly in accordance with the WBS. Delays occur, and unknown or unexpected dependencies develop among tasks.

The coordination problem is increased because software is pure thought-stuff. When constructing a new house, electricians install wiring in the walls as they exist; it is impossible to do otherwise. No electrician can install wiring in the wall as designed 6 months ago, before a change. In software, such physical constraints do not exist. It is entirely possible for a team to develop a set of application programs to process a database using an obsolete database design. When the database design was changed, all involved parties should have been notified, but this may not have occurred. Wasted hours, increased cost, and poor morale are the result.

As mentioned in Chapter 10, another problem is diseconomies of scale. Adding more people to a project increases coordination requirements. The number of possible interactions among team members rises exponentially with the number of team members. Ultimately, no matter how well managed a project is, diseconomies of scale will set in. According to Brooks' Law, adding more people to a late software project makes it later.

As the project proceeds, controlling the configuration of the work product becomes difficult. Consider requirements, for example. The development team produces an initial statement of requirements. Meetings with users produce an adjusted set of requirements. Suppose an event then occurs that necessitates a change to requirements. After deliberation, assume the team decides to ignore a large portion of the changes to the requirements resulting from the event. At this point, there are four different versions of the requirements. If the changes to requirements are not carefully managed, changes from the four versions will be mixed up, and confusion and disorder will result. No one will know which requirements are the correct, current requirements.

Similar problems occur with designs, program code, database data, and other system components. The term **configuration control** refers to a set of management policies, practices, and tools that developers use to maintain control over the project's resources. Such resources include documents, schedules, designs, program code, test suites, and any other shared resource needed to complete the project. Configuration control is vital; a loss of control over a project's configuration is so expensive and disruptive that it can result in termination for senior project managers.

The last major challenge to IS project management is unexpected events. The larger and longer the project, the greater the chance of disruption due to an unanticipated event. Critical people can change companies; even whole teams have been known to pack up and join a competitor. The organization can be acquired, and new management may have different priorities. Congress can change applicable law; Sarbanes-Oxley is a good example of a law that affected not only financial systems, but also other systems whose resources were taken to comply with the new law. Natural disasters such as hurricanes can destroy offices or significantly affect employees' lives.

Because software is thought-stuff, team morale is crucial. I once managed two strong-headed software developers who engaged in a heated argument over the design of a program feature. The argument ended when one threw a chair at the other. The rest of the team divided its loyalties between the two developers, and work came to a standstill as subgroups sneered and argued with one another when they met in hallways or at the coffee pot. How do you schedule that event in your WBS? As a project manager, you never know what strange event is heading your way. Such unanticipated events make project management challenging, but also incredibly fascinating!

WHAT IS THE SINGLE MOST IMPORTANT TASK FOR USERS ON A SYSTEMS DEVELOPMENT PROJECT?

Taking responsibility for requirements is the single most important task you, a future user or manager of users, can perform for a large-scale development project. Taking responsibility goes beyond participating in requirements meetings and stating your opinion on how things should work. Taking responsibility means understanding that the information system is built for your business function and managing requirements accordingly.

"There are no IT projects," says former Kaiser-Permanente CIO Cliff Dodd. Rather, he says, "Some business projects have an IT component."[2] Dodd is right. Information systems exist to help organizations achieve their goals and objectives. Information systems exist to facilitate business processes and to improve decision making. Every information system is simply a part of some larger business project.

When investigating the problems in the IRS modernization program, the IRS Oversight Board stated, "The IRS business units must take direct leadership and ownership of the

---

[2]Quoted in Steve Ulfelder, "How to Talk to Business," *www.computerworld.com/managementtopics/management /story/0,10801,109403,00.html*, March 13, 2006, accessed June 2012.

Modernization program and its projects. In particular this must include defining the scope of each project, preparing realistic and attainable business cases, and controlling scope changes throughout each project's life cycle."[3]

Users cannot be passive recipients of the IS department's services. Instead, users are responsible for ensuring that requirements are complete and accurate. Users must ask only for what they need and must avoid creating requirements that cannot possibly be constructed within the available budget. Because users may not know what is difficult or unrealistic, requirements definition can occur only through an extended conversation among the users and the development team.

Once the requirements are known, the development team will create a project WBS and will initiate management activities for each of the nine knowledge areas in Figure CE15-3. It will fill staff positions, begin the design process, and, later, implement the stated requirements. If users subsequently change their minds about what is needed, considerable rework and waste will occur. **Requirements creep** is the process by which users agree to one set of requirements, then add a bit more ("It won't take too much extra work"), then add a bit more, and so forth. Over time, the requirements creep so much that they describe a completely new project, but the development team is left with the budget and plan of the original project.

Users must take responsibility for managing requirements changes and for avoiding requirements creep. Some requirements change is inevitable; but if changes become extensive, if requirements creep cannot be avoided, start a new project. Don't try to turn a doghouse into a skyscraper, one small change at a time. In that course of action, disaster is the only outcome.

A final part of the users' responsibility for requirements concerns *testing*. You and those who work for you may be asked to help in several different ways. You may be asked to specify testing criteria. If so, you need to help define testable conditions that determine whether a feature or function is complete and operational. Testing may occur in several stages during the project. For example, you may be asked to test design components; evaluating a data model is a good example. Or you may be asked to provide sample data and sample scenarios for program and systems testing. You may be asked to participate in the testing of beta versions. Because only the users can know if a feature works correctly, testing is part of requirements management.

Once more: Taking responsibility for system requirements is the single most important task you can perform on a large-scale development project!

---

[3]IRS Oversight Board, "Independent Analysis of IRS Business Systems Modernization Special Report," www .irsoversightboard.treas.gov, accessed June 2012.

ACTIVE REVIEW

Use this Active Review to verify that you understand the ideas and concepts that answer this chapter extension's study questions.

Q1 WHY IS FORMALIZED PROJECT MANAGEMENT NECESSARY?

Summarize the characteristics of large-scale information systems development projects. Explain why these characteristics make large-scale projects hard to manage. Give two examples of large-scale systems development projects.

Q2 WHAT ARE THE TRADE-OFFS IN REQUIREMENTS, COST, AND TIME?

Describe two meanings for the term *scope*. Describe how requirements affect cost and time. Describe the trade-offs that exist between requirements and time. Explain the trade-offs that exist between time and cost. Describe circumstances in which increasing cost reduces time. Explain circumstances in which increasing cost increases time. Describe circumstances in which time extensions reduce costs.

Q3 WHAT ARE THE DIMENSIONS OF PROJECT MANAGEMENT?

Describe the difference between development processes such as the SDLC and project management. Summarize the activities of the PMI. Describe the contents of the *PMBOK® Guide*. Name the five process groups and the nine knowledge areas. Briefly explain the focus of each management area. Explain how you can use Figure CE15-3.

Q4 HOW DOES A WORK BREAKDOWN STRUCTURE DRIVE PROJECT MANAGEMENT?

State the key strategy for large-scale systems development. Explain why each task needs to produce one or more deliverables. Define *work breakdown structure,* and give an example. In Figure CE15-4, explain the numeric notation under task 1.3.

Define *Gantt chart*, and describe its contents. Explain how task dependencies influence project work. Define *critical path analysis*, and, using your own words, explain what it means. Describe two ways managers can use critical path analysis. Summarize how the WBS can be used to estimate costs. Define *baseline WBS*, and explain how the baseline can be used to monitor a project.

Q5 WHAT IS THE BIGGEST CHALLENGE FOR PLANNING A SYSTEMS DEVELOPMENT PROJECT?

Name the biggest challenge for systems development planning. Explain why this is so. Describe how the logical-poetry nature of software development affects scheduling. Summarize the three approaches to the systems development scheduling challenge that organizations can take. Describe two ways of estimating time to write computer programs. Describe how you can use the knowledge about systems development scheduling that you have.

Q6 WHAT ARE THE BIGGEST CHALLENGES FOR MANAGING A SYSTEMS DEVELOPMENT PROJECT?

Name four factors that create challenges for managing systems development. Give an example of each factor. Define *configuration control*.

Q7 WHAT IS THE SINGLE MOST IMPORTANT TASK FOR USERS ON A SYSTEMS DEVELOPMENT PROJECT?

State and describe the single most important task for users on a systems development project. Explain why, as Dodd put it, there are no IT projects. Summarize user responsibilities for managing requirements. Define *requirements creep*. Describe the action that should occur if requirements creep cannot be stopped. Summarize the users' role for systems testing.

KEY TERMS AND CONCEPTS

Baseline 562

Baseline WBS 566

Configuration control 569

Cost 561

Critical path 565

Critical path analysis 566

Deliverables 564

Diseconomies of scale 561

Function points 568

Gantt chart 564

Lines of code 568

Project Management Institute (PMI) 562

Project Management Professional
  (PMP) 563

Requirements 561

Requirements creep 570

Scope 564

Time 561

Trade-off 561

Work breakdown structure (WBS) 564

USING YOUR KNOWLEDGE

1. Consider two projects: one to track the assignment of people to one of 12 teams in a soccer league, and the second to upgrade the reservations system for Alaska Airlines. Explain how the general characteristics of these two systems development projects differ.

2. Consider the development of an iOS application for PRIDE. Explain the trade-offs that can be made among requirements, cost, and schedule. For a given set of requirements, explain how cost and schedule can be traded off.

3. Consider the process of an election campaign—say, a campaign to elect one of your fellow students for the position of student government president (or similar office at your university):
   a. Develop a WBS for the election campaign.
   b. Explain how knowledge of the critical path could help you plan the campaign.
   c. Explain two ways you can use critical path analysis for planning the campaign.
   d. Explain how you can use critical path analysis for executing and monitoring the campaign progress.
   e. If you have access to Microsoft Project (or other planning software):

   i. Input your WBS to Microsoft Project.
   ii. Assign durations to tasks in your project.
   iii. Specify task dependencies.
   iv. Identify the critical path.

4. Suppose you have a computer virus that is so severe you must reformat your hard drive:
   a. Develop a WBS for the process for recovering your computer.
   b. Estimate the time it will take you to perform each task.
   c. Neither lines of code nor function point estimation pertains to this task. Explain one other way you can improve the quality of your estimate.
   d. Suppose you suspect that your estimate for the time of recovery could be low by as much as 200 percent. How could you use this knowledge?

5. What is the single most important task for users on a systems development project? Do you agree? Why or why not? Why must requirements emerge as a result of a conversation between users and IT professionals?

Chapter 10 provides the background for this Extension.

Agile Development

 Q1 ## WHY IS THE SDLC LOSING CREDIBILITY?

The systems development life cycle (SDLC) process that you learned in Chapter 10 is falling out of favor in the systems development community, primarily for two reasons. First, the nature of the SDLC denies what every experienced developer knows is true: systems requirements are fuzzy and always changing. They change because they need to be corrected, or more is known, or users, once they see a part of the application, change their minds. Other reasons are that business needs change, or technology offers other possibilities.

According to the SDLC, however, progress goes in a linear sequence from requirements to design to implementation. Sometimes this is called the **waterfall method** because the assumption is that once you've finished a phase, you never go back. Requirements are done. Then you do design. Design is done; then you implement. However, experience has shown that it just doesn't work that way.

The SDLC gained popularity when the U.S. Department of Defense stipulated that it would be used for all software development contracts. They did so because they had enjoyed success with a process like the SDLC for building physical things. If you're going to build a runway for example, you specify how long it needs to be, how much weight the surface must withstand, and so forth. Then you design it and next you build it. The waterfall model works.

However, software, information systems, and business processes are not physical; they're social. They're built for people to use to inform themselves and achieve their goals. People and social systems are incredibly malleable; they adapt. That characteristic enables humans to do many amazing things, but it also means that requirements change and the waterfall development process cannot work.

Also, as stated in Chapter 10, requirements change in response to new technology. While technology does change when building physical objects, the rate of change is much less than for information systems.

Another reason that the SDLC is falling out of favor is that it is very risky. The people for whom the system is being constructed cannot see what they have until the end. At that point, if something is wrong, all the money and time has already been spent. Furthermore, what if, as frequently happens, the project runs out of money or time before it is completed? The result is a form of management blackmail in which the developers say, "Well, it's not done yet, but give us another $100,000 or another 6 months, and *then* we'll have it done." If management declines, which it might because the time or money at that point is sunk, they are left not only with the loss but also with the unmet need that caused them to start the process in the first place.

In short, the SDLC assumes that requirements don't change, which everyone who has ever been within 10 feet of a development project knows is not true; it's very risky for the business that sponsors it as well.

CE16

- Expect, even welcome, changes in requirements
- Frequently deliver *working* version of the product
- Work closely with customer, for the duration
- Design as you go
- Test as you go
- Team knows best how it's doing/how to change
- Can be used for applications, information systems, and business process development

WHAT ARE THE PRINCIPLES OF AGILE DEVELOPMENT METHODOLOGIES?

Over the past 40 years, numerous alternatives to the SDLC have been proposed, including *rapid application development*, the *unified process, extreme programming, scrum*, and others. All of these techniques addressed the problems of the SDLC and, by the turn of the century, their philosophy had coalesced into what has come to be known as **agile development**, which means a development process that conforms to the principles in Figure CE16-1.

The first principle is that the development process should expect, and even welcome, change. Given the nature of social systems, *expect* is not a surprise, but why *welcome*? Isn't welcoming requirements change a bit like welcoming a good case of the flu? No, because systems are created to help organizations and people achieve their strategies, and the more the requirements change, the closer they come to facilitating strategies. The result is better and more satisfying for both the users and the development team.[1]

Second, agile development processes are designed to frequently deliver a *working* version of the product. Frequently means something in the range of 1 to several weeks, sometimes as long as 8 weeks, but not longer. This frequency means that management is at risk only for whatever costs and time are used in that period. At its end they will be able to use some product version that has some value to them.

Thus, unlike the SDLC, agile techniques deliver benefits early and often. The initial benefits might be small, but they are positive and increase throughout the process. With the SDLC, no value is generated until the very end. Considering the time value of money, this characteristic alone makes agile techniques more desirable.

The third principle in Figure CE16-1 is that the development team will work closely with the customer until the project ends. Someone who knows the business requirements must be made available to the development team and must be able and willing to clarify and elaborate on requirements. Also, customers need to be available to test the evolving work product and provide guidance on how well new features work.

The fourth principle is a tough one for many developers to accept. Rather than design the complete, overall system at the beginning, only those portions of the design that are needed to complete the current work are done. Sometimes this is called **just-in-time design**. Designing in this way means that the design is constantly changing, and existing designs may need to be revised, along with substantial revision to the work product produced so far. On the surface, it is inefficient. However, experience has shown that far too many teams have constructed elaborate, fanciful, and complete designs that turned out to be glamorous fiction as the requirements changed.

Test as you go, which is the next principle, is obvious if the team is going to be delivering working versions. Testing is initially conducted among members of the team, but involves the business customer as well.

---

[1]Assuming those who are specifying requirements are competent and behave sanely. Alas, this is not always true, but we will leave that situation as an exception here.

Development teams know how well they're doing. You could go into any development environment today and ask the team how it's doing and, once the team understood you were not about to inflict a new management program on them, you would find they know their strengths, weaknesses, bottlenecks, and process problems quite well. That principle is part of agile development methodologies. At the end of every deliverable or some other (short) milestone, the team meets to assess how it's doing and how it can improve.

Finally, agile development methodologies are generic. They can be applied to the creation of applications, information systems, and business processes. They are applicable to other team projects as well, but that subject is beyond the scope of this text.

 WHAT IS THE SCRUM PROCESS?

Scrum is an agile development methodology developed by Jeff Sutherland, Jeff McKenna, and John Scumniotales for a project at the Easel Corporation[2] and extended by others over the past 15 years. *Scrum* is a rugby term, first used for teamwork in a *Harvard Business Review* article written by Hirotaka Takeuchi and Ikujiro Nonaka.[3] In rugby, a *scrum* is a gathering of a team into a circle to restart play after a foul or other interruption. Think of it as a huddle in American football.

SCRUM ESSENTIALS

Scrum is an agile development process that follows the principles shown in Figure CE16-2. First, the process is driven by a prioritized list of requirements created by the users and business sponsors of the new system. Work is divided into scrum work periods, which can be as short as a week but never longer than 8 weeks. From 2 to 4 weeks is recommended. Each work period, the

Figure CE16-2
Scrum Essentials

- **Requirements list drives process**
- **Each work period (1 to 4–8 weeks):**
  - Select requirements to consider
  - Determine tasks to perform—select requirements to deliver
  - Team meets daily for 15 min (stand-up)
    - What I did yesterday
    - What I'm going to do today
    - What's blocking me
  - Test frequently
  - Paired work possible
  - Minimal documentation
  - Deliver (something) that works
  - Evaluate team's work process at end of period (and say thanks)
- **Rinse and repeat until**
  - Customer says we're done
  - Out of time
  - Out of money
- **Three principal roles**
  - Product Owner (business professional)
  - Scrum Master
  - Team Members (7 ± 2 people)

---

[2]Chris Sims and Hillary Louise Johnson. *The Elements of Scrum*. Dymaxcon, 2011, pp. 65, 66.
[3]Hirotaka Takeuchi and Ikujiro Nonaka, "New New Product Development Game," *Harvard Business Review*, Jan 1, 1986. Available for purchase at http://hbr.org.

team selects the top priority items that it will commit to delivering during that time. Each work-day begins with a **stand-up**, which is a 15-minute meeting in which each team member states:

• What he or she has done in the past day

• What he or she will do in the coming day

• Any factors that are blocking his or her progress

The purpose of the stand-up is to achieve accountability for team members' progress and to give public forum for blocking factors. Often one team member will have expertise to help another blocked team member resolve the blocking issue.

Testing is done frequently, possibly many times per day. Sometimes the business owner of the project is involved in daily testing as well. In some cases, team members work in pairs; in **paired programming**, for example, two members share the same computer and write a computer program together. Sometimes, one programmer will provide a test, and the other will either demonstrate that the code passes that test or alter the code so that it will. Then, the two members switch roles. Other types of paired work are possible as well.

Minimal documentation is prepared. The result of the team's work is not design or other documents, but rather, a product that is a working version of the requirements that were selected at the start of the scrum period.

At the end of the scrum period, the working version of the product is delivered to the customer, who can, if desired, put it to work at that time, even in its not fully finished state. After the product is delivered, the team meets to evaluate its own process and to make changes as needed. Team members are given an opportunity to express thanks and receive recognition for superior work at these meetings. (Review the criteria for team success in Chapter Extension 1 and you will see how scrum adheres to the principles of a successful team.)

Figure CE16-3 summarizes the scrum process.

WHEN ARE WE DONE?

Work continues in a repeating cycle of scrum periods until one of three conditions is met:

• The customer is satisfied with the product created and decides to accept the work product, even if some requirements are left unsatisfied.

• The project runs out of time.

• The project runs out of money.

Figure CE16-3
Scrum Process

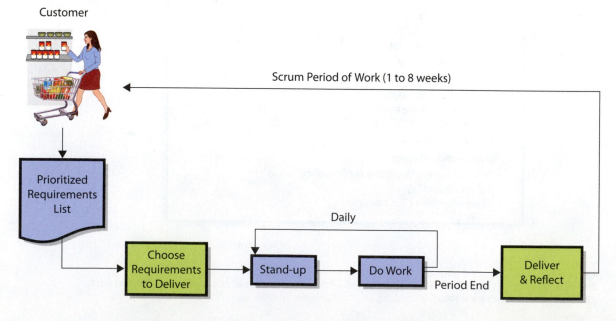

Unlike the SDLC, if a scrum project terminates because of time or budget limitations, the customer will still have a useful, working result for the time and money expended. It may not be the fully functioning version that was desired, but it is something that, assuming requirements are defined and prioritized correctly, can generate value for the project sponsors.

KEY ROLES

Scrum defines three key roles. The **product owner** is the business professional who provides the requirements and is available for clarification and testing. The product owner is the only person on a scrum team who has the authority to add, delete, or change requirements and their priority.

A **scrum master** is an expert in scrum processes who helps to keep the process organized and operating. The scrum master is not the boss; he or she is more like a coach or even a referee. The scrum master steps in when meetings go too long, when team members are misusing meeting time, when the product sponsor isn't doing his or her job, and when other situations are not working. The scrum master is also the guardian of team members' time. If distractions occur, the scrum master steps in to eliminate them. If someone other than the product sponsor attempts to change requirements or priorities, the scrum master negates that attempt.

Finally, **team members** are the programmers, systems analysts, business analysts, database designers, cloud engineers, PQA testing personnel, and any other staff needed to build the work product. Scrum teams are small; five to nine team members are recommended. If work requires more personnel, then the work is reorganized to be accomplished by multiple scrum teams working in parallel. It's not clear that scrum works well for exceedingly large projects, but then again, it's not clear that any other development process works well for them, either.

HOW DO REQUIREMENTS DRIVE THE SCRUM PROCESS?

Scrum is distinguished from other agile development methodologies, in part, by the way that it uses requirements to drive planning and scheduling. First, requirements are specified in a particular manner. One common format is to express requirements in terms of *who* does *what* and *why*.

For example, on the PRIDE system, a requirement could be expressed as:

"As a doctor, I want to view the patient's exercise records so I can make sure he is not doing too much"

Or,

"As a doctor, I want to view the patient's exercise records so I can make sure she is following her prescription."

Each of these requirements specifies who (the doctor) does what (view a patient's exercise data) and why (make sure she is following her prescription). It's not surprising that the requirement includes *who* and *what*, but the need for *why* may surprise you. The purpose of the why clause of the requirement is to set a context for the value that will be delivered by the requirement. Including it increases the likelihood that the product will deliver business value and not just blindly meet the requirement.

As stated, the product owner creates requirements and prioritizes them. For example, one of the two requirements above will be judged higher in importance than the other. All other things being equal, the team will satisfy the higher priority requirement first. This means, too, that if the project runs out of time or money, at least the highest priority requirements will have been completed.

Requirement:

"As a doctor, I want to view the patient's exercise records so I can make sure she is following her prescription."

Tasks:

1. Authenticate the doctor.
2. Obtain patient identifying data from doctor.
3. Determine this doctor is authorized to view this patient's records.
4. Read the database to obtain exercise records.
5. Read the database to obtain most recent prescription record.
6. Format the data into a generic format.
7. Determine the type of mobile device the doctor is using.
8. Format the generic report into a report for that mobile device.

CREATING REQUIREMENTS TASKS

Given a requirement, the team meets to create tasks that must be accomplished to meet that requirement. In Figure CE16-3, this work is done in the *Choose requirements to deliver* activity.

Figure CE16-4 shows eight tasks that need to be done to accomplish this requirement. In this activity, tasks for additional requirements that might be implemented in this scrum period are also created.

Tasks are created as a group, in a team meeting because the team can iterate, and members give feedback to one another. One team member will think of a task that needs to be done of which other members may not be aware. Or, a member may realize that a particular task is incomplete, or is doable in some other way.

SCHEDULING TASKS

As described so far, scrum is good idea, one of many agile processes that might be used. What makes scrum particularly innovative, however, is the way that tasks are scheduled.

Scrum methodology recognizes that developers are terrible, even wretched, at determining how long a task will take. However, developers are quite good at comparing how long something will take in comparison to something else. So, while a developer may be poor at estimating how long it will take to do, say, Task 2 in Figure CE16-4, he or she will likely be accurate when saying that Task 2 will take twice as long as Task 1, or determining some other ratio.

So, according to the scrum process, once the tasks are known for a given set of requirements, the next step is to assign each task a difficulty point score, called *points*. The easiest task has a point score of 1. A task that will take five times longer is given a point score of 5, and so on. For reasons that are beyond the scope of this discussion, points are expressed in values from a sequence of integers known as the Fibonacci sequence: {1, 2, 3, 5, 8, 13, 21, 34, 55, 89, 144, and ?}. The question mark is used because any number larger than 144 is meaningless. Most likely 89 and 144 are meaningless as well. Tasks with such point scores should be subdivided into multiple requirements. When all tasks have received points, the points are summed to a total for the requirement.

Scrum includes several different techniques for assigning points. Team estimation and planning poker are two. You can learn more about them in *The Elements of Scrum*.[4] The gist of these techniques is applying the team's expertise in an iterative, feedback-generating process to obtain team scores.

---

[4]Chris Sims and Hillary Louise Johnson. *The Elements of Scrum*. Dymaxcon, 2011, pp. 125–133.

Figure CE16-5
Summary of Scrum
Estimation Technique

> 1. Team assigns 1 point to simplest task.
>
> 2. Times to deliver working tasks are compared to each other and assigned points (Points are Fibonacci numbers). Use:
>   - a. Team estimation
>   - b. Planning poker
>   - c. Other
>
> 3. Using past experience, team computes its velocity … number of points it can accomplish per scrum period.
>
> 4. Working with product owner, team selects tasks for the upcoming scrum period, constrained by its velocity.

COMMITTING TO FINISH TASKS

As teams work together, they will learn the total number of points of work they can accomplish each scrum period. That term is called the team's **velocity**. The team uses its velocity to determine how many requirements it can commit to accomplishing in the next scrum period. Of course, at first the team will not know its velocity. In that case, senior members will need to make a guess. That guess may be far off, but it will get better as the team gains experience. Unlike the SDLC, there is at least well-founded hope that over time, estimating will improve.

For example, suppose the five requirements on the prioritized requirements list total 125 points. If a team knows its velocity is 100 points per scrum period, they know they cannot do all five. However, if the top four total, say 80 points, they can commit to doing those four, plus something else. In this case, the team would go back to the product owner and ask if there is a requirement lower on the priority list that can be done for the available 20 points of capacity. The scrum estimation process is summarized in Figure CE16-5.

HOCUS-POCUS?

If you haven't participated in software or systems development, this process may sound like so much hocus-pocus. However, it has two very important characteristics that make it not so. First, it is a methodology that incorporates team iteration and feedback for scheduling and tasking, which, as you know by now, is a way a team can create something together that far exceeds what each member can do individually. Second, it provides a framework for process learning. As a team works more scrum periods together, it learns how to assign points more accurately, and it increasingly learns what its true velocity is.

However, as Don Nilson, a certified scrum master with years of experience at Microsoft and other companies says, "Scrum is a good technique. However, it is not magic. You cannot use it to obtain a $500,000 result for $150,000, nor can you use it to obtain a 24 person-year labor result for 12 person-years. You are, however, less likely to lose a lot of time or money than with the traditional SDLC."[5]

---

[5]Personal correspondence with the author, June 3, 2012.

ACTIVE REVIEW

Use this Active Review to verify that you understand the ideas and concepts that answer the chapter extension's study questions.

Q1 WHY IS THE SDLC LOSING CREDIBILITY?

Describe the two reasons that the SDLC is falling out of favor. Explain why the U.S. Department of Defense believed that it was a workable process. Explain the nature of social systems development. Explain what happens when an incomplete SDLC project runs out of time or money.

Q2 WHAT ARE THE PRINCIPLES OF AGILE DEVELOPMENT METHODOLOGIES?

Define *agile development*. In your own words, explain the benefits of each of the principles in Figure CE16-1. Explain why just-in-time design is difficult for some developers to accept. Describe the projects for which agile development is appropriate.

Q3 WHAT IS THE SCRUM PROCESS?

In sports, what is a scrum? Explain the origin of the term as it pertains to teamwork. In your own words, explain the benefits of the principles in Figure CE16-2. Define scrum period and state the recommended length for such periods. Define *stand-up* and explain what happens in a stand-up. Define *paired programming*. Explain the activities and flows in Figure CE16-3. State conditions that cause a scrum project to finish. Summarize the difference between an SDLC project that runs out of money and a scrum project that runs out of money. Name and define three key roles for scrum.

Q4 HOW DO REQUIREMENTS DRIVE THE SCRUM PROCESS?

Explain the format for stating requirements in scrum. Why is *why* needed? Give two examples of scrum-style requirements not in this text. Summarize the process for creating a task list for accomplishing a scrum requirement. Explain what scheduling activity developers do poorly and what scheduling activity they do well. Explain what points are, and summarize how points are assigned to tasks and computed for requirements. Define *velocity* and explain how it is determined. Explain how velocity is used to plan work for a scrum period. In your own words, explain the meaning of, "Unlike the SDLC, there is at least well-founded hope that over time, estimating will improve." Summarize the characteristics of scrum that make this statement true.

KEY TERMS AND CONCEPTS

Agile development 574
Just-in-time design 574
Paired programming 576

Product owner 577
Scrum master 577
Stand-up 576

Team members 577
Velocity 579
Waterfall method 573

USING YOUR KNOWLEDGE

1. Read the criteria for team success in Chapter Extension 1. Explain scrum characteristics that support achieving team success.

2. Read the opening to Chapter 11. Explain how Dr. Flores and Maggie could use a scrum process for managing Ajit. Describe how doing so would reduce the risk of failure.

3. Suppose that you suggest that an information system be developed for your department, using scrum. Further suppose that your management is dubious. Write a one-page memo to justify using scrum.

4. Choose an important project type in a business discipline of interest to you. In accounting, it could be an audit; in marketing, it could be a plan for using social media; in operations, it could be a project of opening a new warehouse. Choose a major activity that is important and that you find interesting. Compare and contrast the use of a process such as the SDLC to a process such as scrum for your project. Which process would you recommend? Justify your recommendation.

Business Process Management

 **STUDY QUESTIONS**

Q1 WHY DO ORGANIZATIONS NEED TO MANAGE BUSINESS PROCESSES?

Q2 WHAT ARE THE STAGES OF BUSINESS PROCESS MANAGEMENT (BPM)?

Q3 HOW DO BUSINESS PROCESSES AND INFORMATION SYSTEMS RELATE?

Q4 WHICH COMES FIRST, BUSINESS PROCESSES OR INFORMATION SYSTEMS?

Q5 HOW IS BPM PRACTICED IN THE REAL WORLD?

Q1 WHY DO ORGANIZATIONS NEED TO MANAGE BUSINESS PROCESSES?

As defined in Chapter 2, a *business process* is a network of activities, actors, roles, repositories, and data and sequence flows that interact to accomplish a business function. To review, activities are something that an actor takes to perform a part of the business function. Actors are either people, or computer programs, or both. You can think of roles as job titles. Example roles are *salesperson*, *credit manager*, *inventory supervisor*, and the like. Repositories are collections of something of value; for us, repositories are collections of data. Data flows represent the movement of data items among activities and repositories, and sequence flows depict the logical flow from one activity to another.

To set the stage for discussing business process management, consider a simple, but representative, example.

A SAMPLE ORDERING BUSINESS PROCESS

Suppose that you work in sales for a company that sells equipment and supplies to the hotel industry. Your products include hotel furniture, cleaning equipment, and supplies, such as towels, linens, and staff uniforms. Processing an order involves the five steps shown in Figure CE17-1. You are one of many actors who perform the salesperson role.

As a salesperson, you do not perform all of the activities shown; rather, you orchestrate their performance. You are the customer's representative within the firm. You ensure that the operations department verifies that the product is available and can be delivered to the customer on the requested schedule. You check with Accounting to verify the credit required to process the order, and you check with your boss, a sales manager, to approve any special terms the customer might request (discounts, free shipping, extended return policy, and so forth). We will document this process further in Q2.

WHY DOES THIS PROCESS NEED MANAGEMENT?

When you joined the firm, they taught you to follow this process, and you've been using it for two years. It seems to work, so why does it require management? The basic answer to this question is that processes are dynamic and often need to be changed. This need can arise because of a process quality problem, a change in technology, or a change in some business fundamental.

CE17

Improve Process Quality

As you learned in Chapter 2, process quality has two dimensions: efficiency (use of resources) and effectiveness (accomplish strategy). The most obvious reason for changing a process is that it has efficiency or effectiveness problems. Consider a sales process. If the organization's goal is to provide high-quality service, then if the process takes too long or if it rejects credit inappropriately it is ineffective and needs to be changed.

With regard to efficiency, the process may use its resources poorly. For example, according to Figure CE17-1, salespeople verify product availability before checking customer credit. If checking availability means nothing more than querying an information system for inventory levels, that sequence makes sense. But suppose that checking availability means that someone in operations needs not only verify inventory levels, but also verify that the goods can be shipped to arrive on time. If the order delivery is complex, say the order is for a large number of beds that have to be shipped from three different warehouses, an hour or two of labor may be required to verify shipping schedules.

After verifying shipping, the next step is to verify credit. If it turns out the customer has insufficient credit and the order is refused, the shipping-verification labor will have been wasted. So, it might make sense to check credit before checking availability.

Similarly, if the customer's request for special terms is disapproved, the cost of checking availability and credit is wasted. If the customer has requested special terms that are not normally approved, it might make sense to obtain approval of special terms before checking availability or credit. Your boss might not appreciate being asked to consider special terms for orders in which the items are not available or for customers with bad credit.

As you can see, it's not easy to determine what process structure is best. The need to monitor process quality and adjust process design, as appropriate, is one reason that processes need to be managed.

Change in Technology

Changing technology is a second reason for managing processes. For example, suppose the company selling the goods in the process in Figure CE17-1 invests in new technology that enables it to provide next-day availability to customers. That capability will be of limited value, however, if the existing credit-checking process requires 2 days. "I can get the goods to you tomorrow, but I can't verify your credit until next Monday" will not be satisfying to either customers or salespeople.

Thus, when new technology changes any of a process' activities in a significant way, the entire process needs to be evaluated. That evaluation is another reason for managing processes.

Change in Business Fundamentals

A third reason for managing business processes is a change in business fundamentals. A substantial change in any of the following factors might result in the need to modify business processes:

- Market (e.g., new customer category, change in customer characteristics)
- Product lines
- Supply chain
- Company policy
- Company organization (e.g., merger, acquisition)
- Internationalization
- Business environment

To understand the implications of such changes, consider just the sequence of verifying availability and checking credit in Figure CE17-1. A new category of customers could mean that the credit-check process needs to be modified; perhaps a certain category of customers is too risky to be extended credit. All sales to such customers must be cash. A change in product lines might require different ways of checking availability. A change in the supply chain might mean that the company no longer stocks some items in inventory but ships directly from the manufacturer instead.

Or, the company might make broad changes to its credit policy. It might, for example, decide to accept more risk and sell to companies with lower credit scores. In this case, approval of special terms becomes more critical than checking credit, and the sequence of those two activities might need to be changed.

Of course, a merger or acquisition will mean substantial change in the organization and its products and markets, as will moving portions of the business offshore or engaging in international commerce. Finally, a substantial change in the business environment, say the onset of a recession, might mean that credit checking becomes vitally important and needs to be moved to first place in this process.

 WHAT ARE THE STAGES OF BUSINESS PROCESS MANAGEMENT (BPM)?

The factors just discussed will necessitate changes in business processes, whether the organization recognizes that need or not. Organizations can either plan to develop and modify business processes, or they can wait and let the need for change just happen to them. In the latter case, the business will continually be in crisis, dealing with one process emergency after another.

Figure CE17-2 shows the basic activities in **business process management (BPM)**, a cyclical process for systematically creating, assessing, and altering business processes. This cycle begins by creating models of business processes. The business users who have expertise and are involved in the particular process (this could be you!) adjust and evaluate those models. Usually teams build an **as-is model** that documents the current situation. Depending on the nature of the problem, new process models are then created, as we will discuss in Q5.

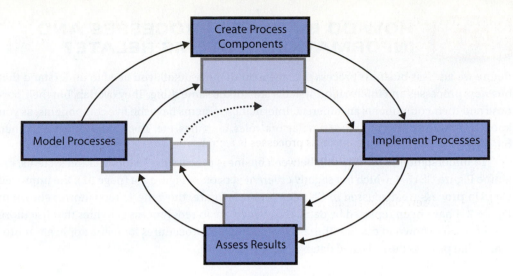

Given the proposed model, the next step is to create process components. If the solution involves an information system, then it is created or adapted at this point. Finally, the new or changed business processes, along with any necessary IS, are implemented.

Well-managed organizations don't stop there. Instead, they create policy, procedures, and committees to continually assess business process effectiveness. The Information Systems Audit and Control Association has created a set of standard practices called **COBIT (Control Objectives for Information and related Technology)** that are often used in the assessment stage of the BPM cycle. Explaining these standards is beyond the scope of this discussion, but you should know that they exist. See *www.isaca.org/cobit* for more information.

When the assessment process indicates that a significant need for change has arisen, the BPM cycle is repeated. Adjusted and new process models are developed, and components are created, implemented, and assessed.

Business process management has the same scope as discussed for information systems in Chapter 7: departmental, enterprise, and inter-enterprise. As shown in Figure CE17-3, BPM becomes more difficult as the scope of the underlying processes increases.

Finally, do not assume that business process management applies only to commercial, profit-making organizations. Nonprofit and government organizations have all three types of processes shown in Figure CE17-3, but most of these processes are service-oriented rather than revenue-oriented. Your state's Department of Labor, for example, has a need to manage its processes, as does the Girl Scouts of America. BPM applies to all types of organizations.

Figure CE17-3
Scope of Business Process Management

Scope	Description	Example	BPM Role
Departmental	Business process resides within a single business function.	Accounts payable	BPM authority belongs to a single departmental manager who has authority to resolve BPM issues.
Enterprise	Business process crosses into multiple departments within a single organization.	Customer relationship management (CRM); enterprise resource management (ERP)	BPM authority shared across several or many departments. Problem resolution via committee and policy.
Inter-enterprise	Business process crosses into multiple organizations.	Supply chain management (SCM)	BPM authority shared by multiple companies. Problem resolution via negotiation and contract.

HOW DO BUSINESS PROCESSES AND INFORMATION SYSTEMS RELATE?

Before we address business process management in more detail, you need to understand that business processes and information systems are not the same thing. They overlap, but their purpose and their components are different. Information systems have the five components, as you know by now. Business processes have actors, roles, activities, etc. The two relate to each other, but how?

To understand the relationship between business processes and information systems, examine Figure CE17-4, which is a slightly different version of Figure 2-4 (page 31), the improved GearUp process we discussed in Chapter 2. In this figure, the generic repositories shown in Figure 2-4 have been replaced by databases, which are in red. Process activities that use those databases are shown in orange. These activities include procedures for using application programs that process the indicated databases.

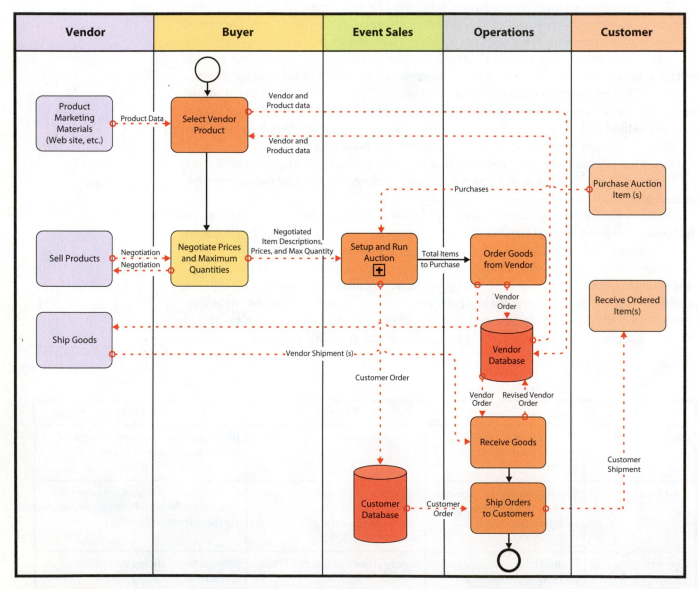

Figure CE17-4
GearUp Ordering Process

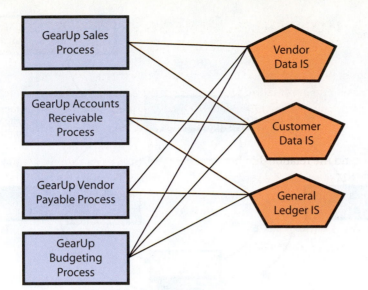

Figure CE17-5
Many-to-many Relationship
of Business Processes and
Information Systems

By the way, be careful with the words *process* and *procedure*. They sound the same, but are not. *Process* refers to the overall business process, like that in Figure CE17-4. A *procedure* is a component of an IS and is embedded within a process activity. Thus, in Figure CE17-4, a procedure for adding Vendor Orders to the Vendor Database is part of the Order Goods from Vendor activity, within the GearUp sales business process.

We can deduce three important principles from this figure. First, information system elements are embedded within business processes, but some activities in business processes are not part of any information system. Again, business processes and information systems overlap, but they are different. Second, this business process uses two separate information systems, and, in general, a business process can use zero, one, or more information systems.

The third principle is not visible in Figure CE17-4, but we can infer it. The information system that processes the Customer Database will be used by other business processes. Accounting, for example, will use it when billing customers or approving customer credit. Similarly, the information system that processes the Vendor Database will be used by other processes, such as an accounts payable process. Thus, a particular information system may be used by one or more business processes.

Recalling the cardinality principles from Chapter 5, we can say that the relationship of business processes and information systems is many-to-many, as illustrated in Figure CE17-5. For example, the GearUp sales process uses two information systems (many), and, at the same time, the General Ledger IS is used by three different processes (also many).

So, business processes and information systems overlap; procedures for using an information system are part of the activities of a business process, but there are activities that involve no IS. Finally, the relationship between business processes is many-to-many.

WHICH COMES FIRST, BUSINESS PROCESSES OR INFORMATION SYSTEMS?

Why do we care about this? What difference does it make? It turns out that the many-to-many relationship between business processes and information systems poses a dilemma when it comes time to build them. Which should we do first? Should we specify one or more business processes and then build the information systems that they require? Or, do we attempt to determine, in the abstract, all of the ways that someone might use an information system, build it, and then construct the business processes around it?

Figure CE17-6
BPM and Systems
Development

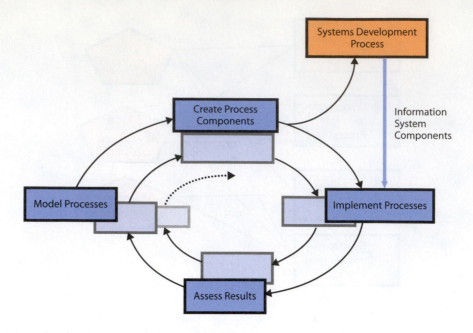

If you reflect on this situation, you can see why ERP systems, which promise to do everything, are both wonderful and terrible. They're wonderful because they include all the business processes and all the system components that an organization will need, at least as determined by the ERP vendor. They're terrible because, to implement ERP, an organization must attempt to do everything at once.

But, for non-ERP business processes and information systems, and for small organizations like GearUp, which should come first? Consider the alternatives.

BUSINESS PROCESSES FIRST

Suppose we decide to design business processes first and then build information system components as a consequence of that process design. If we take this approach, we'll have a development process that looks like that in Figure CE17-6. The organization will engage in business process management and construct system components in the create process components stage of the BPM cycle.

This approach works well for the business processes that are being constructed, but what about others in the future? Suppose the Vendor Database information system is constructed to record vendor orders, shipments received, order shortages, and other data needed for this process. But, what if Accounting wants to use this same information system to verify shipments received in an activity in its Accounts Payable process? Accounts Payable requirements were no part of the original requirements for the Vendor Database IS, and it will only be great fortune if that IS can support Accounting's needs for verification.

So, starting from processes and working toward information systems is likely to work well for the business processes under consideration, but will cause problems later for other processes that use the same information systems. So, what if we start with the information system?

INFORMATION SYSTEM FIRST

To start with systems first, a development team would talk with representative future users of the system and attempt to determine all of the needs that someone at GearUp might have for vendor data. In this case, business and systems analysts would meet with buyers, operations, accounting, and any other personnel that might have an interest in such data. From those requirements, they would then design components and construct the system.

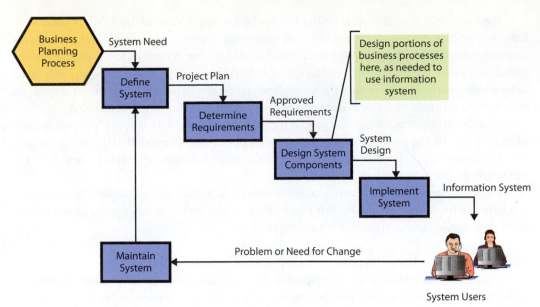

Figure CE17-7 shows a modification to the SDLC that you studied in Chapter 10. As you can see, the processes that use this system are designed as part of Design System Components. This development process makes business processes a poor stepchild of the information systems development process. The focus is on hardware, software, data, procedures (for using the system only), and user training. Some aspects of business processes will be constructed as part of the system implementation; but, as you saw in Figure CE17-4, business processes can include many activities that are not part of the information system. Those activities are unlikely to be considered when the system is constructed.

ANOTHER FACTOR: OFF-THE-SHELF SOFTWARE

A missing factor in this discussion is off-the-shelf software. Few organizations today can afford to create computer programs and design databases in-house. It is unlikely that GearUp, for example, will do so. Instead, most organizations attempt to license software off-the-shelf and adapt it to their needs, or adapt their needs to it.

So, if an organization knows that it most likely will license off-the-shelf software, is it better to design processes first or to develop information systems first? Unfortunately, again, there is no demonstrably correct answer. If an organization starts with business processes first, it is likely to choose a package that will work well for the processes being developed, but that may not work well for other processes that may come along later (like Accounting wanting to use the Vendor Database to verify receipt of goods). However, if it starts with information systems and collects all the requirements, it is likely to find a package that will work better for all users, but, again, business processes will receive short shrift.

AND THE ANSWER IS . . .

In theory, it is better to start with business processes. As discussed in Chapter 3, business processes are closer to the organization's competitive strategy and other goals and objectives. Starting with processes and working toward systems is more likely to result in processes and systems that are aligned with the organization's strategy and direction.

In practice, however, the answer is not clear. Organizations today take both approaches. Sometimes the same organization takes one approach with one set of processes and systems and a second approach with a different set.

The factor that overtakes all is off-the-shelf software. The vendor of the software knows the features that are most commonly needed by its customers. Therefore, if an organization starts with business processes and selects an application that works for those processes, it is likely that the application will also include features and functions that will be needed by other business processes to be designed in the future. At GearUp, an application that can be used to track vendor shipments is likely to be adaptable enough to also serve accounting's need to verify goods received.

Usually, an application software vendor includes procedures for using that software as part of its offering. So, the procedure components in Figure CE17-4 (included in the orange activities) are most likely part of the package. However, the entire business process in Figure CE17-4 is unlikely to be part of the vendor's package.

Therefore, in most cases, if an organization is likely to license an application from a vendor, it is better to begin with processes. This rule is not ironclad, however. You should expect to find both approaches used in organizations during your career.

Not Possible to Buy Processes or Systems Off-the-Shelf

Before we continue with systems development, do not be misled by the last few paragraphs. As stated in Chapter 10, it is possible to buy an off-the-shelf computer application, but the system that uses it is always in-house because the procedures and employees that use that application are in-house. Furthermore, even if the vendor of the application includes business processes as part of the package, as ERP vendors do, those business processes are not yours until you have integrated them into your business and trained your employees. Thus, neither information systems nor business processes can be purchased off-the-shelf.

Keep this in mind when you manage a department that is to receive a new information system or an upgrade. You need to allow time for such integration and training, and you should expect there will be mistakes and problems as the new application is first put into use.

HOW IS BPM PRACTICED IN THE REAL WORLD?

For the rest of the discussion in this chapter extension, we will assume that processes are to be created first, with systems developed during process creation, as shown in Figure CE17-6. Although the stages in this figure are known and accepted in industry, in the real world, it doesn't work out as neatly as is diagrammed. We will consider some of the reasons in this question.

First, this figure implies that an organization has a group of business professionals who perpetually assess processes and wait to pounce on any process that is judged to need improvement. In some very large organizations that have fully endorsed COBIT or other similar alignment standard, it may work like that. But, the reality for most organizations is that the need for process change comes from a problem or unmet need. Business requirements force the stages of the BPM cycle. In such organizations, no one thinks about a process until it's broken.

DEFINING THE PROCESS PROBLEM

As stated in Q1, process problems arise from process quality, from changes in technology, and from changes in the business fundamentals. At GearUp, costs were considered be too high (quality/efficiency problem). With PRIDE, doctors couldn't give the quality care they wanted to give because they didn't have reliable patient exercise data (quality/effectiveness). In the PRIDE case, the solution only became possible because of new cloud technology, so PRIDE was partly the result of new technology as well as the effectiveness quality problem.

Whatever the source of the problem, the task of solving it is ideally given to a team of business analysts, professionals who specialize in business process management. Business analysts are well versed in Porter's models, organizational strategy, and systems alignment theory like COBIT. Business analysts understand the role of technology and information

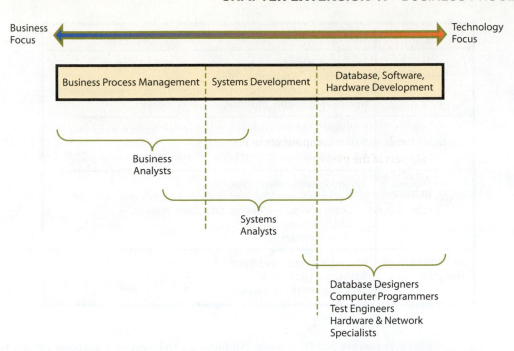

Figure CE17-8
Focus of Personnel Involved in BPM and Systems Development

systems, though they are not technical experts. Business analysts may work in the IS Department, but they are equally likely to work in a business specialty such as operations or accounting. If the process problem involves information systems, the BPM team is augmented with systems analysts and technical personnel as they are needed. Figure CE17-8 shows the focus of these job categories.

Smaller companies may not employ any business analysts or, indeed, anyone with a background in process management. Instead, process problems are addressed by operational, usually nontechnical, business professionals. Often they are given the task to solve a process problem on a part-time, temporary basis.

As shown in Figure CE17-6, the first task is to assess the existing processes by creating an as-is model as described in Q2 by using Business Process Modeling Notation (BPMN). In practice, BPMN is used primarily by larger organizations that have professional and experienced business analysts. Other professionals who are filling the business analyst role for the purpose of a particular problem may not know about BPMN and how to use it, so they may draw less formal, process schematics like that in Figure CE17-1.

Depending on the sophistication of the organization, the difficulty of creating the as-is process diagram varies from easy to hard. An as-is diagram may already exist because it was produced when the existing process was created. On the other hand, the business process may have simply evolved, and it's possible that no one knows the entire process; they just know the particular part they play. This situation is typical in new ventures like those at GearUp.

Other complications include the fact that people disagree on what the existing process is, and sometimes, for a variety of reasons, people want to hide their portions of processes from others. One way or another, however, the job of the business analyst is to understand and document the existing business process. These real-world issues are summarized in Figure CE17-9.

DESIGNING THE NEW PROCESS

Given the as-is model, the next step is to specify alternatives for fixing the problem. As stated in Chapter 2, two fundamental actions are possible:

- Adjust role resources
- Change process structure

Of course, both can be done at the same time.

Figure CE17-9
Real-world BPM Issues

Activity	Real-world Issues
Define Process Problem	Process change driven by problems and unmet needs. Business analysts not available. As-is process unknown, partially understood, viewed differently by different people, misunderstood, or hidden.
Designing the New Process	Simulations of alternatives expensive and often not worth it. Best solution not obvious. Un-doing process changes difficult and expensive.

Create Process Components	Systems development risks:
	    Requirements difficult to specify or evolving
	    Scheduling & budgeting difficulties
	    Changing technology
	    Diseconomies of scale

Implement New Processes	Process migration awkward. Resistance to change. Lack of authority (enterprise and inter-enterprise).

Regarding the resources assigned to roles, possibilities are to increase or decrease the number of employees performing a role, to move the role to employees in a different department, to hire employees with different skill sets, to give employees additional training, to change employee management, and so forth. Additionally, and of more relevance to MIS, information systems can be constructed to augment employee activity or even to replace employee activities with automation. If employees are already using an IS, another way of adjusting role resources is to improve the information system so as to facilitate the new process.

The second alternative is to change the process structure. Recall from Chapter 2 that the GearUp order process was changed to that in Figure CE17-4 in order to enable the the Select Vendor Product in response to a process problem that required the Select Vendor Product, the Order Goods from Vendor, and the Receive Goods activities to share the same database.

Given solution alternatives, the next task is to evaluate and select one. Sometimes the solution to a process problem is obvious, but more often, two or more alternatives are, at least in theory, good solutions. Consider the process in Figure CE17-1. What is the proper order for the middle three activities? Should credit or availability be checked first? In more sophisticated organizations, computer simulations using historical data are used to estimate the impact of different process alternatives Simulations are expensive, however, and the simplified assumptions they necessitate make the results suspect.

In the real world, most companies form a team to develop and evaluate alternatives. The most promising alternative is chosen for implementation by discussion among the team members. Consideration of the four dimensions of feasibility used in the SDLC (cost, technical, schedule, and organizational) can help to eliminate some alternatives. Qualified, talented business analysts are highly valued for this work because it is difficult and expensive to undo process changes that don't work. If processes interest you, becoming a business analyst can be a rewarding career choice.

CREATE PROCESS COMPONENTS

Once one of the process alternatives is selected, the next step is to create components. Insofar as MIS is concerned, this means to create new, or adapt existing, information systems. The real-world risks that we discussed in Chapter 10 apply equally here: Requirements are difficult to specify and may change during the development process; schedules and budgets are difficult to estimate; technology can change while the project is underway; and if schedule delays occur, remedies are difficult because of diseconomies of scale. Refer to Chapter 10 and also Chapter Extension 16 for more on these risks.

IMPLEMENT NEW PROCESSES

The problems of implementing a new or changed process are similar to the problems for implementing a new IS, but possibly greater. Migrating from an existing process to a new process is exceedingly awkward. Employees are unsure exactly what they are to do. "Are we using the new way or the old way on this one?" is a common question. Furthermore, old habits die hard. Others in the organization not involved in the process change will be unaware of the new process and will attempt to do things the "old way." Similar comments pertain to customers, suppliers, and other partners.

As we discussed for ERP systems, some employees will actively resist change, or comply, but do so viciously. Some employees resist because they do not believe in the new process or because they are uncertain that they can succeed in it, or because they do not understand it. Whatever the source of the resistance, it is a real factor when implementing process change. Finally, the resolution of implementation problems can be difficult for enterprise and inter-enterprise processes because there is no recognized authority, no boss, to enforce solutions. In the case of enterprise systems, the CEO or other senior executive does have such authority, but that person is seldom available to enforce low-level process solutions. With inter-enterprise processes, there is no such person; resolution occurs by agreement, negotiation, and even litigation. This authority problem is similar to that for enterprise and inter-enterprise IS.

None of this is to say, however, that business process management is too impractical to succeed. High-quality business processes are critical to the success of every organization. Somehow, one way or another, these challenges need to be overcome. It's just that in many situations it's more a matter of muddling through a messy situation than the diagram in Figure CE17-6 would lead you to believe.

ACTIVE REVIEW

Use this Active Review to verify that you understand the ideas and concepts that answer the chapter extension's study questions.

Q1 WHY DO ORGANIZATIONS NEED TO MANAGE BUSINESS PROCESSES?

Define business process. Define activities, roles, actors, repositories, data flow, and sequence flows. Summarize three reasons that processes need to be changed and give an example of each.

Q2 WHAT ARE THE STAGES OF BUSINESS PROCESS MANAGEMENT (BPM)?

Describe the need for BPM and explain why it is a cycle. Name the four stages of the BPM process and summarize the activities in each. Explain the role of COBIT.

Q3 HOW DO BUSINESS PROCESSES AND INFORMATION SYSTEMS RELATE?

Explain how information systems and business processes differ. Give an example, other than one in this text, of a business process that uses two or more information systems. Give an example, other than one in this text, of an information system that is part of two or more business processes. Explain how the relationship of business processes and information systems is many-to-many.

Q4 WHICH COMES FIRST, BUSINESS PROCESSES OR INFORMATION SYSTEMS?

Explain the problems that occur if we develop business processes first, with IS as a component. Explain the problems that occur if we develop information systems first, with business processes as a component. Explain the differences between Figures CE17-6 and CE17-7. Summarize the issues to address when answering which comes first. Explain why it is not possible to buy processes or systems off-the-shelf.

Q5 HOW IS BPM PRACTICED IN THE REAL WORLD?

Explain how the perpetual assessing of business processes is unrealistic. Name two factors that drive process change. Name and describe three factors that cause process problems. Define business analyst, describe the background of a business analyst, and differentiate business analysts from systems analysts. Summarize real-world issues for defining the process problem, designing the new process, creating process and system components, and implementing new processes.

KEY TERMS AND CONCEPTS

As-is model 584
Business process management
  (BPM) 584

COBIT (Control Objectives for
  Information and related
  Technology) 585

USING YOUR KNOWLEDGE

1. Compare and contrast the initial GearUp process, shown in Figure 2-4 with the version shown in Figure CE17-4. (Treat the parallelograms in Figure 2-4 as databases.)

   a. Summarize the problems that existed in the original process and explain how the adjusted process enables a solution to those problems.

b. Summarize the changes to information systems that will need to be made to implement the process change in Figure CE17-4. Consider each of the five information system components.

c. Which actors (employees) are the primary beneficiaries of the process change?

d. Suppose some employees who are not beneficiaries of a process change are required to do their work differently. Summarize management challenges you can expect. Describe how you would deal with those challenges.

2. Suppose you are starting a business that is similar to GearUp.

a. Should you start with business processes first or information systems first? Defend your answer.

b. Most likely, you will obtain off-the-shelf software and alter it for your applications. How does this fact influence whether you start first with processes or IS?

c. Identify issues in Figure CE17-9 that apply to the GearUp situation. Explain the impact of those issues.

3. Suppose you are starting a venture similar to PRIDE Systems.

a. Should you start with business processes first or information systems first? Defend your answer.

b. All of your mobile applications will be custom-developed. How does this fact influence whether you start first with processes or IS?

c. Identify issues in Figure CE17-9 that apply to the PRIDE Systems situation. Explain the impact of those issues.

4. As explained in Chapter Extension 4, Database Design, in order to represent a many-to-many relationship using the relational model, it is necessary to create an intersection table. If that table has non key data, that data represents something particular about the combination of one entity with another. For example, the relationship between Students and Classes is many-to-many, and Grade is an intersection table that represents the combination of a particular student with a particular class. What is the analog to the intersection table in the relationship between business processes and information systems? Where, for example, in Figure CE17-4 is there evidence of a particular IS application being used in a process?

5. Search Google or Bing using the phrase "what is a business analyst." Investigate several of the links that you find and answer the following questions:

a. What are the primary job responsibilities of a business analyst?

b. What knowledge do business analysts need?

c. What skills/personal traits do business analysts need?

d. Would a career as a business analyst be interesting to you? Explain why or why not.

chapter extension 18

This chapter extension is a capstone of all 12 chapters of this book.

International MIS

Q1 HOW DOES THE GLOBAL ECONOMY AFFECT ORGANIZATIONS AND PROCESSES?

Businesses compete today in a global market. International business has been increasing at a rapid pace since the middle of the 20th century. After World War II, the Japanese and other Asian economies exploded when those countries began to manufacture and sell goods to the West. The rise of the Japanese auto industry and the semiconductor industry in southeastern Asia greatly expanded international trade. At the same time, the economies of North America and Europe became closely integrated.

Since then, a number of other factors have caused international business to skyrocket. The fall of the Soviet Union opened the economies of Russia and Eastern Europe to the world market. More important, the telecommunications boom during the dot-com heyday caused the world to be encircled many times over by optical fiber that can be used for data and voice communications.

After the dot-com bust, optical fiber was largely underused and could be purchased for pennies on the dollar. Plentiful, cheap telecommunications enabled people worldwide to participate in the global economy. Before the advent of the Internet, for a young Indian professional to participate in the Western economy, he or she had to migrate to the West—a process that was politicized and limited. Today, that same young Indian professional, such as Ajit in Chapter 11, can sell his or her goods or services over the Internet without leaving home. During this same period, the Chinese economy became more open to the world, and it, too, benefits from plentiful, cheap telecommunications.

Columnist and author Thomas Friedman estimates that from 1991 until 2007 some 3 billion people were added to the world economy.[1] Not all of those people speak English, and not all of them are well enough educated (or equipped) to participate in the world economy. But even if just 10 percent are, then 300 million people were added to the English-speaking world economy.

But this discussion has a U.S./North American bias. The strengthening world economy is important in its own right, and not just because of the way that it affects the United States. As of 2012, auto manufacturing in the European Union (EU) and North America is in the doldrums, but it is booming in the developing economies of China, India, and Brazil. Economic activity and trade among those nations prosper outside the sphere of the EU and the United States. It remains to be seen whether this activity is strong enough to overcome the consumption slowdown in the developed world, but, in 2012, many EU- and U.S.-based companies find their greatest opportunities outside their national markets.

---

[1]Thomas L. Friedman, *The World Is Flat: A Brief History of the Twenty-First Century 3.0* (New York: Farrar, Strauss and Giroux, 2007).

HOW DOES THE GLOBAL ECONOMY CHANGE THE COMPETITIVE ENVIRONMENT?

To understand the effect of globalization, consider each of the elements in Figure CE18-1. The enlarged and Internet-supported world economy has altered every one of the five competitive forces. Suppliers have to reach a wider range of customers, and customers can consider a wider range of vendors. Suppliers and customers benefit not just from the greater size of the economy, but also by the ease with which businesses can learn about each other using tools such as Google and Bing.

Because of the information available on the Internet, customers can more easily learn of substitutions. The Internet has enabled new market entrants, although not in all cases. Amazon.com, Yahoo!, and Google, for example, have garnered such a large market share that it would be difficult for any new entrant to challenge them. Still, in other industries the global economy facilitates new entrants. Finally, the global economy has intensified rivalry by increasing product and vendor choices and by accelerating the flow of information about price, product, availability, and service.

HOW DOES THE GLOBAL ECONOMY CHANGE COMPETITIVE STRATEGY?

Today's global economy changes thinking about competitive strategies in two major ways. First, the sheer size and complexity of the global economy means that any organization that chooses a strategy allowing it to compete industry-wide is taking a very big bite! Competing in many different countries, with products localized to the language and culture of those countries, is an enormous and expensive task.

For example, to promote Windows worldwide, Microsoft must produce a version of Windows in dozens of different languages. Even in English, Microsoft produces a U.K. version, a U.S. version, an Australian version, and so forth. The problem for Microsoft is even greater, because different countries use different character sets. In some languages, writing flows from left to right. In other languages, it flows from right to left. When Microsoft set out to sell Windows worldwide, it embarked on an enormous project.

The second major way today's world economy changes competitive strategies is that its size, combined with the Internet, enables unprecedented product differentiation. If you choose to produce the world's highest quality and most exotic oatmeal—and if your production costs require you to sell that oatmeal for $350 a pound—your target market might contain only 200 people worldwide. The Internet allows you to find them—and them to find you.

The decision involving a global competitive strategy requires the consideration of these two changing factors.

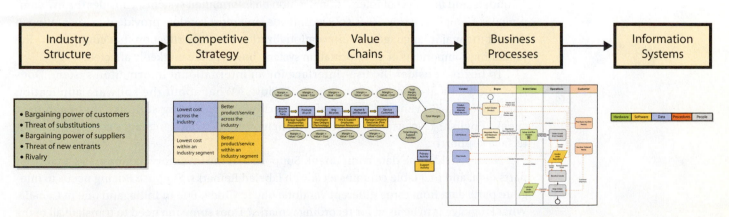

Figure CE18-1
Organizational Strategy Determines Information Systems

HOW DOES THE GLOBAL ECONOMY CHANGE VALUE CHAINS AND BUSINESS PROCESSES?

Because of information systems, any or all of the value chain activities in Figure CE18-1 can be performed anywhere in the world. An international company can conduct sales and marketing efforts locally, for every market in which it sells. 3M divisions, for example, sell in the United States with a U.S. sales force, in France with a French sales force, and in Argentina with an Argentinean sales force. Depending on local laws and customs, those sales offices may be owned by 3M, or they may be locally owned entities with which 3M contracts for sales and marketing services. 3M can coordinate all of the sales efforts of these entities using the same CRM system. When 3M managers need to roll up sales totals for a sales projection, they can do so using an integrated, worldwide system.

Manufacturing of a final product is frequently distributed throughout the world. Components of the Boeing 787 are manufactured in Italy, China, England, and numerous other countries and delivered to Washington and South Carolina for final assembly. Each manufacturing facility has its own inbound logistics, manufacturing, and outbound logistics activities, but those activities are linked together via information systems.

For example, Rolls-Royce manufactures an engine and delivers that engine to Boeing via its outbound logistics activity. Boeing receives the engine using its inbound logistics activity. All of this activity is coordinated via shared, inter-enterprise information systems. Rolls-Royce's CRM is connected with Boeing's supply processes, using techniques such as CRM and enterprise resource planning (ERP).

Because of the abundance of low-cost, well-educated, English-speaking professionals in India, many organizations have chosen to outsource their service and support functions to India. Some accounting functions are outsourced to India as well.

World time differences enable global virtual companies to operate 24/7. Boeing engineers in Los Angeles can develop a design for an engine support strut and send that design to Rolls-Royce in England at the end of their day. The design will be waiting for Rolls-Royce engineers at the start of their day. They review the design, make needed adjustments, and send it back to Boeing in Los Angeles, where the reviewed, adjusted design arrives at the start of the workday in Los Angeles. The ability to work around the clock by moving work into other time zones increases productivity.

WHAT ARE THE CHARACTERISTICS OF INTERNATIONAL IS COMPONENTS?

To understand the effect of internationalization on information systems, consider the five components. Computer hardware is sold worldwide, and most vendors provide documentation in at least the major languages, so internationalization has little effect on that component. The remaining components of an information system, however, are markedly affected.

To begin, consider the user interface for an international information system. Does it include a local-language version of Windows? What about the software application itself? Does an inventory system used worldwide by Boeing suppose that each user speaks English? If so, at what level of proficiency? If not, what languages must the user interface support?

Next, consider the data component. Suppose that the inventory database has a table for parts data, and that table contains a column labeled Remarks. Suppose Boeing needs to integrate parts data from three different vendors: one in China, one in India, and one in Canada. What language is to be used for recording remarks? Does someone need to translate all of the remarks into one language? Into three languages?

The human components—procedures and people—are obviously affected by language and culture. As with business processes, information systems procedures need to reflect local cultural values and norms. For systems users, job descriptions and reporting relationships must be appropriate for the setting in which the system is used. We will say more about this in Q5.

WHAT'S REQUIRED TO LOCALIZE SOFTWARE?

The process of making a computer program work in a second language is called **localizing**. It turns out to be surprisingly hard to do. To localize a document or a Web page, all you need to do is hire a translator to convert your document or page from one language to another. The situation is much more difficult for a computer program, however.

Consider a program you use frequently—say, Microsoft Word—and ask what would translation to a different language entail? The entire user interface would need to be translated. The menu bar and the commands on the menu bar would require translation. It is possible that some of the icons (the small graphics on a menu bar) would need to be changed, because some graphic symbols that are harmless in one culture are confusing or offensive in another.

What about a CRM application program that includes forms, reports, and queries? The labels on each of these would need to be translated. Of course, not all labels translate into words of the same length, and so the forms and reports might need to be redesigned. The questions and prompts for queries, such as "Enter part number for back order," would also require translation.

All of the documentation would need to be translated. That should be just a matter of hiring a translator, except that all of the illustrations in the documentation would need to be redrawn in the second language.

Think, too, about error messages. When someone attempts to order more items than there are in inventory, your application produces an error message. All of those messages would need to be translated. There are other issues as well. Sorting order is one. Spanish uses accents on certain letters, and it turns out that an accented *ó* will sort after *z* when you use the computer's default sort ordering. Figure CE18-2 summarizes the factors to address when localizing software.

Programming techniques can be used to simplify and reduce the cost of localization. However, those techniques must be used in the beginning. For example, suppose that when a certain condition occurs, the program is to display the message "Insufficient quantity in stock." If the programmer codes all such messages into the computer program, then, to localize that program, the programmer will have to find every such message in the code and then ask a translator to change that code. A preferred technique is to give every error message a number and to place the number and text of the error message into a separate file. Then, the code is written to display a particular error number from that file. During localization, translators simply translate the file of error messages into the second language.

- Translate the user interface, including menu bars and commands.
- Translate, and possibly redesign, labels in forms, reports, and query prompts.
- Translate all documentation and help text.
- Redraw and translate diagrams and examples in help text.
- Translate all error messages.
- Translate text in all message boxes.
- Adjust sorting order for different character set.
- Fix special problems in Asian character sets and in languages that read and write from right to left.

Figure CE18-2
Factors to Address When Localizing a Computer Program

The bottom line for you, as a future manager, is to understand two points: (1) Localizing computer programs is much more difficult, expensive, and time consuming than translating documents. (2) If a computer program is likely to be localized, then plan for that localization from the beginning. In addition, when considering the acquisition of a company in a foreign country, be sure to budget time and expense for the localization of information systems.

WHAT ARE THE PROBLEMS AND ISSUES OF GLOBAL DATABASES?

When we discussed CRM and ERP in Chapter 7 and Chapter Extension 11, you learned of the advantage of having all data stored in a single database. In brief, a single database reduces data integrity problems and makes it possible to have an integrated view of the customer or the organization's operations.

International companies that have a single database must, however, declare a single language for the company. Every Remark or Comment or other text field needs to be in a single language. If not, the advantages of a single database disappear. This is not a problem for companies that commit to a single company language. For example, Thomas Keidel, retired CEO of the Mahr Group (*www.mahr.com*), states, "We standardized on English as the official company language; we use English in our meetings, in our emails, and in other correspondence. We have to do this because we have factories in 14 countries, and it would be impossible to make any decision otherwise. We chose English because it is a language that most business professionals have in common." For a company like this, standardizing on a language for database contents is not a problem.

A single database is not possible, however, for companies that use multiple languages. Such companies often decide to give up on the benefits of a single database to let divisions in different countries use different databases, with data in local languages. For example, an international manufacturer might allow a component manufacturing division in South Korea to have a database in Korean and a final assembly division in Brazil to have a different database in Portuguese. In this scenario, the company needs applications to export and import data among the separated databases.

Besides language, performance is a second issue that confronts global databases. Oftentimes, data transmission speeds are too slow to process data from a single geographic location. If so, companies sometimes distribute their database in locations around the world.

Distributed database processing refers to the processing of a single database that resides in multiple locations. If the distributed database contains the same data, it is called a **replicated database**. If the distributed database does not contain copies of the same data, but rather divides the database into nonoverlapping segments, it is called a **partitioned database**. In most cases, querying either type of distributed database can improve performance without too much development work. However, updating a replicated database so that changes are correctly made to all copies of the data is full of challenges that require highly skilled personnel to solve. Still, companies like Amazon.com, which operates call centers in the United States, India, and Ireland, have invested in applications that are able to successfully update distributed databases, worldwide.

WHAT ARE THE CHALLENGES OF INTERNATIONAL ENTERPRISE APPLICATIONS?

As you learned in Chapter 7 and Chapter Extension 11, functional business processes and applications support particular activities within a single workgroup or department. Because the systems operate independently, the organization suffers from islands of automation. Sales and marketing data, for example, are not integrated with operations or manufacturing data.

You learned that many organizations eliminate the problems of information silos by creating enterprise systems. With international IS, however, such systems may not be worthwhile.

ADVANTAGES OF FUNCTIONAL SYSTEMS

Lack of integration is disadvantageous in many situations, but it has *advantages*, however, for international organizations and international systems. Because an order-processing functional system located in, say, the United States is separate from, and independent of, the manufacturing systems located in, say, Taiwan, it is unnecessary to accommodate language, business, and cultural differences in a single system. U.S. order-processing systems can operate in English and reflect the practices and culture of the United States. Taiwanese manufacturing information systems can operate in Chinese and reflect the business practices and culture of Taiwan. As long as there is an adequate data interface between the two systems, they can operate independently, sharing data when necessary.

Enterprise, integrated systems, such as ERP, solve the problems of data isolation by integrating data into a database that provides a comprehensive and organization-wide view. However, as discussed in Q2, that advantage requires that the company standardize on a single language. Otherwise, separate functional databases are needed.

PROBLEMS OF INHERENT PROCESSES

Inherent processes are even more problematic. Each software product assumes that the software will be used by people filling particular roles and performing their actions in a certain way. ERP vendors justify this standardization by saying that their procedures are based on industry-wide best practices and that the organization will benefit by following these standard processes. That statement may be true, but some inherent processes may conflict with cultural norms. If they do, it will be very difficult for management to convince the employees to follow those inherent processes. Or at least it will be difficult in some cultures to do so.

Differences in language, culture, norms, and expectations compound the difficulties of international process management. Just creating an accurate as-is model is difficult and expensive; developing alternative international processes and evaluating them can be incredibly challenging. With cultural differences, it can be difficult just to determine what criteria should be used for evaluating the alternatives, let alone performing the evaluation.

Because of these challenges, in the future it is likely that international business processes will be developed more like inter-enterprise business processes. A high-level process will be defined to document the service responsibilities of each international unit. Then the cloud and Internet standards will be used to connect those services into an integrated, enterprise, international system. The only obligation of an international unit will be to deliver its defined service. One service can be delivered using procedures based on autocratic management policies, and another can be delivered using procedures based on collaborative management policies. The differences will not matter to a cloud-based enterprise system.

 ## HOW DO INTER-ENTERPRISE IS FACILITATE GLOBALIZATION?

As stated, the Internet played a major role in facilitating international commerce. Along with the Internet, however, another major factor has been the rise of international interorganizaitonal systems. Two examples are supply chain and manufacturing systems, as we discuss next. At some point, social media systems may have a positive effect as well, although it is not yet clear how.

HOW DO GLOBAL INFORMATION SYSTEMS AFFECT SUPPLY CHAIN PROFITABILITY?

In short, global information systems increase supply chain profitability. As you learned in Chapter Extension 10, supply chain performance is driven by four factors: facilities, inventories, transportation, and information. Every one of these drivers is positively affected by global information systems. Because of these systems, facilities can be located anywhere in the world. If Amazon.com finds it economically advantageous to warehouse books in Iceland, it can do so. If Rolls-Royce can manufacture its engine turbine blades more cheaply in Poland, it can do so.

Furthermore, information systems reduce inventories and hence save costs. They can be used to reduce or eliminate the **bullwhip effect**, a phenomenon in which the variability in the size and timing of orders increases at each stage of the supply chain. They also support just-in-time (JIT) inventory techniques worldwide. Using information systems, the order of a Dell computer from a user in Bolivia triggers a manufacturing system at Dell, which, in turn, triggers the order of a component from a warehouse in Taiwan—all automatically.

To underscore this point, consider the inventories that exist at this moment in time, worldwide. Every component in one of those inventories represents a waste of the world's resources. Any product or component sitting on a shelf is not being used and is adding no value to the global economy. In the perfect world, a customer would think, "I want a new tablet," and that thought would trigger systems all over the world to produce and assemble necessary components, instantly. Given that we live in a world bound by time and space, instantaneous production is forever unreachable. But the goal of worldwide information systems for supply chain inventory management is to come as close to instantaneous as possible.

Consider transportation, the third driver. When you order a book from Amazon.com, you are presented with at least four shipping options. You can choose the speed and attendant price that is appropriate for your needs. Similar systems for businesses allow them to choose the delivery option that optimizes the value they generate. Further, automated systems enable suppliers and customers to track the shipment's location, 24/7, worldwide.

Finally, global information systems produce comprehensive, accurate, and timely information. Information systems produce data at prodigious rates, worldwide. That data facilitates operations as just discussed, but it also produces information for planning, organizing, deciding, and other analyses.

WHAT IS THE ECONOMIC EFFECT OF GLOBAL MANUFACTURING?

Henry Ford pioneered modern manufacturing methods, and in the process he reduced the price of automobiles to the point where they were no longer the playthings of the very rich but were affordable to the general population. In 1914, Ford took the unprecedented step of unilaterally increasing his workers' pay from $2.50 per day for 10 hours' work to $5 per day for 8 hours' work. As a consequence, many of his workers could soon afford to purchase an automobile. By paying his workers more, Ford increased demand.

The increase in demand was not due only to purchases by his workers, of course. Because of what economists call the **accelerator effect**, a dollar spent will contribute two or three dollars of activity to the economy. Ford's workers spent their increased pay not just on autos, but also on goods and services in their local community, which benefited via the accelerator effect. That benefit enabled non–Ford workers also to afford an auto. Further, because of the positive publicity he achieved with the pay increase, the community was strongly disposed to purchase a Ford automobile.

Consider those events in light of global manufacturing. For example, if Boeing manufactures airplanes entirely in the United States, the U.S. economy will be the sole beneficiary of that economic activity. If an Italian airline chooses to buy a Boeing plane, the transaction will be a cost to the Italian economy. There will be no accelerator effect, and the transaction will have no consequence on Italians' propensity to fly.

However, if Boeing purchases major components for its airplanes from Italian companies, then that purchase will generate an accelerator effect for the Italian economy. By buying in Italy, Boeing contributes to Italy's economy, and ultimately increases Italians' propensity to fly. That foreign-component purchase will, of course, reduce economic activity in the United States, but if it induces Italians to purchase sufficiently more Boeing airplanes, then it is possible that the loss will be compensated by the increase in airplane sales volume. That purchase will also benefit Boeing's image among Italians and increase the likelihood of sales to the Italian government.

The same phenomenon pertains to Dell computers, Cisco routers, and Microsoft programmers.

HOW DOES SOCIAL MEDIA AFFECT INTERNATIONAL BUSINESS?

In truth, we do not know, at least not yet, how social media affects international business, nor do we know the effectiveness of Enterprise 2.0 in multinational companies. It is possible that social media is so culturally biased that it works only in the culture in which it originates. A Facebook social graph of a young college woman in Japan is unlikely to connect in any meaningful way with a similar graph of a male business student in India. Each will have his or her own social network, but they will be domestic, not international.

Similar comments can be made about user-generated content. Teenagers in Chicago are unlikely to be influenced by user-generated tennis shoe designs that are popular in Hanover, Germany. Or are they? Is there a business opportunity for some innovative company to foster user-generated designs in one culture with the express purpose of marketing those designs in another culture? As of June 2012, we do not know.

Opportunities like this will exist for you and your classmates to explore early in your careers. As you use Facebook or Twitter and as you consume or create UGC, think about the international aspects of your activity. Both international social media and international Enterprise 2.0 seem to be ripe for innovation.

 WHAT ARE THE CHALLENGES OF INTERNATIONAL IS MANAGEMENT?

Size and complexity make international IT management challenging. International information systems are larger and more complex. Projects to develop them are larger and more complicated to manage. International IT departments are bigger and composed of people from many cultures with many different native languages. International organizations have more IS and IT assets, and those assets are exposed to more risk and greater uncertainty. Because of the complexity of international law, security incidents are more complicated to investigate.

WHY IS INTERNATIONAL INFORMATION SYSTEMS DEVELOPMENT MORE CHALLENGING?

The factors that affect international information systems development are more challenging than those that affect international software development. If the *system* is truly international, if many people from many different countries will be using the system, then the development project is exceedingly complicated.

To see why, consider the five components. Running hardware in different countries is not a problem, and localizing software is manageable, assuming programs were designed to be

Figure CE18-3
Phases in the SDLC

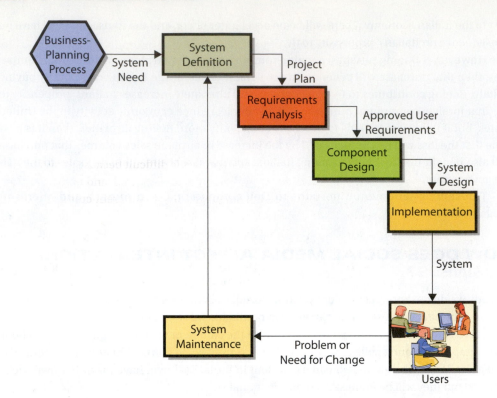

localized. Databases pose more difficulties. First, is a single database to be used, and if so, is it to be distributed? If so, how will updates be processed? Also, what language, currency, and units of measure will be used to store data? If multiple databases are to be used, how are data going to be transported among them? Some of these problems are difficult, but they are solvable with technical solutions.

The same cannot be said for the procedure and people components. An international system is used by people who live and work in cultures that are vastly different from one another. The way that customers are treated in Japan differs substantially from the way that customers are treated in Spain, which differs substantially from the way that customers are treated in the United States. The procedures for using a CRM will be correspondingly different.

Consider the phases of the SDLC as shown in Figure CE18-3. During system definition, we are supposed to determine the purpose and scope of the system. As you know by now, information systems should facilitate the organization's competitive strategy by supporting business processes. But what if the underlying processes differ? Again, customer support in Japan and customer support in Spain may involve completely different processes and activities.

Even if the purpose and scope can be defined in some unified way, how are requirements to be determined? Again, if the underlying business processes differ, then the specific requirements for the information system will differ. Managing requirements for a system in one culture is difficult, but managing requirements for international systems can be many times more difficult.

There are two responses to such challenges: (1) either define a set of standard business processes or (2) develop alternative versions of the system that support different processes in different countries. Both responses are problematic. The first response requires conversion of the organization to different work processes, and, as you learned in Chapter Extension 12, such conversion can be exceedingly difficult. People resist change, and they will do so with vehemence if the change violates cultural norms.

The second response is easier to implement, but it creates system design challenges. It also means that, in truth, there is not one system, but many.

In spite of the problems, both responses are used. For example, SAP, Oracle, and other ERP vendors define standard business processes via the inherent procedures in their software products. Many organizations attempt to enforce those standard procedures. When it becomes organizationally infeasible to do so, organizations develop exceptions to those inherent procedures and develop programs to handle the exceptions. This choice means high maintenance expense.

WHAT ARE THE CHALLENGES OF INTERNATIONAL PROJECT MANAGEMENT?

Managing a global information systems development project is difficult because of project size and complexity. Requirements are complex, many resources are required, and numerous people are involved. Team members speak different languages, live in different cultures, work in different time zones, and seldom meet face-to-face.

One way to understand how these factors affect global project management is to consider each of the project management knowledge areas as set out by the international Project Management Institute's document, the *PMBOK® Guide* (*http://marketplace.pmi.org/Pages/ProductDetail .aspx?GMProduct=00101095501*). Figure CE18-4 summarizes challenges for each knowledge area. Project integration is more difficult because international development projects require the complex integration of results from distributed workgroups. Also, task dependencies can span teams working in different countries, increasing the difficulty of task management.

The scope and requirements definition for international IS is more difficult, as just discussed. Time management is more difficult because teams in different cultures and countries work at different rates. Some cultures have a 35-hour workweek, and some have a 60-hour workweek. Some cultures expect 6-week vacations, and some expect 2 weeks. Some cultures thrive on efficiency of labor, and others thrive on considerate working relationships. There is no standard rate of development for an international project.

In terms of cost, different countries and cultures pay vastly different labor rates. Using critical path analysis, managers may choose to move a task from one team to another. Doing so, however, may substantially increase costs. Thus, management may choose to accept a delay

Knowledge Areas	Challenge
Project integration	Complex integration of results from distributed workgroups. Management of dependencies of tasks from physically and culturally different workgroups.
Scope (requirements)	Need to support multiple versions of underlying business processes. Possibly substantial differences in requirements and procedures.
Time	Development rates vary among cultures and countries.
Cost	Cost of development varies widely among countries. Two members performing the same work in different countries may be paid substantially different rates. Moving work among teams may dramatically change costs.
Quality	Quality standards vary among cultures. Different expectations of quality may result in an inconsistent system.
Human resources	Worker expectations differ. Compensation, rewards, work conditions vary widely.
Communications	Geographic, language, and cultural distance among team members impedes effective communication.
Risk	Development risk is higher. Easy to lose control.
Procurement	Complications of international trade.

Figure CE18-4
Challenges for International IS Project Management

rather than move work to an available (but more expensive) team. The complex trade-offs that exist between time and cost become even more complex for international projects.

Quality and human resources are also more complicated for international projects. Quality standards vary among countries. The IT industry in some nations, like India, has invested heavily in development techniques that increase program quality. Other countries, like the United States, have been less willing to invest in quality. In any case, the integration of programs of varying quality results in an inconsistent system.

Worker expectations vary among cultures and nations. Compensation, rewards, and worker conditions vary, and these differences can lead to misunderstandings, poor morale, and project delays.

Because of these factors, effective team communication is exceedingly important for international projects, but because of language and culture differences and geographic separation, such communication is difficult. Effective communication is also more expensive. Consider, for example, just the additional expense of maintaining a team portal in three or four languages.

If you consider all of the factors in Figure CE18-4, it is easy to understand why project risk is high for international IS development projects. So many things can go wrong. Project integration is complex; requirements are difficult to determine; cost, time, and quality are difficult to manage; worker conditions vary widely; and communication is difficult. Finally, project procurement is complicated by the normal challenges of international commerce.

WHAT ARE THE CHALLENGES OF INTERNATIONAL IT MANAGEMENT?

Chapter 11 defined the four primary responsibilities of the IT department: plan, operate, develop, and protect information systems and IT infrastructure. Each of these responsibilities becomes more challenging for international IT organizations.

Regarding planning, the principal task is to align IT and IS resources with the organization's competitive strategy. The task does not change character for international companies; it just becomes more complex and difficult. Multinational organizations and operations are complicated, and the business processes that support their competitive strategies tend also to be complicated. Further, changes in global economic factors can mean dramatic changes in processes and necessitate transformations in IS and IT support. Technology adoption can also cause remarkable change. The increasing use of cell phones in developing countries, for example, alters the requirements for local information systems. The rising price of oil will also change international business processes. Thus, planning tasks for international IT are larger and more complex.

Three factors create challenges for international IT operations. First, conducting operations in different countries, cultures, and languages adds complexity. Go to the Web site of any multinational corporation, say *www.3m.com* or *www.dell.com*, and you'll be asked to click on the country in which you reside. When you click, you are likely to be directed to a Web server running in some other country. Those Web servers need to be managed consistently, even though they are operated by people living in different cultures and speaking different languages.

The second operational challenge of international IS is the integration of similar, but different, systems. Consider inventory. A multinational corporation might have dozens of different inventory systems in use throughout the world. To enable the movement of goods, many of these systems need to be coordinated and integrated.

Or consider customer support that operates from three different support centers in three different countries. Each support center may have its own information system, but the data among those systems will need to be exported or otherwise shared. If not, then a customer who contacts one center will be unknown to the others.

The third complication for operations is outsourcing. Many organizations have chosen to outsource customer support, training, logistics, and other backroom activities. International outsourcing is particularly advantageous for customer support and other functions that must be operational 24/7. Many companies outsource logistics to UPS, because doing so offers comprehensive, worldwide shipping and logistical support. The organization's information systems usually need to be integrated with outsource vendors' information systems, and this may need to be done for different systems, all over the world.

The fourth IT department responsibility is protecting IS and IT infrastructure. We consider that function in the next question.

HOW DOES THE INTERNATIONAL DIMENSION AFFECT COMPUTER SECURITY RISK MANAGEMENT?

Computer security risk management is more difficult and complicated for international information systems. First, IT assets are subject to more threats. Infrastructure will be located in sites all over the world, and those sites differ in the threats to which they are exposed. Some will be subject to political threats, others to the threat of civil unrest, others to terrorists, and still others will be subject to threats of natural disasters of every conceivable type. Place your data center in Kansas, and it's subject to tornados. Place your data center internationally, and it's potentially subject to typhoons/hurricanes, earthquakes, floods, volcanic eruption, or mudslides. And don't forget epidemics that will affect the data center employees.

Second, the likelihood of a threat is more difficult to estimate for international systems. What is the likelihood that the death of Fidel Castro will cause civil unrest and threaten your data center in Havana? How does an organization assess that risk? What is the likelihood that a computer programmer in India will insert a Trojan horse into code that she writes on an outsourcing contract?

In addition to risk, international information systems are subject to far greater uncertainty. Uncertainty reflects the likelihood that something that "we don't know that we don't know" will cause an adverse outcome. Because of the multitudinous cultures, religions, nations, beliefs, political views, and crazy people in the world, uncertainty about risks to IS and IT infrastructure is high. Again, if you place your data center in Kansas, you have some idea of the magnitude of the uncertainty to which you are exposed, even if you don't know exactly what it is. Place a server in a country on every continent of the world, and you have no idea of the potential risks to which they are exposed.

Technical and data safeguards do not change for international information systems. Because of greater complexity there may be a need for more safeguards or for more complex ones, but the technical and data safeguards described in Chapter 1 all work for international systems. Human safeguards are another matter. For example, can an organization depend on the control of separation of duties and authorities in a culture for which graft is an accepted norm? Or, what is the utility of a personal reference in a culture in which it is considered exceedingly rude to talk about someone when they are not present? Because of these differences, human safeguards need to be chosen and evaluated on a culture-by-culture basis.

In short, risk management for both international information systems and IT infrastructure is more complicated, more difficult, and subject to greater uncertainty.

ACTIVE REVIEW

Use this Active Review to verify that you understand the ideas and concepts that answer the chapter extension's study questions.

Q1 HOW DOES THE GLOBAL ECONOMY AFFECT ORGANIZATIONS AND PROCESSES?

Describe how the global economy has changed since the mid-20th century. Explain how the dot-com bust influenced the global economy and changed the number of workers worldwide. Summarize the ways in which today's global economy influences the five competitive forces. Explain how the global economy changes the way organizations assess industry structure. How does the global economy change competitive strategy? How do global information systems benefit the value chain? Using Figure 3-5 (page 54) as a guide, explain how each primary value chain activity can be performed anywhere in the world.

Q2 WHAT ARE THE CHARACTERISTICS OF INTERNATIONAL IS COMPONENTS?

Explain how internationalization affects the five components of an IS. What does it mean to localize software? Summarize the work required to localize a computer program. In your own words, explain why it is better to design a program to be localized rather than attempt to adapt an existing single-language program to a second language. Explain the problems of having a single database for an international IS. Define *distributed database, replicated database,* and *partitioned database.* State a source of problems for processing replicated databases.

Q3 WHAT ARE THE CHALLENGES OF INTERNATIONAL ENTERPRISE APPLICATIONS?

Summarize the advantages of functional systems for international companies. Summarize the issues of inherent processes for multinational ERP. Explain how the cloud and Internet standards could be used to address the problems of international enterprise applications.

Q4 HOW DO INTER-ENTERPRISE IS FACILITATE GLOBALIZATION?

State the short answer to this question. Name the four drivers of supply chain profitability. Discuss how global information systems affect each driver. Explain how inventories represent waste. Summarize the effect that Henry Ford's act of increasing his workers' pay had on Ford auto sales. Explain how this same phenomenon pertains to Boeing acquiring major subsystems from manufacturers in Italy or to Toyota building autos in the United States. Explain how social media and Enterprise 2.0 affect international companies. Explain the meaning of the following sentence: "It's possible that social media technologies are so culturally biased that they work only in the culture in which they originate." Describe how this situation may create opportunities for businesses.

Q5 WHAT ARE THE CHALLENGES OF INTERNATIONAL IS MANAGEMENT?

State the two characteristics that make international IT management challenging. Explain the difference between international systems development and international software development. Using the five-component framework, explain why international systems development is more difficult. Give an example of one complication for each knowledge area in Figure CE18-4. State the four responsibilities for IT departments. Explain how each of these responsibilities is more challenging for international IT organizations. Describe three factors that create challenges for international IT operations. Explain why international IT assets are subject to more threats. Give three examples. Explain why the likelihood of international threats is more difficult to determine. Describe uncertainty, and explain why it is higher for international IT organizations. Explain how technical, data, and human safeguards differ for international IT organizations. Give two examples of problematic international human safeguards.

KEY TERMS AND CONCEPTS

Accelerator effect 602

Bullwhip effect 602

Distributed database processing 600

Localizing 599

Partitioned database 600

Replicated database 600

USING YOUR KNOWLEDGE

1. Suppose that you are about to have a job interview with a multinational company, such as 3M, Starbucks, or Coca-Cola. Further suppose that you wish to demonstrate an awareness of the changes for international commerce that the Internet and modern information technology have made. Using the information in Q1, create a list of three questions that you could ask the interviewer regarding the company's use of IT in its international business.

2. Suppose you work for a large business that is contemplating acquiring a company in Mexico. Assume you are a junior member of a team that is analyzing the desirability of this acquisition. Your boss, who is not technically savvy, has asked you to prepare a summary of the issues that she should be aware of regarding the merging of the two companies' information systems. She wants your summary to include a list of questions that she should ask of both your IS department and the IS department personnel in the prospective acquisition. Prepare that summary.

3. Using the information in this chapter extension, as well as in Chapter 7, summarize the strengths and weaknesses of functional systems, CRM, ERP, and EAI. How do the advantages and disadvantages of each change in an international setting? For your answer, create a table with strength and weakness columns and a row for each of the four system types.

4. Suppose that you are a junior member of a newly formed, international team that will meet regularly for the next year. You have team members in Europe, North and South America, Japan, Hong Kong, Singapore, Australia, and India. All of your team meetings will be virtual; some will be synchronous, but many will be asynchronous. The team leader has asked you to help prepare the environment for these meetings. In particular, he asked you to summarize the challenges that will occur in conducting these team meetings. He also wants you to assess the strengths and weaknesses of the three collaboration tool sets described in Chapter Extension 2. Use this chapter extension as well as information in Chapter Extensions 1 and 2, in your assessment.

APPLICATION EXERCISES

PART 1

CHAPTER 1: QUALITY OF INFORMATION WITH EXCEL

1. The spreadsheet in Microsoft Excel file **EMIS 4e Ex01** contains records of employee activity on special projects. Open this workbook and examine the data that you find in the three spreadsheets it contains. Assess the accuracy, relevancy, and sufficiency of this data to the following people and problems.

    a. You manage the Denver plant, and you want to know how much time your employees are spending on special projects.

    b. You manage the Reno plant, and you want to know how much time your employees are spending on special projects.

    c. You manage the Quota Computation project in Chicago, and you want to know how much time your employees have spent on that project.

    d. You manage the Quota Computation project for all three plants, and you want to know the total time employees have spent on your project.

    e. You manage the Quota Computation project for all three plants, and you want to know the total labor cost for all employees on your project.

    f. You manage the Quota Computation project for all three plants, and you want to know how the labor-hour total for your project compares to the labor-hour totals for the other special projects.

    g. What conclusions can you make from this exercise?

CHAPTER 1: COMPARING INFORMATION FROM EXCEL AND ACCESS

2. The database in the Microsoft Access file **EMIS 4e Ex02** contains the same records of employee activity on special projects as in Application Exercise 1. Before going any further, open that database and view the records in the Employee Hours table.

    a. Seven queries have been created that process this data in different ways. Using the criteria of accuracy, relevancy, and sufficiency, select the one query that is most appropriate for the information requirements in Application Exercise 1, parts a–f. If no query meets the need, explain why.

    b. What conclusions can you make from this exercise?

    c. Comparing your experiences on these two projects, what are the advantages and disadvantages of spreadsheets and databases?

CHAPTER 2: USE POWERPOINT TO DIAGRAM BUSINESS PROCESS

3. PowerPoint file **EMIS 4e Ex03** contains a copy of Figure 2-2 as well as a collection of spare shapes. Using these shapes, create a business process for the Ship Order to Customer activity. Use your own knowledge and expertise to do this. Assume that the input to the activity are the Customer Order and items as well as a list of items from the Receive Goods activity.

CHAPTER 3: USE EXCEL TO COMPUTE INVENTORY VALUE

4. Figure AE-1 shows an Excel spreadsheet that the resort bicycle rental business uses to value and analyze its bicycle inventory.

    - Examine this figure to understand the meaning of the data. Now use Excel to create a similar spreadsheet. Note the following:

    - The top heading is in 20-point Calibri font. It is centered in the spreadsheet. Cells A1 through H1 have been merged.

    - The second heading, Bicycle Inventory Valuation, is in 18-point Calibri, italics. It is centered in cells A2 through H2, which have been merged.

    - The column headings are set in 11-point Calibri, bold. They are centered in their cells, and the text wraps in the cells.

    a. Make the first two rows of your spreadsheet similar to that in Figure AE-1. Choose your own colors for background and type, however.

    b. Place the current date so that it is centered in cells C3, C4, and C5, which must be merged.

    c. Outline the cells as shown in the figure.

	A	B	C	D	E	F	G	H
1				Resort Bicycle Rental				
2				Bicycle Inventory Valuation				
3				Monday, July 08, 2013				
4	Make of Bike	Bike Cost	Number on Hand	Cost of Current Inventory	Number of Rentals	Total Rental Revenue	Revenue per Bike	Revenue as Percent of Cost of Inventory
5	Wonder Bike	$325	12	$3,900	85	$6,375	$531	163.5%
6	Wonder Bike II	$385	4	$1,540	34	$4,570	$1,143	296.8%
7	Wonder Bike Supreme	$475	8	$3,800	44	$5,200	$650	136.8%
8	LiteLift Pro	$655	8	$5,240	25	$2,480	$310	47.3%
9	LiteLift Ladies	$655	4	$2,620	40	$6,710	$1,678	256.1%
10	LiteLift Racer	$795	3	$2,385	37	$5,900	$1,967	247.4%

Figure AE-1
Worksheet

d. Figure AE-1 uses the following formulas:

Cost of Current Inventory = Bike Cost ×
                              Number on Hand
Revenue per Bike = Total Rental Revenue/
                    Number on Hand
Revenue as a Percent = Total Rental Revenue/
of Cost of Inventory   Cost of Current Inventory

Please use these formulas in your spreadsheet, as shown in Figure AE-1.

e. Format the cells in the columns, as shown.

f. Give three examples of decisions that management of the bike rental agency might make from this data.

g. What other calculation could you make from this data that would be useful to the bike rental management? Create a second version of this spreadsheet in your worksheet document that has this calculation.

CHAPTER EXTENSION 1: MANAGERIAL DECISION MAKING WITH EXCEL

5. Suppose that you have been asked to assist in the managerial decision about how much to increase pay in the next year. Assume you are given a list of the departments in your company, along with the average salary for employees in that department for major companies in your industry. Additionally, you are given the names and salaries of 10 people in each of three departments in your company.

- Assume you have been asked to create a spreadsheet that shows the names of the 10 employees in each department, their current salary, the difference between their current salary and the industry average salary for their department, and the percent their salary would need to be increased to meet the industry average. Your spreadsheet should also compute the average increase

needed to meet the industry average for each department and the average increase, company-wide, to meet industry averages.

a. Use the data in the Word file **EMIS 4e Ex05** and create the spreadsheet.

b. How can you use this analysis to contribute to the employee salary decision? Based on this data, what conclusions can you make?

c. Suppose other team members want to use your spreadsheet. Name three ways you can share it with them and describe the advantages and disadvantages of each.

CHAPTER EXTENSION 1: MANAGERIAL DECISION MAKING WITH ACCESS

6. Suppose that you have been asked to assist in the managerial decision about how much to increase pay in the next year. Specifically, you are tasked to determine if there are significant salary differences among departments in your company.

- You are given an Access database with a table of employee data with the following structure:
- EMPLOYEE (Name, Department, Specialty, Salary)
- Where *Name* is the name of an employee who works in a department, *Department* is the department name, *Specialty* is the name of the employee's primary skill, and *Salary* is the employee's current salary. Assume that no two employees have the same name. You have been asked to answer the following queries:

(1) List the names, department, and salary of all employees earning more than $100,000.

(2) List the names and specialties of all employees in the Marketing department.

(3) Compute the average, maximum, and minimum salary of employees in your company.

(4) Compute the average, minimum, and maximum salary of employees in the Marketing department.

(5) Compute the average, minimum, and maximum salary of employees in the Information Systems department.

(6) *Extra credit:* Compute the average salary for employees in every department. Use *Group By*.

a. Design and run Access queries to obtain the answers to these questions, using the data in the Access file **EMIS 4e Ex06.**

b. Explain how the data in your answer contributes to the salary increase decision.

c. Suppose other team members want to use your Access application. Name three ways you can share it with them, and describe the advantages and disadvantages of each.

CHAPTER EXTENSION 2: FREE AND EASY COLLABORATION TOOLS

7. This exercise requires you to experiment with Google Drive. You will need two Google accounts to complete this exercise. If you have two different email addresses, then set up two Google accounts using those addresses. Otherwise, use your school email address and set up a Google Gmail account. A Gmail account will automatically give you a Google account.

a. In the memo, explain the role of communication in collaboration. Go to *http://drive.google.com/* and sign in with one of your Google accounts. Upload your memo using Google Drive. Save your uploaded document and share it with the email in your second Google account. Sign out of your first Google account.

(If you have access to two computers situated close to each other, use both of them for this exercise. You will see more of the Google Drive functionality by using two computers. If you have two computers, do not sign out of your Google account. Perform step b and all actions for the second account on that second computer. If you are using two computers, ignore the instructions in the following steps to sign out of the Google accounts.)

b. Open a new window in your browser. Access *http://drive.google.com/* from that second window, and sign in using your second Google account. Open the document that you shared in step a.

c. Change the memo by adding a brief description of the need to manage the content in many collaboration projects. Save the document from your second account.

If you are using just one computer, sign out from your second account.

d. Sign in on your first account. Open the most recent version of the memo and add a description of the role of version histories. Save the document. (If you are using two computers, notice how Google warns you that another user is editing the document at the same time. Click *Refresh* to see what happens.) If you are using just one computer, sign out from your first account.

e. Sign in on your second account. Reopen the shared document. From the File menu, save the document as a Word document. Describe how Google processed the changes to your document.

8. This exercise requires you to experiment with Windows Live SkyDrive. You will need two Office Live IDs to complete this exercise. The easiest way to do it is to work with a classmate. If that is not possible, set up two Office Live accounts, using two different Hotmail addresses.

a. Go to *www.skydrive.com*, and sign in with one of your accounts. Create a memo about collaboration tools using the Word Web App. Save your memo. Share your document with the email in your second Office Live account. Sign out of your first account.

(If you have access to two computers situated close to each other, use both of them for this exercise. If you have two computers, do not sign out of your Office Live account. Perform step b and all actions for the second account on that second computer. If you are using two computers, ignore the instructions in the following steps to sign out of the Office Live accounts.)

b. Open a new window in your browser. Access *www.skydrive.com* from that second window, and sign in using your second Office Live account. Open the document that you shared in step a.

c. Change the memo by adding a brief description of content management. Do not save the document yet. If you are using just one computer, sign out from your second account.

d. Sign in on your first account. Attempt to open the memo and note what occurs. Sign out of your first account, and sign back in with your second account. Save the document. Now, sign out of your second account, and sign back in with the first account. Now attempt to open the memo. (If you are using two computers, perform these same actions on the two different computers.)

e. Sign in on your second account. Reopen the shared document. From the File menu, save the document as a Word document. Describe how Google processed the changes to your document.

PART 2

Note: The exercises for the chapter extensions are basically tutorials. Therefore, they are presented first, followed by exercises for Chapters 4–6.

CHAPTER EXTENSION 3: LEARNING EXCEL

9. Complete Chapter Extension 3, Exercise 1, page 387.

10. Complete Chapter Extension 3, Exercise 2, page 387.

11. Complete Chapter Extension 3, Exercise 3, page 388.

CHAPTER EXTENSION 4: DATA MODELING WITH VISIO

12. Complete Chapter Extension 4, Exercise 2, page 403. Use Microsoft Visio to document your entity-relationship design.

13. Complete Chapter Extension 4, Exercise 3, page 403. Use Microsoft Visio to document your entity-relationship design.

CHAPTER EXTENSION 5: APPLY ACCESS SKILLS

14. Complete Chapter Extension 5, Exercise 1, page 422. Requires you to complete Exercise 12 first.

15. Complete Chapter Extension 5, Exercise 2, page 422. Requires you to complete Exercise 13 first.

CHAPTER EXTENSION 6: GETTING THE BEST FEATURES FROM EXCEL AND ACCESS

16. Complete Chapter Extension 6, Exercise 1, page 449.

17. Complete Chapter Extension 6, Exercises 2 and 3, page 449.

18. Complete Chapter Extension 6, Exercise 4, page 449.

19. Complete Chapter Extension 6, Exercise 5, page 449.

CHAPTER 4: USING PARAMETERIZED QUERIES

20. In this exercise, you will learn how to create a query based on data that a user enters and how to use that query to create a data entry form.
    a. Download the Microsoft Access file **EMIS 4e Ex20**. Open the file and familiarize yourself with the data in the Customer table.
    b. Click *Create* in the Access ribbon. On the far right, select *Query Design*. Select the Customer table as the basis for the query. Drag Customer Name, Customer Email, Date Of Last Rental, Bike Last Rented, Total Number Of Rentals, and Total Rental Revenue into the columns of the query results pane (the table at the bottom of the query design window).
    c. In the CustomerName column, in the row labeled Criteria, place the following text:

       [Enter Name of Customer:]

       Type this exactly as shown, including the square brackets. This notation tells Access to ask you for a customer name to query.
    d. In the ribbon, click the red exclamation mark labeled *Run*. Access will display a dialog box with the text "Enter Name of Customer:" (the text you entered in the query Criteria row). Enter the value *Scott, Rex* and click OK.
    e. Save your query with the name *Parameter Query*.
    f. Click the Home tab on the ribbon and click the Design View (upper left-hand button on the Home ribbon). Replace the text in the Criteria row of the CustomerName column with the following text. Type it exactly as shown:

       Like "*" & [Enter part of Customer Name to search by:] & "*"

    g. Run the query by clicking *Run* in the ribbon. Enter *Scott* when prompted *Enter part of Customer Name to search by*. Notice that the two customers who have the name Scott are displayed. If you have any problems, ensure that you have typed the phrase previous shown *exactly* as shown into the Criteria row of the CustomerName column of your query.
    h. Save your query again under the name *Parameter Query*. Close the query window.
    i. Click *Create* in the Access ribbon. Under the Forms group, select the down arrow to the right of More Forms. Choose *Form Wizard*. In the dialog that opens, in the Tables/Queries box, click the down arrow. Select *Parameter Query*. Click the double chevron (>>) symbol, and all of the columns in the query will move to the Selected Fields area.
    j. Click *Next* three times. In the box under *What title do you want for your form?* enter *Customer Query Form* and click *Finish*.
    k. Enter *Scott* in the dialog box that appears. Access will open a form with the values for Scott, Rex. At the bottom of the form, click the right-facing arrow and the data for Scott, Bryan will appear.
    l. Close the form. Select *Object Type* and *Forms* in the Access Navigation Pane. Double-click *Customer Query Form,* and enter the value *James*. Access will display data for all six customers having the value James in their name.

CHAPTER 4: USING EXCEL AND ACCESS TO INFORM COMPUTER UPGRADE DECISIONS

21. You have been asked to help your department decide how to upgrade computers. Let's say, for example, that you want to upgrade all of the computers' operating systems to Windows 8. Furthermore, you want to first upgrade the computers that most need upgrading, but suppose you have a limited budget. To address this situation, you would like to query the data in Figure AE-2, find all computers that do not have Windows 8, and then select those with slower CPUs or smaller memory as candidates for upgrading. To do this, you need to move the data from Excel and into Access.

- Once you have analyzed the data and determined the computers to upgrade, you want to produce a report. In that case, you may want to move the data from Access and back to Excel, or perhaps into Word. In this exercise, you will learn how to perform these tasks.

a. To begin, download the Excel file **EMIS 4e Ex21** from *www.pearsonhighered.com/kroenke* into one of your directories. We will import the data in this file into Access, but before we do so, familiarize yourself with the data by opening it in Excel. Notice that there are three worksheets in this workbook. Close the Excel file.

b. Create a blank Access database. Name the database *Ex21_Answer*. Place it in some directory; it may be the same directory into which you have placed the Excel file, but it need not be. Close the default table that Access creates and delete it.

c. Now we will import the data from the three worksheets in the Excel file **EMIS 4e Ex21** into a single table in your Access database. In the ribbon, select *External Data* and *Import from Excel*. Start the import. For the first worksheet (Denver), you should select *Import the source data into a new table in the current database*. Be sure to click *First Row Contains Column Headings* when Access presents your data. You can use the default Field types and let Access add the primary key. Name your table *Employees* and click *Finish*. There is no need to save your import script.

For the second and third worksheets, again click *External Data, Import Excel*, but this time select *Append a copy of the records to the table Employees*. Import all data.

d. Open the *Employee* table, and examine the data. Notice that Access has erroneously imported a blank line and the *Primary Contact* data into rows at the end of each data set. This data is not part of the employee records, and you should delete it (in three places—once for each worksheet). The *Employee* table should have a total of 40 records.

e. Now, create a parameterized query on this data. Place all of the columns except *ID* into the query. In the *OS* column, set the criteria to select rows for which the value is not *Windows 8*. In the *CPU* (GHz) column, enter the criterion: <=[Enter cutoff value for CPU] and in the *Memory* (GB) column, enter the criterion: <=[Enter cutoff value for Memory]. Test your query. For example, run your query and enter a value of *2* for both CPU and memory. Verify that the correct rows are produced.

	A	B	C	D	E	F	G	H
1	EmpLastName	EmpFirstName	Plant	Computer Brand	CPU (GHz)	Memory (	Disk (GB)	OS
2	Ashley	Jane	Denver	Dell	3	4	400	Windows 7
3	Davidson	Kaye	Denver	Dell	2	3	250	Windows 7
4	Ching	Kam Hoong	Denver	HP	2	3	100	Windows 7
5	Collins	Giovanni	Denver	Dell	1	1	120	Vista
6	Corning	Sandra	Denver	HP	1.2	1	120	Windows 7
7	Scott	Rex	Denver	HP	1.8	2	100	Vista
8	Corovic	Jose	Denver	Dell	3	2	250	Windows 8
9	Lane	Brandon	Denver	Lenova	2	1.512	250	Vista
10	Wei	Guang	Denver	IBM	2	1	120	Windows 7
11	Dixon	Eleanor	Denver	IBM	1	1.512	120	Vista
12	Lee	Brandon	Denver	Dell	0.5	1	80	XP
13	Duong	Linda	Denver	Dell	0.5	0.512	40	XP
14	Bosa	Victor	Denver	HP	1	2	150	Windows 7
15	Drew	Richard	Denver	HP	1	3	100	Windows 7
16	Adams	James	Denver	HP	1	1	80	XP
17	Lunden	Haley	Denver	Lenova	2	2	200	Windows 8
18	Utran	Diem Thi	Denver	Dell	2	1	120	Windows 7
19								
20		Primary Contact:	Kaye Davidson					

Figure AE-2
Employee Computer Data

f. Use your query to find values of CPU and memory that give you as close to a maximum of 15 computers to upgrade as possible.

g. When you have found values of CPU and memory that give you 15, or nearly 15, computers to upgrade, leave your query open. Now click *External data, Word*, and create a Word document that contains the results of your query. Adjust the column widths of the created table so that it fits on the page. Write a memo around this table explaining that these are the computers that you believe should be upgraded.

CHAPTER 5: GRAPHING WITH EXCEL

22. As stated in Chapter Extension 6, a common scenario is to use Microsoft Access with Excel: Users process relational data with Access, import some of the data into Excel, and use Excel's tools for creating professional-looking charts and graphs. You will do exactly that in this exercise.

- Download the Access file **EMIS 4e Ex22** from *www.pearsonhighered.com/kroenke*. Open the database; select *Database Tools/Relationships*. As you can see, there are three tables: *Product, VendorProductInventory*, and *Vendor*. Open each table individually to familiarize yourself with the data.
- For this problem, we will define *InventoryCost* as the product of *IndustryStandardCost* and *QuantityOnHand*. The query *InventoryCost* computes these values for every item in inventory for every vendor. Open that query and view the data to be certain you understand this computation. Open the other queries as well so that you understand the data they produce.

a. Sum this data by vendor and display it in a pie chart. Proceed as follows:

(1) Open Excel and create a new spreadsheet.

(2) Click *Data* on the ribbon, and select *Access* in the *Get External Data* ribbon category.

(3) Navigate to the location in which you have stored the Access file **EMIS 4e Ex22**.

(4) Select the query that contains the data you need for this pie chart.

(5) Import the data into a table.

(6) Format the appropriate data as currency.

(7) Select the range that contains the data, press the function key, and proceed from there to create the pie chart. Name the data and pie chart worksheets appropriately.

b. Follow a similar procedure to create a bar chart. Place the data and the chart in separate worksheets, and name them appropriately.

CHAPTER 5: CLEAN UP THE MESS IN THE SALESPERSON'S SPREADSHEET

23. Reread the Guide on pages 122–123. Suppose you are given the task of converting the salesperson's data into a database. Because that person's data are so poorly structured, it will be a challenge, as you will see.

a. Download the Excel file named **EMIS 4e Ex23** from *www.pearsonhighered.com/kroenke*. This spreadsheet contains data that fit the salesperson's description in the Guide. Open the spreadsheet and view the data.

b. Download the Access file with the same name, **EMIS 4e Ex23**. Open the database, select *Database Tools*, and click *Relationships*. Examine the four tables and their relationships.

c. Somehow, you have to transform the data in the spreadsheet into the table structure in the database. Because so little discipline was shown when creating the spreadsheet, this will be a labor-intensive task. To begin, import the spreadsheet data into a new table in the database; call that table *Sheet1* or some other name.

d. Copy the *Name* data in *Sheet1* onto the clipboard. Then, open the *Customer* table and paste the column of *Name* data into that table.

e. Unfortunately, the task becomes messy at this point. You can copy the *Car Interests* column into *Make or Model of Auto*, but then you will need to straighten out the values by hand. Phone numbers will need to be copied one at a time.

f. Open the *Customer* form and manually add any remaining data from the spreadsheet into each customer record. Connect the customer to his or her auto interests.

g. The data in the finished database are much more structured than the data in the spreadsheet. Explain why this is both an advantage and a disadvantage. Under what circumstances is the database more appropriate? Less appropriate?

CHAPTER 5: ALLOCATE COMPUTERS TO EMPLOYEES WITH ACCESS

24. In this exercise, you will create a two-table database, define relationships, create a form and a report, and use them to enter data and view results.

a. Download the Excel file **EMIS 4e Ex24** from *www.pearsonhighered.com/kroenke*. Open the spreadsheet and review the data in the *Employee* and *Computer* worksheets.

b. Create a new Access database with the name *Ex24_Solution*. Close the table that Access automatically creates and delete it.

c. Import the data from the Excel spreadsheet into your database. Import the *Employee* worksheet into a table named *Employee*. Be sure to check *First Row Contains Column Headings*. Select *Choose my own primary key* and use the ID field as that key.

d. Import the *Computer* worksheet into a table named *Computer*. Check *First Row Contains Column Headings*, but let Access create the primary key.

e. Open the relationships window and add both *Employee* and *Computer* to the design space. Drag ID from *Employee,* and drop it on *EmployeeID* in *Computer*. Check *Enforce Referential Integrity* and the two checkmarks below. Be sure you know what these actions mean.

f. Open the Form Wizard dialog box (under *Create, More Forms*), and add all of the columns for each of your tables to your form. Select *View your data by Employee*. Title your form *Employee* and your subform *Computer*.

g. Open the *Computer* subform and delete *EmployeeID* and *ComputerID*. These values are maintained by Access, and it is just a distraction to keep them. Your form should appear like the one shown in Figure AE-3.

h. Use your form to add two new computers to *Jane Ashley*. Both computers are Dells, and both use Windows 8; one costs $1,750 and the other costs $1,400.

i. Delete the Lenovo computer for Rex Scott.

j. Use the Report Wizard (under *Create*) to create a report having all data from both the *Employee* and *Computer* tables. Play with the report design until you find a design you like. Correct the label alignment if you need to.

CHAPTER 6: INTERNET SPEED: GETTING WHAT YOU PAY FOR?

25. Numerous Web sites are available that will test your Internet data communications speed. You can find a good one at *www.speakeasy.net/speedtest/*. (If that site is no longer active, Google or Bing "What is my Internet speed?" to find another speed-testing site. Use it.)

a. While connected to your university's network, go to Speakeasy and test your speed against servers in Seattle, New York City, and Atlanta. Compute your average upload and download speeds.

b. Run the Speakeasy test again from your home or a public wireless site. Compute your average upload and download speeds. Compare your speed to those listed in Figure 6-3. If you are performing this test at home, are you getting the performance you are paying for?

c. Contact a friend or relative in another state. Ask him or her to run the Speakeasy test against those same three cities.

d. Compare the results in parts a, b, and c. What conclusion, if any, can you make from these tests?

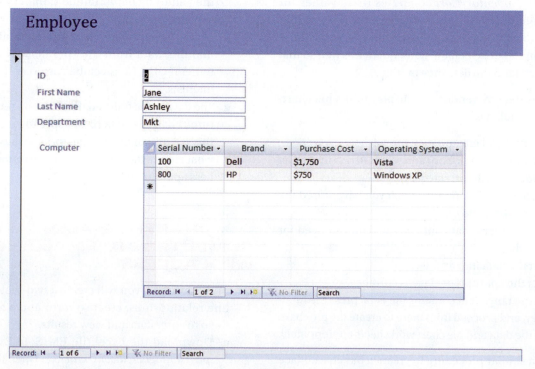

Figure AE-3
Employee Computer Assignment Form

CHAPTER 6: BUDGET NETWORK PROJECTS WITH EXCEL

26. Suppose you work for a company that installs computer networks. Assume that you have been given the task of creating spreadsheets to generate cost estimates, not just for one customer, but for many different clients.

a. Create a spreadsheet to estimate hardware costs. Assume that the user of the spreadsheet will enter the number of pieces of equipment and the standard cost for each type of equipment. Assume that the networks can include the following components: NIC cards; WNIC cards; wireless access points; switches of two types, one faster and one slower, at two different prices; and routers. Also assume that the company will use both UTP and optical fiber cable and that prices for cable are stated as per foot. Use the network in Figure 6-2 as an example.

b. Modify your spreadsheet to include labor costs. Assume there is a fixed cost for the installation of each type of equipment and a per-foot cost for the installation of cable.

c. Give an example of how you might use this spreadsheet for planning network installations. Explain how you could adapt this spreadsheet for project tracking and billing purposes.

CHAPTER 6: ESTIMATING CLOUD COSTS WITH EXCEL

27. Assume you have been asked to create an Office application to estimate cloud computing costs. You decide to create a spreadsheet into which your customers can provide their cloud computing needs and which you can then import into an Access database and use queries to compute cloud computing costs.

Figure AE-4 shows the structure of the spreadsheet into which your customers will input their requirements. You can download this spreadsheet in the Excel file **EMIS 4e Ex27**. Figure AE-5 shows an Access table that has costs corresponding to the requirements in Figure AE-4. You can download this database in the Access file **EMIS 4e Ex27**.

a. Import the spreadsheet data into the Access database.

b. Write queries to compute the cost of each resource.

c. Create a report that shows the cost for each type of resource for each month. Show the total costs for the six-month period for each resource as well. Include a grand total of all the costs.

d. Create a pie chart that breaks out the total costs by resource. *Hint:* You have to move the query data back into Excel.

	A	B	C	D	E	F	G
1		Jan-13	Feb-13	Mar-13	Apr-13	May-13	Jun-13
2	**Compute requirements (hours):**						
3							
4	Extra Small Instance	1800	1800	1800	1800	1800	1800
5	Small Instance	2000	2000	2400	2400	0	0
6	Medium Instance	900	1800	2700	3600	3600	3600
7	Large Instance	0	500	1000	1500	2000	2000
8	Extra Large Instance	0	0	0	1000	1200	1500
9							
10	**Storage requirements:**						
11	Storage Required (GB)	30	35	40	45	50	55
12	Storage Transactions (1000s)	30	30	35	35	40	40
13							
14	**Database requirements (number of instances):**						
15	10GB Database	2	2	2	2	2	2
16	20GB Database	0	3	3	3	3	3
17	30GB Database		4	4	4	4	4
18	40GB Database	0	0	0	3	3	3
19	50GB Database	0	0	2	2	3	0

Figure AE-4
Spreadsheet with Cloud Computing Requirements

Figure AE-5
Access Table Corresponding to Requirements in AE-4

e. Create a pie chart that breaks out the total costs by month. *Hint:* You have to move the query data back into Excel.

f. Assume that processing costs increase by 10 percent across the board. Repeat parts c, d, and e for the changed costs.

PART 3

CHAPTER 7: PRODUCTION PLANNING WITH EXCEL

28. Suppose your manager asks you to create a spreadsheet to compute a production schedule. Your schedule should stipulate a production quantity for seven products that is based on sales projections made by three regional managers at your company's three sales regions.

a. Create a separate worksheet for each sales region. Use the data in the Word file **EMIS 4e Ex28**, which you can download from the text's Web site. This file contains each manager's monthly sales projections for the past year, actual sales results for those same months, and projections for sales for each month in the coming quarter.

b. Create a separate worksheet for each region's data. Import the data from Word into Excel.

c. On each of the worksheets, use the data from the prior four quarters to compute the discrepancy between the actual sales and the sales projections. This discrepancy can be computed in several ways: You could calculate an overall average, or you could calculate an average per quarter or per month. You could also weight recent discrepancies more heavily than earlier ones. Choose a method that you think is most appropriate. Explain why you chose the method you did.

d. Modify your worksheets to use the discrepancy factors to compute an adjusted forecast for the coming quarter. Thus, each of your spreadsheets will show the raw forecast and the adjusted forecast for each month in the coming quarter.

e. Create a fourth worksheet that totals sales projections for all of the regions. Show both the unadjusted forecast and the adjusted forecast for each region and for the company overall. Show month and quarter totals.

f. Create a bar graph showing total monthly production. Display the unadjusted and adjusted forecasts using different colored bars.

CHAPTER 9: THIRD-PARTY COOKIES

29. Open your favorite browser. Go to the options that govern cookies. (On Internet Explorer, go to Tools (the little wheel icon in the upper right-hand corner) / Internet Options / Privacy / Advanced.) If you use another browser and don't know where to go for the privacy settings, search the Internet for your browser name plus the words *disable third-party cookies*. Follow the instructions to find the options page.

a. Disable third-party cookies. Close your browser. Re-open your browser and visit at least five Web sites.

b. Enable third-party cookies. Close your browser. Re-open your browser and visit the same five Web sites.

c. Do you notice any difference in the way the sites you access or your browser behave between a and b? Describe any differences.

d. Go to the same privacy settings location in which you disabled third-party cookies, and select *prompt* rather than *block* third-party cookies. Go to any site you normally visit, or *www.msn.com* if you can't think of any others. Describe what happens.

e. Change your browser's privacy settings back to whatever level of third-party cookie blocking you had when you started this exercise.

f. Summarize your experiences in this exercise.

CHAPTER EXTENSION 8: MAKE YOUR OWN BOM WITH ACCESS

30. Figure CE8-5 (page 473), the sample bill of materials, is a form produced using Microsoft Access. Producing such a form is a bit tricky, so this exercise will guide you through the steps required. You can then apply what you learn to produce a similar report. You can also use Access to experiment on extensions of this form.

a. Create a table named *PART* with columns *PartNumber, Level, Description, QuantityRequired,* and *PartOf*. *Description* and *Level* should be text, *PartNumber* should be AutoNumber, and *QuantityRequired* and *PartOf* should be numeric, long integer. Add the *PART* data shown in Figure CE8-5 to your table.

b. Create a query that has all columns of *PART*. Restrict the view to rows having a value of 1 for *Level*. Name your query *Level1*.

c. Create two more queries that are restricted to rows having values of 2 or 3 for *Level*. Name your queries *Level2* and *Level3*, respectively.

d. Create a form that contains *PartNumber, Level,* and *Description* from *Level1*. You can use a wizard for this if you want. Name the form *Bill of Materials*.

e. Using the subform tool in the Toolbox, create a subform in your form in part d. Set the data on this form to be all of the columns of *Level2*. After you have created the subform, ensure that the Link Child Fields property is set to *PartOf* and that the Link Master Fields property is set to *PartNumber*. Close the *Bill of Materials* form.

f. Open the subform created in part e, and create a subform on it. Set the data on this subform to be all of the columns of *Level3*. After you have created the subform, ensure that the Link Child Fields property is set to *PartOf* and that the Link Master Fields property is set to *PartNumber*. Close the *Bill of Materials* form.

g. Open the *Bill of Materials* form. It should appear as in Figure CE8-5. Open and close the form and add new data. Using this form, add sample BOM data for a product of your own choosing.

h. Following the process similar to that just described, create a *Bill of Materials Report* that lists the data for all of your products.

i. (**Optional, challenging extension**) Each part in the BOM in Figure CE8-5 can be used in, at most, one assembly (there is space to show just one *PartOf* value). You can change your design to allow a part to be used in more than one assembly as follows: First, remove *PartOf* from *PART*. Next, create a second table that has two columns: *AssemblyPartNumber* and *ComponentPartNumber*. The first contains a part number of an assembly and the second a part number of a component. Every component of a part will have a row in this table. Extend the views described above to use this second table and to produce a display similar to Figure CE8-5.

CHAPTER EXTENSION 10: EVALUATE VENDORS WITH ACCESS

31. Assume that you have been given the task of compiling evaluations of vendors made by your company's purchasing agents. Each month, every purchasing agent evaluates all of the vendors that he or she has worked with in the past month on three factors: price, quality, and responsiveness. Assume the ratings are from 1 to 5, with 5 being the best. Because your company has hundreds of vendors and dozens of purchasing agents, you decide to use Access to compile the results.

a. Create a database with three tables: VENDOR (*VendorNumber, Name, Contact*), PURCHASER (*EmpNumber, Name, Email*), and RATING (*EmpNumber, VendorNumber, Month, Year, Price Rating, QualityRating, ResponsivenessRating*). Assume that *VendorNumber* and *EmpNumber* are the keys of VENDOR and PURCHASER, respectively. Decide what you think is the appropriate key for RATING.

b. Create appropriate relationships.

c. Go to this text's companion Web site and import the data in the Excel file **EMIS 4e Ex31**. Note that data for VENDOR, PURCHASER, and RATING are stored in three separate worksheets.

d. Create a query that shows the names of all vendors and their average scores.

e. Create a query that shows the names of all employees and their average scores. *Hint:* In this and in part f, you will need to use the *Group By* function in your query.

f. Create a parameterized query that you can use to obtain the minimum, maximum, and average ratings on each criterion for a particular vendor. Assume you will enter *VendorName* as the parameter.

g. Using the information created by your queries, what conclusions can you make about vendors or purchasers?

CHAPTER EXTENSION 12: MAKE YOUR OWN MARKET-BASKET ANALYSIS WITH ACCESS

32. It is surprisingly easy to create a market-basket report using table data in Access. To do so, however, you will need to enter SQL expressions into the Access query builder. Here, you can just copy SQL statements to type them in. If you take a database class, you will learn how to code SQL statements like those you will use here.

a. Create an Access database with a table named *Order_Data* having columns *OrderNumber*, *ItemName*, and *Quantity*, with data types Number (*LongInteger*), Text (50), and Number (*LongInteger*), respectively. Define the key as the composite (*OrderNumber, ItemName*).

b. Import the data from the Excel file **EMIS 4e Ex32** into the *Order_Data* table.

c. Now, to perform the market-basket analysis, you will need to enter several SQL statements into Access. To do so, click the queries tab and select *Create Query* in Design view. Click *Close* when the Show Table dialog box appears. Right click in the gray section above the grid in the *Select Query* window. Select *SQL View*. Enter the following expression exactly as it appears here:

```
SELECT  T1.ItemName as FirstItem,
        T2.ItemName as SecondItem
FROM    Order_Data T1, Order_Data T2
WHERE   T1.OrderNumber =
        T2.OrderNumber
AND     T1.ItemName <> T2.ItemName;
```

Click the red exclamation point in the toolbar to run the query. Correct any typing mistakes and, once it works, save the query using the name *TwoItemBasket*.

d. Now enter a second SQL statement. Again, click the queries tab and select *Create Query* in Design view. Click *Close* when the Show Table dialog box appears. Right click in the gray section above the grid in the *Select Query* window. Select *SQL View*. Enter the following expression exactly as it appears here:

```
SELECT  TwoItemBasket.FirstItem,
        TwoItemBasket.SecondItem,
        Count(*) AS SupportCount
FROM    TwoItemBasket
GROUP BY TwoItemBasket.FirstItem,
        TwoItemBasket.SecondItem;
```

Correct any typing mistakes and, once it works, save the query using the name *SupportCount*.

e. Examine the results of the second query, and verify that the two query statements have correctly calculated the number of times that two items have appeared together. Explain further calculations you need to make to compute support.

f. Explain the calculations you need to make to compute lift. Although you can make those calculations using SQL, you need more SQL knowledge to do it, and we will skip that here.

g. Explain, in your own words, what the query in part c seems to be doing. What does the query in part d seem to be doing? Again, you will need to take a database class to learn how to code such expressions, but this exercise should give you a sense of the kinds of calculations that are possible with SQL.

CHAPTER EXTENSION 13: REPORTING WITH ACCESS

33. In this exercise, you'll have an opportunity to practice creating reports in Access using the data shown in Figure CE13-1.

a. Open Access, create a new database, and import the data in the text file **EMIS 4e Ex33**. Notice that the data includes an identifier; the four fields in Figure CE13-1; and a sixth field, called Quarter, that represents the calendar quarter in which the sale was made.

b. Use Access to create a report that sorts the data and presents it as shown in Figure CE13-2, except exclude sales less than $75. To do so, first create a query that has this data and then create a report based on that query. Format your report professionally.

c. Modify your report in part b to include subtotals for each customer.

d. Create a query to present the data as shown in Figure CE13-3. Produce a professionally formatted report of this data.

e. Create a query to compute the average of Amount for each Quarter.

f. Create a second table named QUARTER_DATA with fields *QuarterNumber* and *Average_Amount*. Place four rows in this table, one for each quarter and average amount.

g. Create a report that lists the sale data in ascending order of *CustomerName*. In your report, include the date and amount of each sale, as well as the amount of the sale divided by the average amount of a sale for that quarter.

h. Explain how all of the work you have done has been the result of the simple operations of filtering, sorting, grouping, and calculating.

CHAPTER EXTENSION 13: OLAP AND PIVOT WITH EXCEL

34. OLAP cubes are very similar to Microsoft Excel pivot tables. For this exercise, assume that your organization's purchasing agents rate vendors, similar to the situation described in Application Exercise 31.

    a. Open Excel and import the data in the worksheet named *Vendors* from the Excel file **EMIS 4e Ex34**, which you can find on the text's Web site. The spreadsheet will have the following column names: *VendorName*, *EmployeeName*, *Date*, *Year*, and *Rating*.

    b. Under the *Insert* ribbon in Excel, click *Pivot Table*. A wizard will open. Select *Excel* and *Pivot Table* in the first screen. Click *Next*.

    c. When asked to provide a data range, drag your mouse over the data you imported so as to select all of the data. Be sure to include the column headings. Excel will fill in the range values in the open dialog box. Place your pivot table in a separate spreadsheet.

    d. Excel will create a field list on the right-hand side of your spreadsheet. Drag and drop the field named *VendorName* onto the words "Drop Row Fields Here." Drag and drop *EmployeeName* onto the words "Drop Column Fields Here." Now drag and drop the field named *Rating* onto the words "Drop Data Items Here." Voilà! You have a pivot table.

    e. To see how the table works, drag and drop more fields on the various sections of your pivot table. For example, drop *Year* on top of *Employee*. Then move *Year* below *Employee*. Now move *Year* below *Vendor*. All of this action is just like an OLAP cube, and, in fact, OLAP cubes are readily displayed in Excel pivot tables. The major difference is that OLAP cubes are usually based on thousands or more rows of data.

PART 4

CHAPTER 10: PLANNING PROJECT COSTS WITH EXCEL

35. Suppose you are given the task of keeping track of the number of labor hours invested in meetings for systems development projects. Assume your company uses the traditional SDLC and that each phase requires two types of meetings: working meetings and review meetings. *Working meetings* involve users, systems analysts, programmers, and PQA test engineers. *Review meetings* involve all of those people, plus level-1 and level-2 managers of both user departments and the IS department.

    a. Import the data in the Word file **EMIS 4e Ex35** from this text's Web site into a spreadsheet.

    b. Modify your spreadsheet to compute the total labor hours invested in each phase of a project. When a meeting occurs, assume you enter the project phase, the meeting type, the start time, the end time, and the number of each type of personnel attending. Your spreadsheet should calculate the number of labor hours and should add the meeting's hours to the totals for that phase and for the project overall.

    c. Modify your spreadsheet to include the budgeted number (in the source data) of labor hours for each type of employee for each phase. In your spreadsheet, show the difference between the number of hours budgeted and the number actually consumed.

    d. Change your spreadsheet to include the budgeted cost and actual cost of labor. Assume that you enter, once, the average labor cost for each type of employee, as stipulated in the source data.

CHAPTER 10: TRACKING SYSTEMS FAILURES WITH ACCESS

36. Use Access to develop a failure-tracking database application. Use the data in the Excel file **EMIS 4e Ex36** for this exercise. The file includes columns for the following:

    FailureNumber
    DateReported
    FailureDescription
    ReportedBy (the name of the PQA engineer reporting the failure)
    ReportedBy_email (the email address of the PQA engineer reporting the failure)
    FixedBy (the name of the programmer who is assigned to fix the failure)
    FixedBy_email (the email address of the programmer assigned to fix the failure)
    DateFailureFixed
    FixDescription
    DateFixVerified
    VerifiedBy (the name of the PQA engineer verifying the fix)
    VerifiedBy_email (the email address of the PQA engineer verifying the fix)

    a. The data in the spreadsheet have not been normalized. When you enter (or, better, import) the data, normalize it by creating a *Failure* table, a *PQA Engineer* table, and a *Programmer* table. Add other appropriate columns to each table. Create appropriate relationships.

    b. Create one or more forms that can be used to report a failure, to report a failure fix, and to report a failure verification. Create the form(s) so that the user can just pull down the name of a PQA engineer or programmer from the appropriate table to fill in the *ReportedBy*, *FixedBy*, and *VerifiedBy* fields.

c. Construct a report that shows all failures sorted by *ReportedBy* and then by *Date Reported*.

d. Construct a report that shows only fixed and verified failures.

e. Construct a report that shows only fixed but unverified failures.

CHAPTERS 10 AND 11: KEEPING TRACK OF REQUESTS

37. Tracking requests is a common need for both systems development projects and also for IS departments, and, indeed, with any service department. With accurate request tracking, management can get involved when requests are repeatedly made for the same problem or when too many problems are being reported for the same facility or piece of equipment, or too many problems are being reported by the same user.

   • In this exercise, you will create such a system for an IS department that wants to track system problems and responses.

   • Suppose an organization keeps the following data about requests:

   Ticket#
   Date_Submitted
   Date_Opened
   Date_Closed
   Type (new or repeat)
   Reporting_ Employee_Name
   Reporting_Employee_Division
   Technician_Name Problem_System
   Problem_DescriptionONE

   • You can find sample ticket data in the Excel file **EMIS 4e Ex37** on this text's Web site.

   • However, managers often need more information. Among their needs are information that will help them learn who are their best- and worst-performing technicians, how different systems compare in terms of number of problems reported and the time required to fix those problems, how different divisions compare in terms of problems reported and the time required to fix them, which technicians are the best and worst at solving problems with particular systems, and which technicians are best and worst at solving problems from particular divisions.

   a. Use either Access or Excel, or a combination of the two, to produce the information listed above from the data

in the Excel file **EMIS 4e Ex37**. In your answer, you may use queries, formulas, reports, forms, graphs, pivot tables, pivot charts, or any other type of Access or Excel display. Choose the best display for the type of information you are producing.

   b. Explain how you would use these different types of information to manage your department.

   c. Specify any additional information that you would like to have produced from this data to help you manage your department.

   d. Use either Access or Excel or a combination to produce the information in part c.

CHAPTER 12: HOW EASY IS PHISHING?

38. This is an easy exercise with a major lesson!

   a. Open any HTML editor, such as Dreamweaver or Expression Web.

   b. Create a Web page with the title "Phishing Examples" and the subtitle "Go to These Sites."

   c. Under the subtitle, create a hyperlink that will display the text "*www.msn.com.*" However, set the target of this link to be *www.yahoo.com*.

   d. Create a second hyperlink that will display the text "*www.Google.com.*" However, set the target of this link to *www.bing.com*.

   e. Test your Web page. Click each link and observe where your browser goes.

   f. Explain how this exercise pertains to phishing.

CHAPTER 12: COMPUTING THE COST OF A VIRUS

39. Develop a spreadsheet model of the cost of a virus attack in an organization that has three types of computers: employee workstations, data servers, and Web servers. Assume that the number of computers affected by the virus depends on the severity of the virus. For the purposes of your model, assume that there are three levels of virus severity: *Low-severity* incidents affect fewer than 30 percent of the user workstations and none of the data or Web servers. *Medium-severity* incidents affect up to 70 percent of the user workstations, up to half of the Web servers, and none of the data servers. *High-severity* incidents can affect all organizational computers.

   • Assume that 50 percent of the incidents are low severity, 30 percent are medium severity, and 20 percent are high severity.

   • Assume that employees can remove viruses from workstations themselves, but that specially trained technicians are required to repair the servers. The time to eliminate a virus from an infected computer depends on the computer type. Let the time to remove the virus from each type be an input into your model. Assume that when users eliminate the virus themselves, they are unproductive for twice the time required for the removal. Let the average employee hourly labor cost be an input to your model. Let the average cost of a technician also be an input into your model. Finally, let the total number of user computers, data servers, and Web servers be inputs into your model.

- Run your simulation 10 times. Use the same inputs for each run, but draw a random number (assume a uniform distribution for all random numbers) to determine the severity type. Then, draw random numbers to determine the percentage of computers of each type affected, using the constraints detailed earlier. For example, if the attack is of medium severity, draw a random number between 0 and 70 to indicate the percentage of infected user workstations and a random number between 0 and 50 to indicate the percentage of infected Web servers.
- For each run, calculate the total of lost employee hours, the total dollar cost of lost employee labor hours, the total hours of technicians to fix the servers, and the total

cost of technician labor. Finally, compute the total overall cost. Show the results of each run. Show the average costs and hours for the 10 runs.

CHAPTER EXTENSION 17: PROCESS MODELING WITH VISIO

40. In this exercise, you will use Visio to create process diagrams in BPMN notation.

   a. Download the Visio file **EMIS 4e Ex40** from this text's support site. Open the file and familiarize yourself with this diagram. Match the diagram to the correct figure in Chapter Extension 18.

   b. Notice that Visio includes the BPMN shapes. Go to the Shape organizer to see other types of flowchart shapes that Visio supports.

   c. Create a new Visio diagram. Add BPMN shapes that you may want to use.

   d. Model the customer process Respond to Quotation. Make sure your process accepts the inputs shown in **EMIS 4e Ex40** and produces the outputs shown in that figure. Create your process so that your company checks prices and delivery dates and requests changes, if appropriate. Include other logic, if necessary.

   e. Show your work by saving your document as a PDF file.

10/100/1000 Ethernet A type of Ethernet that conforms to the IEEE 802.3 protocol and allows for transmission at a rate of 10, 100, or 1,000 Mbps (megabits per second). p. 133

32-bit processor A processor that can effectively use up to 4GB of main memory. p. 78

64-bit processor A processor that can use more than 4GB of memory; in fact, for all practical purposes, it can use an almost unlimited amount of main memory. p. 78

Abstract reasoning The ability to make and manipulate models. p. 7

Accelerator effect An economic theory that states that a dollar spent will contribute more than a dollar of activity to the economy. p. 602

Access A popular personal and small workgroup DBMS product from Microsoft. p. 113

Access point (AP) A point in a wireless network that facilitates communication among wireless devices and serves as a point of interconnection between wireless and wired networks. The AP must be able to process messages according to both the 802.3 and 802.11 standards, because it sends and receives wireless traffic using the 802.11 protocol and communicates with wired networks using the 802.3 protocol. p. 133

Accounting applications Applications that support accounting functions, such as budgeting, cash management, accounts payable and receivable, and financial reporting. p. 476

Active lurker Someone who reads, consumes, and observes activity in one social medium and then transmits it in another medium. p. 509

Activities The parts of a business process that transform resources and information of one type into resources and information of another type; can be manual or automated. p. 29

Actor In a business process, a person, group, department, or organization. p. 29

Advanced Persistent Threat (APT) A sophisticated, possibly long-running, computer hack that is perpetrated by large, well-funded organizations like governments. APTs are a means to engage in cyberwarfare. p. 313

Adware Programs installed on the user's computer without the user's knowledge or permission that reside in the background and, unknown to the user, observe the user's actions and keystrokes, modify computer activity, and report the user's activities to sponsoring organizations. Most adware is benign in that it does not perform malicious acts or steal data. It does, however, watch user activity and produce pop-up ads. pp. 94, 323

Agile development An adaptive project management process based on the principles listed in Figure CE16-1. Can be used for the management of many types of projects; in this text it applied to the development of information systems. p. 574

Alert A form of report, often requested by recipients, that tells them some piece of usually time-related information, such as notification of the time for a meeting. p. 532

Analysis paralysis When too much time is spent documenting project requirements. p. 271

Android A mobile operating system that is a version of Linux. Android runs on the Google Nexus 7, the Amazon Kindle Fire, as well as many other mobile devices. p. 83

Application software Programs that perform a business function. Some application programs are general purpose, such as Excel or Word. Other application programs are specific to a business function, such as accounts payable. p. 86

ARM A computer architecture and instruction set that is designed for portable devices such as smart phones and tablets. p. 83

As-is model A business process model that documents the current business process; teams then change that model to make adjustments necessary to solve process problems. pp. 485, 584

Asymmetric encryption An encryption method whereby different keys are used to encode and to decode the message; one key encodes the message, and the other key decodes the message. Symmetric encryption is simpler and much faster than asymmetric encryption. p. 321

Asynchronous communication Information exchange that occurs when all members of a work team do not meet at the same time, such as those who work different shifts or at different locations. p. 356

Attribute (1) A variable that provides properties for an HTML tag. Each attribute has a standard name. For example, the attribute for a hyperlink is *href*, and its value indicates which Web page is to be displayed when the user clicks the link. (2) Characteristics of an entity. Example attributes of *Order* would be *OrderNumber, OrderDate, SubTotal, Tax, Total*, and so forth. Example attributes of *Salesperson* would be *SalespersonName, Email, Phone*, and so forth. pp. 146, 391

Authentication The process whereby an information system approves (authenticates) a user by checking the user's password. p. 319

Automated Clearing House (ACH) A network of information systems that provides for the interbank clearing of electronic payments. p. 494

Baseline An initial plan for the development of an information system. p. 562

Baseline WBS The final work breakdown structure plan that shows the planned tasks, dependencies, durations, and resource assignments of a large-scale development project. p. 566

Beta testing The process of allowing future system users to try out the new system on their own. Used to locate program failures just prior to program shipment. p. 267

BI analysis The process of creating business intelligence. The four fundamental categories of BI analysis are reporting, data mining, BigData analysis, and knowledge management. p. 224

BI application The software component of a BI system. p. 223

BI server A computer program that delivers BI application results in a variety of formats to various devices for consumption by BI users. p. 240

BigData A term used to describe data collections that are characterized by huge volume, rapid velocity, and great variety. p. 236

Bigtable A nonrelational data store developed by Google. p. 118

Bill of materials (BOM) A list of the materials that comprise a product. p. 473

Binary digits The means by which computers represent data; also called *bits*. A binary digit is either a zero or a one. p. 76

Biometric authentication The use of personal physical characteristics, such as fingerprints, facial features, and retinal scans, to authenticate users. p. 320

Bits The means by which computers represent data; also called *binary digits*. A bit is either a zero or a one. p. 76

BlackBerry OS One of the most successful early mobile operating systems and is used primarily by business users on BlackBerry devices. p. 83

Blogs (Web-log) Online journals, which use technology to publish news and opinions over the Internet. p. 508

Bluetooth A common wireless protocol designed for transmitting data over short distances; used to replace cables. p. 134

Bring Your Own Device (BYOD) Policy An organizational policy that states employees' permissions and responsibilities when using personal mobile devices for organizational business. p. 463

Broadband Internet communication lines that have speeds in excess of 256 Kbps. DSL and cable modems provide broadband access. p. 135

Brooks' Law The famous adage that states: *Adding more people to a late project makes the project later*. Brooks' Law is true not only because a larger staff requires increased coordination, but also because new people need training. The only people who can train the new employees are the existing team members, who are thus taken off productive tasks. The costs of training new people can overwhelm the benefit of their contribution. p. 258

Brute force attack A password-cracking threat that obtains passwords by trying every possible combination of characters. p. 316

Bullwhip effect Phenomenon in which the variability in the size and timing of orders increases at each stage up the supply chain, from customer to supplier. pp. 498, 602

Bus Means by which the CPU reads instructions and data from main memory and writes data to main memory. p. 77

Business analyst A person who specializes in understanding business needs, strategies, and goals and who helps businesses use IT and implement systems to accomplish organizational strategies. p. 261

Business Intelligence (BI) The processing of operational data to create information that exposes patterns, relationships, and trends of importance to the organization. p. 223

Business intelligence (BI) system A system that provides the right information, to the right user, at the right time. A tool produces the information, but the system ensures that the right information is delivered to the right user at the right time. p. 223

Business process A network of activities for accomplishing a business function. p. 27

Business process management (BPM) The systematic process of creating, assessing, and altering business processes. p. 584

Business Process Modeling Notation (BPMN) A standard set of terms and graphical notations for documenting business processes, created by the Object Management Group (OMG). p. 28

Business process reengineering The activity of altering and designing business processes to take advantage of new information systems. p. 171

Bytes (1) Characters of data. (2) 8-bit chunks. pp. 77, 108

Cable lines Cable television lines that provide high-speed data transmission. p. 135

Cache A file on a domain name resolver that stores domain names and IP addresses that have been resolved. Then, when someone else needs to resolve that same domain name, there is no need to go through the entire resolution process. Instead, the resolver can supply the IP address from the local file. p. 77

Capital The investment of resources with the expectation of future returns in the marketplace. p. 202

Cassandra A durable, nonrelational data store that operates over hundreds or thousands of servers. Originally developed by Facebook but later transferred to the open-source community and has become an Apache Top-Level Project. p. 118

Cell In a spreadsheet, the intersection of a row and a column. p. 372

Central processing unit (CPU) The portion of a computer that selects instructions, processes them, performs arithmetic and logical comparisons, and stores results of operations in memory. p. 75

Charms In Windows 8 applications, icons that slide in from the right of the display. p. 460

Chief information officer (CIO) The title of the principal manager of the IT department. Other common titles are *vice president of information services*, *director of information services*, and, less commonly, *director of computer services*. p. 284

Chief technology officer (CTO) The head of the technology group. The CTO sorts through new ideas and products to identify those that are most relevant to the organization. The CTO's job requires deep knowledge of information technology and the ability to envision how new IT will affect the organization over time. p. 284

Choropleth map A map that displays colors, shades, or patterns in accordance with category values of underlying data. p. 554

Chrome A term that refers to visual overhead such as menus, status bars, and scroll bars in a computer display. p. 458

Client A computer that provides word processing, spreadsheets, database access, and usually a network connection. p. 79

Client-server applications Applications that process code on both the client and the server. p. 86

Closed source A project in which the source code is highly protected and only available to trusted employees and carefully vetted contractors. p. 92

Cloud A term that refers to pooled computer resources that are accessed via the Internet using Internet protocols. p. 147

Cloud computing Computing services that provide processing, data storage, and specific application functions over the Internet. p. 130

Cluster analysis An unsupervised data mining technique whereby statistical techniques are used to identify groups of entities that have similar characteristics. A common use for cluster analysis is to find groups of similar customers in data about customer orders and customer demographics. p. 235

COBIT (Control Objectives for Information and related Technology) A set of standard practices created by the Information Systems Audit and Control Association that are used in the assessment stage of the BPM cycle to determine how well an information system complies with an organization's strategy. p. 585

Collaboration A group of people working together to achieve a common goal via a process of feedback and iteration. pp. 7, 341

Collaboration information system An information system that supports collaboration. p. 350

Collaboration tool The program component of a collaboration system. For the tool to be useful, it must be surrounded by the other four components of an information system. p. 351

Columns Also called *fields*, or groups of bytes. A database table has multiple columns that are used to represent the attributes of an entity. Examples are *PartNumber*, *EmployeeName*, and *SalesDate*. p. 108

Comma-delimited file An exported data file in which field values are separated by commas. p. 424

Commerce server A computer that operates Web-based programs that display products, support online ordering, record and process payments, and interface with inventory-management applications. p. 145

Communities In social media, groups of people related by common interests. Also referred to as hives or tribes. p. 193

Competitive strategy The strategy an organization chooses as the way it will succeed in its industry. According to Porter, the four fundamental competitive strategies are: cost leadership across an industry or within a particular industry segment and differentiation across an industry or within a particular industry segment. p. 52

Component design phase The third phase in the SDLC, in which developers determine hardware and software specifications, design the database (if applicable), design procedures, and create job descriptions for users and operations personnel. p. 259

Computer-based information system An information system that includes a computer. p. 10

Confidence In market-basket terminology, the probability estimate that two items will be purchased together. p. 521

Configuration control Use by developers of a set of management policies, practices, and tools to maintain control over a project's resources. p. 569

Connection data In social media systems, data about relationships. p. 197

Content data In social media systems, data and responses to data that are contributed by users and SM sponsors. p. 197

Content management systems Information systems that track organizational documents, Web pages, graphics, and related materials. p. 511

Context-sensitive chrome Chrome that pops up in the display only when needed and appropriate. p. 459

Cookie A small data file that is stored on the user's computer by a browser. Cookies can be used for authentication, for storing shopping cart contents and user preferences, and for other legitimate purposes. Cookies can also be used to implement spyware. pp. 248, 317

Cooperation A group of people working together, all performing the same type of work, to accomplish a job. p. 341

Cost The dollar amount required to develop an information system from start to finish; one of the critical drivers in large-scale IS development, which typically involves trade-offs with requirements and time. p. 561

Cost feasibility The dimension of system feasibility that assesses whether a new system is likely to generate benefits sufficient to justify the system's cost. p. 260

Critical path The sequence of activities that determine the earliest date by which a project can be completed; takes into account task dependencies. p. 565

Critical path analysis The planning and management of the tasks on the critical path. Tasks on the critical path cannot be allowed to run late; those not on the critical path can run late to the point at which they become part of the critical path. p. 566

Cross-selling The sale of related products; salespeople try to get customers who buy product *X* to also buy product *Y*. p. 520

Crowdsourcing The process by which organizations use social media technologies such as user-generated content to involve their users in the design and marketing of their products. p. 201

Crow's foot A line on an entity-relationship diagram that indicates a 1:N relationship between two entities. p. 392

Crow's-foot diagram A type of entity-relationship diagram that uses a crow's foot symbol to designate a 1:N relationship. p. 393

Custom-developed software Tailor-made software. p. 88

Customer life cycle Taken as a whole, the processes of marketing, customer acquisition, relationship management, and loss/churn that must be managed by CRM systems. p. 172

Customer relationship management system (CRM) An information system that supports business processes for attracting, selling, managing, and supporting customers. p. 171

Data acquisition In business intelligence systems, the process of obtaining, cleaning, organizing, relating, and cataloging source data. p. 224

Data administration A staff function that pertains to *all* of an organization's data assets. Typical data administration tasks are setting data standards, developing data policies, and providing for data security. p. 324

Data channel Means by which the CPU reads instructions and data from main memory and writes data to main memory. p. 77

Data flows Movements of data items from one activity to another activity or to or from a repository. p. 30

Data integrity In a database or a collection of databases, the condition that exists when data values are consistent and in agreement with one another. pp. 30, 167

Data integrity problem In a database or a collection of databases, the situation that exists when data items disagree with one another. An example is two different names for the same customer. p. 394

Data mart A facility that prepares, stores, and manages data for reporting and data mining for specific business functions. p. 233

Data mining The application of statistical techniques to find patterns and relationships among data and to classify and predict. p. 235

Data model A logical representation of the data in a database that describes the data and relationships that will be stored in the database. Akin to a blueprint. p. 390

Data safeguards Steps taken to protect databases and other organizational data by means of data administration and database administration. p. 324

Data warehouse A facility that prepares, stores, and manages data specifically for reporting and data mining. p. 231

Database A self-describing collection of integrated records. p. 108

Database administration A staff function that refers to the protection and effective use of a particular database and its related applications. (Contrast with data administration). Database administration responsibilities include protecting the data, controlling changes to database structure as well as to the supporting DBMS, monitoring and improving performance, and ensuring effective procedures for using the database exist. pp. 114, 324

Database application A collection of forms, reports, queries, and application programs that process a database. p. 114

Database application system An information system having the standard five components, that make database data more accessible and useful. Users employ a database application that consists of forms, formatted reports, queries, and application programs. Each of these, in turn, calls on the database management system (DBMS) to process the database tables. p. 114

Database management system (DBMS) A program used to create, process, and administer a database. p. 113

Database marketing The application of data business intelligence systems to the planning and execution of marketing programs. p. 518

Database tier In the three-tier architecture, the tier that runs the DBMS and receives and processes SQL requests to retrieve and store data. p. 144

Datum A set of elevations based on particular values of the earth's radii. p. 546

DB2 A popular, enterprise-class DBMS product from IBM. p. 113

Decision support systems BI systems that support decision-making. Some authors define business intelligence (BI) systems as supporting decision making only, in which case they use this older term as a synonym for BI systems. p. 223

Decision tree A hierarchical arrangement of criteria for classifying customers, items, and other business objects. p. 521

Defenders of belief In social media, a community that shares a common strongly held belief; such groups seek conformity and want to convince others of the correctness and wisdom of their belief. p. 198

Deliverables Tasks that compose one of many measurable or observable steps in a development project. p. 564

Denial of service (DOS) Security problem in which users are not able to access an information system; can be caused by human errors, natural disaster, or malicious activity. p. 312

Departmental information systems Workgroup information systems that support a particular department. p. 165

Desktop programs Client applications, such as Word, Excel, or Acrobat, that run on a personal computer and do not require a connection to a server. p. 86

Desktop virtualization (also called client virtualization) The process of storing a user's desktop on a remote server. It enables users to run their desktops from many different client computers. p. 84

Digital dashboard An electronic display that is customized for a particular user. p. 532

Digital subscriber line (DSL) A data transmission line that shares telephone lines with voice communication. Used primarily in homes and small businesses. Provides download speeds up to 6.5 Mbps and slower upload speeds, in the neighborhood of 512 Kbps. p. 135

Dimension A characteristic of an OLAP measure; purchase date, customer type, customer location, and sales region are examples of dimensions. p. 534

Dimensional database A database structured to support OLAP processing. p. 537

Discussion forums Forms of asynchronous communication in which one group member posts an entry and other group members respond. A better form of group communication than email, because it is more difficult for the discussion to go off track. p. 358

Diseconomies of scale The added cost that will eventually occur as more people are added to an IS development project. p. 561

Distributed database processing The processing of a database that resides in whole, or in part, in multiple locations. p. 600

Distributed systems Systems in which application processing is distributed across multiple computing devices. p. 178

Domain name The registered, human-friendly valid name in the domain name system (DNS). The process of changing a name into its IP address is called *resolving the domain name*. p. 141

Drill down With an OLAP report, to further divide the data into more detail. p. 535

Drive-by sniffer A person who takes a computer with a wireless connection through an area and searches for unprotected wireless networks in an attempt to gain free Internet access or to gather unauthorized data. p. 311

Dual processor A computer with two CPUs. p. 76

Durability Once data is committed to a data store, it won't be lost, even in the presence of failure. p. 128

Dynamic reports Reports that are generated at the time of request; the reporting system reads the most current data and generates the report using that fresh data. A report on sales today and a report on current stock prices are both dynamic reports. pp. 239, 531

Dynamo A nonrelational data store developed by Amazon.com. p. 118

Effective business process A business process that enables the organization to accomplish its strategy. p. 30

Efficiency The ratio of benefits to costs. p. 31

Elastic In cloud computing, the situation that exists when the amount of resource leased can be dynamically increased or decreased, programmatically, in a short span of time, and organizations pay for just the resource that they use. This terms was first used in this way by Amazon.com. p. 147

Email A form of asynchronous communication in which participants send comments and attachments electronically. As a form of group communication, it can be disorganized, disconnected, and easy to hide from. p. 357

Email spoofing A synonym for *phishing*. A technique for obtaining unauthorized data that uses pretexting via email. The *phisher* pretends to be a legitimate company and sends email requests for confidential data, such as account numbers, Social Security numbers, account passwords, and so forth. Phishers direct traffic to their sites under the guise of a legitimate business. p. 311

Encryption The process of transforming clear text into coded, unintelligible text for secure storage or communication. p. 320

Encryption algorithms Algorithms used to transform clear text into coded, unintelligible text for secure storage or communication. Commonly used methods are DES, 3DES, and AES. p. 320

Enterprise 2.0 The application of Web 2.0 technologies, collaboration systems, social networking, and related technologies to facilitate the cooperative work within organizations. p. 201

Enterprise application integration (EAI) An information system that supports cross-functional business processes by integrating existing functional applications. Unlike CRM or ERP, the organization need not replace existing applications; instead layers of software are created to integrate those applications. p. 175

Enterprise DBMS A product that processes large organizational and workgroup databases. These products support many users, perhaps thousands, and many different database applications. Such DBMS products support 24/7 operations and can manage databases that span dozens of different magnetic disks with hundreds of gigabytes or more of data. IBM's DB2, Microsoft's SQL Server, and Oracle's Oracle Database are examples of enterprise DBMS products. p. 118

Enterprise information system An information system that supports activities in multiple departments. p. 166

Enterprise resource planning (ERP) product A suite of applications, a database, and a set of inherent processes for supporting consolidated business processes with a single information system. p. 479

Enterprise resource planning (ERP) applications Cross-functional, enterprise-wide applications that integrate the primary value-chain activities with the functions of human resources and accounting. p. 479

Enterprise resource planning (ERP) system An information system based on an ERP product. p. 174

Entity In the E-R data model, a representation of some thing that users want to track. Some entities represent a physical object; others represent a logical construct or transaction. p. 391

Entity-relationship (E-R) data model An abstraction of data, based on the E-R model, that defines the categories of things that will be stored, the relationships of those categories (entities), and their attributes. p. 390

Entity-relationship (E-R) diagram A diagram used by database designers to document entities and their relationships to each other. p. 392

ERP system An information system based on an ERP product. p. 479

Ethernet Another name for the IEEE 802.3 protocol, Ethernet is a network protocol that operates at Layers 1 and 2 of the TCP/IP-OSI architecture. Ethernet, the world's most popular LAN protocol, is used on WANs as well. p. 133

Exabyte 10^{18} bytes. p. 77

Exception reports Reports produced when something out of predefined bounds occurs. p. 235

Experimentation Making a reasoned analysis of an opportunity, envisioning potential solutions, evaluating those possibilities, and developing the most promising ones, consistent with the resources you have. p. 8

Expert system Knowledge-sharing system that is created by interviewing experts in a given business domain and codifying the rules used by those experts. p. 510

Expert system shell A program in an expert system that processes a set of rules, typically many times, until the values of the variables no longer change, at which point the system reports the results. p. 511

F score In RFM analysis, a number rating that indicates in which fifth a customer ranks in terms of ordering *frequency*. p. 519

Fields Also called *columns*, groups of bytes in a database table. A database table has multiple columns that are used to represent the attributes of an entity. Examples are *PartNumber*, *EmployeeName*, and *SalesDate*. p. 108

File A group of rows or records having the same columns. In a database, sometimes called a *table*. p. 108

File server A server computer that stores files. p. 359

Firewalls Computing devices located between an organization's internal and external networks that prevent unauthorized access to or from the internal network. A firewall can be a special-purpose computer or it can be a program on a general-purpose computer or on a router. p. 322

Firmware Computer software that is installed into devices such as printers, print services, and various types of communication devices. The software is coded just like other software, but it is installed into special, programmable memory of the printer or other device. p. 89

Five-component framework The five fundamental components of an information system—computer hardware, software, data, procedures, and people—that are present in every information system, from the simplest to the most complex. p. 10

Five forces model Model proposed by Michael Porter that assesses industry characteristics and profitability by means of five competitive forces—bargaining power of suppliers, threat of substitution, bargaining power of customers, rivalry among firms, and threat of new entrants. p. 50

Folksonomy Content structure that has emerged from the processing of many user tags. p. 201

Foreign keys A column or group of columns used to represent relationships. Values of the foreign key match values of the primary key in a different (foreign) table. p. 110

Form Data entry forms are used to read, insert, modify, and delete database data. p. 116

FTP (File Transfer Protocol) A Layer-5 TCP/IP protocol used to copy files from one computer to another. In interorganizational transaction processing, FTP enables users to easily exchange large files. pp. 139, 359

Function points Estimating technique that attempts to schedule a development project by the number of function points in a project, using each function point to determine the number of lines of code and the time for the project. p. 568

Functional application Software that provides features and functions necessary to support a particular business activity (function). p. 468

Functional information system Workgroup information systems that support a particular business function. p. 165

Functional systems Information systems that support a single enterprise function, within a single department or other workgroup. p. 468

Gantt chart A project management chart that shows tasks and their dependencies on each other and schedules them in an optimal way so as to reduce the time it takes to complete them. p. 564

Geocoding A process by which the GIS application needs to convert all of the location identifiers to a common scheme. p. 548

Geofence A geographic boundary set up within a GIS. p. 551

Geographic coordinates Coordinates based on latitude and longitude. p. 548

Geographic information system (GIS) An information system that captures, stores, analyzes, and displays geospatial data. p. 540

Geospatial data Data that can be ordered in reference to the earth. p. 540

Gigabyte (GB) 1,024 MB. p. 77

GIS application Term used to refer to a computer program that manages geospatial data. p. 541

GNU A self-referential acronym meaning GNU not Unix, originally a set of tools for developing an open-source version of Unix. Used today primarily in conjunction with the GNU public license agreement (which see). p. 89

GNU General Public License (GPL) agreement One of the standard license agreements for open source software. p. 90

Google Drive Version management system for sharing documents and spreadsheet data. Documents are stored on a Google server, from which users can access and simultaneously see and edit the documents. Formerly known as Google Docs. p. 360

Granularity The level of detail in data. Customer name and account balance is large granularity data. Customer name, balance, and the order details and payment history of every customer order is smaller granularity. p. 232

Green computing Environmentally conscious computing consisting of three major components: power management, virtualization, and e-waste management. p. 303

Hacking Occurs when a person gains unauthorized access to a computer system. Although some people hack for the sheer joy of doing it, other hackers invade systems for the malicious purpose of stealing or modifying data. pp. 236, 312

Hadoop An open-source program supported by the Apache Foundation that manages thousands of computers and which implements MapReduce. p. 236

Hardware Electronic components and related gadgetry that input, process, output, store, and communicate data according to instructions encoded in computer programs or software. p. 75

Hives In social media, a group of people related by a common interest. Also referred to as communities and tribes. p. 193

Horizontal-market application Software that provides capabilities common across all organizations and industries; examples include word processors, graphics programs, spreadsheets, and presentation programs. p. 86

Host operating system In virtualization, the operating system that hosts the virtual operating systems. p. 84

Href The attribute of an HTML hyperlink element that specifies the URL of target of the link. See also *hyperlinks*. p. 146

HTML (Hypertext Markup Language) A language that defines the structure and layout of Web page content. An HTML tag is a notation used to define a data element for display or other purposes. p. 146

HTTP (Hypertext Transport Protocol) A Layer-5 TCP/IP protocol used to process Web pages. p. 138

HTTPS An indication that a Web browser is using the SSL/TLS protocol to provide secure communications. pp. 139, 321

Human capital The investment in human knowledge and skills with the expectation of future returns in the marketplace. p. 202

Human resources applications Applications that support recruitment, compensation, evaluation, and professional development of employees and affiliated personnel. p. 475

Human safeguards Steps taken to protect against security threats by establishing appropriate procedures for users to follow during system use. p. 325

Hyperlinks Pointers on Web pages to other Web pages. A hyperlink contains an href element that specifies the URL of the Web page to access when the user clicks the hyperlink. The URL can reference a page on the Web server that generated the page containing the hyperlink, or it can reference a page on another server. p. 145

Hyper-social knowledge management The application of social media and related applications for the management and delivery of organizational knowledge resources. p. 514

Hyper-social organization An organization that uses social media to transform its interactions with customers, employees, and partners into mutually satisfying relationships with them and their communities. pp. 198, 505

ICANN (Internet Corporation for Assigned Names and Numbers) A public agency that establishes procedures and authorizes organizations to association names with public IP addresses. p. 140

Identification The process whereby an information system identifies a user by requiring the user to sign on with a user name and password. p. 319

Identifier An attribute (or group of attributes) whose value is associated with one and only one entity instance. p. 391

IEEE 802.3 protocol This standard, also called *Ethernet*, is a network protocol that operates at Layers 1 and 2 of the TCP/IP–OSI architecture. Ethernet, the world's most popular LAN protocol, is used on WANs as well. p. 133

IEEE 802.11 protocol A wireless communications standard, widely used today, that enables cable-free access within a few hundred feet. The most popular version of this standard is IEEE 802.11g, which allows wireless transmissions of up to 54 Mbps. p. 134

If/then rules Format for rules derived from a decision tree (data mining) or by interviewing a human expert (expert systems). p. 510

Implementation phase The fourth phase in the SDLC, in which developers build and integrate system components, test the system, and convert to the new system. p. 238

Import/export The process of transferring data from one computer application to another. p. 423

Industry-specific solution An ERP template that is designed to serve the needs of companies or organizations in specific industries. Such solutions save time and decrease risk; their existence has spurred ERP growth. p. 486

Information (1) Knowledge derived from data, where *data* is defined as recorded facts or figures. (2) Data presented in a meaningful context. (3) Data processed by summing, ordering, averaging, grouping, comparing, or other similar operations. (4) A difference that makes a difference. p. 33

Information silo A condition that exists when data are isolated in separated information systems. pp. 33, 166

Information system (IS) A group of components that interact to produce information. p. 10

Information technology (IT) The products, methods, inventions, and standards that are used for the purpose of producing information. p. 13

Infrastructure as a service (IaaS) The cloud hosting of a bare server computers or storage device. p. 151

Inherent processes The procedures that must be followed to effectively use licensed software. For example, the processes inherent in MRP systems assume that certain users will take specified actions in a particular order. In most cases, the organization must conform to the processes inherent in the software. p. 171

Input hardware Hardware devices that attach to a computer; includes keyboards, mouse, document scanners, and bar-code (Universal Product Code) scanners. p. 75

Inter-enterprise information system An information system that is shared by two or more independent organizations. pp. 147, 166

Internal firewalls Firewalls that sit inside the organizational network. p. 322

Internet When spelled with a small *i*, as in *internet*, a private network of networks. When spelled with a capital *I*, as in *Internet*, the public internet known as the Internet. p. 131

Internet protocols and standards Additions to TCP/IP that enable cloud-hosting vendors to provide processing capabilities in flexible, yet standardized ways. p. 147

Internet service provider (ISP) An ISP provides users with Internet access. An ISP provides a user with a legitimate Internet address; it serves as the user's gateway to the Internet; and it passes communications back and forth between the user and the Internet. ISPs also pay for the Internet. They collect money from their customers and pay access fees and other charges on the users' behalf. p. 134

Inter-enterprise process A business process that crosses not only departmental boundaries, but organizational boundaries as well. Such processes involve activities among organizations having different owners. p. 177

Intranet A private internet (note small *i*) used within a corporation or other organization. p. 131

Intrusion detection system (IDS) A computer program that senses when another computer is attempting to scan the disk or otherwise access a computer. p. 315

Inventory applications Applications that help control and manage inventory and support inventory policy. p. 472

iOS The operating system used on the iPhone, iPod Touch, and iPad. p. 83

IP (Internet Protocol) A Layer-3 TCP/IP protocol. As the name implies, IP is used on the Internet, but it is used on many other internets as well. The chief purpose of IP is to route packets across an internet, which is a network of networks. p. 139

IP address A series of dotted decimals in a format like 192.168.2.28 that identifies a unique device on a network or internet. With the *IPv4* standard, IP addresses have 32 bits. With the *IPv6* standard, IP addresses have 128 bits. Today, IPv4 is more common but will likely be supplanted by IPv6 in the future. With IPv4, the decimal between the dots can never exceed 255. p. 140

IP spoofing A type of spoofing whereby an intruder uses another site's IP address as if it were that other site. p. 311

IPv4 A standard for internet addressing that uses a four decimal digit notation like 65.193.123.253. Gradually being replaced by IPv6. p. 141

IPv6 A standard for internet addressing that uses a long (128 bit) scheme for internet addresses and provides other benefits over IPv4 as well. Gradually overtaking IPv4. p. 141

Just-in-time data Data delivered to the user at the precise time it is needed. p. 453

Just-in-time design Rather than design the complete, overall system at the beginning, only those portions of the design that are needed to complete the current work are done. Common for agile development techniques such as scrum. p. 574

Just-in-time (JIT) inventory policy A policy that seeks to have production inputs (both raw materials and work-in-process) delivered to the manufacturing site just as they are needed. By scheduling delivery of inputs in this way, companies are able to reduce inventories to a minimum. p. 473

Key (1) A column or group of columns that identifies a unique row in a table. (2) A number used to encrypt data. The encryption algorithm applies the key to the original message to produce the coded message. Decoding (decrypting) a message is similar; a key is applied to the coded message to recover the original text. pp. 109, 320

Key escrow A control procedure whereby a trusted party is given a copy of a key used to encrypt database data. p. 325

Key users Users trained to perform social media (SM) engagement and management tasks. p. 508

Kilobyte (K) 1,024 bytes. p. 77

Knowledge management (KM) The process of creating value from intellectual capital and sharing that knowledge with employees, managers, suppliers, customers, and others who need that capital. p. 509

LAN device A computing device that includes important networking components, including a switch, a router, a DHCP server, and other elements. p. 132

Lead-generation applications Sales and marketing applications that send mailings (postal or email) for the purpose of generating sales prospects. Also called *prospect-generation* applications. p. 469

Lead-tracking applications Sales and marketing applications that record data on sales prospects and keep records of customer contacts. p. 469

Libraries In version-control collaboration systems, shared directories that allow access to various documents by means of *permissions*. p. 363

License Agreement that stipulates how a program can be used. Most specify the number of computers on which the program can be installed and sometimes the number of users that can connect to and use the program remotely. Such agreements also stipulate limitations on the liability of the software vendor for the consequences of errors in the software. p. 85

Lift In market-basket terminology, the ratio of confidence to the base probability of buying an item. Lift shows how much the base probability changes when other products are purchased. If the lift is greater than 1, the change is positive; if it is less than 1, the change is negative. p. 521

Lines of code Estimating technique that attempts to schedule a development project by the number of lines of code developers must write for the project. p. 568

Linkages Process interactions across value chains. Linkages are important sources of efficiencies and are readily supported by information systems. p. 54

Linux A version of Unix that was developed by the open-source community. The open-source community owns Linux, and there is no fee to use it. Linux is a popular operating system for Web servers. p. 83

Local area network (LAN) A network that connects computers that reside in a single geographic location on the premises of the company that operates the LAN. The number of connected computers can range from two to several hundred. p. 131

Localizing The process of making a computer program work in a second language. p. 599

Lost-update problem An issue in multi-user database processing in which two or more users try to make changes to the data but the database cannot make the changes because it was not designed to process changes from multiple users. p. 117

M score In RFM analysis, a number rating that indicates in which fifth a customer ranks in terms of *amount spent* per order. p. 519

Mac OS An operating system developed by Apple Computer, Inc., for the Macintosh. The current version is Mac OS X. Macintosh computers are used primarily by graphic artists and workers in the arts community. Mac OS was developed for the Power PC, but as of 2006 could runs on Intel processors as well. p. 82

Machine code A sequence of bits that represent computer instructions and data that can be processed by a computer. p. 90

Main memory A set of cells in which each cell holds a byte of data or instruction; each cell has an address, and the CPU uses the addresses to identify particular data items. p. 76

Maintenance phase A phase of the systems development life-cycle in which the information systems is either a) made to function as it was supposed to in the first place (failure fixing) or b) adapted to changes in requirements. p. 259

Malware Viruses, worms, Trojan horses, spyware, and adware. p. 323

Malware definitions Patterns that exist in malware code. Antimalware vendors update these definitions continuously and incorporate them into their products in order to better fight against malware. p. 323

Management information system (MIS) An information system that helps businesses achieve their strategies. p. 10

Managerial decision Decision that concerns the allocation and use of resources. p. 346

Manufacturing applications Applications that support one or more aspects of manufacturing processes, including planning, scheduling, inventory integration, quality control, and related processes. p. 472

Manufacturing resource planning (MRP II) A follow-on to MRP that includes the planning of materials, personnel, and machinery. It supports many linkages across the organization, including linkages with sales and marketing via the development of a master production schedule. It also includes the capability to perform what-if analyses on variances in schedules, raw materials availabilities, personnel, and other resources. p. 474

Many-to-many (N:M) relationship Relationships involving two entity types in which an instance of one type can relate to many instances of the second type, and an instance of the second type can relate to many instances of the first. For example, the relationship between Student and Class is N:M. One student may enroll in many classes and one class may have many students. Contrast with *one-to-many relationships.* p. 392

MapReduce A two-phase technique for harnessing the power of thousands of computers working in parallel. During the first phase, the Map phase, computers work on a task in parallel; during the second phase, the Reduce phase, the work of separate computers is combined, eventually obtaining a single result. p. 236

Margin The difference between value and cost. p. 53

Market-basket analysis A data mining technique for determining sales patterns. A market-basket analysis shows the products that customers tend to buy together. p. 520

Master production schedule (MPS) A plan for producing products. To create the MPS, the company analyzes past sales levels and makes estimates of future sales. This process is sometimes called a *push manufacturing process*, because the company pushes the products into sales (and customers) according to the MPS. p. 474

Materials requirements planning (MRP) An information system that plans the need for materials and inventories of materials used in the manufacturing process. Unlike MRP II, MRP does not include the planning of personnel, equipment, or facilities requirements. p. 474

Maximum cardinality The maximum number of entities that can be involved in a relationship. Common examples of maximum cardinality are 1:N, N:M, and 1:1. p. 393

Measure The data item of interest on an OLAP report. It is the item that is to be summed, averaged, or otherwise processed in the OLAP cube. Total sales, average sales, and average cost are examples of measures. p. 534

Megabyte (MB) 1,024 KB. p. 77

Memory swapping The movement of programs and data into and out of memory. If a computer has insufficient memory for its workload, such swapping will degrade system performance. p. 78

Metadata Data that describe data. p. 111

Metro-style applications Applications that are touch-screen oriented and minimize non-user data by providing context-sensitive, pop-up menus. They can also be used with a mouse and keyboard. Introduced with Windows 8. p. 82

Microsoft Windows The most popular nonmobile client operating system. Also refers to Windows Server, a popular server operating system that competes with Linux. p. 82

Military Grid Reference System (MGRS) Coordinate system that divides the earth into 60 north-south segments, like segments in an orange and provides a means for specifying locations within those segments. p. 548

Minimum cardinality The minimum number of entities that must be involved in a relationship, typically zero or one. p. 393

Mobile device A small, lightweight, power-conserving, computing device that is capable of wireless access. p. 450

Mobile device management (MDM) software Products that install and update mobile-device software, backup and restore mobile devices, wipe software and data from devices in the event the device is lost or the employee leaves the company. Such products also report usage and provide other mobile device management data. p. 450

Mobile systems Information systems that support users in motion. p. 450

Modifiable areal unit problem (MAUP) A condition that occurs when point-based spatial data are aggregated into regions and the results depend on how the regions are defined. pp. 450, 556

Modules A suite of applications. p. 479

Moore's Law A law, created by Gordon Moore, stating that the number of transistors per square inch on an integrated chip doubles every 18 months. Moore's prediction has proved generally accurate in the 40 years since it was made. Sometimes this law is stated that the performance of a computer doubles every 18 months. Although not strictly true, this version gives the gist of the idea. p. 5

Multi-user processing When multiple users process the database at the same time. p. 117

MySQL A popular open-source DBMS product that is license-free for most applications. p. 113

Named range A subset of the cells in a worksheet that has a unique name. p. 439

Narrowband Internet communication lines that have transmission speeds of 56 Kbps or less. A dial-up modem provides narrowband access. p. 135

Native application A thick-client application that is designed to work with a particular operating system, and sometimes even designed to work only with a particular mobile device that runs that operating system. p. 454

Network A collection of computers that communicate with one another over transmission lines. p. 131

Network interface card (NIC) A hardware component on each device on a network (computer, printer, etc.) that connects the device's circuitry to the communications line. The NIC works together with programs in each device to implement Layers 1 and 2 of the TCP/IP–OSI hybrid protocol. p. 133

Nonvolatile Memory that preserves data even when not powered (e.g., magnetic and optical disks). With such devices, you can turn the computer off and back on, and the contents will be unchanged. p. 79

Normal form A classification of tables according to their characteristics and the kinds of problems they have. p. 395

Normalization The process of converting poorly structured tables into two or more well-structured tables. p. 394

NoSQL DBMS Software data management products that support very high transaction rates processing relatively simple data structures, replicated on many, even thousands of, servers in the cloud. *NotRelational DBMS* is a more appropriate term. p. 119

Object oriented When referring to languages, ones that can be used to create difficult, complex applications, and, if used properly, will result in high-performance code that is easy to alter when requirements change. p. 454

Off-the-shelf software Software that can be used without having to make any changes. p. 88

Off-the-shelf with alterations software Software bought off-the-shelf but altered to fit the organization's specific needs. p. 88

Office Web Apps License-free, Web-based versions of Word, Excel, PowerPoint, and OneNote available on SkyDrive. p. 361

OLAP See *Online analytical processing.* p. 534

OLAP cube A presentation of an OLAP measure with associated dimensions. The reason for this term is that some products show these displays using three axes, like a cube in geometry. Same as *OLAP report.* p. 534

OLAP servers Computer servers running software that performs OLAP analyses. An OLAP server reads data from an operational database, performs preliminary calculations, and stores the results of those calculations in an OLAP database. p. 537

Onboard NIC A built-in NIC. p. 133

One-of-a-kind application Software that is developed for a specific, unique need, usually for a particular company's operations. p. 86

One-to-many (1:N) relationship Relationships involving two entity types in which an instance of one type can relate to many instances of the second type, but an instance of the second type can relate to at most one instance of the first. For example, the relationship between Department and Employee is 1:N. A department may relate to many employees, but an employee relates to at most one department. p. 392

Online analytical processing (OLAP) A dynamic type of reporting system that provides the ability to sum, count, average, and perform other simple arithmetic operations on groups of data. Such reports are dynamic because users can change the format of the reports while viewing them. p. 534

Operating system (OS) A computer program that controls the computer's resources: It manages the contents of main memory, processes keystrokes and mouse movements, sends signals to the display monitor, reads and writes disk files, and controls the processing of other programs. p. 77

Operational decisions Decisions that concern the day-to-day activities of an organization. p. 346

Operations applications Applications that maintain data on finished goods inventory and the movements of goods from inventory to the customer. p. 471

Optical fiber cables Types of cable used to connect the computers, printers, switches, and other devices on a LAN. The signals on such cables are light rays, and they are reflected inside the glass core of the optical-fiber cable. The core is surrounded by a *cladding* to contain the light signals, and the cladding, in turn, is wrapped with an outer layer to protect it. p. 133

Oracle Database A popular, enterprise-class DBMS product from Oracle Corporation. p. 113

Organizational feasibility The dimension of system feasibility that assesses whether a new system is likely to be acceptable according to the laws, ethics, and culture of an organization. p. 261

Output hardware Hardware that displays the results of the computer's processing. Consists of video displays, printers, audio speakers, overhead projectors, and other special-purpose devices, such as large flatbed plotters. p. 76

Outsourcing The process of hiring another organization to perform a service. Outsourcing is done to save costs, to gain expertise, and to free up management time. p. 288

Packet A small piece of an electronic message that has been divided into chunks; these chunks are sent separately and then reassembled at their destination. p. 140

Packet analyzer Program used for appropriate purposes to read, record, and display all of the wireless packets that are broadcast in the vicinity of the computer running the analyzer. p. 152

Packet sniffer Program used for inappropriate purposes to read, record, and display all of the wireless packets that are broadcast in the vicinity of the computer running the sniffer. p. 152

Packet-filtering firewall A firewall that examines each packet and determines whether to let the packet pass. To make this decision, it examines the source address, the destination addresses, and other data. p. 322

Paired programming The situation in which two computer programmers share the same computer and develop a computer program together. p. 576

Parallel installation A type of system conversion in which the new system runs in parallel with the old one for a while. Parallel installation is expensive because the organization incurs the costs of running both systems. p. 268

Partitioned database A database that is divided into nonoverlapping segments, and two or more segments are distributed into different geographic locations. p. 600

Patch A group of fixes for high-priority failures that can be applied to existing copies of a particular product. Software vendors supply patches to fix security and other critical problems. p. 269

Payload The program code of a virus that causes unwanted or hurtful actions, such as deleting programs or data, or, even worse, modifying data in ways that are undetected by the user. p. 323

PC virtualization Synonym for *desktop virtualization*. p. 84

Perimeter firewall A firewall that sits outside the organizational network; it is the first device that Internet traffic encounters. p. 322

Personal DBMS DBMS products designed for smaller, simpler database applications. Such products are used for personal or small workgroup applications that involve fewer than 100 users, and normally fewer than 15. Today, Microsoft Access is the only prominent personal DBMS. p. 118

Personal identification number (PIN) A form of authentication whereby the user supplies a number that only he or she knows. p. 118, 320

Personal information system Information systems used by a single individual. p. 165

Petabyte 10^{15} bytes. p. 77

Phased installation A type of system conversion in which the new system is installed in pieces across the organization(s). Once a given piece works, then the organization installs and tests another piece of the system, until the entire system has been installed. p. 268

Phisher An individual or organization that spoofs legitimate companies in an attempt to illegally capture personal data, such as credit card numbers, email accounts, and driver's license numbers. p. 311

Phishing A technique for obtaining unauthorized data that uses pretexting via email. The *phisher* pretends to be a legitimate company and sends an email requesting confidential data, such as account numbers, Social Security numbers, account passwords, and so forth. p. 311

Pig Query language used with Hadoop. p. 237

Pilot installation A type of system conversion in which the organization implements the entire system on a limited portion of the business. The advantage of pilot implementation is that if the system fails, the failure is contained within a limited boundary. This reduces exposure of the business and also protects the new system from developing a negative reputation throughout the organization(s). p. 267

PixelSense The Microsoft product formerly known as Surface. It allows many users to process the same table-top touch interface. Primarily used in hotels and entertainment centers. p. 100

Platform as a service (PaaS) Category of cloud hosting in which vendors provide hosted computers, an operating system, and possibly a DBMS. p. 150

Plunge installation Sometimes called *direct installation*, a type of system conversion in which the organization shuts off the old system and starts the new system. If the new system fails, the organization is in trouble: Nothing can be done until either the new system is fixed or the old system is reinstalled. Because of the risk, organizations should avoid this conversion style if possible. p. 268

Pooled The situation in which many different organizations use the same physical hardware. p. 147

Power The utility that one gains from a software product. p. 367

Power curve A graph that shows the relationship of the power (the utility that one gains from a software product) as a function of the time using that product. p. 367

Pretexting A security threat in which someone or some program or device deceives by pretending to be someone or something that it is not. Phishing is a good example. p. 311

Primary activities In Porter's value chain model, the fundamental activities that create value—inbound logistics, operations, outbound logistics, marketing/sales, and service. p. 53

Primary key A column in a relation whose values identify a unique row of that relation. p. 109

Private cloud In-house hosting, delivered via Web service standards, which can be dynamically configured. p. 150

Private IP address A type of IP address used within private networks and internets. Private IP addresses are assigned and managed by the company that operates the private network or internet. p. 140

Problem A *perceived* difference between what is and what ought to be. p. 347

Process blueprint In an ERP product, a comprehensive set of inherent processes for organizational activities. p. 483

Product and brand management applications Marketing applications that import records of past sales from order processing or accounts receivable systems and compare those data to projections and sales estimates, in order to assess the effectiveness of promotions, advertising, and general success of a product brand. p. 471

Product owner On a Scrum project, the business professional who provides the requirements and is available for clarification and testing. The only person on a scrum team who has the authority to add, delete, or change requirements and their priority. p. 577

Product quality assurance (PQA) The testing of a system. PQA personnel usually construct a test plan with the advice and assistance of users. PQA test engineers perform testing, and they also supervise user-test activity. Many PQA professionals are programmers who write automated test programs. p. 267

Project data Data that is part of a collaboration's work product. p. 350

Project metadata Data that is used to manage a project. Schedules, tasks, budgets, and other managerial data are examples. p. 350

Project Management Institute (PMI) International organization focused on disseminating best practices in project management. p. 562

Project Management Professional (PMP) Certification awarded by the Project Management Institute to IT professionals who meet the organization's standards of practice and pass an examination. p. 563

Protected data Data about candidates' sex, race, religion, sexual orientation, and disabilities that is illegal to use for hiring decisions. p. 214

Protocol A standardized means for coordinating an activity between two or more entities. p. 131

Public IP address An IP address used on the Internet. Such IP addresses are assigned to major institutions in blocks by the Internet Corporation for Assigned Names and Numbers (ICANN). Each IP address is unique across all computers on the Internet. p. 140

Public key/private key A special version of asymmetric encryption that is popular on the Internet. With this method, each site has a public key for encoding messages and a private key for decoding them. p. 321

Publish results The process of delivering business intelligence to the knowledge workers who need it. p. 225

Pull data Data that mobile or other computing devices request from the server. p. 462

Pull manufacturing process A manufacturing process whereby products are pulled through manufacturing by demand. Items are manufactured in response to signals from customers or other production processes that products or components are needed. p. 474

Pull publishing In business intelligence (BI) systems, the mode whereby users must request BI results. p. 225

Pull report A report that the user must request. To obtain a pull report, a user goes to a Web portal or digital dashboard and clicks a link or button to cause the reporting system to produce and deliver the report. p. 533

Push data Data that the server sends to or pushes onto mobile or other computing devices. p. 462

Push manufacturing process A plan for producing products whereby the company analyzes past sales levels, makes estimates of future sales, and creates a master production schedule. Products are produced according to that schedule and pushed into sales (and customers). p. 474

Push publishing In business intelligence (BI) systems, the mode whereby the BI system delivers business intelligence according to a schedule, or as a result of an event or particular data condition. The users need not specifically request push BI results. p. 225

Push report Reports sent to users according to a preset schedule. Users receive the report without any activity on their part. p. 533

Quad processor A computer with four CPUs. p. 76

Query A request for data from a database. p. 116

Query report Report that is prepared in response to data entered by users. p. 531

R score In RFM analysis, a number rating that indicates in which fifth a customer ranks in terms of *most recent* order. p. 519

RAM Stands for *random access memory*, which is main memory consisting of cells that hold data or instructions. Each cell has an address that the CPU uses to read or write data. Memory locations can be read or written in any order, hence the term *random access*. p. 76

Raster map A map image that consists of pixels, each of which has some value, often that value is a color, but it could also be a data value like elevation or temperature. Contrast with vector map. p. 544

Records Also called *rows*, groups of columns in a database table. p. 108

Regression analysis A type of supervised data mining that estimates the values of parameters in a linear equation. Used to determine the relative influence of variables on an outcome and also to predict future values of that outcome. p. 235

Relation The more formal name for a database table. p. 110

Relational database Database that carries its data in the form of tables and that represents relationships using foreign keys. p. 110

Relationship An association among entities or entity instances in an E-R model or an association among rows of a table in a relational database. p. 392

Replicated database A database that contains duplicated records. Processing of such a database is complex if users want to be able to update the same items at the same time without experiencing *lost-update problems*. p. 600

Report A presentation of data in a structured, meaningful context. p. 116

Report authoring The process of connecting to data sources, creating the report structure, and formatting the report. p. 533

Report delivery The function of reporting systems that determines that reports are pushed or pulled, in the right form, and to the right people at the right time. p. 534

Report management The function of reporting systems that defines who receives what reports, when, and by what means. p. 534

Report media In reporting systems, the channels by which reports are delivered, such as in paper form or electronically. p. 532

Report mode In reporting systems, the categorization of reports into either *push reports* or *pull reports*. p. 533

Report type In reporting systems, the categorization of reports as either *static* or *dynamic*. p. 531

Reporting analysis A business intelligence application that formats data by applying reporting tools to the data. p. 234

Reporting system A system that creates information from disparate data sources and delivers that information to the proper users on a timely basis. p. 528

Repository A collection of business records, usually implemented as a database. p. 30

Requirements The characteristics of an information system; one of the critical drivers in large-scale IS development, which typically involves trade-offs with cost and time. p. 561

Requirements analysis phase The second phase in the SDLC, in which developers conduct user interviews; evaluate existing systems; determine new forms/reports/ queries; identify new features and functions, including security; and create the data model. p. 259

Requirements creep The process in which users agree to one set of requirements, and then add more over time. p. 570

RFM analysis A way of analyzing and ranking customers according to the recency, frequency, and monetary value of their purchases. p. 518

Ribbon The wide bar of tools and selections that appears just under the tabs in an Excel workbook. p. 373

Rich directory An employee directory that includes not only the standard name, email, phone, and address, but also, expertise, organizational relationships, and other employee data. p. 514

Roaming Occurs when users move their activities, especially long-running transactions, across devices. p. 461

Role In a business process, a set of activities performed by a job type or computer system. p. 29

Router A special-purpose computer that moves network traffic from one node on a network to another. p. 140

Rows In the relational model, collections of columns or attribute values that refer to a single entity instance. Also called records or tuples. Just think of a row of a table and you'll be fine! p. 108

Safeguard Any action, device, procedure, technique, or other measure that reduces a system's vulnerability to a threat. p. 309

Schedule feasibility The dimension of system feasibility that assesses whether a new system is likely to be finished in time to meet minimum essential schedule requirements. p. 261

Scope In the discipline of project management, the characteristics needed to be built into an information system; same as the term *requirements*. In the Systems Development Life Cycle (SDLC), *scope* means to define the system boundaries. p. 564

Screen-sharing applications Applications that offer users the ability to view the same whiteboard, application, or other display over a network. p. 356

Scrum master An expert in scrum processes whose function is to keep the development process on track and to protect team members from external distractions and influences. p. 577

SEAMS In social media, a process for transitioning organizational messaging from a structured to a dynamic process. Acronym for Sense, Engage, Activate, Measure, Story tell. p. 507

Secure Socket Layer (SSL) A protocol that uses both asymmetric and symmetric encryption. SSL is a protocol layer that works between Levels 4 (transport) and 5 (application) of the TCP-OSI protocol architecture. When SSL is in use, the browser address will begin with *https://*. The most recent version of SSI is called TLS. p. 321

Seekers of the truth In social media, a community that shares a common desire to learn something, solve a problem, or make something happen. p. 199

Self-efficacy A person's belief that he or she can be successful at his or her job. p. 177

Semantic security Concerns the unintended release of protected information through the release of a combination of reports or documents that are independently not protected. p. 244

Sequence flows A solid arrow in a BPMN diagram that indicates the order of activities in a business process. p. 30

Server farm A large collection of servers that coordinates the activities of the servers, usually for commercial purposes. p. 79

Server tier In the three-tier architecture, the tier that consists of computers that run Web servers to generate Web pages and other data in response to requests from browsers. Web servers also process application programs. p. 144

Server virtualization The process of running two or more operating system instances on the same server. The host operating system runs virtual operating system instances as applications. p. 84

Servers Computers that provide some type of service, such as hosting a database, running a blog, publishing a Web site, or selling goods. Server computers are faster, larger, and more powerful than client computers. p. 79

Service pack A large group of fixes that solve low-priority software problems. Users apply service packs in much the same way that they apply patches, except that service packs typically involve fixes to hundreds or thousands of problems. p. 269

Site license A license purchased by an organization to equip all the computers on a site with certain software. p. 85

SLATES An acronym for Enterprise 2.0 that refers to Search, Links, Authoring, Tags, Extensions, and Signals. See Figure 8-10. p. 201

Small office/home office (SOHO) A business office with usually fewer than 10 employees, often located in the business professional's home. p. 132

Smart cards Plastic cards similar to credit cards that have a microchip. The microchip, which holds much more data than a magnetic strip, is loaded with identifying data. Normally require a PIN. p. 320

SMTP (Simple Mail Transfer Protocol) A Layer-5 architecture used to send email. Normally used in conjunction with other Layer-5 protocols (POP3, IMAP) for receiving email. p. 139

Sniffing A technique for intercepting computer communications. With wired networks, sniffing requires a physical connection to the network. With wireless networks, no such connection is required. p. 311

Social capital The investment in social relations with expectation of future returns in the marketplace. p. 203

Social CRM CRM that includes social networking elements and gives the customer much more power and control in the customer–vendor relationship. p. 199

Social media (SM) The use of information technology to support the sharing of content among networks of users. p. 193

Social media application providers Companies that operate social media sites. Facebook, Twitter, LinkedIn, and Google are all social media application providers. p. 196

Social media information system (SMIS) An information system that supports the sharing of content among networks of users. p. 193

Social media policy A statement that delineates employees' rights and responsibilities when generating social media content. p. 207

Social media sponsors Companies and other organizations that choose to support a presence on one or more social media sites. p. 195

Software as a service (SaaS) Business model whereby companies (such as Google, Amazon.com, and eBay) provide services based on their software, rather than providing software as a product (by means of software-usage licenses). Salesforce.com is an example. p. 150

Source code Computer code as written by humans and that is understandable by humans. p. 90

Speed The dollar-value rate at which goods are exchanged in a given period of time within a supply chain. p. 499

Spoofing When someone pretends to be someone else with the intent of obtaining unauthorized data. If you pretend to be your professor, you are spoofing your professor. p. 311

Spreadsheet A table of data having rows and columns. Computer-based spreadsheets, such as those processed by Excel, include formulas and sophisticated graphics and offer other capabilities. p. 371

Spyware Programs installed on the user's computer without the user's knowledge or permission that reside in the background and, unknown to the user, observe the user's actions and keystrokes, modify computer activity, and report the user's activities to sponsoring organizations. Malicious spyware captures keystrokes to obtain user names, passwords, account numbers, and other sensitive information. Other spyware is used for marketing analyses, observing what users do, Web sites visited, products examined and purchased, and so forth. p. 94, 323

SQL injection attack The situation that occurs when a user enters a SQL statement into a form in which they are supposed to enter a name or other data. p. 324

SQL Server A popular enterprise-class DBMS product from Microsoft. p. 113

Stand-up In scrum, a 15-minute meeting in which each team member states what he/she has done in the past day, what he/she will do in the coming day, and any factors that are blocking his/her progress. p. 576

Static reports Reports that are prepared once from the underlying data and that do not change. A report of the past year's sales, for example, is a static report. pp. 239, 531

Steering committee A group of senior managers from a company's major business functions that works with the CIO to set the IS priorities and decide among major IS projects and alternatives. p. 288

Storage hardware Hardware that saves data and programs. Magnetic disk is by far the most common storage device, although optical disks, such as CDs and DVDs, also are popular. p. 76

Stored procedure A computer program stored in the database that is used to enforce business rules. p. 483

Strategic decisions Decisions that concern broader-scope, organizational issues. p. 346

Strength of a relationship The likelihood that the entity (person or other organization) in a relationship will do something that benefits entities in the relationship. p. 206

Strong password A password with the following characteristics: ten or more characters; does not contain the user's user name, real name, or company name; does not contain a complete dictionary word, in any language; is different from the user's previous passwords; and contains both upper- and lowercase letters, numbers, and special characters. p. 14

Structured data Data in the form of rows and columns. p. 234

Structured decision A type of decision for which there is a formalized and accepted method for making the decision. p. 347

Structured Query Language (SQL) An international standard language for processing database data. p. 114

Subscriptions User requests for particular business intelligence results on a stated schedule or in response to particular events. p. 239

SUM A built-in arithmetic function in Excel that sums the values in a row or column. p. 384

Supervised data mining A form of data mining in which data miners develop a model prior to the analysis and apply statistical techniques to data to estimate values of the parameters of the model. p. 235

Supply chain A network of organizations and facilities that transforms raw materials into products delivered to customers. p. 494

Supply chain profitability The difference between the sum of the revenue generated by the supply chain and the sum of the costs that all organizations in the supply chain incur to obtain that revenue. p. 497

Support In market-basket terminology, the probability that two items will be purchased together. p. 520

Support activities In Porter's value chain model, the activities that contribute indirectly to value creation—procurement, technology, human resources, and the firm's infrastructure. p. 53

Surface a) Until 2012, a Microsoft hardware–software product that enables people to interact with data on the surface of a table, renamed PixelSense. b) After 2012, the name of Microsoft's tablet computing device. p. 91

Swimlane format A type of business process diagram. Like swim lanes in a swimming pool, each role is shown in its own horizontal rectangle. Swimlane format can be used to simplify process diagrams and to draw attention to interactions among components of the diagram. p. 29

Switch A special-purpose computer that receives and transmits data across a network. p. 132

Switching costs Business strategy of locking in customers by making it difficult or expensive to change to another product or supplier. p. 57

Symbian A principal mobile operating system that is popular on phones in Europe and the Far East, but less so in North America. p. 83

Symmetric encryption An encryption method whereby the same key is used to encode and to decode the message. p. 320

Synchronous communication Information exchange that occurs when all members of a work team meet at the same time, such as face-to-face meetings or conference calls. p. 356

System A group of components that interact to achieve some purpose. p. 10

System conversion The process of *converting* business activity from the old system to the new. p. 267

System definition phase The first phase in the SDLC, in which developers, with the help of eventual users, define the new system's goals and scope, assess its feasibility, form a project team, and plan the project. p. 259

Systems analysis and design The process of creating and maintaining information systems. It is sometimes called *systems development*. p. 255

Systems analysts IS professionals who understand both business and technology. They are active throughout the systems development process and play a key role in moving the project from conception to conversion and, ultimately, maintenance. Systems analysts integrate the work of the programmers, testers, and users. p. 261

Systems development The process of creating and maintaining information systems. It is sometimes called *systems analysis and design*. p. 255

Systems development life cycle (SDLC) The classical process used to develop information systems. These basic tasks of systems development are combined into the following phases: system definition, requirements analysis, component design, implementation, and system maintenance (fix or enhance). p. 258

Systems thinking The ability to model the components of the system, to connect the inputs and outputs among those components into a sensible whole that reflects the structure and dynamics of the phenomenon observed. p. 7

Tab-delimited file An exported file in which data values are separated by tab characters. p. 424

Table Also called a *file*, a group of similar rows or records in a database. p. 108

Tag In markup languages such as HTML and XML, notation used to define a data element for display or other purposes. p. 145

Target The asset that is desired by a security threat. p. 309

Task list In SharePoint, a special type of list that is pre-configured to store data such as task title, description, assigned to, due date, status, predecessor tasks and other useful task data. p. 365

TCP (Transmission Control Protocol) The most popular Layer-4 protocol in the TCP/IP protocol architecture. As a transport protocol, TCP has many functions. One is to break messages into pieces, called *segments*, and provide reliable transport for each segment. p. 139

TCP/IP protocol architecture A protocol architecture having five layers that evolved as a hybrid of the TCP/IP and the OSI architecture. This architecture is used on the Internet and on most internets. p. 138

Team members The programmers, systems analysts, business analysts, database designers, cloud-engineers, PQA testing personnel, and any other staff needed to develop an information system. p. 577

Team surveys Forms of asynchronous communication in which one team member creates a list of questions and other team members respond. Microsoft SharePoint has built-in survey capability. p. 358

Technical feasibility The dimension of system feasibility that assesses whether the requirements for a new system can likely be met within existing, available technology. pp. 240, 261

Technical safeguards Safeguards that involve the hardware and software components of an information system. p. 319

Terabyte (TB) 1,024 GB. p. 77

Test plan Groups of sequences of actions that users will take when using the new system. p. 267

The Internet The public internet. p. 131

The Singularity A point in time in which computer systems become able to design and code themselves. At that point, computer systems will surpass the ability of humans to comprehend them. See www.Singularity.com. p. 238

Thematic map A map that shows themes about geographic locations. p. 554

Thick client application A software application that requires programs other than just a browser on a user's computer. Thick client applications must go through an installation process, either by a human or via remote, programmatic installers, to be used. p. 86

Thin client application A software application that requires nothing more than a browser. Installation of thin clients is automatic. p. 86

Third-party cookie A cookie created by a site other than the one visited. p. 248

Threat A person or organization that seeks to obtain data or other assets illegally, without the owner's permission and often without the owner's knowledge. p. 309

Three-tier architecture Architecture used by most web sites and Internet applications. The tiers refer to three different classes of computers. The user tier consists of users' computers that have browsers that request and process Web pages. The server tier consists of computers that run Web servers and in the process generate Web pages and other data in response to requests from browsers. Web servers also process application programs. The third tier is the database tier, which runs the DBMS that processes the database. p. 144

Time The duration from start to finish to develop an IS; one of the critical drivers in large-scale IS development, which typically involves trade-offs with cost and requirements. p. 561

Trade-off A decision that must be made to favor one thing over another; in project development, a company might choose a trade-off of cost over scope or schedule. p. 561

Train the trainer Training sessions in which vendors train the organization's employees, called Super Users, to become in-house trainers in order to improve training quality and reduce training expenses. p. 483

Transport Layer Security (TLS) A protocol, using both asymmetric and symmetric encryption, that works between Levels 4 (transport) and 5 (application) of the TCP–OSI protocol architecture. TLS is the new name for a later version of SSL. pp. 289, 321

Tribes In social media, a group of people related by a common interest. Also referred to as communities or hives. p. 193

Trigger A computer program stored within the database that runs to keep the database consistent. p. 483

Trojan horses Viruses that masquerade as useful programs or files. The name refers to the gigantic mock-up of a horse that was filled with soldiers and moved into Troy during the Peloponnesian Wars. A typical Trojan horse appears to be a computer game, an MP3 music file, or some other useful, innocuous program. pp. 94, 323

Tunnel A virtual, private pathway over a public or shared network from the VPN client to the VPN server. p. 142

Unified Modeling Language (UML) A series of diagramming techniques that facilitates OOP development. UML has dozens of different diagrams for all phases of system development. UML does not require or promote any particular development process. p. 390

Universal Serial Bus (USB) A standard for connecting computers and external devices such as printers, scanners, keyboards, and mice. A USB device is a peripheral device that conforms to the USB standard. p. 76

Unix An operating system developed at Bell Labs in the 1970s. It has been the workhorse of the scientific and engineering communities since then. p. 83

Unshielded twisted pair (UTP) cable A type of cable used to connect the computers, printers, switches, and other devices on a LAN. A UTP cable has four pairs of twisted wire. A device called an RJ-45 connector is used to connect the UTP cable into NIC devices. p. 133

Unstructured decision A type of decision for which there is no agreed-on decision-making process. p. 347

Unsupervised data mining A form of data mining whereby the analysts do not create a model or hypothesis before running the analysis. Instead, they apply the data mining technique to the data and observe the results. With this method, analysts create hypotheses after the analysis to explain the patterns found. p. 235

URL (Uniform Resource Locator) A document's address on the Web. URLs begin on the right with a top-level domain, and, moving left, include a domain name and then are followed by optional data that locates a document within that domain. p. 141

User experience (UX) A term that refers not only to the user interface (UI), but also to the way that the application behaves within that UI. p. 458

User-generated content (UGC) In Web 2.0, data and information that is provided by users. Examples are product ratings, product problem solutions, product designs, and marketing data. p. 208

User interface (UI) The presentation format of an application that consists of windows, menus, icons, dialog boxes, toolbars, etc., as well as user content. p. 458

User tier In the three-tier architecture, the tier that consists of computers that have browsers that request and process Web pages. p. 144

Usurpation Occurs when unauthorized programs invade a computer system and replace legitimate programs. Such unauthorized programs typically shut down the legitimate system and substitute their own processing. p. 312

Value The amount of money that a customer is willing to pay for a resource, product, or service. p. 53

Value chain A network of value-creating activities. p. 53

Value of social capital Value of a social network, which is determined by the number of relationships in a social network, by the strength of those relationships, and by the resources controlled by those related. p. 203

Vector map Map with features that consist of points, lines, and shapes. Vector maps can be scaled up and down without loss of fidelity. Contrast with *raster map*. p. 545

Velocity In scrum, the total number of points of work that a team can accomplish in each scrum period. p. 579

Version control Use of software to control access to and configuration of documents, designs, and other electronic versions of products. p. 362

Version management Use of software to control configuration of documents, designs, and other electronic versions of products. p. 360

Vertical-market application Software that serves the needs of a specific industry. Examples of such programs are those used by dental offices to schedule appointments and bill patients, those used by auto mechanics to keep track of customer data and customers' automobile repairs, and those used by parts warehouses to track inventory, purchases, and sales. p. 86

Videoconferencing Technology that combines a conference call with video cameras. p. 357

Viral hook A characteristic of a marketing program that causes one person to pass a marketing message on to others. The viral hook might be a humorous or outrageous video or story, or something of value to be exchanged. p. 195

Virtual machines (vm) Computer programs that present the appearance of independent operating systems within a second, host operating system. The host can support multiple virtual machines, each of which is assigned assets such as disk space, devices, network connections, over which it has control. p. 84

Virtual meetings Meetings in which participants do not meet in the same place and possibly not at the same time. p. 356

Virtual private network (VPN) A WAN connection alternative that uses the Internet or a private internet to create the appearance of private point-to-point connections. In the IT world, the term *virtual* means something that appears to exist that does not exist in fact. Here, a VPN uses the public Internet to create the appearance of a private connection. p. 142

Virtualization The process whereby multiple operating systems run as clients on a single host operating system. Gives the appearance of many computers running on a single computer. p. 84

Virus A computer program that replicates itself. pp. 94, 323

Volatile Data that will be lost when the computer or device is not powered. p. 79

Vulnerability An opening or a weakness in a security system. Vulnerabilities exist because there are no safeguards or because the existing safeguards are ineffective. p. 309

WAN wireless A wide area network that provides network connections for computing devices such as smartphones, Kindles, or iPads using cell phone technology. p. 135

Waterfall method The fiction that one phase of the SDLC can be completed in its entirety and the project can progress, without any backtracking, to the next phase of the SDLC. Projects seldom are that simple; backtracking is normally required. pp. 270, 573

Web farm A facility that runs multiple Web servers. Work is distributed among the computers in a Web farm so as to maximize throughput. p. 145

Web page A document encoded in HTML that is created, transmitted, and consumed using the World Wide Web. p. 144

Web server A program that processes the HTTP protocol and transmits Web pages on demand. Web servers also process application programs. p. 145

Web service standards SOA (service-oriented architecture) standards that use HTTP and are used to specify how computers interoperate. p. 149

Webinar A virtual meeting in which attendees can view the same computer desktop and communicate via phone and possibly via camera. p. 356

Web-logs See *Blogs*. p. 508

Wide area network (WAN) A network that connects computers located at different geographic locations. p. 131

Windows An operating system designed and sold by Microsoft. It is the most widely used operating system. p. 82

Windows Live SkyDrive A cloud-based facility that provides for the storage and sharing of Office documents and other files. SkyDrive offers free storage of up to 25GB and provides ready access to Office Web Applications for Word, Excel, PowerPoint, and OneNote. p. 361

Windows RT A version of Windows 8 that is specifically designed to provide a touch-based interface for devices that use ARM architecture, including phones, tablets, and some computers. p. 83

Windows Server A version of Windows that has been specifically designed and configured for server use. It has much more stringent and restrictive security procedures than other versions of Windows and is popular on servers in organizations that have made a strong commitment to Microsoft. p. 83

Wireless NIC (WNIC) Devices that enable wireless networks by communicating with wireless access points. Such devices can be cards that slide into the PCMA slot or they can be built-in, onboard devices. WNICs operate according to the 802.11 protocol. p. 133

Work breakdown structure (WBS) A hierarchy of the tasks required to complete a project; for a large project, it might involve hundreds or thousands of tasks. p. 564

Workbook In Microsoft Excel, one or more worksheets. p. 371

Workflow control Use of information systems to monitor the execution of a work team's processes; to ensure that actions are taken at appropriate times and to prohibit the skipping of steps or tasks. p. 363

Workgroup information system An information system that is shared by a group of people for a particular purpose. p. 165

Worksheet A spreadsheet in Microsoft Excel. p. 371

Worm A virus that propagates itself using the Internet or some other computer network. Worm code is written specifically to infect another computer as quickly as possible. p. 94, 323